POWER, PRIVILEGE AND LAW

A CIVIL RIGHTS READER

By

Leslie Bender
Professor of Law
Syracuse University

Daan Braveman
Dean and Professor of Law
Syracuse University

AMERICAN CASEBOOK SERIES®

WEST PUBLISHING CO.
ST. PAUL, MINN., 1995

ABOUT THE COVER

Our cover image consists of two panels of The Amistad murals, painted by Hale Woodruff in 1939 to tell the story of the Amistad mutiny trial. The murals decorate the walls of the Savery Library, Talladega College, Talladega, Alabama, and we are grateful to Mrs. Frances Dates and the library staff for giving us permission to use the images.

In 1839 a shipload of 54 African captives leaving Havana, Cuba, revolted against their Spanish captors. While in transport, the slaves rose up against the ship's master, killed him and others, but spared two Spaniards, Montez and Ruiz, so that they could steer the ship back to Africa. The Spaniards tried to deceive the mutinous slaves and instead of travelling east to Africa travelled north. After two months at sea, the ship was sighted off Long Island, New York and boarded by officers of a U.S. ship, the Washington. The Spaniards begged for the aid of the Americans and told the story of the mutiny. The crew of the Washington hauled the ship to New London, Connecticut, took custody of the remaining 49 Africans, and then sued in libel for salvage costs. The Amistad case is an action in admiralty with multiple parties claiming the value of the ship, the costs of salvage, the cargo and the slaves. This admiralty case in New Haven, Connecticut was anything but simple however, because the major value of the cargo was the value of the slaves. The Spanish government claimed that by treaty, the U.S. has agreed to give back to its rightful owner the property or cargo that it captures by salvaging a pirated ship. If the slaves are Spanish property, they must be returned. If they were found to be free people and not slaves, then neither international law nor treaty require their return to captivity. So, the crux of the case is whether or not the Africans are slaves and property of the Spanish or free people.

At the trial and on appeal to the U.S. Supreme Court, former president, John Quincy Adams, and Roger Baldwin, defended the captives' right to mutiny or revolt against captivity based on principles of justice and natural law. The mutiny and trial became the centerpiece of abolitionist work and attention. Abolitionist and black church groups provided resources for legal counsel, food and clothing, a translator, education, and eventually for the return voyage after the captives won their freedom. The Amistad incident was a strong force in bringing together abolitionist forces that pressed for freedom for African descendants through the Dred Scott case and the Civil War.

This scene of the trial shows Cinque, the African leader, standing proud against the accusations of the Spaniards. Woodruff included himself with the otherwise all white, all male jury. For more information on the Amistad mutiny trial, see HOWARD JONES, MUTINY ON THE AMISTAD (Oxford, 1987); CHRISTOPHER MARTIN, THE AMISTAD AFFAIR (Abelard-Schuman, 1970); ROBERT M. COVER, JUSTICE ACCUSED: ANTISLAVERY AND THE JUDICIAL PROCESS 109-116 (Yale, 1975).

American Casebook Series and the WP symbol are registered trademarks of West Publishing Co. Registered in U.S. Patent and Trademark Office.

COPYRIGHT © 1995 By WEST PUBLISHING CO.
610 Opperman Drive
P.O. Box 64526
St. Paul, MN 55164–0526
1–800–328–9352

Library of Congress Cataloging-in-Publication Data

Braveman, Daan.
  Power, privilege and law : a civil rights reader / by Daan
Braveman, Leslie Bender.
    p.   cm. — (American casebook series)
  Includes index.
  ISBN 0–314–04577–5
  1. Civil rights—United States—Cases. 2. Critical legal studies—
United States—Cases. 3. Social justice—Cases. I. Bender,
Leslie, 1952–   . II. Title. III. Series.
KF4748.B73 1995
342.73'085—dc20
[347.30285]

94–42836
CIP

ISBN 0–314–04577–5

For Peter Allan Sandwall, who brings love and art to my life,
and for my children, Benjamin and Rachael Saller Bender,
who inspire my struggles for justice and enrich my soul

L.B.

For Lorraine and Adam

D.B.

*

Preface

Preparing these materials was a labor of love. We have developed and taught from different versions of them over the years. A few years ago, when we were in an earlier stage of this project, we wrote an essay about one incarnation of this course that may offer a potential teacher a fuller understanding of what vision animated our collection of materials. Rather than include that essay in this book, we refer you to it. Leslie Bender & Daan Braveman, *Impassioning a Civil Rights Course*, 16 Vermont L. Rev. 943 (Spring 1992). Much has changed since that version of the course and much has remained the same. Although these edited cases, readings, essays, questions, and comments still seem to us to be a work-in-progress, we know that by the time you get them, they will look like a finished product. We consider them part of an ongoing conversation about power, privilege, and law. We are happy to share them with you and hope that they will brighten your teaching and learning experiences. We enthusiastically invite you, as a student, teacher, or scholar involved with these materials and issues, to write to us and share your thoughts about additional materials that ought to be included and about your experiences teaching from them. Thank you for taking the time to seriously consider using our work.

This book can be used in various course settings. We have used different versions in a year long seminar, in one semester courses with different amounts of credit (and different names), and in a year long course. We have co-taught the course and taught it individually We used materials in this book in courses entitled Civil Rights, Contemporary Legal Theories, Social Justice and Law, Jurisprudence, first year and upper-level Constitutional Law Courses, and Lawyers' Role. This book can also be used as a main text or supplemental readings in any law courses designed to address issues of gender, race, class, sexual orientation, ethnicity, or disability, as well as any courses taking critical approaches to law. This reader would easily complement constitutional law courses. We also believe that these materials would work well in seminars and classes in other departments of the university where students are examining law in relation to issues in their disciplines. We encourage you to share these materials with colleagues who teach graduate and upper-level undergraduate courses in Women's Studies, African–American Studies, interdisciplinary courses about race, gender, sexuality, identity, legal history, Political Theory and Science courses, Sociology or Social Theory courses, courses on rhetoric and textual studies, and courses in Philosophy of Law or Psychology and Law.

OVERVIEW OF POWER, PRIVILEGE AND LAW

This book is a collection of cases, transdisciplinary readings (articles, essays, literature, and book excerpts), commentaries, and questions focusing on the role of law in producing, replicating, and disrupting hierarchies of power and privilege, particularly those based on racial groupings, gender, social and economic class, sexual orientations, and disabilities. Our primary goal is to enable students to read law critically with a special sensitivity to the ways in which legal techniques, rhetorical strategies, and legal practices reproduce patterns of power and privilege that work to subordinate people based on categories of identity. The materials are designed to reveal these strategies through close readings of the language and underlying assumptions in judicial opinions. Students are encouraged to examine legal opinions for their similarities and differences in approaches to power and privilege across identity categories and to compare them with insights garnered from the wide range of multi-disciplinary scholarly excerpts surrounding the case texts.

After an introduction that describes our project as one of looking at the liberatory potential within notions like civil rights, we explain how our pedagogical approach of legal critique is fashioned to lead to student empowerment. For a law course that is structured so differently from many typical law courses, we felt it was important to share with students some reasons for our teaching/learning strategies. The introduction closes with various readings that encourage students to examine the role and power of law in society and to understand law as a potential instrument of social justice.

Part II examines the meaning of power and privilege, on a personal level and on a structural level, through powerful narrative and theoretical writings. How is one's daily life experiences affected by being identified as "white" or "male" or "able-bodied"? What are the structures or systems of power that deprive certain groups of people of equal opportunities to improve the quality of their own lives? Our hope in Part II is to begin to make visible some of the hidden assumptions of our social lives and law.

Part III, addressing the construction of exclusion in the law, is the most extensive component of the book. We introduce these materials with an essay we have written describing techniques and assumptions the law uses to justify the denial of power and privilege to certain groups, and then we invite the students to read through the following materials with an eye toward these techniques and others they might discern. We have selected primarily Supreme Court cases spanning a century to show how these techniques are repeatedly employed, much in the same way in the past as today and often in the same way to exclude different groups of peoples from legal and social privileges. Students are encouraged to read for much more than the result or rule. We ask them to look at the types of arguments, the kinds of language, and the strategic approaches used in cases that divide groups of people based on their racial, sexual, or class-based identities. We have separate subsections on racial groups (specifically including African–Americans, European–Americans, Hispanic–Americans, Native Americans and Asian–Americans), gender, sexual orientation, poverty or wealth-based classifications, and disabilities. Each subsection includes newer and older cases, and either law review article excerpts or essays. Many of the selected cases are shocking for their blatant discrimination and blindness to justice (not color-blindness, but intentional ignorance), yet they were written by justices on our highest court. Perhaps by learning how courts argued and justified these decisions in the past (both distant and recent), students can develop strategies to expose similar flaws in arguments being made today and tomorrow. In each of the subsections, students can see repeated patterns and new patterns in the legal treatment of "others", while they learn more about the history and quality of discrimination experienced by different identity groups.

Part IV looks at alternative constructions of identity that subvert the law's typical categories. Each of us has multiple aspects of our identities that combine and have different valences in different contexts or environments. Readings reveal the inadequacy of our current legal analyses and propose alternatives. How might we talk about identity in ways that recognize our multiplicity, but do not undermine our possibilities for coalitions and solidarity? Can we make law compatible with these newer, more satisfying understandings of identity, power, and privilege?

The final section, Part V entitled Visions of Justice, gives students examples of positive strategies of resistance and for change that lawyers have used or proposed. We recognize that a concentrated study of ways in which the law has failed us in our struggles for equality and justice can be depressing and can feel disempowering for students. In Part V we have brought together examples of what can be done once lawyers and social activists have gained deeper understandings about power and privilege. In the last part we also invite students to understand law as only one tool in the struggle for justice and emphasize the need to employ multiple tools simultaneously in order to achieve social change.

*

Acknowledgements

We owe our thanks to many people for their help in writing and compiling this book. First, and most important, we want to express our sincere appreciation to the students who have used previous versions of the materials. Their willingness to reexamine and challenge personal understandings of these difficult issues was refreshing. Their insights and suggestions were invaluable as we proceeded with this project.

We also greatly appreciate the assistance provided by Carla DiMarco and Neil Phillips, our research assistants, and Kimmberly Bulkley and Brynja McDivitt who helped proofing the manuscript. Peter Sandwall and Frances Dates deserve special thanks for their roles in securing the image used on the cover of the book.

Finally, others have helped us in our research and our own understandings of the topics. We each thank Syracuse University College of Law for summer research grants that helped us make progress on this book. People on the WMST-L and FEMJUR listservs gave us very helpful ideas for further research. We also read many articles that we were unable to include in the book. The authors of these articles helped shape our thinking about the materials, and we thank them as well.

Leslie Bender
Professor, Syracuse University
College of Law & Women's Studies Program
(315) 443-4462
lbender@mailbox.syr.edu

Daan Braveman
Dean and Professor, Syracuse
University College of Law
(315) 443-2540
braveman@law.syr.edu

*

Summary of Contents

*

Table of Contents

Table of Cases

The principal cases are in bold type. Cases cited or discussed in the text are roman type. References are to pages. Cases cited in principal cases and within other quoted materials are not included.

Table of Authorities

POWER, PRIVILEGE
AND LAW

A CIVIL RIGHTS READER

*

Chapter One

INTRODUCTION

Silver Writes

It is true—
I've always loved
the daring
           ones
Like the black young
man
Who tried
to crash
All barriers
at once,
      wanted to
swim
At a white
beach (in Alabama)
Nude.[1]

Silver Writes is Alice Walker's favorite poem of the many she wrote during the civil rights struggles of the 1960s. In her book, In Search of Our Mothers' Gardens, Walker stated that she liked the poem because it not only revealed something about her own motivations for joining the movement but also exposed why the term "civil rights" could not adequately capture "our longings and our dreams, or those of the non-black people who stood among us." The term, Walker wrote, is "totally lacking in color" and "has no poetry." She explained:

> "Civil Rights" is a term that did not evolve out of black culture, but, rather, out of American law. As such, it is a term of limitation. It speaks only to physical possibilities—necessary and treasured, of course—but not of the spirit. Even as it promises assurance of greater freedoms it narrows the area in which people might expect to find them....
>
> When one reads the poems, especially, of the period, this becomes very clear. The poems, like the songs of that time, reveal an entirely different *quality of imagination and spirit* than the term

---

1. Alice Walker, In Search of Our Mothers' Gardens 335 (Harvest/HBJ, 1983).

"Civil Rights" describes. The poems are full of protest and "civil disobedience," yes, but they are also full of playfulness and whimsicality, an attraction to world families and the cosmic sea—full of a lot of naked people longing to swim free.

This book is designed with the spirit of Alice Walker's poem in mind. In a very real sense, *Silver Writes* was our guide in developing materials that provide a range of perspectives on issues relating to race, gender, class, sexuality, and disability. The material in the following chapters will hopefully provide opportunities to develop critical understanding of the way law works to perpetuate, or displace, existing patterns of power and privilege.

We begin with an excerpt about the educational process generally, and its role in developing an understanding of issues related to privilege and power.

bell hooks, TOWARD A REVOLUTIONARY FEMINIST PEDAGOGY

in Talking Back 49–54 (South End Press, 1989).

My favorite teacher in high school was Miss Annie Mae Moore, a short, stout black woman. She had taught my mama and her sisters. She could tell story after story about their fast ways, their wildness. She could tell me ways I was like mama, ways I was most truly my own self. She could catch hold of you and turn you around, set you straight (these were the comments folk made about her teaching)—so that we would know what we were facing when we entered her classroom. Passionate in her teaching, confident that her work in life was a pedagogy of liberation (words she would not have used but lived instinctively), one that would address and confront our realities as black children growing up in the segregated South, black children growing up within a white-supremacist culture. Miss Moore knew that if we were to be fully self-realized, then her work, and the work of all our progressive teachers, was not to teach us solely the knowledge in books, but to teach us an oppositional world view—different from that of our exploiters and oppressors, a world view that would enable us to see ourselves not through the lens of racism or racist stereotypes but one that would enable us to focus clearly and succinctly, to look at ourselves, at the world around us, critically—analytically—to see ourselves first and foremost as striving for wholeness, for unity of heart, mind, body, and spirit.

It was as a student in segregated black schools called Booker T. Washington and Crispus Attucks that I witnessed the transformative power of teaching, of pedagogy. In particular, those teachers who approached their work as though it was indeed a pedagogy, a science of teaching, requiring diverse strategies, approaches, explorations, experimentation, and risks, demonstrated the value—the political power—of teaching. Their work was truly education for critical consciousness. In these segregated schools, the teachers were almost all black women.

Many of them had chosen teaching at a historical moment when they were required by custom to remain single and childless, to have no visible erotic or sexual life. Among them were exceptional teachers who gave to their work a passion, a devotion that made it seem a true calling, a true vocation. They were the teachers who conceptualized opposition- al world views, who taught us young black women to exult and glory in the power and beauty of our intellect. They offered to us a legacy of liberatory pedagogy that demanded active resistance and rebellion against sexism and racism. They embodied in their work, in their lives (for none of them appeared as tortured spinsters estranged and alienated from the world around them) a feminist spirit. They were active participants in black community, shaping our futures, mapping our intellectual terrains, sharing revolutionary fervor and vision. I write these words, this essay to express the honor and respect I have for them because they have been my pedagogical guardians. Their work has had a profound impact on my consciousness, on my development as a teacher.

During years of graduate school, I waited for that phase of study when we would focus on the meaning and significance of pedagogy, when we would learn about teaching, about how to teach. That moment never arrived. For years I have relied on those earlier models of excellent teaching to guide me. Most specifically, I understood from the teachers in those segregated schools that the work of any teacher committed to the full self-realization of students was necessarily and fundamentally radical, that ideas were not neutral, that to teach in a way that liberates, that expands consciousness, that awakens, is to challenge domination at its very core. It is this pedagogy that Paulo Freire calls "education as the practice of freedom." In his introduction to Freire's *Pedagogy of the Oppressed*, Richard Shaull writes:

> Education either functions as an instrument which is used to facilitate the integration of the younger generation into the logic of the present system and bring about conformity to it, or it becomes "the practice of freedom," the means by which men and women deal critically and creatively with reality and discover how to participate in the transformation of their world.

A liberatory feminist movement aims to transform society by eradi- cating patriarchy, by ending sexism and sexist oppression, by challenging the politics of domination on all fronts. Feminist pedagogy can only be liberatory if it is truly revolutionary because the mechanisms of appro- priation within white-supremacist, capitalist patriarchy are able to co-opt with tremendous ease that which merely appears radical or subversive. Within the United States, contemporary feminist movement is sustained in part by the efforts academic women make to constitute the university setting as a central site for the development and dissemination of feminist thought. Women's Studies has been the location of this effort. Given the way universities work to reinforce and perpetuate the status quo, the way knowledge is offered as commodity, Women's Studies can easily become a place where revolutionary feminist thought and feminist activism are submerged or made secondary to the goals of academic careerism. Without diminishing in any way our struggle as academics striving to succeed in institutions, such effort is fully compatible with liberatory feminist struggle only when we consciously, carefully, and strategically link the two. When this connection is made initially but not sustained, or when it is never evident, Women's Studies becomes either an exotic terrain for those politically chic few seeking affirmation or a small settlement within the larger institutional structure where women (and primarily white women) have a power base, which rather than being oppositional simply mirrors the status quo. When feminist struggle is the central foundation for feminist education, Women's Studies and the feminist classroom (which can exist outside the domain of Women's Studies) can be places where education is the practice of freedom, the place for liberatory pedagogy.

At this historical moment, there is a crisis of engagement within universities, for when knowledge becomes commoditized, then much authentic learning ceases. Students who want to learn hunger for a space where they can be challenged intellectually. Students also suffer, as many of us who teach do, from a crisis of meaning, unsure about what has value in life, unsure even about whether it is important to stay alive. They long for a context where their subjective needs can be integrated with study, where the primary focus is a broader spectrum of ideas and modes of inquiry, in short a dialectical context where there is serious and rigorous critical exchange. This is an important and exciting time for feminist pedagogy because in theory and practice our work meets these needs.

Feminist education—the feminist classroom—is and should be a place where there is a sense of struggle, where there is visible acknowledgement of the union of theory and practice, where we work together as teachers and students to overcome the estrangement and alienation that have become so much the norm in the contemporary university. Most importantly, feminist pedagogy should engage students in a learning process that makes the world "more rather than less real." In my classrooms, we work to dispel the notion that our experience is not a "real world" experience. This is especially easy since gender is such a pressing issue in contemporary life. Every aspect of popular culture alerts us to the reality that folks are thinking about gender in both reactionary and progressive ways. What is important is that they are thinking critically. And it is this space that allows for the possibility of feminist intervention, whether it be in our classroom or in the life of students outside the classroom. Lately, there has been a truly diverse body of students coming to my classes and other feminist classes at universities all around the United States. Many of us have been wondering "what's going on" or "why are all these men, and white men in the class." This changing student body reflects the concern about gender issues, that it is one of the real important issues in people's private lives that is addressed academically. Freire writes, "Education as the practice of freedom—as opposed to education as the practice of domination—denies that we are abstract, isolated, independent, and unattached to the world; it also denies that the world exists as a reality apart from us."

To make a revolutionary feminist pedagogy, we must relinquish our ties to traditional ways of teaching that reinforce domination. This is very difficult. Women's Studies courses are often viewed as not seriously academic because so much "personal stuff" is discussed. Fear that their courses will be seen as "gut" classes has led many feminist professors to rely more on traditional pedagogical styles. This is unfortunate. Certainly, the radical alternative to the status quo should never have been simply an inversion. That is to say, critical of the absence of any focus on personal experience in traditional classrooms, such focus becomes the central characteristic of the feminist classroom. This model must be viewed critically because a class can still be reinforcing domination, not transforming consciousness about gender, even as the "personal" is the ongoing topic of conversation.

To have a revolutionary feminist pedagogy we must first focus on the teacher-student relationship and the issue of power. How do we as feminist teachers use power in a way that is not coercive, dominating? Many women have had difficulty asserting power in the feminist classroom for fear that to do so would be to exercise domination. Yet we must acknowledge that our role as teacher is a position of power over others. We can use that power in ways that diminish or in ways that enrich and it is this choice that should distinguish feminist pedagogy from ways of teaching that reinforce domination. One simple way to alter the way one's "power" as teacher is experienced in the classroom is to elect not to assume the posture of all-knowing professors. This is also difficult. When we acknowledge that we do not know everything, that we do not have all the answers, we risk students leaving our classrooms and telling others that we are not prepared. It is important to make it clear to students that we are prepared and that the willingness to be open and honest about what we do no know is a gesture of respect for them.

To be oppositional in the feminist classroom one must have a standard of valuation that differs from the norm. Many of us tried new ways of teaching without changing the standards by which we evaluated our work. We often left the classroom feeling uncertain about the learning process or even concerned that we were failing as teachers. Let me share a particular problem I have faced. My classroom style is very confrontational. It is a model of pedagogy that is based on the assumption that many students will take courses from me who are afraid to assert themselves as critical thinkers, who are afraid to speak (especially students from oppressed and exploited groups). The revolutionary hope that I bring to the classroom is that it will become a space where they can come to voice. Unlike the stereotypical feminist model that suggests women best come to voice in an atmosphere of safety (one in which we are all going to be kind and nurturing), I encourage students to work at coming to voice in an atmosphere where they may be afraid or see themselves at risk. The goal is to enable all students, not just an assertive few, to feel empowered in a rigorous, critical discussion. Many students find this pedagogy difficult, frightening, and very demanding. They do not usually come away from my class talking about how much they enjoyed the experience.

One aspect of traditional models of teaching I had not surrendered was that longing for immediate recognition of my value as a teacher, and immediate affirmation. Often I did not feel liked or affirmed and this was difficult for me to accept. I reflected on my student experiences and the reality that I often learned the most in classes that I did not enjoy and complained about, which helped me to work on the traditional assumption that immediate positive feedback is the signifier of worth. Concurrently, I found that students who often felt they hated a class with me would return later to say how much they learned, that they understood that it was the different style that made it hard as well as the different demands. I began to see that courses that work to shift paradigms, to change consciousness, cannot necessarily be experienced immediately as fun or positive or safe and this was not a worthwhile criteria to use in evaluation.

In the feminist classroom, it is important to define the terms of engagement, to identify what we mean when we say that a course will be taught from a feminist perspective. Often the initial explanations about pedagogy will have a serious impact on the way students experience a course. It is important to talk about pedagogical strategy. For a time, I assumed that students would just get the hang of it, would see that I was trying to teach in a different way and accept it without explanation. Often, that meant I explained after being criticized. It is important for feminist professors to explain not only what will differ about the classroom experience but to openly acknowledge that students must consider whether they wish to be in such a learning space. On a basic level, students are often turned off by the fact that I take attendance, but because I see the classroom experience as constituting a unique learning experience, to miss class is to really lose a significant aspect of the process. Whether or not a student attends class affects grading and this bothers students who are not accustomed to taking attendance seriously. Another important issue for me has been that each student participate in classroom discussion, that each student have a voice. This is a practice I think is important not because every student has something valuable to say (this is not always so), but often students who do have meaningful comments to contribute are silent. In my classes, everyone's voice is heard as students read paragraphs which may explore a particular issue. They do not have the opportunity to refuse to read paragraphs. When I hear their voices, I become more aware of information they may not know that I can provide. Whether a class is large or small, I try to talk with all students individually or in small groups so that I have a sense of their needs. How can we transform consciousness if we do not have some sense of where the students are intellectually, psychically?

Concern with how and what students are learning validates and legitimates a focus, however small, on personal confession in classroom discussions. I encourage students to relate the information they are learning to the personal identities they are working to socially construct, to change, to affirm. If the goal of personal confession is not narcissism, it must take place within a critical framework where it is related to material that is being discussed. When, for example, I am teaching Toni Morrison's novel, *The Bluest Eye,* I may have students write personal paragraphs about the relationship between race and physical beauty, which they read in class. Their paragraphs may reveal pain, woundedness as they explore and express ways they are victimized by racism and sexism, or they may express ideas that are racist and sexist. Yet the paragraphs enable them to approach the text in a new way. They may read the novel differently. They may be able to be more critical and analytical. If this does not happen, then the paragraphs fail as a pedagogical tool. To make feminist classrooms the site of transformative learning experiences, we must constantly try new methods, new approaches.

Finally, we cannot have a revolutionary feminist pedagogy if we do not have revolutionary feminists in the classroom. Women's Studies courses must do more than offer a different teaching style; we must really challenge issues of sexism and sexist oppression both by what we teach and how we teach. This is truly a collective effort. We must learn from one another, sharing ideas and pedagogical strategies. Although I have invited feminist colleagues to come and participate in my classes, they do not. Classroom territoriality is another traditional taboo. Yet if we are to learn from one another, if we are to develop a concrete strategy for radicalizing our classrooms, we must be more engaged as a group. We must be willing to deconstruct this power dimension, to challenge, change, and create new approaches. If we are to move toward a revolutionary feminist pedagogy, we must challenge ourselves and one another to restore to feminist struggle its radical and subversive dimension. We must be willing to restore the spirit of risk—to be fast, wild, to be able to take hold, turn around, transform.

Notes and Questions

1. Have your educational experiences functioned as means of conforming you to the "logic of the present system?" Or, have they encouraged you to "deal critically and creatively with reality and discover how to participate in the transformation of [the] world?" Consider bell hooks' observation:

> In the introduction to a conversation with Paulo Freire published in *idac,* emphasis is placed on an educative process that is not based on an authoritarian, dominating model where knowledge is transferred from a powerful professor to a powerless student. Education, it was suggested, could be a space for the development of critical consciousness, where there could be dialogue and mutual growth of both student and professor:

If we accept education in this richer and more dynamic sense of acquiring a critical capacity and intervention in reality, we immediately know that there is no such thing as neutral education. All education has an intention, a goal, which can only be political. Either it mystifies reality by rendering it impenetrable and obscure—which leads people to a blind march through incomprehensible labyrinths or it unmasks the economic and social structures which are determining the relationships of exploitation and oppression among persons, knocking down labyrinths and allowing people to walk their own road. So we find ourselves confronted with a clear option: to educate for liberation or to educate for domination.

In retrospect, it seems that my most radical professors were still educating for domination. And I wondered if this was so because we could not imagine how to educate for liberation in the corporate university. In Freire's case, he speaks as a white man of privilege who stands and acts in solidarity with oppressed and exploited groups, especially in their efforts to establish literacy programs that emphasize education for critical consciousness. In my case, as a black woman from a working-class background, I stand and act as a member of an oppressed, exploited group, who has managed to acquire a degree of privilege. While I choose to educate for liberation, the site of my work has been within the walls of universities peopled largely by privileged white students and a few non-white students. Within those walls, I have tried to teach literature and Women's Studies courses in a way that does not reinforce structures of domination: imperialism, racism, sexism, and class exploitation.

bell hooks, "Pedagogy and Political Commitment: A Comment" in Talking Back 101 (South End Press, 1989).

2. How might a course be designed to facilitate "education as the practice of freedom?" What are the implications for selection of course materials and teaching methods, for examples?

3. How might the classroom itself be used to better understand issues of power and privilege?

4. In what ways might the study of privilege and power cause conflict and pain?

5. Do hooks' observations about education generally apply to legal education specifically? Consider the following.

PAUL CARRINGTON, OF LAW AND THE RIVER
34 J. Legal Educ. 222, 226–27 (1984).

. . . One cannot believe in the worth of one's professional skill and judgment as a lawyer unless one also has some minimal belief in the idea of law and the institutions that enforce it. The river is complex and changing, but it is tangible, a wet experience to refresh the pilot's conviction that his knowledge pertains to reality in nature. The law, in contrast, is a mere hope that people who apply the lash of power will seek to obey the law's command. Let us not be modest: it is an act of considerable courage to maintain belief in such a hope.

There are many familiar reasons why lawyers may disbelieve in their own professionalism. Lawyers everywhere and always must have known that the law cannot deliver all that is promised in its behalf. For the law to be applied, facts must be known, and facts can be very elusive. The law is itself obscure in many of its specific applications; its meaning must be found if at all in the conduct of officials. But officials are people and that means they are vulnerable to the attractions of self-aggrandizement, and to other influences. Even if they are altruistic, they may use power to pursue social and political agendas not embodied in the law. So law will reflect the tastes of that class of persons from whom the officials are drawn. And, if this be so, then perhaps as some of our colleagues may be heard to say, law is a mere deception by which the powerful weaken the resistance of the powerless. Thus, enforcement and even obedience may be morally degenerate. Faced with such impediments to belief in law, who can fail to have doubts about the validity of their professionalism as lawyers?

Such disbelief threatens competence. More than a few lawyers lack competence because they have lost, or never acquired, the needed confidence that law matters. Lawyers lacking confidence that legal principles actually influence the exercise of power have no professional tools with which to do their work. In due course they must abandon whatever professionalism they have, to choose between simple neglect of their work or the application of common cunning, such techniques as bribery and intimidation in all their many forms.

Moreover, there is dread in disbelief. A lawyer who succumbs to legal nihilism faces a far greater danger than mere professional incompetence. He must contemplate the dreadful reality of government by cunning and a society in which the only right is might. Such a fright can sustain belief in many that law is at least possible and must matter.

The professionalism and intellectual courage of lawyers does not require rejection of Legal Realism and its lesson that who decides also matters. What it cannot abide is the embrace of nihilism and its lesson that who decides is everything, and principle nothing but cosmetic. Persons espousing the latter view, however honestly held, have a substantial ethical problem as teachers of professional law students. The nihilist teacher threatens to rob his or her students of the courage to act on such professional judgment as they may have acquired. Teaching cynicism may, and perhaps probably does, result in the learning of the skills of corruption: bribery and intimidation. In an honest effort to proclaim a need for revolution, nihilist teachers are more likely to train crooks than radicals. If this risk is correctly appraised, the nihilist who must profess that legal principle does not matter has an ethical duty to depart the law school, perhaps to seek a place elsewhere in the academy. . . .

This article provoked a number of responses, including the following.

ROBERT GORDON, "OF LAW AND THE RIVER," AND OF NIHILISM AND ACADEMIC FREEDOM

35 J. Legal Educ. 1, 13–16 (1985).

1. When you speak of the professional as one who believes in the law, it is not clear how you are using "law." You could mean: the body of current professional practices. Or: the utopian norms of fair process, restraint-of-power, equality, "dialogue" ..., or whatever, embodied in law but only imperfectly realized in the current professional practices. It makes a lot of difference. One position is: "A true professional complacently subscribes to the going system, whatever it is." Another is: "A true professional should work to bring the practice of law into closer harmony with its utopian norms." I should have thought that if law teachers had any ethical duty to teach either of these positions, it would be the second. The academic wing of the profession in particular is *supposed* to be reformist in its aspirations: if lawyers or judges or legislators are doing bad things, the professors should point that out and try to get them to change. This seems to be your own stance. It seems to me a good stance; and if law students and lawyers often respond to it with cynicism or indifference, that is no reason to abandon it.

More specifically: is it wrong for law teachers to try to discourage their students from doing what they plan to do? It depends, surely. I agree with you that if a law teacher starts thinking that all lawyers do more harm than good, believes nothing can be done to change that situation even slightly, and counsels all his students to abandon the law, he is in the wrong job and ought to get out. But what if he wants his students to change current practices, rather than abandon them? ... If people in the law school do not engage in critical reflection on what lawyers do, who will?

2. When you speak of the belief that law *matters,* it is not clear in what sense you mean "matters". You could mean: (1) Law is more than just a mask for, or rationalization of, naked power and self-interest: its norms, rules, procedures, reasoning processes, etc. have an autonomous content, have an independent influence upon the actions of legal officials and ordinary persons in society.... (2) Legal rules are not infinitely manipulable: they do constrain outcomes. (This is a complex assertion, which would obviously have to be considerably expanded and refined before anyone could evaluate it: it is too shorthand to constitute a *credo* for an intelligent professional.) (3) The current system of rules in force, and practices of the officials and lawyers who apply them, is basically a good one, if not close to the best attainable system in an imperfect world, at least on the whole more good than bad. (This is obviously a political judgment, which if made a criterion of a good

professional arbitrarily excludes critical idealists who believe the system embodies many serious evils and could be made a good deal better than it is.)

Perhaps you do not mean any of these things, but something else entirely. The point is that you have been repeating the phrase "law matters" as if it has a transparent and accepted meaning to your audience; whereas it is really very indefinite.

3. What is "nihilism", anyway? That of course depends on how one understands its opposite, the belief that "law matters".…

4. Finally, the relationship of "nihilism" to "corruption". Quite honestly I would not expect to be able to find much of any correlation between a set of jurisprudential or political beliefs abstractly described (as contrasted with the inspiriting or dispiriting force of a teacher's personal presence or example) and the behavior in practice of law graduates exposed to such beliefs. But if there are such correlations, my intuitions about them run opposite to yours. Is it not somewhat more plausible that corruption in students will be promoted by that kind of resignation to current practices that so frequently passes as worldly wisdom—that is, by teachers who believe in nothing but the inevitability of the *status quo?* …

Notes and Questions

1. Is Paul Carrington suggesting that the role of legal education is to facilitate the integration of students into the logic of the existing system?

2. Does Robert Gordon see a greater transformative function for legal education?

3. Can legal education prepare people for the profession while serving as a "practice of freedom?" For an additional critique of legal education, see Angela Harris and Marjorie Shultz, *"A(nother) Critique of Pure Reason": Toward Civic Virtue in Legal Education,* 45 Stan.L.Rev. 1773 (1993).

Both Carrington and Gordon speak of the belief that "law matters." In this book, we examine the ways in which law might matter in inflicting, or rectifying, the injustices suffered by those traditionally excluded from social, economic, and political positions of privilege. The power of law in this regard is the subject of the next two excerpts.

ROBERT COVER, VIOLENCE AND THE WORD

95 Yale L.J. 1601, 1601–18 (1986).

I. Introduction: The Violence of Legal Acts

Legal interpretation takes place in a field of pain and death. This is true in several senses. Legal interpretive acts signal and occasion the imposition of violence upon others: A judge articulates her understanding of a text, and as a result, somebody loses his freedom, his property, his children, even his life. Interpretations in law also constitute justifications for violence which has already occurred or which is about to occur. When interpreters have finished their work, they frequently leave behind victims whose lives have been torn apart by these organized, social practices of violence. Neither legal interpretation nor the violence it occasions may be properly understood apart from one another. This much is obvious, though the growing literature that argues for the centrality of interpretive practices in law blithely ignores it.

Taken by itself, the word "interpretation" may be misleading. "Interpretation" suggests a social construction of an interpersonal reality through language. But pain and death have quite other implications. Indeed, pain and death destroy the world that "interpretation" calls up. That one's ability to construct interpersonal realities is destroyed by death is obvious, but in this case, what is true of death is true of pain also, for pain destroys, among other things, language itself. Elaine Scarry's brilliant analysis of pain makes this point:

> [F]or the person, in pain, so incontestably and unnegotiably present is it that "having pain" may come to be thought of as the most vibrant example of what it is to "have certainty," while for the other person it is so elusive that hearing about pain may exist as the primary model of what it is "to have doubt." Thus pain comes unshareably into our midst as at once that which cannot be denied and that which cannot be confirmed. Whatever pain achieves, it achieves in part through its unshareability, and it ensures this unshareability in part through its resistance to language.... Prolonged pain does not simply resist language but actively destroys it, bringing about an immediate reversion to a state anterior to language, to the sounds and cries a human being makes before language is learned.

The deliberate infliction of pain in order to destroy the victim's normative world and capacity to create shared realities we call torture. The interrogation that is part of torture, Scarry points out, is rarely designed to elicit information. More commonly, the torturer's interrogation is designed to demonstrate the end of the normative world of the victim—the end of what the victim values, the end of the bonds that constitute the community in which the values are grounded. Scarry thus concludes that "in compelling confession, the torturers compel the prisoner to record and objectify the fact that intense pain is world-destroying." That is why torturers almost always require betrayal—a demonstration that the victim's intangible normative world has been crushed by the material reality of pain and its extension, fear. The torturer and victim do end up creating their own terrible "world," but this world derives its meaning from being imposed upon the ashes of another. The logic of that world is complete domination, though the objective may never be realized....

II. THE ACTS OF JUDGES: INTERPRETATIONS, DEEDS AND ROLES

We begin, then, not with what the judges say, but with what they do.

The judges deal pain and death.

That is not all that they do. Perhaps that is not what they usually do. But they *do* deal death, and pain. From John Winthrop through Warren Burger they have sat atop a pyramid of violence, dealing....

In this they are different from poets, from critics, from artists. It will not do to insist on the violence of strong poetry, and strong poets. Even the violence of weak judges is utterly real—a naive but immediate reality, in need of no interpretation, no critic to reveal it. Every prisoner displays its mark. Whether or not the violence of judges is justified is not now the point—only that it exists in fact and differs from the violence that exists in literature or in the metaphoric characterizations of literary critics and philosophers. I have written elsewhere that judges of the state are jurispathic—that they kill the diverse legal traditions that compete with the State. Here, however, I am not writing of the jurispathic quality of the office, but of its homicidal potential.

The dual emphasis on the *acts* of judges and on the violence of these acts leads to consideration of three characteristics of the interpretive dimension of judicial behavior. Legal interpretation is (1) a practical activity, (2) designed to generate credible threats and actual deeds of violence, (3) in an effective way. In order to explore the unseverable connection between legal interpretation and violence, each of these three elements must be examined in turn.

A. Legal Interpretation as a Practical Activity

Legal interpretation is a form of practical wisdom. At its best it seeks to "impose *meaning* on the institution ... and then to restructure it in the light of that meaning." There is, however, a persistent chasm between thought and action. It is one thing to understand what ought to be done, quite another thing to do it. Doing entails an act of will and may require courage and perseverance. In the case of an individual's actions, we commonly think such qualities are functions of motivation, character, or psychology.

Legal interpretation is practical activity in quite another sense, however. The judicial word is a mandate for the deeds of others. Were that not the case, the practical objectives of the deliberative process could be achieved, if at all, only through more indirect and risky means. The context of a judicial utterance is institutional behavior in which others, occupying preexisting roles, can be expected to act, to implement, or otherwise to respond in a specified way to the judge's interpretation. Thus, the institutional context ties the language act of practical understanding to the physical acts of others in a predictable, though not logically necessary, way. These interpretations, then, are not only "practical," they are, themselves, practices....

B. Interpretation Within a System Designed to Generate Violence

The gulf between thought and action widens wherever serious violence is at issue, because for most of us, evolutionary, psychological, cultural and moral considerations inhibit the infliction of pain on other people. Of course, these constraints are neither absolute nor universal.

There are some deviant individuals whose behavior is inconsistent with such inhibitions. Furthermore, almost all people are fascinated and attracted by violence, even though they are at the same time repelled by it. Finally, and most important for our purposes, in almost all people social cues may overcome or suppress the revulsion to violence under certain circumstances. These limitations do not deny the force of inhibitions against violence. Indeed, both together create the conditions without which law would either be unnecessary or impossible. Were the inhibition against violence perfect, law would be unnecessary; were it not capable of being overcome through social signals, law would not be possible.

Because legal interpretation is as a practice incomplete without violence—because it depends upon the social practice of violence for its efficacy—it must be related in a strong way to the cues that operate to bypass or suppress the psycho-social mechanisms that usually inhibit people's actions causing pain and death. Interpretations which occasion violence are distinct from the violent acts they occasion. When judges interpret the law in an official context, we expect a close relationship to be revealed or established between their words and the acts that they mandate. That is, we expect the judges' words to serve as virtual triggers for action. We would not, for example, expect contemplations or deliberations on the part of jailers and wardens to interfere with the action authorized by judicial words. But such a routinization of violent behavior requires a form of organization that operates simultaneously in the domains of action and interpretation. In order to understand the violence of a judge's interpretive act, we must also understand the way in which it is transformed into a violent deed despite general resistance to such deeds; in order to comprehend the meaning of this violent deed, we must also understand in what way the judge's interpretive act authorizes and legitimates it . . . .

Persons who act within social organizations that exercise authority act violently without experiencing the normal inhibitions or the normal degree of inhibition which regulates the behavior of those who act autonomously. When judges interpret, they trigger agentic behavior within just such an institution or social organization. On one level judges may appear to be, and may in fact be, offering their understanding of the normative world to their intended audience. But on another level they are engaging a violent mechanism through which a substantial part of their audience loses its capacity to think and act autonomously.

C. *Interpretation and the Effective Organization of Violence*

A third factor separates the authorization of violence as a deliberative, interpretive exercise from the deed. Deeds of violence are rarely suffered by the victim apart from a setting of domination. That setting may be manifestly coercive and violent or it may be the product of a history of violence which conditions the expectations of the actors. The imposition of violence depends upon the satisfaction of the social preconditions for its effectiveness. Few of us are courageous or foolhardy enough to *act* violently in an uncompromisingly principled fashion without attention to the likely responses from those upon whom we would impose our wills.

If legal interpretation entails action in a field of pain and death, we must expect, therefore, to find in the act of interpretation attention to the *conditions of effective domination*. To the extent that effective domination is not present, either our understanding of the law will be adjusted so that it will require only that which can reasonably be expected from people in conditions of reprisal, resistance and revenge, or there will be a crisis of credibility. The law may come over time to bear only an uncertain relation to the institutionally implemented deeds it authorizes. . . .

D. *Legal Interpretation as Bonded Interpretation*

Legal interpretation, therefore, can never be "free"; it can never be the function of an understanding of the text or word alone. Nor can it be a simple function of what the interpreter conceives to be merely a reading of the "social text," a reading of all relevant social data. Legal interpretation must be capable of transforming itself into action; it must be capable of overcoming inhibitions against violence in order to generate its requisite deeds; it must be capable of massing a sufficient degree of violence to deter reprisal and revenge.

In order to maintain these critical links to effective violent behavior, legal interpretation must reflexively consider its own social organization. In so reflecting, the interpreter thereby surrenders something of his independence of mind and autonomy of judgment, since the legal meaning that some hypothetical Hercules (Hyporcules) might construct out of the sea of our legal and social texts is only one element in the institutional practice we call law. Coherent legal meaning is an element in legal interpretation. But it is an element potentially in tension with the need to generate effective action in a violent context. And neither effective action nor coherent meaning can be maintained, separately or together, without an entire structure of social cooperation. Thus, legal interpretation is a form of bonded interpretation, bound at once to practical application (to the deeds it implies) and to the ecology of jurisdictional roles (the conditions of effective domination). The bonds are reciprocal. For the deeds of social violence as we know them also require that they be rendered intelligible—that they be both subject to interpretation and to the specialized and constrained forms of behavior that are "roles." And the behavior within roles that we expect can neither exist without the interpretations which explain the otherwise meaningless patterns of strong action and inaction, nor be intelligible without understanding the deeds they are designed to effectuate.

Legal interpretation may be the act of judges or citizens, legislators or presidents, draft resisters or right-to-life protesters. Each kind of interpreter speaks from a distinct institutional location. Each has a differing perspective on factual and moral implications of any given understanding of the Constitution. The understanding of each will vary as roles and moral commitments vary. But considerations of word, deed, and role will always be present in some degree. The relationships among these three considerations are created by the practical, violent context of the practice of legal interpretation, and therefore constitute the most significant aspect of the legal interpretive process....

MARTHA MINOW, PARTIAL JUSTICE AND MINORITIES

in The Fate of Law 68–77 (Austin Sarat & Thomas
Kearns, eds., U.Mich. Press, 1991).

I would like to pursue the insights of either the insider and outsider narratives—and both of them together. This means recognizing that law is a set of practices and institutions situated within more than one narrative of human history and more than one social experience. Law itself should not be misunderstood to be a shared language. That would revive a myth of rational consensus that the competing narratives belie. Rather than using a legal language or a language of theory that speaks on a universal plane, my own conclusion is that I should work on legal theory by working on problems in specific contexts. According to old criteria, this would not be recognized as legal doctrine, or as jurisprudence. The challenge, then, includes resisting the temptation to seek approval according to established mores and prestige values. My theoretical understandings would be deepened by sustained looks at concrete social problems, while attending to the larger questions they open. This means pursuing a theory in practice and a theory that is at once pluralist, heterogeneous, and localist.

What do I mean by pluralist, heterogeneous, and localist? By pluralist, I mean acting on the insight that perspectives are partial by seeking out alternative views, and by conditioning assertions of any one view with deliberate efforts to see its limits from a perspective beyond itself....

By seeking pluralist understandings in these settings, I hope a judge would do more than nod blankly with the statement that my own viewpoint is partial. Instead, the judge should seek out an understanding of contrasting viewpoints, at least until glimpsing how incomprehensible her own view must be to some others. Knowing the partiality of her own knowledge, information, and normative scheme may not change the outcome in some cases, but it should make the process of decision problematic. Further, by understanding the partiality of her own view, the judge may reach different conclusions some of the time.

By heterogeneity, I mean facing up to the multiplicity of discourses and frameworks for analysis that occupy legal spaces currently.... We each can learn to craft an analysis based on deontological rights theories, another couched in the economic vocabulary of utility maximization and cost-benefit analysis, and still another that looks to symbolic meanings, textual understandings, and communal stories. Arguments that persuade a given judge may well draw on all three strands. Importantly, each framework is not reducible to the others. Breathing vitality into multiple frameworks matters because the experiences and dilemmas we articulate in legal settings are too complex and multiple to be captured in any single framework. We are moved and we move others by articulating claims and theories that resonate with prior commitments or hopes, and the discourse of law should not predetermine the range of commitments and hopes to which we can appeal. Yet, to borrow an idea from economics, I think that anyone using one framework should internalize its costs—its undervaluing of what is valued by other frameworks—rather than imposing these costs as the externalities of its use. The damage to symbolic human dignity from cost-benefit analysis, for example, should be addressed within the context of cost-benefit analysis, not left as an attack by outsiders.

But if I only explore pluralist and heterogeneous approaches to concrete social problems, there will be something unacceptably lacking from the legal theories I propose.... An understanding of the partiality of all perspectives does not make them all equally plausible or equally acceptable. Moral relativism of this sort is a mistake, not an answer.

Some say moral relativism results if we solicit and celebrate the view of those who have been excluded, degraded, or oppressed. Surely, this celebration of multiplicity topples the hierarchy that canonized one set of experiences as the norm. Yet the demand for that kind of pluralism does not and should not suspend the critique of power relationships that motivate it. When those from the margin seek tolerance and pluralism, we do not treat beliefs with indifference. We instead demand respect for difference. This is not the simple liberal commitment to tolerance either, for that approach leaves those with privilege too complacent about the comfortable place from which they are asked to tolerate or put up with those who are different. Instead, the struggle waged by the outsiders is for a process of continually dealing with difference in ways that enlarge people's understanding of the partiality of their own perspective. And while this struggle may seem a new assertion of a universal truth, I do not mean it to be so, for even this commitment to understanding the perspectives of others must remain contingent, partial, subject to challenge, and subject to change.

Given the Holocaust, Pol Pot, and other instances of genocide in recent memory, it should be hard to forget that, in ripe social circumstances, a "true belief" can mobilize people to do anything in the name of that belief. Yet we must remain equally vigilant against a kind of mutual acceptance and indifference that places oppression on an equal footing with any other human activity. For law, the problem comes in several layers. Treating a theory of legal authority as well grounded and demanding obedience may mean losing sight of the partiality of those perspectives that capture legal authority. Yet, encouraging skepticism and resistance toward legal authority may undermine a tool for redressing historical inequalities and restraints—and confuse the sense of some stopping points, some authoritative judgments, about issues of interpersonal, social, and political disagreement.

Thus, in addition to the several frameworks already visible in legal scholarship and judicial and legislative acts, I think we need to elaborate and refine what is as yet only an inchoate framework—a language we could use to describe and criticize power relations between people and between groups and also to examine the influence of social and economic structures in individual self-perception and choice.

Lawyers and judges, and anyone using legal notions, should be better equipped to articulate and evaluate the material, institutional settings that make some people marginal and some people more comfortable with society's rules and benefits. We need more, not fewer, words and ideas about these things, and we need to make legal inquiries that can challenge rather than obscure how legal notions themselves contributed to this process of dividing the marginal and the comfortable.

Finally, when I urge a legal theory that is contextual, I am arguing for concrete sites for theory. Rather than starting with abstract concepts and looking for examples or illustrations, legal theory should start with actual problems, as defined and experienced by the people living through them. . . .

A commitment to local, concrete inquiries would switch the focus from, for example, questions about the fate of law if individual judgments cannot be reconciled, or if abstract concepts, like rights, no longer seem coherent or bounded. Those concerns are too stylized to convey how they implicate and construct human experience. Centralized, governmental authority may govern people whose own normative commitments rest on incommensurate premises; people may comply, people may resist, people may live quietly with conflicts, and people may bring their conflicts into spheres of public attention and debate. We must not pretend that the law provides one comprehensive scheme that orchestrates all the legal relationships among subgroups and between the central government and each group; instead, law provides multiple languages and institutions within which to play out struggles. . . .

What I suggest here is a way to treat law as our folding tents and tools for making temporary shelters before we break-up camp and move on to the next problem. Alternatively, for those who find that metaphor too free of conflict, we should view legal institutions and legal language as terrains for struggle over situated problems. It might be more comforting to think of law as a set of right answers, or a set of trump cards to play to resolve otherwise perpetual games. But recognition of partiality, I think, demands more of us. . . . The enterprise can be put this way: can we make law a tool for helping us remake a world of distinctions so that people do not oppress one another? The inquiry can be generalized in this question: if we pursue partial justice, how can we make the instruments of a centralized legal system respect the settings where people make meaning without abandoning people to the power relations in which they find themselves? . . . Wherever you find yourself in the debates I have described, you are implicated in them. If you hang onto steady certainties, you have closed off challenges that may not

persuade you—but that mean a great deal to those who think you do not
see their perspective. If you concede that there are multiple, irreconcilable perspectives, you may feed a complacency that further entrenches
the particular perspectives that currently prevail. If you pursue the
tensions between these positions, however, and engage with the possibilities that you may not be right, you still may persuasively find some
answers quite wrong. By engaging with what surprises you, by encountering the bend of your own thought, you may move someone else to let
loose of a rigid belief; you may supply the room for another to make
room for you. You may help the partiality of justice become its virtue
rather than its hypocrisy.

Notes and Questions

1. What are the ways, suggested by Robert Cover, that law causes pain
yet appears removed from the very act of inflicting that pain?

2. Is Robert Cover's proposition that "law is violent" limited to instances of criminal punishment? Consider the following:

> Law's violence is not coextensive with law's malevolence; rather, it is
> inflicted wherever legal will is imposed on the world, wherever a legal
> edict, a judicial decision, or a legislative act cuts, wrenches, or excises
> life from its social context. So conceived, law's violence is hardly
> separable from the rule of law itself, from the deadening normalcy of
> bureaucratic abstractions and routine interpretive acts that claim for
> law a position beyond positioning and a universality made plausible only
> by the systematic privileging of some voices and silencing of others.
> Thus law's interpretive violence is presented as impersonal and even-
> handed rule following, the crushing consequence of law's inexorable will.
> Law is first implicated in violence only at the level of interpretation, in
> the cerebral effort to give voice to law and to make rules work.

Austin Sarat and Thomas Kearns, "A Journey Through Forgetting: Toward
a Jurisprudence of Violence" in The Fate of Law 210–11 (Austin Sarat &
Thomas Kearns, eds., U.Mich. Press, 1991)

3. Elizabeth Iglesias has written that the violence of law is derived not
only from the interpretative process but also from institutional arrangements which determine "*who* must be persuaded to listen to whom in the
many contexts that construct our social reality and regulate our daily lives."
*Structures of Subordination: Women of Color at the Intersection of Title VII
and the NLRA. Not!*, 28 Harv.Civ.R.–Civ.L.L.Rev. 394, 396 (1993). She
invokes "the concept of structural violence" to examine the oppression
resulting from "the socially constructed categories of race and gender." Id.
at 397.

4. Some scholars have argued that the interpretative process is, or at
least should be, neutral and objective. See, e.g. Herbert Wechsler, *Toward
Neutral Principles of Constitutional Law,* 73 Colum.L.Rev. 1, 15 (1959) ("I
put it to you that the main constituent of the judicial process is precisely
that it must be genuinely principled, resting with respect to every step that
is involved in reaching judgment on analysis and reasons quite transcending
the immediate result that is achieved.") Under such an approach, decisions

are purportedly reached independent of the judges' personal preferences, and are based on principles that apply notwithstanding the context. For a discussion and critique of that approach, *see* Erwin Chermerinsky, *Foreword: The Vanishing Constitution,* 103 Harv.L.Rev. 43 (1989).

In what ways do both Robert Cover and Martha Minow question the notion of law's objectivity and neutrality?

5. Can you recall any examples where law served as a tool for maintaining oppression? For eliminating it?

6. Do you think law can be made a tool for remaking "a world of distinctions so that people do not oppress one another?"

7. Do you see any common threads in Alice Walker's poem, bell hooks' articles, and the Robert Cover and Martha Minow excerpts?

Chapter Two

MEANINGS OF PRIVILEGE
AND POWER

A. ON A PERSONAL LEVEL

An interesting property of privilege is the way it often is invisible to its holders, while appearing sharp and well-defined to those denied it. A first step in addressing problems of inequality and unjustifiable privilege in law is learning to recognize ways privilege manifests itself, how it looks rightfully earned or as "the norm" to its holders, and how unjust and oppressive it feels to differently situated people. We begin this learning process with an exercise that should precede your reading of the subsequent text.

EXERCISE

Write a short essay or list about the privileges of each of the following: being male, being white, being middle- or upper-class, being heterosexual, and being able-bodied in the U.S. While all of us occupy race, gender, class, sexuality, age, and health/ableness identities simultaneously, try to separate the privileges attributable to each category if you can.

When you have finished your essay or list of privileges attributable to each aspect of one's identity, compare your essay with that written by someone from a different identity category than yourself.

The excerpts that follow explore some aspects of what it means to have privilege at a personal level. We begin with a story shared by Professor Alan Freeman, a law professor at Buffalo. While interweaving personal narrative, exegesis of Supreme Court opinions and statutes, and complex critical legal theories to examine the civil rights movement and civil rights law, Freeman uses the following anecdote to bring evidence of race-based privilege home to law students:

ALAN FREEMAN, RACISM, RIGHTS AND THE QUEST FOR EQUALITY OF OPPORTUNITY: A CRITICAL LEGAL ESSAY

23 Harv.C.R.–C.L.L.Rev. 295, 330–31 (1988).

I recall witnessing a revolting scene just outside my own law school building a couple of summers ago. The first day of the two-day New York bar exam had just ended and the exhausted examinees were streaming out of the building toward cars and buses to get away from our architecturally stark suburban campus. As I walked toward the parking lot, I saw a tall black man, similar in age and appearance to the other bar examinees, repeatedly saying "Excuse me" to individual passersby, only to be unanswered and treated as if he were not there at all.

What I saw was a person obviously seeking help but instead being treated as a source of fear and annoyance by others. I witnessed some eight or ten such instances before I reached him from across the wide plaza. It turned out that he was a Syracuse law graduate who was taking the bar exam in Buffalo. He had been given a ride in the morning by his aunt and uncle, with whom he was staying downtown, and they had left directions for the trip home. He was uncertain whether he had enough bus fare, since the campus bus does not go all the way downtown. I gave him a ride to make his downtown bus connection, and learned during the ten-minute trip that he was nervous, scared, alienated by Buffalo and shaken by the callous treatment inflicted by the others. I tell the story to students when they announce complacently that racism is no longer a problem.

———

In 1988, Dr. Peggy McIntosh used her experience and understanding of gender-based privilege to help her identify and analyze her own race-based privileges. Her work was ground-breaking.

PEGGY McINTOSH, WHITE PRIVILEGE AND MALE PRIVILEGE: A PERSONAL ACCOUNT OF COMING TO SEE CORRESPONDENCES THROUGH WORK IN WOMEN'S STUDIES*

Working Paper No. 189, Wellesley College Center for Research on Women, 1988.

Through work to bring materials and perspectives from Women's Studies into the rest of the curriculum, I have often noticed men's unwillingness to grant that they are overprivileged in the curriculum, even though they may grant that women are disadvantaged. Denials that amount to taboos surround the subject of advantages that men gain from women's disadvantages. These denials protect male privilege from being fully recognized, acknowledged, lessened, or ended.

* ©Peggy McIntosh, 1988. Permission to reproduce must be obtained from the author.

Thinking through unacknowledged male privilege as a phenomenon with a life of its own, I realized that since hierarchies in our society are interlocking, there was most likely a phenomenon of white privilege that was similarly denied and protected, but alive and real in its effects. As a white person, I realized I had been taught about racism as something that puts others at a disadvantage, but had been taught not to see one of its corollary aspects, white privilege, which puts me at an advantage.

I think whites are carefully taught not to recognize white privilege, as males are taught not to recognize male privilege. So I have begun in an untutored way to ask what it is like to have white privilege. This paper is a partial record of my personal observations and not a scholarly analysis. It is based on my daily experiences within my particular circumstances.

I have come to see white privilege as an invisible package of unearned assets that I can count on cashing in each day, but about which I was "meant" to remain oblivious. White privilege is like an invisible weightless knapsack of special provisions, assurances, tools, maps, guides, codebooks, passports, visas, clothes, compass, emergency gear, and blank checks.

Since I have had trouble facing white privilege, and describing its results in my life, I saw parallels here with men's reluctance to acknowledge male privilege. Only rarely will a man go beyond acknowledging that women are disadvantaged to acknowledging that men have unearned advantage, or that unearned privilege has not been good for men's development as human beings, or for society's development, or that privilege systems might ever be challenged and *changed*.

I will review here several types or layers of denial that I see at work protecting, and preventing awareness about, entrenched male privilege. Then I will draw parallels, from my own experience, with the denials that veil the facts of white privilege. Finally, I will list forty-six ordinary and daily ways in which I experience having white privilege, by contrast with my African American colleagues in the same building. This list is not intended to be generalizable. Others can make their own lists from within their own life circumstances.

Writing this paper has been difficult, despite warm receptions for the talks on which it is based.[1] For describing white privilege makes one newly accountable. As we in Women's Studies work reveal male privilege and ask men to give up some of their power, so one who writes about having white privilege must ask, "Having described it, what will I do to lessen or end it?"

The denial of men's overprivileged state takes many forms in discussions of curriculum change work. Some claim that men must be

---

1. This paper was presented at the Virginia Women's Studies Association conference in Richmond in April, 1986 and the American Educational Research Association conference in Boston in October, 1986 and discussed with two groups of participants in the Dodge Seminars for Secondary School Teachers in New York and Boston in the spring of 1987.

central in the curriculum because they have done most of what is important or distinctive in life or in civilization. Some recognize sexism in the curriculum but deny that it makes male students seem unduly important in life. Others agree that certain *individual* thinkers are male oriented but deny that there is any *systemic* tendency in disciplinary frameworks or epistemology to overempower men as a group. Those men who do grant that male privilege takes institutionalized and embedded forms are still likely to deny that male hegemony has opened doors for them personally. Virtually all men deny that male overreward alone can explain men's centrality in all the inner sanctums of our most powerful institutions. Moreover, those few who will acknowledge that male privilege systems have overempowered them usually end up doubting that we could dismantle these privilege systems. They may say they will work to improve women's status, in the society or in the university, but they can't or won't support the idea of lessening men's. In curricular terms, this is the point at which they say that they regret they cannot use any of the interesting new scholarship on women because the syllabus is full. When the talk turns to giving men less cultural room, even the most thoughtful and fair-minded of the men I know will tend to reflect, or fall back on, conservative assumptions about the inevitability of present gender relations and distributions of power, calling on precedent or sociobiology and psychobiology to demonstrate that male domination is natural and follows inevitably from evolutionary pressures. Others resort to arguments from "experience" or religion or social responsibility or wishing and dreaming.

After I realized, through faculty development work in Women's Studies, the extent to which men work from a base of unacknowledged privilege, I understood that much of their oppressiveness was unconscious. Then I remembered the frequent charges from women of color that white women whom they encounter are oppressive. I began to understand why we are justly seen as oppressive, even when we don't see ourselves that way. At the very least, obliviousness of one's privileged state can make a person or group irritating to be with. I began to count the ways in which I enjoy unearned skin privilege and have been conditioned into oblivion about its existence, unable to see that it put me "ahead" in any way, or put my people ahead, overrewarding us and yet also paradoxically damaging us, or that it could or should be changed.

My schooling gave me no training in seeing myself as an oppressor, as an unfairly advantaged person, or as a participant in a damaged culture. I was taught to see myself as an individual whose moral state depended on her individual moral will. At school, we were not taught about slavery in any depth; we were not taught to see slaveholders as damaged people. Slaves were seen as the only group at risk of being dehumanized. My schooling followed the pattern which Elizabeth Minnich has pointed out: whites are taught to think of their lives as morally neutral, normative, and average, and also ideal, so that when we work to benefit others, this is seen as work that will allow "them" to be more like "us." I think many of us know how obnoxious this attitude can be in men.

After frustration with men who would not recognize male privilege, I decided to try to work on myself at least by identifying some of the daily effects of white privilege in my life. It is crude work, at this stage, but I will give here a list of special circumstances and conditions I experience that I did not earn but that I have been made to feel are mine by birth, by citizenship, and by virtue of being a conscientious law-abiding "normal" person of goodwill. I have chosen those conditions that I think in my case *attach somewhat more to skin-color privilege* than to class, religion, ethnic status, or geographical location, though these other privileging factors are intricately intertwined. As far as I can see, my Afro–American co-workers, friends, and acquaintances with whom I come into daily or frequent contact in this particular time, place, and line of work cannot count on most of these conditions.

1. I can, if I wish, arrange to be in the company of people of my race most of the time.

2. I can avoid spending time with people whom I was trained to mistrust and who have learned to mistrust my kind or me.

3. If I should need to move, I can be pretty sure of renting or purchasing housing in an area which I can afford and in which I would want to live.

4. I can be reasonably sure that my neighbors in such a location will be neutral or pleasant to me.

5. I can go shopping alone most of the time, fairly well assured that I will not be followed or harassed by store detectives.

6. I can turn on the television or open to the front page of the paper and see people of my race widely and positively represented.

7. When I am told about our national heritage or about "civilization," I am shown that people of my color made it what it is.

8. I can be sure that my children will be given curricular materials that testify to the existence of their race.

9. If I want to, I can be pretty sure of finding a publisher for this piece on white privilege.

10. I can be fairly sure of having my voice heard in a group in which I am the only member of my race.

11. I can be casual about whether or not to listen to another woman's voice in a group in which she is the only member of her race.

12. I can go into a book shop and count on finding the writing of my race represented, into a supermarket and find the staple foods that fit with my cultural traditions, into a hairdresser's shop and find someone who can deal with my hair.

13. Whether I use checks, credit cards, or cash, I can count on my skin color not to work against the appearance that I am financially reliable.

14. I could arrange to protect our young children most of the time from people who might not like them.

15. I did not have to educate our children to be aware of systemic racism for their own daily physical protection.

16. I can be pretty sure that my children's teachers and employers will tolerate them if they fit school and workplace norms; my chief worries about them do not concern others' attitudes toward their race.

17. I can talk with my mouth full and not have people put this down to my color.

18. I can swear, or dress in secondhand clothes, or not answer letters, without having people attribute these choices to the bad morals, the poverty, or the illiteracy of my race.

19. I can speak in public to a powerful male group without putting my race on trial.

20. I can do well in a challenging situation without being called a credit to my race.

21. I am never asked to speak for all the people of my racial group.

22. I can remain oblivious to the language and customs of persons of color who constitute the world's majority without feeling in my culture any penalty for such oblivion.

23. I can criticize our government and talk about how much I fear its policies and behavior without being seen as a cultural outsider.

24. I can be reasonably sure that if I ask to talk to "the person in charge," I will be facing a person of my race.

25. If a traffic cop pulls me over or if the IRS audits my tax return, I can be sure I haven't been singled out because of my race.

26. I can easily buy posters, postcards, picture books, greeting cards, dolls, toys, and children's magazines featuring people of my race.

27. I can go home from most meetings of organizations I belong to feeling somewhat tied in, rather than isolated, out of place, outnumbered, unheard, held at a distance, or feared.

28. I can be pretty sure that an argument with a colleague of another race is more likely to jeopardize her chances for advancement than to jeopardize mine.

29. I can be fairly sure that if I argue for the promotion of a person of another race, or a program centering on race, this is not likely to cost me heavily within my present setting, even if my colleagues disagree with me.

30. If I declare there is a racial issue at hand, or there isn't a racial issue at hand, my race will lend me more credibility for either position than a person of color will have.

31. I can choose to ignore developments in minority writing and minority activist programs, or disparage them, or learn from them, but in any case, I can find ways to be more or less protected from negative consequences of any of these choices.

32. My culture gives me little fear about ignoring the perspectives and powers of people of other races.

33. I am not made acutely aware that my shape, bearing, or body odor will be taken as a reflection on my race.

34. I can worry about racism without being seen as self-interested or self-seeking.

35. I can take a job with an affirmative action employer without having my co-workers on the job suspect that I got it because of my race.

36. If my day, week, or year is going badly, I need not ask of each negative episode or situation whether it has racial overtones.

37. I can be pretty sure of finding people who would be willing to talk with me and advise me about my next steps, professionally.

38. I can think over many options, social, political, imaginative, or professional, without asking whether a person of my race would be accepted or allowed to do what I want to do.

39. I can be late to a meeting without having the lateness reflect on my race.

40. I can choose public accommodation without fearing that people of my race cannot get in or will be mistreated in the places I have chosen.

41. I can be sure that if I need legal or medical help, my race will not work against me.

42. I can arrange my activities so that I will never have to experience feelings of rejection owing to my race.

43. If I have low credibility as a leader, I can be sure that my race is not the problem.

44. I can easily find academic courses and institutions that give attention only to people of my race.

45. I can expect figurative language and imagery in all of the arts to testify to experiences of my race.

46. I can choose blemish cover or bandages in "flesh" color and have them more or less match my skin.

   I repeatedly forgot each of the realizations on this list until I wrote it down. For me, white privilege has turned out to be an elusive and fugitive subject. The pressure to avoid it is great, for in facing it I must give up the myth of meritocracy. If these things are true, this is not such a free country; one's life is not what one makes it; many doors open for certain people through no virtues of their own. These perceptions mean also that my moral condition is not what I had been led to believe. The appearance of being a good citizen rather than a troublemaker comes in large part from having all sorts of doors open automatically because of my color....

A further paralysis of nerve comes from literary silence protecting privilege. My clearest memories of finding such analysis are in Lillian Smith's unparalleled *Killers of the Dream* and Margaret Andersen's review of Karen and Mamie Fields' *Lemon Swamp*. Smith, for example, wrote about walking toward black children on the street and knowing they would step into the gutter; Andersen contrasted the pleasure that she, as a white child, took on summer driving trips to the south with Karen Fields' memories of driving in a closed car stocked with all necessities lest, in stopping, her black family should suffer "insult, or worse." Adrienne Rich also recognizes and writes about daily experiences of privilege, but in my observation, white women's writing in this area is far more often on systemic racism than on our daily lives as light-skinned women.[2]

In unpacking this invisible knapsack of white privilege, I have listed conditions of daily experience that I once took for granted, as neutral, normal, and universally available to everybody, just as I once thought of a male-focused curriculum as the neutral or accurate account that can speak for all. Nor did I think of any of these perquisites as bad for the holder. I now think that we need a more finely differentiated taxonomy of privilege, for some of these varieties are only what one would want for everyone in a just society, and others give license to be ignorant, oblivious, arrogant, and destructive. Before proposing some more finely tuned categorization, I will make some observations about the general effects of these conditions on my life and expectations.

In this potpourri of examples, some privileges make me feel at home in the world. Others allow me to escape penalties or dangers that others suffer. Through some, I escape fear, anxiety, insult, injury, or a sense of not being welcome, not being real. Some keep me from having to hide, to be in disguise, to feel sick or crazy, to negotiate each transaction from the position of being an outsider or, within my group, a person who is suspected of having too close links with a dominant culture. Most keep me from having to be angry.

I see a pattern running through the matrix of white privilege, a pattern of assumptions that were passed on to me as a white person. There was one main piece of cultural turf; it was my own turf, and I was among those who could control the turf. I could measure up to the cultural standards and take advantage of the many options I saw around me to make what the culture would call a success of my life. *My skin*

2. Andersen, Margaret, "Race and the Social Science Curriculum: A Teaching and Learning Discussion." *Radical Teacher,* November, 1984, pp. 17–20. Smith, Lillian, *Killers of the Dream*, New York, 1949.

color was an asset for any move I was educated to want to make. I could think of myself as "belonging" in major ways and of making social systems work for me. I could freely disparage, fear, neglect, or be oblivious to anything outside of the dominant cultural forms. Being of the main culture, I could also criticize it fairly freely. My life was reflected back to me frequently enough so that I felt, with regard to my race, if not to my sex, like one of the real people.

Whether through the curriculum or in the newspaper, the television, the economic system, or the general look of people in the streets, I received daily signals and indications that my people counted and that others *either didn't exist or must be trying, not very successfully, to be like people of my race.* I was given cultural permission not to hear voices of people of other races or a tepid cultural tolerance for hearing or acting on such voices. I was also raised not to suffer seriously from anything that darker-skinned people might say about my group, "protected," though perhaps I should more accurately say *prohibited,* through the habits of my economic class and social group, from living in racially mixed groups or being reflective about interactions between people of differing races.

In proportion as my racial group was being made confident, comfortable, and oblivious, other groups were likely being made unconfident, uncomfortable, and alienated. Whiteness protected me from many kinds of hostility, distress, and violence, which I was being subtly trained to visit in turn upon people of color.

For this reason, the word "privilege" now seems to me misleading. Its connotations are too positive to fit the conditions and behaviors which "privilege systems" produce. We usually think of privilege as being a favored state, whether earned, or conferred by birth or luck. School graduates are reminded they are privileged and urged to use their (enviable) assets well. The word "privilege" carries the connotation of being something everyone must want. Yet some of the conditions I have described here work to systemically overempower certain groups. Such privilege simply *confers dominance,* gives permission to control, because of one's race or sex. The kind of privilege that gives license to some people to be, at best, thoughtless and, at worst, murderous should not continue to be referred to as a desirable attribute. Such "privilege" may be widely desired without being in any way beneficial to the whole society.

Moreover, though "privilege" may confer power, it does not confer moral strength. Those who do not depend on conferred dominance have traits and qualities that may never develop in those who do. Just as Women's Studies courses indicate that women survive their political circumstances to lead lives that hold the human race together, so "underprivileged" people of color who are the world's majority have survived their oppression and lived survivors' lives from which the white global minority can and must learn. In some groups, those dominated have actually become strong through *not* having all of these unearned advantages, and this gives them a great deal to teach the others. Members of so-called privileged groups can seem foolish, ridiculous, infantile, or dangerous by contrast.

I want, then, to distinguish between earned strength and unearned power conferred systemically. Power from unearned privilege can look like strength when it is, in fact, permission to escape or to dominate. But not all of the privileges on my list are inevitably damaging. Some, like the expectation that neighbors will be decent to you, or that your race will not count against you in court, should be the norm in a just society and should be considered as the entitlement of everyone. Others, like the privilege not to listen to less powerful people, distort the humanity of the holders as well as the ignored groups. Still others, like finding one's staple foods everywhere, may be a function of being a member of a numerical majority in the population. Others have to do with not having to labor under pervasive negative stereotyping and mythology.

We might at least start by distinguishing between positive advantages that we can work to spread, to the point where they are not advantages at all but simply part of the normal civic and social fabric, and negative types of advantage that unless rejected will always reinforce our present hierarchies. For example, the positive "privilege" of belonging, the feeling that one belongs within the human circle, as Native Americans say, fosters development and should not be seen as privilege for a few. It is, let us say, an entitlement that none of us should have to earn; ideally it is an *unearned entitlement*. At present, since only a few have it, it is an *unearned advantage* for them. The negative "privilege" that gave me cultural permission not to take darker-skinned Others seriously can be seen as arbitrarily conferred dominance and should not be desirable for anyone. This paper results from a process of coming to see that some of the power that I originally saw as attendant on being a human being in the United States consisted in *unearned advantage* and *conferred dominance,* as well as other kinds of special circumstance not universally taken for granted.

In writing this paper I have also realized that white identity and status (as well as class identity and status) give me considerable power to choose whether to broach this subject and its trouble. I can pretty well decide whether to disappear and avoid and not listen and escape the dislike I may engender in other people through this essay, or interrupt, answer, interpret, preach, correct, criticize, and control to some extent what goes on in reaction to it. Being white, I am given considerable power to escape many kinds of danger or penalty as well as to choose which risks I want to take.

There is an analogy here, once again, with Women's Studies. Our male colleagues do not have a great deal to lose in supporting Women's Studies, but they do not have a great deal to lose if they oppose it either. They simply have the power to decide whether to commit themselves to more equitable distributions of power. They will probably feel few penalties whatever choice they make; they do not seem, in any obvious short-term sense, the ones at risk, though they and we are all at risk because of the behaviors that have been rewarded in them.

Through Women's Studies work I have met very few men who are truly distressed about systemic, unearned male advantage and conferred dominance. And so one question for me and others like me is whether we will be like them, or whether we will get truly distressed, even outraged, about unearned race advantage and conferred dominance and if so, what we will do to lessen them. In any case, we need to do more work in identifying how they actually affect our daily lives. We need more down-to-earth writing by people about these taboo subjects. We need more understanding of the ways in which white "privilege" damages white people, for these are not the same ways in which it damages the victimized. Skewed white psyches are an inseparable part of the picture, though I do not want to confuse the kinds of damage done to the holders of special assets and to those who suffer the deficits. Many, perhaps most, of our white students in the United States think that racism doesn't affect them because they are not people of color; they do not see "whiteness" as a racial identity. Many men likewise think that Women's Studies does not bear on their own existences because they are not female; they do not see themselves as having gendered identities. Insisting on the universal "effects" of "privilege" systems, then, becomes one of our chief tasks, and being more explicit about the *particular* effects in particular contexts is another. Men need to join us in this work.

In addition, since race and sex are not the only advantaging systems at work, we need to similarly examine the daily experience of having age advantage, or ethnic advantage, or physical ability, or advantage related to nationality, religion, or sexual orientation. Professor Marnie Evans suggested to me that in many ways the list I made also applies directly to heterosexual privilege. This is a still more taboo subject than race privilege: the daily ways in which heterosexual privilege makes some persons comfortable or powerful, providing supports, assets, approvals, and rewards to those who live or expect to live in heterosexual pairs. Unpacking that content is still more difficult, owing to the deeper imbeddedness of heterosexual advantage and dominance and stricter taboos surrounding these.

But to start such an analysis I would put this observation from my own experience: The fact that I live under the same roof with a man triggers all kinds of societal assumptions about my worth, politics, life, and values and triggers a host of unearned advantages and powers. After recasting many elements from the original list I would add further observations like these:

1. My children do not have to answer questions about why I live with my partner (my husband).

2. I have no difficulty finding neighborhoods where people approve of our household.

3. Our children are given texts and classes that implicitly support our kind of family unit and do not turn them against my choice of domestic partnership.

4. I can travel alone or with my husband without expecting embarrassment or hostility in those who deal with us.

5. Most people I meet will see my marital arrangements as an asset to my life or as a favorable comment on my likability, my competence, or my mental health.

6. I can talk about the social events of a weekend without fearing most listeners' reactions.

7. I will feel welcomed and "normal" in the usual walks of public life, institutional and social.

8. In many contexts, I am seen as "all right" in daily work on women because I do not live chiefly with women.

Difficulties and dangers surrounding the task of finding parallels are many. Since racism, sexism, and heterosexism are not the same, the advantages associated with them should not be seen as the same. In addition, it is hard to isolate aspects of unearned advantage that derive chiefly from social class, economic class, race, religion, region, sex, or ethnic identity. The oppressions are both distinct and interlocking, as the Combahee River Collective Statement of 1977 continues to remind us eloquently.[3]

One factor seems clear about all of the interlocking oppressions. They take both active forms that we can see and embedded forms that members of the dominant group are taught not to see. In my class and place, I did not see myself as racist because I was taught to recognize racism only in individual acts of meanness by members of my group, never in invisible systems conferring racial dominance on my group from birth. Likewise, we are taught to think that sexism or heterosexism is carried on only through intentional, individual acts of discrimination, meanness, or cruelty, rather than in invisible systems conferring unsought dominance on certain groups. Disapproving of the systems won't be enough to change them. I was taught to think that racism could end if white individuals changed their attitudes; many men think sexism can be ended by individual changes in daily behavior toward women. But a man's sex provides advantage for him whether or not he approves of the way in which dominance has been conferred on his group. A "white" skin in the United States opens many doors for whites whether or not we approve of the way dominance has been conferred on us. Individual acts can palliate, but cannot end, these problems. To redesign social systems, we need first to acknowledge their colossal unseen dimensions. The silences and denials surrounding privilege are the key political tool here. They keep the thinking about equality or equity incomplete,

3. "A Black Feminist Statement," The Combahee River Collective, pp. 13–22 in Hull, Scott, Smith, eds., *All the Women Are White, All the Blacks Are Men, But Some of Us Are Brave: Black Women's Studies.* The Feminist Press, 1982.

protecting unearned advantage and conferred dominance by making these taboo subjects. Most talk by whites about equal opportunity seems to me now to be about equal opportunity to try to get into a position of dominance while denying that *systems* of dominance exist.

Obliviousness about white advantage, like obliviousness about male advantage, is kept strongly inculturated in the United States so as to maintain the myth of meritocracy, the myth that democratic choice is equally available to all. Keeping most people unaware that freedom of confident action is there for just a small number of people props up those in power and serves to keep power in the hands of the same groups that have most of it already. Though systemic change takes many decades, there are pressing questions for me and I imagine for some others like me if we raise our daily consciousness on the perquisites of being light-skinned. What will we do with such knowledge? As we know from watching men, it is an open question whether we will choose to use unearned advantage to weaken invisible privilege systems and whether we will use any of our arbitrarily awarded power to try to reconstruct power systems on a broader base.

Notes and Questions

1. Have you experienced events similar to the one that Freeman observed? If you were the recipient of the treatment received by the bar examinee, in what ways would the daily or cumulative effect of those experiences affect your ability to succeed?

2. Did the essay or list of privileges you created in response to the exercise address the same kinds of concerns that McIntosh did? What did she leave out that is important to you? Did she cause you to understand notions of privilege differently? Should we even use the term "privilege" or is that too loaded, as McIntosh suggests?

3. Few could ever equal poet and essayist Audre Lorde's way with words as she describes the race-based differences of privilege between African–American and white women: "Some problems we share as women, some we do not. You fear your children will grow up to join the patriarchy and testify against you, we fear our children will be dragged from a car and shot down in the street, and you will turn your backs upon the reasons they are dying." Audre Lorde, Age, Race, Class, and Sex: Women Redefining Difference, in Sister/Outsider 119 (Crossing Press, 1984).

4. White privilege. Cheryl Harris explains how the law constructs whiteness as property, with all the concomitant privileges or rights that accompany property. Cheryl Harris, *Whiteness as Property,* 106 Harv.L.Rev. 1709 (1993). Neil Gotanda asks his readers to interrogate whiteness in his powerful article about the way whiteness is privileged in our notion of a colorblind constitution. Neil Gotanda, *A Critique of "Our Constitution is Colorblind,"* 44 Stan.L.Rev. 1 (1991). In the next two excerpts, Barbara Flagg discusses the transparency of white privilege and Patricia Williams reveals the functioning of white and male privilege through a story from her own experience.

BARBARA FLAGG, "WAS BLIND, BUT NOW I SEE": WHITE RACE CONSCIOUSNESS AND THE RE-QUIREMENT OF DISCRIMINATORY INTENT

91 Mich.L.Rev. 953, 970–3 (1993).

White people externalize race. For most whites, most of the time, to think or speak about race is to think or speak about people of color, or perhaps, at times, to reflect on oneself (or other whites) in relation to people of color. But we tend not to think of ourselves or our racial cohort as racially distinctive. Whites' "consciousness" of whiteness is predominantly unconsciousness of whiteness. We perceive and interact with other whites as individuals who have no significant racial characteristics. In the same vein, the white person is unlikely to see or describe himself in racial terms, perhaps in part because his white peers do not regard him as racially distinctive. Whiteness is a transparent quality when whites interact with whites in the absence of people of color. Whiteness attains opacity, becomes apparent to the white mind, only in relation to, and contrast with, the "color" of nonwhites.

I do not mean to claim that white people are oblivious to the race of other whites. Race is undeniably a powerful determinant of social status and so is always noticed, in a way that eye color, for example, may not be. However, whites' social dominance allows us to relegate our own racial specificity to the realm of the subconscious. Whiteness is the racial norm. In this culture the black person, not the white, is the one who is different. The black, not the white, is racially distinctive. Once an individual is identified as white, his distinctively racial characteristics need no longer be conceptualized in racial terms; he becomes effectively raceless in the eyes of other whites. Whiteness is always a salient personal characteristic, but once identified, it fades almost instantaneously from white consciousness into transparency.

The best "evidence" for the pervasiveness of the transparency phenomenon will be the white reader's own experience: critically assessing our habitual ways of thinking about ourselves and about other white people should bring transparency into full view. The questions that follow may provide some direction for the reader's reflections.

In what situations do you describe yourself as white? Would you be likely to include white on a list of three adjectives that describe you? Do you think about your race as a factor in the way other whites treat you? For example, think about the last time some white clerk or salesperson treated you deferentially, or the last time the first taxi to come along stopped for you. Did you think, "That wouldn't have happened if I weren't white"? Are you conscious of yourself as white when you find yourself in a room occupied only by white people? What if there are people of color present? What if the room is mostly nonwhite?

Do you attribute your successes or failures in life to your whiteness? Do you reflect on the ways your educational and occupational opportunities have been enhanced by your whiteness? What about the life courses of others? In your experience, at the time of Justice Souter's nomination, how much attention did his race receive in conversations among whites about his abilities and prospects for confirmation? Did you or your white acquaintances speculate on the ways his whiteness might have contributed to his success, how his race may have affected his character and personality, or how his whiteness might pre-dispose him to a racially skewed perspective on legal issues?

If your lover or spouse is white, how frequently do you reflect on that fact? Do you think of your white friends as your white friends, other than in contrast with your friends who are not white? Do you try to understand the ways your shared whiteness affects the interactions between yourself and your white partner, friends, and acquaintances? For example, perhaps you have become aware of the absence of people of color on some occasion. Did you move beyond that moment of recognition to consider how the group's uniform whiteness affected its interactions, agenda, process, or decisions? Do you inquire about the ways white persons you know have dealt with the fact, and privilege, of their whiteness?

PATRICIA WILLIAMS, THE ALCHEMY OF RACE AND RIGHTS

146–148 (Harv.U.Press, 1991).

Some time ago, Peter Gabel and I taught a contracts class together. (He was one of the first to bring critical theory to legal analysis and so is considered a "founder" of Critical Legal Studies.) Both recent transplants from California to New York, each of us hunted for apartments in between preparing for class. Inevitably, I suppose, we got into a discussion of trust and distrust as factors in bargain relations. It turned out that Peter had handed over a $900 deposit in cash, with no lease, no exchange of keys, and no receipt, to strangers with whom he had no ties other than a few moments of pleasant conversation. He said he didn't need to sign a lease because it imposed too much formality. The handshake and the good vibes were for him indicators of trust more binding than a form contract. At the time I told Peter he was mad, but his faith paid off. His sublessors showed up at the appointed time, keys in hand, to welcome him in. There was absolutely nothing in my experience to prepare me for such a happy ending. (In fact I remain convinced that, even if I were of a mind to trust a lessor with this degree of informality, things would not have worked out so successfully for me: many Manhattan lessors would not have trusted a black person enough to let me in the door in the first place, paperwork, references, and credit check notwithstanding.)

I, meanwhile, had friends who found me an apartment in a building they owned. In my rush to show good faith and trustworthiness, I signed a detailed, lengthily negotiated, finely printed lease firmly establishing me as the ideal arm's-length transactor.

As Peter and I discussed our experiences, I was struck by the similarity of what each of us was seeking, yet with such polar approaches. We both wanted to establish enduring relationships with the people in whose houses we would be living; we both wanted to enhance trust of ourselves and to allow whatever closeness was possible. This similarity of desire, however, could not reconcile our very different relations to the tonalities of law. Peter, for example, appeared to be extremely self-conscious of his power potential (either real or imagistic) as white or male or lawyer authority figure. He therefore seemed to go to some lengths to overcome the wall that image might impose. The logical ways of establishing some measure of trust between strangers were an avoidance of power and a preference for informal processes generally.

On the other hand, I was raised to be acutely conscious of the likelihood that no matter what degree of professional I am, people will greet and dismiss my black femaleness as unreliable, untrustworthy, hostile, angry, powerless, irrational, and probably destitute. Futility and despair are very real parts of my response. So it helps me to clarify boundary; to show that I can speak the language of lease is my way of enhancing trust of me in my business affairs. As black, I have been given by this society a strong sense of myself as already too familiar, personal, subordinate to white people. I am still evolving from being treated as three-fifths of a human, a subpart of the white estate. I grew up in a neighborhood where landlords would not sign leases with their poor black tenants, and demanded that rent be paid in cash; although superficially resembling Peter's transaction, such informality in most white-on-black situations signals distrust, not trust. Unlike Peter, I am still engaged in a struggle to set up transactions at arm's length, as legitimately commercial, and to portray myself as a bargainer of separate worth, distinct power, sufficient *rights* to manipulate commerce.

Peter, I speculate, would say that a lease or any other formal mechanism would introduce distrust into his relationships and he would suffer alienation, leading to the commodification of his being and the degradation of his person to property. For me, in contrast, the lack of formal relation to the other would leave me estranged. It would risk a figurative isolation from that creative commerce by which I may be recognized as whole, by which I may feed and clothe and shelter myself, by which I may be seen as equal—even if I am stranger. For me, stranger-stranger relations are better than stranger-chattel....

———

Nowhere are stories about wealth and class-based privilege more poignant than when we compare children's lives. Journalist Alex Kotlowitz introduces us to Pharoah and Lafeyette Rivers, pre-teen and young teenage boys who were growing up in the Henry Horner Homes public housing complex in Chicago in the mid-to-late 1980s:

ALEX KOTLOWITZ, THERE ARE NO CHILDREN HERE

8–10, 12–14, 17–18, 26–28, 43–50 (Doubleday, 1991).

THE CHILDREN called home "Hornets" or, more frequently, "the projects" or, simply, the "jects" (pronounced *jets*). Pharoah called it "the graveyard." But they never referred to it by its full name: the Governor Henry Horner Homes.

Nothing here, the children would tell you, was as it should be. Lafeyette and Pharoah lived at 1920 West Washington Boulevard, even though their high-rise sat on Lake Street. Their building had no enclosed lobby; a dark tunnel cut through the middle of the building, and the wind and strangers passed freely along it. Those tenants who received public aid had their checks sent to the local currency exchange, since the building's first-floor mailboxes had all been broken into. And since darkness engulfed the building's corridors, even in the daytime, the residents always carried flashlights, some of which had been handed out by a local politician during her campaign.

Summer, too, was never as it should be. It had become a season of duplicity.

On June 13, [1985] . . . Lafeyette celebrated his twelfth birthday. Under the gentle afternoon sun, yellow daisies poked through the cracks in the sidewalk as children's bright faces peered out from behind their windows. Green leaves clothed the cottonwoods, and pastel cotton shirts and shorts, which had sat for months in layaway, clothed the children. And like the fresh buds on the crabapple trees, the children's spirits blossomed with the onset of summer.

Lafeyette and his nine-year-old cousin Dede danced across the worn lawn outside their building, singing the lyrics of an L.L. Cool J rap, their small hips and spindly legs moving in rhythm. The boy and girl were on their way to a nearby shopping strip, where Lafeyette planned to buy radio headphones with $8.00 he had received as a birthday gift.

Suddenly, gunfire erupted. The frightened children fell to the ground. "Hold your head down!" Lafeyette snapped, as he covered Dede's head with her pink nylon jacket. If he hadn't physically re-strained her, she might have sprinted for home, a dangerous action when the gangs started warring. "Stay down," he ordered the trembling girl.

The two lay pressed to the beaten grass for half a minute, until the shooting subsided. Lafeyette held Dede's hand as they cautiously crawled through the dirt toward home. When they finally made it inside, all but fifty cents of Lafeyette's birthday money had trickled from his pockets.

Lafeyette's summer opened the way it would close, with gunshots. For Lafeyette and Pharoah, these few months were to be a rickety bridge to adolescence.

If the brothers had one guidepost in their young lives these few months, though, it was their mother, LaJoe. They depended on her; she depended on them. The boys would do anything for their mother.

A shy, soft-spoken woman, LaJoe was known for her warmth and generosity, not only to her own children but to her children's friends. Though she received Aid to Families with Dependent Children, neighbors frequently knocked on her door to borrow a can of soup or a cup of flour. She always obliged. LaJoe had often mothered children who needed advice or comforting. Many young men and women still called her "Mom." She let so many people through her apartment, sometimes just to use the bathroom, that she hid the toilet paper in the kitchen because it had often been stolen. . . .

To LaJoe, the neighborhood had become a black hole. She could more easily recite what wasn't there than what was. There were no banks, only currency exchanges, which charged customers up to $8.00 for every welfare check cashed. There were no public libraries, movie theaters, skating rinks, or bowling alleys to entertain the neighborhood's children. For the infirm, there were two neighborhood clinics, the Mary Thompson Hospital and the Miles Square Health Center, both of which teetered on the edge of bankruptcy and would close by the end of 1989. Yet the death rate of newborn babies exceeded infant mortality rates in a number of Third World countries, including Chile, Costa Rica, Cuba, and Turkey. And there was no rehabilitation center, though drug abuse was rampant.

According to a 1980 profile of the Twenty-seventh Ward—a political configuration drawn, ironically, in the shape of a gun and including both Henry Horner and Rockwell Gardens, a smaller but no less forbidding public housing complex—60,110 people lived here, 88 percent of them black, 46 percent of them below the poverty level. It was an area so impoverished that when Mother Teresa visited it in 1982, she assigned nuns from her Missionaries of Charity to work at Henry Horner. They had set up a soup kitchen, a shelter for women and children, and an afterschool program. Where there used to be thirteen social service agencies there were now only three: the Missionaries of Charity, the Boys Club, and the Chicago Commons Association. The latter two provided recreational activities as well as tutoring, counseling, and day care, but they had limited funds. A Chicago Commons' program called Better Days for Youth targeted children under thirteen who were having problems in school or with the police, but there was money to serve only twenty-eight children at a time. . . .

Her three oldest children, to whom she felt she'd given everything she could, had all disappointed her. All had dropped out of school. All had been in jail at least once. All had been involved with drugs. The oldest, LaShawn, a slender twenty-year-old, was so delicately featured some called her "China Doll." She worked as a prostitute from time to time to support her drug habit. The next oldest, nineteen-year-old Paul, named after his father, had served time in an Indiana prison for burglary. Terence, now seventeen, had been the most troublesome problem for LaJoe and, because of their extraordinary closeness, her biggest disappointment. He began selling drugs at the age of eleven and had been in and out, usually in, trouble with the law ever since.

LaJoe also had a set of four-year-old triplets: Timothy, Tiffany, and Tammie. The two girls so resembled each other that not even their father could tell them apart.

All eight children had the same father, Paul, to whom LaJoe had been married for seventeen years. But the two had long ago fallen out of love. He lived at home only sporadically.

LaJoe wanted it to be different for Lafeyette and Pharoah, different from the way it had been for her three oldest children and different from the way it had been for her. . . .

Lafeyette had promised his mother he wouldn't let anything happen to Pharoah. But for a brief moment, he thought he had lost him.

Three days after Lafeyette's birthday, gunfire once again filled the air. It was two-thirty in the afternoon; school had just let out. As Lafeyette and his mother hustled the triplets onto the floor of the apartment's narrow hallway, a drill they now followed almost instinctually, they caught glimpses through the windows of young gunmen waving their pistols about. One youth toted a submachine gun.

The dispute had started when two rival drug gangs fired at each other from one high-rise to another.

From his first-floor apartment, Lafeyette, who had left his fifth-grade class early that day, watched hopefully for Pharoah as the children poured out of the Henry Suder Elementary School, just a block away. Panicking, many of the youngsters ran directly toward the gunfire. Lafeyette and his mother screamed at the children to turn back. But they kept coming, clamoring for the shelter of their homes.

Lafeyette finally spotted his brother, first running, then walking, taking cover behind trees and fences. But then he lost sight of him. "Mama, lemme go get him. Lemme go," Lafeyette begged. He was afraid that Pharoah would run straight through the gunfire. Pharoah would later say he had learned to look both ways and that's why he'd started walking. "My mama told me when you hear the shooting, first to walk because you don't know where the bullets are coming," he explained. LaJoe refused Lafeyette's request to let him go after his brother. She couldn't even go herself. The guns kept crackling.

Lafeyette's friend James, who was cowering behind a nearby tree, sprinted for the Riverses' apartment. Pharoah saw him and ran, too. The two frantically pounded with their fists on the metal door. "Let us in!" James wailed. "Let us in! It's James and Pharoah!" James's heart was beating so hard that he could hear it above the commotion. But with all the noise, no one heard their frenzied pleas, and the two ran to a friend's apartment upstairs.

Meanwhile, the police, who at first thought they were the targets of the shooting, had taken cover in their cars and in the building's breezeway. Passersby lay motionless on the ground, protected by parked vehicles and a snow-cone vending stand. Then, as suddenly as it began, the battle ended. No one, amazingly, had been hurt. Lafeyette learned later that one errant bullet pierced a friend's third-floor window with such force that it cut through a closet door and lodged in the cinder-block wall.

The police made no arrests. And when a reporter called the police department's central headquarters the next day, he was told that there was no record of the shoot-out.

But Lafeyette knew. So did Pharoah. . . .

Inside their apartment's hallway, Lafeyette and Pharoah huddled on the floor, sweating in the early July heat. Pharoah shook with each gun pop, his big eyes darting nervously from one end of the long hallway to the other. He clutched a garbage bag filled with aluminum cans he'd collected; his small body was curled up against the security of the cool concrete wall.

The muscles in Lafeyette's face tensed. He had his hands full, watching over Pharoah and the triplets. The young ones knew enough to stay in the windowless corridor away from possible stray bullets, but they chattered and fought until Tiffany, too restless to sit still for long, stood up. Lafeyette shoved her back down.

"We wanna go," whined Tiffany.

"Be quiet," admonished her brother. "You crazy?"

The narrow hall of their four-bedroom apartment had become their fallout shelter. Stray bullets had zipped through their apartment before, once leaving two holes the size of nickels in the olive-green living room curtains. Another time a bullet found its way into the hallway; it had traveled through a bedroom window and the bedroom door, missing Terence by inches. The children now knew enough to sit away from the doorways.

The five children squatted on the musty floor long after the shooting subsided. LaJoe, who huddled with them, could sit still no longer. Wearing a T-shirt that read WIPE OUT GRAFFITI, she walked into the kitchen and began to sweep the floors. Cleaning house was the only way she could clear her mind, to avoid thinking about what might happen or what might have been. It was cathartic in demanding focus and concentration. She scrubbed and washed and rearranged furniture, particularly when things got tense—with family problems, shootings, and deaths. The kids knew to stay out of her way, except for Lafeyette, who, like his mother, also found cleaning a useful distraction.

"Lemme help you," he begged, still sitting by the wall. "You figuring to start cleaning up 'cause you upset. You figuring to start cleaning up." LaJoe didn't hear him. "Mama, let me help you. Ain't nobody gonna get killed out there today."

"Stay there, Lafie. Someone's gotta watch the triplets," LaJoe said.

Lafeyette shrugged, but resigned to his duties, he slithered down the wall, resting on the floor as he kept the triplets in check and watched his mother work.

For LaJoe, cleaning the apartment seemed nearly hopeless. The apartment never looked perfectly neat and orderly: a chair always faced in the wrong direction or a rug's edge curled up or under itself. Eight people lived in the apartment—LaJoe, her five youngest children, and the two older brothers, Terence and Paul. It swelled to nine if the children's father stayed over. He would sleep on the couch or, on occasion, in the double bed with the triplets. A stack of food-caked dishes, waiting to be washed, often filled the kitchen sink, or the plastic garbage container overflowed with leftovers and paper. Roaches were everywhere. Even when the housing authority sprayed, the roaches came back. Once a small colony of them took refuge from the pesticides in a small portable radio that belonged to one of the older children. The insects were discovered days later, thriving. Maggots nested in the building, mostly by the undersized incinerator, which overflowed with garbage. . . .

But the apartment's two bathrooms were in the worst shape of all. Neither had a window, and the fans atop the building, which had provided much needed air circulation, had been stolen. In the first bathroom, a horrible stench, suggesting raw, spoiled meat, periodically rose from the toilet. On such days, LaJoe and the family simply avoided using that bathroom. Sometimes she would pour ammonia in the toilet to mitigate the smell. LaJoe had heard rumors that the previous tenants had performed abortions there, and she attributed the smell to dead fetuses.

The second bathroom housed the family's one bathtub. There was no shower, a luxury the children had never experienced. The tub doubled as a clothes washer, since the building's laundry was long ago abandoned, and the closest one was now a mile away. The tub's faucet couldn't be turned off. A steady stream of scalding hot water cascaded into the tub day and night. The boys had learned to sleep through the noise, but the constant splashing drove LaJoe batty. She had considered muffling it by placing a towel under the faucet, but then she realized that the bath would overflow. Instead, she used the towel to wedge shut the bathroom door, which was missing a knob. . . .

BIRD LEG LOVED DOGS. And for that reason, Lafeyette loved Bird Leg. His real name was Calvin Robinson, and though he was three years older than Lafeyette, he let the younger boy tag along with him, in part because he had few friends. The older boys made fun of his obsession with dogs; the younger ones seemed to understand it.

Bird Leg and Lafeyette hunted for German shepherds, mutts, and even pit bulls in the small, fenced-in back yards of the Hispanic and white neighborhoods just north of the housing project. Ordinarily, the dogs growled and fought with Lafeyette and other strangers, but Bird

Leg could communicate with them in ways the other children found uncanny. As he climbed into the back yards, he talked to them, consoled them, cajoled them, lured them, until they sidled up to him, drooling on their newfound friend. Then he unchained them, lifted them over the yard fence, and brought them home.

"The dogs would always come with him," recalls one boy, with a combination of amazement and respect. "He had more dogs than he did friends."

With Lafeyette's assistance, Bird Leg kept his assortment of canines—some stolen, some strays, some raised from birth—in an abandoned garage catty-corner from Lafeyette's building. Bird Leg often got down on his hands and knees to speak to his companions. Sometimes he kissed them on their sloppy chops, a practice the other children shook their heads at in disbelief. A few nights a week, Bird Leg scrounged through the trash bins behind the nearby Kentucky Fried Chicken, and collected half-finished meals to feed his pets. Lafeyette often helped.

Bird Leg occasionally spent the night with his animals in the worn, leaning garage, huddling among them for warmth. On one unusually cold fall night, Bird Leg, only twelve at the time, built a fire by the garage door, fueling it with cardboard and rags. The heat, he hoped, would warm his shivering friends. Instead, the old wooden building, without much coaxing, quickly caught fire and burned to the ground. The police brought Bird Leg to his mother, who, though angry, couldn't help laughing at her son's misguided intentions. It was the first of what were to be many brushes with the law.

As Bird Leg got older, he became involved with the Vice Lords, and he and Lafeyette grew apart. Lafeyette was too young and too wary to join the gangs, but he cherished all that Bird Leg had taught him about dogs. And he missed him.

Bird Leg, his mother suspects, sought protection from the gang in the same way he sought love from his dogs. Jimmie Lee, said his mother, had become like a big brother, though Bird Leg didn't run drugs for him. In fact, many of Lee's older workers didn't even know Bird Leg. Also, a close relative was a Vice Lord, which meant that Bird Leg, who lived on the western edge of Horner, Disciples' territory, frequently had to withstand a beating just to enter his building. Uncles' and cousins' associations with a particular gang can mark children too young to have chosen their own affiliation.

As a teenager, Bird Leg became increasingly reckless and hard-headed. By the age of fourteen, he had for all intents and purposes dropped out of school. Friends say he would sometimes borrow a shotgun from a friend and randomly shoot at Disciples, a practice not uncommon among the very young gang members. He also started raising his pit bulls to fight. His favorite was a light brown muscular terrier named Red. "I was scared of that dog," Alberta Robinson said later. "I once went to hit Bird Leg for something he did and that dog just about bit me." The police eventually confiscated the starving and scarred terrier; Bird Leg had used it to threaten an officer.

Bird Leg had always lived on the edge and, indeed, earned his nickname when at the age of four he chased a tennis ball into a busy street and was struck by a speeding, drunk driver. The doctors had to insert pins in one knee and ankle. When the chest-high cast came off after many weeks, his leg was so thin and fragile-looking that his grandmother started calling him Bird Leg.

In the summer of 1986, while shooting dice with some friends, he was approached by a man with a shotgun demanding his money, and Bird Leg, in his youthful defiance, ran. The man emptied a cartridge of buckshot into Bird Leg's shoulder. That incident, added to the intensifying war between the gangs, caused his mother to move her family into an apartment on the city's far north side. But, as is often the case when families move, Bird Leg and his brothers kept returning to Horner to visit friends.

Sometimes at Henry Horner you can almost smell the arrival of death. It is the odor of foot-deep pools of water that, formed from draining fire hydrants, become fetid in the summer sun. It is the stink of urine puddles in the stairwell corners and of soiled diapers dumped in the grass. It is the stench of a maggot-infested cat carcass lying in a vacant apartment and the rotting food in the overturned trash bins. It is, in short, the collected scents of summer.

In mid-August of the summer of 1987, the Vice Lords and their rivals reached a temporary truce. Because of the season's violence, the police had increased their presence at Horner. The gangs knew that more police would only disrupt their drug transactions, so they agreed among themselves to stop, in their own word, "clowning." But for young members like Bird Leg, such business acumen seemed at odds with what had become almost instinctual for young gang members: Vice Lords got along with neither Gangster Stones nor Disciples. Truce or no truce.

On a Thursday night late in August, a rival gang member shot Bird Leg in the arm with buckshot. After being treated at the hospital, he joked with his older brother and cousin that if he were to die he wanted to be buried in his white jogging suit. They laughed and told him they would oblige him.

The next evening, August 21, Bird Leg, despite his mother's protestations, left his north side apartment to visit friends at Horner. As he sat in the late day's heat and watched two friends play basketball, a group of young Disciples started taunting him, tossing bricks and bottles at his feet. His thirteen-year-old sister, who also was at Horner visiting friends, pleaded with Bird Leg to come inside the building to their cousins' apartment. "Get your ass upstairs," Bird Leg ordered her. "I'm gonna kill some of these punks today or they're gonna kill me." It was tough talk for a fifteen-year-old; his sister ran inside, crying. By the time she climbed the six floors to her cousins' apartment, a single pistol shot had echoed from below.

Twenty-four-year-old Willie Elliott had stepped from between two parked cars and aimed a pistol at Bird Leg. Only two feet away, the boy froze like a deer caught in the glare of a car's headlights. The bullet tore through Bird Leg's chest. He clutched his wound and ran through the breezeway of one highrise. "Man, I've been shot!" he hollered in disbelief. He appeared to be heading for the safety of a busy street. He didn't make it. The bullet, which had hit him at point-blank range, entered his chest and spiraled through his body like an out-of-control drill, lacerating his heart, lungs, spleen, and stomach. Bird Leg, struggling to breathe, collapsed beneath an old cottonwood, where, cooled by its shade, he died.

Word of death spreads fast in Henry Horner. Sometimes the killing happens late at night when most people are asleep. Then, since few witnesses are around, the incident can take on mythic proportions. A stabbing becomes a butchering. A shooting becomes an execution. Sometimes it can take days for the correct name of the victim to surface. But a daytime killing here draws a crowd, and as Bird Leg lay against the tree, a young boy mounted his bike to deliver the news.

From a friend's second-floor window, Lafeyette heard the boy's breathless rendering of the fight, but he decided not to join the other children who ran across Damen Avenue to the crime scene. "I just didn't want to go," he said later. He had already seen enough.

James, however, more adventurous, sprinted across Damen and snaked through the crowd that had already gathered around Bird Leg. He later told Lafeyette what he saw. On the grass, only ten feet from a small playground filled with young children, lay Bird Leg, his white jogging suit stained with blood. Wrapped around one of his closed fists was his only weapon, his belt.

"I was just shocked," James told Lafeyette. "The eyes just rolled to the back of his head and he was gone."

Within minutes after Bird Leg died, Jimmie Lee stepped through the crowd. It was, said one, like Moses parting the waters. People stepped back to let him through. He looked down at Bird Leg's limp body, said nothing, and then walked back through the crowd, where he assembled a band of thirty teenagers. With Lee at their flank, the young militia marched west, looking for revenge. James and the rest of the crowd scattered.

Charlie Toussas, the plainclothes officer who knew Lee well, confronted Lee and his army. "Jimmie, this isn't a good time for this." Lee, according to Toussas, silently turned to his followers, lifted his hand, and pointed to the other side of Damen; and the contingent of Vice Lords, as if manipulated by puppeteers, turned and marched back to their own turf. In the weeks to come, Disciples were the targets of gunfire.

When someone at Henry Horner is killed, mimeographed sheets usually go up in the buildings' hallways, giving details of the funeral. Bird Leg's family, though, avoided this procedure. Having heard that the Disciples planned to storm the funeral home and turn over the casket, they didn't want to publicize the funeral's location. They not only moved it from a nearby mortuary to a distant south side church, they also called the police, who assigned two plainclothesmen to sit through the service and, in effect, keep watch over the dead.

Bird Leg's swollen face made him look twice his age. But the new red-trimmed white jogging suit, which his mother had bought to honor his wishes, and a small gold friendship pin bearing his initials were reminders that Bird Leg had been only fifteen.

Lafeyette, Pharoah, and James were the first to file up to the open casket, where Lafeyette ran his fingers along Bird Leg's jogging suit. At first hesitantly and then with great affection, he caressed the boy's puffy face. James also gently touched the body, pulling back before his fingers reached his friend's rounded cheeks. Pharoah, barely tall enough to see into the casket, stood on tiptoe but kept his hands to his side. He had hardly known Bird Leg; he was here to be with his big brother.

"It looks like he's breathing," James whispered to Lafeyette, desperately wanting to be told he was wrong.

"He ain't breathing," Lafeyette assured him.

James glanced at Bird Leg again and, to no one in particular, muttered, "I'm figuring to cry." He wiped the tears from his face with the back of his hand.

Except for its plush red-cushioned pews, the one-story Zion Grove Baptist church, formerly a barbershop and before that a grocery store, seemed tired and worn. It adjoined an abandoned hamburger stand and faced a vacant lot. Inside, the church was sparsely decorated. A nearly lifesize rendering of *The Last Supper* covered the back wall; an American flag, wrapped around its pole, was draped in clear plastic.

The low ceiling and cinder-block walls did little to discourage the late August heat. The two bright floral arrangements, one at each end of the casket, struggled to retain their beauty through the hour-long service. Friends and relatives and fellow gang members, about 150 in all, shifted uncomfortably in the pews, fanning themselves with the mimeographed programs in a futile attempt to keep from perspiring.

The humidity put everyone on edge. Bird Leg's sister, in her grief, wailed in a pained, high-pitched voice that echoed through the small church like a stiff wind through a canyon. "I wanna kiss him. He ain't dead. He ain't dead," she cried. Months later, her protestations would echo in Pharoah's head; it was the one moment he would vividly recall from the funeral.

The three boys found seats off to the side, positioned so that one of the numerous thin pillars wouldn't obstruct their view of the lectern. Lafeyette wore faded gray corduroy pants and a shimmery silver-colored nylon jacket; Pharoah wore matching navy blue corduroy pants and sweatshirt. Both outfits were in sharp contrast to the tight suits and carefully cocked fedoras of most of the men. James himself looked like a young man, in his own purple high-waisted suit and black fedora. Three of Bird Leg's relatives, including a brother, wore T-shirts that read I [LOVE] BIRD LEG. Jimmie Lee, dressed in a charcoal-black sport coat, sat unobtrusively in the crowd. He had been asked to be a pall-bearer.

To the deep, sorrowful spirituals played on the church's organ, the Reverend C.H. Stimage, an elderly minister who had been preaching here for over thirty years, climbed to the lectern. "God needs some young soldiers among the old soldiers," he consoled the gathered mourners. His message in funerals for the young was usually the same: he warned of the evils of drinking and drugs, and sometimes, when he felt comfortable about it, cautioned them against the lure of the gangs. When young gang members die, other youngsters attend church; it was, reasoned the minister, the only time he could preach to them about the love of God.

Carla Palmore, a sturdy, self-assured seventeen-year-old who had been a friend of Bird Leg's, followed the minister to the lectern. Carla wanted to be upbeat, to be hopeful, and, as if to proclaim her intent, sported a matching pink skirt and blouse that, amid the mourners' somber suits and dark dresses, seemed all the more cheerful. Despite her efforts, though, her speech underlined the general feeling among her peers that many of them, like Bird Leg, might not make it to adulthood. During her impromptu sermon, Lafeyette and James and the others in the church nodded in assent.

"Tomorrow is not promised for us. So let's take advantage of today," she urged them. "Sometimes we take tomorrow for granted. Oh, I'll do this tomorrow or tomorrow this will happen. And we forget that tomorrow's not promised to us and we never get a chance to tell those people that we love them or how we feel about them and then, when they're gone, there's so much pain that you feel because you didn't get to do that." Carla caught her breath; her audience remained silent and attentive.

"Bird Leg wasn't a perfect person, but he wasn't a terrible person, and people are going to say that he was a great person or some people are going to say he deserved it, that he was a terrible person. We can't pass judgment on him, because whatever he's doing, there's somebody who's doing more or somebody who's doing less. He cared about his family and I don't think he was deep into it as much as people thought. All of you are here to pay your tribute to him as Bird Leg or as a gang member and maybe you're here for both or either one of them, but it could be you. You take tomorrow for granted and it could be you tomorrow. We just never know what's going to happen. You all need to get your lives together before it's too late."

Jimmie Lee hugged her as she stepped down. "You did a good job," he told her. "I appreciate what you said. I heard you." Meanwhile, another family friend led the congregation in a spirited rendition of the pop song "Lean on Me," a song that always stirred Pharoah's emotions. Here, in the company of other sobbing children and adults, large tears slid down his plump cheeks. He clutched his rolled-up sweatshirt to his chest for security, and, as often happened to him in tense situations, he found himself battling a piercing headache.

James cried too. It looked to some as if he might be doubled over in pain, but he hid his teary face in his black felt hat, which he held between his legs so that others wouldn't see him cry. Lafeyette stared hard at the whirling blades of the long-stemmed electric fan behind the lectern, his eyes sad and vacant, his right arm slung over the pew in front of him so that he could hold the hand of his two-year-old nephew, Terence's child, Snuggles. "Look," Snuggles said to his young uncle, "Bird Leg's asleep." Lafeyette shushed him, his chin buried in his free hand. "I cried on the inside," he said later. "I didn't have enough in me to cry."

As the service closed and the mourners moved forward to pass the casket for one last look at the body, Pharoah, still gripping his balled-up sweatshirt, asked of Lafeyette, "What's up in heaven? Do they have stores?"

"Shut up," Lafeyette said. "You don't know what you talking 'bout."

As the boys waited to file out of their aisle, they heard a mother, two rows back, scold her son: "That could have been you if I'd let you go over there. They would have killed you, too." When gang members passed the casket for the last time, they flashed the hand signal of the Conservative Vice Lords at Bird Leg's stiff body, their thumbs and index fingers forming the letter C. The boys didn't speak until they were outside the church.

"We're gonna die one way or the other by killing or plain out," James said to Lafeyette. "I just wanna die plain out."

Lafeyette nodded. "Me too."

————

Jonathan Kozol and Theresa Funiciello present stories from the lives and thoughts of poverty-stricken women and their children.

JONATHAN KOZOL, RACHEL AND HER CHILDREN

62–71 (Crown, 1988).

Angelina is twelve years old, Stephen is eleven, Erica is nine. The youngest child, eleven months, is sitting on the floor. A neighbor's child, six years old, sits in my lap and leans her head against my chest; she holds her arms around my neck. Her name or nickname (I do not know which) is Raisin. When she likes she puts her fingers on my mouth and interrupts the conversation with a tremolo of rapid words. There are two rooms. Rachel disappears into the second room, then returns and stands, uneasy, by the door.

Angie: "Ever since August we been livin' here. The room is either very hot or freezin' cold. When it be hot outside it's hot in here. When it be cold outside we have no heat. We used to live with my aunt but then it got too crowded there so we moved out. We went to welfare and they sent us to the shelter. Then they shipped us to Manhattan. I'm scared of the elevators. 'Fraid they be stuck. I take the stairs."

Raisin: "Elevator might fall down and you would die."

Rachel: "It's unfair for them to be here in this room. They be yellin'. Lots of times I'm goin' to walk out. Walk out on the street and give it up. No, I don't do it. BCW [Bureau of Child Welfare] come to take the children. So I make them stay inside. Once they walk outside that door they are in danger."

Angie: "I had a friend Yoki. They was tryin' to beat her. I said: 'Leave her.' They began to chase me. We was runnin' to the door. So we was runnin'. I get to the door. The door was stuck. I hit my eye and it began to bleed. So I came home and washed the blood. Me and my friends sat up all night and prayed. Prayin' for me. 'Dear Lord, can you please help me with my eye? If you do I promise to behave.' I was askin' God why did this happen. I wish someone in New York could help us. Put all of the money that we have together and we buy a building. Two or three rooms for every family. Everybody have a kitchen. Way it is, you frightened all the time. I think this world is coming to the end."

Stephen: "This city is rich."

Angie: "Surely is!"

Erica: "City and welfare, they got something goin'. Pay $3,000 every month to stay in these here rooms ..."

Rachel: "I believe the City Hall got something goin' here. Gettin' a cut. They got to be. My children, they be treated like chess pieces. Send all of that money off to Africa? You hear that song? They're not thinking about people starvin' here in the United States. I was thinkin': Get my kids and all the other children here to sing, 'We are the world. We live here too.' How come do you care so much for people you can't see? Ain't we the world? Ain't we a piece of it? We are so close they be afraid to see. Give us a shot at something. We are something! Ain't we *something*? I'm depressed. But we are *something*! People in America don't want to see."

Angie: "Christmas is sad for everyone. We have our toys. That's not the reason why. They givin' you toys and that do help. I would rather that we have a place to be."

Erica: "I wrote a letter to Santa Claus. Santa say that he don't have the change."

Raisin: "I saw Santa on the street. Then I saw Santa on another street. I pulled his beard and he said something nasty."

Angie: "There's one thing I ask: a home to be in with my mother. That was my only wish for Christmas. But it could not be."

Raisin: "I saw Mr. Water Bug under my mother's bed. Mr. Rat be livin' with us too."

Angie: "It's so cold right now you got to use the hot plate. Plug it in so you be warm. You need to have a hot plate. Are you goin' to live on cold bologna all your life?"

Raisin: "Mr. Rat came in my baby sister's crib and bit her. Nobody felt sorry for my sister. Then I couldn't go to sleep. I started crying. All of a sudden I pray and went to sleep and then I woke up in the mornin', make my bed, and took a bath, and ate, and went to school. So I came back and did my homework. And all of a sudden there was something *irritatin'* at my hand. I looked out the window and the moon was goin' up. And then—I had a dream. I went to sleep and I was dreamin' and I dreamed about a witch that bit me. I felt *dead*. When I woke back up I had a headache."

Angie: "School is bad for me. I feel ashamed. They know we're not the same. My teacher do not treat us all the same. They know which children live in the hotel."

Erica: "My teacher isn't like that. She treats all of us the same. We all get smacked. We all get punished the same way."

Stephen: "I'm in sixth grade. When I am a grown-up I be a computer."

Erica: "You're in the fifth. You lie."

Raisin: "When I grow up I want to be multiplication and subtraction and division."

Angie: "Last week a drug addict tried to stab me. With an ice pick. Tried to stab my mother too. Older girls was botherin' us. They try to make us fight. We don't fight. We don't start fires. They just pickin' on us. We ran home and got our mother. They ran home and got their mother."

Raisin: "Those girls upstairs on the ninth floor, they be bad. They sellin' crack."

Erica: "Upstairs, ninth floor, nine-o-five, they sellin' crack."

Raisin: "A man was selling something on the street. He had some reefers on him and the po-lice caught him and they took him to the jail. You know where the junkies put the crack? Put the crack inside the pipe. Smoke it like that. They take a torch and burn the pipe and put it in their mouth. They go like this." [Puffs.]

I ask: "Why do they do it?"

Erica: "Feel good! Hey! Make you feel fine!"

Angie: "This girl I know lives in a room where they sell drugs. One day she asks us do we want a puff. So we said: 'No. My mother doesn't let us do it.' One day I was walkin' in the hall. This man asked me do I want some stuff. He said: 'Do you want some?' I said no and I ran home."

Raisin: "One day my brother found these two big plastic bags inside his teddy bear. Po-lice came up to my room and took that teddy bear." She's interrupted. "I ain't finished! And they took it. One day we was by my uncle's car and this man came and he said: 'Do you want some?' We said no. We told my uncle and he went and found the man and he ran to the bar and went into the women's bathroom in the bar. And so we left."

Angie: "I think this world is ending. Yes. Ending. Everybody in this city killin' on each other. Countries killin' on each other. Why can't people learn to stick together? It's no use to fightin'. Fightin' over nothin'. What they fightin' for? A flag! I don't know what we are fightin' for. President Reagan wants to put the rockets on the moon. What's he doin' messin' with the moon? If God wanted man and woman on the moon He would of put us there. They should send a camera to the moon and feed the people here on earth. Don't go messin' there with human beings. Use that money to build houses. Grow food! Buy seeds! Weave cloth! Give it to the people in America!"

Erica: "When we hungry and don't have no food we borrow from each other. Her mother [Raisin's] give us food. Or else we go to Crisis. In the mornin' when we wake up we have a banana or a cookie. If the bus ain't late we have our breakfast in the school. What I say to President Reagan: Give someone a chance! I believe he be a selfish man. Can't imagine how long he been president."

Raisin: "Be too long."

Angie: "Teacher tell us this be a democracy. I don't know. I doubt it. Rich people, couldn't they at least give us a refund?"

Raisin: "This man say his son be gettin' on his nerves. He beat his little son 'bout two years old. A wooden bat. He beat him half to death. They took him to the hospital and at five-thirty he was dead. A little boy. [Interrupted.] Let me talk!"

Erica: "The little boy. He locked himself into the bathroom. He was scared. After he died police came and his father went to jail. His mother, she went to the store."

Raisin, in a tiny voice: "People fight in here and I don't like it. Why do they do it? 'Cause they're sad. They fight over the world. I ain't finished!"

Erica: "One time they was two cops in the hall. One cop pulled his gun and he was goin' shoot me. He said did I live there? I said no. So I came home."

Raisin: "I was in this lady room. She be cryin' because her baby died. He had [mispronounced] pneumonia. He was unconscious and he died." Soft voice: "Tomorrow is my birthday."

The children are tended by a friend. In the other bedroom, Rachel, who is quieter now, paces about and finally sits down.

"Do you know why there's no carpet in the hall? If there was a carpet it would be on fire. Desperate people don't have no control. You have to sleep with one eye open. Tell the truth, I do not sleep at night.

"Before we lived here we were at the Forbell shelter [barracks shelter on Forbell Street in Brooklyn]. People sleep together in one room. You sleep across. You have to dress in front of everybody. Men and women. When you wake, some man lookin' at you puttin' on your clothes. Lookin' at your children too. Angelina, she be only twelve years old. . . .

"There's one thing. My children still are pure. They have a concept of life. Respect for life. But if you don't get 'em out of here they won't have anything for long. If you get 'em out right now. But if you don't . . . My girls are innocent still. They are unspoiled. Will they be that way for long? Try to keep 'em in the room. But you can't lock 'em up for long.

"When we moved here I was forced to sign a paper. Everybody has to do it. It's a promise that you will not cook inside your room. So we lived on cold bologna. Can you feed a child on that? God forgive me but nobody shouldn't have to live like this. I can't even go downstairs and get back on the elevator. Half the time it doesn't work. Since I came into this place my kids begun to get away from me.". . .

"Most of us are black. Some Puerto Rican. Some be white. They suffer too. Can you get the government to know that we exist? I know that my children have potential. They're intelligent. They're smart. They need a chance. There's nothin' wrong with them for now. But not for long. My daughter watches junkies usin' needles. People smokin' crack in front a them. Screwin' in front a them. They see it all. They see it everywhere. What is a man and woman gonna do when they are all in the same room?

"I met a girl the other day. She's twelve years old. Lives on the fourteenth floor. She got a baby the same age as mine. Her mother got five children of her own. I don't want my daughter havin' any baby. She's a child. Innocent. Innocent. No violence. She isn't bitter. But she's scared. You understand? This is America. These children growin' up too fast. We have no hope. And you know why? Because we all feel just the same way deep down in our hearts. Nowhere to go . . . I'm not a killer. My kids ain't no killers. But if they don't learn to kill they know they're goin' to die.

"They didn't go to school last week. They didn't have clean clothes. Why? Because the welfare messed my check. It's supposed to come a week ago. It didn't come. I get my check today. I want my kids to go to school. They shouldn't miss a day. How they gonna go to school if they don't got some clothes? I couldn't wash. I didn't have the money to buy food.

"Twice the welfare closed my case. When they do it you are s'posed to go for a fair hearing. Take some papers, birth certificates. So I went out there in the snow. Welfare worker wasn't there. They told me to come back. Mister, it ain't easy to be beggin'. I went to the Crisis. And I asked her, I said, 'Give me somethin' for the kids to eat. Give me *somethin'!* Don't turn me away when I am sittin' here in front of you and askin' for your help!' She said she had nothin'. So my kids went out into the street. That's right! Whole night long they was in Herald Square panhandlin'. Made five dollars. So we bought bologna. My kids is good to me. We had bread and bologna.

"Welfare, they are not polite. They're personal. 'Did you do this? Did you do that? Where your husband at?' Understand me? 'Cause they sittin' on the other side of this here desk, they think we're stupid and we do not understand when we're insulted. 'Oh, you had another baby?' Yeah! I had another baby! What about it? Are you goin' to kill that baby? I don't say it, but that's what I feel like sayin'. You learn to be humble.

"I'm here five miserable months. So I wonder: Where I'm goin'? Can't the mayor give us a house? A part-time job? I am capable of doin' *somethin'.*

"You go in the store with food stamps. You need Pampers. You're not s'posed to use the stamps for Pampers. Stores will accept them. They don't care about the law. What they do is make you pay a little extra. They know you don't have no choice. So they let you buy the Pampers for two dollars extra.

"Plenty of children livin' here on nothin' but bread and bologna. Peanut butter. Jelly. Drinkin' water. You buy milk. I bought one gallon yesterday. Got *this* much left. They drink it fast. Orange juice, they drink it fast. End up drinkin' Kool Aid.

"Children that are poor are used like cattle. Cattle or horses. They are owned by welfare. They know they are bein' used—for what? Don't *use* them! Give 'em somethin'!

"In this bedroom I'm not sleepin' on a bed. They won't give me one. You can see I'm sleepin' on a box spring. I said to the manager: 'I need a bed instead of sleepin' on a spring.' Maid give me some blankets. Try to make it softer." . . .

"Before they shipped us here we lived for five years in a basement. Five years in a basement with no bathroom. One small room. You had to go upstairs two floors to use the toilet. No kitchen. It was fifteen people in five rooms. Sewer kept backing up into the place we slept. Every time it flooded I would have to pay one hundred dollars just to get the thing unstuck. There were all my children sleepin' in the sewage. So you try to get them out and try to get them somethin' better. But it didn't get no better. I came from one bad place into another. But the difference is this is a place where I cannot get out.

"If I can't get out of here I'll give them up. I have asked them: 'Do you want to go away?' I love my kids and, if I did that, they would feel betrayed. They love me. They don't want to go. If I did it, I would only do it to protect them. They'll live anywhere with me. They're innocent. Their minds are clean. They ain't corrupt. They have a heart. All my kids love people. They love life. If they got a dime, a piece of bread, they'll share it. Letting them panhandle made me cry. I had been to welfare, told the lady that my baby ain't got Pampers, ain't got nothing' left to eat. I got rude and noisy and it's not my style to do that but you learn that patience and politeness get you nowhere.

"When they went out on the street I cried. I said: 'I'm scared. What's gonna happen to them?' But if they're hungry they are goin' to do *something*. They are gonna find their food from somewhere. Where I came from I was fightin' for my children. In this place here I am fightin' for my children. I am tired of fightin'. I don't want to fight. I want my kids to live in peace.

"I was thinkin' about this. If there was a place where you could sell part of your body, where they buy an arm or somethin' for a thousand dollars, I would do it. I would do it for my children. I would give my life if I could get a thousand dollars. What would I lose? I lived my life. I want to see my children grow up to live theirs.

"A lot of women do not want to sell their bodies. This is something that good women do not want to do. I will sell mine. I *will*. I will solicit. I will prostitute if it will feed them."

I ask: "Would you do it?"

"Ain't no 'would I?' I would do it." Long pause ... "Yes. I *did*.

"I had to do it when the check ain't come. Wasn't no one gonna buy my arm for any thousand dollars. But they's plenty gonna pay me twenty dollars for my body. What was my choice? Leave them out there on the street, a child like Angelina, to panhandle? I would take my life if someone found her dead somewhere. I would go crazy. After she did it that one time I was ashamed. I cried that night. All night I cried and cried. So I decided I had one thing left. In the mornin' I got up out of this bed. I told them I was goin' out. Out in the street. Stand by the curb. It was a cold day. Freezin'! And my chest is bad. I'm thirty-eight years old. Cop come by. He see me there. I'm standin' out there cryin'. Tells me I should go inside. Gives me three dollars. 'It's too cold to be outside.' Ain't many cops like that. Not many people either ...

"After he's gone a man come by. Get in his car. Go with him where he want. Takin' a chance he crazy and he kill me. Wishin' somehow that he would.

"So he stop his car. And I get in. I say a price. That's it. Go to a room. It's some hotel. He had a lot of money so he rented a deluxe.

Asked me would I stay with him all night. I tell him no I can't 'cause I have kids. So, after he done ... whatever he did ... I told him that I had to leave. Took out a knife at me and held it at my face. He made me stay. When I woke up next day I was depressed. Feel so guilty what I did. I feel real scared. I can understand why prostitutes shoot drugs. They take the drugs so they don't be afraid.

"When he put that knife up to my throat, I'm thinkin' this: What is there left to lose? I'm not goin' to do any better in this life. If I be dead at least my kids won't ever have to say that I betrayed them. I don't like to think like that. But when things pile up on you, you do. 'I'm better if I'm dead.'

"So I got me twenty dollars and I go and buy the Pampers for the baby and three dollars of bologna and a loaf of bread and everyone is fed. . . .

"All that I want is somethin' that's my own. I got four kids. I need four plates, four glasses, and four spoons. Is that a lot? I know I'm poor. Don't have no bank account, no money, or no job. Don't have no nothin'. No foundation. Then and yet my children have a shot in life. They're innocent. They're pure. They have a chance."

THERESA FUNICIELLO, THE POVERTY INDUSTRY
Ms. Magazine, 33–36, 40 (November/December 1990).

Firefighters returning from a false alarm in Queens, New York, one beautiful October day in 1989 were gazing into the sky when they passed an apartment complex. Ten stories up, a body was dangling from the window. Hector Faberlle and his coworkers yelled up front to get the rig turned around. Just as it arrived back at the building, a little girl, naked, hit the ground. Faberlle ran to resuscitate her as two other firefighters dashed into the building.

According to Faberlle, "We tried to stabilize her. Just as she was breathing on her own, I heard people screaming. I looked up and saw another small child spinning down." Witnesses said a woman had seemed to dangle him before she let go of him. Hussein, age three, fell on his seven-year-old sister. "After that we couldn't get a pulse from her and blood was spilling from her mouth."

Ameenah Abdus–Salaam, a 32–year–old black middle-class Muslim housewife, was trying to send all five of her children back to Allah, through their apartment window. Her daughter Zainab was pronounced dead at the hospital. Hussein survived and a year later is still in rehabilitation. Just as Ms. Abdus–Salaam was about to toss out her one-year-old, firefighters burst in. As they were overtaking her, she urged the children to go quickly, as if they would go on their own. All were naked. According to one news report, she said, "We came into this world with nothing and that's how we're going to leave." Three children and their mother, who intended to jump when she completed the task, were rescued.

Ms. Abdus–Salaam was charged with murder, attempted murder, first- and second-degree assault, reckless endangerment, and endangering the welfare of a child. Neighbors said the mother was loving and the children were always polite and clean, as if that rendered the occurrence more mysterious. And then Ameenah Abdus–Salaam and her children vanished from our collective memory.

When I was young I could not possibly have understood or forgiven (as if it were mine to forgive) the acts of Ameenah Abdus–Salaam on October 5, 1989. Some of that youth I spent as a Muslim—drapes for clothes, virtually nonstop prayers, my two feet of hair cordoned with a bolt of white cloth bound so tightly I could never forget it was there. I took this religion as seriously as those that preceded it, starting with Catholicism (I went to *that* church every day until I was 18). My religion was as solid as a rock mountain pervious only to centuries of dripping water. (Latent feminism finally crept up on me.)

In Islam, everything is ritualized, from sex to eating. That's how I know what Ameenah Abdus–Salaam was doing calmly while she held Hussein out of the window before letting go. She was praying.

In form and function, as in other patriarchal religions, Muslim women are buried alive in contradictions. They are equal; no, superior; no, inferior—to men, to snakes, to witches. Make no mistake: an Islamic woman without a man, especially a woman with children, isn't remotely like a fish without a bicycle.

This woman had five children, aged one to eight years, and was recently separated from her husband. She had trouble making her last month's rent. She surely feared a descent into poverty and probably homelessness. (As of this writing she is not granting interviews.) Ahead lay the streets. Welfare. Welfare hotels. Drugs, prostitution, guns, knives, gambling, drunkenness, and all manner of spiritual death. But for a woman with the option of deliverance, it wasn't inevitable.

Some years after shedding my Muslim garb, I had a baby and ended up homeless and on welfare myself. Not long after, I organized a welfare rights center, where we (the mothers trapped in this system) tried, among other things, to sort out the differences between "us" and "them" (mothers not on welfare). One subject was the stereotype of child abuse. It was something each of us understood at some terribly private gut level, but never articulated outside our circle; even then, we were cautious.

My own revelation came when my daughter was about a year old. At one point, she was sick and cried almost nonstop for a week. I was experiencing severe sleep deprivation coupled with the trauma of being unable to comfort her. For one horrible moment, I felt like hurling her against the wall. Fortunately, my mother came by unexpectedly and held the baby for a couple of hours, giving me time to gather composure. My daughter's fever broke and we both survived. But ever since, I have understood child abuse. And any parent who claims not to understand it in that context, ain't hardly trying.

I had been very close to where Ameenah Abdus–Salaam was. On another level, our circumstances were very different. A homeless mother of five (I had only one) has virtually no chance of being taken in by friends or family for more than a night or two. A homeless mother of four or more has only a 16 percent chance of keeping her children together. If she stays in an abandoned building with them and gets caught, they'll be taken away for "neglect." Still, there are commonalities shared by women of all races and religions, from rural to urban poverty. The merciless anxiety, the humiliation of being shuttled back and forth like herded animals, the stress of keeping kids in school, are constant. Only the details vary.

In New York City, if she were able to keep them together, at some point they would approach an Emergency Assistance Unit (EAU), which is obligated to shelter them in some way. This would mean waiting for hours, sometimes even days, on plastic chairs or the bare floor. If the family didn't eat pork, they'd eat nothing, since baloney sandwiches are about all they'd get for several meals. Some nights they might be moved (often after midnight) to a roach, lice, and rat infested welfare hotel for a few hours. In the morning the family would be shuttled back to wait again.

If they were lucky, after some days they would finally be placed in a welfare hotel or "transitional" shelter. These often provide less space per family member than that required for jail cells. Because the family was large, they wouldn't even get apartment referrals from city workers until after they'd been in this hell for months. (One rural homeless mother told me her family was placed in a motel with bars instead of windows and not one store or school within walking distance. She was at the mercy of a barely functional shuttle system for the homeless.)

At first, many mothers try to continue taking children to their previous schools. In New York City, this usually means traveling with them (other babies in tow) to another borough in the morning and returning for them in the afternoon. When one child is too sick to travel, none go to school. After a while, the mother might try to place the children in a school closer to the shelter. Legal, yes. Easy, no. If the mother does accomplish this, other kids in the new school will soon realize her children are "untouchables." School life will become anathema to her kids. They'll begin to adopt the coping mechanisms of other homeless kids who *will* associate with them.

Night brings scant respite. Police sirens. Gunshots from outside or down the hall. Families fighting. Too many people and too few beds, often with neither sheets nor blankets, much less pillows. The mattresses have long since burst like pastry puffs. Bedbugs pinch.

Those of us who are lucky have a little stove in the room. I'll never forget the first time I used one in a welfare hotel. I had just added eggs to the frying pan when swarms of roaches scrambled out of the lit burner in every direction—including into the frying pan. It was days before I could bring myself to try it again. All the things most people take for granted become little horrors.

If the Abdus–Salaam family emerged from the "temporary" shelter intact and were placed in an apartment, the world would think their problems solved. But now they would be a welfare family. Overnight she would switch from homeless victim to society's victimizer. Her living conditions would not improve nor her stress diminish, but she would join the larger class of poor women—despised abusers of the system—welfare mothers. To have come this far would have been a heroic feat, but what would be said of her is that she's a drain on national resources, has too many children she shouldn't have had if she couldn't afford to, and she doesn't "work."

On welfare, the chances of having enough money to live in a remotely decent neighborhood and pay for basic human needs are laughable—even in New York, where welfare benefits are "high." On the day when the Abdus–Salaam family almost came to total halt, the *maximum* monthly grant in New York City for a mother and five children was $814.20—or *less than three fifths of the federal poverty threshold for the same size family*. The *average* New York grant for six was $655 per month. (In January 1990 there was a slight, almost negligible increase in aggregate benefits.) Assuming the family received the maximum, the rent allotment would have been $349. Assuming the absurd—that they could find habitable housing for that price in New York or most any other U.S. city—they would be left with $465.20, or about $2.50 per person, per day, for most of their food. (Food stamps would provide less than two weeks of nutritionally adequate food for the month.) That same $2.50 must cover some of their medical expenses, and *all* their utilities, toothpaste, toilet paper, furniture, soap, baby bottles, diapers, laundry, transportation, kitchen utensils, and clothing. If Ms. Abdus–Salaam lived in South Dakota, she'd have had just about $1.88 for all those things. If she were a single mother living in California aged 25 or less, she'd have a 98 percent chance of landing on welfare. In New York, if she took one subway ride in search of an elusive job, she'd use up over 90 percent of her daily ration. If she's menstruating and needs to buy a box of sanitary napkins, she'd have to dip into her children's share. Like millions of women, she has at her disposal only one commodity guaranteed to produce sufficient income to keep her family together: her body. For some women that's unthinkable; for example, to a devout Muslim, even survival does not justify such a damning act. Yet to kill herself—only herself—would be to act irresponsibly to her children. Had *Mr.* Abdus–Salaam died instead of leaving the family, everything would have been different.

Ameenah would have been the recipient of sympathy and support. As a widow with minor children, she would become a Social Security recipient instead of a welfare mother. (The maximum family benefit for survivor families on Social Security in 1989—$1,898.90 per month—could be enough to continue living modestly where she was. While this sum is hardly lavish, the family would remain above poverty.) No social policy experts would go nuts because she didn't have a "job." In fact, she would be thought a good mother for taking care of her children full-time, "at least while they're small." If and when she did get a paying job, she could earn thousands of dollars without a reduction in her Social Security check. (On welfare, a job would be taxed at 100 percent. Outside of minimal work-related expenses, for the most part her welfare check would be reduced one dollar for every dollar she was paid.) The message: the needs and rights of women and children are determined by the nature of their prior relationship to a man; the only difference between "survivor" families and "welfare" families is the imprimatur of the father. How did such a cruel policy come to be? . . .

If any woman reading this were penniless today and went to apply for welfare to feed her children, she would not receive her first welfare check for about a month. Not because the welfare is prohibited from giving her money sooner, but because they are allowed to take 30 days to determine the obvious: that she is poor. The 30-day deadline might come and go with no relief. Or destructive policies plus bureaucratic bungling might prevent a check from ever coming. If she did make it onto the rolls, she might—like at least one million needy U.S. citizens every year—be cut off despite being still legally entitled to welfare. This process has been given the name "churning" by the welfare department, as needy people are routinely cut off and sometimes put back on months later.

One ghastly result of such U.S. social policy is that far more children die from poverty than slip away at the hands of mothers like Ameenah Abdus–Salaam. Twelve times as many poor children die in fires than do nonpoor children. Eight times as many die of disease, according to a study done by the state of Maine—where, by the way, 98 percent of the population is white. Thirty times as many low birth weight babies die as do normal weight babies. In 1987, one in two homeless mothers in New York reported *losing* weight during pregnancy. Even at the bottom luck plays a role: whose kid is hit by a stray bullet, the kitchen stove explodes because it was used nonstop as the only source of heat in a frozen apartment, whose infant dies of pneumonia. Poverty is the number one killer of children in the U.S.A. Murder by malfeasance.

Children are poor because their mothers are poor.

Ameenah Abdus–Salaam's tragic acts may not be so mysterious, after all. The miracle is that more women, facing similar anguish, don't do the same.

On September 19, 1990, I attended a court hearing. Ameenah Abdus–Salaam's male attorney had pleaded her "not responsible by reason of mental disease or defect." Two court-appointed psychiatrists agreed, and recommended she be released—no longer a danger to herself or anyone else. District Attorney John Santucci's office refused to accept the recommendation until another psychiatrist, of the D.A.'s choosing, can evaluate her. The case could drag on indefinitely. The male judge has consistently refused to set bail. Ameenah herself was not "produced" for the proceedings. All four walls of the courtroom are of elaborately carved wood. Above the judge's throne, in raised gold letters, gleam the words *In God We Trust*. However misguided it may seem to outsiders, that was the one thing Ameenah Abdus–Salaam intended to do.

Notes and Questions

1. If you had grown up to the sounds of bullets whizzing over your head and the funerals of your friends killed in gang warfare or by drugs, or if you had had to go to school from homeless shelters or rat-infested single-room occupancy buildings without adequate clothing or nourishment, would you be where you are now? How much of your success and opportunity to be in school is attributable to some form of privilege?

2. What does Ms. Funiciello's poverty story tell us about the intersections of wealth-based and culture-based privileges?

3. The Census Bureau reports that in 1992, there were 36.9 million poor Americans, 1.2 million more than the year before. *Census Bureau Report,* 10/04/93. To be considered poor by the Census Bureau, a family of four must have under $14,335/year and someone living alone must have less than $7,143/year. Because the poverty line is set so artificially low, the true number of poor Americans greatly exceeds this data. When the poverty data is broken down by race, Blacks constitute 33.3 percent of the poor and Hispanic peoples are 29.3 percent. Children fare particularly badly. Even using the government's low figures, 21.9 percent of our nation's children live below the poverty line. Children under 18 constitute forty percent of the poor, but only 26 percent of the nation's population. See also Daan Braveman, *Children, Poverty and State Constitutions,* 38 Emory L.J. 577 (1989).

4. The growing number of women and their children living in poverty has been labelled the "feminization of poverty." Diana Pearce, *The Feminization of Poverty: Women, Work and Welfare,* 11 Urban and Social Change Rev. 28 (1978); Sara McLanahan, Annemette Sorenson, & Dorothy Watson, *Sex Differences in Poverty, 1950–1980,* 15 Signs 102 (1989); Johanna Brenner, *Feminist Political Discourses: Radical versus Liberal Approaches to the Feminization of Poverty and Comparable Worth,* in Women, Class, and the Feminist Imagination: A Socialist–Feminist Reader 491, 495–498 (Karen V. Hansen & Ilene J. Philipson, eds., Temple, 1990); Julianne Malveaux, *Gender Difference and Beyond: An Economic Perspective on Diversity and Commonality among Women,* in Theoretical Perspectives on Sexual Difference 226–238 (Deborah L. Rhode, ed., Yale, 1990). See also Diana M. Pearce & Kelley Ellsworth, *Welfare and Women's Poverty: Reform or Reinforcement?,* 16 J.Legis. 141 (1990); Teresa L. Amott & Julie A. Matthaei, Race, Gender & Work: A Multicultural Economic History of Women in the United States (South End Press, 1991).

B. ON A STRUCTURAL LEVEL

Learning about the workings of privilege and power from narratives, personal stories, and individual reflections helps us better understand these phenomena. Yet our understandings can be greatly increased by exposure to theoretical or structural analyses about power and privilege. One of the terms frequently used by theorists in discussing power and privilege is oppression. Professors Marilyn Frye and Iris Young introduce us to metaphorical and theoretical ways of understanding this concept.

MARILYN FRYE, OPPRESSION

in The Politics of Reality: Essays in Feminist Theory 1–16 (Crossing Press, 1983).

... The statement that women are oppressed is frequently met with the claim that men are oppressed too. We hear that oppressing is oppressive to those who oppress as well as to those they oppress. Some men cite as evidence of their oppression their much-advertised inability to cry. It is tough, we are told, to be masculine. When the stresses and frustrations of being a man are cited as evidence that oppressors are oppressed by their oppressing, the word 'oppression' is being stretched to meaninglessness; it is treated as though its scope includes any and all human experience of limitation or suffering, no matter the cause, degree or consequence. Once such usage has been put over on us, then if ever we deny that any person or group is oppressed, we seem to imply that we think they never suffer and have no feelings. We are accused of insensitivity; even of bigotry. For women, such accusation is particularly intimidating, since sensitivity is one of the few virtues that has been assigned to us. If we are found insensitive, we may fear we have no redeeming traits at all and perhaps are not real women. Thus are we silenced before we begin: the name of our situation drained of meaning and our guilt mechanisms tripped.

But this is nonsense. Human beings can be miserable without being oppressed, and it is perfectly consistent to deny that a person or group is oppressed without denying that they have feelings or that they suffer.

We need to think clearly about oppression, and there is much that mitigates against this. I do not want to undertake to prove that women are oppressed (or that men are not), but I want to make clear what is being said when we say it. We need this word, this concept, and we need it to be sharp and sure.

The root of the word 'oppression' is the element 'press'. *The press of the crowd; pressed into military service; to press a pair of pants; printing press; press the button.* Presses are used to mold things or flatten them or reduce them in bulk, sometimes to reduce them by squeezing out the gasses or liquids in them. Something pressed is something caught between or among forces and barriers which are so related to each other that jointly they restrain, restrict or prevent the thing's motion or mobility. Mold. Immobilize. Reduce.

The mundane experience of the oppressed provides another clue. One of the most characteristic and ubiquitous features of the world as experienced by oppressed people is the double bind—situations in which options are reduced to a very few and all of them expose one to penalty, censure or deprivation. For example, it is often a requirement upon oppressed people that we smile and be cheerful. If we comply, we signal our docility and our acquiescence in our situation. We need not, then, be taken note of. We acquiesce in being made invisible, in our occupying no space. We participate in our own erasure. On the other hand, anything but the sunniest countenance exposes us to being perceived as mean, bitter, angry or dangerous. This means, at the least, that we may be found "difficult" or unpleasant to work with, which is enough to cost one one's livelihood; at worst, being seen as mean, bitter, angry or dangerous has been known to result in rape, arrest, beating and murder. One can only choose to risk one's preferred form and rate of annihilation.

Another example: It is common in the United States that women, especially younger women, are in a bind where neither sexual activity nor sexual inactivity is all right. If she is heterosexually active, a woman is open to censure and punishment for being loose, unprincipled or a whore. The "punishment" comes in the form of criticism, snide and embarrassing remarks, being treated as an easy lay by men, scorn from her more restrained female friends. She may have to lie and hide her behavior from her parents. She must juggle the risks of unwanted pregnancy and dangerous contraceptives. On the other hand, if she refrains from heterosexual activity, she is fairly constantly harassed by men who try to persuade her into it and pressure her to "relax" and "let her hair down"; she is threatened with labels like "frigid," "uptight," "manhater," "bitch" and "cocktease." The same parents who would be disapproving of her sexual activity may be worried by her inactivity because it suggests she is not or will not be popular, or is not sexually normal. She may be charged with lesbianism. If a woman is raped, then if she has been heterosexually active she is subject to the presumption that she liked it (since her activity is presumed to show that she likes sex), and if she has not been heterosexually active, she is subject to the presumption that she liked it (since she is supposedly "repressed and frustrated"). Both heterosexual activity and heterosexual nonactivity are likely to be taken as proof that you wanted to be raped, and hence, of course, weren't *really* raped at all. You can't win. You are caught in a bind, caught between systematically related pressures.

Women are caught like this, too, by networks of forces and barriers that expose one to penalty, loss or contempt whether one works outside the home or not, is on welfare or not, bears children or not, raises children or not, marries or not, stays married or not, is heterosexual, lesbian, both or neither. Economic necessity; confinement to racial and/or sexual job ghettos; sexual harassment; sex discrimination; pressures of competing expectations and judgments about *women, wives* and *mothers* (in the society at large, in racial and ethnic subcultures and in one's own mind); dependence (full or partial) on husbands, parents or the state; commitment to political ideas; loyalties to racial or ethnic or other "minority" groups; the demands of self-respect and responsibilities to others. Each of these factors exists in complex tension with every other, penalizing or prohibiting all of the apparently available options. And nipping at one's heels, always, is the endless pack of little things. If one dresses one way, one is subject to the assumption that one is advertising one's sexual availability; if one dresses another way, one appears to "not care about oneself" or to be "unfeminine." If one uses "strong language," one invites categorization as a whore or slut; if one does not, one invites categorization as a "lady"—one too delicately constituted to cope with robust speech or the realities to which it presumably refers.

The experience of oppressed people is that the living of one's life is confined and shaped by forces and barriers which are not accidental or occasional and hence avoidable, but are systematically related to each other in such a way as to catch one between and among them and restrict or penalize motion in any direction. It is the experience of being caged in: all avenues, in every direction, are blocked or booby trapped.

Cages. Consider a birdcage. If you look very closely at just one wire in the cage, you cannot see the other wires. If your conception of what is before you is determined by this myopic focus, you could look at that one wire, up and down the length of it, and be unable to see why a bird would not just fly around the wire any time it wanted to go somewhere. Furthermore, even if, one day at a time, you myopically inspected each wire, you still could not see why a bird would have trouble going past the wires to get anywhere. There is no physical property of any one wire, *nothing* that the closest scrutiny could discover, that will reveal how a bird could be inhibited or harmed by it except in the most accidental way. It is only when you step back, stop looking at the wires one by one, microscopically, and take a macroscopic view of the whole cage, that you can see why the bird does not go anywhere; and then you will see it in a moment. It will require no great subtlety of mental powers. It is perfectly *obvious* that the bird is surrounded by a network of systematically related barriers, no one of which would be the least hindrance to its flight, but which, by their relations to each other, are as confining as the solid walls of a dungeon.

It is now possible to grasp one of the reasons why oppression can be hard to see and recognize: one can study the elements of an oppressive structure with great care and some good will without seeing the structure as a whole, and hence without seeing or being able to understand that one is looking at a cage and that there are people there who are caged, whose motion and mobility are restricted, whose lives are shaped and reduced.

. . .

As the cageness of the birdcage is a macroscopic phenomenon, the oppressiveness of the situations in which women live our various and different lives is a macroscopic phenomenon. Neither can be *seen* from a microscopic perspective. But when you look macroscopically you can see it—a network of forces and barriers which are systematically related and which conspire to the immobilization, reduction and molding of women and the lives we live.

The image of the cage helps convey one aspect of the systematic nature of oppression. Another is the selection of occupants of the cages, and analysis of this aspect also helps account for the invisibility of the oppression of women.

It is as a woman (or as a Chicana/o or as a Black or Asian or lesbian) that one is entrapped.

"Why can't I go to the park; you let Jimmy go!"

"Because it's not safe for girls."

"I want to be a secretary, not a seamstress; I don't

want to learn to make dresses."

"There's no work for negroes in that line; learn a

skill where you can earn your living."

When you question why you are being blocked, why this barrier is in your path, the answer has not to do with individual talent or merit, handicap or failure; it has to do with your membership in some category understood as a "natural" or "physical" category. The "inhabitant" of the "cage" is not an individual but a group, all those of a certain category. If an individual is oppressed, it is in virtue of being a member of a group or category of people that is systematically reduced, molded, immobilized. Thus, to recognize a person as oppressed, one has to see that individual *as* belonging to a group of a certain sort.

There are many things which can encourage or inhibit perception of someone's membership in the sort of group or category in question here. In particular, it seems reasonable to suppose that if one of the devices of restriction and definition of the group is that of physical confinement or segregation, the confinement and separation would encourage recognition of the group as a group. This in turn would encourage the macroscopic focus which enables one to recognize oppression and encourages the individuals' identification and solidarity with other individuals of the group or category. But physical confinement and segregation of the group as a group is not common to all oppressive structures, and when an oppressed group is geographically and demographically dispersed the perception of it as a group is inhibited. There may be little or nothing in the situations of the individuals encouraging the macroscopic focus which would reveal the unity of the structure bearing down on all members of that group.

A great many people, female and male and of every race and class, simply do not believe that *woman* is a category of oppressed people, and I think that this is in part because they have been fooled by the dispersal and assimilation of women throughout and into the systems of class and race which organize men. Our simply being dispersed makes it difficult for women to have knowledge of each other and hence difficult to recognize the shape of our common cage. The dispersal and assimilation of women throughout economic classes and races also divides us against each other practically and economically and thus attaches *interest* to the inability to see: for some, jealousy of their benefits, and for some, resentment of the others' advantages.

To get past this, it helps to notice that in fact women of all races and classes *are* together in a ghetto of sorts. There is a women's place, a sector, which is inhabited by women of all classes and races, and it is not defined by geographical boundaries but by function. The function is the service of men and men's interests as men define them, which includes the bearing and rearing of children. The details of the service and the working conditions vary by race and class, for men of different races and classes have different interests, perceive their interests differently, and express their needs and demands in different rhetorics, dialects and languages. But there are also some constants.

Whether in lower, middle or upper-class home or work situations, women's service work always includes personal service (the work of maids, butlers, cooks, personal secretaries), sexual service (including provision for his genital sexual needs and bearing his children, but also including "being nice," "being attractive for him," etc.), and ego service (encouragement, support, praise, attention). Women's service work also is characterized everywhere by the fatal combination of responsibility and powerlessness: we are held responsible and we hold ourselves responsible for good outcomes for men and children in almost every respect though we have in almost no case power adequate to that project. The details of the subjective experience of this servitude are local. They vary with economic class and race and ethnic tradition as well as the personalities of the men in question. So also are the details of the forces which coerce our tolerance of this servitude particular to the different situations in which different women live and work.

All this is not to say that women do not have, assert and manage sometimes to satisfy our own interests, nor to deny that in some cases and in some respects women's independent interests do overlap with men's. But at every race/class level and even across race/class lines men do not serve women as women serve men. "Women's sphere" may be understood as the "service sector," taking the latter expression much more widely and deeply than is usual in discussions of the economy.

It seems to be the human condition that in one degree or another we all suffer frustration and limitation, all encounter unwelcome barriers, and all are damaged and hurt in various ways. Since we are a social species, almost all of our behavior and activities are structured by more than individual inclination and the conditions of the planet and its atmosphere. No human is free of social structures, nor (perhaps) would happiness consist in such freedom. Structure consists of boundaries, limits and barriers; in a structured whole, some motions and changes are possible, and others are not. If one is looking for an excuse to dilute the word 'oppression', one can use the fact of social structure as an excuse and say that everyone is oppressed. But if one would rather get clear about what oppression is and is not, one needs to sort out the sufferings, harms and limitations and figure out which are elements of oppression and which are not.

From what I have already said here, it is clear that if one wants to determine whether a particular suffering, harm or limitation is part of someone's being oppressed, one has to look at it *in context* in order to tell whether it is an element in an oppressive structure: one has to see if it is part of an enclosing structure of forces and barriers which tends to the immobilization and reduction of a group or category of people. One has to look at how the barrier or force fits with others and to whose benefit or detriment it works. As soon as one looks at examples, it becomes obvious that not everything which frustrates or limits a person is oppressive, and not every harm or damage is due to or contributes to oppression. . . .

Another example: The boundaries of a racial ghetto in an American city serve to some extent to keep white people from going in, as well as to keep ghetto dwellers from going out. A particular white citizen may be frustrated or feel deprived because s/he cannot stroll around there and enjoy the "exotic" aura of a "foreign" culture, or shop for bargains in the ghetto swap shops. In fact, the existence of the ghetto, of racial segregation, does deprive the white person of knowledge and harm her/his character by nurturing unwarranted feelings of superiority. But this does not make the white person in this situation a member of an oppressed race or a person oppressed because of her/his race. One must look at the barrier. It limits the activities and the access of those on both sides of it (though to different degrees). But it is a product of the intention, planning and action of whites for the benefit of whites, to secure and maintain privileges that are available to whites generally, as members of the dominant and privileged group. Though the existence of the barrier has some bad consequences for whites, the barrier does not exist in systematic relationship with other barriers and forces forming a structure oppressive to whites; quite the contrary. It is part of a structure which oppresses the ghetto dwellers and thereby (and by white intention) protects and furthers white interests as dominant white culture understands them. This barrier is not oppressive to whites, even though it is a barrier to whites.

Barriers have different meanings to those on opposite sides of them, even though they are barriers to both. The physical walls of a prison no more dissolve to let an outsider in than to let an insider out, but for the insider they are confining and limiting while to the outsider they may mean protection from what s/he takes to be threats posed by insiders— freedom from harm or anxiety. A set of social and economic barriers and forces separating two groups may be felt, even painfully, by members of both groups and yet may mean confinement to one and liberty and enlargement of opportunity to the other.

The service sector of the wives/mommas/assistants/girls is almost exclusively a woman-only sector; its boundaries not only enclose women but to a very great extent keep men out. Some men sometimes encounter this barrier and experience it as a restriction on their movements, their activities, their control or their choices of "lifestyle." Thinking they might like the simple nurturant life (which they may imagine to be quite free of stress, alienation and hard work), and feeling deprived since it seems closed to them, they thereupon announce the discovery that they are oppressed, too, by "sex roles." But that barrier is erected and maintained by men, for the benefit of men. It consists of cultural and economic forces and pressures in a culture and economy controlled by men in which, at every economic level and in all racial and ethnic subcultures, economy, tradition—and even ideologies of liberation—work to keep at least local culture and economy in male control....

One is marked for application of oppressive pressures by one's membership in some group or category. Much of one's suffering and frustration befalls one partly or largely because one is a member of that category. In the case at hand, it is the category, *woman*. Being a woman is a major factor in my not having a better job than I do; being a woman selects me as a likely victim of sexual assault or harassment; it is my being a woman that reduces the power of my anger to a proof of my insanity. If a woman has little or no economic or political power, or achieves little of what she wants to achieve, a major causal factor in this is that she is a woman. For any woman of any race or economic class, being a woman is significantly attached to whatever disadvantages and deprivations she suffers, be they great or small.

None of this is the case with respect to a person's being a man. Simply being a man is not what stands between him and a better job; whatever assaults and harassments he is subject to, being male is not what selects him for victimization; being male is not a factor which would make his anger impotent—quite the opposite. If a man has little or no material or political power, or achieves little of what he wants to achieve, his being male is no part of the explanation. Being male is something he has going *for* him, even if race or class or age or disability is going against him.

Women are oppressed, *as women*. Members of certain racial and/or economic groups and classes, both the males and the females, are oppressed *as* members of those races and/or classes. But men are not oppressed *as men*.

... and isn't it strange that any of us should have been confused and mystified about such a simple thing?

IRIS MARION YOUNG, FIVE FACES OF OPPRESSION

in Rethinking Power 174–195 (Thomas Wartenberg, ed., SUNY Press, 1992).

... Oppression in the structural sense is part of the basic fabric of a society, not a function of a few people's choice or policies. You won't eliminate this structural oppression by getting rid of the rules or making some new laws, because oppressions are systematically reproduced in major economic, political, and cultural institutions. Thus, one reason that "oppression" is not commonly used to describe injustice in our society is that the prevailing political discourse does not have a place in its social ontology for structuration and social groups.

Mirroring majority political discourse, philosophical discussions of justice and injustice rarely use the term "oppression," using instead the term "discrimination" to refer to some of the injustices radicals call oppression. Even radical philosophers tend to avoid the term "oppression." Although his analysis is clearly influenced by Black Marxism and Black Power movements, Bernard Boxill, for example, consistently uses the term "discrimination" to designate the injustice that blacks have suffered and continue to suffer in U.S. society. This is a symptom of the hold majority political discourse has over our thinking, perhaps especially over philosophers, who in turn help legitimate that discourse by using it and giving it technical precision. By "discrimination" I mean conscious actions and policies by which members of a group are excluded from institutions or confined to inferior positions. Discrimination is often an instrument of oppression, and discriminatory practices are certainly part of some oppressions, but the concept of oppression is neither coincident with nor reducible to discrimination.

Discrimination is a methodologically individualist concept. In recent years most courts have found that there has been discrimination only if particular victims of discrimination can be individually identified, that a particular agent can be identified as responsible for discrimination, and it can be shown that the agent knew its actions or policies were discriminatory. To be sure, the concept of discrimination can make reference to groups insofar as a discriminatory policy excludes a whole class of persons from some position or activity. Even when concerning groups, however, discrimination is usually an individualist concept insofar as it presupposes an identifiable agent who discriminates, and that the sum of discrimination is the sum of discriminatory acts.

The difference between the concept of discrimination and the concept of oppression emerges most clearly with the insight that oppression often exists in the absence of overt discrimination. Though actions and policies that explicitly discriminated against members of particular groups were common in the United States not long ago and have by no means disappeared, legislation and litigation in the past twenty years have greatly lessened overt policies of discrimination against most groups, with the outrageous exception of lesbians and gay men. Socialists, feminists, antiracism activists, insist, however, that this serious reduction in overt and conscious policies of exclusion and segregation has done little to reduce the oppression that many groups have suffered and continue to suffer. This concept cites the vast and deep injustices some groups suffer as a consequence of frequently unconscious assumptions and reactions of well-meaning people in ordinary interactions, media and cultural stereotypes, and structural features of bureaucratic hierarchy and market mechanisms, in short, the normal ongoing processes of everyday life. As Marilyn Frye puts it, oppression refers to "an enclosing structure of forces and barriers which tends to be the immobilization and reduction of a group or category of people." . . .

Insofar as economic location and occupation significantly determine a person's self-understanding, perception of social relations and others, and insofar as such economic location in our society tends to be reproduced across generations, classes are certainly social groups in the sense I have discussed. Just how class will be defined will depend on the uses of the definition, for example, to understand the structural imperatives of accumulation or to understand the motivation of particular persons to support certain policies.

Group differentiation does not necessarily imply oppression, however; groups can exist that are not oppressed. In the United States, Catholics are a group in the sense I have discussed, but they are no longer an oppressed group. In Northern Ireland, on the other hand, Catholics are an oppressed group. Whether a group is oppressed depends on whether it is subject to one or more of the five conditions I shall discuss below. Despite the modern myth of a decline of parochial attachments and ascribed identities, I think that group differentiation is both an inevitable and desirable aspect of modern social processes. Social justice, then, requires not the melting away of differences, but institutions that promote reproduction of and respect for group difference without oppression.

I have suggested that oppression is the inhibition of a group through a vast network of everyday practices, attitudes, assumptions, behaviors, and institutional rules; it is structural or systemic. The systemic character of oppression implies that an oppressed group need not have a correlate oppressing group. While structural oppression in our society involves relations among groups, these relations do not generally fit the paradigm of one group's consciously and intentionally keeping another down. Foucault suggests that to understand the meaning and operation of power in modern society we should look beyond the model of power as "sovereignty," a dyadic relation of ruler and subject, and instead analyze the exercise of power as the effect of liberal and humanized practices of education, bureaucratic administration, production and distribution of consumer goods, medical practice, and so on. The conscious actions of many individuals daily contribute to maintaining and reproducing oppression, but those people are usually simply doing their jobs or living their lives, not understanding themselves as agents of oppression. Defining oppression as structural is an innovation of the new left usage of the term to describe our society. Many people understand oppression to refer only to a conscious tyranny of one individual or group over another and for that reason will not use the term to describe injustices in our own society.

By denying that structural oppression is perpetrated by an identifiable agent of oppression I do not mean to suggest that within this system of oppression individual persons do not intentionally do things to harm others in oppressed groups. The raped woman, the beaten black youth, the locked-out worker, and the gay man harassed on the street are victims of intentional behavior by identifiable agents. Nor do I mean to suggest that specific groups are not beneficiaries of the oppression of other groups, and thus have an interest in their continued oppression. On the contrary, for every oppressed group there is a group that is *privileged* in relation to that group.

The concept of oppression has been used among radicals since the 1960s, partly in reaction to some Marxist attempts to reduce the injustices of racism and sexism, for example, to the effects of class domination or bourgeois ideology. Racism, sexism, ageism, and homophobia, some social movements asserted, are distinct forms of oppression with their own dynamics apart from the dynamics of class, even though they might interact with class oppression. From often heated discussions among socialists, feminists, and antiracism activists in the last ten years, a consensus is emerging that many different groups must be said to be oppressed in our society, and that no group's or form of oppression can claim causal or moral primacy. The same discussion has also come to understand that group differences cross individual lives in a multiplicity of ways that can entail privilege and oppression for the same person in different respects. Only a plural explication of the concept of oppression can appropriately capture these insights.

Accordingly, in the following sections I offer an explication of five faces of oppression as a useful set of categories and distinctions that I believe is comprehensive, in the sense that it covers all the groups said by new left social movements to be oppressed and covers all the ways they are oppressed. I derive the five faces of oppression from reflection on the condition of these groups. Because different factors, or combinations of factors, constitute the oppression of different groups, making their oppression irreducible, I believe it is not possible to have one essential definition of oppression. With the following five categories, however, the oppression of any group can be described, as well as its similarities with and differences from the oppression of other groups.

EXPLOITATION

The central function of Marx's theory of exploitation is to explain how class structure can exist in the absence of legally and normatively sanctioned class distinctions. In precapitalist societies domination is overt and carried on through direct political means. In both slave society and feudal society the right to appropriate the product of the labor of others partly defines class privilege, and these societies legitimate class distinctions with ideologies of natural superiority and inferiority.

Capitalist society, on the other hand, removes traditional juridically enforced class distinctions and promotes a belief in the legal freedom of persons. Workers freely contract with employers, receive a wage, and no formal mechanisms of law or custom force them to work for that employer or any employer. Thus, the mystery of capitalism arises:

when everyone is formally free, how can there be class domination? Why does there continue to be class distinction between the wealthy, who own the means of production, and the mass of people, who work for them? The theory of exploitation answers this question.

Profit, the basis of capitalist power and wealth, is a mystery if we assume that in the market goods exchange at their values. Marx's use of the labor theory of value, however, dispels this mystery. Every commodity's value is a function of the labor time necessary for the production of labor power. Labor power is the one commodity that in the process of being consumed produces new value. Profit then comes from the difference between the actual labor and the value of that capacity to labor that the capitalist purchases and puts to work. The owner of capital appropriates this surplus value, which accounts for the possibility of realizing a profit....

The central insight expressed with the concept of exploitation, then, is that domination occurs through a steady process of the transfer of the results of the labor of some people to benefit others. The injustice of class division does not consist only in the fact that some people have great wealth while most people have little and some are severely deprived. The theory of exploitation shows that this relation of power and inequality is produced and reproduced through a systematic process in which the energies of the have-nots are continuously expended to maintain and augment the power, status, and wealth of the haves.

Many writers have cogently argued that the Marxian concept of exploitation is too narrow to encompass all forms of domination and oppression. In particular, by confining itself to examining class domination and oppression, the Marxist concept of exploitation does not contribute to an understanding of such group oppressions as sexism and racism. The question, then, is whether the concept of exploitation can be broadened to include other ways that the labor and energy expenditure of one group benefits another, thus reproducing a relation of domination between them.

Feminists have had little difficulty showing that women's oppression consists partly in a systematic and unreciprocated transfer of powers from women to men. Women's oppression consists not merely in an inequality of status, power, and wealth resulting from men's excluding women from privileged activities. The freedom, power, status, and self-realization of men is possible precisely because women work for them. Gender exploitation has two aspects, transfer of the fruits of material labor to men, and the transfer of nurturing and sexual energies to men....

Most feminist theories of gender exploitation have concentrated on the institutional structure of the patriarchal family. Recently, however, feminists have begun to theorize relations of gender exploitation enacted in the contemporary workplace and through the state. Carol Brown argues that as men have removed themselves from responsibility for children, many women have become dependent on the state for subsistence as they continue to bear nearly total responsibility for child rearing. This creates a new system of the exploitation of women's domestic labor mediated by those state institutions, which she calls public patriarchy.

In twentieth-century capitalist economies, the workplaces that women have been entering in increasing numbers serve as another important site of gender exploitation. David Alexander argues that most typically feminine jobs have gender tasks involving sexual labor, nurturing, caring for a person's body, or smoothing over relations through personality. In these ways, women's energies are expended in workplaces that enhance the status of, please, or comfort others, usually men; and these gender-based labors of waitresses, clerical workers, nurses, and other caretakers often go unnoticed and undercompensated.

To summarize, women are exploited in the Marxian sense to the degree that they are wage workers. Some have argued that women's domestic labor is also a form of capitalist class exploitation insofar as it is labor covered by the wages a family receives. As a class, however, women undergo specific forms of gender exploitation--ways the energies and power of women are expended, often unnoticed and unacknowledged, usually to benefit men by releasing them for more important and creative work, enhancing their status or the environment around them, or providing men with sexual or emotional service.

Race is a structure of oppression at least as basic as class or gender. Are there, then, racially specific forms of exploitation? This is different from the question of whether racial groups are subjected to intense capitalist exploitation. Racial groups in the United States, especially blacks and Latinos, are oppressed through capitalist superexploitation resulting from a segmented labor market that tends to reserve skilled, high-paying, unionized jobs for whites. There is wide disagreement about whether such superexploitation benefits whites as a group or only benefits the capitalist class, and I do not intend to resolve that dispute here.

However one answers the question about capitalist superexploitation of racial groups, is it also possible to conceptualize a form of exploitation that is racially specific on analogy with the gender-specific forms I have discussed? The category of *menial* labor might provide an opening for such conceptualization. In its derivation "menial" means the labor of servants. Wherever there is racism, including the United States today, there is the assumption, more or less enforced, that members of the oppressed racial groups are or ought to be servants of those, or some of those, in the privileged group. In white racist societies this generally means that many white people have dark- or yellow-skinned domestic servants, and in the United States today there remains significant race structuring of private household service.

In the United States today much service labor has gone public: anybody can have servants if they go to a good hotel, a good restaurant, or hire a cleaning service. Servants often attend the daily—and nightly—activities of business executives, government officials, and other high-status professionals. In our society there remains strong cultural pressure to fill servant jobs—like bell hop, porter, chamber maid, bus boy, and so on—with black and Latin workers. These jobs entail a transfer of energies whereby the servers enhance the status of the served, to place them in an aristocracy—the rule of the best.

Menial labor today refers to more than service, however; it refers to any servile, unskilled, low-paying work lacking in autonomy, and in which a person is subject to orders from several people. Menial work tends to be auxiliary work, instrumental to another person's work, in which that other person receives primary recognition for doing the job. Laborers on a construction site, for example, are at the beck and call of welders, electricians, carpenters, and other skilled workers, who receive recognition for the job done. In the history of the United States, explicit racial discrimination reserved menial work for blacks, Chicanos, American Indians, and Chinese, and menial work still tends to be linked to black and Latino workers. I offer this category of menial labor as a form of racially specific exploitation, only as a proposal, however, that needs discussion.

MARGINALIZATION

Increasingly in the United States, racial oppression occurs more in the form of marginalization than exploitation. Marginals are people the system of labor markets cannot or will not employ. Not only in Third World capitalist countries, but also in most Western capitalist societies, there is a growing underclass of people permanently confined to lives of social marginality, the majority of whom are racially marked—blacks or Indians in Latin America, blacks, East Indians, Eastern Europeans, or North Africans in Europe.

Marginalization is by no means the fate only of racially marked groups, however. In the United States a shamefully large proportion of the population is marginal: old people, and increasingly people who are not very old but get laid off from their jobs and cannot find new work; young people, especially black or Latino, who cannot find first or second jobs; many single mothers and their children; other people involuntarily unemployed; many mentally or physically disabled people; and American Indians, especially those on reservations.

Marginalization is perhaps the most dangerous form of oppression. A whole category of people is expelled from useful participation in social life, then potentially subject to severe material deprivation and even extermination. The material deprivation marginalization often causes certainly is unjust, especially in a society in which others have plenty. Contemporary advanced capitalist societies in principle have acknowledged the injustice of material deprivation caused by marginalization, and have taken some steps to address it by providing welfare payments and services. The continuance of this welfare state is by no means assured, and in most welfare-state societies, especially the United States, benefits are not sufficient to eliminate large-scale suffering and deprivation.

Material deprivation, which can be addressed by redistributive social policies, is not, however, the extent of the harm caused by marginalization. Two categories of injustice beyond distribution are associated with marginality in advanced capitalist societies. The provision of welfare itself produces new injustice when it deprives dependent persons of rights and freedoms that others have. If justice requires that every person have the opportunity to develop and exercise his or her capacities, finally, then marginalization is unjust primarily because it blocks such opportunity to exercise capacities in socially defined and recognized ways.

Liberalism traditionally asserts the right of all rational autonomous agents to equal citizenship. Early bourgeois liberalism made explicit that citizenship excluded all those whose reason was questionable or not fully developed and all those not independent. Thus, poor people, women, the mad and the feeble-minded, and children were explicitly excluded from citizenship, and many of these were housed in institutions modeled on the modern prison: poor houses, insane asylums, schools.

In our own society the exclusion of dependent persons from equal citizenship rights is only barely hidden beneath the surface. Because they are dependent on bureaucratic institutions for support or services, old people, poor people, and mentally or physically disabled people are subject to patronizing, punitive, demeaning, and arbitrary treatment by the policies and people associated with welfare bureaucracies. Being a dependent in this society implies being legitimately subject to often arbitrary and invasive authority of social service providers and other public and private bureaucrats, who enforce rules with which the marginal must comply, and otherwise exercise power over the conditions of his or her life. In meeting needs of the marginalized, with the aid of social scientific disciplines, the welfare agencies also construct the needs themselves. Medical and social service professionals know what is good for those they serve, and the marginals and dependents themselves do not have the right to claim to know what is good for them. Dependency thus implies in this society, as it has in all liberal societies, a sufficient condition to suspend rights to privacy, respect, and individual choice.

Although dependency thus produces conditions of injustice in our society, dependency in itself should not and need not be oppressive. We cannot imagine a society in which some people would not need to be dependent on others at least some of the time: children, sick people, women recovering from childbirth, old people who have become frail, and depressed or otherwise emotionally needy persons have the moral right to be dependent on others for subsistence and support.

An important contribution of feminist moral theory has consisted in questioning the deeply held assumption that moral agency and full citizenship require that a person be autonomous and independent. Feminists have exposed such an assumption as inappropriately individualistic and derived from a specifically male experience of social relations, valuing competition and solitary achievement. Female experience of social relations, arising both from women's typical domestic care responsibilities and from the kinds of paid work that many women do, tends to recognize dependence as a basic human condition. Whereas in the autonomy model a just society would as much as possible give people the opportunity to be independent, the feminist model instead envisions justice as according respect and decision-making participation to those who are dependent as well as those who are independent. Dependence should not be a reason to be deprived of choice and respect, and much of the oppression many marginals experience would diminish if a less individualistic model of rights prevailed.

Marginalization does not cease to be oppressive when one has shelter and food. Many old people, for example, have sufficient means to live comfortably but remain oppressed in their marginal status. Even if marginals were provided a comfortable material life within institutions that respected their freedom and dignity, injustices of marginality would remain in the form of uselessness, boredom, and lack of self-respect. Most of this society's productive and recognized activities take place in contexts of organized social cooperation, and social structures and processes that close persons out of participation in such social cooperation are unjust.

The fact of marginalization raises basic structural issues of justice. In particular, we must consider what is just about a connection between participation in productive activities of social cooperation, on the one hand, and acquisition of the means of consumption, on the other. As marginalization is increasing, with no sign of abatement, some social policy analysts have introduced the idea of a "social wage" as a socially provided, guaranteed income not tied to the wage system. Restructuring activities of production and service provision to ensure that everyone able and willing has socially recognized work to do, moreover, also implies organization of socially productive activity at least partly outside of a wage system.

POWERLESSNESS

As I have indicated, the Marxian idea of class is important because it helps reveal the structure of exploitation: that some people have their power and wealth because they profit from the labor of others. For this reason I reject the claim of some that a traditional class exploitation model fails to capture the structure of contemporary society. It is still the case that the labor of most people in the society augments the power of a few; whatever their differences from nonprofessional workers, most professional workers share with them not being members of the capitalist class.

An adequate conception of oppression, however, cannot ignore the experience of social division colloquially referred to as the difference between the "middle class" and the "working class," a division structured by the social division of labor between professionals and nonprofessionals. Rather than expanding or revising the Marxian concept of class to take account of this experience, as some writers do, I suggest that we follow Weber and describe this as a difference in *status* rather than class. Being a professional entails occupying a status position that nonprofessionals lack, creating a condition of oppression that nonprofessionals suffer. I shall call this kind of oppression "powerlessness."

The absence of genuine democracy in the United States means that most people do not participate in making decisions that regularly affect the conditions of their lives and actions. In this sense most people lack significant power. Powerlessness, however, describes the lives of people who have little or no work autonomy, exercise little creativity or judgment in their work, have no technical expertise or authority, express themselves awkwardly, especially in public or bureaucratic settings, and do not command respect. Powerlessness names the oppressive situations Sennet and Cobb describe in their famous study of working class men.

The clearest way for me to think of this powerless status is negatively: the powerless lack the status and sense of self that professionals tend to have. There are three aspects of status privilege that professionals have, the lack of which produces oppression for nonprofessionals.

First, acquiring and practicing a profession has an expansive, progressive character. Being professional usually requires a college education and learning a specialized knowledge that entails working with symbols and concepts. In acquiring one's profession, a person experiences progress in learning the necessary expertise, and usually when one begins practicing one enters a career, that is, a working life of growth or progress in professional development. The life of the nonprofessional by comparison is powerless in the sense that it lacks this orientation toward the progressive development of one's capacities.

Second, while most professionals have supervisors and do not have power to affect many decisions or the action of very many people, most nevertheless have considerable day-to-day work autonomy. Professionals usually have some authority over others, moreover, either over workers they supervise or over auxiliaries or clients. Nonprofessionals, on the other hand, lack autonomy, and both in their working lives and in their consumer-client lives, they often stand under the authority of professionals.

Though having its material basis in a division of labor between mental and manual work, the group division between middle class and working class designates not a division only in working life, but also in nearly all aspects of social life. Professionals and nonprofessionals belong to different cultures in the United States. The two groups tend to live in segregated neighborhoods or even different towns, not least because of the actions and decisions of real estate people. They tend to have different tastes in food, decor, clothes, music, and vacations. Members of the two groups socialize for the most part with others in the same status group. While there is some intergroup mobility between generations, for the most part the children of professionals become professionals and the children of nonprofessionals do not.

Thus, third, the privileges of the professional extend beyond the workplace to elevate a whole way of life, which consists in being "respectable." To treat someone with respect is to be prepared to listen to what they have to say or to do what they request because they have some authority, expertise, or influence.

The norms of respectability in our society are associated specifically with professional culture. Professional dress, speech, tastes, and demeanor all connote respectability. Generally professionals expect and receive respect from others. In restaurants, banks, hotels, real estate offices, and many other such public places, professionals typically receive more respectful treatment than nonprofessionals. For this reason nonprofessionals seeking a loan or a job, or to buy a house or a car, will often try to look "professional" and "respectable" in these settings. The privilege of this professional respectability starkly appears in the dynamics of racism and sexism. In daily interchange women and men of color must prove their respectability. At first they are often not treated by strangers with respectful distance or deference. Once people discover that this woman or that Puerto Rican man is a college teacher or a business executive, however, people often behave more respectfully toward her or him. Working-class white men, on the other hand, are often treated with respect until their working class status is revealed.

Cultural Imperialism

Exploitation, marginality, and powerlessness all refer to relations of power and oppression that occur by virtue of the social division of labor: who works for whom, who does not work, and how the content of work in one position is defined in relation to others. These three categories refer to the structural and institutional relations that delimit people's material lives, including but not limited to the resources they have access to, the concrete opportunity they have or do not have to develop and exercise capacities in involving, socially recognized ways that enhance rather than diminish their lives. These kinds of oppression are a matter of concrete power in relation to others, who benefits from whom, and who is dispensable.

Exploitation, marginality, and powerlessness all refer to relations of power and oppression that occur by virtue of the social division of labor: who works for whom, who does not work, and how the content of work in one position is defined in relation to others. These three categories refer to the structural and institutional relations that delimit people's material lives, including but not limited to the resources they have access to, the concrete opportunity they have or do not have to develop and exercise capacities in involving, socially recognized ways that enhance rather than diminish their lives. These kinds of oppression are a matter of concrete power in relation to others, who benefits from whom, and who is dispensable.

Recent theorists of movements of group liberation, especially feminists and black liberation theorists, have also given prominence to a rather different experience of oppression, which I shall call cultural imperialism. This is the experience of existing in a society whose dominant meanings render the particular perspectives and point of view of one's own group invisible at the same time as they stereotype one's group and mark it out as "other."

Cultural imperialism consists in the universalization of one group's experience and culture and its establishment as the norm. Some groups have exclusive or primary access to what Nancy Fraser calls the means of interpretation and communication in a society. As a result, the dominant cultural products of the society, that is, those most widely disseminated, express the experience, values, goals, and achievements of the groups that produce them. The cultural products also express their perspective on and interpretation of events and elements in the society, including the other groups in the society, insofar as they are noticed at all. Often without noticing they do so, the dominant groups project their own experience as representative of humanity as such.

An encounter with groups different from the dominant group, however, challenges its claim to universality. The dominant group saves its position by bringing the other group under the measure of its dominant norms. Consequently, the difference of women from men, Native Americans or Africans from Europeans, Jews from Christians, homosexuals from heterosexuals, or workers from professionals becomes reconstructed as deviance and inferiority. The dominant groups and their cultural expressions are the normal, the universal, and thereby unremarkable. Since the dominant group's cultural expressions are the only expressions that receive wide dissemination, the dominant groups construct the differences that some groups exhibit as lack and negation in relation to the norms, and those groups become marked out as "other."

Victims of cultural imperialism experience a paradoxical oppression in that they are both marked out by stereotypes and rendered invisible. As remarkable, deviant beings, the culturally dominated are stamped with an essence. In contrast, the privileged are indefinable because they are individual; each is whatever he or she wants to be, they are what they do, and by their doings they are judged. The stereotype marks and defines the culturally dominated, confines them to a nature that is usually attached in some way to their bodies, and thus that cannot easily be denied. These stereotypes so permeate the society that they are not noticed as contestable. Just as everyone knows that the earth goes around the sun, so everyone knows that gay people are promiscuous, that Indians are alcoholics, and that women are good with children.

Those living under cultural imperialism find themselves defined from the outside, positioned, and placed by a system of dominant meanings they experience as arising from elsewhere, from those with whom they do not identify and who do not identify with them. The dominant culture's stereotyped, marked, and inferiorized images of the group must be internalized by group members at least to the degree that they are forced to react to behaviors of others that express or are influenced by those images. This creates for the culturally oppressed the experience that W.E.B. DuBois called "double consciousness." "This sense of always looking at one's self through the eyes of others, of measuring one's soul by the tape of a world that looks on in amused contempt and pity." This consciousness is double because the oppressed subject refuses to coincide with these devalued, objectified, stereotyped visions of herself or himself. The subject desires recognition as human, capable of activity, full of hope and possibility, but receives from the dominant culture only the judgment that he or she is different, marked, or inferior.

People in culturally oppressed groups often maintain a sense of positive subjectivity because they can affirm and recognize one another as sharing similar experiences and perspectives on social life. The group defined by the dominant culture as deviant, as a stereotyped other, *is* culturally different from the dominant group because the status of otherness creates specific experiences not shared by the dominant group and because culturally oppressed groups also are often socially segregated and occupy specific positions in the social division of labor. They express their specific group experiences and interpretations of the world to one another, developing and perpetuating their own culture. Double consciousness, then, occurs because one finds one's being defined by two cultures: a dominant and a subordinate culture.

Cultural imperialism involves the paradox of experiencing oneself as invisible at the same time that one is marked out and noticed as different. The perspectives of other groups dominate the culture without their noticing it as a perspective, and their cultural expressions are widely disseminated. These dominant cultural expressions often simply pay no attention to the existence and experience of those other groups, only to mention or refer to them in stereotyped or marginalized ways. This, then, is the injustice of cultural imperialism: that the oppressed group's experience and interpretation of social life finds no expression that touches the dominant culture, while that same culture imposes on the oppressed group its experience and interpretations of social life.

VIOLENCE

Finally, many groups suffer the oppression of systematic and legitimized violence. The members of some groups live with the fear of random, unprovoked attacks on their persons or property, which have no motive but to damage, humiliate, or destroy them. In U.S. society women, blacks, Asians, Arabs, gay men, and lesbians live under such threats of violence, and in at least some regions Jews, Puerto Ricans, Chicanos, and other Spanish-speaking Americans must fear such violence as well. Violation may also take the form of name-calling or petty harassment intended to degrade or humiliate, and always signals an underlying threat of physical attack.

Such violence is systematic because it is directed at any member of the group simply because he or she is a member of that group. Any woman, for example, has reason to fear rape. The violence to which these oppressed groups are subject, moreover, is usually legitimate in the sense that most people regard it as unsurprising, and so it usually goes unpunished. Police beatings or killings of black youths, for example, are rarely publicized, rarely provoke moral outrage on the part of most white people, and rarely receive punishment.

An important aspect of the kind of random but systematic violence I am referring to here is its utter irrationality. Xenophobic violence is different from the violence of state or ruling-class repression. Repressive violence has a rational, though evil, motive: rulers use it as a coercive tool to maintain their power. Many accounts of racist, sexist, or homophobic violence try to explain it as motivated by a desire to maintain group privilege or domination. I agree that fear of violence functions to help keep these oppressed groups subordinate. I think the causes of such violence must be traced to unconscious structures of identity formation that project onto some groups the fluid, bodily aspect of the subject that threatens the rigid unity of that identity.

Conclusion

The five faces of oppression that I have explicated here function as criteria of oppression, not as a full theoretical account of oppression. With them we can tell whether a group is oppressed, according to objective social structures and behaviors. Being subject to any one of these five conditions is sufficient for calling a group oppressed. Most of the groups I listed earlier as oppressed in U.S. society experience more than one of these forms, and some experience all five.

Nearly all, if not all, groups said by contemporary social movements to be oppressed in our society suffer cultural imperialism. Which other oppressions are experienced by which groups, however, is quite variable. Working-class people are exploited and powerless, for example, but if employed and white do not experience marginalization and violence. Gay men, on the other hand, are not *qua* gay exploited or powerless, but they experience severe cultural imperialism and violence. Similarly, Jews and Arabs as groups are victims of cultural imperialism and violence, though many members of these groups also suffer exploitation or powerlessness. Old people are oppressed by marginalization and cultural imperialism, and this is also true of physically or mentally disabled people. As a group women are subject to gender-based exploitation, powerlessness, cultural imperialism, and violence. Racism in the United States associates blacks and Latinos with marginalization, even though many members of these groups escape that condition; members of these groups often suffer all five forms of oppression.

With these criteria I have specifically avoided defining structures and kinds of oppression according to the groups oppressed: racism, classism, sexism, heterosexism, ageism. The forms of group oppression these terms name are not homologous, and the five criteria can help describe how and why not. The five criteria also help show that while no group oppression is reducible to or explained by any other group oppression, the oppression of one group is not a closed system with its own attributes, but overlaps with the oppression of other groups. With these criteria, moreover, we can claim that one group is more oppressed than another, insofar as it is subject to more of these five conditions, without thereby theoretically privileging a particular form of oppression or one oppressed group.

Notes and Questions

1. Large numbers of men and women in our society deny that women are oppressed or treated inequitably in the 1990s. Does Professor Frye's bird cage metaphor offer an easily understandable approach for explaining why so many people deny that women are oppressed? Professor Frye also discusses the "double bind". How does the double bind affect different racial minorities in the U.S.?

2. There are many kinds of structural oppressions—racism, sexism, heterosexism, classism, ableism, ageism and more. While there are similarities between how these oppressive structures function, the experiences and roots of these oppressions differ. There can be both strengths and pitfalls in trying to compare experiences of oppression to build solidarity between and among identity groups. Professor Young, by breaking down oppression into five different varieties, ameliorates one of the serious problems that occurs when oppressions are compared—the oppression sweepstakes.

3. While Frye and Young take more philosophical and political approaches to understanding oppressions, Professor Charles Lawrence uses psychology to argue that systemic oppressions, like racism, are so virulent because they are unconscious. Charles Lawrence, III, *The Id, the Ego and Equal Protection: Reckoning with Unconscious Racism*, 39 Stan.L.Rev. 317 (1987). In order to build his argument about why the "intent" standard is fallacious for determining whether racially discriminatory conduct violates the equal protection clause of the fourteenth amendment, Professor Lawrence explains:

CHARLES LAWRENCE, III, THE ID, THE EGO AND EQUAL PROTECTION: RECKONING WITH UNCONSCIOUS RACISM
39 Stan.L.Rev. 317, 321–23 (1987).

Much of one's inability to know racial discrimination when one sees it results from a failure to recognize that racism is both a crime and a disease. This failure is compounded by a reluctance to admit that the illness of racism infects almost everyone. Acknowledging and understanding the malignancy are prerequisites to the discovery of an appropriate cure. But the diagnosis is difficult, because our own contamination with the very illness for which a cure is sought impairs our comprehension of the disorder.

Americans share a common historical and cultural heritage in which racism has played and still plays a dominant role. Because of this shared experience, we also inevitably share many ideas, attitudes, and beliefs that attach significance to an individual's race and induce negative feelings and opinions about nonwhites. To the extent that this cultural belief system has influenced all of us, we are all racists. At the same time, most of us are unaware of our racism. We do not recognize the ways in which our cultural experience has influenced our beliefs about race or the occasions on which those beliefs affect our actions. In other words, a large part of the behavior that produces racial discrimination is influenced by unconscious racial motivation.

There are two explanations for the unconscious nature of our racially discriminatory beliefs and ideas. First, Freudian theory states that the human mind defends itself against the discomfort of guilt by denying or refusing to recognize those ideas, wishes, and beliefs that conflict with what the individual has learned is good or right. While our historical experience has made racism an integral part of our culture, our society has more recently embraced an ideal that rejects racism as immoral. When an individual experiences conflict between racist ideas and the societal ethic that condemns those ideas, the mind excludes his racism from consciousness.

Second, the theory of cognitive psychology states that the culture—including, for example, the media and an individual's parents, peers, and authority figures—transmits certain beliefs and preferences. Because these beliefs are so much a part of the culture, they are not experienced as explicit lessons. Instead, they seem part of the individual's rational ordering of her perceptions of the world. The individual is unaware, for example, that the ubiquitous presence of a cultural stereotype has influenced her perception that blacks are lazy or unintelligent. Because racism is so deeply ingrained in our culture, it is likely to be transmitted by tacit understandings: Even if a child is not told that blacks are inferior, he learns that lesson by observing the behavior of others. These tacit understandings, because they have never been articulated, are less likely to be experienced at a conscious level.

In short, requiring proof of conscious or intentional motivation as a prerequisite to constitutional recognition that a decision is race-dependent ignores much of what we understand about how the human mind works. It also disregards both the irrationality of racism and the profound effect that the history of American race relations has had on the individual and collective unconscious.

––––––

Professors Richard Delgado and Jean Stefancic illustrate how cultural images have reinforced the structures of oppression and perpetuated racism and other social ills in our society. We give you this excerpt and encourage you to peruse the extensive footnoted materials and detailed bibliography that follow the article in its original published form.

RICHARD DELGADO AND JEAN STEFANCIC, IMAGES OF THE OUTSIDER IN AMERICAN LAW AND CULTURE: CAN FREE EXPRESSION REMEDY SYSTEMIC SOCIAL ILLS?

77 Cornell L.Rev. 1258, 1261–75 (1992).

I.

IMAGES OF THE OUTSIDER

A small but excellent literature chronicles the depiction in popular culture of each of the major minority subgroups of color—African–Americans, Mexicans, Native Americans, and Asians. In this Part, we summarize that history and draw parallels among the ways that society has traditionally depicted the four groups.

A. African–Americans

Early in our history, as everyone knows, slave traders rounded up African villagers and transported them to the New World in chains. En route, many died; those who survived were sold and forced to work in the fields and houses of a colonial nation bent on economic development and expansion. By the end of the Civil War, over 4,000,000 African–Americans were condemned to exist in some form of this American Nightmare.

Slave codes regulated behavior, deterring rebellion and forbidding intermarriage. They also prohibited Southern blacks from learning to read and write, thereby denying them access to the world of print then replete with arguments about "the rights of man." The dominant image of blacks in the popular theater and literature of the late eighteenth century was that of the docile and contented slave—child-like, lazy, illiterate, and dependent on the protection and care of a white master. The first appearance of Sambo, a "comic Negro" stereotype, occurred in 1781 in a play called The Divorce. This black male character, portrayed by a white in blackface, danced, sang, spoke nonsense, and acted the buffoon. The black man's potential as a sexual and economic competitor was minimized by portraying him as an object of laughter.

Blackface minstrelsy found a new popularity in the 1830s when Thomas D. Rice created Jim Crow, modeled on an elderly crippled black slave who shuffle-danced and sang. It is thought that Rice even borrowed the old man's shabby clothes for a more authentic stage performance. Rice's performance of Jump Jim Crow won him immediate success in the United States and England. By the 1840s minstrel shows were standard fare in American music halls. In these shows, whites in blackface created and disseminated stereotypes of African–Americans as inept urban dandies or happy child-like slaves. Probably more whites—at least in the North—received their understanding of African–American culture from minstrel shows than from first hand acquaintance with blacks or their ideas.

Because laws forbade slaves to learn to read or write, slave culture was primarily oral. Thus, it is highly significant that former slaves such as Frederick Douglass and William Wells Brown published accounts of captivity, life on plantations, and escapes to freedom. These early slave narratives, published in the North and circulated among abolitionist societies, presented counterimages to the prevailing myths of the dominant culture. The abolitionist movement reached its apogee with the publication of Harriet Beecher Stowe's Uncle Tom's Cabin. Though Stowe was successful in presenting the slave master as villain, her portrayal of Uncle Tom changed the stereotype of the black slave only a little: Previously he had been docile, content, or comic, while in her depiction he became gentle, long-suffering, and imbued with Christian piety.

After the Civil War, the black image bifurcated. The "good slave" image continued, but was soon joined by an ominous "shadow" figure. The Uncle Tom character became romanticized, a black mouthpiece espousing an apologia for the beliefs of the old genteel white Confederacy. Though never overtly sexual, his masculine form re-emerged as the avuncular storyteller Uncle Remus, as well as various other "uncles." His feminine form evolved into a "mammy" figure—cook, washerwoman, nanny, and all-round domestic servant—responsible for the comfort of the Southern white household. With no life of her own, imbued with practical wisdom, she took an intense interest in the welfare and well-being of the white family she cared for. During the tumultuous Reconstruction period, the sexuality denied to uncles and mammies found a crude outlet in a new stereotype of the recently freed male Negro as brutish and bestial. The Ku Klux Klan and other illegal raiding parties justified their reign of terror as necessary to control newly freed blacks whom they believed ready to force sex on any white woman they might encounter. This stereotype, appearing in novels with titles like The Negro as Beast, was offered to justify the widespread lynching that took 2,500 black lives between 1885 and 1900.

The myth of the out of control ambitious black was fueled by currents prevalent in the marketplace of Western thought during the late nineteenth century. Some of these ideas have been identified by Catherine Silk and John Silk: 1) the growth of American imperialism; 2) the absorption of "inferior races;" 3) the white man's burden mentality—the white South bearing the burden in the U.S.; 4) the manifest destiny belief of the Anglo–Saxons; and 5) the new social science theory concerning genetic inferiority.

Many of these ideas found expression in the powerful, crass, and influential writings of Thomas Dixon. His work represented an effort to satisfy his two goals in life: making money and converting people to racism. He believed that whites, both Northern and Southern, were duty bound to protect the Anglo–Saxon heritage, particularly white women, who were destined to produce a superior race. In 1905, Dixon wrote The Clansman, a tale of two families, one Northern and one Southern, united through marriage. It proved a sensation, particularly in the South. Ten years later, film-maker D.W. Griffith used the plots of this and another of Dixon's novels for his epic three-hour film, The Birth of a Nation.

The film transformed Dixon's novels into vivid visual images, featuring uncles, mammies, buffoons, an interfering mulatto mistress, and a chase scene in which a black man with animal-like traits pursues a young white woman until she leaps to her death from a pedestal-like perch at the edge of a cliff. The film played to audiences throughout the country. New white immigrants from Eastern and Southern Europe saw the film in numerous movie houses in poor neighborhoods, where it played for almost a year. In the South it played for fifteen years. A special screening was held at the White House for Dixon's former classmate, President Woodrow Wilson, his guests, and the entire Supreme Court. Wilson later described the film as "like writing history with lightning."

Blacks could do little to confront the overwhelming popularity of The Birth of a Nation. The NAACP, by then established with its own newspaper, mobilized opposition. But the film's momentum was unstoppable. Film critics, many of them liberal, though decrying its racism, praised the film for its technical and artistic merits.

In contrast, efforts to present the story of Reconstruction from a black point of view were unsuccessful. Novelist Albion Tourgee, a white superior court judge and activist, used black characters who spoke in their own voices to show the freed man as a person who worked hard and attempted to succeed, but was victimized by the Ku Klux Klan. Tourgee believed the answer to racism lay in portraying blacks as normal—like everyone else. His novel, Bricks Without Straw, attracted a devoted but small audience; the South's treatment of blacks no longer interested many Northerners, and few Southerners were willing to listen. Black writers suffered a similar fate. While Charles Chesnutt, author of The Conjure Woman, was included in a list of "the foremost storytellers of the time," his publisher refused to release his next novel because the previous two about racial themes had been commercially unsuccessful. As Silk and Silk point out, "[M]essages only reach those people who are willing to listen. Only when a later audience became receptive . . . could [their] tales be . . . appreciated."

Although blacks had gained formal legal equality, the Supreme Court, in 1896, upheld segregation in Plessy v. Ferguson. Lynchings continued; racist stereotypes prevailed. Blacks had little access to the press or the film industry and could do little to change the racism that both industries promulgated. Nevertheless, blacks joined the army in droves during World War I. Segregation in the ranks was rigidly enforced, however, and many blacks returned angry and disheartened. After the war, unrest in the country led to at least twenty-five urban race riots, many in the previously peaceful North. Repressive images immediately increased and prevailed for a little over a decade. Then, as the disruption abated, a few writers, such as Eugene O'Neill and Sinclair

Lewis, portrayed blacks and their plight sympathetically. Black writers and artists in New York created the Harlem Renaissance. Blacks' image metamorphosed yet again. Whites, excited and enthusiastic over this new artistic rapprochement with blacks, quickly praised them and their work for elements of the exoticism and primitivism popularized by Gauguin. Echoing early images of good-natured, happy-go-lucky blacks, white society began to regard African–Americans as musically talented, rhythmical, passionate, and entertaining. Although these developments heralded a somewhat more positive image of blacks, nevertheless the new images retained elements of condescension and previous stereotypes. The majority-race critics, intellectuals, and artists who were entranced by the Renaissance may have intended no harm, yet they perpetuated views of African–Americans as the exotic other.

With World War II, black soldiers and workers were needed for the war effort; the more virulent forms of racism were held in abeyance. However, when the war ended and the soldiers returned, racial hostilities again sharpened. Having experienced a relatively racism-free environment during the war, black workers and soldiers were not prepared to return to lives of menial work and subservience to whites. For many, expectations of improvement were fed by war propaganda depicting the U.S. as fighting for freedom. Activism sprang up; the Civil Rights movement began, and once again the dominant image of blacks took on new forms: the cocky, street-smart black who knows his rights; the unreasonable, opportunistic community leader and militant; the safe, comforting, cardigan-wearing ("nice") black of TV sitcoms; and the Black Bomber of superstud films, all mutations of, and permutations of, old familiar forms.

B. Other Groups

1. Native Americans

The experience of other groups parallels that of blacks. For example, when the colonists arrived in Virginia and Massachusetts in the seventeenth century, they brought with them images of the Indian created in England and Europe. Early explorers described native peoples of the "new world" as innocent, ingenuous, friendly, and naked. At first, relations between the two groups were cordial. Later, however, more settlers arrived, bringing with them English concepts of property—land transfer, titles, deeds—that were foreign to Indian thought. Indians who did not cooperate with the settlers' plans were forced off their lands; eventually hostilities broke out, resulting in a conflict that lasted over two centuries.

Early writings about Native Americans reflected two romanticized images—"the Indian princess," incarnated most notably in Pocahantas, and "the man Friday," found in Robinson Crusoe, earlier as the troublesome servant Caliban, later as the faithful loyal Chingachgook, and in the twentieth century the buffoon and sidekick Tonto. The first instance of the "captivity narrative" appeared in Massachusetts in 1682 with Mary Rowlandson's "Captivity and Restoration." Early fiction portrayed Indians as looters, burners, and killers—but not rapists, because New Englanders knew that Indians rarely committed rape. But the erotic elements of Rowlandson's story, although mild and subordinated to her religious message, made it the prototype for later captivity tales that emphasized sexual aggression directed toward Simon-pure captives.

Other writers followed suit without Rowlandson's delicacy, portraying Indians as animal-like and sub-human, a characterization whose roots go back to Paracelsus (1493–1541), who proposed that Indians were not among "the sons of Adam." Shakespeare explored this theme when he wrote The Tempest and created a servant for Prospero—Caliban—whose name was an anagram of the newly coined word "cannibal." Cotton Mather and other Puritan writers called Indians wolves, lions, sorcerers, and demons possessed by Satan. By the nineteenth century, Indians had become savage, barbarous, and half-civilized. In early movies restless natives and jungle beasts were practically interchangeable elements. No wonder, then, that Indians were removed, with little protest from the dominant society, to reservations, just as wild and rare beasts were confined to animal reserves.

Later movies of the "cowboys and Indians" genre built on these images when they featured war dances, exotic dress, drunkenness, surprise attacks, scalping, raiding, raping, tomahawks, tomtoms, and torture. D.W. Griffith, creator of Birth of a Nation, incorporated these elements and more in The Battle of Elderbush Gulch (1913). In that movie, a white woman, trapped in a cabin surrounded by Indians, awaits her fate, not knowing whether the Indian attackers will kill her or whether one of her white defenders will shoot her before letting the Indians take her alive. By 1911, portrayal of Indians in film had become so demeaning that representatives of four western tribes protested to President William Howard Taft and to Congress. But little change occurred until World War II, when Hollywood transferred the enemy role to the Japanese and Germans. Many of these early Indian movies are still shown on television, feeding the psyches of new generations of Americans with the familiar stereotypes.

Shortly after the end of the war, Hollywood released Broken Arrow (1950), the first movie ever to feature an Indian as hero—Cochise of the Apaches. Though artistically and historically flawed, it was widely praised. Other "noble savage" films reversed the stereotype in the opposite direction, portraying Native Americans with exaggerated nobleness—a striking parallel to the treatment adulating whites gave black writers during the Harlem Renaissance.

In 1969, N. Scott Momaday, a Kiowa–Cherokee writer, won the Pulitzer Prize for his novel House Made of Dawn. In 1972, PBS ran a BBC production of The Last of the Mohicans. In each of these cases, much of the audience was struck by the intelligence of the Native American voice—a far cry from the earlier steady diet (still heard today) of chiefs saying "ugh," braves shrieking war whoops, and Tonto saying "me gettum." It was not always so. Thomas Jefferson wished Congress could speak half as well as orators of Indian nations. William Penn praised the Lenni Lanape language of the Delaware for its subtlety. Yet, speech of the Indians—as well as that of African–Americans, Mexicans, and Asians—has been mangled, blunted and rendered inarticulate by whites who then became entitled to speak for them. Like the other groups of color, Native Americans have been disempowered by the very element which, they are told, will save them.

2. *Asian–Americans*

With Asian–Americans, we find the same pattern we found elsewhere: the dominant depiction in popular culture is negative—although rarely seen as such at the time—and the stereotype shifts to accommodate society's changing needs.

In the middle years of the nineteenth century, Chinese were welcomed into the land for their labor: They were needed to operate the mines, build railroads, and carry out other physical tasks necessary to the country's development. The industrious immigrants soon, however, began to surpass white American workers. They opened small businesses, succeeded in making profitable mines that others had abandoned. Not surprisingly, Chinese became the scapegoats for the 1870s Depression. Unionists and writers exaggerated negative traits thought associated with them—opium smoking, gambling—and succeeded in having anti-Chinese legislation enacted. By 1882 public sentiment had been mobilized sufficiently so that Congress was able to pass an Exclusion Act, which reduced the number of Chinese in the U.S. from 105,000 in 1880 to 65,000 in 1908.

During this period, Japan's international position was on the rise, yet U.S. writers and politicians depicted all Asians as inferior, unassimilable, willing to work inhuman hours at low wages, and loyal to foreign despots. When Japan defeated first China and then Russia, it began to replace China as the "yellow peril." By 1924, all Asians were barred, an exclusion the Supreme Court had upheld for the Chinese in 1889. During a period of increasing tensions between the two countries, the film industry portrayed Japanese and other Asians—during this period few distinctions were made—in unremittingly negative terms. As with African–Americans and Native Americans, Asian men were depicted as cunning, savage, and as potential rapists interested in defiling white women. (In sharp contrast, white male actors were seen as having legitimate access to Asian women.)

As U.S. militancy grew, films began to devalue Asian—principally Japanese—life. Not even they valued life, the narratives of the day said. Why should we value theirs? During earlier periods, when racism against Asians was relatively quiescent, writers and film-makers employed the stock character of the Charlie Chan—the hapless, pidgin-talking Asian, in many respects the functional equivalent of the Sambo or uncle. But as anti-Japanese sentiment increased, we began depicting even domestic Asians as foul and tricky. Anti–Asian films were easy to produce and profitable; Hollywood would often assign a Japanese actor to play a Chinese villain and vice versa.

W.R. Hearst sponsored Patria, an anti-Asian film serial that began in 1919 and continued for several years, depicting Asians as a Yellow Menace. At one point, Woodrow Wilson became disturbed by the virulence of Hearst's production and wrote asking him to soften it. Hearst responded by changing the series so that it became dominantly anti-Mexican. In the period immediately preceding and following World War II, anti-Japanese images continued to proliferate. A stock character was the master Oriental criminal, often played by Anglo actors in make-up. By this time, films and novels were distinguishing between Chinese (who were good), and Japanese (who were bad). After Pearl Harbor, intense anti-Japanese propaganda resulted in federal action to intern 110,000 Japanese Americans, many of whom had lived in the United States all their lives. Many lost farms, houses, and other property. It later came to light that much of the evidence of likely sabotage and fifth column activities had been fabricated.

Following World War II, depictions of blacks and Indians were upgraded to some extent, but those of Asians only a little. Many of James Bond's villains, for example, have been Asian. In recent days, Japan has once again become a serious economic rival of the United States, producing automobiles, computers and other products at a price and quality American industry has proven unable to match. Predictably, a further wave of anti-Asian sentiment and stereotyping is re-emerging.

3. Mexican–Americans

Images of Mexican–Americans ("Chicanos") fall into three or four well-delineated stereotypes—the greaser, the conniving, treacherous bandido, the happy-go-lucky shiftless lover of song, food, and dance, and the tragic, silent "Spanish" tall, dark, and handsome type of romantic fiction—which change according to society's needs. As with blacks, Asians, and Indians, most Americans have relatively few interpersonal contacts with Mexican–Americans; therefore, these images become the individual's only reality. When such a person meets an actual Mexican–American, he or she tends to place the other in one of the ready-made categories. Stereotyping thus denies members of both groups the opportunity to interact with each other on anything like a complex, nuanced human level.

During and just after the conquest, when the U.S. was seizing and then settling large tracts of Mexican territory in the Southwest, "Western" or "conquest" fiction depicted Anglos bravely displacing shifty, brutal, and treacherous Mexicans. After the war ended and control of the Southwest passed to American hands, a subtle shift occurred. Anglos living and settling in the new regions were portrayed as Protestant, independent, thrifty, industrious, mechanically resourceful, and interested in progress; Mexicans, as traditional, sedate, lacking in mechanical resourcefulness and ambition. Writers both on and off the scene created the same images of indolent, pious Mexicans—ignoring the two centuries of enterprising farmers and ranchers who withstood or negotiated with Apaches and Comanches and built a sturdy society with irrigation, land tenure, and mining codes.

In the late conquest period, depiction of this group bifurcated. As happened at a different period with African–Americans, majority-race writers created two images of the Mexican: the "good" (loyal) Mexican peon or sidekick, and the "bad" fighter/greaser Mexican who did not know his place. The first was faithful and domestic; the second, treacherous and evil. As with other groups, the second ("bad") image had sexual overtones: the greaser coveted Anglo women and would seduce or rape them if given the opportunity. Children's books of this time, like the best-selling Buffalo Bill series, were full of Mexican stereotypes used to reinforce moral messages to the young: They are like this, we like that. The series ended in 1912.

The first thirty years of this century saw heavy Mexican immigration of mainly poor workers. The first Bracero programs—official, temporary importation of field hands—appeared. With increasing numbers, white-only signs, segregated housing and schools appeared, aimed now at Mexicans in addition to blacks. Since there was now an increased risk of interaction and intermarriage, novels and newspaper writing reinforced the notion of these immigrants' baseness, simplicity, and inability to become assimilated.

The movies of this period depicted Latins as buffoons, sluts, or connivers; even some of the titles were disparaging: for example, The Greaser's Gauntlet. Films featured brown-skinned desperadoes stealing horses or gold, lusting after pure Anglo women, shooting noble Saxon heroes in the back, or acting the part of hapless buffoons. Animated cartoons and short subjects, still shown on television, featured tequila-drinking Mexicans, bullfighters, Speedy Gonzalez and Slowpoke Rodriguez, and clowns—as well as Castilian caballeras, light-skinned, upper class, and prone to wearing elaborate dresses and carrying castanets.

World War II brought the need for factory and agricultural workers and a new flood of immigrants. Images softened to include "normal," or even noble, Mexicans, like the general of Marlon Brando's Viva Zapata. Perhaps realizing it had overstepped, America diminished the virulence of its anti-Mexican imagery. Yet the Western genre, with Mexican villains and bandits, continues; and the immigrant speaking gibberish still makes an appearance. Even the most favorable novel and film of the post-war period, The Milagro Beanfield War, ends in stereotypes.

A few writers found their own culture alienating or sick and sought relief in a more serene Southwest culture. As with the Harlem Renaissance, these creative artists tended to be more generous to Mexicans, but nevertheless retained the Anglo hero as the central figure or Samaritan who uplifts the Mexican from his or her traditional ignorance.

Notes and Questions

1. Professors Delgado and Stefancic primarily tell us about cultural images from film and television. Can you think of harmful stereotypes in cultural images of the outsider in commercials and advertisements? in music and literature? in visual arts?

Can you think of negative *gender* stereotypes in film, television, advertising and other media? How about negative cultural images of gays and lesbians?

2. Do you think these images influence our unconscious and perpetuate structures of oppression? How could we test the reliability of that hypothesis?

3. Do cultural images like the ones reported by Delgado and Stefancic infuse legal doctrines and writings? Is this a reciprocal relationship—do legal constructs and writings affect our cultural images?

4. The materials in this section have illustrated the subtle ways in which structures of privilege and power affect an individual's experiences and understandings of the world. These structures affect law as well in both subtle and overt ways. Privilege and power in the legal system are often located in the power to name what is relevant to resolving a dispute. Professor Gerald Torres and Kathryn Milun select the Mashpee Indian Case as an example of the ways that the "power to name" and the "power to define the rules of the game" skew the fairness of our legal system. In *Translating Yonnondio by Precedent and Evidence: The Mashpee Indian Case,* 1990 Duke L.J. 625, the authors tell how a land dispute between the Mashpee Indians and town of Mashpee turned on the legal question of whether the Mashpee Indians were a tribe, because only tribes were entitled to the protection of the federal Non–Intercourse Act. The Mashpees considered themselves a tribe, but when the court applied the definitions of tribes from earlier case law and anthropological experts, the Mashpees failed to meet the formalistic definitions. Experts and precedent demanded that tribes be racially pure, have authoritarian leadership, and maintain consistent territorial occupancy. The Mashpees had entirely different conceptions of land ownership and appropriate leadership styles than those imposed upon by them by the anthropological definition, and several centuries earlier they had rejected the idea of racial purity in determining tribe membership. The two understandings of tribal membership, the Mashpees' and the precedents', were alien to one another and incompatible. If only one definition can apply legally, those with the power to decide "what constitutes a tribe" will prevail. Who ought to be able to decide whether a people are a tribe—those peoples for themselves or others who observe them? Torres and Milun see a glaring "disjunction between the ethno-legal categories and the Mashpee's lived experience" and fault the legal system for the ways it used notions of relevance and precedent to exclude the Mashpees' experience. Id. at 628–9.

And finally for this section, last but not least, Professor Martha Minow offers us illustrations of how the concept of difference with its unstated assumptions is used by those in power to subordinate others.

MARTHA MINOW, MAKING ALL THE DIFFERENCE

49–78 (Cornell U. Press, 1990).

Dilemmas of difference appear unresolvable. The risk of nonneutrality—the risk of discrimination—accompanies efforts both to ignore and to recognize difference in equal treatment and special treatment. Difference can be recreated in color or gender blindness and in affirmative action; in governmental neutrality and in governmental preferences; and in discretionary decisions and in formal constraints on discretion. Why does difference seem to pose choices each of which undesirably revives difference or the stigma or disadvantage associated with it?

In this last question lies a clue to the problem. The possibility of reiterating difference, whether by acknowledgment or nonacknowledgment, arises as long as difference itself carries stigma and precludes equality. Buried in the questions about difference are assumptions that difference is linked to stigma or deviance and that sameness is a prerequisite for equality. Perhaps these assumptions themselves must be identified and assessed if we are to escape or transcend the dilemmas of difference.

If to be equal one must be the same, then to be different is to be unequal or even deviant. But any assignment of deviance must be made from the vantage point of some claimed normality: a position of equality implies a contrasting position used to draw the relationship—and it is a relationship not of equality and inequality but of superiority and inferiority. To be different is to be different in relationship to someone or something else—and this point of comparison must be so taken for granted, so much the "norm," that it need not even be stated.

At least five closely related but unstated assumptions underlie difference dilemmas. Once articulated and examined, these assumptions can take their proper place among other choices about how to treat difference, and we can consider what we might do to challenge or renovate them.

FIVE UNSTATED ASSUMPTIONS

First, we often assume that "differences" are intrinsic, rather than viewing them as expressions of comparisons between people on the basis of particular traits. Each of us is different from everyone else in innumerable ways. Each of these differences is an implicit comparison we draw. And the comparisons themselves depend upon and reconfirm the selection of particular traits as the ones that assume importance in the comparison process. An assessment of difference selects out some traits and makes them matter; indeed, it treats people as subject to categorization rather than as manifesting multitudes of characteristics.

Second, we typically adopt an unstated point of reference when assessing others. It is from the point of reference of this norm that we determine who is different and who is normal. The hearing-impaired student is different in comparison to the norm of the hearing student—yet the hearing student differs from the hearing-impaired student as much as she differs from him, and the hearing student undoubtedly has other traits that distinguish him from other students. Unstated points of reference may express the experience of a majority or may express the perspective of those who have had greater access to the power used in naming and assessing others. Women are different in relation to the unstated male norm. Blacks, Mormons, Jews, and Arabs are different in relation to the unstated white Christian norm. Handicapped persons are different in relation to the unstated norm of able-bodiedness or, as some have described it, the vantage point of "Temporarily Able Persons."

The unstated point of comparison is not general but particular, and not inevitable but only seemingly so when left unstated. The unstated reference point promotes the interests of some but not others; it can remain unstated because those who do not fit have less power to select the norm than those who fit comfortably within the one that prevails.

A reference point for comparison purposes is central to a notion of equality. Equality asks, equal compared with whom? A notion of equality that demands disregarding a "difference" calls for assimilation to an unstated norm. To strip away difference, then, is often to remove or ignore a feature distinguishing an individual from a presumed norm—such as that of a white, able-bodied, Christian man—but leaving that norm in place as the measure for equal treatment. The white person's supposed compliment to a black friend, "I don't even think of you as black," marks a failure to see the implicit racism in ignoring a "difference" and adopting an unstated and potentially demeaning point of comparison. As historian J.R. Pole has explained, constitutional notions of equality in the United States rest on the idea that people are equal because they could all take one another's places in work, intellectual exchange, or political power if they were disassociated from their contexts of family, religion, class, or race and if they had the same opportunities and experiences. This concept of equality makes the recognition of differences a basis for denying equal treatment. In view of the risk that difference will mean deviance or inequality, stigmatization from difference, once identified, is not surprising.

Third, we treat the person doing the seeing or judging as without a perspective, rather than as inevitably seeing and judging from a particular situated perspective. Although a person's perspective does not collapse into his or her demographic characteristics, no one is free from perspective, and no one can see fully from another's point of view.

Fourth, we assume that the perspectives of those being judged are either irrelevant or are already taken into account through the perspective of the judge. This assumption is a luxury of those with more power or authority, for those with less power often have to consider the views of people unlike themselves. As a novelist has wryly observed, horses "have always understood a great deal more than they let on. It is difficult to be sat on all day, every day, by some other creature, without forming an opinion about them. On the other hand, it is perfectly possible to sit all day, every day, on top of another creature and not have the slightest thought about them whatsoever." Moreover, this assumption treats a person's self-conception or world view as unrelated to how others treat him or her.

Finally, there is an assumption that the existing social and economic arrangements are natural and neutral. If workplaces and living arrangements are natural, they are inevitable. It follows, then, that differences in the work and home lives of particular individuals arise because of personal choice. We presume that individuals are free, unhampered by the status quo, when they form their own preferences and act upon them. From this view, any departure from the status quo risks nonneutrality and interference with free choice.

These interrelated assumptions, once made explicit, can be countered with some contrary ones. Consider these alternative starting points. Difference is relational, not intrinsic. Who or what should be taken as the point of reference for defining differences is debatable. There is no single, superior perspective for judging questions of difference. No perspective asserted to produce "the truth" is without a situated perspective, because any statement is made by a person who has a perspective. Assertions of a difference as "the truth" may indeed obscure the power of the person attributing a difference while excluding important competing perspectives. Difference is a clue to the social arrangements that make some people less accepted and less integrated while expressing the needs and interests of others who constitute the presumed model. And social arrangements can be changed. Arrangements that assign the burden of "differences" to some people while making others comfortable are historical artifacts. Maintaining these historical patterns embedded in the status quo is not neutral and cannot be justified by the claim that everyone has freely chosen to do so. . . .

Assumption 1: Difference is Intrinsic, Not Comparison

Legal analysis, cast in a judicial mode, typically asks whether a given situation "fits" in a category defined by a legal rule or instead belongs outside it. . . . For example, are Jews a race? Is a contagious disease a handicap? Other questions take the form "Is doing x really doing y?" For example, is offering a statutory guarantee of job reinstatement after maternity leave really engaging in gender discrimination? Is denying unemployment benefits to someone who left work because of pregnancy also really discriminating on the basis of gender? As Martin Golding has explained, these may appear to be simple factual questions with clear answers, but they are also "questions about the application of a name, to which any answer is arbitrary." Edward Levi, a leading expositor of the nature of legal reasoning, has explained the three steps involved: "Similarity is seen between cases; next the rule of law inherent in the first case is announced; then the rule of law is made applicable to the second case.... The finding of similarity or difference is the key step in the legal process."

Again, as critics have noted for nearly a century, these patterns of legal analysis imply that legal reasoning yields results of its own accord, beyond human control. But differences between people and between problems and between legal concepts or precedents are statements of relationships; they express a comparison with another person, problem, concept, or precedent. A difference cannot be understood except as a contrast between instances, or between a norm and an example. Assessing similarities and differences is a basic cognitive process in organizing the world; it depends on comparing a new example with an older one. Legal analysis depends on the process of comparing this case with other cases, a process of drawing similarities and differences. Ann Scales has noted: "To characterize similarities and differences among situations is a key step in legal judgments. That step, however, is not a mechanistic manipulation of essences. Rather, that step always has a moral crux." The very act of classification remakes the boundaries of the class, moving the line to include rather than exclude this instance. Indeed, many categories used to describe people's differences are invented only at the moment when summoned into the service of defining someone. Acknowledging this means acknowledging that difference is not discovered but humanly invented.

Sometimes, courts have made such acknowledgments. For example, when asked whether Jews and Arabs are distinct races for the purposes of civil rights statutes, the Supreme Court in 1987 reasoned that objective, scientific sources could not resolve this question, essentially acknowledging that racial identity is socially constructed. Yet, oddly, the justices then turned to middle and late nineteenth-century notions of racial identity, prevalent when the remedial statutes were adopted, rather than examining contemporary assumptions and current prejudices. The problem for the litigants was whether to invoke categories that had been used to denigrate them in order to obtain legal protection. As these cases illustrate, groups that seek to challenge assigned categories and stigma run into this dilemma: "How do you protest a socially imposed categorization, except by organizing around the category?" Moreover, a label of difference accentuates one over all other characteristics and may well carry a web of negative associations. Perceptions and assessments of difference pick out the traits that do not fit comfortably within dominant social arrangements, even when those traits could easily be made irrelevant by different social arrangements or different rules about what traits should be allowed to matter.

Legislatures on occasion demonstrate an understanding of the labeling process that assigns some people to categories based on traits that may be only imagined by others. The federal Rehabilitation Act forbids discrimination against handicapped persons—and also against persons perceived by others to be handicapped.

Some have argued that the assignment of differences in Western thought entails not just relationships and comparisons but also the imposition of hierarchies. To explore this idea, we need the next unstated assumption: the implicit norm or reference point for the comparison through which difference is assigned.

Assumption 2: The Norm Need Not Be Stated

To treat someone as different means to accord him treatment that is different from the treatment of someone else; to describe someone as "the same" implies "the same as" someone else. When differences are discussed without explicit reference to the person or trait on the other side of the comparison, an unstated norm remains. Usually, this default reference point is so powerful and well established that specifying it is not thought necessary.

When women argue for rights, the implicit reference point used in discussions of sameness and difference is the privilege accorded some men—typically, white men who are well established in the society. It is misleading to treat the implicit norm as consisting of all men, as rhetoric for women's rights tends to do, for that obscures historical racial and class differences in the treatment of men themselves. But the reference point of privileged men can present powerful arguments for overcoming the exclusion of women from activities and opportunities. Reform efforts on behalf of women during the nineteenth and twentieth centuries asserted women's fundamental similarities to the men who were allowed to vote, sit on juries, engage in business, and participate in essential political and economic institutions. Declarations of rights in the federal Constitution and other basic legal documents used universal terms, and advocates for women's rights argued that women fit those terms as well as privileged men did. Unfortunately for the reformers, embracing the theory of "sameness" meant that any sign of difference between women and the men used for comparison could be used to justify treating women differently from those men.

A prominent "difference" assigned to women, by implicit comparison with men, is pregnancy—especially pregnancy experienced by women working for pay outside their homes. The Supreme Court's treatment of issues concerning pregnancy and the workplace highlights the power of the unstated norm in analyses of problems of difference. In 1975 the Court accepted an appeal to a male norm in striking down a Utah statute that disqualified a woman from receiving unemployment compensation for a specified period surrounding childbirth, even if her reasons for leaving work were unrelated to the pregnancy. Although the capacity to become pregnant is a difference between women and men, this fact alone did not justify treating women and men differently on matters unrelated to pregnancy. Using men as the norm, the Court reasoned that any woman who can perform like a man can be treated like a man. A woman could not be denied unemployment compensation for different reasons than a man would.

What, however, is equal treatment for the woman who is correctly identified within the group of pregnant persons, not simply stereotyped as such, and temporarily unable to work outside the home for that reason? The Court first grappled with these issues in two cases that posed the question of whether discrimination on the basis of pregnancy—that is, employers' denial of health benefits—amounted to discrimination on the basis of sex. In both instances the Court answered negatively, reasoning that the employers drew a distinction not on the forbidden basis of sex but only on the basis of pregnancy; and since women could be both pregnant and nonpregnant, these were not instances of sex discrimination. Only from a point of view that regards pregnancy as a strange occurrence, rather than an ongoing bodily potential, would its relationship to female experience be made so tenuous; and only from a vantage point that regards men as the norm would the exclusion of pregnancy from health insurance coverage seem unproblematic and free from gender discrimination.

Congress responded by enacting the Pregnancy Discrimination Act, which amended Title VII (the federal law forbidding gender discrimination in employment) to include discrimination on the basis of pregnancy within the range of impermissible sex discrimination. Yet even under these new statutory terms, the power of the unstated male norm persists in debates over the definition of discrimination. Indeed, a new question arose under the Pregnancy Discrimination Act: if differential treatment on the basis of pregnancy is forbidden, does the statute also forbid any state requirement for pregnancy or maternity leaves—which are, after all, distinctions drawn on the basis of pregnancy, even though drawn to help women?

A collection of employers launched a lawsuit in the 1980s arguing that even favorable treatment on the basis of pregnancy violated the Pregnancy Discrimination Act. The employers challenged a California statute that mandated a limited right to resume a prior job following an unpaid pregnancy disability leave. The case—California Federal Savings & Loan Association v. Guerra, which became known as "Cal/Fed"—in a real and painful sense divided the community of advocates for women's rights. Writing briefs on opposing sides, women's rights groups went public with the division. Some maintained that any distinction on the basis of pregnancy—any distinction on the basis of sex—would perpetuate the negative stereotypes long used to demean and exclude women. Others argued that denying the facts of pregnancy and the needs of new mothers could only hurt women; treating women like men in the workplace violated the demands of equality. What does equality demand—treating women like men, or treating women specially?

What became clear in these arguments was that a deeper problem had produced this conundrum: a work world that treats as the model worker the traditional male employee who has a full-time wife and mother to care for his home and children. The very phrase "special treatment," when used to describe pregnancy or maternity leave, posits men as the norm and women as different or deviant from that norm.

The problem was not women, or pregnancy, but the effort to fit women's experiences and needs into categories forged with men in mind.

The case reached the Supreme Court. Over a strenuous dissent, a majority of the justices reconceived the problem and rejected the presumption of the male norm which had made the case seem like a choice between "equal treatment" and "special treatment." Instead, Justice Marshall's opinion for the majority shifted from a narrow workplace comparison to a broader comparison of men and women in their dual roles as workers and as family members. The Court found no conflict between the Pregnancy Discrimination Act and the challenged state law that required qualified reinstatement of women following maternity leaves, because "California's pregnancy disability leave statute allows women, as well as men, to have families without losing their jobs." The Court therefore construed the federal law to permit states to require that employers remove barriers in the workplace that would disadvantage pregnant people compared with others. Moreover, reasoned the majority, if there remains a conflict between a federal ban against sex-based discrimination and a state law requiring accommodation for women who take maternity leaves, that conflict should be resolved by the extension to men of benefits comparable to those available to women following maternity or pregnancy leaves. Here, the Court used women's experiences as the benchmark and called for treating men equally in reference to women, thus reversing the usual practice. The dissenters, however, remained convinced that the federal law prohibited preferential treatment on the basis of pregnancy; they persisted in using the male norm as the measure for equal treatment in the workplace.

There remains a risk of using the child-rearing couple as a new unstated reference point and failing then to recognize the burdens of workers who need accommodation to care for a dependent parent or to take care of some other private need. A new norm may produce new exclusions and assign the status of "difference" to still someone else. Unstated references appear in many other contexts. The assumption of able-bodiedness as the norm is manifested in architecture that is inaccessible to people who use wheelchairs, canes, or crutches to get around. Implicit norms often work subtly, through categories manifested in language. Reasoning processes tend to treat categories as clear, bounded, and sharp edged; a given item either fits within the category or it does not. Instead of considering the entire individual, we often select one characteristic as representative of the whole. George Lakoff has illustrated this phenomenon with the term "mother." Although "mother" appears to be a general category, with subcategories such as "working mother" and "unwed mother," the very need for modifying adjectives demonstrates an implicit prototype that structures expectations about and valuations of members of the general category, yet treats these expectations and valuations as mere reflections of reality. If the general category is religion but the unstated prototype is Christianity, a court may have trouble recognizing as a religion a group lacking, for example, a minister.

Psychologist Jerome Bruner wrote, "There is no seeing without looking, no hearing without listening, and both looking and listening are shaped by expectancy, stance, and intention." Unstated reference points lie hidden in legal discourse, which is full of the language of abstract universalism. The U.S. Constitution, for example, included general language to describe persons protected by it, even when it excluded black slaves and white women from its intended reach. Legal language seeks universal applicability, regardless of the particular traits of an individual, yet abstract universalism often "takes the part for the whole, the particular for the universal and essential, the present for the eternal." Legal reasoning feels rational, according to one theorist, when "particular metaphors for categorizing likeness and difference in the world have become frozen, or institutionalized as common sense." Making explicit the unstated points of reference is the first step in addressing this problem; the next is challenging the presumed neutrality of the observer, who in fact sees inevitably from a situated perspective.

Assumption 3: The Observer Can See Without a Perspective

This assumption builds on the others. Differences are intrinsic, and anyone can see them; there is one true reality, and impartial observers can make judgments unaffected and untainted by their own perspective or experience. The facts of the world, including facts about people's traits, are knowable truly only by someone uninfluenced by social or cultural situations. Once legal rules are selected, regardless of prior disputes over the rules themselves, society may direct legal officials to apply them evenhandedly and to use them to discover and categorize events, motives, and culpability as they exist in the world. This aspiration to impartiality in legal judgments, however, is just that—an aspiration, not a description. The aspiration even risks obscuring the inevitable perspective of any given legal official, or of anyone else, and thereby makes it harder to challenge the impact of perspective on the selection of traits used to judge legal consequences.

The ideal of objectivity itself suppresses the coincidence between the viewpoints of the majority and what is commonly understood to be objective or unbiased. For example, in an employment discrimination case the defendant, a law firm, sought to disqualify Judge Constance Baker Motley from sitting on the case because she, as a black woman who had once represented plaintiffs in discrimination cases, would identify with those who suffer race or sex discrimination. The defendant assumed that Judge Motley's personal identity and her past political work had made her different, lacking the ability to perceive without a perspective. Judge Motley declined, however, to recuse herself and explained: "If background or sex or race of each judge were, by definition, sufficient grounds for removal, no judge on this court could hear this case, or many others, by virtue of the fact that all of them were attorneys, of a sex, often with distinguished law firm or public service backgrounds."

Because of the aspiration to impartiality and the prevalence of universalist language in law, most observers of law have been reluctant to confront the arguments of philosophers and psychologists who challenge the idea that observers can see without a perspective. Philosophers such as A.J. Ayer and W.V. Quine note that although we can alter the theory we use to frame our perceptions of the world, we cannot see the world unclouded by preconceptions. What interests us, given who we are and where we stand, affects our ability to perceive.

The impact of the observer's unacknowledged perspective may be crudely oppressive. When a municipality includes a nativity creche in its annual Christmas display, the majority of the community may perceive no offense to non-Christians in the community. If the practice is challenged in court as a violation of the Constitution's ban against establishment of religion, a judge who is Christian may also fail to see the offense to anyone and merely conclude, as the Supreme Court did in 1984, that Christmas is a national holiday. Judges may be peculiarly disabled from perceiving the state's message about a dominant religious practice because judges are themselves often members of the dominant group and therefore have the luxury of seeing their perspectives mirrored and reinforced in major social and political institutions. Similarly, members of a racial majority may miss the impact of their own race on their perspective about the race of others.

The power of unacknowledged perspectives permeated a recent Supreme Court analysis of the question of whether a federal statute exempting religious organizations from rules against religious discrimination in employment decisions violates the establishment clause of the First Amendment. A majority for the Court endorsed this legislative grant of discretion to religious organizations, and rejected a discharged employee's claims that such accommodation of religion unconstitutionally promotes religious organizations at the price of individual religious liberty. The majority reasoned that the preference for religion was exercised not by the government but rather by the church. Here, the justices suggested that the government could remain neutral even while exempting religious organizations from otherwise universal prohibitions against discriminating on the basis of religion in employment decisions.

Justice Sandra Day O'Connor pointed out in her concurring opinion that allowing a private decision-maker to use religion in employment decisions inevitably engaged the government in that discrimination. For her, the question for the Court was how an "objective observer" would perceive a government policy of approving such religion-based employment decisions. She challenged the justices in the majority to admit that the law was not neutral and to explore the meaning of this nonneutrality to someone not involved in the dispute. The aspiration to impartiality infuses her analysis, yet the meaning of objectivity almost dissolves in application: "To ascertain whether the statute [exempting religious organizations from the ban against religious discrimination in employment] conveys a message of endorsement, the relevant issue is how it would be perceived by an objective observer, acquainted with the text, legislative history, and implementation of the statute."

What could "objective" mean here? First, it acknowledges the limited perspective of the government representatives. Second, it rejects the viewpoint of the religious group as too biased or embedded in the problem. So at a minimum, "objective" means "free from the biases of the litigating parties." But is there anyone who has no perspective on this issue? Justice O'Connor described a judge as someone capable of filling the shoes of the "objective observer," yet she acknowledged that she was answering from her own perspective: *"In my view* the objective observer should perceive the government action as an accommodation of the exercise of religion rather than as a government endorsement of religion." Although at other times, Justice O'Connor has indicated a sensitive awareness of perspectives other than her own, here she failed to consider that no one can achieve a perspective free from a particular viewpoint. Her conclusion in this case—like her rejection of a religious-freedom challenge to a military regulation punishing servicemen for the wearing of religious headgear—did not consider the possibility that her own perspective matches the perspective of a majority group and neglects the perspective of a minority. The comfort of finding one's perspective widely shared does not make it any less a perspective, especially in the face of evidence that other people perceive the world from a different perspective.

Justice Antonin Scalia's dissenting opinion in an affirmative action case reveals both considerable shrewdness about the effect of the observer's hidden perspective and surprising unawareness about the impact of his own perspective. He predicted that the majority's approval of an affirmative action employment plan would lead many employers to engage in voluntary affirmative action plans that employ only minimally capable employees rather than risk litigation challenging their employment practices as discriminatory: "This situation is more likely to obtain, of course, with respect to the least skilled jobs—perversely creating an incentive to discriminate against precisely those members of the nonfavored groups *least* likely to have profited from societal discrimination in the past." Justice Scalia thus implied, without quite saying, that the perspective of the justices had influenced their development of a rule promoting affirmative action plans in a setting that could never touch members of the Court or people like them.

Yet in another respect his opinion manifests, rather than exposes, the impact of the observer's perspective on the observed. He provided a generous and sympathetic view of the male plaintiff, Johnson, but demonstrated no comparable understanding of Joyce, the woman promoted ahead of him; his description of the facts of the case offered more details about Johnson's desires and efforts to advance his career. In effect, Justice Scalia tried to convey Johnson's point of view that the promotion of Joyce represented discrimination against Johnson. Unlike the majority of the court, Justice Scalia provided no description of Joyce's career aspirations and her efforts to fulfill them; he thus betrayed a critical lack of sympathy for those most injured by social discrimination in the past. Most curious was his apparent inability to imagine that Joyce and other women working in relatively unskilled jobs are, even more so than Johnson, people "*least* likely to have profited from societal discrimination in the past." Operating under the apparent assumption that people fall into one of two groups—women and blacks on the one hand; white, unorganized, unaffluent, and unknown persons on the other—Justice Scalia neglected the women who have been politically powerless and in need of the Court's protection. Although his opinion reveals that the Court may neglect the way it protects professional jobs from the affirmative action it prescribes for nonprofessionals, he himself remained apparently unaware of the effects of his own perspective on his ability to sympathize with some persons but not others.

A classic instance of unselfconscious immersion in a perspective that harms others appears in the Supreme Court's majority opinion in Plessy v. Ferguson, which upheld the rationale of "separate but equal" in rejecting a challenge to legislated racial segregation in public railway cars. This is the decision ultimately overturned by the Court in Brown v. Board of Education. A majority of the Court reasoned in *Plessy* that if any black people felt that segregation stamped them with a badge of inferiority, "it is not by reason of anything found in the [legislation], but solely because the colored race chooses to put that construction upon it."

Homer Plessy's attorney had urged the justices to imagine themselves in the shoes of a black person: "Suppose a member of this court, nay, suppose every member of it, by some mysterious dispensation of providence should wake to-morrow with a black skin and curly hair . . . and in traveling through that portion of the country where the 'Jim Crow Car' abounds, should be ordered into it by the conductor. It is easy to imagine what would be the result. . . . What humiliation, what rage would then fill the judicial mind!" But the justices in the Court's majority in 1896 remained unpersuaded and, indeed, seemed unable to leave the perspective of a dominant group even when they offered their own imagined shift in perspectives. They posed the hypothetical situation of a state legislature dominated by blacks which adopted the same law commanding racial segregation in railway cars that was then before the Court. The justices reasoned that certainly whites "would not acquiesce in [the] assumption" that this law "relegate[d] the white race to an inferior position." Even in their effort to imagine how they would feel if the racial situation were reversed, the justices thereby manifested their viewpoint as members of a dominant and powerful group, which would never feel stigmatized by segregation.

Demonstrating that it was not impossible at that time to imagine a perspective other than that of the majority, however, Justice John Harlan dissented. He declared that the arbitrary separation of the races amounted to "a badge of servitude wholly inconsistent with the civil freedom and the equality before the law." He specifically rebutted the majority's claim about the meaning of segregation: "Everyone knows that the statute in question had its origins in the purpose, not so much to exclude white persons from railroad cars occupied by blacks, as to exclude colored people from coaches occupied by or assigned to white persons."

Justices to this day often fail to acknowledge their own perspective and its influence in the assignment of difference in relation to some unstated norm. Veiling the standpoint of the observer conceals its impact on our perception of the world. Denying that the observer's perspective influences perception leads to the next assumption: that all other perspectives are either presumptively identical to the observer's own or do not matter.

Assumption 4: Other Perspectives Are Irrelevant

In her short story "Meditations on History," Sherley Ann Williams illustrates how people can assume that their perspective is the truth, ignore other perspectives, and thereby miss much of what is going on. In the story a pregnant slave woman waits to be hanged for running away from her master and killing a white man. The owner has confined her in detention until her baby is born; then he will take the baby, to make up for the loss of his grown slave. A white man who is writing a book about managing slaves interviews the slave woman and seems satisfied that he is able to understand her. He concludes that she is basically stupid and confused; he grows especially irritated as she hums and sings during their interview, never considering that she is in this way communicating with other slaves about a rescue plan. When she escapes, with the help of her friends, the writer is baffled; he never comes to understand how incomplete was his understanding of her.

Many people who judge differences in the world reject as irrelevant or relatively unimportant the experience of "different people." William James put it this way: "We have seen the blindness and deadness to each other which are our natural inheritance." People often use stereotypes as though they were real and complete, thereby failing to see the complex humanity of others. Stereotyped thinking is one form of the failure to imagine the perspective of another. Glimpsing contrasting perspectives may alter assumptions about the world, as well as about the meaning of difference.

When judges consider the situation of someone they think is very much unlike themselves, there is a risk that they will not only view that person's plight from their own vantage point but also fail to imagine that there might be another vantage point. When a criminal defendant charged racial discrimination in the administration of the death penalty in Georgia's criminal justice system, the Supreme Court split between those justices who treated alternative perspectives as irrelevant and those who tried to imagine them. The defendant's lawyer submitted a statistical study of over 2,000 murder cases in Georgia during the 1970s, and the Court assumed it to be valid. According to the study, a defendant's likelihood of receiving the death sentence correlated with the victim's race and, to a lesser extent, with the defendant's race: black defendants convicted of killing white victims had the greatest likelihood of receiving the death penalty, and defendants of either race who killed black victims had considerably less chance of being sentenced to death. A majority of the Court concluded that even taking this evidence as true, the defendant had failed to show that the decision-makers in his case had acted with a discriminatory purpose.

Moreover, reasoned Justice Lewis Powell for the majority, recognizing the defendant's claim would open the door "to claims based on unexplained discrepancies that correlate to membership in other minority groups, and even to gender" or physical appearance. This argument, perhaps meant in part to trivialize the charge of race discrimination by linking it with physical appearance, implied that discrepancies in criminal sentences are random and too numerous to control. This formulation took the vantage point of such decision-makers as the reviewing court and the jury but not the perspective of the criminal defendant. Scholars of discrimination law have argued that the effect of discrimination on minorities is the same whether or not the majority group members intended it.

What would happen if the Court in a case like this considered an alternative perspective? Justice William Brennan explored this possibility in his dissent. Perhaps knowing that neither he nor many of his readers could fully grasp the defendant's perspective, he tried to look through the eyes of the defense attorney who is asked by Warren McCleskey, the black defendant in the case, about the chances of a death sentence. Adopting that viewpoint, Justice Brennan concluded that "counsel would feel bound to tell McCleskey, that defendants charged with killing white victims in Georgia are 4.3 times as likely to be sentenced to death as defendants charged with killing blacks ... [and] there was a significant chance that race would play a prominent role in determining if he lived or died." Moreover, he wrote, "enhanced willingness to impose the death sentence on black defendants, or diminished willingness to render such a sentence when blacks are victims, reflects a devaluation of the lives of black persons." Under these circumstances, he concluded, the judicial system had, in fact, considered race and produced judgments "completely at odds with [the] concern that an individual be evaluated as a unique human being."

To the majority's fear of widespread challenges to all aspects of criminal sentence Justice Brennan responded: "Taken at its face, such a statement seems to suggest a fear of too much justice.... The prospect that there may be more widespread abuse than McCleskey documents may be dismaying, but it does not justify complete abdication of our judicial role." To the majority of the Court, acknowledging discrimination in this case looked like a management problem for the courts rather than a means of reducing potential injustices suffered by defendants.

Randall Kennedy has emphasized still another perspective deflected by the majority, the perspective of the black communities "whose welfare is slighted by criminal justice systems that respond more forcefully to the killing of whites than the killing of blacks." In this view, black communities are denied equal access to a public good: punishment of those who injure members of that community. Taken seriously, this perspective could lead to the execution of more black defendants who have killed black victims. Kennedy concludes that "race-based devaluations of human life constitute simply one instance of a universal phenomenon: the propensity for persons to sympathize more fully with those with whom they can identify."

It may be impossible to take the perspective of another completely, but the effort to do so can help us recognize that our own perspective is partial. Searching especially for the viewpoint of minorities not only helps those in the majority shake free of their unstated assumptions but also helps them develop a better normative sense in light of the experience of those with less power. Members of minority groups have often had to become conversant with the world view of the majority while also trying to preserve their own. W.E.B. Du Bois's famous statement in his *Souls of Black Folk* describes that effort: "It is a peculiar sensation, this double-consciousness, this sense of always looking at one's self through the eyes of others, of measuring one's soul by the tape of the world that looks on in amused contempt and pity. One ever feels his twoness—an American, a Negro." More recently, bell hooks explained her perception of how she and other women of color came to understand the world: "Living as we did—on the edge—we developed a particular way of seeing reality. We looked both from the outside in and from the inside out. We focused our attention on the center as well as on the margin. We understood both." Works of fiction have often powerfully evoked the multiple worlds inhabited by members of minorities and thereby helped to convey the partiality of even a majority world view that presents itself as the one reality.

Judges have sometimes demonstrated an acute awareness of the perspective of religious persons or groups, contrasted with the view of a secular employer or the government. In Sherbert v. Verner, the Supreme Court considered the claims of a member of the Seventh–Day Adventists who had been discharged by her employer because she would not work on Saturday—the Sabbath observed by her church—and was unable to find other work that allowed her to observe her Sabbath. When she applied for state unemployment compensation, the state commission rejected her claim on the ground that she had refused to accept suitable work. The commission argued that it employed a neutral rule, denying benefits to anyone who failed without good cause to accept suitable work when offered. The Supreme Court reasoned that this rule was not neutral; that from the woman's point of view it burdened her religious beliefs. Indeed, reasoned the Court, the government's failure to accommodate religion, within reasonable limits, amounted to hostility toward religion.

Similarly, in Wisconsin v. Yoder, a majority of the Supreme Court refused enforcement of compulsory school laws against members of an Amish community who claimed that their religious way of life would be burdened if their adolescent children had to attend school beyond the eighth grade. Even though compulsory school laws serve widely supported public purposes, and even though the Amish way of life seemed unfamiliar to the Court, the justices were able to imagine the intrusion represented by compulsory schooling. Yet Justice William O. Douglas, in partial dissent, reminded the Court of another perspective often ignored: the viewpoint of the children, who might have preferred the chance to continue their formal education.

A perspective may go unstated because it is so unknown to those in charge that they do not recognize it as a perspective. Judges in particular often presume that the perspective they adopt is either universal or superior to others. Indeed, a perspective may go unstated because it is so powerful and pervasive that it may be presumed without defense. It has been said that Aristotle could have checked out—and corrected—his faulty assertion that women have fewer teeth than men. He did not do so, however, because he thought he knew. Presumptions about whose perspective ultimately matters arise from the fifth typically unarticulated assumption, that the status quo is the preferred situation.

Assumption 5: The Status Quo Is Natural, Uncoerced, and Good

Connected with many of the other assumptions is the idea that critical features of the status quo—general social and economic arrangements—are natural and desirable. From this assumption follow three propositions. First, the goal of governmental neutrality demands the status quo because existing societal arrangements are assumed to be neutral. Second, governmental actions that change the status quo have a different status from omissions, or failures to act, that maintain the status quo. Third, prevailing societal arrangements are not forced on anyone. Individuals are free to make choices and to assume responsibility for those choices. These propositions are rarely stated, both because they are deeply entrenched and because they treat the status quo as good, natural, and freely chosen—and thus not in need of discussion.

Difference may seem salient, then, not because of a trait intrinsic to the person but because the dominant institutional arrangements were designed without that trait in mind—designed according to an unstated norm reconfirmed by the view that alternative perspectives are irrelevant or have already been taken into account. The difference between buildings built without considering the needs of people in wheelchairs and buildings that are accessible to people in wheelchairs reveals that institutional arrangements define whose reality is to be the norm and what is to seem natural. Sidewalk curbs are not neutral or natural but humanly constructed obstacles. Interestingly, modifying what has been the status quo often brings unexpected benefits as well. Inserting curb cuts for the disabled turns out to help many others, such as bike riders and parents pushing baby strollers. (They can also be positioned to avoid endangering a visually impaired person who uses a cane to determine where the sidewalk ends.)

Yet the weight of the status quo remains great. Existing institutions and language already shape the world and already express and recreate attitudes about what counts as a difference, and who or what is the relevant point of comparison. Assumptions that the status quo is natural, good, and uncoerced make proposed changes seem to violate the commitment to neutrality, predictability, and freedom. ...

Sometimes, judges have challenged the assumption that the status quo is natural and good; they have occasionally approved public and private decisions to take difference into account in efforts to alter existing conditions and to remedy their harmful effects. But for the most part, unstated assumptions work in subtle and complex ways. They fill a basic human need to simplify and make our world familiar and unsurprising, yet by their very simplification, assumptions exclude contrasting views. Moreover, they contribute to the dilemma of difference by frustrating legislative and constitutional commitments to change the treatment of differences in race, gender, ethnicity, religion, and handicap.

As the following excerpts suggest, existing patterns of privilege and power can be maintained by positioning historically excluded groups, or members within such groups, against each other.

NEIL GOTANDA, ASIAN AMERICAN RIGHTS AND THE "MISS SAIGON SYNDROME"

in Asian Americans and the Supreme Court 1087–91 (Hyung–
Chan Kim, ed., Greenwood Press, 1992).

INTRODUCTION

In July, 1990, playwright David Henry Hwang and actor B.D. Wong, both Tony award winners for the Broadway production of Hwang's Madame Butterfly, wrote to the Screen Actors Guild to protest the casting of Jonathan Pryce as the lead in the planned Broadway production of *Miss Saigon*. Cameron Mackintosh, the enormously successful producer of such international successes as *Cats, Phantom of the Opera* and *Les Miseràbles,* had chosen Pryce, of Welsh descent, to reprise his widely-praised London portrayal of a Eurasian Saigon pimp.

Hwang and B.D. Wong complained that the choice of a white actor, with only the pretense of an effort to find an Asian actor for the role, was insensitive and racially discriminatory. Surprisingly, the actors union supported the protest and demanded that Pryce be replaced. In the past, the union had not been particularly responsive to Asian American complaints of discrimination in casting.

This protest, while newsworthy, was not a major news story until Cameron Mackintosh adopted a confrontational tactic. Instead of negotiating seriously with the union, Mackintosh cancelled the entire New

York production, purportedly forfeiting millions of dollars in advance ticket sales. The result was front-page coverage of the ensuing international shouting match, and a controversy which continues well after *Miss Saigon's* Broadway opening on April 11, 1991. The reaction from the press and general public was all but unanimous against the Asian American protest. Newspaper editorials, theater critics, intellectuals, actors, and radio talk-show hosts charged David Hwang and B.D. Wong with reverse racism and undermining racial progress in the theater.

While these charges of race discrimination vs. reverse racism, and artistic freedom vs. union assertion of actor's rights have generated important discussions, this article will focus upon the angry tone of the mainstream reaction to the Asian American protest. My interpretation of the vehement reaction against the protesters is that the reaction reflects a widespread popular belief that racism directed against Asian Americans is insignificant or *does not exist*. This denial of the existence of racism against Asian Americans is what I will call the "Miss Saigon Syndrome." I provide a name for the phenomenon of the controversy surrounding *Miss Saigon* not only because of the widespread attention, but because my assessment is that the mainstream denial of racism towards Asian Americans is a pervasive and deeply held belief.

In this article, I will not attempt to respond directly and argue that racism against Asian Americans really does exist. Other authors have explored the various dimensions of this form of American racism. The question addressed in this paper is how this erroneous perception—the Miss Saigon Syndrome—can continue to be maintained and reproduced when it seems so intuitively and obviously incorrect to Asian Americans. Many interpretive perspectives are possible to examine the Miss Saigon Syndrome. This paper will focus upon American racial legal ideology with special attention to the decisions of the U.S. Supreme Court. I will examine the interactions of the model minority image, and the Supreme Court's creation of dual identities of "alien" and "racial minority" for Asian Americans.

Besides addressing the ideology of race as it applies to Asian Americans, another purpose of this article is to show that addressing the question of race at the ideological level is an integral part of general anti-racist struggles. In the ideological dimension of anti-racist efforts, the ideology of the law and the ideology of race can be linked together politically.

RACIAL STRATIFICATION AND THE MODEL MINORITY

This section examines the model minority image to discern the racial character and the principal components of this stereotype. I argue that the notion of the model minority carries an implied racial context of racial stratification and that there are distinct ideological messages implicit within the model minority image and racial stratification. Further, racial stratification implies an altered legal vision of race. The multi-level conception of race implicit in a racial stratification model is a sharp change from the Black–White model of race used in legal discrimination theory.

The image of Asians as model minority is a distinctly racial conceptualization. The perception of economic gains of Asian American small businesses (especially the image of the "Korean grocer"), the dramatic presence of Asians at U.S. colleges and universities, and Japanese automobile sales are blended together in a confusing mix. These various images of the successful Asian have only the Asian racial image in common. For example, economic ties between small businesses and Nissan Motors are non-existent. Small Asian American business and giant Asian corporations share no political allegiances. Similarly, ties of cultural tradition are irrelevant to the business enterprise. The common linkages are solely in the mainstream perception of racial similarity.

The development of the model minority image is traced in Su Sun Bai's recent examination of the political exclusion of Asian Americans from the political process. He locates its beginning in a 1966 *New York Times* article entitled, *"Success Story, Japanese American Style."* Continuing through the present, there has been presented a consistent theme: a racial minority *can* succeed in the U.S. The comparison with African Americans is sometimes implied and sometimes explicit. From this theme, Su Sun Bai cites with approval an analysis finding three functional political messages: a "benefit denying" function, a "system preserving" function and a "minority blaming" function. My analysis of these three functions suggests that they operate to support the Miss Saigon Syndrome.

The first functional message is one which points to the various "successes" of Asian Americans and concludes that there remain few if any genuine issues of racism. Had there been continued racism, Asian Americans would not have been able to demonstrate any visible achievement. Without an issue of racism, there is no basis for remedial benefits.

The second message suggests that even if Asian Americans demonstrate or prove racial discrimination, such a showing is not to be taken seriously. Since the perceived conditions of Asian Americans are clearly not as serious as those of African Americans in the urban centers, such claims of racial discrimination are simply a "sour grapes" complaint. This impression functions to preserve the status quo and limit any remedial change.

An example of this "sour grapes" response can be seen in media comments on the Miss Saigon controversy. Frank Rich, the extremely influential theater critic for the *New York Times* only grudgingly conceded that Asian American actors and actresses had some genuine racial grievances. After making that concession, he later gave Miss Saigon a very favorable review in which he made no mention of complaints about Miss Saigon's demeaning Oriental stereotypes. Rich and other reviewers were implicitly anxious to preserve the status quo.

The third message, minority-blaming, is directed not at Asian Americans, but at African Americans. Since model minority Asian Americans have succeeded, the message of minority-blaming points to African Americans as themselves responsible for their situation. Without directly denying that Asian Americans have faced racism, minority-blaming significantly blunts efforts to redress racial grievances. Taken together, these three "messages" within the model minority myth function to support the Miss Saigon syndrome.

This conception of the model minority, a successful non-White minority within the American racial scheme, is a relatively new addition to American racial thought. Past discussions of race used a two-category Black/White framework for almost all analysis. There have been notable studies of individual racial groups, incidents or periods. But almost all general discussions of race in the legal literature, even those which were couched in terms of "minorities" or "ethnicity" have focused upon African American and White bi-polar racial relations.

While there has not yet appeared a substantial body of writing on the comparative role of non-Black racial minorities, I have the distinct impression that only after World War II, and especially since the expansion of Asian and Western Hemisphere immigration in the early 1960's, has the theme of racial stratification emerged in discussions about race.

Racial stratification has occurred within America both as a sociological development and at the level of racial ideology. As an empirical matter, one can point to rising average income levels of Asian Americans, the extraordinarily high levels of participation by Asian Americans in higher education, and the visible appearance of Asian Americans in elite circles of finance, politics, education, and the arts. These are clear signposts of economic achievement. However, these observations remain racialized in their underlying character since they utilize a racial category—Asian American—as the basis for the sociological model.

This use of racial categories is the first level of racial ideology found in racial stratification. A more explicitly ideological use of racial stratification is to compare Asian Americans with African Americans, often as part of an analysis of African American poverty. The conservative versions of such an analysis attempt to show how race does not explain the deep levels of economic poverty found among African Americans in the central cities. One example of this approach is conservative economist Thomas Sowell's discussion in his book, Race and Economics. Sowell compares in passing, "Negroes, Jews, Irishmen, Italians, West Indians, Japanese, Puerto Ricans, and Mexicans."

The ideological effect of this emergent racial stratification has been to reinterpret economic and social disparities within the U.S. Racial stratification suggests that the economic rungs of the socio-economic ladder—with Whites at the top, African Americans at the bottom and Asians and Latinos in between—are the product of "natural" and "normal" socio-economic forces. This contrasts with the earlier two-race model, in which the sharp economic disparity between African Americans and Whites was regarded as an aberration. The conclusion that the Black–White economic disparity was too sharp and therefore represented a social problem requiring repair was the ideological assumption underlying much of our anti-discrimination legislation. This has been especially true in interpretations of Title VII of the Civil Rights Act of 1964, where there has developed an understanding that a business or employment practice which resulted in eliminating more minorities than whites was racial discrimination and a violation of Title VII.

Under the model of racial stratification, however, the economic disparities between Black and White, while clearly present and of demonstrable severity, do not appear to be a genuine social problem. The presence of more successful Asian Americans and Latinos, located between Whites and African Americans, proves that the social and economic barriers can be overcome and are not rooted in "race." Thus racial stratification serves to justify and legitimate existing racial disparities.

This ideological dimension to racial stratification operates to support the model minority image. The perception of Asian American success when combined with the lack of relative economic success for African Americans proves that Asian Americans are a successful minority and do not "really" suffer from racism. . . .

ALICE WALKER, ADVANCING LUNA—
AND IDA B. WELLS

in You Can't Keep a Good Woman Down 85–104.
(Harcourt, Brace, Jovanovich, 1981).

I met Luna the summer of 1965 in Atlanta where we both attended a political conference and rally. It was designed to give us the courage, as temporary civil rights workers, to penetrate the small hamlets farther south. I had taken a bus from Sarah Lawrence in New York and gone back to Georgia, my home state, to try my hand at registering voters. It had become obvious from the high spirits and sense of almost divine purpose exhibited by black people that a revolution was going on, and I did not intend to miss it. Especially not this summery, student-studded version of it. And I thought it would be fun to spend some time on my own in the South.

Luna was sitting on the back of a pickup truck, waiting for someone to take her from Faith Baptist, where the rally was held, to whatever gracious black Negro home awaited her. I remember because someone who assumed I would also be traveling by pickup introduced us. I remember her face when I said, "No, no more back of pickup trucks for me. I know Atlanta well enough, I'll walk." She assumed of course (I guess) that I did not wish to ride beside her because she was white, and I was not curious enough about what she might have thought to explain it to her. And yet I was struck by her passivity, her *patience* as she sat on the truck alone and ignored, because someone had told her to wait there quietly until it was time to go.

This look of passively waiting for something changed very little over the years I knew her. It was only four or five years in all that I did. It seems longer, perhaps because we met at such an optimistic time in our lives. John Kennedy and Malcolm X had already been assassinated, but King had not been and Bobby Kennedy had not been. Then too, the lethal, bizarre elimination by death of this militant or that, exiles, flights to Cuba, shoot-outs between former Movement friends sundered forever by lies planted by the FBI, the gunning down of Mrs. Martin Luther King, Sr., as she played the Lord's Prayer on the piano in her church (was her name Alberta?), were still in the happily unfathomable future.

We believed we could change America because we were young and bright and held ourselves *responsible* for changing it. We did not believe we would fail. That is what lent fervor (revivalist fervor, in fact; we would *revive* America!) to our songs, and lent sweetness to our friendships (in the beginning almost all interracial), and gave a wonderful fillip to our sex (which, too, in the beginning, was almost always interracial).

What first struck me about Luna when we later lived together was that she did not own a bra. This was curious to me, I suppose, because she also did not need one. Her chest was practically flat, her breasts like those of a child. Her face was round, and she suffered from acne. She carried with her always a tube of that "skin-colored" (if one's skin is pink or eggshell) medication designed to dry up pimples. At the oddest times—waiting for a light to change, listening to voter registration instructions, talking about her father's new girlfriend, she would apply the stuff, holding in her other hand a small brass mirror the size of her thumb, which she also carried for just this purpose.

We were assigned to work together in a small, rigidly segregated South Georgia town that the city fathers, incongruously and years ago, had named Freehold. Luna was slightly asthmatic and when overheated or nervous she breathed through her mouth. She wore her shoulder-length black hair with bangs to her eyebrows and the rest brushed behind her ears. Her eyes were brown and rather small. She was attractive, but just barely and with effort. Had she been the slightest bit overweight, for instance, she would have gone completely unnoticed, and would have faded into the background where, even in a revolution, fat people seem destined to go. I have a photograph of her sitting on the steps of a house in South Georgia. She is wearing tiny pearl earrings, a dark sleeveless shirt with Peter Pan collar, Bermuda shorts, and a pair of those East Indian sandals that seem to adhere to nothing but a big toe.

The summer of '65 was as hot as any other in that part of the South. There was an abundance of flies and mosquitoes. Everyone complained about the heat and the flies and the hard work, but Luna complained less than the rest of us. She walked ten miles a day with me up and down those straight Georgia highways, stopping at every house that looked black (one could always tell in 1965) and asking whether anyone needed help with learning how to vote. The simple mechanics: writing one's name, or making one's "X" in the proper column.   And then, though we were required to walk, everywhere, we were empowered to offer prospective registrants a car in which they might safely ride down to the county courthouse.   And later to the polling places.   Luna, almost overcome by the heat, breathing through her mouth like a dog, her hair plastered with sweat to her head, kept looking straight ahead, and walking as if the walking itself was her reward.

I don't know if we accomplished much that summer.   In retrospect, it seems not only minor, but irrelevant.   A bunch of us, black and white, lived together.   The black people who took us in were unfailingly hospitable and kind.   I took them for granted in a way that now amazes me.   I realize that at each and every house we visited I *assumed* hospitality, I *assumed* kindness.   Luna was often startled by my "boldness."   If we walked up to a secluded farmhouse and half a dozen dogs ran up barking around our heels and a large black man with a shotgun could be seen whistling to himself under a tree, she would become nervous, I, on the other hand, felt free to yell at this stranger's dogs, slap a couple of them on the nose, and call over to him about his hunting.

That month with Luna of approaching new black people every day taught me something about myself I had always suspected: I thought black people superior people.   Not simply superior to white people, because even without thinking about it much, I assumed almost everyone was superior to them; but to everyone.   Only white people, after all, would blow up a Sunday-school class and grin for television over their "victory," *i.e.*, the death of four small black girls.   Any atrocity, at any time, was expected from them.   On the other hand, it never occurred to me that black people *could* treat Luna and me with anything but warmth and concern.   Even their curiosity about the sudden influx into their midst of rather ignorant white and black Northerners was restrained and courteous.   I was treated as a relative, Luna as a much welcomed guest.

Luna and I were taken in by a middle-aged couple and their young school-age daughter.   The mother worked outside the house in a local canning factory, the father worked in the paper plant in nearby Augusta.   Never did they speak of the danger they were in of losing their jobs over keeping us, and never did their small daughter show any fear that her house might be attacked by racists because we were there.   Again, I did not expect this family to complain, no matter what happened to them because of us.   Having understood the danger, they had assumed the risk.   I did not think them particularly brave, merely typical.

I think Luna liked the smallness—only four rooms—of the house. It was in this house that she ridiculed her mother's lack of taste.   Her yellow-and-mauve house in Cleveland, the eleven rooms, the heated garage, the new car every year, her father's inability to remain faithful to her mother, their divorce, the fight over the property, even more bitter than over the children.   Her mother kept the house and the children.   Her father kept the car and his new girlfriend, whom he wanted Luna to meet and "approve." I could hardly imagine anyone disliking her mother so much. Everything Luna hated in her she summed up in three words: *"yellow and mauve."*

I have a second photograph of Luna and a group of us being bullied by a Georgia state trooper. This member of Georgia's finest had followed us out into the deserted countryside to lecture us on how misplaced—in the South—was our energy, when "the Lord knew" the North (where he thought all of us lived, expressing disbelief that most of us were Georgians) was just as bad. (He had a point that I recognized even then, but it did not seem the point where we were.) Luna is looking up at him, her mouth slightly open as always, a somewhat dazed look on her face. I cannot detect fear on any of our faces, though we were all afraid. After all, 1965 was only a year after 1964 when three civil rights workers had been taken deep into a Mississippi forest by local officials and sadistically tortured and murdered. Luna almost always carried a flat black shoulder bag. She is standing with it against her side, her thumb in the strap.

At night we slept in the same bed. We talked about our schools, lovers, girlfriends we didn't understand or missed. She dreamed, she said, of going to Goa. I dreamed of going to Africa. My dream came true earlier than hers: an offer of a grant from an unsuspected source reached me one day as I was writing poems under a tree. I left Freehold, Georgia, in the middle of summer, without regrets, and flew from New York to London, to Cairo, to Kenya, and, finally, to Uganda, where I settled among black people with the same assumptions of welcome and kindness I had taken for granted in Georgia. I was taken on rides down the Nile as a matter of course, and accepted all invitations to dinner, where the best local dishes were superbly prepared in my honor. I became, in fact, a lost relative of the people, whose ancestors had foolishly strayed, long ago, to America.

I wrote to Luna at once.

But I did not see her again for almost a year. I had graduated from college, moved into a borrowed apartment in Brooklyn Heights, and was being evicted after a month. Luna, living then in a tenement on East 9th Street, invited me to share her two-bedroom apartment. If I had seen the apartment before the day I moved in I might never have agreed to do so. Her building was between Avenues B and C and did not have a front door. Junkies, winos, and others often wandered in during the night (and occasionally during the day) to sleep underneath the stairs or to relieve themselves at the back of the first-floor hall.

Luna's apartment was on the third floor. Everything in it was painted white. The contrast between her three rooms and kitchen (with its red bathtub) and the grungy stairway was stunning. Her furniture consisted of two large brass beds inherited from a previous tenant and stripped of paint by Luna, and a long, high-backed church pew which she had managed somehow to bring up from the South. There was a simplicity about the small apartment that I liked. I also liked the notion of extreme contrast, and I do to this day. Outside our front window was the decaying neighborhood, as ugly and ill-lit as a battle-ground. (And allegedly as hostile, though somehow we were never threatened with bodily harm by the Hispanics who were our neighbors, and who seemed, more than anything, *bewildered* by the darkness and filth of their surroundings.) Inside was the church pew, as straight and spare as Abe Lincoln lying down, the white walls as spotless as a monastery's, and a small, unutterably pure patch of blue sky through the window of the back bedroom. (Luna did not believe in curtains, or couldn't afford them, and so we always undressed and bathed with the lights off and the rooms lit with candles, causing rather nun-shaped shadows to be cast on the walls by the long-sleeved high-necked nightgowns we both wore to bed.)

Over a period of weeks, our relationship, always marked by mutual respect, evolved into a warm and comfortable friendship which provided a stability and comfort we both needed at that time. I had taken a job at the Welfare Department during the day, and set up my typewriter permanently in the tiny living room for work after I got home. Luna worked in a kindergarten, and in the evenings taught herself Portuguese.

It was while we lived on East 9th Street that she told me she had been raped during her summer in the South. It is hard for me, even now, to relate my feeling of horror and incredulity. This was some time before Eldridge Cleaver wrote of being a rapist/revolutionary; of "practicing" on black women before moving on to white. It was also, unless I'm mistaken, before LeRoi Jones (as he was then known; now of course Imamu Baraka, which has an even more presumptuous meaning than "the King") wrote his advice to young black male insurrectionaries (women were not told what to do with *their* rebelliousness): "Rape the white girls. Rape their fathers." It was clear that he meant this literally and also as: to rape a white girl *is* to rape her father. It was the misogynous cruelty of this latter meaning that was habitually lost on black men (on men in general, actually), but nearly always perceived and rejected by women of whatever color.

"Details?" I asked.

She shrugged. Gave his name. A name recently in the news, though in very small print.

He was not a Movement star or anyone you would know. We had met once, briefly. I had not liked him because he was coarse and spoke of black women as "our" women. (In the early Movement, it was pleasant to think of black men wanting to own us as a group; later it became clear that owning us meant exactly *that* to them.) He was physically unattractive, I had thought, with something of the hoodlum about him: a swaggering, unnecessarily mobile walk, small eyes, rough skin, a mouthful of wandering or absent teeth. He was, ironically, among the first persons to shout the slogan everyone later attributed solely to Stokeley Carmichael—Black Power! Stokeley was chosen as the originator of this idea by the media, because he was physically beautiful and photogenic and articulate. Even the name—Freddie Pye—was diminutive, I thought, in an age of giants.

"What did you do?"

"Nothing that required making a noise."

"Why didn't you scream?" I felt I would have screamed my head off.

"You know why."

I did. I had seen a photograph of Emmett Till's body just after it was pulled from the river. I had seen photographs of white folks standing in a circle roasting something that had talked to them in their own language before they tore out its tongue. I knew why, all right.

"What was he trying to prove?"

"I don't know. Do you?"

"Maybe you filled him with unendurable lust," I said.

"I don't think so," she said.

Suddenly I was embarrassed. Then angry. Very, very angry. *How dare she tell me this!* I thought.

Who knows what the black woman thinks of rape? Who has asked her? Who *cares*? Who has even properly acknowledged that *she* and not the white woman in this story is the most likely victim of rape? Whenever interracial rape is mentioned, a black woman's first thought is to protect the lives of her brothers, her father, her sons, her lover. A history of lynching has bred this reflex in her. I feel it as strongly as anyone. While writing a fictional account of such a rape in a novel, I read Ida B. Wells's autobiography three times, as a means of praying to her spirit to forgive me.

My prayer, as I turned the pages, went like this: *"Please forgive me. I am a writer."* (This self-revealing statement alone often seems to me sufficient reason to require perpetual forgiveness; since the writer is guilty not only of always wanting to know—like Eve—but also of trying—again like Eve—to find out.) "I cannot write contrary to what life reveals to me. I wish to malign no one. But I must struggle to understand at least my own tangled emotions about interracial rape. I know, Ida B. Wells, you spent your whole life protecting, and trying to protect, black men accused of raping white women, who were lynched by white mobs, or threatened with it. You know, better than I ever will, what it means for a whole people to live under the terror of lynching. Under the slander that their men, where white women are concerned, are creatures of uncontrollable sexual lust. You made it so clear that the black men accused of rape in the past were innocent victims of white criminals that I grew up believing black men literally did not rape white women. At all. Ever. Now it would appear that some of them, the very twisted, the terribly ill, do. What would you have me write about them?"

Her answer was: *"Write nothing. Nothing at all. It will be used against black men and therefore against all of us. Eldridge Cleaver and LeRoi Jones don't know who they're dealing with. But you remember. You are dealing with people who brought their children to witness the murder of black human beings, falsely accused of rape. People who handed out, as trophies, black fingers and toes. Deny! Deny! Deny!"*

And yet, I have pursued it: *"Some black men themselves do not seem to know what the meaning of raping someone is. Some have admitted rape in order to denounce it, but others have accepted rape as a part of rebellion, of 'paying whitey back.' They have gloried in it."*

"They know nothing of America," she says. *"And neither, apparently, do you. No matter what you think you know, no matter what you feel about it, say nothing. And to your dying breath!"*

Which, to my mind, is virtually useless advice to give to a writer. Freddie Pye was the kind of man I would not have looked at then, not even once. (Throughout that year I was more or less into exotica: white ethnics who knew languages were a peculiar weakness; a half-white hippie singer; also a large Chinese mathematician who was a marvelous dancer and who taught me to waltz.) There was no question of belief.

But, in retrospect, there was a momentary *suspension* of belief, a kind of *hope* that perhaps it had not really happened; that Luna had made up the rape, "as white women have been wont to do." I soon realized this was unlikely. I was the only person she had told.

She looked at me as if to say: "I'm glad *that* part of my life is over." We continued our usual routine. We saw every interminable, foreign, depressing, and poorly illuminated film ever made. We learned to eat brown rice and yogurt and to tolerate kasha and odd-tasting teas. My half-black hippie singer friend (now a well-known reggae singer who says he is from "de I-lands" and not Sheepshead Bay) was "into" tea and kasha and Chinese vegetables.

And yet the rape, the knowledge of the rape, out in the open, admitted, pondered over, was now between us. (And I began to think that perhaps—whether Luna had been raped or not—it had always been so; that her power over my life was exactly the power *her word on rape* had over the lives of black men, over *all* black men, whether they were guilty or not, and therefore over my whole people.)

Before she told me about the rape, I think we had assumed a lifelong friendship. The kind of friendship one dreams of having with a person one has known in adversity; under heat and mosquitoes and immaturity and the threat of death. We would each travel, we would write to each other from the three edges of the world.

We would continue to have an "international list" of lovers whose amorous talents or lack of talents we would continue (giggling into our dotage) to compare. Our friendship would survive everything, be truer than everything, endure even our respective marriages, children, husbands—assuming we *did*, out of desperation and boredom someday, marry, which did not seem a probability, exactly, but more in the area of an amusing idea.

But now there was a cooling off of our affection for each other. Luna was becoming mildly interested in drugs, because everyone we knew was. I was envious of the openendedness of her life. The financial backing to it. When she left her job at the kindergarten because she was tired of working, her errant father immediately materialized. He took her to dine on scampi at an expensive restaurant, scolded her for living on East 9th Street, and looked at me as if to say: "Living in a slum of this magnitude must surely have been your idea." As a cullud, of course.

For me there was the welfare department every day, attempting to get the necessary food and shelter to people who would always live amid the dirty streets I knew I must soon leave. I was, after all, a Sarah Lawrence girl "with talent." It would be absurd to rot away in a building that had no front door.

I slept late one Sunday morning with a painter I had met at the Welfare Department. A man who looked for all the world like Gene Autry, the singing cowboy, but who painted wonderful surrealist pictures of birds and ghouls and fruit with *teeth*. The night before, three of us— me, the painter, and "an old Navy buddy" who looked like his twin and who had just arrived in town—had got high on wine and grass.

That morning the Navy buddy snored outside the bedrooms like a puppy waiting for its master. Luna got up early, made an immense racket getting breakfast, scowled at me as I emerged from my room, and left the apartment, slamming the door so hard she damaged the lock. (Luna had made it a rule to date black men almost exclusively. My insistence on dating, as she termed it, "anyone" was incomprehensible to her, since in a politically diseased society to "sleep with the enemy" was to become "infected" with the enemy's "political germs." There is more than a grain of truth in this, of course, but I was having too much fun to stare at it for long. Still, coming from Luna it was amusing, since she never took into account the risk her own black lovers ran by sleeping with "the white woman," and she had apparently been convinced that a summer of relatively innocuous political work in the South had cured her of any racial, economic, or sexual political disease.)

Luna never told me what irked her so that Sunday morning, yet I remember it as the end of our relationship. It was not, as I at first feared, that she thought my bringing the two men to the apartment was inconsiderate. The way we lived allowed us to *be* inconsiderate from time to time. Our friends were varied, vital, and often strange. Her friends especially were deeper than they should have been into drugs.

The distance between us continued to grow. She talked more of going to Goa. My guilt over my dissolute if pleasurable existence coupled with my mounting hatred of welfare work, propelled me in two directions: south and to West Africa. When the time came to choose, I discovered that *my* summer in the South had infected me with the need to return, to try to understand, and write about, the people I'd merely lived with before.

We never discussed the rape again. We never discussed, really, Freddie Pye or Luna's remaining feelings about what had happened. One night, the last month we lived together, I noticed a man's blue denim jacket thrown across the church pew. The next morning, out of Luna's bedroom walked Freddie Pye. He barely spoke to me—possibly because as a black woman I was expected to be hostile toward his presence in a white woman's bedroom. I was too surprised to exhibit hostility, however, which was only a part of what I felt, after all. He left.

Luna and I did not discuss this. It is odd, I think now, that we didn't. It was as if he was never there, as if he and Luna had not shared the bedroom that night. A month later, Luna went alone to Goa, in her solitary way. She lived on an island and slept, she wrote, on the beach. She mentioned she'd found a lover there who protected her from the local beachcombers and pests.

Several years later, she came to visit me in the South and brought a lovely piece of pottery which my daughter much later dropped and broke, but which I glued back together in such a way that the flaw improves the beauty and fragility of the design.

Afterwords, Afterwards Second Thoughts

That is the "story." It has an "unresolved" ending. That is because Freddie Pye and Luna are still alive, as am I. However, one evening while talking to a friend, I heard myself say that I had, in fact, written *two* endings. One, which follows, I considered appropriate for such a story published in a country truly committed to justice, and the one above, which is the best I can afford to offer a society in which lynching is still reserved, at least subconsciously, as a means of racial control.

I said that if we in fact lived in a society committed to the establishment of justice for everyone ("justice" in this case encompassing equal housing, education, access to work, adequate dental care, et cetera), thereby placing Luna and Freddie Pye in their correct relationship to each other, i.e., that of brother and sister, *compañeros,* then the two of them would be required to struggle together over what his rape of her had meant.

Since my friend is a black man whom I love and who loves me, we spent a considerable amount of time discussing what this particular rape meant to us. Morally wrong, we said, and not to be excused. Shameful; politically corrupt. Yet, as we thought of what might have happened to an indiscriminate number of innocent young black men in Freehold, Georgia, had Luna screamed, it became clear that more than a little of Ida B. Wells's fear of probing the rape issue was running through us, too. The implications of this fear would not let me rest, so that months and years went by with most of the story written but with me incapable, or at least unwilling, to finish or to publish it.

In thinking about it over a period of years, there occurred a number of small changes, refinements, puzzles, in angle. Would these shed a wider light on the continuing subject? I do not know. In any case, I returned to my notes, hereto appended for the use of the reader.

LUNA: IDA B. WELLS—DISCARDED NOTES

Additional characteristics of Luna: At a time when many in and out of the Movement considered "nigger" and "black" synonymous, and indulged in a sincere attempt to fake Southern "hip" speech, Luna resisted. She was the kind of WASP who could not easily imitate another's ethnic style, nor could she even exaggerate her own. She was what she was. A very straight, clear-eyed, coolly observant young woman with no talent for existing outside her own skin.

IMAGINARY KNOWLEDGE

Luna explained the visit from Freddie Pye in this way:

"He called that evening, said he was in town, and did I know the Movement was coming north? I replied that I did know that."

When could he see her? he wanted to know.

"Never," she replied.

He had burst into tears, or something that sounded like tears, over the phone. He was stranded at wherever the evening's fund-raising event had been held. Not in the place itself, but outside, in the street. The "stars" had left, everyone had left. He was alone. He knew no one else in the city. Had found her number in the phone book. And had no money, no place to stay.

Could he, he asked, crash? He was tired, hungry, broke—and even in the South had had no job, other than the Movement, for months. Et cetera.

When he arrived, she had placed our only steak knife in the waist-band of her jeans.

He had asked for a drink of water. She gave him orange juice, some cheese, and a couple of slices of bread. She had told him he might sleep on the church pew and he had lain down with his head on his rolled-up denim jacket. She had retired to her room, locked the door, and tried to sleep. She was amazed to discover herself worrying that the church pew was both too narrow and too hard.

At first he muttered, groaned, and cursed in his sleep. Then he fell off the narrow church pew. He kept rolling off. At two in the morning she unlocked her door, showed him her knife, and invited him to share her bed.

Nothing whatever happened except they talked. At first, only he talked. Not about the rape, but about his life.

"He was a small person physically, remember?" Luna asked me. (She was right. Over the years he had grown big and, yes, burly, in my imagination, and I'm sure in hers.) "That night he seemed tiny. A child. He was still fully dressed, except for the jacket and he, literally, hugged his side of the bed. I hugged mine. The whole bed, in fact, was between us. We were merely hanging to its edges."

At the fund-raiser—on Fifth Avenue and 71st Street, as it turned out—his leaders had introduced him as the unskilled, barely literate, former Southern fieldworker that he was. They had pushed him at the rich people gathered there as an example of what "the system" did to "the little people" in the South. They asked him to tell about the thirty-seven times he had been jailed. The thirty-five times he had been beaten. The one time he had lost consciousness in the "hot" box. They told him not to worry about his grammar. "Which, as you may recall," said Luna, "was horrible." Even so, he had tried to censor his "ain'ts" and his "us'es." He had been painfully aware that he was on exhibit, like Frederick Douglass had been for the Abolitionists. But unlike Douglass he had no oratorical gift, no passionate language, no silver tongue. He knew the rich people and his own leaders perceived he was nothing: a broken man, unschooled, unskilled at anything. . . .

Yet he had spoken, trembling before so large a crowd of rich, white Northerners—who clearly thought their section of the country would never have the South's racial problems—begging, with the painful stories of his wretched life, for their money.

At the end, all of them—the black leaders, too—had gone. They left him watching the taillights of their cars, recalling the faces of the friends come to pick them up: the women dressed in African print that shone, with elaborately arranged hair, their jewelry sparkling, their perfume exotic. They were so beautiful, yet so strange. He could not imagine that one of them could comprehend his life. He did not ask for a ride, because of that, but also because he had no place to go. Then he had remembered Luna.

Soon Luna would be required to talk. She would mention her confusion over whether, in a black community surrounded by whites with a history of lynching blacks, she had a right to scream as Freddie Pye was raping her. For her, this was the crux of the matter.

And so they would continue talking through the night.

This is another ending, created from whole cloth. If I believed Luna's story about the rape, and I did (had she told anyone else I might have dismissed it), then this reconstruction of what might have happened is as probable an accounting as any is liable to be. Two people have now become "characters."

I have forced them to talk until they reached the stumbling block of the rape, *which they must remove themselves*, before proceeding to a place from which it will be possible to insist on a society in which Luna's word alone on rape can never be used to intimidate an entire people, and in which an innocent black man's protestation of innocence of rape is unprejudicially heard. Until such a society is created, relationships of affection between black men and white women will always be poisoned—from within as from without—by historical fear and the threat of violence, and solidarity among black and white women is only rarely likely to exist.

POSTCRIPT: HAVANA, CUBA, NOVEMBER 1976

I am in Havana with a group of other black American artists. We have spent the morning apart from our Cuban hosts bringing each other up to date on the kind of work (there are no apolitical artists among us) we are doing in the United States. I have read "Luna."

High above the beautiful city of Havana I sit in the Havana Libre pavilion with the muralist/photographer in our group. He is in his mid-thirties, a handsome, brown, erect individual whom I have known casually for a number of years. During the sixties he designed and painted street murals for both SNCC and the Black Panthers, and in an earlier discussion with Cuban artists he showed impatience with their explanation of why we had seen no murals covering some of the city's rather dingy walls: Cuba, they had said, unlike Mexico, has no mural tradition. "But the point of a revolution," insisted Our Muralist, "is to make new traditions!" And he had pressed his argument with such passion for the *usefulness,* for revolutionary communication, of his craft, that the Cubans were both exasperated and impressed. They drove us around the city for a tour of their huge billboards, all advancing socialist thought and the heroism of men like Lenin, Camilo, and Che Guevara, and said, "These, *these* are our 'murals'!"

While we ate lunch, I asked Our Muralist what he'd thought of "Luna." Especially the appended section.

"Not much," was his reply. "Your view of human weakness is too biblical," he said. "You are unable to conceive of the man without conscience. The man who cares nothing about the state of his soul because he's long since sold it. In short," he said, "you do not understand that some people are simply evil, a disease on the lives of other people, and that to remove the disease altogether is preferable to trying to interpret, contain, or forgive it. Your 'Freddie Pye,'" and he laughed, "was probably raping white women on the instructions of his government."

Oh ho, I thought. Because, of course, for a second, during which I stalled my verbal reply, this comment made both very little and very much sense.

"I *am* sometimes naive and sentimental," I offered. I am sometimes both, though frequently by design. Admission in this way is tactical, a stimulant to conversation.

"And shocked at what I've said," he said, and laughed again. "Even though," he continued, "you know by now that blacks could be hired to blow up other blacks, and could be hired *by someone* to shoot down Brother Malcolm, and hired *by someone* to provide a diagram of Fred Hampton's bedroom so the pigs could shoot him easily while he slept, you find it hard to believe a black man could be hired *by someone* to rape white women. But think a minute, and you will see why it is the perfect disruptive act. Enough blacks raping or accused of raping enough white women and any political movement that cuts across racial lines is doomed.

"Larger forces are at work than your story would indicate," he continued. "You're still thinking of lust and rage, moving slowly into aggression and purely racial hatred. But you should be considering money—which the rapist would get, probably from your very own tax dollars, in fact—and a maintaining of the status quo; which those hiring the rapist would achieve. I know all this," he said, "because when I was broke and hungry and selling my blood to buy the food and the paint that allowed me to work, I was offered such 'other work.'"

"But you did not take it."

He frowned. "There you go again. How do you know I didn't take it? It paid, and I was starving."

"You didn't take it," I repeated.

"No," he said. "A black and white 'team' made the offer. I had enough energy left to threaten to throw them out of the room."

"But even if Freddie Pye *had been* hired *by someone* to rape Luna, that still would not explain his second visit."

"Probably nothing will explain that," said Our Muralist. "But assuming Freddie Pye *was* paid to disrupt—by raping a white woman— the black struggle in the South, he may have wised up enough later to comprehend the significance of Luna's decision not to scream."

"So you are saying he *did have* a conscience?" I asked.

"Maybe," he said, but his look clearly implied I would never understand anything about evil, power, or corrupted human beings in the modern world.

But of course he is wrong.

Notes and Questions

1. How does the model minority concept perpetuate racism against both Asian Americans and other racial groups? Can you think of recent incidents in which excluded groups were pitted against each other?

2. What is the significance of Luna's decision not to scream? Which groups are pitted against each other in interracial rape incidents?

3. In writing about the conflict in Los Angeles between African Americans and Korean Americans, Professor Lisa Ikemoto observed: "Although the conflict as constructed does not directly speak of dominant white society, it arranges the various racial identities so as to preserve the authority of whiteness and devalue difference. The differences between Blacks and Asians emerge as a tale of relative nonwhiteness. When racial identity is

constructed oppositionally, conflict becomes inevitable and coalition becomes unimaginable, and both groups are publicly debilitated and exposed." Lisa Ikemoto, *Traces of the Master Narrative in the Story of African American/Korean American Conflict: How We Construct "Los Angeles"*, 66 S.Cal.L.Rev. 1581, 1583 (1993).

4. Professor Derrick Bell has written that existing patterns of privilege and power are maintained by pitting individuals within outsider groups against each other. His "rules of racial standing" include the following:

THIRD RULE

Few blacks avoid diminishment of racial standing, most of their statements about racial conditions being diluted and their recommendations of other blacks taken with a grain of salt. The usual exception to this rule is the black person who publicly disparages or criticizes other blacks who are speaking or acting in ways that upset whites. Instantly, such statements are granted "enhanced standing" even when the speaker has no special expertise or experience in the subject he or she is criticizing.

FOURTH RULE

When a black person or group makes a statement or takes an action that the white community or vocal components thereof deem "outrageous," the latter will actively recruit blacks willing to refute the statement or condemn the action. Blacks who respond to the call for condemnation will receive superstanding status. Those blacks who refuse to be recruited will be interpreted as endorsing the statements and action and may suffer political or economic reprisals.

Derrick Bell, "The Rules of Racial Standing" in Faces at the Bottom of the Well 114, 118 (Basic Books, 1992).

Chapter Three

CONSTRUCTION OF EXCLUSION IN LAW

A. INTRODUCTION: WHO "WE THE PEOPLE" WERE NOT

The Constitution begins with the majestic phrase, "We the People of the United States, in Order to form a more perfect Union, establish Justice, insure domestic Tranquility, provide for the common defense, promote the general Welfare, and secure the Blessings of Liberty to ourselves and our Posterity, do ordain and establish this Constitution for the United States of America." When the framers wrote these words, however, they did not intend to include many groups of peoples within "We the People." Justice and the blessings of liberty were to be conferred on some, but certainly not all peoples.

In this Chapter, we will examine who "we the people" aren't; who was excluded. Specifically, we will explore how courts have constructed legal challenges about exclusion on the basis of race, gender, class, sexuality, and disability. To begin, we have included an excerpt from Derrick Bell's book, And We Are Not Saved, which invites us to see the work of the framers through the eyes of Geneva Crenshaw, a prominent black woman civil rights lawyer, who travels back in time to the Constitutional Convention.

DERRICK BELL, THE REAL STATUS OF BLACKS TODAY: THE CHRONICLE OF THE CONSTITUTIONAL CONTRADICTION

in And We Are Not Saved 26–38, 41–42 (Basic Books, 1987).

AT THE END of a journey back millions of light-years, I found myself standing quietly at the podium at the Constitutional Convention of 1787. It was late afternoon, and hot in that late summer way that makes it pleasant to stroll down a shaded country lane, but mighty oppressive in a large, crowded meeting room, particularly one where the doors are closed and locked to ensure secrecy.

The three dozen or so convention delegates looked tired. They had doubtless been meeting all day and now, clustered in small groups, were caucusing with their state delegations. So intense were their discussions that the few men who looked my way did not seem to see me. They knew this was a closed meeting, and thus could not readily take in the appearance, on what had just been an empty platform, of a tall stranger—a stranger who was not only a woman but also, all too clearly, black.

Though I knew I was protected by extraordinary forces, my hands were wet with nervous perspiration. Then I remembered why I was there. Taking a deep breath, I picked up the gavel and quickly struck the desktop twice, hard.

"Gentlemen," I said, "my name is Geneva Crenshaw, and I appear here to you as a representative of the late twentieth century to test whether the decisions you are making today might be altered if you were to know their future disastrous effect on the nation's people, both white and black."

For perhaps ten seconds, there was a shocked silence. Then the chamber exploded with shouts, exclamations, oaths. I fear the delegates' expressions of stunned surprise did no honor to their distinguished images. A warm welcome would have been too much to expect, but their shock at my sudden presence turned into an angry commotion unrelieved by even a modicum of curiosity.

The delegates to the Constitutional Convention were, in the main, young and vigorous. When I remained standing, unmoved by their strong language and dire threats, several particularly robust delegates charged toward the platform, determined to carry out the shouted orders: "Eject the Negro woman at once!"

Suddenly the hall was filled with the sound of martial music, blasting trumpets, and a deafening roll of snare drums. At the same time—as the delegates were almost upon me—a cylinder composed of thin vertical bars of red, white, and blue light descended swiftly and silently from the high ceiling, nicely encapsulating the podium and me.

The self-appointed ejection party neither slowed nor swerved, a courageous act they soon regretted. As each man reached and tried to pass through the transparent light shield, there was a loud hiss, quite like the sound that electrified bug zappers make on a warm summer evening. While not lethal, the shock each attacker received was sufficiently strong to knock him to the floor, stunned and shaking.

The injured delegates all seemed to recover quickly, except one who had tried to pierce the light shield with his sword. The weapon instantly glowed red hot and burned his hand. At that point, several delegates tried to rush out of the room either to escape or to seek help—but neither doors nor windows would open.

"Gentlemen," I repeated, but no one heard me in the turmoil of shouted orders, cries of outrage, and efforts to sound the alarm to those outside. Scanning the room, I saw a swarthy delegate cock his long pistol, aim carefully, and fire directly at me. But the ball hit the shield, ricocheted back into the room, and shattered an inkwell, splattering my intended assassin with red ink.

At that, one of the delegates, raising his hand, roared, "Silence!" and then turned to me. "Woman! Who are you and by what authority do you interrupt this gathering?"

"Gentlemen," I began, "delegates"—then paused and, with a slight smile, added, "fellow citizens, I—like some of you—am a Virginian, my forefathers having labored on the land holdings of your fellow patriot, the Honorable Thomas Jefferson. I have come to urge that, in your great work here, you not restrict the sweep of Mr. Jefferson's self-evident truths that all men are equal and endowed by the Creator with inalienable rights, including 'Life, Liberty and the pursuit of Happiness.'" It was, I thought, a clever touch to invoke the name of Thomas Jefferson who, then serving as American minister to France, was not a member of the Virginia delegation. But my remark could not overcome the offense of my presence.

"How dare you insert yourself in these deliberations?" a delegate demanded.

"I dare," I said, "because slavery is an evil that Jefferson, himself a slave owner and unconvinced that Africans are equal to whites, nevertheless found involved 'a perpetual exercise of the most boisterous passions, the most unremitting despotism on the one part, and degrading submissions on the other.' Slavery, Jefferson has written, brutalizes slave owner as well as slave and, worst of all, tends to undermine the 'only firm basis' of liberty, the conviction in the minds of the people that liberty is 'the gift of God.'

"Gentlemen, it was also Thomas Jefferson who, considering the evil of slavery, wrote: 'I tremble for my country when I reflect that God is just; that his justice cannot sleep forever.'"

There was a hush in the group. No one wanted to admit it, but the ambivalence on the slavery issue expressed by Jefferson obviously had meaning for at least some of those in the hall. It seemed the right moment to prove both that I was a visitor from the future and that Jefferson's troubled concern for his country had not been misplaced. In quick, broad strokes, I told them of the country's rapid growth, of how slavery had expanded rather than withered of its own accord, and finally of how its continued presence bred first suspicion and then enmity between those in the South who continued to rely on a plantation economy and those Northerners committed to industrial development using white wage workers. The entry into the Union of each new state, I explained, further dramatized the disparity between North and South. Inevitably, the differences led to armed conflict—a civil war that, for all its bloody costs, did not settle those differences, and they remain divisive even as we celebrate our two-hundredth anniversary as one nation.

"The stark truth is that the racial grief that persists today," I ended, "originated in the slavery institutionalized in the document you are drafting. Is this, gentlemen, an achievement for which you wish to be remembered?"

Oblivious to my plea, a delegate tried what he likely considered a sympathetic approach. "Geneva, be reasonable. Go and leave us to our work. We have heard the petitions of Africans and of abolitionists speaking in their behalf. Some here are sympathetic to these pleas for freedom. Others are not. But we have debated this issue at length, and after three months of difficult negotiations, compromises have been reached, decisions made, language drafted and approved. The matter is settled. Neither you nor whatever powers have sent you here can undo what is done."

I was not to be put off so easily. "Sirs," I said, "I have come to tell you that the matter of slavery will not be settled by your compromises. And even when it is ended by armed conflict and domestic turmoil far more devastating than that you hope to avoid here, the potential evil of giving priority to property over human rights will remain. Can you not address the contradiction in your words and deeds?"

"There is no contradiction," replied another delegate. "Gouverneur Morris of Pennsylvania, the Convention's most outspoken opponent of slavery, has admitted that 'life and liberty were generally said to be of more value, than property, ... [but] an accurate view of the matter would nevertheless prove that property was the main object of Society.' "

"A contradiction," another delegate added, "would occur were we to follow the course you urge. We are not unaware of the moral issues raised by slavery, but we have no response to the delegate from South Carolina, General Charles Cotesworth Pinckney, who has admonished us that 'property in slaves should not be exposed to danger under a Govt. instituted for the protection of property.' "

"Of what value is a government that does not secure its citizens in their persons and their property?" inquired another delegate. "Government, as Mr. Pierce Butler from South Carolina has maintained here, 'was instituted principally for the protection of property and was itself ... supported by property.' Property, he reminded us, was 'the great object of government; the great cause of war; the great means of carrying it on.' And the whole South Carolina delegation joined him in making clear that 'the security the Southern states want is that their negroes may not be taken from them.' "

"Your deliberations here have been secret," I replied. "And yet history has revealed what you here would hide. The Southern delegates have demanded the slavery compromises as their absolute precondition to forming a new government."

"And why should it not be so?" a delegate in the rear called out. "I do not represent the Southern point of view, and yet their rigidity on the slavery issue is wholly natural, stemming as it does from the commitment of their economy to labor-intensive agriculture. We are not surprised by the determined bargaining of the Georgia and South Carolina delegations, nor distressed that our Southern colleagues, in seeking the protection they have gained, seem untroubled by doubts about the policy and morality of slavery and the slave trade."

"Then," I countered, "you are not troubled by the knowledge that this document will be defended by your Southern colleagues in the South Carolina ratification debates, by admissions that 'Negroes were our wealth, our only resource'?"

"Why, in God's name," the delegate responded, "should we be troubled by the truth, candidly stated? They have said no less in these chambers. General Charles Cotesworth Pinckney has flatly stated that 'South Carolina and Georgia cannot do without slaves.' And his cousin and fellow planter, Charles Pinckney, has added, 'The blacks are the laborers, the peasants of the Southern states.' "

At this, an elderly delegate arose and rapped his cane on his chair for attention. "Woman, we would have you gone from this place. But if a record be made, that record should show that the economic benefits of slavery do not accrue only to the South. Plantation states provide a market for Northern factories, and the New England shipping industry and merchants participate in the slave trade. Northern states, moreover, utilize slaves in the fields, as domestics, and even as soldiers to defend against Indian raids."

I shook my head. "Here you are then! Representatives from large and small states, slave states and those that have abolished slavery, all of you are protecting your property interests at the cost of your principles."

There was no response. The transparent shield protected my person, served as a language translator smoothing the differences in English usage, and provided a tranquilizing effect as it shimmered softly in the hot and humid room. Evidently, even this powerful mechanism could not bring the delegates to reassess their views on the slavery issue.

I asked, "Are you not concerned with the basic contradiction in your position: that you, who have gathered here in Philadelphia from each state in the confederacy, in fact represent and constitute major property holders? Do you not mind that your slogans of liberty and individual rights are basically guarantees that neither a strong government nor the masses will be able to interfere with your property rights and those of your class? This contradiction between what you espouse and what you here protect will be held against you by future citizens of this nation."

"Unless we continue on our present course," a delegate called out, "there will be no nation whose origins can be criticized. These sessions were called because the country is teetering between anarchy and bankruptcy. The nation cannot meet its debts. And only a year ago, thousands of poor farmers in Massachusetts and elsewhere took up arms against the government."

"Indeed," I said, "I am aware of Shay's Rebellion, led by Daniel Shay, a former officer who served with distinction in the war against England. According to historians of my time, the inability of Congress to respond to Massachusetts's appeal for help provided 'the final argument to sway many Americans in favor of a stronger federal government.' I understand the nature of the crisis that brings you here, but the compromises you make on the slavery issue are—"

"Young woman!" interrupted one of the older delegates. "Young woman, you say you understand. But I tell you that it is 'nearly impossible for anybody who has not been on the spot to conceive (from any description) what the delicacy and danger of our situation ... [has] been. I am President of this Convention, drafted to the task against my wishes. I am here and I am ready to embrace any tolerable compromise that ... [is] competent to save us from impending ruin.' "

While so far I had recognized none of the delegates, the identity of this man—seated off by himself, and one of the few who had remained quiet through the bedlam that broke out after my arrival—was unmistakable.

"Thank you, General Washington," I responded. "I know that you, though a slave owner, are opposed to slavery. And yet you have said little during these meetings—to prevent, one may assume, your great prestige from unduly influencing debate. Future historians will say of your silence that you recognize that for you to throw the weight of your opinion against slavery might so hearten the opponents of the system, while discouraging its proponents, as to destroy all hope of compromise. This would prevent the formation of the Union, and the Union, for you, is essential."

"I will not respond to these presumptions," said General Washington, "but I will tell you now what I will say to others at a later time. There are in the new form some things, I will readily acknowledge, that never did, and I am persuaded never will, obtain my cordial approbation; but I did then conceive, and do now most firmly believe, that in the aggregate it is the best constitution, that can be obtained at this epoch, and that this, or a dissolution, awaits our choice, and is the only alternative."

"Do you recognize," I asked, "that in order to gain unity among yourselves, your slavery compromises sacrifice freedom for the Africans who live amongst you and work for you? Such sacrifices of the rights of one group of human beings will, unless arrested here, become a difficult-to-break pattern in the nation's politics."

"Did you not listen to the general?" This man, I decided, must be James Madison. As the delegates calmed down, he had returned to a prominent seat in the front of the room directly in front of the podium. It was from this vantage point that he took notes of the proceedings which, when finally released in 1840, became the best record of the Convention.

"I expect," Madison went on, "that many will question why I have agreed to the Constitution. And, like General Washington, I will answer: 'because I thought it safe to the liberties of the people, and the best that could be obtained from the jarring interests of States, and the miscellaneous opinions of Politicians; and because experience has proved that the real danger to America & to liberty lies in the defect of *energy & stability* in the present establishments of the United States.' "

"Do not think," added a delegate from Massachusetts, "that this Convention has come easily to its conclusions on the matter that concerns you. Gouverneur Morris from Pennsylvania has said to us in the strongest terms: 'Domestic slavery is the most prominent feature in the aristocratic countenance of the proposed Constitution.' He warned again and again that 'the people of Pennsylvania will never agree to a representation of Negroes.'

"Many of us shared Mr. Morris's concern about basing apportionment on slaves as insisted by the Southern delegates. I recall with great sympathy his questions:

> Upon what principle is it that the slaves shall be computed in the representation? Are they men? Then make them citizens & let them vote? Are they property? Why then is no other property included? . . .

> The admission of slaves into the Representation when fairly explained comes to this: that the inhabitant of Georgia and S.C. who goes to the Coast of Africa, and in defiance of the most sacred laws of humanity tears away his fellow creatures from their dearest connections & damns them to the most cruel bondages, shall have more votes in a Govt. instituted for protection of the rights of mankind, then the Citizen of Pa or N. Jersey who views with a laudable horror, so nefarious a practice.

"I tell you, woman, this Convention was not unmoved at these words of Mr. Morris's only a few weeks ago."

"Even so," I said, "the Convention has acquiesced when representatives of the Southern states adamantly insisted that the proposed new government not interfere with their property in slaves. And is it not so that, beyond a few speeches, the representatives of the Northern states have been, at best, ambivalent on the issue?"

"And why not?" interjected another delegate. "Slavery has provided the wealth that made independence possible. The profits from slavery funded the Revolution. It cannot be denied. At the time of the Revolution, the goods for which the United States demanded freedom were produced in very large measure by slave labor. Desperately needing assistance from other countries, we purchased this aid from France with tobacco produced mainly by slave labor. The nation's economic well-being depended on the institution, and its preservation is essential if the Constitution we are drafting is to be more than a useless document. At least, that is how we view the crisis we face."

To pierce the delegates' adamant front, I called on the oratorical talents that have, in the twentieth century, won me both praise and courtroom battles: "The real crisis you face should not be resolved by your recognition of slavery, an evil whose immorality will pollute the nation as it now stains your document. Despite your resort to euphemisms like *persons* to keep out of the Constitution such words as *slave* and *slavery,* you cannot evade the consequences of the ten different provisions you have placed in the Constitution for the purpose of protecting property in slaves.*

"Woman!" a delegate shouted from the rear of the room. "Explain to us how you, a black, have gotten free of your chains and gained the audacity to come here and teach white men anything."

I smiled, recognizing the eternal question. "Audacity," I replied, "is an antidote to your arrogance. Be assured: my knowledge, despite my race, is far greater than yours."

"But if my race and audacity offend you, then listen to your contemporaries who have opposed slavery in most moving terms. With all due respect, there are few in this company whose insight exceeds that of Abigail Adams who wrote her husband, John, during the Revolutionary War: 'I wish most sincerely there was not a slave in the province; it always appeared a most iniquitous scheme to me to fight ourselves for what we are daily robbing and plundering from those who have as good a right to freedom as we have.' Mrs. Adams's wish is, as you know, shared by many influential Americans who denounce slavery as a corrupting and morally unjustifiable practice.

"Gentlemen," I continued, "how can you disagree with the view of the Maryland delegate Luther Martin that the slave trade and 'three-fifths' compromises 'ought to be considered as a solemn mockery of, and insult to that God whose protection we had then implored, and ... who views with equal eye the poor African slave and his American master'? I can tell you that Mr. Martin will not only abandon these deliberations

---

* The historian William Wiecek has listed the following direct and indirect accommodations to slavery contained in the Constitution:

1. Article I, Section 2: representatives in the House were apportioned among the states on the basis of population, computed by counting all free persons and three-fifths of the slaves (the "federal number," or "three-fifths," clause);

2. Article I, Section 2, and Article I, Section 9: two clauses requiring, redundantly, that direct taxes (including capitations) be apportioned among the states on the foregoing basis, the purpose being to prevent Congress from laying a head tax on slaves to encourage their emancipation;

3. Article I, Section 9: Congress was prohibited from abolishing the international slave trade to the United States before 1808;

4. Article IV, Section 2: the states were prohibited from emancipating fugitive slaves, who were to be returned on demand of the master;

5. Article I, Section 8: Congress empowered to provide for calling up the states' militias to suppress insurrections, including slave uprisings;

6. Article IV, Section 4: the federal government was obliged to protect the states against domestic violence, including slave insurrections;

7. Article V: the provisions of Article I, Section 9, clauses 1 and 4 (pertaining to the slave trade and direct taxes) were made unamendable;

8. Article I, Section 9, and Article I, Section 10: these two clauses prohibited the federal government and the states from taxing exports, one purpose being to prevent them from taxing slavery indirectly by taxing the exported product of slave labor.

and refuse to sign the Constitution but also oppose its ratification in Maryland. And further, he will, in his opposition, expose the deal of the committee on which he served, under which New England states agreed to give the slave trade a twenty-year immunity from federal restrictions in exchange for Southern votes to eliminate restrictions on navigation acts. What is more, he will write that, to the rest of the world, it must appear 'absurd and disgraceful to the last degree, that we should *except* from the exercise of that power [to regulate commerce], the *only branch of commerce* which is *unjustifiable in its nature,* and *contrary* to the rights of *mankind.*' "

"Again, woman," a Northern delegate assured me, "we have heard and considered all those who oppose slavery. Despite the remonstrations of the abolitionists—of whom few, I must add, believe Negroes to be the equal of white men, and even fewer would want the blacks to remain in this land were slavery abandoned—we have acted as we believe the situation demands."

"I cannot believe," I said, "that even a sincere belief in the superiority of the white race should suffice to condone so blatant a contradiction of your hallowed ideals."

"It should be apparent by now," said the delegate who had shot at me, but had now recovered his composure and shed his ink-stained coat, "that we do not care what you think. Furthermore, if your people actually had the sensitivities of real human beings, you would realize that you are not wanted here and would have the decency to leave."

"I will not leave!" I said steadily, and waited while the delegates conferred.

Finally, a delegate responded to my challenge. "You have, by now, heard enough to realize that we have not lightly reached the compromises on slavery you so deplore. Perhaps we, with the responsibility of forming a radically new government in perilous times, see more clearly than is possible for you in hindsight that the unavoidable cost of our labors will be the need to accept and live with what you call a contradiction."

The delegate had gotten to his feet, and was walking slowly toward me as he spoke. "This contradiction is not lost on us. Surely we know, even though we are at pains not to mention it, that we have sacrificed the rights of some in the belief that this involuntary forfeiture is necessary to secure the rights for others in a society espousing, as its basic principle, the liberty of all."

He was standing directly in front of the shield now, ignoring its gentle hum, disregarding its known danger. "It grieves me," he continued, "that your presence here confirms my worst fears about the harm done to your people because the Constitution, while claiming to speak in an unequivocal voice, in fact promises freedom to whites and condemns blacks to slavery. But what alternative do we have? Unless we here frame a constitution that can first gain our signatures and then win ratification by the states, we shall soon have no nation. For better or worse, slavery has been the backbone of our economy, the source of much of our wealth. It was condoned in the colonies and recognized in the Articles of Confederation. The majority of the delegates to this convention own slaves and must have that right protected if they and their states are to be included in the new government."

He paused and then asked, more out of frustration than defiance, "What better compromise on this issue can you offer than that which has been fashioned over so many hours of heated debate?"

The room was silent. The delegate, his statement made, his question presented, turned and walked slowly back to his seat. A few from his state touched his hand as he passed. Then all eyes turned to me.

I thanked the delegate for his question and then said, "The processes by which Northern states are even now abolishing slavery are known to you all. What is lacking here is not legislative skill but the courage to recognize the evil of holding blacks in slavery—an evil that would be quickly and universally condemned were the subjects of bondage members of the Caucasian race. You fear that unless the slavery of blacks is recognized and given protection, the nation will not survive. And my message is that the compromises you are making here mean that the nation's survival will always be in doubt. For now in my own day, after two hundred years and despite bloody wars and the earnest efforts of committed people, the racial contradiction you sanction in this document remains and threatens to tear this country apart."

"Mr. Chairman," said a delegate near the podium whose accent indicated that he was from the deep South, "this discussion grows tiresome and I resent to my very soul the presence in our midst of this offspring of slaves. If she accurately predicts the future fate of her race in this country, then our protection of slave property, which we deem essential for our survival, is easier to justify than in some later time when, as she implies, negroes remain subjugated even without the threats we face."

"Hear! Hear!" shouted a few delegates. "Bravo, Colonel!"

"It's all hypocrisy!" the Colonel shouted, his arms flailing the air, "sheer hypocrisy! Our Northern colleagues bemoan slavery while profiting from it as much as we in the South, meanwhile avoiding its costs and dangers. And our friends from Virginia, where slavery began, urge the end of importation—not out of humanitarian motivations, as their speeches suggest, but because they have sufficient slaves, and expect the value of their property will increase if further imports are barred.

"Mr. George Mason, of the Virginia delegation, in his speech opposing the continued importation of slaves expressed fear that, if not barred, the people of Western lands, already crying for slaves, could get them through South Carolina and Georgia. He moans that: 'Slavery discourages arts & manufactures. The poor despise labor when performed by slaves. They prevent the immigration of Whites, who really enrich & strengthen a Country. They produce the most pernicious effect on manners.' Furthermore, according to Mr. Mason, 'every master of slaves is born a petty tyrant. They bring the judgment of heaven on a Country ... [and] by an inevitable chain of causes & effects providence punishes national sins, by national calamities.'

"This, Mr. Chairman, is nothing but hypocrisy or, worse, ignorance of history. We speak easily today of liberty, but the rise of liberty and equality in this country has been accompanied by the rise of slavery. The negress who has seized our podium by diabolical force charges that we hold blacks slaves because we view them as inferior. Inferior in every way they surely are, but they were not slaves when Virginia was a new colony 150 years ago. Or, at least, their status was hardly worse than the luckless white indentured servants brought here from debtors' prisons and the poverty-ridden streets of England. Neither slave nor servant lived very long in that harsh, fever-ridden clime." ...

"In effect," I concluded, "what I call a contradiction here was deemed a solution then. Slavery enabled the rich to keep their lands, arrested discontent and repression of other Englishmen, strengthened their rights and nourished their attachment to liberty. But the solution, ... put an end to the process of turning Africans into Englishmen. The rights of Englishmen were preserved by destroying the rights of Africans.'" ...

"Woman! We implore you to allow us to continue our work. While we may be inconsistent about the Negro problem, we are convinced that this is the only way open to us. You asked that we let your people go. We cannot do that and still preserve the potential of this nation for good—a potential that requires us to recognize here and now what later generations may condemn as evil. And as we talk I wonder—are the problems of race in your time equally paradoxical?"

I longed to continue the debate, but never got the chance. Apparently someone outside had finally understood the delegates' signals for help, and had summoned the local militia. Hearing some commotion beyond the window, I turned to see a small cannon being rolled up, pointing straight at me. Then, in quick succession, the cannoneer lighted the fuse; the delegates dived under their desks; the cannon fired; and, with an ear-splitting roar, the cannonball broke against the light shield and splintered, leaving me and the shield intact.

I knew then my mission was over, and I returned to the twentieth century....

Notes and Questions

1. Professor Bell entitled this chapter, "The Chronicle of the Constitutional Contradiction." What is the "constitutional contradiction?"

2. Is there any continuing legacy of that contradiction?

3. Can you think of any recent examples of a similar constitutional contradiction?

4. Are all political decisions pragmatic products of compromise? Are judicial decisions similar? If so, should they be?

5. On the 200th anniversary of the Constitution, Justice Thurgood Marshall reflected on the celebration of a document which, in its original form, excluded groups of peoples.

THURGOOD MARSHALL, REFLECTIONS ON THE BICENTENNIAL OF THE UNITED STATES CONSTITUTION

101 Harv.L.Rev. 1, 1–5 (1987).

The year 1987 marks the 200th anniversary of the United States Constitution. A Commission has been established to coordinate the celebration. The official meetings, essay contests, and festivities have begun.

The planned commemoration will span three years, and I am told 1987 is "dedicated to the memory of the Founders and the document they drafted in Philadelphia." We are to "recall the achievements of our Founders and the knowledge and experience that inspired them, the nature of the government they established, its origins, its character, and its ends, and the rights and privileges of citizenship, as well as its attendant responsibilities."

Like many anniversary celebrations, the plan for 1987 takes particular events and holds them up as the source of all the very best that has followed. Patriotic feelings will surely swell, prompting proud proclamations of the wisdom, foresight, and sense of justice shared by the framers and reflected in a written document now yellowed with age. This is unfortunate—not the patriotism itself, but the tendency for the celebration to oversimplify, and overlook the many other events that have been instrumental to our achievements as a nation. The focus of this celebration invites a complacent belief that the vision of those who debated and compromised in Philadelphia yielded the "more perfect Union" it is said we now enjoy.

I cannot accept this invitation, for I do not believe that the meaning of the Constitution was forever "fixed" at the Philadelphia Convention. Nor do I find the wisdom, foresight, and sense of justice exhibited by the framers particularly profound. To the contrary, the government they devised was defective from the start, requiring several amendments, a civil war, and momentous social transformation to attain the system of constitutional government, and its respect for the individual freedoms and human rights, that we hold as fundamental today. When contemporary Americans cite "The Constitution," they invoke a concept that is vastly different from what the framers barely began to construct two centuries ago.

For a sense of the evolving nature of the Constitution we need look no further than the first three words of the document's preamble: "We the People." When the Founding Fathers used this phrase in 1787, they did not have in mind the majority of America's citizens. "We the People" included, in the words of the framers, "the whole Number of free Persons." On a matter so basic as the right to vote, for example, Negro slaves were excluded, although they were counted for representational purposes—at three-fifths each. Women did not gain the right to vote for over a hundred and thirty years.

These omissions were intentional. The record of the framers' debates the slave question is especially clear: the Southern states acceded to the demands of the New England states for giving Congress broad power to regulate commerce, in exchange for the right to continue the slave trade. The economic interests of the regions coalesced: New Englanders engaged in the "carrying trade" would profit from transporting slaves from Africa as well as goods produced in America by slave labor. The perpetuation of slavery ensured the primary source of wealth in the Southern states.

Despite this clear understanding of the role slavery would play in the new republic, use of the words "slaves" and "slavery" was carefully avoided in the original document. Political representation in the lower House of Congress was to be based on the population of "free Persons" in each state, plus three-fifths of all "other Persons." Moral principles against slavery, for those who had them, were compromised, with no explanation of the conflicting principles for which the American Revolutionary War had ostensibly been fought: the self-evident truths "that all men are created equal, that they are endowed by their Creator with certain unalienable Rights, that among these are Life, Liberty and the pursuit of Happiness."

It was not the first such compromise. Even these ringing phrases from the Declaration of Independence are filled with irony, for an early draft of what became that declaration assailed the King of England for suppressing legislative attempts to end the slave trade and for encouraging slave rebellions. The final draft adopted in 1776 did not contain this criticism. And so again at the Constitutional Convention eloquent objections to the institution of slavery went unheeded, and its opponents eventually consented to a document which laid a foundation for the tragic events that were to follow. . . .

As a result of compromise, the right of the Southern states to continue importing slaves was extended, officially, at least until 1808. We know that it actually lasted a good deal longer, as the framers possessed no monopoly on the ability to trade moral principles for self-interest. But they nevertheless set an unfortunate example. Slaves could be imported, if the commercial interests of the North were protected. To make the compromise even more palatable, customs duties would be imposed at up to ten dollars per slave as a means of raising public revenues.

No doubt it will be said, when the unpleasant truth of the history of slavery in America is mentioned during this bicentennial year, that the Constitution was a product of its times, and embodied a compromise which, under other circumstances, would not have been made. But the effects of the framers' compromise have remained for generations. They arose from the contradiction between guaranteeing liberty and justice to all, and denying both to Negroes.

The original intent of the phrase, "We the People," was far too clear for any ameliorating construction. Writing for the Supreme Court in 1857, Chief Justice Taney penned the following passage in the Dred Scott case, on the issue of whether, in the eyes of the framers, slaves were "constituent members of the sovereignty," and were to be included among "We the People":

> We think they are not, and that they are not included, and were not intended to be included....

> They had for more than a century before been regarded as beings of an inferior order, and altogether unfit to associate with the white race ...; and so far inferior, that they had no rights which the white man was bound to respect; and that the negro might justly and lawfully be reduced to slavery for his benefit....

> . . .

> [A]ccordingly, a negro of the African race was regarded ... as an article of property, and held, and bought and sold as such.... [N]o one seems to have doubted the correctness of the prevailing opinion of the time.

And so, nearly seven decades after the Constitutional Convention, the Supreme Court reaffirmed the prevailing opinion of the framers regarding the rights of Negroes in America. It took a bloody civil war before the thirteenth amendment could be adopted to abolish slavery, though not the consequences slavery would have for future Americans.

While the Union survived the civil war, the Constitution did not. In its place arose a new, more promising basis for justice and equality, the fourteenth amendment, ensuring protection of the life, liberty, and property of all persons against deprivations without due process, and guaranteeing equal protection of the laws. And yet almost another century would pass before any significant recognition was obtained of the rights of black Americans to share equally even in such basic opportunities as education, housing, and employment, and to have their votes counted, and counted equally. In the meantime, blacks joined America's military to fight its wars and invested untold hours working in its factories and on its farms, contributing to the development of this country's magnificent wealth and waiting to share in its prosperity.

What is striking is the role legal principles have played throughout America's history in determining the condition of Negroes. They were enslaved by law, emancipated by law, disenfranchised and segregated by law; and, finally, they have begun to win equality by law. Along the way, new constitutional principles have emerged to meet the challenges of a changing society. The progress has been dramatic, and it will continue.

The men who gathered in Philadelphia in 1787 could not have envisioned these changes. They could not have imagined, nor would they have accepted, that the document they were drafting would one day be construed by a Supreme Court to which had been appointed a woman and the descendent of an African slave. "We the People" no longer enslave, but the credit does not belong to the framers. It belongs to those who refused to acquiesce in outdated notions of "liberty," "justice," and "equality," and who strived to better them.

And so we must be careful, when focusing on the events which took place in Philadelphia two centuries ago, that we not overlook the momentous events which followed, and thereby lose our proper sense of perspective. Otherwise, the odds are that for many Americans the bicentennial celebration will be little more than a blind pilgrimage to the shrine of the original document now stored in a vault in the National Archives. If we seek, instead, a sensitive understanding of the Constitution's inherent defects, and its promising evolution through 200 years of history, the celebration of the "Miracle at Philadelphia" will, in my view, be a far more meaningful and humbling experience. We will see that the true miracle was not the birth of the Constitution, but its life, a life nurtured through two turbulent centuries of our own making, and a life embodying much good fortune that was not.

Thus, in this bicentennial year, we may not all participate in the festivities with flag-waving fervor. Some may more quietly commemorate the suffering, struggle, and sacrifice that has triumphed over much of what was wrong with the original document, and observe the anniversary with hopes not realized and promises not fulfilled. I plan to celebrate the bicentennial of the Constitution as a living document, including the Bill of Rights and the other amendments protecting individual freedoms and human rights....

B. RHETORIC OF EXCLUSION

The materials in this Chapter will consider the rhetorical devices and assumptions used by courts to justify the exclusion and subordination of various groups of peoples. We will focus not only on what the court may have concluded in a specific case, but also on the techniques and assumptions used by the court to reach the conclusion. We ask that you analyze word choices, metaphors, analogies, organizations of arguments, historical and social contexts, constructed dichotomies between social realities and legal rights, and reliance on economic or property interests to curb civil rights. As you study the material you may find that patterns emerge, indicating that courts use similar kinds of arguments to rationalize the exclusion of groups of peoples from the benefits associated with privilege and power. Specifically, look for the following styles of argumentation by the courts:

1. *Rhetoric of self/other.* The court may use the language and assumptions of difference to sanction existing structures of privilege. With regard to racism, for example, it has been suggested that the discursive strategy includes four essential elements: (a) stressing real or

imaginary differences between the racist and victim; (b) assigning values to these differences to the detriment of the victim; (c) making the differences absolutes by generalizing from them; and (d) justifying present or possible privilege.[1] As you read the cases on race discrimination, consider whether they include these elements. Do the cases involving other forms of exclusion also adopt this discursive strategy?

2. *Explicit group-targeted difference language and stereotyping.* Related to the rhetoric of self/other is the use of language that is explicitly racist, sexist, homophobic, or otherwise demeaning and hateful. Can you find examples of such language in the cases? How is that language used to justify the results?

3. *Naming.* In some instances, the court may legitimate exclusion by the way it names, or describes, the group affected by the challenged conduct. What appears as race or gender discrimination to some, for example, may be described as not really involving those classifications.

4. *Metaphor.* The court may also use metaphors to sanction the continued exclusion of groups from "We the People." Consider, for example, whether the cases create artificial we/they categories through metaphors about family and citizenship.

5. *Blame the victim.* In some instances the court may blame the targeted group for its own predicament. Are such arguments effective devices for perpetuating existing patterns of privilege and power? Do they allow the court and other branches of government to avoid responsibility for the results?

6. *Racial stratification.* This technique involves comparison and ranking of targeted groups. Consider how this technique works to maintain exclusion of those groups.

7. *Framers' intent.* Another way to transfer responsibility is to suggest that the framers of the Constitution intended the result, and that the court is bound by that intent. When this argument is offered, examine the strength of the evidence of the framers' intent? What kind of language is used to describe the framers? Does the court deify them and, if so, what effect does this have in strengthening the court's conclusion? Perhaps most importantly, consider why we should be bound by that intent.

8. *Structure of government.* The court may justify its conclusion by suggesting that responsibility lies with some governmental entity other than the court itself. Specifically, the court may use separation of power arguments to find that the proper recourse, if any, is with the legislature or executive. Similarly, the court may invoke federalism concerns in concluding that the states, not the federal government, are responsible for the specific problem. Consider whether the suggested

1. A. Memmi, *Attempt at Definition in Dominated Man: Notes Toward a Portrait* 186 (Pub.1986) quoted in Robert Williams, *Documents of Barbarism: The Contempo-* *rary Legacy of European Racism and Colonialism in the Narrative Traditions of Federal Indian Law,* 31 Ariz.L.Rev. 237, 262 (1989).

alternatives provide realistic avenues to redress the deprivations in the specific case. Also, consider the message that is heard when some people are told that their complaints will be entertained by the court while others are told to take them elsewhere.

9. *In the nature of things.* The court may attempt to explain the subordination of a group by arguing that the oppressive condition is natural, or just part of the way things are. When you see this kind of argument, consider what is the stated, or more often unstated, norm.

10. *Hidden norms and universalizing dominant perspectives.* A related technique involves the use of arguments and language that convey the impression that the court's position is objective and neutral, not the product of a partial perspective. It is important to examine such arguments and language for hidden norms. Is the court seeing the issue from a perspective, and whose perspective is it?

11. *Trivializing the harm.* In still other instances the court may construct the legal struggle by trivializing the actual harm to the members of the subordinated group. This technique may be accomplished directly by describing the actual effect of the challenged practice or policy as minimal, or by using words and phrases (e.g., "mere _____") that convey the same message. In what way is this an effective device to persuade the reader to agree with the court's ultimate decision upholding the infliction of the harm?

12. *Decontextualizing.* This technique involves consideration of a problem without regard to its social, historical, or political context. How does such decontextualizing make it easier for the court to justify its conclusion?

13. *Social, not legal, problem.* In a number of cases, the court constructs the specific issue as a social problem and, thus, not appropriate for the "law" to resolve. What distinguishes a "social" problem from a legal one? Does the court offer any real criteria for distinguishing between the two? Does the specific issue in the case strike you as a social one, not subject to resolution by the apparatus of law?

14. *Slippery slope.* A common form of legal argumentation is the slippery slope argument that if a certain position is adopted a parade of horribles will follow. How do the cases invoke this technique to support continued subordination of peoples? Will the parade necessarily follow the adoption of the position? Are you persuaded that the parade, even if it follows, contains real horribles?

15. *Precedent and reliance on historical discrimination.* The court may also justify an existing injustice by invoking prior cases and history that relied on biases and assumptions to disempower groups of people; cases that used the techniques described above to perpetuate the very injustice. Does this use of precedent and history enable the court to convey the impression that its current decision is somehow compelled? Does it enable the court to hide responsibility for the harm that results from its decision?

16. *Cumulative effect or overkill.* In many of the cases the courts do not use only one of these techniques, but instead invoke a number of them. What is the cumulative effect? Does the whole become greater than the sum of the individual parts?

C. RACIAL CLASSIFICATIONS

1. The Concept of "Race"

In this section, we will explore how law has constructed legal challenges to the exclusion of racial groups and has thereby perpetuated, or displaced, existing patterns of power and privilege with respect to those groups. At the outset, we want to consider the concept of race itself. In the following cases, the courts attempt to develop understandings of what is meant by that concept. Again, we ask that you consider not only the precise holdings of the cases but also the techniques and assumptions used by the courts to reach their understandings.

PEOPLE v. HALL

Supreme Court of California, 1854.
4 Cal. 399.

MR. CH. J. MURRAY delivered the opinion of the Court.

The appellant, a free white citizen of this State, was convicted of murder upon the testimony of Chinese witnesses.

The point involved in this case, is the admissibility of such evidence.

The 394th section of the Act Concerning Civil Cases, provides that no Indian or Negro shall be allowed to testify as a witness in any action or proceeding in which a White person is a party.

The 14th section of the Act of April 16th, 1850, regulating Criminal Proceedings, provides that "No Black, or Mulatto person, or Indian, shall be allowed to give evidence in favor of, or against a white man."

The true point at which we are anxious to arrive, is the legal signification of the words, "Black, Mulatto, Indian and White person," and whether the Legislature adopted them as generic terms, or intended to limit their application to specific types of the human species.

Before considering this question, it is proper to remark the difference between the two sections of our Statute, already quoted, the latter being more broad and comprehensive in its exclusion, by use of the word "Black," instead of Negro.

Conceding, however, for the present, that the word "Black," as used in the 14th section, and "Negro," in 394th, are convertible terms, and that the former was intended to include the latter, let us proceed to inquire who are excluded from testifying as witnesses under the term "Indian."

When Columbus first landed upon the shores of this continent, in his attempt to discover a western passage to the Indies, he imagined that he had accomplished the object of his expedition, and that the Island of

San Salvador was one of those Islands of the Chinese sea, lying near the extremity of India, which had been described by navigators.

Acting upon this hypothesis, and also perhaps from the similarity of features and physical conformation, he gave to the Islanders the name of Indians, which appellation was universally adopted, and extended to the aboriginals of the New World, as well as of Asia.

From that time, down to a very recent period, the American Indians and the Mongolian, or Asiatic, were regarded as the same type of the human species.

In order to arrive at a correct understanding of the intention of our Legislature, it will be necessary to go back to the early history of legislation on this subject, our Statute being only a transcript of those of older States.

At the period from which this legislation dates, those portions of Asia which include India proper, the Eastern Archipelago, and the countries washed by the Chinese waters, as far as then known, were denominated the Indies, from which the inhabitants had derived the generic name of Indians.

Ethnology, at that time, was unknown as a distinct science, or if known, had not reached that high point of perfection which it has since attained by the scientific inquiries and discoveries of the master minds of the last half century. Few speculations had been made with regard to the moral or physical differences between the different races of mankind. These were general in their character, and limited to those visible and palpable variations which could not escape the attention of the most common observer.

The general, or perhaps universal opinion of that day was, that there were but three distinct types of the human species, which, in their turn, were subdivided into varieties or tribes. This opinion is still held by many scientific writers, and is supported by Cuvier, one of the most eminent naturalists of modern times.

Many ingenious speculations have been resorted to for the purpose of sustaining this opinion. It has been supposed, and not without plausibility, that this continent was first peopled by Asiatics, who crossed Behring's Straits, and from thence found their way down to the more fruitful climates of Mexico and South America. Almost every tribe has some tradition of coming from the North, and many of them, that their ancestors came from some remote country beyond the ocean....

The similarity of the skull and pelvis, and the general configuration of the two races; the remarkable resemblance in eyes, beard, hair, and other peculiarities, together with the contiguity of the two Continents, might well have led to the belief that this country was first peopled by the Asiatics, and that the difference between the different tribes and the parent stock was such as would necessarily arise from the circumstances of climate, pursuits, and other physical causes, and was no greater than that existing between the Arab and the European, both of whom were supposed to belong to the Caucasian race.

Although the discoveries of eminent Archeologists, and the researches of modern Geologists, have given to this Continent an antiquity of thousands of years anterior to the evidence of man's existence, and the light of modern science may have shown conclusively that it was not peopled by the inhabitants of Asia, but that the Aborigines are a distinct type, and as such claim a distinct origin, still, this would not, in any degree, alter the meaning of the term, and render that specific which was before generic.

We have adverted to these speculations for the purpose of showing that the name of Indian, from the time of Columbus to the present day, has been used to designate, not alone the North American Indian, but the whole of the Mongolian race, and that the name, though first applied probably through mistake, was afterwards continued as appropriate on account of the supposed common origin.

That this was the common opinion in the early history of American legislation, cannot be disputed, and, therefore, all legislation upon the subject must have borne relation to that opinion.

Can, then, the use of the word "Indian," because at the present day it may be sometimes regarded as a specific, and not as a generic term, alter this conclusion? We think not; because at the origin of the legislation we are considering, it was used and admitted in its common and ordinary acceptation, as a generic term, distinguishing the great Mongolian race, and as such, its meaning then became fixed by law, and in construing Statutes the legal meaning of words must be preserved.

Again: the words of the Act must be construed in *pari materia*. It will not be disputed that "White" and "Negro," are generic terms, and refer to two of the great types of mankind. If these, as well as the word "Indian," are not to be regarded as generic terms, including the two great races which they were intended to designate, but only specific, and applying to those Whites and Negroes who were inhabitants of this Continent at the time of the passage of the Act, the most anomalous consequences would ensue. The European white man who comes here would not be shielded from the testimony of the degraded and demoralized caste, while the Negro, fresh from the coast of Africa, or the Indian of Patagonia, the Kanaka, South Sea Islander, or New Hollander, would be admitted, upon their arrival, to testify against white citizens in our courts of law.

To argue such a proposition would be an insult to the good sense of the Legislature.

The evident intention of the Act was to throw around the citizen a protection for life and property, which could only be secured by removing him above the corrupting influences of degraded castes.

It can hardly be supposed that any Legislature would attempt this by excluding domestic Negroes and Indians, who not unfrequently have correct notions of their obligations to society, and turning loose upon the community the more degraded tribes of the same species, who have nothing in common with us, in language, country or laws.

We have, thus far, considered this subject on the hypothesis that the 14th section of the Act Regulating Criminal Proceedings, and the 394th section of the Practice Act, were the same.

As before remarked, there is a wide difference between the two. The word "Black" may include all Negroes, but the term "Negro" does not include all Black persons.

By the use of this term in this connection, we understand it to mean the opposite of "White," and that it should be taken as contradistinguished from all White persons.

In using the words, "No Black, or Mulatto person, or Indian shall be allowed to give evidence for or against a White person," the Legislature, if any intention can be ascribed to it, adopted the most comprehensive terms to embrace every known class or shade of color, as the apparent design was to protect the White person from the influence of all testimony other than that of persons of the same caste. The use of these terms must, by every sound rule of construction, exclude every one who is not of white blood. . . .

We are not disposed to leave this question in any doubt. The word "White" has a distinct signification, which *ex vi termini,* excludes black, yellow, and all other colors. It will be observed, by reference to the first section of the second article of the Constitution of this State, that none but white males can become electors, except in the case of Indians, who may be admitted by special Act of the Legislature. On examination of the constitutional debates, it will be found that not a little difficulty existed in selecting these precise words, which were finally agreed upon as the most comprehensive that could be suggested to exclude all inferior races.

If the term "White," as used in the Constitution, was not understood in its generic sense as including the Caucasian race, and necessarily excluding all others, where was the necessity of providing for the admission of Indians to the privilege of voting, by special legislation?

We are of the opinion that the words "White," "Negro," "Mulatto," "Indian," and "Black person," wherever they occur in our Constitution and laws, must be taken in their generic sense, and that, even admitting the Indian of this Continent is not of the Mongolian type, that the words "Black person," in the 14th section must be taken as contradistinguished from White, and necessarily excludes all races other than the Caucasian.

We have carefully considered all the consequences resulting from a different rule of construction, and are satisfied that even in a doubtful case we would be impelled to this decision on grounds of public policy.

The same rule which would admit them to testify, would admit them to all the equal rights of citizenship, and we might soon see them at the polls, in the jury box, upon the bench, and in our legislative halls.

This is not a speculation which exists in the excited and over-heated imagination of the patriot and statesman, but it is an actual and present danger.

The anomalous spectacle of a distinct people, living in our community, recognizing no laws of this State except through necessity, bringing with them their prejudices and national feuds, in which they indulge in open violation of law; whose mendacity is proverbial; a race of people whom nature has marked as inferior, and who are incapable of progress or intellectual development beyond a certain point, as their history has shown; differing in language, opinions, color, and physical conformation; between whom and ourselves nature has placed an impassable difference, is now presented, and for them is claimed, not only the right to swear away the life of a citizen, but the further privilege of participating with us in administering the affairs of our Government.

These facts were before the Legislature that framed this Act, and have been known as matters of public history to every subsequent Legislature.

There can be no doubt as to the intention of the Legislature, and that if it had ever been anticipated that this class of people were not embraced in the prohibition, then such specific words would have been employed as would have put the matter beyond any possible controversy.

For these reasons, we are of opinion that the testimony was inadmissible.

The judgment is reversed and the cause remanded.

MR. JUSTICE WELLS dissented.

UNITED STATES v. THIND

Supreme Court of the United States, 1922.
261 U.S. 204, 43 S.Ct. 338, 67 L.Ed. 616.

MR. JUSTICE SUTHERLAND delivered the opinion of the Court.

This cause is here upon a certificate from the Circuit Court of Appeals requesting the instruction of this Court in respect of the following questions:

"1. Is a high-caste Hindu, of full Indian blood, born at Amritsar, Punjab, India, a white person within the meaning of section 2169, Revised Statutes?

"2. Does the Act of February 5, 1917 (39 Stat. 875, § 3), disqualify from naturalization as citizens those Hindus now barred by that act, who had lawfully entered the United States prior to the passage of said act?"

The appellee was granted a certificate of citizenship by the District Court of the United States for the District of Oregon, over the objection of the Naturalization Examiner for the United States. A bill in equity was then filed by the United States, seeking a cancellation of the certificate on the ground that the appellee was not a white person and therefore not lawfully entitled to naturalization. The District Court, on motion, dismissed the bill and an appeal was taken to the Circuit Court of Appeals. No question is made in respect of the individual qualifications of the appellee. The sole question is whether he falls within the class designated by Congress as eligible.

Section 2169, Revised Statutes (Comp.St. § 4358), provides that the provisions of the Naturalization Act "shall apply to aliens being free white persons and to aliens of African nativity and to persons of African descent."

If the applicant is a white person, within the meaning of this section, he is entitled to naturalization; otherwise not. In Ozawa v. United States, 260 U.S. 178, we had occasion to consider the application of these words to the case of a cultivated Japanese and were constrained to hold that he was not within their meaning. As there pointed out, the provision is not that any particular class of persons shall be excluded, but it is, in effect, that only white persons shall be included within the privilege of the statute. "The intention was to confer the privilege of citizenship upon that class of persons whom the fathers knew as white, and to deny it to all who could not be so classified. It is not enough to say that the framers did not have in mind the brown or yellow races of Asia. It is necessary to go farther and be able to say that had these particular races been suggested the language of the act would have been so varied as to include them within its privileges".... Following a long line of decisions of the lower Federal courts, we held that the words imported a racial and not an individual test and were meant to indicate only persons of what is *popularly* known as the Caucasian race. But, as there pointed out, the conclusion that the phrase "white persons" and the word "Caucasian" are synonymous does not end the matter. It enabled us to dispose of the problem as it was there presented, since the applicant for citizenship clearly fell outside the zone of debatable ground on the negative side; but the decision still left the question to be dealt with, in doubtful and different cases, by the "process of judicial inclusion and exclusion." Mere ability on the part of an applicant for naturalization to establish a line of descent from a Caucasian ancestor will not ipso facto and necessarily conclude the inquiry. "Caucasian" is a conventional word of much flexibility, as a study of the literature dealing with racial questions will disclose, and while it and the words "white persons" are treated as synonymous for the purposes of that case, they are not of identical meaning—idem per idem.

In the endeavor to ascertain the meaning of the statute we must not fail to keep in mind that it does not employ the word "Caucasian," but the words "white persons," and these are words of common speech and not of scientific origin. The word "Caucasian," not only was not employed in the law, but was probably wholly unfamiliar to the original framers of the statute in 1790. When we employ it, we do so as an aid to the ascertainment of the legislative intent and not as an invariable substitute for the statutory words. Indeed, as used in the science of ethnology, the connotation of the word is by no means clear, and the use of it in its scientific sense as an equivalent for the words of the statute, other considerations aside, would simply mean the substitution of one perplexity for another. But in this country, during the last half century especially, the word by common usage has acquired a popular meaning, not clearly defined to be sure, but sufficiently so to enable us to say that its popular as distinguished from its scientific application is of appreciably narrower scope. It is in the popular sense of the word, therefore, that we employ it as an aid to the construction of the statute, for it would be obviously illogical to convert words of common speech used in a statute into words of scientific terminology when neither the latter nor the science for whose purposes they were coined was within the contemplation of the framers of the statute or of the people for whom it was framed. The words of the statute are to be interpreted in accordance with the understanding of the common man from whose vocabulary they were taken.

They imply, as we have said, a racial test; but the term "race" is one which, for the practical purposes of the statute, must be applied to a group of living persons *now* possessing in common the requisite characteristics, not to groups of persons who are supposed to be or really are descended from some remote, common ancestor, but who, whether they both resemble him to a greater or less extent, have, at any rate, ceased altogether to resemble one another. It may be true that the blond Scandinavian and the brown Hindu have a common ancestor in the dim reaches of antiquity, but the average man knows perfectly well that there are unmistakable and profound differences between them today; and it is not impossible, if that common ancestor could be materialized in the flesh, we should discover that he was himself sufficiently differentiated from both of his descendants to preclude his racial classification with either. The question for determination is not, therefore, whether by the speculative processes of ethnological reasoning we may present a probability to the scientific mind that they have the same origin, but whether we can satisfy the common understanding that they are now the same or sufficiently the same to justify the interpreters of a statute— written in the words of common speech, for common understanding, by unscientific men—in classifying them together in the statutory category as white persons. In 1790 the Adamite theory of creation—which gave a common ancestor to all mankind—was generally accepted, and it is not at all probable that it was intended by the legislators of that day to submit the question of the application of the words "white persons" to the mere test of an indefinitely remote common ancestry, without regard to the extent of the subsequent divergence of the various branches from such common ancestry or from one another.

The eligibility of this applicant for citizenship is based on the sole fact that he is of high-caste Hindu stock, born in Punjab, one of the extreme northwestern districts of India, and classified by certain scientific authorities as of the Caucasian or Aryan race. The Aryan theory as a racial basis seems to be discredited by most, if not all, modern writers on the subject of ethnology. A review of their contentions would serve no useful purpose. . . .

The term "Aryan" has to do with linguistic, and not at all with physical, characteristics, and it would seem reasonably clear that mere resemblance in language, indicating a common linguistic root buried in remotely ancient soil, is altogether inadequate to prove common racial origin. There is, and can be, no assurance that the so-called Aryan language was not spoken by a variety of races living in proximity to one another. Our own history has witnessed the adoption of the English tongue by millions of negroes, whose descendants can never be classified racially with the descendants of white persons, notwithstanding both may speak a common root language.

The word "Caucasian" is in scarcely better repute. It is at best a conventional term, with an altogether fortuitous origin, which under scientific manipulation, has come to include far more than the unscientific mind suspects. It includes not only the Hindu, but some of the Polynesians (that is, the Maori, Tahitians, Samoans, Hawaiians, and others), the Hamites of Africa, upon the ground of the Caucasic cast of their features, though in color they range from brown to black. We venture to think that the average well-informed white American would learn with some degree of astonishment that the race to which he belongs is made up of such heterogeneous elements.

The various authorities are in irreconcilable disagreement as to what constitutes a proper racial division. . . .

It may be, therefore, that a given group cannot be properly assigned to any of the enumerated grand racial divisions. The type may have been so changed by intermixture of blood as to justify an intermediate classification. Something very like this has actually taken place in India. Thus, in Hindustan and Berar there was such an intermixture of the "Aryan" invader with the dark-skinned Dravidian.

In the Punjab and Rajputana, while the invaders seem to have met with more success in the effort to preserve their racial purity, intermarriages did occur producing an intermingling of the two and destroying to a greater or lesser degree the purity of the "Aryan" blood. The rules of caste, while calculated to prevent this intermixture, seem not to have been entirely successful.

It does not seem necessary to pursue the matter of scientific classification further. We are unable to agree with the District Court, or with other lower federal courts, in the conclusion that a native Hindu is eligible for naturalization under section 2169. The words of familiar speech, which were used by the original framers of the law, were intended to include only the type of man whom they knew as white. The immigration of that day was almost exclusively from the British Isles and Northwestern Europe, whence they and their forebears had come. When they extended the privilege of American citizenship to "any alien being a free white person" it was these immigrants—bone of their bone and flesh of their flesh—and their kind whom they must have had affirmatively in mind. The succeeding years brought immigrants from Eastern, Southern and Middle Europe, among them the Slavs and the dark-eyed, swarthy people of Alpine and Mediterranean stock, and these were received as unquestionably akin to those already here and readily amalgamated with them. It was the descendants of these, and other immigrants of like origin, who constituted the white population of the country when section 2169, re-enacting the naturalization test of 1790, was adopted, and, there is no reason to doubt, with like intent and meaning.

What, if any, people of primarily Asiatic stock come within the words of the section we do not deem it necessary now to decide. There is much in the origin and historic development of the statute to suggest that no Asiatic whatever was included.... The words of the statute, it must be conceded, do not readily yield to exact interpretation, and it is probably better to leave them as they are than to risk undue extension or undue limitation of their meaning by any general paraphrase at this time.

What we now hold is that the words "free white persons" are words of common speech, to be interpreted in accordance with the understanding of the common man, synonymous with the word "Caucasian" only as that word is popularly understood. As so understood and used, whatever may be the speculations of the ethnologist, it does not include the body of people to whom the appellee belongs. It is a matter of familiar observation and knowledge that the physical group characteristics of the Hindus render them readily distinguishable from the various groups of persons in this country commonly recognized as white. The children of English, French, German, Italian, Scandinavian, and other European parentage, quickly merge into the mass of our population and lose the distinctive hallmarks of their European origin. On the other hand, it cannot be doubted that the children born in this country of Hindu parents would retain indefinitely the clear evidence of their ancestry. It is very far from our thought to suggest the slightest question of racial superiority or inferiority. What we suggest is merely racial difference, and it is of such character and extent that the great body of our people instinctively recognize it and reject the thought of assimilation.

It is not without significance in this connection that Congress, by the Act of February 5, 1917, 39 Stat. 874, c. 29, § 3 has now excluded from admission into this country all natives of Asia within designated limits of latitude and longitude, including the whole of India. This not only constitutes conclusive evidence of the congressional attitude of opposition to Asiatic immigration generally, but is persuasive of a similar attitude toward Asiatic naturalization as well, since it is not likely that Congress would be willing to accept as citizens a class of persons whom it rejects as immigrants.

It follows that a negative answer must be given to the first question, which disposes of the case and renders an answer to the second question unnecessary, and it will be so certified.

Answer to question No. 1, No.

SAINT FRANCIS COLLEGE v. AL–KHAZRAJI

Supreme Court of the United States, 1987.
481 U.S. 604, 107 S.Ct. 2022, 95 L.Ed.2d 582.

JUSTICE WHITE delivered the opinion of the Court.

Respondent, a citizen of the United States born in Iraq, was an associate professor at St. Francis College, one of the petitioners here. In January 1978, he applied for tenure; the Board of Trustees denied his request on February 23, 1978. He accepted a 1–year, nonrenewable contract and sought administrative reconsideration of the tenure decision, which was denied on February 6, 1979. He worked his last day at the college on May 26, 1979....

We granted certiorari, ... limited to the ... question whether a person of Arabian ancestry was protected from racial discrimination under § 1981 ...

Section 1981 provides:

"All persons within the jurisdiction of the United States shall have the same right in every State and Territory to make and enforce contracts, to sue, be parties, give evidence, and to the full and equal benefit of all laws and proceedings for the security of persons and property as is enjoyed by white citizens, and shall be subject to like punishment, pains, penalties, taxes, licenses, and exactions of every kind, and to no other."

Although § 1981 does not itself use the word "race," the Court has construed the section to forbid all "racial" discrimination in the making of private as well as public contracts. *Runyon v. McCrary,* 427 U.S. 160, 168 (1976). Petitioner college, although a private institution, was therefore subject to this statutory command. There is no disagreement among the parties on these propositions. The issue is whether respondent has alleged *racial* discrimination within the meaning of § 1981.

Petitioners contend that respondent is a Caucasian and cannot allege the kind of discrimination § 1981 forbids....

Petitioner's submission rests on the assumption that all those who might be deemed Caucasians today were thought to be of the same race when § 1981 became law in the 19th century; and it may be that a variety of ethnic groups, including Arabs, are now considered to be within the Caucasian race.[4] The understanding of "race" in the 19th

---

4. There is a common popular understanding that there are three major human races—Caucasoid, Mongoloid, and Negroid. Many modern biologists and anthropolo- gists, however, criticize racial classifications as arbitrary and of little use in understanding the variability of human beings. It is said that genetically homogeneous popula-

century, however, was different. Plainly, all those who might be deemed Caucasian today were not thought to be of the same race at the time § 1981 became law.

In the middle years of the 19th century, dictionaries commonly referred to race as a "continued series of descendants from a parent who is called the *stock*," "[t]he lineage of a family," or "descendants of a common ancestor," The 1887 edition of Webster's expanded the definition somewhat: "The descendants of a common ancestor; a family, tribe, people or nation, believed or presumed to belong to the same stock." It was not until the 20th century that dictionaries began referring to the Caucasian, Mongolian, and Negro races, or to race as involving divisions of mankind based upon different physical characteristics. Even so, modern dictionaries still include among the definitions of race "a family, tribe, people, or nation belonging to the same stock."

Encyclopedias of the 19th century also described race in terms of ethnic groups, which is a narrower concept of race than petitioners urge....

These dictionary and encyclopedic sources are somewhat diverse, but it is clear that they do not support the claim that for the purposes of § 1981, Arabs, Englishmen, Germans, and certain other ethnic groups are to be considered a single race. We would expect the legislative history of § 1981 ... to reflect this common understanding, which it surely does. The debates are replete with references to the Scandinavian races, as well as the Chinese, Latin, Spanish, and Anglo–Saxon races. Jews, Mexicans, blacks, and Mongolians, were similarly categorized. Gypsies were referred to as a race. Likewise, the Germans ...

There was a reference to the Caucasian race, but it appears to have been referring to people of European ancestry.

The history of the 1870 Act reflects similar understanding of what groups Congress intended to protect from intentional discrimination. It is clear, for example, that the civil rights sections of the 1870 Act provided protection for immigrant groups such as the Chinese. This view was expressed in the Senate. In the House, Representative Bingham described § 16 of the Act, part of the authority for § 1981, as declaring "that the States shall not hereafter discriminate against the immigrant from China and in favor of the immigrant from Prussia, nor against the immigrant from France and in favor of the immigrant from Ireland."

tions do not exist and traits are not discontinuous between populations; therefore, a population can only be described in terms of relative frequencies of various traits. Clear-cut categories do not exist. The particular traits which have generally been chosen to characterize races have been criticized as having little biological significance. It has been found that differences between individuals of the same race are often greater than the differences between the "average" individuals of different races. These observations and others have led some, but not all, scientists to conclude that racial classifications are for the most part sociopolitical, rather than biological, in nature....

Based on the history of § 1981, we have little trouble in concluding that Congress intended to protect from discrimination identifiable classes of persons who are subjected to intentional discrimination solely because of their ancestry or ethnic characteristics. Such discrimination is racial discrimination that Congress intended § 1981 to forbid, whether or not it would be classified as racial in terms of modern scientific theory. The Court of Appeals was thus quite right in holding that § 1981, "at a minimum," reaches discrimination against an individual "because he or she is genetically part of an ethnically and physiognomically distinctive sub-grouping of *homo sapiens.*" It is clear from our holding, however, that a distinctive physiognomy is not essential to qualify for § 1981 protection. If respondent on remand can prove that he was subjected to intentional discrimination based on the fact that he was born an Arab, rather than solely on the place or nation of his origin, or his religion, he will have made out a case under § 1981....

JUSTICE BRENNAN, concurring.

Pernicious distinctions among individuals based solely on their ancestry are antithetical to the doctrine of equality upon which this Nation is founded. Today the Court upholds Congress' desire to rid the Nation of such arbitrary and invidious discrimination, and I concur in its opinion and judgment. I write separately only to point out that the line between discrimination based on "ancestry or ethnic characteristics," and discrimination based on "place or nation of ... origin," is not a bright one. It is true that one's ancestry—the ethnic group from which an individual and his or her ancestors are descended—is not necessarily the same as one's national origin—the country "where a person was *born,* or, more broadly, the country from which his or her ancestors *came.*" Often, however, the two are identical as a factual matter: one was born in the nation whose primary stock is one's own ethnic group. Moreover, national origin claims have been treated as ancestry or ethnicity claims in some circumstances.... I therefore read the Court's opinion to state only that discrimination based on *birthplace alone* is insufficient to state a claim under § 1981.

FRANCESCHI v. HYATT CORPORATION

United States District Court, District of Puerto Rico, 1992.
782 F.Supp. 712.

PEREZ-GIMENEZ, DISTRICT JUDGE.

In this case, the Court considers an issue of considerable import to civil rights, namely, whether 42 U.S.C. § 1981 prohibits the exclusion, on the basis of race, ancestry, or ethnic background of non-registered guests to a privately owned hotel with a facially neutral "no visitors policy," but which allegedly excludes guests on impermissible grounds. The Court also considers the novel question whether intraracial discrimination is actionable under § 1981. This Court answers both questions in the affirmative....

On March 26, 1987, Ms. Castro and Ms. Nogueras registered as guests of the Hotel purportedly to attend an important 936 conference. Ms. Castro invited Mr. Nogueras and Ms. Blanco to spend the afternoon at the Hotel and remain for dinner at the Hotel's restaurant. Co-plaintiffs Nogueras and Blanco allege that upon arrival, they were denied entrance to the Hotel's premises by the guard on duty. According to co-plaintiffs, the guard informed them of the Hotel's no visitors policy and denied them access to the premises. They were also informed that in order to contact Ms. Castro, they would have to drive to a public telephone down the road from the Hotel.

Mr. Nogueras begrudgingly complied. He reached the public phone, contacted Ms. Castro at the Hotel, and explained the situation. After telling Mr. Nogueras that she would take care of the matter, Ms. Castro proceeded to the front desk of the Hotel. At the front desk, Ms. Castro informed the clerk on duty that her son and daughter were at the gate, that they had been denied access to the premises, and that they were her invitees for the afternoon. Ms. Castro was then informed of the Hotel's no visitors policy.

Unsatisfied with the explanation, Ms. Castro asked to see the manager, Ms. Carmen Garcia, who in essence repeated the Hotel's policy and reiterated that her invitees could not enter the premises. Ms. Castro, a lawyer, protested that these were her guests and added that, pursuant to both state and federal law, they could not be denied access to a public accommodation such as the Hotel.

It is here that the nub of the controversy and therefore the more hotly debated sequence of events allegedly took place. After contacting Ms. Castro, Mr. Nogueras and Ms. Blanco returned to the guard post at the entrance of the Hotel premises to await further instructions from Ms. Castro. Co-plaintiffs allege that while waiting at the gate, ... the guard would consistently admit anyone whose main language was English and denied admittance to Spanish speaking visitors thus enhancing co- plaintiffs [sic] humiliation of being denied access to the hotel's premises on the basis of their ethnic origin and language. Nogueras was also informed by an employee of the hotel that "This management is prejudiced agaisnt [sic] people of our race" (meaning Puerto Ricans).

Defendant, Hyatt Hotels of Puerto Rico, strenuously denies allegations that the Hotel, its management, officers or agents have ever had a hotel policy of racial or ethnic discrimination on the basis of visitors' hispanic ancestry and categorically denies that its management has ever excluded or denied access to anyone on the basis of the same. The Hotel emphasizes that 90% of its registered guests are of Puerto Rican descent. Because of this fact, it submits that it is illogical to assert that the Hotel has ever had a discriminatory hotel admission policy....

... Defendant argues that even if race-based exclusions are actionable under § 1981, plaintiffs may not obtain relief because their claims state discrimination on the basis of nationality as Puerto Ricans and not on the basis of race. Therefore, defendant contends, plaintiff is unable to obtain relief because discrimination on the basis of nationality is not actionable under § 1981.

Defendant also contends that even if this Court finds that plaintiff's allegations state a claim of discrimination, they may not recover because Puerto Ricans are not a race for purposes of § 1981.

Defendant further asserts that, even if Puerto Ricans admit of classification as a race, plaintiffs in particular do not fall under the protection afforded by the statute because they are "white, convinced they are of European ancestry, and do not have a skin color or ethnic characteristics which could be classified into a race (Puerto Rico) protected by section 1981."

Finally, defendant affirms that, even if plaintiffs state a cause of action under § 1981, the action must still be dismissed because intra-racial discrimination is not actionable pursuant to § 1981. We address each argument in seriatim.

1. NATIONALITY

While it has been recognized that birthplace alone is insufficient to state a cause of action under § 1981, courts have noted that particular groups may be the subject of double discrimination, that is, discrimination on the basis of more than one ground.... In Shaare [Tefila Congregation v. Cobb] ... it was recognized that persons of Jewish descent could be the subject of intertwined racial and religious discrimination. Shaare ... recognized the possibility that discrimination on the basis of race could exist side by side with religious persecution.

This court is convinced that the logic ... in Shaare is equally applicable and persuasive in the case at bar. In this respect, this Court considers the words of Justice Brennan in this respect particularly illuminating: It is true that one's ancestry—the ethnic group from which an individual and his or her ancestors are descended—is not necessarily the same as one's national origin—the country "where a person was born, or, more broadly, the country from which his or her ancestors came." ... Often, however, the two are identical as a factual matter: one was born in the nation whose primary stock is one's own ethnic group. Saint Francis, 481 U.S. at 614.

In their Amended Complaint, plaintiff explicitly alleges that the guard on duty stated that the Hotel's management was "prejudiced against people of our race." We find that Puerto Ricans may indeed be the subject of discrimination on the basis of nationality as well as race or ethnicity and we so hold today.

2. PUERTO RICANS AS A RACE

Defendants also take the position that, at the time of § 1981's enactment, Puerto Ricans were not recognized as a distinct race and thus do not enjoy the protection of the statute. Defendant forgets that, although divided on the issue, courts have recognized that discrimination against Hispanics is actionable under § 1981. Manzanares v. Safeway Stores, Inc., 593 F.2d 968 (10th Cir.1979) (recognizing the need to include people of Hispanic origin within the protection of § 1981); Cubas v. Rapid American Corp., 420 F.Supp. 663 (E.D.Pa.1976) (Cuban–Americans); Budinsky v. Corning Glass Works, 425 F.Supp. 786 (W.D.Pa.1977) (Hispanics); Gonzalez v. Stanford Applied Engineering, Inc., 597 F.2d 1298 (9th Cir.1979) (Mexican–American).

Defendant cites a series of cases for the proposition that Hispanics, as opposed to other groups, do not enjoy the protection of § 1981. Motion In Compliance at pp. 8–10, citing Davis v. Boyle–Midway, Inc., 615 F.Supp. 560 (N.D.Ga.1985) ("... it would be a mistake to conclude from this that all Hispanics, as a group, are subject to racial discrimination."); Petrone v. City of Reading, 541 F.Supp. 735 (E.D.Pa.1982) (where there was no allegation that an Italian plaintiff was generally perceived as non-white, he could not state a claim under § 1981); and Martinez v. Hazelton Research Animals Inc., 430 F.Supp. 186 (D.Md. 1977) ("... this court finds that the allegation that the plaintiff is an Hispanic male, without more, is an insufficient allegation of racial background to support an allegation of racial discrimination and thus fails to state a cause of action under 42 U.S.C. 1981.").

As regards these cases, only two remarks need be made by this Court. First, two of the cases are, strictly speaking, inapposite to the case at bar. The Petrone and Martinez cases only hold that the mere assertion of discrimination on the basis of race is not enough to state a cause of action. In the case at bar, plaintiffs do not allege merely that they were denied access on the basis of their race, they contend that it is the Hotel's policy to exclude visitors on a racial basis. The Davis holding fares no better. The basis for the court's finding that not all Hispanics are the subject of discrimination is that some Hispanics appear and consider themselves white. Therefore, the court surmises, Hispanics, as a group, may not enjoy the protection of § 1981. The court's heavy reliance on the different appearance of Hispanics is no longer persuasive in light of Saint Francis' admonition that physiognomic characteristics are no longer the telltale of sign of racial discrimination.

This Court will not engage in a patronizing discourse over what constitutes the physiognomic, social and cultural characteristics that make up and define Puerto Ricans as a distinct race or ethnic group. Suffice it to say that given our rich heritage, Puerto Ricans of all colors, sizes and ethnic backgrounds abound. It is a generally accepted fact, and this Court takes judicial notice, that Puerto Ricans are of Taino Indian, Black, European and, more recently, Anglo–American ancestry (to name a few) and, more often than not, a mixture of two or more of the above. To simplistically and ignorantly argue that "Hispanics are by definition of Spanish or Portuguese descent, and therefore biologically caucasians," and to conclude that Puerto Ricans, as a race, admit of a definition of white, is to ignore the obvious.

We simply re-state that discrimination against Hispanics has been found actionable and that skin color is not determinative. Even if, as defendants propose, "... all Hispanics, as a group, [may not be] subject to racial discrimination," Mr. Nogueras may have been the subject of discrimination because of his race—regardless of his color or appearance—because he was identified as a Puerto Rican in just the same manner that the Supreme Court held that Mr. Al–Khazraji could maintain a suit for racial discrimination under § 1981 if he established that he was identified as an Arab by his employer even though he appeared Caucasian. Mr. Nogueras is thus entitled to make his case to the jury.

3. DEFENDANT'S APPEARANCE

Defendant insists that because plaintiff's appearance is that of a Caucasian, plaintiffs may not bring an action pursuant to § 1981. Defendant candidly admits, however, that the protection against racial discrimination afforded by § 1981 has recently been expanded "beyond persons of the black race." ...[14]

It is well settled that a person's distinctive physiognomy—one which clearly and unambiguously identifies a person as a member of protected group—is not determinative in § 1981 actions. Saint Francis....

As in the case of Mr. Al–Khazraji in Saint Francis, it may be the case that Mr. Nogueras appears Caucasian. In fact, it may even be the case that, following a genealogical study of Mr. Nogueras' forbearers, this Court would conclude that he descends from a strictly white European lineage. According to Mr. Nogueras, however, the guard had no difficulty in identifying him as Puerto Rican. In light of Saint Francis and its interpretation of McDonald, this Court finds that physiognomic characteristics are not determinative and thus plaintiffs may recover if it is established that they were subject to discrimination because they were Puerto Ricans and were identified as such by the entrance guard.

4. INTRA-RACIAL DISCRIMINATION

Defendants contend that intra-racial discrimination is not actionable under § 1981. In so doing, defendant glosses over decisions that clearly stand for the proposition that intra-racial discrimination is actionable under the statute. LaFlore v. Emblem Tape & Label Co., 448 F.Supp. 824 (D.Colo.1978) (Intra-racial claims by one caucasian against another are actionable under § 1981 so long as they flow from racial discrimination).... As recognized by LaFlore and implicit in Saint Francis: "It is irrelevant that the plaintiff is herself Caucasian so long as she was discriminated against as if she belonged to a minority." [T]he LaFlore decision "define[s] the statutory term 'white citizens' to mean 'most

14. Defendant's interpretation of Saint Francis, although not incorrect, is slightly off the mark. It is more correct to say that Saint Francis stands for the proposition that a person's physical appearance as a caucasian is not determinative in discrimination cases. It is the perception, by the discriminator, of the discriminatees' race that is important for purposes of § 1981. Thus, Saint Francis obviates the need to determine the race or ethnicity of the discriminatee and focuses instead on the perception of that person by the discriminator.

favored group,' and reads section 1981 to entitle all persons to the rights and benefits enjoyed by the most favored."

This approach represents a re-thinking of how courts go about making a determination of discrimination in a given case.... [C]ourts should focus on defendant's perceptions of plaintiff's ethnic and racial differences rather than on plaintiff's racial status. The focus would then shift to the racial content of defendant's actions as a means of ascertaining defendant's perceptions....

This Court recognizes that prior to the Supreme Court's decision in Saint Francis, other courts, scared by the potential task of distinguishing among a myriad of color shades, physiognomic and cultural characteristics, have shied away from grappling with cases that deal with subtle degrees of intra-racial discrimination.

This Court agrees with the proposition that courts should not be placed in the "unsavory business" of measuring skin color. We note however, that the holding in Saint Francis effectively lays to rest this quandary by eliminating color as a determinative factor. It is true, as defendant points out, that "the Court's opinion was based on the fact that the term 'race'" is of "doubtful sociological validity." But that is precisely the import of the decision: the recognition that physiognomic characteristics are no longer considered the indispensable magic recipient for a cause of action under the statute. Rather, it is the subjection of a person to intentional discrimination—because of the belief that he or she belongs to a given race—that renders such behavior actionable....

Notes and Questions

1. How would you describe the concept of race advanced in *Hall?* What techniques and assumptions were used to justify the court's conclusion that a Chinese individual was prohibited from giving evidence against a white person?

2. Did the Supreme Court adopt a similar concept of race in *Thind?* Did the Court use similar rhetorical techniques and assumptions? One commentator observed that *Thind* "moved race out of the scientific realm by establishing two subjective grounds for citizenship. First, that a potential citizen be 'white' in the popular sense. And second, that he be assimilable. In short, assimilation now became a legal criteria in the 'desirable race' equation." Jeff Lesser, Always "Outsiders": Asians, Naturalization, and the Supreme Court, 12 *Amerasia J.* 83, 88 (1985–86). Do you agree with this assessment of the decision?

3. The Court in *Thind* states that it is suggesting "merely racial difference" and not "racial superiority or inferiority." Are you persuaded? Why would "the great body of our people ... reject the thought of assimilation" of racially different people if they did not assign some significance to the difference? By the way, who is "our people?"

4. What is the test adopted by the Court in *St. Francis College* for determining which groups constitute a "race" for purposes of Section 1981?

Would Jews be considered a race under that test. *See* Shaare Tefila Congregation v. Cobb, 481 U.S. 615, 107 S.Ct. 2019, 95 L.Ed.2d 594 (1987) (Whatever the current understanding, Jews were considered a distinct race when Congress enacted the post-Civil War civil rights acts.) Is the Court's test limited to that statute? If Mr. Al–Khazraji had been denied tenure by a state school would he have been able to assert a race discrimination claim under the Fourteenth Amendment?

5. Is the Court's method for defining a racial group in *St. Francis College* different from the method it used in *Thind?*

6. What is the approach used in *Franceschi* to determine whether conduct is race-based? Is that approach required by *St. Francis College?* Whether or not required, does it confront the issues of privilege and power that are associated with race discrimination?

7. Consider the story of Susie Guillory Phipps, a 43 year old woman who thought she was white, had been married twice to white men, went to white schools, and lived in a white neighborhood in Louisiana. In the course of applying for a passport, she obtained a copy of her birth certificate which indicated that she and her parents had been designated as "colored." Phipps was quoted as saying that this information caused her to be "sick for days." Her husband encouraged her to fight the designation all the way to the Supreme Court, saying "What the hell do you want to drop it for? Are you a nigger?" Phipps did challenge the designation in court but was unsuccessful in her attempts to change the racial classification on her birth certificate from colored to white. *See* Doe v. State, Department of Health & Human Resources, 479 So.2d 369 (La.App. 4 Cir.1985), writ denied 485 So.2d 60 (La.1986); Lauren Austin, The Meaning of Race in Sections 1981 and 1982: The Subtext of Color 2–3 (unpublished paper 1993).

Does the Phipps story confirm the following observation of Langston Hughes:

> "That one drop of Negro blood—because just one drop of black blood makes a man colored. One drop—you are a Negro! Now, why is that? Why is Negro blood so much more powerful than any other kind of blood in the world? If a man has Irish blood in him, people will say, 'He's part Irish.' If he has a little Jewish blood, they'll say, 'He's half Jewish.' But if he has just a small bit of colored blood in him bam!— He's a Negro!' Not, 'He's part Negro.'" No, be it ever so little, if that blood is black, 'He's a Negro!' Now, that is what I do not understand— why our one drop is so powerful.... Black is powerful. You can have ninety-nine drops of white blood in your veins down South—but if that other one drop is black, shame on you! Even if you look white, you're black. That drop is powerful."

Langston Hughes, Simple Takes a Wife 85 (1953) (quoted in Neil Gotanda, *A Critique of "Our Constitution is Color–Blind"*, 44 Stan. L.Rev. 1, 26 n. 101 (1991).

MICHAEL OMI & HAROLD WINANT, RACIAL FORMATIONS

in Paula Rothenberg, Race, Class & Gender in the United
States 26–33 (2d ed., St. Martin's Press, 1992).

The Phipps case illustrates the continuing dilemma of defining race and establishing its meaning in institutional life. Today, to assert that variations in human physiognomy are racially based is to enter a constant and intense debate. *Scientific* interpretations of race have not been alone in sparking heated controversy; *religious* perspectives have done so as well. Most centrally, of course, race has been a matter of *political* contention. This has been particularly true in the United States, where the concept of race has varied enormously over time without ever leaving the center stage of US history.

WHAT IS RACE?

Race consciousness, and its articulation in theories of race, is largely a modern phenomenon. When European explorers in the New World "discovered" people who looked different than themselves, these "natives" challenged then existing conceptions of the origins of the human species, and raised disturbing questions as to whether *all* could be considered in the same "family of man." Religious debates flared over the attempt to reconcile the Bible with the existence of "racially distinct" people. Arguments took place over creation itself, as theories of polygenesis questioned whether God had made only one species of humanity ("monogenesis"). Europeans wondered if the natives of the New World were indeed human beings with redeemable souls. At stake were not only the prospects for conversion, but the types of treatment to be accorded them. The expropriation of property, the denial of political rights, the introduction of slavery and other forms of coercive labor, as well as outright extermination, all presupposed a worldview which distinguished Europeans—children of God, human beings, etc.—from "others." Such a worldview was needed to explain why some should be "free" and others enslaved, why some had rights to land and property while others did not. Race, and the interpretation of racial differences, was a central factor in that worldview.

In the colonial epoch science was no less a field of controversy than religion in attempts to comprehend the concept of race and its meaning. Spurred on by the classificatory scheme of living organisms devised by Linnaeus in *Systema Naturae,* many scholars in the eighteenth and nineteenth centuries dedicated themselves to the identification and ranking of variations in humankind. Race was thought of as a *biological* concept, yet its precise definition was the subject of debates which, as we have noted, continue to rage today. Despite efforts ranging from Dr. Samuel Morton's studies of cranial capacity to contemporary attempts to base racial classification on shared gene pools, the concept of race has defied biological definition. . . .

Attempts to discern the *scientific meaning* of race continue to the present day. Although most physical anthropologists and biologists have abandoned the quest for a scientific basis to determine racial categories, controversies have recently flared in the area of genetics and educational psychology. For instance, an essay by Arthur Jensen which argued that hereditary factors shape intelligence not only revived the "nature or nurture" controversy, but raised highly volatile questions about racial equality itself. Clearly the attempt to establish a *biological* basis of race has not been swept into the dustbin of history, but is being resurrected in various scientific arenas. All such attempts seek to remove the concept of race from fundamental social, political, or economic determination. They suggest instead that the truth of race lies in the terrain of innate characteristics, of which skin color and other physical attributes provide only the most obvious, and in some respects most superficial, indicators.

RACE AS A SOCIAL CONCEPT

The social sciences have come to reject biologistic notions of race in favor of an approach which regards race as a *social* concept. Beginning in the eighteenth century, this trend has been slow and uneven, but its direction clear. In the nineteenth century Max Weber discounted biological explanations for racial conflict and instead highlighted the social and political factors which engendered such conflict. The work of pioneering cultural anthropologist Franz Boas was crucial in refuting the scientific racism of the early twentieth century by rejecting the connection between race and culture, and the assumption of a continuum of "higher" and "lower" cultural groups. Within the contemporary social science literature, race is assumed to be a variable which is shaped by broader societal forces.

Race is indeed a pre-eminently *sociohistorical* concept. Racial categories and the meaning of race are given concrete expression by the specific social relations and historical context in which they are embedded. Racial meanings have varied tremendously over time and between different societies.

In the United States, the black/white color line has historically been rigidly defined and enforced. White is seen as a "pure" category. Any racial intermixture makes one "nonwhite." In the movie *Raintree County*, Elizabeth Taylor describes the worst of fates to befall whites as "havin' a little Negra blood in ya'—just one little teeny drop and a person's all Negra." This thinking flows from what Marvin Harris has characterized as the principle of *hypo-descent:*

> By what ingenious computation is the genetic tracery of a million years of evolution unraveled and each man [sic] assigned his proper social box? In the United States, the mechanism employed is the rule of hypo-descent. This descent rule requires Americans to believe that anyone who is known to have had a Negro ancestor is a Negro. We admit nothing in between. . . . "Hypo-descent" means affiliation with the subordinate rather than the superordinate group

in order to avoid the ambiguity of intermediate identity.... The rule of hypo-descent is, therefore, an invention, which we in the United States have made in order to keep biological facts from intruding into our collective racist fantasies.

The Susie Guillory Phipps case merely represents the contemporary expression of this racial logic.

By contrast, a striking feature of race relations in the lowland areas of Latin America since the abolition of slavery has been the relative absence of sharply defined racial groupings. No such rigid descent rule characterizes racial identity in many Latin American societies. Brazil, for example, has historically had less rigid conceptions of race, and thus a variety of "intermediate" racial categories exist. Indeed, as Harris notes, "One of the most striking consequences of the Brazilian system of racial identification is that parents and children and even brothers and sisters are frequently accepted as representatives of quite opposite racial types." Such a possibility is incomprehensible within the logic of racial categories in the US.

To suggest another example: the notion of "passing" takes on new meaning if we compare various American cultures' means of assigning racial identity. In the United States, individuals who are actually "black" by the logic of hypo-descent have attempted to skirt the discriminatory barriers imposed by law and custom by attempting to "pass" for white. Ironically, these same individuals would not be able to pass for "black" in many Latin American societies.

Consideration of the term "black" illustrates the diversity of racial meanings which can be found among different societies and historically within a given society. In contemporary British politics the term "black" is used to refer to all nonwhites. Interestingly this designation has not arisen through the racist discourse of groups such as the National Front. Rather, in political and cultural movements, Asian as well as Afro–Caribbean youth are adopting the term as an expression of self-identity. The wide-ranging meanings of "black" illustrate the manner in which racial categories are shaped politically.

The meaning of race is defined and contested throughout society, in both collective action and personal practice. In the process, racial categories themselves are formed, transformed, destroyed and re-formed. We use the term *racial formation* to refer to the process by which social, economic and political forces determine the content and importance of racial categories, and by which they are in turn shaped by racial meanings. Crucial to this formulation is the treatment of race as a *central axis* of social relations which cannot be subsumed under or reduced to some broader category or conception.

RACIAL IDEOLOGY AND RACIAL IDENTITY

The seemingly obvious, "natural" and "common sense" qualities which the existing racial order exhibits themselves testify to the effectiveness of the racial formation process in constructing racial meanings and racial identities.

One of the first things we notice about people when we meet them (along with their sex) is their race. We utilize race to provide clues about *who* a person is. This fact is made painfully obvious when we encounter someone whom we cannot conveniently racially categorize— someone who is, for example, racially "mixed" or of an ethnic/racial group with which we are not familiar. Such an encounter becomes a source of discomfort and momentarily a crisis of racial meaning. Without a racial identity, one is in danger of having no identity.

Our compass for navigating race relations depends on preconceived notions of what each specific racial group looks like. Comments such as, "Funny, you don't look black," betray an underlying image of what black should be. We also become disoriented when people do not act "black," "Latino," or indeed "white." The content of such stereotypes reveals a series of unsubstantiated beliefs about who these groups are and what "they" are like.

In US society, then, a kind of "racial etiquette" exists, a set of interpretative codes and racial meanings which operate in the interactions of daily life. Rules shaped by our perception of race in a comprehensively racial society determine the "presentation of self," distinctions of status, and appropriate modes of conduct. "Etiquette" is not mere universal adherence to the dominant group's rules, but a more dynamic combination of these rules with the values and beliefs of subordinated groupings. This racial "subjection" is quintessentially ideological. Everybody learns some combination, some version, of the rules of racial classification, and of their own racial identity, often without obvious teaching or conscious inculcation. Race becomes "common sense"—a way of comprehending, explaining and acting in the world.

Racial beliefs operate as an "amateur biology," a way of explaining the variations in "human nature." Differences in skin color and other obvious physical characteristics supposedly provide visible clues to differences lurking underneath. Temperament, sexuality, intelligence, athletic ability, aesthetic preferences and so on are presumed to be fixed and discernible from the palpable mark of race. Such diverse questions as our confidence and trust in others (for example, clerks or salespeople, media figures, neighbors), our sexual preferences and romantic images, our tastes in music, films, dance, or sports, and our very ways of talking, walking, eating and dreaming are ineluctably shaped by notions of race. Skin color "differences" are thought to explain perceived differences in intellectual, physical and artistic temperaments, and to justify distinct treatment of racially identified individuals and groups.

The continuing persistence of racial ideology suggests that these racial myths and stereotypes cannot be exposed as such in the popular imagination. They are, we think, too essential, too integral, to the maintenance of the US social order. Of course, particular meanings, stereotypes and myths can change, but the presence of a *system* of racial meanings and stereotypes, of racial ideology, seems to be a permanent feature of US culture.

Film and television, for example, have been notorious in disseminating images of racial minorities which establish for audiences what people from these groups look like, how they behave, and "who they are." The power of the media lies not only in their ability to reflect the dominant racial ideology, but in their capacity to shape that ideology in the first place. D.W. Griffith's epic *Birth of a Nation,* a sympathetic treatment of the rise of the Ku Klux Klan during Reconstruction, helped to generate, consolidate and "nationalize" images of blacks which had been more disparate (more regionally specific, for example) prior to the film's appearance. In US television, the necessity to define characters in the briefest and most condensed manner has led to the perpetuation of racial caricatures, as racial stereotypes serve as shorthand for scriptwriters, directors and actors, in commercials, etc. Television's tendency to address the "lowest common denominator" in order to render programs "familiar" to an enormous and diverse audience leads it regularly to assign and reassign racial characteristics to particular groups, both minority and majority.

These and innumerable other examples show that we tend to view race as something fixed and immutable—something rooted in "nature." Thus we mask the historical construction of racial categories, the shifting meaning of race, and the crucial role of politics and ideology in shaping race relations. Races do not emerge full-blown. They are the results of diverse historical practices and are continually subject to challenge over their definition and meaning.

RACIALIZATION: THE HISTORICAL DEVELOPMENT OF RACE

In the United States, the racial category of "black" evolved with the consolidation of racial slavery. By the end of the seventeenth century, Africans whose specific identity was Ibo, Yoruba, Fulani, etc., were rendered "black" by an ideology of exploitation based on racial logic—the establishment and maintenance of a "color line." This of course did not occur overnight. A period of indentured servitude which was not rooted in racial logic preceded the consolidation of racial slavery. With slavery, however, a racially based understanding of society was set in motion which resulted in the shaping of a specific *racial* identity not only for the slaves but for the European settlers as well. Winthrop Jordan has observed: "From the initially common term *Christian,* at mid-century there was a marked shift toward the terms *English* and *free.* After about 1680, taking the colonies as a whole, a new term of self-identification appeared—*white.*"

We employ the term *racialization* to signify the extension of racial meaning to a previously racially unclassified relationship, social practice or group. Racialization is an ideological process, an historically specific one. Racial ideology is constructed from pre-existing conceptual (or, if one prefers, "discursive") elements and emerges from the struggles of competing political projects and ideas seeking to articulate similar elements differently. An account of racialization processes that avoids the pitfalls of US ethnic history remains to be written.

Particularly during the nineteenth century, the category of "white" was subject to challenges brought about by the influx of diverse groups who were not of the same Anglo–Saxon stock as the founding immigrants. In the nineteenth century, political and ideological struggles emerged over the classification of Southern Europeans, the Irish and Jews, among other "non-white" categories. Nativism was only effectively curbed by the institutionalization of a racial order that drew the color line *around*, rather than *within*, Europe.

By stopping short of racializing immigrants from Europe after the Civil War, and by subsequently allowing their assimilation, the American racial order was reconsolidated in the wake of the tremendous challenge placed before it by the abolition of racial slavery. With the end of Reconstruction in 1877, an effective program for limiting the emergent class struggles of the later nineteenth century was forged: the definition of the working class *in racial terms*—as "white." This was not accomplished by any legislative decree or capitalist maneuvering to divide the working class, but rather by white workers themselves. Many of them were recent immigrants, who organized on racial lines as much as on traditionally defined class lines. The Irish on the West Coast, for example, engaged in vicious anti-Chinese race-baiting and committed many pogrom-type assaults on Chinese in the course of consolidating the trade union movement in California.

Thus the very political organization of the working class was in important ways a racial project. The legacy of racial conflicts and arrangements shaped the definition of interests and in turn led to the consolidation of institutional patterns (e.g., segregated unions, dual labor markets, exclusionary legislation) which perpetuated the color line *within* the working class. Selig Perlman, whose study of the development of the labor movement is fairly sympathetic to this process, notes that:

> The political issue after 1877 was racial, not financial, and the weapon was not merely the ballot, but also "direct action"—violence. The anti-Chinese agitation in California, culminating as it did in the Exclusion Law passed by Congress in 1882, was doubtless the most important single factor in the history of American labor, for without it the entire country might have been overrun by Mongolian [sic] labor and *the labor movement might have become a conflict of races instead of one of classes.*

More recent economic transformations in the US have also altered interpretations of racial identities and meanings. The automation of southern agriculture and the augmented labor demand of the postwar boom transformed blacks from a largely rural, impoverished labor force to a largely urban, working-class group by 1970. When boom became bust and liberal welfare statism moved rightwards, the majority of blacks came to be seen, increasingly, as part of the "underclass," as state "dependents." Thus the particularly deleterious effects on blacks of global and national economic shifts (generally rising unemployment rates, changes in the employment structure away from reliance on labor intensive work, etc.) were explained once again in the late 1970s and 1980s (as they had been in the 1940s and mid–1960s) as the result of defective black cultural norms, of familial disorganization, etc. In this way new racial attributions, new racial myths, are affixed to "blacks." Similar changes in racial identity are presently affecting Asians and Latinos, as such economic forces as increasing Third World impoverishment and indebtedness fuel immigration and high interest rates, Japanese competition spurs resentments, and US jobs seem to fly away to Korea and Singapore. . . .

Once we understand that race overflows the boundaries of skin color, superexploitation, social stratification, discrimination and prejudice, cultural domination and cultural resistance, state policy (or of any other particular social relationship we list), once we recognize the racial dimension present to some degree in *every* identity, institution and social practice in the United States—once we have done this, it becomes possible to speak of *racial formation.* This recognition is hard-won; there is a continuous temptation to think of race as an *essence,* as something fixed, concrete and objective, as (for example) one of the categories just enumerated. And there is also an opposite temptation: to see it as a mere illusion, which an ideal social order would eliminate.

In our view it is crucial to break with these habits of thought. The effort must be made to understand race as *an unstable and "decentered" complex of social meanings constantly being transformed by political struggle* . . . .

2. *Exclusion Based on Race*

JOHNSON v. McINTOSH

Supreme Court of the United States, 1823.
21 U.S. 543, 5 L.Ed. 681.

MARSHALL, CH. J., delivered the opinion of the court.—The plaintiffs in this cause claim the land in their declaration mentioned, under two grants, purporting to be made, the first in 1773, and the last in 1775, by the chiefs of certain Indian tribes, constituting the Illinois and the Piankeshaw nations; and the question is, whether this title can be recognised in the courts of the United States? The facts, as stated in the case agreed, show the authority of the chiefs who executed this conveyance, so far as it could be given by their own people; and likewise show, that the particular tribes for whom these chiefs acted were in rightful possession of the land they sold. The inquiry, therefore, is, in a great measure, confined to the power of Indians to give, and of private individuals to receive, a title, which can be sustained in the courts of this country.

As the right of society to prescribe those rules by which property may be acquired and preserved is not, and cannot, be drawn into question; as the title to lands, especially, is, and must be, admitted, to depend entirely on the law of the nation in which they lie; it will be necessary, in pursuing this inquiry, to examine, not simply those principles of abstract justice, which the Creator of all things has impressed on the mind of his creature man, and which are admitted to regulate, in a great degree, the rights of civilized nations, whose perfect independence is acknowledged; but those principles also which our own government has adopted in the particular case, and given us as the rule for our decision.

On the discovery of this immense continent, the great nations of Europe were eager to appropriate to themselves so much of it as they could respectively acquire. Its vast extent offered an ample field to the ambition and enterprise of all; and the character and religion of its inhabitants afforded an apology for considering them as a people over whom the superior genius of Europe might claim an ascendency. The potentates of the old world found no difficulty in convincing themselves, that they made ample compensation to the inhabitants of the new, by bestowing on them civilization and Christianity, in exchange for unlimited independence. But as they were all in pursuit of nearly the same object, it was necessary, in order to avoid conflicting settlements, and consequent war with each other, to establish a principle, which all should acknowledge as the law by which the right of acquisition, which they all asserted, should be regulated, as between themselves. This principle was, that discovery gave title to the government by whose subjects, or by whose authority, it was made, against all other European governments, which title might be consummated by possession. The exclusion of all other Europeans, necessarily gave to the nation making the discovery the sole right of acquiring the soil from the natives, and establishing settlements upon it. It was a right with which no Europeans could interfere. It was a right which all asserted for themselves, and to the assertion of which, by others, all assented. Those relations which were to exist between the discoverer and the natives, were to be regulated by themselves. The rights thus acquired being exclusive, no other power could interpose between them.

In the establishment of these relations, the rights of the original inhabitants were, in no instance, entirely disregarded; but were, necessarily, to a considerable extent, impaired. They were admitted to be the rightful occupants of the soil, with a legal as well as just claim to retain possession of it, and to use it according to their own discretion; but their rights to complete sovereignty, as independent nations, were necessarily diminished, and their power to dispose of the soil, at their own will, to whomsoever they pleased, was denied by the original fundamental principle, that discovery gave exclusive title to those who made it. While the different nations of Europe respected the right of the natives, as occupants, they asserted the ultimate dominion to be in themselves; and claimed and exercised, as a consequence of this ultimate dominion, a power to grant the soil, while yet in possession of the natives. These grants have been understood by all, to convey a title to the grantees, subject only to the Indian right of occupancy.

The history of America, from its discovery to the present day, proves, we think, the universal recognition of these principles. . . .

By the treaty which concluded the war of our revolution, Great Britain relinquished all claim, not only to the government, but to the "propriety and territorial rights of the United States," whose boundaries were fixed in the second article. By this treaty, the powers of government, and the right to soil, which had previously been in Great Britain, passed definitively to these states. We had before taken possession of them, by declaring independence; but neither the declaration of independence, nor the treaty confirming it, could give us more than that which we before possessed, or to which Great Britain was before entitled. It has never been doubted, that either the United States, or the several states, had a clear title to all the lands within the boundary lines described in the treaty, subject only to the Indian right of occupancy, and that the exclusive power to extinguish that right, was vested in that government which might constitutionally exercise it. . . . .

Although we do not mean to engage in the defence of those principles which Europeans have applied to Indian title, they may, we think, find some excuse, if not justification, in the character and habits of the people whose rights have been wrested from them. The title by conquest is acquired and maintained by force. The conqueror prescribes its limits. Humanity, however, acting on public opinion, has established, as a general rule, that the conquered shall not be wantonly oppressed, and that their condition shall remain as eligible as is compatible with the objects of the conquest. Most usually, they are incorporated with the victorious nation, and become subjects or citizens of the government with which they are connected. The new and old members of the society mingle with each other; the distinction between them is gradually lost, and they make one people. Where this incorporation is practicable, humanity demands, and a wise policy requires, that the rights of the conquered to property should remain unimpaired; that the new subjects should be governed as equitably as the old, and that confidence in their security should gradually banish the painful sense of being separated from their ancient connections, and united by force to strangers. When the conquest is complete, and the conquered inhabitants can be blended with the conquerors, or safely governed as a distinct people, public opinion, which not even the conqueror can disregard, imposes these restraints upon him; and he cannot neglect them, without injury to his fame, and hazard to his power.

But the tribes of Indians inhabiting this country were fierce savages, whose occupation was war, and whose subsistence was drawn chiefly from the forest. To leave them in possession of their country, was to leave the country a wilderness; to govern them as a distinct people, was impossible, because they were as brave and as high-spirited as they were fierce, and were ready to repel by arms every attempt on their independence. . . .

That law which regulates, and ought to regulate in general, the relations between the conqueror and conquered, was incapable of application to a people under such circumstances. The resort to some new and different rule, better adapted to the actual state of things, was unavoidable. Every rule which can be suggested will be found to be attended with great difficulty. However extravagant the pretension of converting the discovery of an inhabited country into conquest may appear; if the principle has been asserted in the first instance, and afterwards sustained; if a country has been acquired and held under it; if the property of the great mass of the community originates in it, it becomes the law of the land, and cannot be questioned. So too, with respect to the concomitant principle, that the Indian inhabitants are to be considered merely as occupants, to be protected, indeed, while in peace, in the possession of their lands, but to be deemed incapable of transferring the absolute title to others. However this restriction may be opposed to natural right, and to the usages of civilized nations, yet, if it be indispensable to that system under which the country has been settled, and be adapted to the actual condition of the two people, it may, perhaps, be supported by reason, and certainly cannot be rejected by courts of justice. . . .

After bestowing on this subject a degree of attention which was more required by the magnitude of the interest in litigation, and the able and elaborate arguments of the bar, than by its intrinsic difficulty, the court is decidedly of opinion, that the plaintiffs do not exhibit a title which can be sustained in the courts of the United States; and that there is no error in the judgment which was rendered against them in the district court of Illinois.

Notes and Questions

1. Which techniques and assumptions did the Supreme Court use in *Johnson* in concluding that Indians did not have power to convey title to their own land? Does Chief Justice Marshall concede that the discovery doctrine may lead to an unjust result but nevertheless conclude that it must be applied to deprive the Indians of their lands? Is *Johnson* another example of the "constitutional contradiction?" See *Bell*, supra at 124.

2. "We the people" was certainly meant to exclude the Native Americans. Indeed, the Constitution provided that in apportioning representatives, "Indians, not taxed" would be excluded from the count. U.S. Const., art. I, § 2. In 1884, the Supreme Court ruled that an Indian, who had been born in the United States and had severed ties with his tribe, was not a citizen within the meaning of the Fourteenth Amendment. Elk v. Wilkins, 112 U.S. 94 (1884). Congress did not enact a general grant of citizenship for Indians until 1924. 8 U.S.C. § 1401(a)(2).

3. Although the *Johnson* decision dealt specifically with land title issues, it has served as the foundation for the much larger proposition that the federal government has plenary power over Indian affairs. The follow-

ing excerpt examines the extent to which *Johnson* has led to the disempow-
erment of Indian peoples and infliction of harm on them.

ROBERT WILLIAMS, JR., THE AMERICAN INDIAN IN WESTERN LEGAL THOUGHT

325–328 (Oxford University Press, 1990).

The conquest of the earth is not a pretty thing when you look into it
too much. The history of the American Indian in Western legal thought
reveals that a will to empire proceeds most effectively under a rule of
law. In the United States, and in the other Western settler-colonized
states, that rule begins with the Doctrine of Discovery and its discourse
of conquest, which denies fundamental human rights and self-determination to indigenous tribal peoples. For the native peoples of the United
States, Latin America, Canada, Australia, and New Zealand, therefore,
the end of the history of their colonization begins by denying the
legitimacy of and respect for the rule of law maintained by the racist
discourse of conquest of the Doctrine of Discovery. This medievally
grounded discourse, reaffirmed in Western colonizing law by Chief
Justice John Marshall in *Johnson v. McIntosh*, vests superior rights of
sovereignty over non-Western indigenous peoples and their territories in
European-descended governments. The Doctrine of Discovery and its
discourse of conquest assert the West's lawful power to impose its vision
of truth on non-Western peoples through a racist, colonizing rule of law.

In the United States, the doctrine has proved itself to be a perfect
instrument of empire. Under the rules and principles of federal Indian
law derived from the doctrine, the United States acquired a continent
"in perfect good faith" that its wars and acts of genocide directed
against Indian people accorded with the rule of law. Supreme Court
decisions interpreting the doctrine have extended to the federal government plenary power to control Indian affairs unrestrained by normal
constitutional limitations. In case after case, the Supreme Court in the
late nineteenth and early twentieth centuries simply refused to check
Congress's free rein in matters where it was thought that broad discretionary powers were vital to the solution of the immensely difficult
"Indian problem." Treaties promising tribes a reserved homeland in
perpetuation were wantonly violated; tribes were relocated to distant,
barren regions to accommodate white expansion; and tribal lands and
resources were repeatedly confiscated to satisfy the needs and destiny of
a superior civilization.

Besides justifying unquestioned abrogation and unilateral determination of tribal treaty and property rights, the discourse of conquest
derived from the Doctrine of Discovery has been interpreted to permit
the denial of other fundamental human rights of Indian tribal peoples in
the United States. Violent suppression of Indian religious practices and
traditional forms of government, separation of Indian children from
their homes, wholesale spoliation of treaty-guaranteed resources, forced
assimilative programs, and involuntary sterilization of Indian women

represent but a few of the practical extensions of a racist discourse of conquest that at its core regards tribal peoples as normatively deficient and culturally, politically, and morally inferior. And the United States, it is conceded, possesses one of the most "liberal" and "progressive" reputations among the Western nations respecting its treatment of native peoples under the Doctrine of Discovery. For other Western colonial states, the history of indigenous peoples' fate under the West's rule of law, grounded in the Doctrine of Discovery and its denial of human rights to non-Western tribal peoples, is indeed the stuff of black legend.

For half a millennium, whether inscribed in United States Indian law and its central Doctrine of Discovery, in the Spanish jurist Victoria's Law of Nations, or in Lord Coke's English common law, Western legal thought has sought to erase the difference presented by the American Indian in order to sustain the privileges of power it accords to Western norms and value structures. Animated by a central orienting vision of its own universalized, hierarchical position among all other discourses, the West's archaic, medievally derived legal discourse respecting the American Indian is ultimately genocidal in both its practice and its intent.

The Doctrine of Discovery was nothing more than the reflection of a set of Eurocentric racist beliefs elevated to the status of a universal principle—one culture's argument to support its conquest and colonization of a newly discovered, alien world. In its form as articulated by Western legal thought and discourse today, however, the peroration of this Eurocentric racist argument is no longer declaimed. Europe during the Discovery era refused to recognize any meaningful legal status or rights for indigenous tribal peoples because "heathens" and "infidels" were legally presumed to lack the rational capacity necessary to assume an equal status or to exercise equal rights under the West's medievally derived colonizing law.

Today, principles and rules generated from this Old World discourse of conquest are cited by the West's domestic and international courts of law to deny indigenous nations the freedom and dignity to govern themselves according to their own vision. Thus as a first step toward the decolonization of the West's law respecting the American Indian, the Doctrine of Discovery must be rejected. It permits the West to accomplish by law and in good conscience what it accomplished by the sword in earlier eras: the physical and spiritual destruction of indigenous people.

The reconstruction of the West's Indian law so that it would be grounded in a vision rejecting the discourse of conquest contained in the Doctrine of Discovery could begin its search for foundations in New World soil. The principles inherent in the Gus–Wen–Tah, an indigenously articulated New World discourse of peace, suggest the beginnings of a differently oriented vision of a law to govern the relations between the West and non-Western peoples.

The principles embodied in the Gus–Wen–Tah, the Two Row Wampum, were the basis for all treaties and agreements between the great nations of the Haudenosaunee Confederacy (called the Confederated Iroquois Nations by the European colonial powers) and the great nations of Europe. These basic principles were the covenant chain linking these two different peoples by which each agreed to respect the other's vision.

When the Haudenosaunee first came into contact with the European nations, treaties of peace and friendship were made. Each was symbolized by the Gus–Wen–Tah, or Two Row Wampum. There is a bed of white wampum which symbolizes the purity of the agreement. There are two rows of purple, and those two rows have the spirit of your ancestors and mine. There are three beads of wampum separating the two rows and they symbolize two paths or two vessels, travelling down the same river together. One, a birch bark canoe, will be for the Indian people, their laws, their customs and their ways. The other, a ship, will be for the white people and their laws, their customs and their ways. We shall each travel the river together, side by side, but in our own boat. Neither of us will try to steer the other's vessel.

The vision of the Gus–Wen–Tah can be found inscribed throughout the *corpora* of documents relating the American Indians' legal and political thought and discourse. At the core of this Americanized vision of law is the idea that freedom requires different peoples to respect each other's vision of how their respective vessels should be steered.

The Doctrine of Discovery, with its denial of territorial and self-determination rights for indigenous peoples equal to the rights of Western peoples, works to deny respect to the Indians' visions in numerous ways. Certainly one of the most threatening is its denial of their right to an equal voice as peoples on the world stage. Under the Doctrine of Discovery, indigenous peoples' complaints of human-rights abuses and demands for territorial protection and self-determination are regarded as matters of exclusive domestic concern within the conqueror's courts and political system. Thus the West's present rule of law denies indigenous peoples an international status in their struggles for survival in the modern world. Such a status could provide indigenous peoples with ready and immediate access to international legal and political forums. Then, indigenous peoples themselves could voice their visions of their rights before the world and seek protection and preservation through means other than those provided by a conqueror's rule of law and its discourses of conquest.

History records that acts of genocide are most easily concealed in a world atmosphere of complicitous silence; a people is extinguished with a whimper, not a bang. An equal voice would certainly not necessarily guarantee the continued protection and preservation of the centuries-old visions of tribal peoples. Denying that voice, however, would most assuredly assist the efforts of those in power who seek the silent liquidation of colonized tribal peoples.

Whether from stupidity or shame, those Western-derived colonial sovereignties that continue to rely on Western-derived legal discourse as a shield against tribal peoples' assertions of abuses of fundamental human rights would conveniently have the world forget that the anachronistic premises at the core of their discursive practices once unquestioningly legitimated the use of the sword against indigenous nations. That tribal nations have not forgotten the history of conquest justified by Western legal thought and discourse explains why indigenous peoples now seek to redefine radically the conceptions of their rights and status in international and domestic legal forums. Pushed to the brink of extinction by the premises inherent in the West's vision of the world and the Indians' lack of a place in that world, contemporary tribalism recognizes the compelling necessity of articulating and defining its own vision within the global community. Only then, in the free play by which a shared global discourse may evolve, can tribalism's differently oriented vision be fairly considered as something other than an anachronistic inconvenience to the West's relentless, consumption-oriented world view. But such a discourse, with its potential for broadening perspectives on our human condition, is currently suppressed by a set of medievally derived prior restraints. Discourses of conquest, grounded in archaic, racist ideas that, once revealed, could not be redeemed by those who relied on them, continue to be asserted today by the West to deny respect to the Indians' vision.

SCOTT v. SANDFORD

Supreme Court of the United States, 1856.
60 U.S. 393, 15 L.Ed. 691.

MR. CHIEF JUSTICE TANEY delivered the opinion of the court....

The plaintiff in error, who was also the plaintiff in the court below, was, with his wife and children, held as slaves by the defendant, in the State of Missouri; and he brought this action in the Circuit Court of the United States for that district, to assert the title of himself and his family to freedom.

The declaration ... contains the averment necessary to give the court jurisdiction; that he and the defendant are citizens of different States; that is, that he is a citizen of Missouri, and the defendant a citizen of New York....

The question is simply this: Can a negro, whose ancestors were imported into this country, and sold as slaves, become a member of the political community formed and brought into existence by the Constitution of the United States, and as such become entitled to all the rights, and privileges, and immunities, guarantied by that instrument to the citizen? One of which rights is the privilege of suing in a court of the United States in the cases specified in the Constitution.

It will be observed, that the plea applies to that class of persons only whose ancestors were negroes of the African race, and imported into this country, and sold and held as slaves. The only matter in issue before the court, therefore, is, whether the descendants of such slaves, when they shall be emancipated, or who are born of parents who had become free before their birth, are citizens of a State, in the sense in which the word citizen is used in the Constitution of the United States. And this being the only matter in dispute on the pleadings, the court must be understood as speaking in this opinion of that class only, that is, of those persons who are the descendants of Africans who were imported into this country, and sold as slaves.

The situation of this population was altogether unlike that of the Indian race. The latter, it is true, formed no part of the colonial communities, and never amalgamated with them in social connections or in government. But although they were uncivilized, they were yet a free and independent people, associated together in nations or tribes, and governed by their own laws. Many of these political communities were situated in territories to which the white race claimed the ultimate right of dominion. But that claim was acknowledged to be subject to the right of the Indians to occupy it as long as they thought proper, and neither the English nor colonial Governments claimed or exercised any dominion over the tribe or nation by whom it was occupied, nor claimed the right to the possession of the territory, until the tribe or nation consented to cede it. These Indian Governments were regarded and treated as foreign Governments, as much so as if an ocean had separated the red man from the white; and their freedom has constantly been acknowledged, from the time of the first emigration to the English colonies to the present day, by the different Governments which succeeded each other. Treaties have been negotiated with them, and their alliance sought for in war; and the people who compose these Indian political communities have always been treated as foreigners not living under our Government. It is true that the course of events has brought the Indian tribes within the limits of the United States under subjection to the white race; and it has been found necessary, for their sake as well as our own, to regard them as in a state of pupilage, and to legislate to a certain extent over them and the territory they occupy. But they may, without doubt, like the subjects of any other foreign Government, be naturalized by the authority of Congress, and become citizens of a State, and of the United States; and if an individual should leave his nation or tribe, and take up his abode among the white population, he would be entitled to all the rights and privileges which would belong to an emigrant from any other foreign people....

The words "people of the United States" and "citizens" are synonymous terms, and mean the same thing. They both describe the political body who, according to our republican institutions, form the sovereignty, and who hold the power and conduct the Government through their representatives. They are what we familiarly call the "sovereign people," and every citizen is one of this people, and a constituent member of this sovereignty. The question before us is, whether the class of persons described in the plea in abatement compose a portion of this people, and are constituent members of this sovereignty? We think they are not, and that they are not included, and were not intended to be included, under the word "citizens" in the Constitution, and can therefore claim none of the rights and privileges which that instrument provides for and secures to citizens of the United States. On the contrary, they were at that time considered as a subordinate and inferior class of beings, who had been subjugated by the dominant race, and, whether emancipated or not, yet remained subject to their authority, and had no rights or privileges but such as those who held the power and the Government might choose to grant them.

It is not the province of the court to decide upon the justice or injustice, the policy or impolicy, of these laws. The decision of that question belonged to the political or law-making power; to those who formed the sovereignty and framed the Constitution. The duty of the court is, to interpret the instrument they have framed, with the best lights we can obtain on the subject, and to administer it as we find it, according to its true intent and meaning when it was adopted.

In discussing this question, we must not confound the rights of citizenship which a State may confer within its own limits, and the rights of citizenship as a member of the Union....

It is very clear, ... that no State can, by any act or law of its own, passed since the adoption of the Constitution, introduce a new member into the political community created by the Constitution of the United States. It cannot make him a member of this community by making him a member of its own. And for the same reason it cannot introduce any person, or description of persons, who were not intended to be embraced in this new political family, which the Constitution brought into existence, but were intended to be excluded from it.

The question then arises, whether the provisions of the Constitution, in relation to the personal rights and privileges to which the citizen of a State should be entitled, embraced the negro African race, at that time in this country, or who might afterwards be imported, who had then or should afterwards be made free in any State; and to put it in the power of a single State to make him a citizen of the United States, and endue him with the full rights of citizenship in every other State without their consent? Does the Constitution of the United States act upon him whenever he shall be made free under the laws of a State, and raised there to the rank of a citizen, and immediately clothe him with all the privileges of a citizen in every other State, and in its own courts?

The court think the affirmative of these propositions cannot be maintained. And if it cannot, the plaintiff in error could not be a citizen of the State of Missouri, within the meaning of the Constitution of the United States, and, consequently, was not entitled to sue in its courts.

It is true, every person, and every class and description of persons, who were at the time of the adoption of the Constitution recognised as citizens in the several States, became also citizens of this new political body; but none other; it was formed by them, and for them and their posterity, but for no one else. And the personal rights and privileges guarantied to citizens of this new sovereignty were intended to embrace those only who were then members of the several State communities, or who should afterwards by birthright or otherwise become members, according to the provisions of the Constitution and the principles on which it was founded. It was the union of those who were at that time members of distinct and separate political communities into one political family, whose power, for certain specified purposes, was to extend over the whole territory of the United States. And it gave to each citizen rights and privileges outside of his State which he did not before possess, and placed him in every other State upon a perfect equality with its own citizens as to rights of person and rights of property; it made him a citizen of the United States.

It becomes necessary, therefore, to determine who were citizens of the several States when the Constitution was adopted. And in order to do this, we must recur to the Governments and institutions of the thirteen colonies, when they separated from Great Britain and formed new sovereignties, and took their places in the family of independent nations. We must inquire who, at that time, were recognised as the people or citizens of a State, whose rights and liberties had been outraged by the English Government; and who declared their independence, and assumed the powers of Government to defend their rights by force of arms.

In the opinion of the court, the legislation and histories of the times, and the language used in the Declaration of Independence, show, that neither the class of persons who had been imported as slaves, nor their descendants, whether they had become free or not, were then acknowledged as a part of the people, nor intended to be included in the general words used in that memorable instrument.

It is difficult at this day to realize the state of public opinion in relation to that unfortunate race, which prevailed in the civilized and enlightened portions of the world at the time of the Declaration of Independence, and when the Constitution of the United States was framed and adopted. But the public history of every European nation displays it in a manner too plain to be mistaken.

They had for more than a century before been regarded as beings of an inferior order, and altogether unfit to associate with the white race, either in social or political relations; and so far inferior, that they had no rights which the white man was bound to respect; and that the negro might justly and lawfully be reduced to slavery for his benefit. He was bought and sold, and treated as an ordinary article of merchandise and traffic, whenever a profit could be made by it. This opinion was at that time fixed and universal in the civilized portion of the white race. It was regarded as an axiom in morals as well as in politics, which no one thought of disputing, or supposed to be open to dispute; and men in every grade and position in society daily and habitually acted upon it in their private pursuits, as well as in matters of public concern, without doubting for a moment the correctness of this opinion.

And in no nation was this opinion more firmly fixed or more uniformly acted upon than by the English Government and English people. They not only seized them on the coast of Africa, and sold them or held them in slavery for their own use; but they took them as ordinary articles of merchandise to every country where they could make a profit on them, and were far more extensively engaged in this commerce than any other nation in the world.

The opinion thus entertained and acted upon in England was naturally impressed upon the colonies they founded on this side of the Atlantic. And, accordingly, a negro of the African race was regarded by them as an article of property, and held, and bought and sold as such, in every one of the thirteen colonies which united in the Declaration of Independence, and afterwards formed the Constitution of the United States. The slaves were more or less numerous in the different colonies, as slave labor was found more or less profitable. But no one seems to have doubted the correctness of the prevailing opinion of the time.

The legislation of the different colonies furnishes positive and indisputable proof of this fact.

It would be tedious, in this opinion, to enumerate the various laws they passed upon this subject. It will be sufficient, as a sample of the legislation which then generally prevailed throughout the British colonies, to give the laws of two of them; one being still a large slaveholding State, and the other the first State in which slavery ceased to exist.

The province of Maryland, in 1717, (ch. 13, § 5,) passed a law declaring "that if any free negro or mulatto intermarry with any white woman, or if any white man shall intermarry with any negro or mulatto woman, such negro or mulatto shall become a slave during life, excepting mulattoes born of white women, who, for such intermarriage, shall only become servants for seven years, to be disposed of as the justices of the county court, where such marriage so happens, shall think fit; to be applied by them towards the support of a public school within the said county. And any white man or white woman who shall intermarry as aforesaid, with any negro or mulatto, such white man or white woman shall become servants during the term of seven years, and shall be disposed of by the justices as aforesaid, and be applied to the uses aforesaid."

The other colonial law to which we refer was passed by Massachusetts in 1705, (chap. 6.) It is entitled "An act for the better preventing of a spurious and mixed issue," &c.; and it provides, that "if any negro or mulatto shall presume to smite or strike any person of the English or other Christian nation, such negro or mulatto shall be severely whipped, at the discretion of the justices before whom the offender shall be convicted."

And "that none of her Majesty's English or Scottish subjects, nor of any other Christian nation, within this province, shall contract matrimony with any negro or mulatto; nor shall any person, duly authorized to solemnize marriage, presume to join any such in marriage, on pain of forfeiting the sum of fifty pounds; one moiety thereof to her Majesty, for and towards the support of the government within this province, and the other moiety to him or them that shall inform and sue for the same, in any of her Majesty's courts of record within the province, by bill, plaint, or information."

We give both of these laws in the words used by the respective legislative bodies, because the language in which they are framed, as well as the provisions contained in them, show, too plainly to be misunderstood, the degraded condition of this unhappy race. They were still in force when the Revolution began, and are a faithful index to the state of feeling towards the class of persons of whom they speak, and of the position they occupied throughout the thirteen colonies, in the eyes and thoughts of the men who framed the Declaration of Independence and established the State Constitutions and Governments. They show that a perpetual and impassable barrier was intended to be erected between the white race and the one which they had reduced to slavery, and governed as subjects with absolute and despotic power, and which they then looked upon as so far below them in the scale of created beings, that intermarriages between white persons and negroes or mulattoes were regarded as unnatural and immoral, and punished as crimes, not only in the parties, but in the person who joined them in marriage. And no distinction in this respect was made between the free negro or mulatto and the slave, but this stigma, of the deepest degradation, was fixed upon the whole race.

We refer to these historical facts for the purpose of showing the fixed opinions concerning that race, upon which the statesmen of that day spoke and acted. It is necessary to do this, in order to determine whether the general terms used in the Constitution of the United States, as to the rights of man and the rights of the people, was intended to include them, or to give to them or their posterity the benefit of any of its provisions.

The language of the Declaration of Independence is equally conclusive:

It begins by declaring that, "when in the course of human events it becomes necessary for one people to dissolve the political bands which have connected them with another, and to assume among the powers of the earth the separate and equal station to which the laws of nature and nature's God entitle them, a decent respect for the opinions of mankind requires that they should declare the causes which impel them to the separation."

It then proceeds to say: "We hold these truths to be self-evident: that all men are created equal; that they are endowed by their Creator with certain unalienable rights; that among them is life, liberty, and the pursuit of happiness; that to secure these rights, Governments are instituted, deriving their just powers from the consent of the governed."

The general words above quoted would seem to embrace the whole human family, and if they were used in a similar instrument at this day would be so understood. But it is too clear for dispute, that the enslaved African race were not intended to be included, and formed no part of the people who framed and adopted this declaration; for if the language, as understood in that day, would embrace them, the conduct of the distinguished men who framed the Declaration of Independence would have been utterly and flagrantly inconsistent with the principles they asserted; and instead of the sympathy of mankind, to which they so confidently appealed, they would have deserved and received universal rebuke and reprobation.

Yet the men who framed this declaration were great men—high in literary acquirements—high in their sense of honor, and incapable of asserting principles inconsistent with those on which they were acting. They perfectly understood the meaning of the language they used, and how it would be understood by others; and they knew that it would not in any part of the civilized world be supposed to embrace the negro race, which, by common consent, had been excluded from civilized Governments and the family of nations, and doomed to slavery. They spoke and acted according to the then established doctrines and principles, and in the ordinary language of the day, and no one misunderstood them. The unhappy black race were separated from the white by indelible marks, and laws long before established, and were never thought of or spoken of except as property, and when the claims of the owner or the profit of the trader were supposed to need protection.

This state of public opinion had undergone no change when the Constitution was adopted, as is equally evident from its provisions and language.

The brief preamble sets forth by whom it was formed, for what purposes, and for whose benefit and protection. It declares that it is formed by the people of the United States; that is to say, by those who were members of the different political communities in the several States; and its great object is declared to be to secure the blessings of liberty to themselves and their posterity. It speaks in general terms of the people of the United States, and of citizens of the several States, when it is providing for the exercise of the powers granted or the privileges secured to the citizen. It does not define what description of persons are intended to be included under these terms, or who shall be regarded as a citizen and one of the people. It uses them as terms so well understood, that no further description or definition was necessary.

But there are two clauses in the Constitution which point directly and specifically to the negro race as a separate class of persons, and show clearly that they were not regarded as a portion of the people or citizens of the Government then formed.

One of these clauses reserves to each of the thirteen States the right to import slaves until the year 1808, if it thinks proper. And the importation which it thus sanctions was unquestionably of persons of the race of which we are speaking, as the traffic in slaves in the United States had always been confined to them. And by the other provision the States pledge themselves to each other to maintain the right of property of the master, by delivering up to him any slave who may have escaped from his service, and be found within their respective territories. By the first above-mentioned clause, therefore, the right to purchase and hold this property is directly sanctioned and authorized for twenty years by the people who framed the Constitution. And by the second, they pledge themselves to maintain and uphold the right of the master in the manner specified, as long as the Government they then formed should endure. And these two provisions show, conclusively, that neither the description of persons therein referred to, nor their descendants, were embraced in any of the other provisions of the Constitution; for certainly these two clauses were not intended to confer on them or their posterity the blessings of liberty, or any of the personal rights so carefully provided for the citizen.

No one of that race had ever migrated to the United States voluntarily; all of them had been brought here as articles of merchandise. The number that had been emancipated at that time were but few in comparison with those held in slavery; and they were identified in the public mind with the race to which they belonged, and regarded as a part of the slave population rather than the free. It is obvious that they were not even in the minds of the framers of the Constitution when they were conferring special rights and privileges upon the citizens of a State in every other part of the Union.

Indeed, when we look to the condition of this race in the several States at the time, it is impossible to believe that these rights and privileges were intended to be extended to them.

It is very true, that in that portion of the Union where the labor of the negro race was found to be unsuited to the climate and unprofitable to the master, but few slaves were held at the time of the Declaration of Independence; and when the Constitution was adopted, it had entirely worn out in one of them, and measures had been taken for its gradual abolition in several others. But this change had not been produced by any change of opinion in relation to this race; but because it was discovered, from experience, that slave labor was unsuited to the climate and productions of these States: for some of the States, where it had ceased or nearly ceased to exist, were actively engaged in the slave trade, procuring cargoes on the coast of Africa, and transporting them for sale to those parts of the Union where their labor was found to be profitable, and suited to the climate and productions. And this traffic was openly carried on, and fortunes accumulated by it, without reproach from the people of the States where they resided. And it can hardly be supposed that, in the States where it was then countenanced in its worst form— that is, in the seizure and transportation—the people could have regarded those who were emancipated as entitled to equal rights with themselves.

And we may here again refer, in support of this proposition, to the plain and unequivocal language of the laws of the several States, some passed after the Declaration of Independence and before the Constitution was adopted, and some since the Government went into operation.

We need not refer, on this point, particularly to the laws of the present slaveholding States. Their statute books are full of provisions in relation to this class, in the same spirit with the Maryland law which we have before quoted. They have continued to treat them as an inferior class, and to subject them to strict police regulations, drawing a broad line of distinction between the citizen and the slave races, and legislating in relation to them upon the same principle which prevailed at the time of the Declaration of Independence. As relates to these States, it is too plain for argument, that they have never been regarded as a part of the people or citizens of the State, nor supposed to possess any political rights which the dominant race might not withhold or grant at their pleasure. And as long ago as 1822, the Court of Appeals of Kentucky decided that free negroes and mulattoes were not citizens within the meaning of the Constitution of the United States; . . .

And if we turn to the legislation of the States where slavery had worn out, or measures taken for its speedy abolition, we shall find the same opinions and principles equally fixed and equally acted upon. . . .

It would be impossible to enumerate and compress in the space usually allotted to an opinion of a court, the various laws, marking the condition of this race, which were passed from time to time after the Revolution, and before and since the adoption of the Constitution of the United States. In addition to those already referred to, it is sufficient to say, that Chancellor Kent, whose accuracy and research no one will question, states in the sixth edition of his Commentaries, (published in 1848, 2 vol., 258, note b,) that in no part of the country except Maine, did the African race, in point of fact, participate equally with the whites in the exercise of civil and political rights.

The legislation of the States therefore shows, in a manner not to be mistaken, the inferior and subject condition of that race at the time the Constitution was adopted, and long afterwards, throughout the thirteen States by which that instrument was framed; and it is hardly consistent with the respect due to these States, to suppose that they regarded at that time, as fellow-citizens and members of the sovereignty, a class of beings whom they had thus stigmatized; whom, as we are bound, out of respect to the State sovereignties, to assume they had deemed it just and necessary thus to stigmatize, and upon whom they had impressed such deep and enduring marks of inferiority and degradation; or, that when they met in convention to form the Constitution, they looked upon them as a portion of their constituents, or designed to include them in the provisions so carefully inserted for the security and protection of the liberties and rights of their citizens. It cannot be supposed that they intended to secure to them rights, and privileges, and rank, in the new political body throughout the Union, which every one of them denied within the limits of its own dominion. More especially, it cannot be believed that the large slaveholding States regarded them as included in the word citizens, or would have consented to a Constitution which might compel them to receive them in that character from another State. For if they were so received, and entitled to the privileges and immunities of citizens, it would exempt them from the operation of the special laws and from the police regulations which they considered to be necessary for their own safety. It would give to persons of the negro race, who were recognised as citizens in any one State of the Union, the right to enter every other State whenever they pleased, singly or in companies, without pass or passport, and without obstruction, to sojourn there as long as they pleased, to go where they pleased at every hour of the day or night without molestation, unless they committed some violation of law for which a white man would be punished; and it would give them the full liberty of speech in public and in private upon all subjects upon which its own citizens might speak; to hold public meetings upon political affairs, and to keep and carry arms wherever they went. And all of this would be done in the face of the subject race of the same color, both free and slaves, and inevitably producing discontent and insubordination among them, and endangering the peace and safety of the State.

It is impossible, it would seem, to believe that the great men of the slaveholding States, who took so large a share in framing the Constitution of the United States, and exercised so much influence in procuring its adoption, could have been so forgetful or regardless of their own safety and the safety of those who trusted and confided in them.

Besides, this want of foresight and care would have been utterly inconsistent with the caution displayed in providing for the admission of new members into this political family. For, when they gave to the citizens of each State the privileges and immunities of citizens in the several States, they at the same time took from the several States the power of naturalization, and confined that power exclusively to the Federal Government. No State was willing to permit another State to determine who should or should not be admitted as one of its citizens, and entitled to demand equal rights and privileges with their own people, within their own territories. The right of naturalization was therefore, with one accord, surrendered by the States, and confided to the Federal Government. And this power granted to Congress to establish an uniform rule of naturalization is, by the well-understood meaning of the word, confined to persons born in a foreign country, under a foreign Government. It is not a power to raise to the rank of a citizen any one born in the United States, who, from birth or parentage, by the laws of the country, belongs to an inferior and subordinate class. And when we find the States guarding themselves from the indiscreet or improper admission by other States of emigrants from other countries, by giving the power exclusively to Congress, we cannot fail to see that they could never have left with the States a much more important power—that is, the power of transforming into citizens a numerous class of persons, who in that character would be much more dangerous to the peace and safety of a large portion of the Union, than the few foreigners one of the States might improperly naturalize. The Constitution upon its adoption obviously took from the States all power by any subsequent legislation to introduce as a citizen into the political family of the United States any one, no matter where he was born, or what might be his character or condition; and it gave to Congress the power to confer this character upon those only who were born outside of the dominions of the United States. And no law of a State, therefore, passed since the Constitution was adopted, can give any right of citizenship outside of its own territory. . . .

To all this mass of proof we have still to add, that Congress has repeatedly legislated upon the same construction of the Constitution that we have given. Three laws, two of which were passed almost immediately after the Government went into operation, will be abundantly sufficient to show this. The two first are particularly worthy of notice, because many of the men who assisted in framing the Constitution, and took an active part in procuring its adoption, were then in the halls of legislation, and certainly understood what they meant when they used the words "people of the United States" and "citizen" in that well-considered instrument.

The first of these acts is the naturalization law, which was passed at the second session of the first Congress, March 26, 1790, and confines the right of becoming citizens "to aliens being free white persons."

Now, the Constitution does not limit the power of Congress in this respect to white persons. And they may, if they think proper, authorize the naturalization of any one, of any color, who was born under allegiance to another Government. But the language of the law above quoted, shows that citizenship at that time was perfectly understood to be confined to the white race; and that they alone constituted the sovereignty in the Government.

Congress might, as we before said, have authorized the naturalization of Indians, because they were aliens and foreigners. But, in their then untutored and savage state, no one would have thought of admitting them as citizens in a civilized community. And, moreover, the atrocities they had but recently committed, when they were the allies of Great Britain in the Revolutionary war, were yet fresh in the recollection of the people of the United States, and they were even then guarding themselves against the threatened renewal of Indian hostilities. No one supposed then that any Indian would ask for, or was capable of enjoying, the privileges of an American citizen, and the word white was not used with any particular reference to them.

Neither was it used with any reference to the African race imported into or born in this country; because Congress had no power to naturalize them, and therefore there was no necessity for using particular words to exclude them.

It would seem to have been used merely because it followed out the line of division which the Constitution has drawn between the citizen race, who formed and held the Government, and the African race, which they held in subjection and slavery, and governed at their own pleasure.

Another of the early laws of which we have spoken, is the first militia law, which was passed in 1792, at the first session of the second Congress. The language of this law is equally plain and significant with the one just mentioned. It directs that every "free able-bodied white male citizen" shall be enrolled in the militia. The word white is evidently used to exclude the African race, and the word "citizen" to exclude unnaturalized foreigners; the latter forming no part of the sovereignty, owing it no allegiance, and therefore under no obligation to defend it. The African race, however, born in the country, did owe allegiance to the Government, whether they were slave or free; but it is repudiated, and rejected from the duties and obligations of citizenship in marked language.

The third act to which we have alluded is even still more decisive; it was passed as late as 1813, (2 Stat., 809,) and it provides: "That from and after the termination of the war in which the United States are now engaged with Great Britain, it shall not be lawful to employ, on board of any public or private vessels of the United States, any person or persons except citizens of the United States, or persons of color, natives of the United States."

Here the line of distinction is drawn in express words. Persons of color, in the judgment of Congress, were not included in the word citizens, and they are described as another and different class of persons, and authorized to be employed, if born in the United States.

And even as late as 1820, (chap. 104, sec. 8,) in the charter to the city of Washington, the corporation is authorized "to restrain and prohibit the nightly and other disorderly meetings of slaves, free negroes, and mulattoes," thus associating them together in its legislation; and after prescribing the punishment that may be inflicted on the slaves, proceeds in the following words: "And to punish such free negroes and mulattoes by penalties not exceeding twenty dollars for any one offence; and in case of the inability of any such free negro or mulatto to pay any such penalty and cost thereon, to cause him or her to be confined to labor for any time not exceeding six calendar months." And in a subsequent part of the same section, the act authorizes the corporation "to prescribe the terms and conditions upon which free negroes and mulattoes may reside in the city."

This law, like the laws of the States, shows that this class of persons were governed by special legislation directed expressly to them, and always connected with provisions for the government of slaves, and not with those for the government of free white citizens. And after such an uniform course of legislation as we have stated, by the colonies, by the

States, and by Congress, running through a period of more than a century, it would seem that to call persons thus marked and stigmatized, "citizens" of the United States, "fellow-citizens," a constituent part of the sovereignty, would be an abuse of terms, and not calculated to exalt the character of an American citizen in the eyes of other nations.

The conduct of the Executive Department of the Government has been in perfect harmony upon this subject with this course of legislation. The question was brought officially before the late William Wirt, when he was the Attorney General of the United States, in 1821, and he decided that the words "citizens of the United States" were used in the acts of Congress in the same sense as in the Constitution; and that free persons of color were not citizens, within the meaning of the Constitution and laws; and this opinion has been confirmed by that of the late Attorney General, Caleb Cushing, in a recent case, and acted upon by the Secretary of State, who refused to grant passports to them as "citizens of the United States."

But it is said that a person may be a citizen, and entitled to that character, although he does not possess all the rights which may belong to other citizens; as, for example, the right to vote, or to hold particular offices; and that yet, when he goes into another State, he is entitled to be recognised there as a citizen, although the State may measure his rights by the rights which it allows to persons of a like character or class resident in the State, and refuse to him the full rights of citizenship.

This argument overlooks the language of the provision in the Constitution of which we are speaking.

Undoubtedly, a person may be a citizen, that is, a member of the community who form the sovereignty, although he exercises no share of the political power, and is incapacitated from holding particular offices. Women and minors, who form a part of the political family, cannot vote; and when a property qualification is required to vote or hold a particular office, those who have not the necessary qualification cannot vote or hold the office, yet they are citizens.

So, too, a person may be entitled to vote by the law of the State, who is not a citizen even of the State itself. And in some of the States of the Union foreigners not naturalized are allowed to vote. And the State may give the right to free negroes and mulattoes, but that does not make them citizens of the State, and still less of the United States. And the provision in the Constitution giving privileges and immunities in other States, does not apply to them.

Neither does it apply to a person who, being the citizen of a State, migrates to another State. For then he becomes subject to the laws of the State in which he lives, and he is no longer a citizen of the State from which he removed. And the State in which he resides may then, unquestionably, determine his status or condition, and place him among the class of persons who are not recognised as citizens, but belong to an inferior and subject race; and may deny him the privileges and immunities enjoyed by its citizens.

But so far as mere rights of person are concerned, the provision in question is confined to citizens of a State who are temporarily in another State without taking up their residence there. It gives them no political rights in the State, as to voting or holding office, or in any other respect. For a citizen of one State has no right to participate in the government of another. But if he ranks as a citizen in the State to which he belongs, within the meaning of the Constitution of the United States, then, whenever he goes into another State, the Constitution clothes him, as to the rights of person, will all the privileges and immunities which belong to citizens of the State. And if persons of the African race are citizens of a State, and of the United States, they would be entitled to all of these privileges and immunities in every State, and the State could not restrict them; for they would hold these privileges and immunities under the paramount authority of the Federal Government, and its courts would be bound to maintain and enforce them, the Constitution and laws of the State to the contrary notwithstanding. And if the States could limit or restrict them, or place the party in an inferior grade, this clause of the Constitution would be unmeaning, and could have no operation; and would give no rights to the citizen when in another State. He would have none but what the State itself chose to allow him. This is evidently not the construction or meaning of the clause in question. It guaranties rights to the citizen, and the State cannot withhold them. And these rights are of a character and would lead to consequences which make it absolutely certain that the African race were not included under the name of citizens of a State, and were not in the contemplation of the framers of the Constitution when these privileges and immunities were provided for the protection of the citizen in other States. . . .

MR. JUSTICE MCLEAN dissenting. . . .

There is no averment in this plea which shows or conduces to show an inability in the plaintiff to sue in the Circuit Court. It does not allege that the plaintiff had his domicil in any other State, nor that he is not a free man in Missouri. He is averred to have had a negro ancestry, but this does not show that he is not a citizen of Missouri, within the meaning of the act of Congress authorizing him to sue in the Circuit Court. It has never been held necessary, to constitute a citizen within the act, that he should have the qualifications of an elector. Females and minors may sue in the Federal courts, and so may any individual who has a permanent domicil in the State under whose laws his rights are protected, and to which he owes allegiance.

Being born under our Constitution and laws, no naturalization is required, as one of foreign birth, to make him a citizen. The most general and appropriate definition of the term citizen is "a freeman." Being a freeman, and having his domicil in a State different from that of the defendant, he is a citizen within the act of Congress, and the courts of the Union are open to him. . . .

In the argument, it was said that a colored citizen would not be an agreeable member of society. This is more a matter of taste than of law. Several of the States have admitted persons of color to the right of suffrage, and in this view have recognised them as citizens; and this has been done in the slave as well as the free States.... Our independence was a great epoch in the history of freedom; and while I admit the Government was not made especially for the colored race, yet many of them were citizens of the New England States, and exercised, the rights of suffrage when the Constitution was adopted, and it was not doubted by any intelligent person that its tendencies would greatly ameliorate their condition.

Many of the States, on the adoption of the Constitution, or shortly afterward, took measures to abolish slavery within their respective jurisdictions; and it is a well-known fact that a belief was cherished by the leading men, South as well as North, that the institution of slavery would gradually decline, until it would become extinct. The increased value of slave labor, in the culture of cotton and sugar, prevented the realization of this expectation. Like all other communities and States, the South were influenced by what they considered to be their own interests.

But if we are to turn our attention to the dark ages of the world, why confine our view to colored slavery? On the same principles, white men were made slaves. All slavery has its origin in power, and is against right....

Mr. Justice Curtis dissenting ...

It has been often asserted that the Constitution was made exclusively by and for the white race. It has already been shown that in five of the thirteen original States, colored persons then possessed the elective franchise, and were among those by whom the Constitution was ordained and established. If so, it is not true, in point of fact, that the Constitution was made exclusively by the white race. And that it was made exclusively for the white race is, in my opinion, not only an assumption not warranted by anything in the Constitution, but contradicted by its opening declaration, that it was ordained and established by the people of the United States, for themselves and their posterity. And as free colored persons were then citizens of at least five States, and so in every sense part of the people of the United States, they were among those for whom and whose posterity the Constitution was ordained and established....

It has been further objected, that if free colored persons, born within a particular State, and made citizens of that State by its Constitution and laws, are thereby made citizens of the United States, then, under the second section of the fourth article of the Constitution, such persons would be entitled to all the privileges and immunities of citizens in the several States; and if so, then colored persons could vote, and be eligible to not only Federal offices, but offices even in those States whose

Constitution and laws disqualify colored persons from voting or being elected to office.

But this position rests upon an assumption which I deem untenable. Its basis is, that no one can be deemed a citizen of the United States who is not entitled to enjoy all the privileges and franchises which are conferred on any citizen. That this is not true, under the Constitution of the United States, seems to me clear.

A naturalized citizen cannot be President of the United States, nor a Senator till after the lapse of nine years, nor a Representative till after the lapse of seven years, from his naturalization. Yet, as soon as naturalized, he is certainly a citizen of the United States. Nor is any inhabitant of the District of Columbia, or of either of the Territories, eligible to the office of Senator or Representative in Congress, though they may be citizens of the United States. So, in all the States, numerous persons, though citizens, cannot vote, or cannot hold office, either on account of their age, or sex, or the want of the necessary legal qualifications. The truth is, that citizenship, under the Constitution of the United States, is not dependent on the possession of any particular political or even of all civil rights; and any attempt so to define it must lead to error. To what citizens the elective franchise shall be confided, is a question to be determined by each State, in accordance with its own views of the necessities or expediencies of its condition. What civil rights shall be enjoyed by its citizens, and whether all shall enjoy the same, or how they may be gained or lost, are to be determined in the same way....

The conclusions at which I have arrived ... are:

First. That the free native-born citizens of each State are citizens of the United States.

Second. That as free colored persons born within some of the States are citizens of those States, such persons are also citizens of the United States.

Third. That every such citizen, residing in any State, has the right to sue and is liable to be sued in the Federal courts, as a citizen of that State in which he resides.

Fourth. That as the plea to the jurisdiction in this case shows no facts, except that the plaintiff was of African descent, and his ancestors were sold as slaves, and as these facts are not inconsistent with his citizenship of the United States, and his residence in the State of Missouri....

I dissent, therefore, from that part of the opinion of the majority of the court, in which it is held that a person of African descent cannot be a citizen of the United States....

PLESSY v. FERGUSON

Supreme Court of the United States, 1896.
163 U.S. 537, 16 S.Ct. 1138, 41 L.Ed. 256.

MR. JUSTICE BROWN, delivered the opinion of the court.

This case turns upon the constitutionality of an act of the general assembly of the state of Louisiana, passed in 1890, providing for separate railway carriages for the white and colored races. . . .

The petition for the writ of prohibition averred that petitioner was seven-eighths Caucasian and one-eighth African blood; that the mixture of colored blood was not discernible in him; and that he was entitled to every right, privilege, and immunity secured to citizens of the United States of the white race; and that, upon such theory, he took possession of a vacant seat in a coach where passengers of the white race were accommodated, and was ordered by the conductor to vacate said coach, and take a seat in another, assigned to persons of the colored race, and, having refused to comply with such demand, he was forcibly ejected, with the aid of a police officer, and imprisoned in the parish jail to answer a charge of having violated the above act.

The constitutionality of this act is attacked upon the ground that it conflicts both with the thirteenth amendment of the constitution, abolishing slavery, and the fourteenth amendment, which prohibits certain restrictive legislation on the part of the states.

1. That it does not conflict with the thirteenth amendment, which abolished slavery and involuntary servitude, except as a punishment for crime, is too clear for argument. Slavery implies involuntary servitude,—a state of bondage; the ownership of mankind as a chattel, or, at least, the control of the labor and services of one man for the benefit of another, and the absence of a legal right to the disposal of his own person, property, and services. This amendment was said in the Slaughter–House Cases, 16 Wall. 36, to have been intended primarily to abolish slavery, as it had been previously known in this country, and that it equally forbade Mexican peonage or the Chinese coolie trade, when they amounted to slavery or involuntary servitude, and that the use of the word "servitude" was intended to prohibit the use of all forms of involuntary slavery, of whatever class or name. It was intimated, however, in that case, that this amendment was regarded by the statesmen of that day as insufficient to protect the colored race from certain laws which had been enacted in the Southern states, imposing upon the colored race onerous disabilities and burdens, and curtailing their rights in the pursuit of life, liberty, and property to such an extent that their freedom was of little value; and that the fourteenth amendment was devised to meet this exigency.

So, too, in the Civil Rights Cases, 109 U.S. 3, 3 Sup.Ct. 18, it was said that the act of a mere individual, the owner of an inn, a public conveyance or place of amusement, refusing accommodations to colored people, cannot be justly regarded as imposing any badge of slavery or servitude upon the applicant, but only as involving an ordinary civil injury, properly cognizable by the laws of the state, and presumably subject to redress by those laws until the contrary appears. "It would be running the slavery question into the ground," said Mr. Justice Bradley, "to make it apply to every act of discrimination which a person may see fit to make as to the guests he will entertain, or as to the people he will take into his coach or cab or car, or admit to his concert or theater, or deal with in other matters of intercourse or business."

A statute which implies merely a legal distinction between the white and colored races—a distinction which is founded in the color of the two races, and which must always exist so long as white men are distinguished from the other race by color—has no tendency to destroy the legal equality of the two races, or re-establish a state of involuntary servitude. . . .

2. By the fourteenth amendment, all persons born or naturalized in the United States, and subject to the jurisdiction thereof, are made citizens of the United States and of the state wherein they reside; and the states are forbidden from making or enforcing any law which shall abridge the privileges or immunities of citizens of the United States, or shall deprive any person of life, liberty, or property without due process of law, or deny to any person within their jurisdiction the equal protection of the laws. . . .

The object of the amendment was undoubtedly to enforce the absolute equality of the two races before the law, but, in the nature of things, it could not have been intended to abolish distinctions based upon color, or to enforce social, as distinguished from political, equality, or a commingling of the two races upon terms unsatisfactory to either. Laws permitting, and even requiring, their separation, in places where they are liable to be brought into contact, do not necessarily imply the inferiority of either race to the other, and have been generally, if not universally, recognized as within the competency of the state legislatures in the exercise of their police power. The most common instance of this is connected with the establishment of separate schools for white and colored children, which have been held to be a valid exercise of the legislative power even by courts of states where the political rights of the colored race have been longest and most earnestly enforced. . . .

Laws forbidding the intermarriage of the two races may be said in a technical sense to interfere with the freedom of contract, and yet have been universally recognized as within the police power of the state.

The distinction between laws interfering with the political equality of the negro and those requiring the separation of the two races in schools, theaters, and railway carriages has been frequently drawn by this court. . . .

It is claimed by the plaintiff in error that, in any mixed community, the reputation of belonging to the dominant race, in this instance the white race, is "property," in the same sense that a right of action or of inheritance is property. Conceding this to be so, for the purposes of this case, we are unable to see how this statute deprives him of, or in any way affects his right to, such property. If he be a white man, and assigned to a colored coach, he may have his action for damages against the company for being deprived of his so-called "property." Upon the other hand, if he be a colored man, and be so assigned, he has been deprived of no property, since he is not lawfully entitled to the reputation of being a white man.

In this connection, it is also suggested by the learned counsel for the plaintiff in error that the same argument that will justify the state legislature in requiring railways to provide separate accommodations for the two races will also authorize them to require separate cars to be provided for people whose hair is of a certain color, or who are aliens, or who belong to certain nationalities, or to enact laws requiring colored people to walk upon one side of the street, and white people upon the other, or requiring white men's houses to be painted white, and colored men's black, or their vehicles or business signs to be of different colors, upon the theory that one side of the street is as good as the other, or that a house or vehicle of one color is as good as one of another color. The reply to all this is that every exercise of the police power must be reasonable, and extend only to such laws as are enacted in good faith for the promotion of the public good, and not for the annoyance or oppression of a particular class. . . .

So far, then, as a conflict with the fourteenth amendment is concerned, the case reduces itself to the question whether the statute of Louisiana is a reasonable regulation, and with respect to this there must necessarily be a large discretion on the part of the legislature. In determining the question of reasonableness, it is at liberty to act with reference to the established usages, customs, and traditions of the people, and with a view to the promotion of their comfort, and the preservation of the public peace and good order. Gauged by this standard, we cannot say that a law which authorizes or even requires the separation of the two races in public conveyances is unreasonable, or more obnoxious to the fourteenth amendment than the acts of congress requiring separate schools for colored children in the District of Columbia, the constitutionality of which does not seem to have been questioned, or the corresponding acts of state legislatures.

We consider the underlying fallacy of the plaintiff's argument to consist in the assumption that the enforced separation of the two races stamps the colored race with a badge of inferiority. If this be so, it is not by reason of anything found in the act, but solely because the colored race chooses to put that construction upon it. The argument necessarily assumes that if, as has been more than once the case, and is not unlikely to be so again, the colored race should become the dominant power in the state legislature, and should enact a law in precisely similar terms, it would thereby relegate the white race to an inferior position. We imagine that the white race, at least, would not acquiesce in this assumption. The argument also assumes that social prejudices may be overcome by legislation, and that equal rights cannot be secured to the negro except by an enforced commingling of the two races. We cannot accept this proposition. If the two races are to meet upon terms of social equality, it must be the result of natural affinities, a mutual appreciation of each other's merits, and a voluntary consent of individuals. As was said by the court of appeals of New York in People v. Gallagher, 93 N.Y. 438, 448: "This end can neither be accomplished nor promoted by laws which conflict with the general sentiment of the community upon whom they are designed to operate. When the government, therefore, has secured to each of its citizens equal rights before the law, and equal opportunities for improvement and progress, it has accomplished the end for which it was organized, and performed all of the functions respecting social advantages with which it is endowed." Legislation is powerless to eradicate racial instincts, or to abolish distinctions based upon physical differences, and the attempt to do so can only result in accentuating the difficulties of the present situation. If the civil and political rights of both races be equal, one cannot be inferior to the other civilly or politically. If one race be inferior to the other socially, the constitution of the United States cannot put them upon the same plane.

It is true that the question of the proportion of colored blood necessary to constitute a colored person, as distinguished from a white person, is one upon which there is a difference of opinion in the different states; some holding that any visible admixture of black blood stamps the person as belonging to the colored race; others, that it depends upon the preponderance of blood, and still others, that the predominance of white blood must only be in the proportion of three-fourths. But these are questions to be determined under the laws of each state, and are not properly put in issue in this case. Under the allegations of his petition, it may undoubtedly become a question of importance whether, under the laws of Louisiana, the petitioner belongs to the white or colored race....

MR. JUSTICE HARLAN dissenting.

By the Louisiana statute the validity of which is here involved, all railway companies (other than street-railroad companies) carry passengers in that state are required to have separate but equal accommodations for white and colored persons, "by providing two or more passenger coaches for each passenger train, or by dividing the passenger coaches by a partition so as to secure separate accommodations."...

Only "nurses attending children of the other race" are excepted from the operation of the statute. No exception is made of colored attendants traveling with adults. A white man is not permitted to have his colored servant with him in the same coach, even if his condition of health requires the constant personal assistance of such servant. If a colored maid insists upon riding in the same coach with a white woman whom she has been employed to serve, and who may need her personal attention while traveling, she is subject to be fined or imprisoned for such an exhibition of zeal in the discharge of duty.

While there may be in Louisiana persons of different races who are not citizens of the United States, the words in the act "white and colored races" necessarily include all citizens of the United States of both races residing in that state. So that we have before us a state enactment that compels, under penalties, the separation of the two races in railroad passenger coaches, and makes it a crime for a citizen of either race to enter a coach that has been assigned to citizens of the other race....

However apparent the injustice of such legislation may be, we have only to consider whether it is consistent with the constitution of the United States....

In respect of civil rights, common to all citizens, the constitution of the United States does not, I think, permit any public authority to know the race of those entitled to be protected in the enjoyment of such rights. Every true man has pride of race, and under appropriate circumstances, when the rights of others, his equals before the law, are not to be affected, it is his privilege to express such pride and to take such action based upon it as to him seems proper. But I deny that any legislative body or judicial tribunal may have regard to the race of citizens when the civil rights of those citizens are involved. Indeed, such legislation as that here in question is inconsistent not only with that equality of rights which pertains to citizenship, national and state, but with the personal liberty enjoyed by every one within the United States....

These notable additions [Civil War Amendments] to the fundamental law were welcomed by the friends of liberty throughout the world. They removed the race line from our governmental systems. They had, as this court has said, a common purpose, namely, to secure "to a race recently emancipated, a race that through many generations have been held in slavery, all the civil rights that the superior race enjoy." They declared, in legal effect, this court has further said, "that the law in the states shall be the same for the black as for the white; that all persons, whether colored or white, shall stand equal before the laws of the states; and in regard to the colored race, for whose protection the amendment was primarily designed, that no discrimination shall be made against them by law because of their color." ...

It was said in argument that the statute of Louisiana does not discriminate against either race, but prescribes a rule applicable alike to white and colored citizens. But this argument does not meet the difficulty. Every one knows that the statute in question had its origin in the purpose, not so much to exclude white persons from railroad cars occupied by blacks, as to exclude colored people from coaches occupied by or assigned to white persons....

If a state can prescribe, as a rule of civil conduct, that whites and blacks shall not travel as passengers in the same railroad coach, why may it not so regulate the use of the streets of its cities and towns as to compel white citizens to keep on one side of a street, and black citizens to keep on the other? Why may it not, upon like grounds, punish whites and blacks who ride together in street cars or in open vehicles on a

public road or street? Why may it not require sheriffs to assign whites to one side of a court room, and blacks to the other? And why may it not also prohibit the commingling of the two races in the galleries of legislative halls or in public assemblages convened for the consideration of the political questions of the day? Further, if this statute of Louisiana is consistent with the personal liberty of citizens, why may not the state require the separation in railroad coaches of native and naturalized citizens of the United States, or of Protestants and Roman Catholics?
. . .

The white race deems itself to be the dominant race in this country. And so it is, in prestige, in achievements, in education, in wealth, and in power. So, I doubt not, it will continue to be for all time, if it remains true to its great heritage, and holds fast to the principles of constitutional liberty. But in view of the constitution, in the eye of the law, there is in this country no superior, dominant, ruling class of citizens. There is no caste here. Our constitution is color-blind, and neither knows nor tolerates classes among citizens. In respect of civil rights, all citizens are equal before the law. The humblest is the peer of the most powerful. The law regards man as man, and takes no account of his surroundings or of his color when his civil rights as guarantied by the supreme law of the land are involved. It is therefore to be regretted that this high tribunal, the final expositor of the fundamental law of the land, has reached the conclusion that it is competent for a state to regulate the enjoyment by citizens of their civil rights solely upon the basis of race.

In my opinion, the judgment this day rendered will, in time, prove to be quite as pernicious as the decision made by this tribunal in the Dred Scott Case. . . .

. . . The present decision, it may well be apprehended, will not only stimulate aggressions, more or less brutal and irritating, upon the admitted rights of colored citizens, but will encourage the belief that it is possible, by means of state enactments, to defeat the beneficent purposes which the people of the United States had in view when they adopted the recent amendments of the constitution, by one of which the blacks of this country were made citizens of the United States and of the states in which they respectively reside, and whose privileges and immunities, as citizens, the states are forbidden to abridge. Sixty millions of whites are in no danger from the presence here of eight millions of blacks. The destinies of the two races, in this country, are indissolubly linked together, and the interests of both require that the common government of all shall not permit the seeds of race hate to be planted under the sanction of law. What can more certainly arouse race hate, what more certainly create and perpetuate a feeling of distrust between these races, than state enactments which, in fact, proceed on the ground that colored citizens are so inferior and degraded that they cannot be allowed to sit in public coaches occupied by white citizens? That, as all will admit, is the real meaning of such legislation as was enacted in Louisiana. . . .

There is a race so different from our own that we do not permit those belonging to it to become citizens of the United States. Persons belonging to it are, with few exceptions, absolutely excluded from our country. I allude to the Chinese race. But, by the statute in question, a Chinaman can ride in the same passenger coach with white citizens of the United States, while citizens of the black race in Louisiana, many of whom, perhaps, risked their lives for the preservation of the Union, who are entitled, by law, to participate in the political control of the state and nation, who are not excluded, by law or by reason of their race, from public stations of any kind, and who have all the legal rights that belong to white citizens, are yet declared to be criminals, liable to imprisonment, if they ride in a public coach occupied by citizens of the white race. It is scarcely just to say that a colored citizen should not object to occupying a public coach assigned to his own race. He does not object, nor, perhaps, would he object to separate coaches for his race if his rights under the law were recognized. But he does object, and he ought never to cease objecting, that citizens of the white and black races can be adjudged criminals because they sit, or claim the right to sit, in the same public coach on a public highway.

The arbitrary separation of citizens, on the basis of race, while they are on a public highway, is a badge of servitude wholly inconsistent with the civil freedom and the equality before the law established by the constitution. It cannot be justified upon any legal grounds.

If evils will result from the commingling of the two races upon public highways established for the benefit of all, they will be infinitely less than those that will surely come from state legislation regulating the enjoyment of civil rights upon the basis of race. We boast of the freedom enjoyed by our people above all other peoples. But it is difficult to reconcile that boast with a state of the law which, practically, puts the brand of servitude and degradation upon a large class of our fellow citizens,—our equals before the law. The thin disguise of "equal" accommodations for passengers in railroad coaches will not mislead any one, nor atone for the wrong this day done....

If laws of like character should be enacted in the several states of the Union, the effect would be in the highest degree mischievous. Slavery, as an institution tolerated by law, would, it is true, have disappeared from our country; but there would remain a power in the states, by sinister legislation, to interfere with the full enjoyment of the blessings of freedom, to regulate civil rights, common to all citizens, upon the basis of race, and to place in a condition of legal inferiority a large body of American citizens, now constituting a part of the political community, called the "People of the United States," for whom, and by whom through representatives, our government is administered. Such a system is inconsistent with the guaranty given by the constitution to each state of a republican form of government, and may be stricken down by congressional action, or by the courts in the discharge of their solemn duty to maintain the supreme law of the land, anything in the constitution or laws of any state to the contrary notwithstanding....

Notes and Questions

1. Review the list of techniques and assumptions described above. Which were used in *Scott?* (Or, perhaps we should more appropriately ask: which, if any, were not used?) Find specific examples of the various rhetorical strategies and underlying assumptions.

2. Recall Professor Cover's discussion of the violence of law (p. 11, supra). Is *Scott* an example of how legal interpretation inflicts real pain?

3. After the *Scott* decision and the Civil War, the Constitution was amended to include the Thirteenth Amendment which abolished slavery, and the Fourteenth Amendment which provided that all persons born or naturalized in the United States are citizens of the U.S. and the state where they reside. These Amendments appeared to reconstruct membership in "We the People." Yet, despite the Amendments, the Court upheld the "separate, but equal" law challenged in *Plessy.* Which techniques and assumptions were used by the Court? Did Justice Harlan use some of these in his dissenting opinion? In this regard, is *Plessy* similar to *Scott?*

4. Plessy argued that he was not "colored", but rather was really "white" and, thus, had a property right to the privileges flowing to members of that dominant group. Was his argument similar to Thind's (p. 145, supra)? Why do you think both may have adopted this strategy, rather than one that conceded membership in the targeted group? What does it suggest about issues of privilege and power? For an interesting analysis of the persistence of the property concept of whiteness, *see* Cheryl Harris, *Whiteness as Property,* 106 Harv.L.Rev. 1709 (1993).

You may be wondering how the Railroad officials knew Plessy was "colored", if in fact he was seven-eights Caucasian. For a fascinating account of the design of the case as a test case, *see* Charles Lofgren, The Plessy Case (Oxford University Press, 1987).

5. Justice Harlan maintains in *Plessy* that the Constitution is "color-blind," a metaphor that frequently reappears in more recent cases. See, e.g., Shaw v. Reno, ___ U.S. ___, 113 S.Ct. 2816, 2824, 125 L.Ed.2d 511 (1993); City of Richmond v. J.A. Croson Co., 488 U.S. 469, 109 S.Ct. 706, 102 L.Ed.2d 854 (1989); Metro Broadcasting, Inc. v. Federal Communications Commission, 497 U.S. 547, 602, 110 S.Ct. 2997, 3028, 111 L.Ed.2d 445 (1990) (O'Connor, dissenting). Does the concept of a color-blind constitution displace or perpetuate existing patterns of privilege and power? *See* T. Alexander Aleinikoff, *A Case for Race–Consciousness,* 91 Colum.L.Rev. 1060 (1991); Neil Gotanda, *A Critique of "Our Constitution is Color–Blind",* 44 Stanford L.Rev. 1 (1991) (arguing that the metaphor legitimates and maintains the advantages whites hold over other Americans). Consider also the following.

BARBARA FLAGG, "WAS BLIND, BUT NOW I SEE": WHITE RACE CONSCIOUSNESS AND THE REQUIREMENT OF DISCRIMINATORY INTENT

91 Mich.L.Rev. 953, 961–62, 968–79, 992–93, 1005–17 (1993).

The Supreme Court first set forth the discriminatory intent require-ment in 1976, in Washington v. Davis. [426 U.S. 229] In that case the Court addressed the constitutionality of "Test 21," a written examina-tion developed by the U.S. Civil Service Commission and administered to applicants for positions as officers in the Metropolitan Police Depart-ment of the District of Columbia. Two rejected black applicants argued that Test 21 was racially discriminatory in that its effect was to disquali-fy black applicants at approximately four times the rate of white appli-cants; the plaintiffs did not allege intentional discrimination. The challengers lost in the District Court but were, temporarily, more successful on appeal: the Court of Appeals concluded that the applicable constitutional standard should be borrowed from Griggs v. Duke Power Co., [401 U.S. 424 (1971)] a Title VII case. In Griggs, as it was then understood, the Supreme Court had ruled that disparate impact alone, without proof of discriminatory intent, would be adequate to support the finding of a statutory violation absent proof by the employer that the facially neutral criterion in question was related to job performance. Though the District of Columbia petitioners challenged only the Court of Appeals' application of the Griggs approach, not the standard itself, the Supreme Court viewed the lower court's reliance on Griggs as plain error and set itself the task of correcting the mistake. The constitutional rule, the Court said, is that "the invidious quality of a law claimed to be racially discriminatory must ultimately be traced to a racially discrimina-tory purpose." Facially neutral laws with racially disparate effects, therefore, receive strict scrutiny only on a demonstration of discrimina-tory intent....

One relatively simple explanation for the stability of the require-ment of discriminatory purpose is its intuitive appeal, or more precisely the appeal of the principles it embodies. Colorblindness is extremely attractive to white liberals, and process theory's promise to regulate only the inputs to legislative decisionmaking, but not the substance of the resulting decisions, is extremely attractive to jurists confronting the countermajoritarian difficulty. But there is, I think, another explana-tion: the Davis rule reflects a distinctively white way of thinking about race....

There is a profound cognitive dimension to the material and social privilege that attaches to whiteness in this society, in that the white person has an everyday option not to think of herself in racial terms at all. In fact, whites appear to pursue that option so habitually that it may be a defining characteristic of whiteness: to be white is not to think about it. I label the tendency for whiteness to vanish from whites' self-perception the transparency phenomenon....

At a minimum, transparency counsels that we not accept seemingly neutral criteria of decision at face value. Most whites live and work in settings that are wholly or predominantly white. Thus whites rely on primarily white referents in formulating the norms and expectations that become criteria of decision for white decisionmakers. Given whites' tendency not to be aware of whiteness, it's unlikely that white decisionmakers do not similarly misidentify as race-neutral personal characteristics, traits, and behaviors that are in fact closely associated with whiteness. . . .

I recommend instead that whites adopt a deliberate and thoroughgoing skepticism regarding the race neutrality of facially neutral criteria of decision. This stance has the potential to improve the distribution across races of goods and power that whites currently control. In addition, skepticism may help to foster the development of a positive white racial identity that does not posit whites as superior to blacks.

Operating from a presumption that facially neutral criteria of decision are in fact white-specific may prompt white decisionmakers to engage in the sort of analysis presented earlier, when they would not otherwise have done so. Heightened awareness of formerly overlooked race specificity may, in turn, lead to the formulation of modified criteria of decision that are more attuned to, and more productive of, distributive racial justice. . . .

The skeptical stance may contribute to the development of a positive white racial identity by relativizing white norms. Even whites who do not harbor any conscious or unconscious belief in the superiority of white people participate in the maintenance of white supremacy whenever we impose white norms without acknowledging their whiteness. Any serious effort to dismantle white supremacy must include measures to dilute the effect of whites' dominant status, which carries with it the power to define as well as to decide. Because the skeptical stance prevents the unthinking imposition of white norms, it encourages white decisionmakers to consider adopting nonwhite ways of doing business, so that the formerly unquestioned white-specific criterion of decision becomes just one option among many. The skeptical stance thus can be instrumental in the development of a relativized white race consciousness, in which the white decisionmaker is conscious of the whiteness and contingency of white norms.

Most white people have no experience of a genuine cultural pluralism, one in which whites' perspectives, behavioral expectations, and values are not taken to be the standard from which all other cultural norms deviate. Whites therefore have no experiential basis for assessing the benefits of participating in a pluralist society so defined. On the assumption that prevailing egalitarian mores preclude white supremacy as a justification for the maintenance of the status quo, adopting the skeptical stance in the interest of exploring cultural pluralism seems the most appropriate course of action for any white person who acknowledges the transparency phenomenon. . . .

In outline, the proposed rule calls for heightened scrutiny of governmental criteria of decision that have racially disparate effects. The constitutional challenger bears the burden of persuasion on the question of the existence of racially disparate effects. Once disparate impact is proven, the burden of production shifts to government to articulate the purposes behind the challenged rule of decision. The reviewing court ought to interpret government's purpose(s) in as pluralist a manner as possible, but government has the option of resisting that interpretation in favor of an assimilationist construction of its goals. In that event, government will bear a burden of justification similar to that imposed under traditional intermediate scrutiny. Finally, whether governmental purposes are construed pluralistically or in an assimilationist manner, the constitutional challenger has the obligation to produce alternative means of achieving government's goals. Government must implement the challenger's proposals unless it can demonstrate that those alternatives provide less effective means of implementing its goals than the criteria of decision originally employed.

. . .

B. The Colorblindness Objection

The proposed rule clearly abandons the colorblindness principle, which disapproves any use of any race-specific criterion of decision, no matter what the race of the decisionmaker or of the persons respectively advantaged or burdened by that criterion. First, the proposed rule is founded on the presumption that facially neutral criteria of decision employed by white decisionmakers are in fact race-specific; the rule at least challenges the assumption of the colorblindness perspective that such a thing as a racially neutral criterion of decision is possible. Second, the rule permits government to take responsibility for disparate racial effects by adopting parallel race-conscious criteria of decision in appropriate instances. Finally, though the proposed rule does resemble colorblindness insofar as it mandates heightened scrutiny in the interest of mitigating the race-based effects of some covertly race-specific criteria of decision, it does so only when those effects flow from transparently white-specific bases of decision. That is, the rule contemplates heightened judicial scrutiny only when facially neutral criteria formulated or deployed by white governmental decisionmakers operate to disadvantage nonwhites. It is not symmetrical; heightened scrutiny is not appropriate when black governmental decisionmakers formulate and apply facially neutral criteria that negatively impact whites.

A transparency-conscious disparate impact rule should not be symmetrical because transparency itself is a white-specific phenomenon. In our society only whites have the social power that renders our point of view perspectiveless, that elevates our expectations to the status of "neutral" norms, and that permits us to see ourselves and our race-specific characteristics as raceless. Assuming there are, or can be, meaningful instances in which nonwhites gain the power to formulate as well as to apply governmental rules of decision, the existence of any disparate negative effect on whites would trigger at minimum an immediate inquiry, by whites, into the possible racial components of such facially neutral rules. Nonwhite decisionmaking never benefits from transparency.

Nevertheless, colorblindness is such a powerful norm that many will see its abandonment as a serious defect of the proposed rule. Further reflection will demonstrate, however, that colorblindness is a highly problematic constitutional principle. Justice Scalia, the strictest adherent to the colorblindness principle currently on the Supreme Court, staked out his position in the words of Alexander Bickel: " 'The lesson of the great decisions of the Supreme Court and the lesson of contemporary history have been the same for at least a generation: discrimination on the basis of race is illegal, immoral, unconstitutional, inherently wrong, and destructive of democratic society.' " The remainder of this Part will consider, in turn, the claims that colorblindness is an established constitutional principle, that it is morally self-evident, and that it is instrumental to the attainment of racial justice.

The available evidence suggests that its framers did not understand the Fourteenth Amendment to constitutionalize an abstract colorblindness principle. First, the series of race-conscious Freedmen's Bureau Acts adopted in the same period as the Fourteenth Amendment supports the conclusion that the framers did not oppose race-conscious legislation per se. However, the argument that those measures were directed at aiding the actual victims of prior discrimination dilutes their evidentiary value. The stronger case against the colorblindness interpretation rests, ironically, on the work of Alexander Bickel, who reached the conclusion that the framers did not intend to outlaw segregated public education, antimiscegenation laws, or the exclusion of blacks from jury service and the vote. Bickel concluded that the framers left open the question of giving "greater protection" than the Civil Rights Act of 1866, which for him would have meant extending the prohibition against race-conscious measures, "to be decided another day." The colorblindness principle has become entrenched in doctrine, but rather gradually. As a matter of constitutional precedent, it is quite the new arrival on the block.

Contemporary commentators saw no unequivocal commitment to colorblindness in Brown v. Board of Education, though some argued that the series of per curiam decisions that followed it compelled the conclusion that Brown rested on colorblindness after all. However, subsequent desegregation decisions cut the other way; they tended to rely on racial balancing as a proxy for desegregation and on occasion suggested that race-conscious measures might be permissible outside the remedial context. Though the Court did adopt one rule embodying the colorblindness perspective in 1976—the requirement of discriminatory intent it declined to do the same in the more controversial context of race-specific affirmative action when opportunities arose in 1974 and 1978. The Court did not settle on an explicit doctrine requiring strict scrutiny of all race-specific measures until 1989.

The evolution of the role of colorblindness in equal protection discourse is enlightening. Colorblindness was not in itself especially controversial in the early post-Brown era. Its significance lay in its potential to resolve the process-theoretical difficulties Wechsler had understood Brown to pose. As one might expect, the colorblindness principle became an item of contention in its own right as the debate over affirmative action heated up.... Increasingly, colorblindness was defended in moral and substantive terms, featuring, for example, instrumental arguments that race-conscious measures would ultimately exacerbate racial tensions or that they inevitably stigmatize blacks. This shift in theoretical perspective, from the "neutral" to the avowedly substantive, coincided, of course, with the conceptualization of the "innocent" white "victim" of affirmative action. One has to rephrase Bickel's famous remark: Whose ox was being gored at the time when colorblindness took center stage in the equality debate?

Turning from the legal to the moral realm, the principal foundation of colorblindness seems to be its enormous intuitive appeal. To "judge a person by the color of his skin" just seems wrong. This moral insight may be the visceral rejection of its equally visceral opposite, the tendency of human beings to react negatively to persons of a different color than themselves. However, moral insights are at best problematic sources of constitutional doctrine and must in any event be subject to revision in the light of experience.

The colorblindness principle may also appear morally desirable by virtue of its relation to the liberal value of individual autonomy. Colorblindness often is seen as an expression of individual autonomy, which requires in part that persons not be held responsible or judged for personal characteristics not within their own control. Individuals ought to reap the fruits of their own industry, but they ought neither to benefit nor to be disadvantaged because of characteristics like race or gender that are a matter of birth.

However, colorblindness is at best a paradoxical means of implementing autonomy values. On the one hand, autonomy is not served when the individual is pigeonholed by race; certainly the whole person is much more than the color of her skin. On the other hand, individual autonomy ought to include the power of self-definition, the ability to make fundamental value choices and to select life strategies to implement them. Such choices are not unbounded; for many individuals, to be oneself is to share in the cultural values of a community to which one belongs by birth. Thus, for example, for many black people embracing blackness as an explicit and positive aspect of personal identity is an essential component in the process of self-definition....

Proponents of the existing disparate impact rule appear to believe that individual autonomy is served when decisionmakers "ignore" the race of those affected by their decisions, but the transparency phenomenon, which suggests that colorblindness may operate instead as an opening for the unthinking imposition of white norms and expectations,

belies that view. The proposed rule takes a broader view of personal autonomy and takes seriously the centrality of race to many individuals' self-definition. For those who have to choose between the language, customs, hairstyle, dress, or lifestyle of their own community and a desirable job or other governmental benefit, the autonomy costs of transparently white norms are considerable.

The final category of arguments purporting to support the colorblindness principle may be characterized, loosely, as exemplifying antisubordinationist concerns. Race consciousness—the explicit use of racial classifications as a means of disadvantaging nonwhites—has been the primary vehicle of racial subordination until quite recently. The ideology of opposition to racial hierarchy evolved in reaction to the specific forms in which racial oppression had manifested itself. Rejecting racial distinctions seemed the natural avenue to reversing that history of oppression and achieving racial justice, especially during the "Second Reconstruction" of the 1950s and 1960s; colorblindness appeared to be the exact antithesis of the form of race consciousness that had been the root cause of racial subordination. If "color" had marked an individual as inferior, then the refusal to recognize "color" would be the way to elevate him to equal status with whites. In effect, colorblindness became the rule-like proxy for an underlying, historically based antisubordination principle.

The problem with the colorblindness principle as a strategy for achieving racial justice is that it has not been effective outside the social context in which it arose. Like all rules, colorblindness is both over- and underinclusive with respect to the underlying policy—antisubordination—it is intended to implement. It is underinclusive because the explicit use of racial classifications is no longer the principal vehicle of racial oppression; structural and institutional racism, of the sort illustrated by the transparency phenomenon, now are the predominant causes of blacks' continued inability to thrive in this society. Colorblindness is overinclusive insofar as it regards the explicit use of racial classifications to advantage blacks as equally blameworthy as the historical use of such classifications to blacks' disadvantage. In each respect colorblindness fails to implement racial justice; that it is a failed social policy is evident from the statistics revealing that blacks are scarcely better off today than they were before this ideology took hold in the 1950s and 1960s.

Liberals who wish to implement the goal of racial justice should give up the colorblindness principle in favor of a functional analysis of proposed means of achieving those ends. The proposed rule offers a better prospect for achieving racial equity because it permits nonwhites to engage white-controlled government in a dialogue concerning the scope of government's goals and the range of means that might be effective in attaining them. It requires government to define its goals in ways that do not systematically favor whites, and it also requires government to utilize diverse means of achieving its goals whenever possible. Unlike the inflexible, acontextual, and ahistorical colorblindness principle, the proposed rule offers the opportunity for government to take responsibility for racial justice.

C. AN INSTITUTIONAL OBJECTION

The institutional objection to the proposed rule mirrors the final, and for many, most persuasive argument articulated in Washington v. Davis:

> A rule that a statute designed to serve neutral ends is nevertheless invalid, absent compelling justification, if in practice it benefits or burdens one race more than another would be far reaching and would raise serious questions about, and perhaps invalidate, a whole range of tax, welfare, public service, regulatory, and licensing statutes that may be more burdensome to the poor and to the average black than to the more affluent white.

In short, the proposed rule might require the courts to engage in a form of economic redistribution. . . .

[T]he proposed rule does have, and is intended to have, some racially redistributive effects. The Davis argument points out a core dilemma in liberal egalitarian rhetoric: while we approve and are willing in some respects to foster racial equality, we endorse no similar economic egalitarianism. Thus, because our history of the overt and covert, intentional and thoughtless oppression of blacks by whites has placed the former in a relatively disadvantaged economic position, any attempt at racial reform runs afoul of our at least equally strong resistance to intervention in the existing distribution of economic goods, a resistance that is especially acute when the federal judiciary assumes responsibility to alter the status quo.

The solution to the dilemma, I think, is for white people to acknowledge that taking responsibility for race discrimination does and should cost something. . . . If the status quo results from a long history of the systematic privileging of whites, as it surely does, then one can only expect that a more racially just society would see a different, and more equal, distribution of societal goods.

The proposed rule in fact has relatively modest redistributive effects. It does no more than require government not to pursue thoughtlessly goals that advantage whites, and it permits nonwhites to propose inclusive means of accomplishing permissible goals; it does not mandate absolute distributional equality. It lays some of the burden of formulating more inclusive strategies at the feet of nonwhites, but it requires government to adopt those strategies whenever possible. To that extent, the proposed rule mandates a modest transfer of power as well as a somewhat more racially just distribution of benefits and burdens. We whites should expect no less from any rule that attempts seriously to address the structural racism of which transparency is one manifestation.

Conclusion

White people can do better than to continue to impose our beliefs, values, norms, and expectations on black people under the rubric of race neutrality.   Recognizing transparency for the defining characteristic of whiteness that it is ought to impel us to a radical skepticism concerning the possibility of race-neutral decisionmaking.   Operating from the presumption that facially neutral criteria of decision are in reality race-specific can prompt whites committed to the realization of racial justice to search for and adopt more racially inclusive ways of doing business. In this way, the skeptical stance can be instrumental in the development of a positive white racial identity, one that comprehends whiteness not as the (unspoken) racial norm, but as just one racial identity among many.

Whites who wish to see the destruction of racial hierarchy can hold government to the same standards of transparency consciousness.   We can and ought to expect the institution designed to be representative of all the people not to contribute to the maintenance of white supremacy. The demand that government decisionmakers take responsibility for race discrimination by adopting the skeptical stance can be embodied in the rejection of the discriminatory intent requirement.   A reformed disparate impact rule would prefer pluralist interpretations of government purposes, and it would require implementation through pluralist means whenever possible.   Uncovering, naming, and counteracting the unrecognized whiteness of a white-dominated government and of the criteria of decision it employs is a first, crucial step in the realignment of social power that dismantling white supremacy entails.

KOREMATSU v. UNITED STATES

Supreme Court of the United States, 1944.
323 U.S. 214, 65 S.Ct. 193, 89 L.Ed. 194.

MR. JUSTICE BLACK delivered the opinion of the Court.

The petitioner, an American citizen of Japanese descent, was convicted in a federal district court for remaining in San Leandro, California, a "Military Area", contrary to Civilian Exclusion Order No. 34 of the Commanding General of the Western Command, U.S. Army, which directed that after May 9, 1942, all persons of Japanese ancestry should be excluded from that area.   No question was raised as to petitioner's loyalty to the United States....

It should be noted, to begin with, that all legal restrictions which curtail the civil rights of a single racial group are immediately suspect. That is not to say that all such restrictions are unconstitutional.   It is to say that courts must subject them to the most rigid scrutiny.   Pressing public necessity may sometimes justify the existence of such restrictions; racial antagonism never can....

Exclusion Order No. 34, which the petitioner knowingly and admittedly violated was one of a number of military orders and proclamations, all of which were substantially based upon Executive Order No. 9066, 7 Fed.Reg. 1407. That order, issued after we were at war with Japan, declared that "the successful prosecution of the war requires every possible protection against espionage and against sabotage to national-defense material, national-defense premises, and national-defense utilities. ***"

One of the series of orders and proclamations, a curfew order, which like the exclusion order here was promulgated pursuant to Executive Order 9066, subjected all persons of Japanese ancestry in prescribed West Coast military areas to remain in their residences from 8 p.m. to 6 a.m. As is the case with the exclusion order here, that prior curfew order was designed as a "protection against espionage and against sabotage." In Kiyoshi Hirabayashi v. United States, 320 U.S. 81, 63 S.Ct. 1375, 87 L.Ed. 1774, we sustained a conviction obtained for violation of the curfew order. The Hirabayashi conviction and this one thus rest on the same 1942 Congressional Act and the same basic executive and military orders, all of which orders were aimed at the twin dangers of espionage and sabotage.

The 1942 Act was attacked in the Hirabayashi case as an unconstitutional delegation of power; it was contended that the curfew order and other orders on which it rested were beyond the war powers of the Congress, the military authorities and of the President, as Commander in Chief of the Army; and finally that to apply the curfew order against none but citizens of Japanese ancestry amounted to a constitutionally prohibited discrimination solely on account of race. To these questions, we gave the serious consideration which their importance justified. We upheld the curfew order as an exercise of the power of the government to take steps necessary to prevent espionage and sabotage in an area threatened by Japanese attack.

In the light of the principles we announced in the Hirabayashi case, we are unable to conclude that it was beyond the war power of Congress and the Executive to exclude those of Japanese ancestry from the West Coast war area at the time they did. True, exclusion from the area in which one's home is located is a far greater deprivation than constant confinement to the home from 8 p.m. to 6 a.m. Nothing short of apprehension by the proper military authorities of the gravest imminent danger to the public safety can constitutionally justify either. But exclusion from a threatened area, no less than curfew, has a definite and close relationship to the prevention of espionage and sabotage. The military authorities, charged with the primary responsibility of defending our shores, concluded that curfew provided inadequate protection and ordered exclusion. They did so, as pointed out in our Hirabayashi opinion, in accordance with Congressional authority to the military to say who should, and who should not, remain in the threatened areas.

In this case the petitioner challenges the assumptions upon which we rested our conclusions in the Hirabayashi case. He also urges that by May 1942, when Order No. 34 was promulgated, all danger of

Japanese invasion of the West Coast had disappeared. After careful consideration of these contentions we are compelled to reject them.

Here, as in the Hirabayashi case, "* * * we cannot reject as unfounded the judgment of the military authorities and of Congress that there were disloyal members of that population, whose number and strength could not be precisely and quickly ascertained. We cannot say that the war-making branches of the Government did not have ground for believing that in a critical hour such persons could not readily be isolated and separately dealt with, and constituted a menace to the national defense and safety, which demanded that prompt and adequate measures be taken to guard against it."

Like curfew, exclusion of those of Japanese origin was deemed necessary because of the presence of an unascertained number of disloyal members of the group, most of whom we have no doubt were loyal to this country. It was because we could not reject the finding of the military authorities that it was impossible to bring about an immediate segregation of the disloyal from the loyal that we sustained the validity of the curfew order as applying to the whole group. In the instant case, temporary exclusion of the entire group was rested by the military on the same ground. The judgment that exclusion of the whole group was for the same reason a military imperative answers the contention that the exclusion was in the nature of group punishment based on antagonism to those of Japanese origin. That there were members of the group who retained loyalties to Japan has been confirmed by investigations made subsequent to the exclusion. Approximately five thousand American citizens of Japanese ancestry refused to swear unqualified allegiance to the United States and to renounce allegiance to the Japanese Emperor, and several thousand evacuees requested repatriation to Japan.

We uphold the exclusion order as of the time it was made and when the petitioner violated it. In doing so, we are not unmindful of the hardships imposed by it upon a large group of American citizens. But hardships are part of war, and war is an aggregation of hardships. All citizens alike, both in and out of uniform, feel the impact of war in greater or lesser measure. Citizenship has its responsibilities as well as its privileges, and in time of war the burden is always heavier. Compulsory exclusion of large groups of citizens from their homes, except under circumstances of direst emergency and peril, is inconsistent with our basic governmental institutions. But when under conditions of modern warfare our shores are threatened by hostile forces, the power to protect must be commensurate with the threatened danger. . . .

It is said that we are dealing here with the case of imprisonment of a citizen in a concentration camp solely because of his ancestry, without evidence or inquiry concerning his loyalty and good disposition towards the United States. Our task would be simple, our duty clear, were this a case involving the imprisonment of a loyal citizen in a concentration camp because of racial prejudice. Regardless of the true nature of the assembly and relocation centers—and we deem it unjustifiable to call them concentration camps with all the ugly connotations that term implies—we are dealing specifically with nothing but an exclusion order. To cast this case into outlines of racial prejudice, without reference to the real military dangers which were presented, merely confuses the issue. Korematsu was not excluded from the Military Area because of hostility to him or his race. He was excluded because we are at war with the Japanese Empire, because the properly constituted military authorities feared an invasion of our West Coast and felt constrained to take proper security measures, because they decided that the military urgency of the situation demanded that all citizens of Japanese ancestry be segregated from the West Coast temporarily, and finally, because Congress, reposing its confidence in this time of war in our military leaders—as inevitably it must—determined that they should have the power to do just this. There was evidence of disloyalty on the part of some, the military authorities considered that the need for action was great, and time was short. We cannot—by availing ourselves of the calm perspective of hindsight—now say that at that time these actions were unjustified.

Affirmed.

Mr. Justice Frankfurter, concurring. . . .

. . . The respective spheres of action of military authorities and of judges are of course very different. But within their sphere, military authorities are no more outside the bounds of obedience to the Constitution than are judges within theirs. . . . To recognize that military orders are "reasonably expedient military precautions" in time of war and yet to deny them constitutional legitimacy makes of the Constitution an instrument for dialectic subtleties not reasonably to be attributed to the hard-headed Framers, of whom a majority had had actual participation in war. If a military order such as that under review does not transcend the means appropriate for conducting war, such action by the military is as constitutional as would be any authorized action by the Interstate Commerce Commission within the limits of the constitutional power to regulate commerce. And being an exercise of the war power explicitly granted by the Constitution for safeguarding the national life by prosecuting war effectively, I find nothing in the Constitution which denies to Congress the power to enforce such a valid military order by making its violation an offense triable in the civil courts. To find that the Constitution does not forbid the military measures now complained of does not carry with it approval of that which Congress and the Executive did. That is their business, not ours.

Mr. Justice Roberts, dissenting.

I dissent, because I think the indisputable facts exhibit a clear violation of Constitutional rights.

This is not a case of keeping people off the streets at night as was Kiyoshi Hirabayashi v. United States, nor a case of temporary exclusion of a citizen from an area for his own safety or that of the community, nor a case of offering him an opportunity to go temporarily out of an area where his presence might cause danger to himself or to his fellows. On the contrary, it is the case of convicting a citizen as a punishment for not submitting to imprisonment in a concentration camp, based on his ancestry, and solely because of his ancestry, without evidence or inquiry concerning his loyalty and good disposition towards the United States. If this be a correct statement of the facts disclosed by this record, and facts of which we take judicial notice, I need hardly labor the conclusion that Constitutional rights have been violated. . . .

MR. JUSTICE MURPHY, dissenting.

This exclusion of "all persons of Japanese ancestry, both alien and non-alien," from the Pacific Coast area on a plea of military necessity in the absence of martial law ought not to be approved. Such exclusion goes over "the very brink of constitutional power" and falls into the ugly abyss of racism.

In dealing with matters relating to the prosecution and progress of a war, we must accord great respect and consideration to the judgments of the military authorities who are on the scene and who have full knowledge of the military facts. The scope of their discretion must, as a matter of necessity and common sense, be wide. And their judgments ought not to be overruled lightly by those whose training and duties ill-equip them to deal intelligently with matters so vital to the physical security of the nation.

At the same time, however, it is essential that there be definite limits to military discretion, especially where martial law has not been declared. Individuals must not be left impoverished of their constitutional rights on a plea of military necessity that has neither substance nor support. Thus, like other claims conflicting with the asserted constitutional rights of the individual, the military claim must subject itself to the judicial process of having its reasonableness determined and its conflicts with other interests reconciled. "What are the allowable limits of military discretion, and whether or not they have been overstepped in a particular case, are judicial questions."

The judicial test of whether the Government, on a plea of military necessity, can validly deprive an individual of any of his constitutional rights is whether the deprivation is reasonably related to a public danger that is so "immediate, imminent, and impending" as not to admit of delay and not to permit the intervention of ordinary constitutional processes to alleviate the danger. Civilian Exclusion Order No. 34, banishing from a prescribed area of the Pacific Coast "all persons of Japanese ancestry, both alien and non-alien," clearly does not meet that test. Being an obvious racial discrimination, the order deprives all those within its scope of the equal protection of the laws as guaranteed by the Fifth Amendment. It further deprives these individuals of their constitutional rights to live and work where they will, to establish a home where they choose and to move about freely. In excommunicating them without benefit of hearings, this order also deprives them of all their constitutional rights to procedural due process. Yet no reasonable relation to an "immediate, imminent, and impending" public danger is evident to support this racial restriction which is one of the most sweeping and complete deprivations of constitutional rights in the history of this nation in the absence of martial law.

It must be conceded that the military and naval situation in the spring of 1942 was such as to generate a very real fear of invasion of the Pacific Coast, accompanied by fears of sabotage and espionage in that area. The military command was therefore justified in adopting all reasonable means necessary to combat these dangers. In adjudging the military action taken in light of the then apparent dangers, we must not erect too high or too meticulous standards; it is necessary only that the action have some reasonable relation to the removal of the dangers of invasion, sabotage and espionage. But the exclusion, either temporarily or permanently, of all persons with Japanese blood in their veins has no such reasonable relation. And that relation is lacking because the exclusion order necessarily must rely for its reasonableness upon the assumption that all persons of Japanese ancestry may have a dangerous tendency to commit sabotage and espionage and to aid our Japanese enemy in other ways. It is difficult to believe that reason, logic or experience could be marshalled in support of such an assumption.

That this forced exclusion was the result in good measure of this erroneous assumption of racial guilt rather than bona fide military necessity is evidenced by the Commanding General's Final Report on the evacuation from the Pacific Coast area. In it he refers to all individuals of Japanese descent as "subversive," as belonging to "an enemy race" whose "racial strains are undiluted," and as constituting "over 112,000 potential enemies * * * at large today" along the Pacific Coast. In support of this blanket condemnation of all persons of Japanese descent, however, no reliable evidence is cited to show that such individuals were generally disloyal or had generally so conducted themselves in this area as to constitute a special menace to defense installations or war industries, or had otherwise by their behavior furnished reasonable ground for their exclusion as a group....

Justification for the exclusion is sought, instead, mainly upon questionable racial and sociological grounds not ordinarily within the realm of expert military judgment, supplemented by certain semi-military conclusions drawn from an unwarranted use of circumstantial evidence. Individuals of Japanese ancestry are condemned because they are said to be 'a large, unassimilated, tightly knit racial group, bound to an enemy nation by strong ties of race, culture, custom and religion. They are claimed to be given to "emperor worshipping ceremonies" and to "dual citizenship." Japanese language schools and allegedly pro-Japanese organizations are cited as evidence of possible group disloyalty, together with facts as to certain persons being educated and residing at length in Japan. It is intimated that many of these individuals deliberately resided "adjacent to strategic points," thus enabling them "to carry into execution a tremendous program of sabotage on a mass scale should any considerable number of them have been inclined to do so." The need for protective custody is also asserted. The report refers without identity to "numerous incidents of violence" as well as to other admittedly unverified or cumulative incidents. From this, plus certain other events not shown to have been connected with the Japanese Americans, it is concluded that the "situation was fraught with danger to the Japanese population itself" and that the general public "was ready to take matters into its own hands." Finally, it is intimated, though not directly charged or proved, that persons of Japanese ancestry were responsible for three minor isolated shellings and bombings of the Pacific Coast area, as well as for unidentified radio transmissions and night signalling.

The main reasons relied upon by those responsible for the forced evacuation, therefore, do not prove a reasonable relation between the group characteristics of Japanese Americans and the dangers of invasion, sabotage and espionage. The reasons appear, instead, to be largely an accumulation of much of the misinformation, half-truths and insinuations that for years have been directed against Japanese Americans by people with racial and economic prejudices—the same people who have been among the foremost advocates of the evacuation. A military judgment based upon such racial and sociological considerations is not entitled to the great weight ordinarily given the judgments based upon strictly military considerations. Especially is this so when every charge relative to race, religion, culture, geographical location, and legal and economic status has been substantially discredited by independent studies made by experts in these matters.

The military necessity which is essential to the validity of the evacuation order thus resolves itself into a few intimations that certain individuals actively aided the enemy, from which it is inferred that the entire group of Japanese Americans could not be trusted to be or remain loyal to the United States. No one denies, of course, that there were some disloyal persons of Japanese descent on the Pacific Coast who did all in their power to aid their ancestral land. Similar disloyal activities have been engaged in by many persons of German, Italian and even more pioneer stock in our country. But to infer that examples of individual disloyalty prove group disloyalty and justify discriminatory action against the entire group is to deny that under our system of law individual guilt is the sole basis for deprivation of rights. Moreover, this inference, which is at the very heart of the evacuation orders, has been used in support of the abhorrent and despicable treatment of minority groups by the dictatorial tyrannies which this nation is now pledged to destroy. To give constitutional sanction to that inference in this case, however well-intentioned may have been the military command on the Pacific Coast, is to adopt one of the cruelest of the rationales used by our enemies to destroy the dignity of the individual and to encourage and open the door to discriminatory actions against other minority groups in the passions of tomorrow.

No adequate reason is given for the failure to treat these Japanese Americans on an individual basis by holding investigations and hearings to separate the loyal from the disloyal, as was done in the case of persons of German and Italian ancestry. . . .

I dissent, therefore, from this legalization of racism. Racial discrimination in any form and in any degree has no justifiable part whatever in our democratic way of life. It is unattractive in any setting but it is utterly revolting among a free people who have embraced the principles set forth in the Constitution of the United States. All residents of this nation are kin in some way by blood or culture to a foreign land. Yet they are primarily and necessarily a part of the new and distinct civilization of the United States. They must accordingly be treated at all times as the heirs of the American experiment and as entitled to all the rights and freedoms guaranteed by the Constitution.

Mr. Justice Jackson, dissenting.

Korematsu was born on our soil, of parents born in Japan. The Constitution makes him a citizen of the United States by nativity and a citizen of California by residence. No claim is made that he is not loyal to this country. There is no suggestion that apart from the matter involved here he is not law-abiding and well disposed. Korematsu, however, has been convicted of an act not commonly a crime. It consists merely of being present in the state whereof he is a citizen, near the place where he was born, and where all his life he has lived. . . .

A citizen's presence in the locality, however, was made a crime only if his parents were of Japanese birth. Had Korematsu been one of four—the others being, say, a German alien enemy, an Italian alien enemy, and a citizen of American-born ancestors, convicted of treason but out on parole—only Korematsu's presence would have violated the order. The difference between their innocence and his crime would result, not from anything he did, said, or thought, different than they, but only in that he was born of different racial stock.

Now, if any fundamental assumption underlies our system, it is that guilt is personal and not inheritable. Even if all of one's antecedents had been convicted of treason, the Constitution forbids its penalties to be visited upon him. . . . But here is an attempt to make an otherwise innocent act a crime merely because this prisoner is the son of parents as to whom he had no choice, and belongs to a race from which there is no way to resign. . . .

Much is said of the danger to liberty from the Army program for deporting and detaining these citizens of Japanese extraction. But a judicial construction of the due process clause that will sustain this order is a far more subtle blow to liberty than the promulgation of the order itself. A military order, however unconstitutional, is not apt to last longer than the military emergency. Even during that period a succeeding commander may revoke it all. But once a judicial opinion rationalizes such an order to show that it conforms to the Constitution, or rather rationalizes the Constitution to show that the Constitution sanctions such an order, the Court for all time has validated the principle of racial discrimination in criminal procedure and of transplanting American citizens. The principle then lies about like a loaded weapon ready for the hand of any authority that can bring forward a plausible claim of an urgent need. Every repetition imbeds that principle more deeply in our law and thinking and expands it to new purposes....

ROBERT CHANG, TOWARD AN ASIAN AMERICAN SCHOLARSHIP: CRITICAL RACE THEORY, POST–STRUCTURALISM, AND NARRATIVE SPACE

81 Cal.L.Rev. 1243, 1286–1299 (1993).

Exclusion has many faces. Its harms are insidious and its methods multifarious. One reason that exclusion is so readily able to work its harms is that exclusion, at a certain point, becomes so pervasive that it becomes invisible. In this way, the present-day effects of exclusion become disconnected from the past. As a consequence, the oppressed are blamed for the sins of their oppressors. For example, the dominant group often condemns the existence of ethnic enclaves such as China-towns and decries the unassimilability of Asian Americans. In doing so, the dominant group forgets that their laws and their history helped to create these ghettos. In this way, the past is obscured, and the victim is blamed, or worse, forgotten. But since "[i]nvisibility is not a natural state for anyone," efforts can be made to combat it....

What follows, then, is a story of the past. It is also a story of the present. I tell it now because I do not want it to be a story of the future.

A. EXCLUSION FROM LEGAL AND POLITICAL PARTICIPATION

1. Immigration and Naturalization

America has power, but not justice.

In prison, we were victimized as if we were guilty.

Given no opportunity to explain, it was really brutal.

I bow my head in reflection but there is nothing I can do.

This poem was written by an anonymous Chinese immigrant detained on Angel Island in San Francisco Bay. In the first half of the twentieth century, all Chinese immigrants were detained as suspects until their claims for right of entry were verified by intensive cross-examination. The feeling of powerlessness this poet describes reflects the culmination of discriminatory policies that began soon after the Chinese first arrived in America. Individual and community stories from this period resonate with degradation and despair. But the early history of Asian immigrants is also marked by their determined struggle against anti-Asian discrimination.

Knowledge of the experience of the early Chinese immigrants provides a context for understanding the experiences of all Asian immigrant groups because other Asian immigrants encountered similar violence and discrimination when they arrived. Later arrivals, trying to avoid this discrimination, distanced themselves from earlier arrivals. For example, in an attempt to distinguish themselves from the Chinese, Japanese men wore Western-style suits when they arrived in the United States, and Japanese "picture brides who arrived wearing kimonos and wooden clogs were whisked off upon landing by their husbands to dressmakers and shoemakers to be outfitted with Victorian clothing and shoes." The Koreans "thought that the Chinese and Japanese immigrants before them had provoked white anti-Asian reactions by retaining their old ways and keeping to themselves." They tried to overcome racial discrimination by distancing themselves from the Chinese and Japanese and by becoming more "westernized." Asian Indians were distinguished from other Asians by European and North American scholars, who identified Asian Indians as descendants of the Aryan (white) race; many Asian Indian immigrants embraced this myth. Filipinos distanced themselves from the Chinese by identifying themselves with the Malay rather than the Mongolian race. In essence, the discriminatory laws against the Chinese not only hurt the Chinese immigrants but, by encouraging each group to be more "western" than the next, also prevented the building of coalitions among different Asian American groups. Ironically, despite these efforts by Japanese, Korean, Asian Indian, and Filipino immigrants to "westernize" and to be accepted, they were treated by white Americans as merely different strains of the same "Yellow Peril" first embodied by the Chinese.

The Chinese, along with thousands of other pioneers, were drawn to California by the Gold Rush, with 325 Chinese arriving in 1849, 450 in 1850, 2176 in 1851, and 20,026 in 1852. They were not long in America before they began encountering legal and political opposition. For example, in 1854, the California Supreme Court ruled that Chinese immigrants could not testify against a white person in a court of law. This prohibition profoundly limited the chances for the Chinese, the vast majority of whom lived in California at this time, to obtain justice.

While this prohibition from testifying in California's state courts presented a great barrier to full participation in the American political-legal process, the greatest formal obstacle was the 1790 federal naturalization statute that permitted only "free white persons" to become naturalized. Following the Fourteenth Amendment and the subsequent amendment of the naturalization statute to include persons of African nativity or descent, Asians became the only group of aliens ineligible for citizenship. An 1878 decision by a circuit court in California solidified this bar against naturalization of Chinese aliens. From that point, the Chinese were generally ineligible for naturalization. Opinion was divided with regard to the Japanese and Asian Indians, a few of whom had managed to become naturalized, but the United States Supreme Court eventually decided that "white persons" under the naturalization statutes did not include the Japanese and Asian Indian immigrants.

The decision denying Asian Indians the right to naturalize nullified the citizenship of scores of Asian Indians granted before the decision. . . . Improvements in these discriminatory naturalization statutes began during the 1940s and culminated with the McCarran–Walter Act of 1952.

Besides denying Asians rights generally thought to accompany citizenship, classifying aliens into two groups—those eligible and those ineligible for citizenship—provided the basis for state discrimination. In essence, such classification permitted states to pass statutes that were race-neutral on their faces, and thus immune to equal protection challenges, which nevertheless discriminated on the basis of race. Many states took advantage of this classification to outlaw ownership of land by aliens ineligible for citizenship. States also enacted licensing laws that prevented Asian immigrants, as aliens ineligible for citizenship, from becoming "attorneys, physicians, teachers, pharmacists, veterinarians, hairdressers, cosmetologists, barbers, funeral directors, peddlers, and hunters." In certain parts of the country, children of Asian nativity or Asian ancestry were placed in segregated schools. Asian Americans were thus denied quintessential American rights, such as the right to own property, the right to choose one's profession, and the right to send one's children to public schools.

Yet even through the hard times recounted above, Asian Americans did not passively accept these and other injustices. Most people know about *Brown v. Board of Education* and the cases leading up to it, in which African Americans challenged segregated school systems, but few people know that Asian Americans also challenged the legality of segregated schools. Chinese plaintiffs filed lawsuits challenging segregated schools as violative of their equal protection rights. Japanese immigrants pursued a political solution to the problem of segregated schooling. Although such measures ultimately proved unsuccessful, I mention them now to counter the charge that Asian Americans have not faced discrimination and to challenge the myth that Asian Americans are a passive model minority.

Asian American contributions to the civil rights movement have been largely ignored and are often actively denied. Even significant contributions to civil rights have been forgotten. For example, few people know that the Chinese played an important role in the enactment of Reconstruction-era civil rights legislation.... Test cases brought after the passage of the 1870 Act by the Chinese did remarkably well in challenging discriminatory state and local measures.

However, the Chinese community was unable to effectively challenge the federal government's anti-Chinese measures. These federal measures ultimately had a profound impact on the psyche and development of the Chinese American community. In 1882, the United States government passed the first of a series of Chinese exclusion acts, specifically targeting Chinese by severely restricting Chinese immigration. These acts culminated in the Geary Act of 1892, an act called "the most draconian immigration law ever passed." This Act remained valid for over fifty years. To enforce these exclusionary immigration laws, the government set up a special immigration station in 1910 near San Francisco. Here, hundreds of would-be immigrants were detained for months and were often sent back to China. The Angel Island facility, like Alcatraz Prison nearby, was intended to be escape-proof.

The detainment of Chinese immigrants on Angel Island and the discriminatory treatment they received created a sense of alienation and powerlessness not only in the detainees, but also in those Chinese already in the United States. The detainees were treated like animals or commodities, forced to live in squalid, cramped quarters....

Immigration laws were soon passed which directly attacked the development of existing Chinese communities in the United States. When it appeared that more Chinese women were immigrating, a new immigration law was passed in 1924....

This provision crippled the development of a stable Chinese American community; and in conjunction with antimiscegenation laws in many states, it effectively emasculated an entire generation of male Chinese immigrants. Men in other Asian American groups underwent similar experiences, although the strategies employed were different.

These discriminatory measures remained largely in effect until the passage of the 1952 McCarran–Walter Act, which permitted the naturalization of Asian immigrants and set token immigration quotas. These quotas, based on national origins quotas established in 1921 and codified in the 1924 National Origins Act, were not changed until 1965 when the McCarran–Walter Act was amended to abolish the national origins system as well as the Asiatic barred zone. The 1965 amendments profoundly affected the development—or, as Professor Bill Hing states, the "remaking"—of Asian America....

2. Disfranchisement

When I joined the faculty at my former school, the Dean told me that I could participate in faculty meetings. On the first Tuesday of September, I felt proud to attend my first faculty meeting. I did not know then that it would be the last meeting I would attend that semester. As issues came up for decision, I voted, just like the other faculty members. It was only after the meeting that I was told that, as a legal writing instructor, I was not allowed to vote. My face turned red. I did not return.

The Dean had not lied to me when he told me that I was allowed to participate in faculty meetings; we simply differed in our interpretation of "participation." From my perspective, the Dean's notion of "participation" was impoverished because I included "meaningful" as part of my definition of "participation."

To an outside observer, it might appear that I stopped going because I did not care about faculty meetings. But when you listen to my story, you will understand that this is not so. ...

Systemic disfranchisement—whether at the level of faculty meetings or national elections—discourages many Asian Americans from participating in the political process. This is reflected in the low voter registration statistics which show Asian Americans to be "grossly underrepresented in terms of their voting power in relation to their numbers in the population." This political silence has been attributed to "cultural differences, the difficulty of combining Asian Pacific American subgroups into a cohesive 'minority' group because of their diverse nationalities and generations, and their lack of interest in politics." These reasons, however, are largely myths created to prevent the enfranchisement of Asian Americans.

————

The following cases provide additional examples where the Court concluded that certain conduct that appeared to be race-based was not really a racial classification.

UNITED STATES v. ANTELOPE

Supreme Court of the United States, 1977.
430 U.S. 641, 97 S.Ct. 1395, 51 L.Ed.2d 701.

Mr. Chief Justice Burger delivered the opinion of the Court.

The question presented by our grant of certiorari is whether, under the circumstances of this case, federal criminal statutes violate the Due Process Clause of the Fifth Amendment by subjecting individuals to federal prosecution by virtue of their status as Indians.

On the night of February 18, 1974, respondents, enrolled Coeur d'Alene Indians, broke into the home of Emma Johnson, an 81–year–old non-Indian, in Worley, Idaho; they robbed and killed Mrs. Johnson. Because the crimes were committed by enrolled Indians within the boundaries of the Coeur d'Alene Indian Reservation, respondents were subject to federal jurisdiction under the Major Crimes Act, 18 U.S.C. § 1153. They were, accordingly, indicted by a federal grand jury on charges of burglary, robbery, and murder. Respondent William Davison was convicted of second-degree murder only. Respondents Gabriel Francis Antelope and Leonard Davison were found guilty of all three crimes as charged, including first-degree murder under the felony-murder provisions of 18 U.S.C. § 1111, as made applicable to enrolled Indians by 18 U.S.C. § 1153.

In the United States Court of Appeals for the Ninth Circuit, respondents contended that their felony-murder convictions were unlawful as products of invidious racial discrimination. They argued that a non-Indian charged with precisely the same offense, namely the murder of another non-Indian within Indian country, would have been subject to prosecution only under Idaho law, which in contrast to the federal murder statute, 18 U.S.C. § 1111, does not contain a felony-murder provision. To establish the crime of first-degree murder in state court, therefore, Idaho would have had to prove premeditation and deliberation. No such elements were required under the felony-murder component of 18 U.S.C. § 1111....

The decisions of this Court leave no doubt that federal legislation with respect to Indian tribes, although relating to Indians as such, is not based upon impermissible racial classifications. Quite the contrary, classifications expressly singling out Indian tribes as subjects of legislation are expressly provided for in the Constitution and supported by the ensuing history of the Federal Government's relations with Indians....

Legislation with respect to these "unique aggregations" has repeatedly been sustained by this Court against claims of unlawful racial discrimination. In upholding a limited employment preference for Indians in the Bureau of Indian Affairs, we said in Morton v. Mancari, 417 U.S. 535, 552 (1974): "Literally every piece of legislation dealing with Indian tribes and reservations ... single(s) out for special treatment a constituency of tribal Indians living on or near reservations. If these laws ... were deemed invidious racial discrimination, an entire Title of the United States Code (25 U.S.C.) would be effectively erased...." In light of that result, the Court unanimously concluded in Mancari: "The preference, as applied, is granted to Indians not as a discrete racial group, but, rather, as members of quasi-sovereign tribal entities...." Last Term, in Fisher v. District Court, 424 U.S. 382 (1976), we held that members of the Northern Cheyenne Tribe could be denied access to Montana State courts in connection with an adoption proceeding arising on their reservation. Unlike Mancari, the Indian plaintiffs in Fisher were being denied a benefit or privilege available to non-Indians; nevertheless, a unanimous Court dismissed the claim of racial discrimination: "(W)e reject the argument that denying (the Indian plaintiffs) access to the Montana courts constitutes impermissible racial discrimination. The exclusive jurisdiction of the Tribal Court does not derive from the race of the plaintiff but rather from the quasi-sovereign status of the Northern Cheyenne Tribe under federal law."

Both Mancari and Fisher involved preferences or disabilities directly promoting Indian interests in self-government, whereas in the present case we are dealing, not with matters of tribal self-regulation, but with federal regulation of criminal conduct within Indian country implicating Indian interests. But the principles reaffirmed in Mancari and Fisher point more broadly to the conclusion that federal regulation of Indian affairs is not based upon impermissible classifications. Rather, such regulation is rooted in the unique status of Indians as "a separate people" with their own political institutions. Federal regulation of Indian tribes, therefore, is governance of once-sovereign political communities; it is not to be viewed as legislation of a " 'racial' group consisting of 'Indians'...." Indeed, respondents were not subjected to federal criminal jurisdiction because they are of the Indian race but because they are enrolled members of the Coeur d'Alene Tribe. We therefore conclude that the federal criminal statutes enforced here are based neither in whole nor in part upon impermissible racial classifications....

CITY OF MEMPHIS v. GREENE

Supreme Court of the United States, 1981.
451 U.S. 100, 101 S.Ct. 1584, 67 L.Ed.2d 769.

JUSTICE STEVENS delivered the opinion of the Court.

The question presented is whether a decision by the city of Memphis to close the north end of West Drive, a street that traverses a white residential community, violated § 1 of the Civil Rights Act of 1866, Rev.Stat. § 1978, 42 U.S.C. § 1982, or the Thirteenth Amendment to the United States Constitution. The city's action was challenged by respondents, who resided in a predominantly black area to the north. The Court of Appeals ultimately held the street closing invalid because it adversely affected respondents' ability to hold and enjoy their property. We reverse because the record does not support that holding.

I

Most of the relevant facts concerning the geography, the decision to close the street, and the course of the litigation are not in dispute. The inferences to be drawn from the evidence, however, are subject to some disagreement.

A. GEOGRAPHY

Hein Park, a small residential community in Memphis, Tenn., is bounded on three sides by thoroughfares and on the west by the campus of Southwestern University. West Drive is a two-lane street about a half-mile long passing through the center of Hein Park. Its southern terminus is a short distance from an entrance to Overton Park, a large recreation area containing, among other facilities, the municipal zoo. Its northern terminus is at the intersection of Jackson Ave. and Springdale St., two heavily traveled four-lane avenues. West Drive is one of three streets that enter Hein Park from the north; two streets enter from the east.

The closing will have some effect on both through traffic and local traffic. Prior to the closing, a significant volume of traffic southbound on Springdale St. would continue south on West Drive and then— because of the location of Overton Park to the south of Hein Park— make either a right or a left turn to the next through street a few blocks away, before resuming the southerly route to the center of the city. The closing of West Drive will force this traffic to divert to the east or west before entering Hein Park, instead of when it leaves, but the closing will not make the entire route any longer. With respect to local traffic, the street closing will add some distance to the trip from Springdale St. to the entrance to Overton Park and will make access to some homes in Hein Park slightly less convenient.

The area to the north of Hein Park is predominantly black. All of the homes in Hein Park were owned by whites when the decision to close the street was made....

In summary ... the critical facts established by the record are these: The city's decision to close West Drive was motivated by its interest in protecting the safety and tranquility of a residential neighborhood. The procedures followed in making the decision were fair and were not affected by any racial or other impermissible factors. The city has conferred a benefit on certain white property owners but there is no reason to believe that it would refuse to confer a comparable benefit on black property owners. The closing has not affected the value of property owned by black citizens, but it has caused some slight inconvenience to black motorists.

II

Under the Court's recent decisions the absence of proof of discriminatory intent forecloses any claim that the official action challenged in this case violates the Equal Protection Clause of the Fourteenth Amendment. Petitioners ask us to hold that respondents' claims under § 1982 and the Thirteenth Amendment are likewise barred by the absence of proof of discriminatory purpose. We note initially that the coverage of both § 1982 and the Thirteenth Amendment is significantly different from the coverage of the Fourteenth Amendment. The prohibitions of the latter apply only to official action, or, as implemented by 42 U.S.C. § 1983 (1976 ed., Supp.III), to action taken under color of state law. We have squarely decided, however, that § 1982 is directly applicable to private parties, and it has long been settled that the Thirteenth Amendment "is not a mere prohibition of State laws establishing or upholding slavery, but an absolute declaration that slavery or involuntary servitude shall not exist in any part of the United States." Thus, although respondents challenge official action in this case, the provisions of the law on which the challenge is based cover certain private action as well. Rather than confront prematurely the rather general question whether either § 1982 or the Thirteenth Amendment requires proof of a specific unlawful purpose, we first consider the extent to which either provision applies at all to this street closing case. We of course deal first with the statutory question.

III

Section 1982 provides: "All citizens of the United States shall have the same right, in every State and Territory, as is enjoyed by white citizens thereof to inherit, purchase, lease, sell, hold, and convey real and personal property." To effectuate the remedial purposes of the statute, the Court has broadly construed this language to protect not merely the enforceability of property interests acquired by black citizens but also their right to acquire and use property on an equal basis with white citizens.... Although these cases broadly defined the property rights protected by § 1982, our cases, like the statutory language itself, all concerned the right of black persons to hold and acquire property on an equal basis with white persons and the right of blacks not to have property interests impaired because of their race.

Therefore, as applied to this case, the threshold inquiry under § 1982 must focus on the relationship between the street closing and the property interests of the respondents. As the Court of Appeals correctly noted in its first opinion, the statute would support a challenge to municipal action benefiting white property owners that would be refused to similarly situated black property owners. For official action of that kind would prevent blacks from exercising the same property rights as whites. But respondents' evidence failed to support this legal theory. Alternatively, as the Court of Appeals held in its second opinion, the statute might be violated by official action that depreciated the value of property owned by black citizens. But this record discloses no effect on the value of property owned by any member of the respondent class. Finally, the statute might be violated if the street closing severely restricted access to black homes, because blacks would then be hampered in the use of their property. Again, the record discloses no such restriction.

The injury to respondents established by the record is the requirement that one public street rather than another must be used for certain trips within the city. We need not assess the magnitude of that injury to conclude that it does not involve any impairment to the kind of property interests that we have identified as being within the reach of § 1982. We therefore must consider whether the street closing violated respondents' constitutional rights.

IV

In relevant part, the Thirteenth Amendment provides: "Neither slavery nor involuntary servitude, except as a punishment for crime whereof the party shall have been duly convicted, shall exist within the United States, or any place subject to their jurisdiction." In this case respondents challenge the conferring of a benefit upon white citizens by a measure that places a burden on black citizens as an unconstitutional "badge of slavery." ...

In Jones [v. Alfred H. Mayer Co., 392 U.S. 409 (1968)], the Court left open the question whether § 1 of the Amendment by its own terms did anything more than abolish slavery. It is also appropriate today to leave that question open because a review of the justification for the official action challenged in this case demonstrates that its disparate impact on black citizens could not, in any event, be fairly characterized as a badge or incident of slavery.

In this case the city favored the interests of safety and tranquility. As a matter of constitutional law a city's power to adopt rules that will avoid anticipated traffic safety problems is the same as its power to correct those hazards that have been revealed by actual events. The decision to reduce the flow of traffic on West Drive was motivated, in part, by an interest in the safety of children walking to school....

The residential interest in comparative tranquility is also unquestionably legitimate. That interest provides support for zoning regulations, designed to protect a "quiet place where yards are wide, people few, and motor vehicles restricted...." and for the accepted view that a man's home is his castle. The interest in privacy has the same dignity in a densely populated apartment complex, or in an affluent neighborhood of single-family homes. In either context, the protection of the individual interest may involve the imposition of some burdens on the general public.

Whether the individual privacy interests of the residents of Hein Park, coupled with the interest in safety, should be considered strong enough to overcome the more general interest in the use of West Drive as a thoroughfare is the type of question that a multitude of local governments must resolve every day. Because there is no basis for concluding that the interests favored by the city in its decision were contrived or pretextual, the District Court correctly concluded that it had no authority to review the wisdom of the city's policy decision.

The interests motivating the city's action are thus sufficient to justify an adverse impact on motorists who are somewhat inconvenienced by the street closing. That inconvenience cannot be equated to an actual restraint on the liberty of black citizens that is in any sense comparable to the odious practice the Thirteenth Amendment was designed to eradicate. The argument that the closing violates the Amendment must therefore rest, not on the actual consequences of the closing, but rather on the symbolic significance of the fact that most of the drivers who will be inconvenienced by the action are black.

But the inconvenience of the drivers is a function of where they live and where they regularly drive—not a function of their race; the hazards and the inconvenience that the closing is intended to minimize are a function of the number of vehicles involved, not the race of their drivers or of the local residents. Almost any traffic regulation—whether it be a temporary detour during construction, a speed limit, a one-way street, or a no-parking sign—may have a differential impact on residents of adjacent or nearby neighborhoods. Because urban neighborhoods are so frequently characterized by a common ethnic or racial heritage, a regulation's adverse impact on a particular neighborhood will often have a disparate effect on an identifiable ethnic or racial group. To regard an inevitable consequence of that kind as a form of stigma so severe as to violate the Thirteenth Amendment would trivialize the great purpose of that charter of freedom. Proper respect for the dignity of the residents of any neighborhood requires that they accept the same burdens as well as the same benefits of citizenship regardless of their racial or ethnic origin....

JUSTICE MARSHALL, with whom JUSTICE BRENNAN and JUSTICE BLACKMUN join, dissenting.

This case is easier than the majority makes it appear. Petitioner city of Memphis, acting at the behest of white property owners, has closed the main thoroughfare between an all-white enclave and a predominantly Negro area of the city. The stated explanation for the closing is of a sort all too familiar: "protecting the safety and tranquility of a residential neighborhood" by preventing "undesirable traffic" from entering it. Too often in our Nation's history, statements such as these have been little more than code phrases for racial discrimination. These words may still signify racial discrimination, but apparently not, after today's decision, forbidden discrimination. The majority, purporting to rely on the evidence developed at trial, concludes that the city's stated interests are sufficient to justify erection of the barrier. Because I do not believe that either the Constitution or federal law permits a city to carve out racial enclaves I dissent. . . .

I readily accept much of the majority's summary of the circumstances that led to this litigation. I would, however, begin by emphasizing three critical facts. First, as the District Court found, Hein Park "was developed well before World War II as an exclusive residential neighborhood for white citizens and these characteristics have been maintained." Second, the area to the north of Hein Park, like the "undesirable traffic" that Hein Park wants to keep out, is predominantly Negro. And third, the closing of West Drive stems entirely from the efforts of residents of Hein Park. Up to this point, the majority and I are in agreement. But we part company over our characterizations of the evidence developed in the course of the trial of this case. At the close of the evidence, the trial court described this as "a situation where an all white neighborhood is seeking to stop the traffic from an overwhelmingly black neighborhood from coming through their street." In the legal and factual context before us, I find that a revealing summary of the case. The majority apparently does not. . . .

The majority . . . concedes that the trial court "clearly concluded . . . that the adverse impact on blacks was greater than on whites." The majority suggests, however, that this "impact" is limited to the "inconvenience" that will be suffered by drivers who live in the predominantly Negro area north of Hein Park and who will no longer be able to drive through the subdivision. This, says the majority, is because residents of the area north of Hein Park will still be able to get where they are going; they will just have to go a little out of their way and thus will take a little longer to complete the trip.

This analysis ignores the plain and powerful symbolic message of the "inconvenience." Many places to which residents of the area north of Hein Park would logically drive lie to the south of the subdivision. Until the closing of West Drive, the most direct route for those who lived on or near Springdale St. was straight down West Drive. Now the Negro drivers are being told in essence: "You must take the long way around because you don't live in this 'protected' white neighborhood." Negro residents of the area north of Hein Park testified at trial that this is what they thought the city was telling them by closing West Drive. Even the District Court, which granted judgment for petitioners, conceded that "[o]bviously, the black people north of [Hein Park] . . . are being told to stay out of the subdivision." In my judgment, this message constitutes a far greater adverse impact on respondents than the majority would prefer to believe.

The majority also does not challenge the Sixth Circuit's second finding, that the barrier is being erected at the point of contact of the two communities. Nor could it do so, because the fact is not really in dispute. The Court attempts instead to downplay the significance of this barrier by calling it "a curb that will not impede the passage of municipal vehicles." But that is beside the point. Respondents did not bring this suit to challenge the exclusion of municipal vehicles from Hein Park. Their goal is to preserve access for their own vehicles. But in fact, they may not even be able to preserve access for their own persons. The city is creating the barrier across West Drive by deeding public property to private landowners. Nothing will prevent the residents of Hein Park from excluding "undesirable" pedestrians as well as vehicular traffic if they so choose. What is clear is that there will be a barrier to traffic that is to be erected precisely at the point where West Drive (and thus, all-white Hein Park) ends and Springdale St. (and the mostly Negro section) begins.

The psychological effect of this barrier is likely to be significant. In his unchallenged expert testimony in the trial court, Dr. Marvin Feit, a professor of psychiatry at the University of Tennessee, predicted that the barrier between West Drive and Springdale St. will reinforce feelings about the city's "favoritism" toward whites and will "serve as a monument to racial hostility." ... I cannot subscribe to the majority's apparent view that the city's erection of this "monument to racial hostility" amounts to nothing more than a "slight inconvenience." Thus, unlike the majority, I do not minimize the significance of the barrier itself in determining the harm respondents will suffer from its erection.

The majority does not attempt to question the third conclusion by the Court of Appeals, that the closing of West Drive is intended as a protection of Hein Park against "undesirable" outside influences. Rather, its disagreement with the Court of Appeals is over the inference to be drawn. The majority insists that to the extent that the Court of Appeals found racially discriminatory intent, that finding is not supported by the record. The majority also asserts, that there is "no evidence" that either the residents of Hein Park or the city officials were motivated by any racial considerations. A proper reading of the record demonstrates to the contrary that respondents produced at trial precisely the kind of evidence of intent that we [have] deemed probative....

The term "undesirable traffic" first entered this litigation through the trial testimony of Sarah Terry. Terry, a West Drive resident who opposed the closing, testified that she was urged to support the barrier by an individual who explained to her that "the traffic on the street was undesirable traffic." The majority apparently reads the term "undesirable" as referring to the prospect of having any traffic at all on West Drive. But the common-sense understanding of Terry's testimony must be that the word "undesirable" was meant to describe the traffic that was actually using the street, as opposed to any traffic that might use it.

Of course, the traffic that was both actually using the street and would be affected by the barrier was predominantly Negro....

The testimony of city planning officials, for example, strongly suggests that the city deviated from its usual procedures in deciding to close West Drive. In particular, despite an unambiguous requirement that applications for street closings be signed by "all" owners of property abutting on the thoroughfare to be closed, the city here permitted this application to go through without the signature or the consent of Sarah Terry. Perhaps more important, the city gave no notice to the Negro property owners living north of Hein Park that the Planning Commission was considering an application to close West Drive. The Planning Commission held its hearing without participation by any of the affected Negro residents and it declined to let them examine the file on the West Drive closing. It gave no notice that the City Council would be considering the issue. When respondents found out about it, they sought to state their case. But the Council gave opponents of the proposal only 15 minutes, even though some members objected that that was not enough time. Furthermore, although the majority treats West Drive as just another closing, it is, according to the city official in charge of closings, the only time the city has ever closed a street for traffic control purposes. And it cannot be disputed that all parties were aware of the disparate racial impact of the erection of the barrier. The city of Memphis, moreover, has an unfortunate but very real history of racial segregation—a history that has in the past led to intercession by this Court.... Regardless of whether this evidence is viewed as conclusive, it can hardly be stated with accuracy that "no evidence" exists.

Most important, I believe that the findings of the District Court and the record in this case fully support the Court of Appeals' conclusion that Negro property owners are likely to suffer economic harm as a result of the construction of the barrier. In attempting to demonstrate to the trial court that the closing of West Drive would adversely affect their property, respondents first introduced the testimony of H.C. Moore, a real estate agent with 17 years' experience in the field. Moore began by predicting that after West Drive was closed, Hein Park would become "more or less a Utopia within the city of Memphis," families who had left the inner city for the suburbs would probably return in order to live there, and the property values in Hein Park "would be enhanced greatly." Moore was then asked what effect the closing would have on the property values in the Springdale area. He responded: "From an economic standpoint there would not be a lessening of value in those properties in the Springdale area, but from a psychological standpoint, it would have a tendency to have a demoralizing—." At this point, counsel for petitioners interposed an objection, but Moore was eventually permitted to answer the question, and he testified as follows: "In my opinion, with the 17 years experience in the real estate industry, psychologically it would have a deterring, depressing effect on those individuals who might live north of the Hein Park area. With the closure of the street, the creation of another little haven, the fact that these people are in a lower economic social group and wouldn't be able to actually afford housing with the illustrious price tags of those houses in the Hein Park area, it would be, in my opinion, like the individual looking in the pastry store who doesn't have a dime and who can't afford it. And consequently, as a result of such, their moralistic values on their properties could tend to be such that the upkeep would not be nearly so great and it could have a detrimental effect on the property values in the future." Surely Moore's uncontroverted expert testimony is evidence of an impairment of property values, an impairment directly traceable to the closing of West Drive. The majority dismisses this aspect of Moore's testimony as "speculation." Yet the majority has no trouble crediting Moore's brief and conclusory testimony that the immediate impact of the closing would be negligible. Unlike the majority, I am unable to dismiss so blithely the balance of his comments.

The majority also gives insufficient weight to the testimony of Dr. Feit on this point. Dr. Feit testified, based on his experience as Director of Planning for Allegheny County, Pa., that the shift in traffic patterns as a result of the closing of West Drive would lower the property values for owners living north of Hein Park. He further testified that the closing of West Drive would lead to increased hostility toward Hein Park residents and, ultimately, to increased police harassment of residents of the Springdale area. I would have thought it indisputable that increased police harassment of property owners must be construed as a significant impairment of their property interests....

I can only agree with the Court of Appeals, which viewed the city's action as nothing more than "one more of the many humiliations which society has historically visited" on Negro citizens. In my judgment, respondents provided ample evidence that erection of the challenged barrier will harm them in several significant ways. Respondents are being sent a clear, though sophisticated, message that because of their race, they are to stay out of the all-white enclave of Hein Park and should instead take the long way around in reaching their destinations to the south. Combined with this message are the prospects of increased police harassment and of a decline in their property values. It is on the basis of these facts, all firmly established by the record, that I evaluate the legal questions presented by this case....

The majority concludes that the kind of harm that § 1982 was meant to prohibit does not exist in this case, but as I have stated, a proper reading of the record demonstrates substantial harm to respondents' property rights as a result of the establishment of a barrier at the northern edge of Hein Park. The closing will both burden respondents' ability to enjoy their property and also depress its value, thus falling within the literal language of § 1982. Even the majority concedes that "the statute might be violated by official action that depreciated the value of property owned by [Negro] citizens." I believe that that is precisely what is challenged in this case....

I do not, of course, mean to suggest that the Reconstruction Congress that enacted § 1982 anticipated the precise situation presented by this case. Nor do I wish to imply that the Act prevents government from ever closing a street when the effect is to inflict harm on Negro property owners. But because of our Nation's sad legacy of discrimination and the broad remedial purpose of § 1982, I believe that official actions whose effects fall within its terms ought to be closely scrutinized. When, as here, the decisionmaker takes action with full knowledge of its enormously disproportionate racial impact, I believe that § 1982 requires that the government carry a heavy burden in order to justify its action. Absent such a justification, the injured property owners are entitled to relief. . . .

In sustaining the closing of West Drive, the majority points to petitioners' "[p]roper management of the flow of vehicular traffic within a city," and their exercise of the "unquestionably legitimate" "residential interest in comparative tranquility." Those interests might, as the majority contends, well prove "sufficient to justify an adverse impact on motorists who are somewhat inconvenienced by the street closing," ante, at 1600, but that is not the impact that the city must explain in this case. It must instead justify the substantial injury that it has inflicted on Negro citizens solely for the benefit of the white residents of Hein Park. For that purpose, the proffered explanations are insufficient. . . . It is simply unrealistic to suggest, as does the Court, that the harm suffered by respondents has no more than "symbolic significance," and it defies the lessons of history and law to assert that if the harm is only symbolic, then the federal courts cannot recognize it. Compare Plessy v. Ferguson, 163 U.S. 537, 551, 16 S.Ct. 1138, 1143, 41 L.Ed. 256 (1896) ("We consider the underlying fallacy of the plaintiff's argument to consist in the assumption that the enforced separation of the two races stamps the colored race with a badge of inferiority. If this be so, it is not by reason of anything found in the act, but solely because the colored race chooses to put that construction upon it"), with Brown v. Board of Education, 347 U.S. 483, 494, 74 S.Ct. 686, 691, 98 L.Ed. 873 (1954) ("To separate them from others . . . solely because of their race generates a feeling of inferiority as to their status in the community that may affect their hearts and minds in a way unlikely ever to be undone. . . . Whatever may have been the extent of psychological knowledge at the time of Plessy v. Ferguson, this finding is amply supported by modern authority"). The message the city is sending to Negro residents north of Hein Park is clear, and I am at a loss to understand why the majority feels so free to ignore it. . . .

HERNANDEZ v. NEW YORK

Supreme Court of the United States, 1991.
500 U.S. 352, 111 S.Ct. 1859, 114 L.Ed.2d 395.

JUSTICE KENNEDY announced the judgment of the Court and delivered an opinion in which THE CHIEF JUSTICE, JUSTICE WHITE and JUSTICE SOUTER join.

Petitioner Dionisio Hernandez asks us to review the New York state courts' rejection of his claim that the prosecutor in his criminal trial exercised peremptory challenges to exclude Latinos from the jury by reason of their ethnicity. If true, the prosecutor's discriminatory use of peremptory strikes would violate the Equal Protection Clause.... We must determine whether the prosecutor offered a race-neutral basis for challenging Latino potential jurors and, if so, whether the state courts' decision to accept the prosecutor's explanation should be sustained.

Petitioner and respondent both use the term "Latino" in their briefs to this Court. Amicus briefs on both sides employ instead the term "Hispanic," and the parties referred to the excluded jurors by that term in the trial court. Both words appear in the state court opinions. No attempt has been made at a distinction by the parties and we make no attempt to distinguish the terms in this opinion. We will refer to the excluded venirepersons as Latinos in deference to the terminology preferred by the parties before the Court....

[T]he prosecutor volunteered his reasons for striking the jurors in question. He explained: "Your honor, my reason for rejecting the—these two jurors—I'm not certain as to whether they're Hispanics. I didn't notice how many Hispanics had been called to the panel, but my reason for rejecting these two is I feel very uncertain that they would be able to listen and follow the interpreter." After an interruption by defense counsel, the prosecutor continued: "We talked to them for a long time; the Court talked to them, I talked to them. I believe that in their heart they will try to follow it, but I felt there was a great deal of uncertainty as to whether they could accept the interpreter as the final arbiter of what was said by each of the witnesses, especially where there were going to be Spanish-speaking witnesses, and I didn't feel, when I asked them whether or not they could accept the interpreter's translation of it, I didn't feel that they could. They each looked away from me and said with some hesitancy that they would try, not that they could, but that they would try to follow the interpreter, and I feel that in a case where the interpreter will be for the main witnesses, they would have an undue impact upon the jury." [1] ...

Petitioner contends that the reasons given by the prosecutor for challenging the two bilingual jurors were not race-neutral. In evaluating the race-neutrality of an attorney's explanation, a court must determine whether, assuming the proffered reasons for the peremptory challenges are true, the challenges violate the Equal Protection Clause as a matter of law. A court addressing this issue must keep in mind the fundamental principle that "official action will not be held unconstitutional solely because it results in a racially disproportionate impact....

1. The prosecutor later gave the same explanation for challenging the bilingual potential jurors: "... I felt that from their answers they would be hard pressed to accept what the interpreter said as the final thing on what the record would be, and I even had to ask the Judge to question them on that, and their answers were—I thought they both indicated that they would have trouble, although their final answer was they could do it. I just felt from the hesitancy in their answers and their lack of eye contact that they would not be able to do it."

Proof of racially discriminatory intent or purpose is required to show a violation of the Equal Protection Clause." " 'Discriminatory purpose' . . . implies more than intent as volition or intent as awareness of consequences. It implies that the decisionmaker . . . selected . . . a particular course of action at least in part 'because of,' not merely 'in spite of,' its adverse effects upon an identifiable group."

A neutral explanation in the context of our analysis here means an explanation based on something other than the race of the juror. At this step of the inquiry, the issue is the facial validity of the prosecutor's explanation. Unless a discriminatory intent is inherent in the prosecutor's explanation, the reason offered will be deemed race neutral.

Petitioner argues that Spanish-language ability bears a close relation to ethnicity, and that, as a consequence, it violates the Equal Protection Clause to exercise a peremptory challenge on the ground that a Latino potential juror speaks Spanish. He points to the high correlation between Spanish-language ability and ethnicity in New York, where the case was tried. We need not address that argument here, for the prosecutor did not rely on language ability without more, but explained that the specific responses and the demeanor of the two individuals during voir dire caused him to doubt their ability to defer to the official translation of Spanish-language testimony.

The prosecutor here offered a race-neutral basis for these peremptory strikes. As explained by the prosecutor, the challenges rested neither on the intention to exclude Latino or bilingual jurors, nor on stereotypical assumptions about Latinos or bilinguals. The prosecutor's articulated basis for these challenges divided potential jurors into two classes: those whose conduct during voir dire would persuade him they might have difficulty in accepting the translator's rendition of Spanish-language testimony and those potential jurors who gave no such reason for doubt. Each category would include both Latinos and non-Latinos. While the prosecutor's criterion might well result in the disproportionate removal of prospective Latino jurors, that disproportionate impact does not turn the prosecutor's actions into a per se violation of the Equal Protection Clause. . . .

Unless the government actor adopted a criterion with the intent of causing the impact asserted, that impact itself does not violate the principle of race-neutrality. Nothing in the prosecutor's explanation shows that he chose to exclude jurors who hesitated in answering questions about following the interpreter because he wanted to prevent bilingual Latinos from serving on the jury. . . .

In the context of this trial, the prosecutor's frank admission that his ground for excusing these jurors related to their ability to speak and understand Spanish raised a plausible, though not a necessary, inference that language might be a pretext for what in fact were race-based peremptory challenges. This was not a case where by some rare coincidence a juror happened to speak the same language as a key witness, in a community where few others spoke that tongue. If it were, the explanation that the juror could have undue influence on jury deliberations might be accepted without concern that a racial generalization had come into play. But this trial took place in a community with a substantial Latino population, and petitioner and other interested parties were members of that ethnic group. It would be common knowledge in the locality that a significant percentage of the Latino population speaks fluent Spanish, and that many consider it their preferred language, the one chosen for personal communication, the one selected for speaking with the most precision and power, the one used to define the self.

The trial judge can consider these and other factors when deciding whether a prosecutor intended to discriminate. For example, though petitioner did not suggest the alternative to the trial court here, Spanish-speaking jurors could be permitted to advise the judge in a discreet way of any concerns with the translation during the course of trial. A prosecutor's persistence in the desire to exclude Spanish-speaking jurors despite this measure could be taken into account in determining whether to accept a race-neutral explanation for the challenge.

The trial judge in this case chose to believe the prosecutor's race-neutral explanation for striking the two jurors in question, rejecting petitioner's assertion that the reasons were pretextual....

Deference to trial court findings on the issue of discriminatory intent makes particular sense in this context because ... the finding will "largely turn on evaluation of credibility." In the typical peremptory challenge inquiry, the decisive question will be whether counsel's race-neutral explanation for a peremptory challenge should be believed. There will seldom be much evidence bearing on that issue, and the best evidence often will be the demeanor of the attorney who exercises the challenge....

In the case before us, we decline to overturn the state trial court's finding on the issue of discriminatory intent unless convinced that its determination was clearly erroneous. It "would pervert the concept of federalism" to conduct a more searching review of findings made in state trial court than we conduct with respect to federal district court findings....

We discern no clear error in the state trial court's determination that the prosecutor did not discriminate on the basis of the ethnicity of Latino jurors. We have said that "[w]here there are two permissible views of the evidence, the factfinder's choice between them cannot be clearly erroneous." The trial court took a permissible view of the evidence in crediting the prosecutor's explanation. Apart from the prosecutor's demeanor, which of course we have no opportunity to review, the court could have relied on the facts that the prosecutor defended his use of peremptory challenges without being asked to do so by the judge, that he did not know which jurors were Latinos, and that the ethnicity of the victims and prosecution witnesses tended to undercut any motive to exclude Latinos from the jury. Any of these factors could be taken as evidence of the prosecutor's sincerity. The trial court, moreover, could rely on the fact that only three challenged jurors can with confidence be identified as Latinos, and that the prosecutor had a verifiable and legitimate explanation for two of those challenges. Given these factors, that the prosecutor also excluded one or two Latino venirepersons on the basis of a subjective criterion having a disproportionate impact on Latinos does not leave us with a "definite and firm conviction that a mistake has been committed."

Language permits an individual to express both a personal identity and membership in a community, and those who share a common language may interact in ways more intimate than those without this bond. Bilinguals, in a sense, inhabit two communities, and serve to bring them closer. Indeed, some scholarly comment suggests that people proficient in two languages may not at times think in one language to the exclusion of the other. The analogy is that of a high-hurdler, who combines the ability to sprint and to jump to accomplish a third feat with characteristics of its own, rather than two separate functions.... This is not to say that the cognitive processes and reactions of those who speak two languages are susceptible of easy generalization, for even the term "bilingual" does not describe a uniform category. It is a simple word for a more complex phenomenon with many distinct categories and subdivisions.

Our decision today does not imply that exclusion of bilinguals from jury service is wise, or even that it is constitutional in all cases. It is a harsh paradox that one may become proficient enough in English to participate in trial, ... only to encounter disqualification because he knows a second language as well....

Just as shared language can serve to foster community, language differences can be a source of division. Language elicits a response from others, ranging from admiration and respect, to distance and alienation, to ridicule and scorn. Reactions of the latter type all too often result from or initiate racial hostility. In holding that a race-neutral reason for a peremptory challenge means a reason other than race, we do not resolve the more difficult question of the breadth with which the concept of race should be defined for equal protection purposes. We would face a quite different case if the prosecutor had justified his peremptory challenges with the explanation that he did not want Spanish-speaking jurors. It may well be, for certain ethnic groups and in some communities, that proficiency in a particular language, like skin color, should be treated as a surrogate for race under an equal protection analysis.... And, as we make clear, a policy of striking all who speak a given language, without regard to the particular circumstances of the trial or the individual responses of the jurors, may be found by the trial judge to be a pretext for racial discrimination. But that case is not before us....

JUSTICE O'CONNOR, with whom JUSTICE SCALIA joins, concurring in the judgment.

I agree with the plurality that we review for clear error the trial court's finding as to discriminatory intent, and agree with its analysis of this issue. I agree also that the finding of no discriminatory intent was not clearly erroneous in this case. I write separately because I believe that the plurality opinion goes farther than it needs to in assessing the constitutionality of the prosecutor's asserted justification for his peremptory strikes. . . .

In this case, the prosecutor's asserted justification for striking certain Hispanic jurors was his uncertainty about the jurors' ability to accept the official translation of trial testimony. If this truly was the purpose of the strikes, they were not strikes because of race, and therefore did not violate the Equal Protection Clause under Batson. They may have acted like strikes based on race, but they were not based on race. No matter how closely tied or significantly correlated to race the explanation for a peremptory strike may be, the strike does not implicate the Equal Protection Clause unless it is based on race. That is the distinction between disproportionate effect, which is not sufficient to constitute an equal protection violation, and intentional discrimination, which is.

Disproportionate effect may, of course, constitute evidence of intentional discrimination. The trial court may, because of such effect, disbelieve the prosecutor and find that the asserted justification is merely a pretext for intentional race-based discrimination. But if, as in this case, the trial court believes the prosecutor's nonracial justification, and that finding is not clearly erroneous, that is the end of the matter. Batson does not require that a prosecutor justify a jury strike at the level of a for-cause challenge. It also does not require that the justification be unrelated to race. Batson requires only that the prosecutor's reason for striking a juror not be the juror's race.

JUSTICE STEVENS, with whom JUSTICE MARSHALL joins, dissenting.

. . . The Court mistakenly believes that it is compelled to reach this result because an equal protection violation requires discriminatory purpose. The Court overlooks, however, the fact that the "discriminatory purpose" which characterizes violations of the Equal Protection Clause can sometimes be established by objective evidence that is consistent with a decisionmaker's honest belief that his motive was entirely benign. "Frequently the most probative evidence of intent will be objective evidence of what actually happened," including evidence of disparate impact. The line between discriminatory purpose and discriminatory impact is neither as bright nor as critical as the Court appears to believe.

The Court therefore errs in focusing the entire inquiry on the subjective state of mind of the prosecutor. In jury selection challenges, the requisite invidious intent is established once the defendant makes out a prima facie case. No additional evidence of this intent is necessary unless the explanation provided by the prosecutor is sufficiently powerful to rebut the prima facie proof of discriminatory purpose. By requiring that the prosecutor's explanation itself provide additional, direct evidence of discriminatory motive, the Court has imposed on the defendant the added requirement that he generate evidence of the prosecutor's actual subjective intent to discriminate. . . .

I would reject the prosecutor's explanation without reaching the question whether the explanation was pretextual. . . . Even assuming the prosecutor's explanation in rebuttal was advanced in good faith, the justification proffered was insufficient to dispel the existing inference of racial animus.

The prosecutor's explanation was insufficient for three reasons. First, the justification would inevitably result in a disproportionate disqualification of Spanish-speaking venirepersons. An explanation that is "race-neutral" on its face is nonetheless unacceptable if it is merely a proxy for a discriminatory practice. Second, the prosecutor's concern could easily have been accommodated by less drastic means. As is the practice in many jurisdictions, the jury could have been instructed that the official translation alone is evidence; bilingual jurors could have been instructed to bring to the attention of the judge any disagreements they might have with the translation so that any disputes could be resolved by the court. Third, if the prosecutor's concern was valid and substantiated by the record, it would have supported a challenge for cause. The fact that the prosecutor did not make any such challenge, should disqualify him from advancing the concern as a justification for a peremptory challenge.

Each of these reasons considered alone might not render insufficient the prosecutor's facially neutral explanation. In combination, however, they persuade me that his explanation should have been rejected as a matter of law. Accordingly, I respectfully dissent.

Notes and Questions

1. Although the decisions in *Korematsu, Antelope, Greene,* and *Hernandez* address different forms of racial exclusion, they have a common feature. In each case, the Court concludes that the challenged conduct was not really race-based. What techniques were used?

2. Despite the Court's conclusions, in what ways do the decisions perpetuate patterns of privilege?

3. What was the basis for the military order in *Korematsu* if not race? How do the majority and dissenting opinions differ on this point? What does Justice Jackson mean when he observes that a judicial construction of the Constitution that sustains the military order is a "far more subtle blow to liberty than the promulgation of the order itself"?

4. In *Antelope,* the Court relied on Morton v. Mancari, 417 U.S. 535, 94 S.Ct. 2474, 41 L.Ed.2d 290 (1974), which upheld an employment preference for Indians in the Bureau of Indian Affairs. Is *Morton* easily distinguishable from *Antelope*? Did the Court pay sufficient attention to the different contexts? In what way is *Antelope* very much like *Hernandez*? Should the law treat Indian peoples as a distinct racial group? Compare David

Williams, *The Borders of the Equal Protection Clause: Indians as Peoples*, 38 UCLA L.Rev. 759 (1991) with Carole Goldberg–Ambrose, *Not "Strictly" Racial: A Response to "Indians as Peoples"*, 39 UCLA L.Rev. 169 (1991).

5. Are the majority and dissenting opinions in *Greene* discussing the same case? What explains the different perspectives? Is *Greene* similar in any respects to *Plessy*? Did the Court use rhetorical techniques or assumptions similar to those used in other cases in this section?

6. Do *Hernandez* and *Greene* illustrate the problems that Professor Lawrence (80–81, *supra*) identified with the "intent" standard?

7. In what way does the strike of a juror solely on language differ from one where language and race are connected? Consider the following observation: "[I]f the prosecutor had excluded a blond-haired, blue-eyed Brahmin woman from Long Island whose ancestors arrived in America on the Mayflower, and who was fluent in Spanish because she held a doctorate degree in the Spanish language, that exclusion would be less troubling. A strike truly based *solely* upon language seems quite different from a strike based upon the complex interrelationship between language and race. Language has a distinct meaning for certain racial and ethnic minority groups; it is an affirmative badge of identity signifying a bond to a common culture and history." Deborah Ramirez, *Excluded Voices: The Disenfranchisement of Ethnic Groups From Jury Service*, 1993 Wis.L.Rev. 761, 803.

8. Which of the "faces of oppression" (66, *supra*) appear in the cases in this section on racial exclusion?

D. GENDER AND SEXUALITY

1. *Construction of Gender and Sexuality*

Our cultural, social, political, economic and legal constructions of gender and sexuality privilege the experiences and understandings of males and heterosexuals as the unstated norms. This subsection offers examples of ways that the law has been a formidable player in the production and reproduction of these constructions.

We start with a recent overview explaining the nature/culture understandings of sex and gender based in the psychological literature, but with parallels in many other disciplines. In order to better understand how women have been subordinated in law and society, theorists have articulated a sex/gender model wherein sex is a term used to represent one's biological status, and gender is a term of art representing the social and cultural construction of identity based on roles attached to sexes.

**STEPHANIE RIGER, RETHINKING
THE DISTINCTION BETWEEN
SEX AND GENDER**

(unpublished manuscript)

RETHINKING THE DISTINCTION BETWEEN SEX AND GENDER

The study of sex differences has a long history in psychology. Beginning with the emergence of experimentation at the end of the 19th century, researchers (many of them women) attempted to identify empirically the "true" differences between men and women. At least three obstacles stymied these projects: Some studies found inconsistent results; many studies found no differences between the sexes; and it was impossible to create a non-sexist environment in which the essential natures of males and females could emerge untainted. One way out of the impasse was to shift from the study of cognitive and behavioral sex differences to the exploration of "masculinity" and "femininity" as opposite and complementary substrates of personality. Anne Constantinople's argument that femininity and masculinity were neither unidimensional nor bipolar led to a further shift to the study of androgyny. Acknowledging that an individual could be high in both "masculinity" and "femininity," the concept of androgyny freed personality traits from a corporeal base, although it continued to label some traits as "masculine" and others as "feminine". Moving beyond a focus on personality traits, contemporary approaches highlight the importance of status and power in determining sex differences in behavior and attitudes.

Critical to the evolution of this stream of research is the conceptual distinction of sex (i.e., one's biological properties) from gender (i.e., the cultural expectations of those in a certain sex category). John Money and his colleagues provided one of the earliest distinctions between sex and gender in pointing out that gender identity, one's sense of oneself as male or female, is not bound to biological sex. Separating gender from sex clarifies the assumption that behaviors or personality traits are not inextricably linked to biology; that is, that sex differences may be as much a product of culture as of nature and that there are as many ways of being "female" as there are different cultures. The replacement of the term "gender differences" by the currently popular usage "gender-related differences" further emphasizes the uncoupling of gender from sex. Confusion of the terms "sex" and "gender" reflects conflicting and muddled views about the causes of sex-linked phenomena.

In psychology, Rhoda Unger advocated the adoption of the dual vocabulary of sex and gender not only to limit assumptions of biological causality associated with findings of sex differences but also to highlight the importance of gender as a stimulus variable, i.e., how the label "male" or "female" alters others' expectations and perceptions. Feminist psychology currently emphasizes the way gender is negotiated through interpersonal interactions that reflect and reinforce an unequal distribution of power and resources in society. Sex is important primarily as a static cue that assigns people to a particular gender category, hence biological properties are relevant only as they are socially meaningful.

Distinguishing gender from sex has facilitated feminist research on the social construction of gender, i.e., the cultural, social, political and economic forces that shape relations between men and women. Eschewing biological determinism, much of this research treats culture as if it were completely separate and distinguishable from biology. Some claim that all sex differences other than those engaged in reproduction are socially constructed, suggesting that these differences are infinitely plastic and culturally malleable. From this perspective, bodies are neutral or merely blank slates on which culture inscribes its dictates. This view risks overlooking important, biologically-linked aspects of women's (and men's) experience. A woman's breastfeeding may affect her attitude toward her children, while a stressful occupation may affect women's and men's physiology in different ways. Certainly bodies are subject to cultural interpretation, but an emphasis on gender to the exclusion of sex (or on culture to the exclusion of biology) may disregard potentially important aspects of people's lives. A belief that biology is irrelevant may, indeed, hold women to a male standard of behavior. For example, many organizational policies ignore the fact that a woman's career-building years coincide with her childbearing years. These policies are not neutral; they are instead designed with the expectation that employees are male.

Including biology in a feminist psychology of women requires that we make explicit the assumptions underlying our conceptions of sex and gender. Here I examine problems with the concepts of sex and gender. I then criticize the assumed separation between sex and gender that stems from what I will argue is a false distinction between nature and nurture. Simple dichotomies such as "male/female" or "culture/nature" obscure the complex connections between their two poles while typically giving primacy to one of the pair. I conclude by advocating the use of a transactional model of the relationship between biology and the social environment as a strategy for including biology in the study of women and men.

Problems With the Conceptualization of Sex and Gender

Much of the research using the distinction between sex and gender assumes not only that sex is based on biology and gender on culture, but also that both are dimorphic. That is, two genders are assumed to parallel two sexes. These assumptions are problematic.

Five Sexes, Not Two?

As Unger noted, the division of sex into dichotomous categories is not always self-evident. The hormones associated with sex—androgen, estrogen and progesterone—exist in both males and females, albeit in different proportions. People who have ambiguous or contradictory sex characteristics also challenge our assumption of sexual dimorphism. The external genitalia and internal sex characteristics that occur congruently in most individuals may conflict in as many as 4% of the population. Intersexed individuals provide so many combinations of male and female sex characteristics that geneticist Anne Fausto–Sterling has created three more sex categories to facilitate proper classification. She adds to "male" and "female" the categories "merms" (for those who have testes and some aspects of female genitalia but no ovaries), "ferms" (for those who have ovaries and some aspects of male genitalia but lack testes) and "herms" (hermaphrodites: for those who have one testis and one ovary). Although Western culture rejects the notion of more than two sexes (and backs up that rejection with surgical intervention), some societies, such as the Sambia of Papua New Guinea or those in the Dominican Republic have a third social category for intersexed "females" who become male at puberty. These societies have three sexes (e.g., male, female, and *guevedoche* or "penis at twelve" in the Dominican Republic) but only two genders.

The need to identify the infant's "true sex" as male or female is a fairly modern invention. In the Middle Ages, individuals with hermaphroditic characteristics were free to decide at adolescence which sex to belong to, although they had to stick to that choice or be punished. Today, a general assumption in Western culture is that people have a "primary, profound, determined and determining sexual identity," discoverable at birth. In cases of intersexed infants, doctors assign sex based on the length of the penis, a literal example of phallocentrism. As Suzanne Kessler pointed out, physicians who treat the intersexed engage in a curious semantic reversal. They do not consider the ambiguous genitalia that are present at birth to be natural; rather, surgery restores the body to a "natural" state.

At the heart of the need to identify "true sex" is the belief that one's sex "hides the most secret parts of the individual: the structures of his fantasies, the roots of his ego, the forms of his relationship to reality". Hence, "proper" identification of the intersexed child's biological nature is necessary not only for purposes of sex classification but also because one's psychological essence resides in sex. Not only the blending of bodies is prohibited but also the blending of minds. Without assignment as male or female, and without surgical intervention to reinforce that assignment, an intersexed child has been thought in the modern era to be doomed to be a psychological misfit.

Kessler has argued that physicians undertake genital reconstruction of intersexed infants not because ambiguous genitalia are life-threatening to the child, but because they are threatening to a culture founded on a two-sex system. As Fausto–Sterling points out, laws governing the draft, marriage, the family, and sexuality are posited on a two-sex system; hence the state and the legal system have an interest in maintaining the belief in sexual dimorphism. But such a belief defies nature, since almost all biological aspects of gender exist on a continuum rather than in discrete categories. Males have relatively more "male" sex hormones while females have relatively more "female" ones, yet some individuals have hormone levels below those of their assigned sex but above those of the other sex. Even Fausto–Sterling's categories of "merms" and "ferms" treat as disjunctive differences that actually are continuous.

Perhaps the recognition of multiple sex categories will help break down the dichotomous thinking that pervades attitudes about the sexes. In a five sex system, it is impossible to talk about the "opposite" sex. Parents of two children tend to describe their children in contrasting terms: one is a leader, the other a follower; one is shy, the other aggressive. But parents of three or four children focus on unique aspects of each child in their descriptions, emphasizing diversity rather than opposition. Recognizing that the variables that make up biological sex exist on continua rather than in mutually exclusive categories may help break down the conceptualization of the sexes as paired opposites.

Many Genders—or None?

Gender, likewise, is not a simple dichotomy. Some cultures have a third gender that, like the Zuni "berdache," allows men to combines elements of male and female social roles, although few cultures permit females to act out the male gender role. The prevalence of a belief in a two-sex system obscures the perception of cultural systems which are not binary. Furthermore, gender must be viewed in the context of other demographic variables that have social import, such as race and ethnicity. Feminist theorists have long recognized that we cannot talk about "women", only about women in the context of their ethnicity, social class, and so forth: e.g., African–American women, young women, poor women, etc. The expectations and life experience of women may be defined as much by other demographic factors, such as race or poverty, as by gender. Even the capacity to bear children, sometimes thought a common denominator among women, is not shared by all. Yet women who are infertile are no less women. Ultimately this stream of thought should dissipate "woman"—or any other demographic variable—as a unitary category of analysis.

Many behaviors thought to be related to gender may actually be associated with status or power. What is considered feminine is frequently the product of powerlessness and low status. For example, although Carol Gilligan linked with gender an emphasis on rationality compared to relatedness in moral decision-making, Rachel Hare–Mustin and Jeanne Maracek reframed Gilligan's distinction, making status rather than gender the determining factor. Those in higher positions tend to advocate rules and rationality, while those lower in the hierarchy must focus on connection and communal goals to survive. From this perspective, gender is not the sum of individual personality characteristics attributed to males and females, but the product of interactional processes occurring within particular contexts that reflect and reinforce the distribution of resources in society.

PROBLEMS WITH THE NATURE/NURTURE DISTINCTION

Problems in understanding the relationship between sex and gender stem from an underlying assumption that nature is distinct from culture. This belief is deeply imbedded in our society and in our science. As philosopher of science Sandra Harding observed, "the culture/nature dichotomy structures public policy, institutional and individual social practices, the organization of the disciplines (the social versus the natural sciences), indeed the very way we see the world around us." The distinction between nature and culture—itself a product of culture—has been attacked on several grounds. First, some argue that our views of nature impose cultural stereotypes on the natural world: what we consider to be the "facts" of biology are actually the interpretations generated by culture. Others make the opposite argument, that culture is simply the manifestation of biology. In a third position, which I will argue is the most useful for the study of women and gender, nature and culture are inextricably entwined. Here I examine each of these positions briefly.

Biology as Culture

Some argue that rather than mirroring or even reflecting nature, biology (and indeed, all science) is permeated by cultural stereotypes of male and female that mediate and distort how we see reality. From this perspective, the "facts" purported to be discovered by biologists are merely cultural interpretations invented by them. Critics have challenged the disinterestedness of scientists on many grounds. Science is embedded in, not distinct from, society, and scientists are affected by the values and interests of the times. In biologist Ruth Hubbard's words, "Science is made by people who live at a specific time in a specific place and whose thought patterns reflect the truths that are accepted by the wider society." Feminist critics have pointed out the ways in which theories and practices in science reflect and reinforce a belief in male superiority.

Take, for example, research on the egg and the sperm. As eighth grade biology class taught us, the egg and the sperm unite to create a fertilized egg, the basis of human life. But anthropologist Emily Martin has drawn a convincing picture of how, when scientists study fertilization, they view that process through a lens of stereotypes of masculinity and femininity that colors what they see. Males are seen as *producing* sperm while females *shed* eggs, a less active process; the sperm is described in active terms, such as "burrow" and "penetrate", while the lowly egg "is transported" or even "drifts." The heroic sperm ventures up a dark passageway to find the dormant egg, the prize of its perilous journey. The female is seen as passive in this process, although as biosociologist Alice Rossi reminds us, "inert substances such as dead sperm and even particles of India ink reach the oviducts as rapidly as live sperm do". In short, biologists described the process of fertilization in terms that "feminized" the passive egg and "masculinized" the active, aggressive sperm.

Recently, however, this fairy tale has taken a modern twist: Current research suggests that adhesive molecules on the surface of the egg trap the sperm. Rather than a passive maiden, the egg now is depicted as an aggressive sperm-catcher, and fertilization the result of interaction between the two. But this picture too taints new data with old stereotypes: the egg is now portrayed as engulfing and devouring rather than passive and waiting. The common thread running through these interpretations is the stereotypes about women that they reflect.

Certainly biology is a product of culture, but it is not simply limited to reproducing cultural stereotypes. The socially constructed nature of biology allows the possibility of bias, but it does not mean that bias will predominate. As Fausto–Sterling pointed out, "The activities of scientists are self-deluding *and* self-correcting; they are at once potentially progressive and retrogressive." Strategies exist for minimizing the impact of cultural blinders on science. Biologist Ruth Hubbard, for example, proposed making explicit the implicit assumptions that underlie scientific descriptions and interpretations, while philosopher of science Sandra Harding advocated starting scientific inquiry from the perspective of women and other subordinate groups in order to reduce the distorted vision that comes from a position of dominance.

Culture as Biology

The opposite of the claim that science simply reproduces culture is the proposition that culture is always biologically-bound. One meaning of this claim is that social as well as biological influences are always mediated through the central nervous system. Because the elements of culture that shape our biological beings are themselves experienced biologically, culture is always mediated by biology. Accordingly, as Money acerbically put it, the opposite of our biological selves is not culture, but rather our astral beings.

Biological determinists take a further step, claiming that biology inevitably and inescapably determines relations between the sexes. Drawing on evolutionary theory, for example, sociobiologists claim that social behavior has a biological basis in the need of surviving organisms to perpetuate their genes. As Richard Dawkins put it, "we are survival machines—robot vehicles blindly programmed to preserve the selfish molecules known as genes". Sociobiologists' claims about rape illustrate this view. Applying a form of cost/benefit analysis, they argue that males are genetically programmed to rape when the potential reproductive benefits outweigh the cost of punishment. Yet there is no evidence that rape contributes to the reproductive success of the rapist. Indeed, the examples of same-sex rape in prison, rape-murders that obviously leave the victim unable to reproduce, and rape of girls not of childbearing age or of elderly women counter the argument that rape is reproductively beneficial or motivated.

Some sociobiologists claim that human universals, such as the sexual division of labor, demonstrate a biological basis for behavior. Such a claim has two major flaws. First, the universality of social phenomenon may be the product of ubiquitous social environments. Second, the universality of many behaviors is in dispute. Even though all societies divide labor by sex, for example, the form that division takes varies considerably both within and across cultures. In some societies, men earn the bread while women bake it, but in other cultures women are the merchants and financiers (Fausto–Sterling, 1985). Certainly some physical capacities and experiences of the sexes differ universally: only women experience menstruation, pregnancy, miscarriage, parturition, lactation and menopause; mothers typically take care of their very young children; and men are, on average, larger and stronger than women. Yet these define only central tendencies among human capacities, while the form that these capacities take is heavily dependent on social and cultural conditions. The amazing diversity of social arrangements across cultures and across time, particularly in conditions of rapid technological change, makes generalization fraught with danger.

Perhaps most damning to biological determinism is the shrinking or disappearing of the group differences purported to be explained by biology as our techniques of measurement become more sophisticated. In 1982, Melissa Hines could state with confidence that "Human males and females differ in their expression of several important behaviors, including play patterns, aggression, and certain cognitive abilities such as visuospatial and verbal ability". Such broad generalizations of sex differences can no longer be made.

Twenty years ago, many feminist social scientists rejected the idea of innate sex differences in thought or emotion, emphasizing instead the cultural construction of gender. A hallmark of this perspective was the publication in 1974 of Eleanor Maccoby and Carol Jacklin's encyclopedic *The Psychology of Sex Differences*. In their careful scrutiny of hundreds of studies of personality and abilities, Maccoby and Jacklin identified only a very small number of sex differences that could be considered scientifically reliable. Today, using meta-analytic statistical techniques, even the small number identified by Maccoby and Jacklin has shrunk. But by a decade after the publication of Maccoby and Jacklin's work, a strand of feminism had emerged that celebrates women's difference, exemplified by Carol Gilligan's book published in 1982, *In A Different Voice*.

Although Gilligan did not attribute difference to biology, other feminist social scientists such as Alice Rossi began to raise the question of biology's role in determining women's behavior. Rossi asserted that social factors as well as biology determine behavior, although most of the evidence she presented suggests biology as causal. Others seem to suggest a biological determinism centered on female's procreative capacity or on male's supposedly innate propensity for violence. Whereas sociobiologists and social Darwinists appeal to biology to justify the status quo, some radical feminists look to biology as the basis for challenges to the existing social order. Their arguments, focused primarily on male control of women's sexuality, seem to attribute men's potential for violence and aggression to an innate biological flaw. Ironically, other feminists had deemed sexist the attribution of a personality trait or behavior to women's biology when there is no evidence to support such causality. Unsubstantiated attributions from a reductionistic perspective about the impact of male biology on behavior seem no more persuasive.

Nature Versus Culture: A False Opposition

Perhaps the biggest problem in the nature/nurture distinction is the assumption that these are two independent domains, with biology providing the foundation on which social experiences are overlaid. From this perspective, gender is the social phenomena, diverging widely over place and time, that is imposed on biological difference, whereas biology typically is seen as the First Cause, more primary in its impact than other factors. This "bedrock" view of biology is illustrated in the following claim about sex differences in the brain:

> The die is cast *in utero;* that's when the mind is made up, and the luggage of our bodies, and of society's expectations of us, merely supplements this basic biological fact of life.

This perspective incorrectly implies that social effects are modifiable, while nature is immutable (surgical interventions notwithstanding). Anthropologist Clifford Geertz summarizes this "stratographic" metaphor:

> man *[sic]* is a composite of 'levels,' each superimposed upon those beneath it and underpinning those above it. As one analyzes man, one peels off layer after layer, each such layer being complete and irreducible in itself, revealing another, quite different sort of layer underneath. Strip off the motley forms of culture and one finds the structural and functional regularities of social organization. Peel off these in turn and one finds the underlying psychological factors—"basic need" or what-have-you—that support and make them possible. Peel off psychological factors and one is left with the biological foundations—anatomical, physiological, neurological—of the whole edifice of human life.

Rather than a set of separate levels, however, the relatively general response capacities of human beings are given shape and meaning by culture: "Gender is neither simply the manifestation of sex nor simply an easily dispensible artifact of culture. It is, instead, what a culture makes of sex; it is the cultural transformation of male and female infants into adult men and women". In a parallel fashion, all humans are born with a motor capacity to smile, but what they smile at is shaped by culture. The biological and social aspects of human experience constitute a unitary system, although they can be measured and analyzed separately. There is no such thing as a human nature independent of culture; that is, culture is just as essential an ingredient in human nature as biology, and vice versa. Accordingly, gender and sex are inextricably entwined.

Notes and Questions

1. Is the sex/gender dichotomy useful for understanding the dynamics of sex-based power and privilege in our society? Is there a similar biology/culture model for race? Is racial identity any less attached to biology than gender identity? than sexual identity (heterosexual, bisexual, gay, lesbian, transsexual)? What relevance ought biological factors have? How is the construction of gender identity different from the construction of racial identity that we studied in the last section? Is sexual identity related to or different from gender identity? How?

2. How ought our understanding of whether sex-based differences are biologically determined or culturally constructed affect the development and

application of law? Should the law treat biologically-based sex differences separately from culturally-based sex differences? Does Riger think these can be separated?

Catharine MacKinnon, a leading feminist theorist, has developed her own theory about how the law has understood and ought to address sex difference.

CATHARINE MacKINNON, ON DIFFERENCE AND DOMINANCE

in Feminism Unmodified 32–47 (Harvard U. Press, 1987).

What is a gender question a question of? What is an inequality question a question of? These two questions underlie applications of the equality principle to issues of gender, but they are seldom explicitly asked. I think it speaks to the way gender has structured thought and perception that mainstream legal and moral theory tacitly gives the same answer to them both: these are questions of sameness and difference. The mainstream doctrine of the law of sex discrimination that results is, in my view, largely responsible for the fact that sex equality law has been so utterly ineffective at getting women what we need and are socially prevented from having on the basis of a condition of birth: a chance at productive lives of reasonable physical security, self-expression, individuation, and minimal respect and dignity. Here I expose the sameness/difference theory of sex equality, briefly show how it dominates sex discrimination law and policy and underlies its discontents, and propose an alternative that might do something....

According to the approach to sex equality that has dominated politics, law, and social perception, equality is an equivalence, not a distinction, and sex is a distinction. The legal mandate of equal treatment—which is both a systemic norm and a specific legal doctrine—becomes a matter of treating likes alike and unlikes unlike; and the sexes are defined as such by their mutual unlikeness. Put another way, gender is socially constructed as difference epistemologically; sex discrimination law bounds gender equality by difference doctrinally. A built-in tension exists between this concept of equality, which presupposes sameness, and this concept of sex, which presupposes difference. Sex equality thus becomes a contradiction in terms, something of an oxymoron, which may suggest why we are having such a difficult time getting it.

Upon further scrutiny, two alternate paths to equality for women emerge within this dominant approach, paths that roughly follow the lines of this tension. The leading one is: be the same as men. This path is termed gender neutrality doctrinally and the single standard philosophically. It is testimony to how substance gets itself up as form in law that this rule is considered formal equality. Because this approach mirrors the ideology of the social world, it is considered abstract, meaning transparent of substance; also for this reason it is considered not only to be the standard, but a standard at all. It is so far the leading rule that the words "equal to" are code for, equivalent to, the words "the same as"—referent for both unspecified.

To women who want equality yet find that you are different, the doctrine provides an alternate route: be different from men. This equal recognition of difference is termed the special benefit rule or special protection rule legally, the double standard philosophically. It is in rather bad odor. Like pregnancy, which always calls it up, it is something of a doctrinal embarrassment. Considered an exception to true equality and not really a rule of law at all, this is the one place where the law of sex discrimination admits it is recognizing something substantive. Together with the Bona Fide Occupational Qualification (BFOQ), the unique physical characteristic exception under ERA policy, compensatory legislation, and sex-conscious relief in particular litigation, affirmative action is thought to live here.

The philosophy underlying the difference approach *is* that sex is a difference, a division, a distinction, beneath which lies a stratum of human commonality, sameness. The moral thrust of the sameness branch of the doctrine is to make normative rules conform to this empirical reality by granting women access to what men have access to: to the extent that women are no different from men, we deserve what they have. The differences branch, which is generally seen as patronizing but necessary to avoid absurdity, exists to value or compensate women for what we are or have become distinctively as women (by which is meant, unlike men) under existing conditions.

My concern is not with which of these paths to sex equality is preferable in the long run or more appropriate to any particular issue, although most discourse on sex discrimination revolves about these questions as if that were all there is. My point is logically prior: to treat issues of sex equality as issues of sameness and difference *is to take a particular approach*. I call this the difference approach because it is obsessed with the sex difference. The main theme in the fugue is "we're the same, we're the same, we're the same." The counterpoint theme (in a higher register) is "but we're different, but we're different, but we're different." Its underlying story is: on the first day, difference was; on the second day, a division was created upon it; on the third day, irrational instances of dominance arose. Division may be rational or irrational. Dominance either seems or is justified. Difference *is*.

There is a politics to this. Concealed is the substantive way in which man has become the measure of all things. Under the sameness standard, women are measured according to our correspondence with man, our equality judged by our proximity to his measure. Under the difference standard, we are measured according to our lack of correspondence with him, our womanhood judged by our distance from his measure. Gender neutrality is thus simply the male standard, and the special protection rule is simply the female standard, but do not be deceived: masculinity, or maleness, is the referent for both. Think about it like those anatomy models in medical school. A male body is the human body; all those extra things women have are studied in ob/gyn. It truly is a situation in which more is less. Approaching sex discrimination in this way—as if sex questions are difference questions and equality questions are sameness questions—provides two ways for the law to hold women to a male standard and call that sex equality . . . .

Having been very hard on the difference answer to sex equality questions, I should say that it takes up a very important problem: how to get women access to everything we have been excluded from, while also valuing everything that women are or have been allowed to become or have developed as a consequence of our struggle either not to be excluded from most of life's pursuits or to be taken seriously under the terms that have been permitted to be our terms. It negotiates what we have managed in relation to men. Legally articulated as the need to conform normative standards to existing reality, the strongest doctrinal expression of its sameness idea would prohibit taking gender into account in any way.

Its guiding impulse is: we're as good as you. Anything you can do, we can do. Just get out of the way. I have to confess a sincere affection for this approach. It has gotten women some access to employment and education, the public pursuits, including academic, professional, and blue-collar work; the military; and more than nominal access to athletics. It has moved to change the dead ends that were all we were seen as good for and has altered what passed for women's lack of physical training, which was really serious training in passivity and enforced weakness. It makes you want to cry sometimes to know that it has had to be a mission for many women just to be permitted to do the work of this society, to have the dignity of doing jobs a lot of other people don't even want to do.

The issue of including women in the military draft has presented the sameness answer to the sex equality question in all its simple dignity and complex equivocality. As a citizen, I should have to risk being killed just like you. The consequences of my resistance to this risk should count like yours. The undercurrent is: what's the matter, don't you want me to learn to kill . . . just like you? Sometimes I see this as a dialogue between women in the afterlife. The feminist says to the soldier, "we fought for your equality." The soldier says to the feminist, "oh, no, *we* fought for *your* equality."

Feminists have this nasty habit of counting bodies and refusing not to notice their gender. As applied, the sameness standard has mostly gotten men the benefit of those few things women have historically had—for all the good they did us. Almost every sex discrimination case that has been won at the Supreme Court level has been brought by a man. Under the rule of gender neutrality, the law of custody and divorce has been transformed, giving men an equal chance at custody of children and at alimony. Men often look like better "parents" under gender-neutral rules like level of income and presence of nuclear family, because men make more money and (as they say) initiate the building of family units. In effect, they get preferred because society advantages them before they get into court, and law is prohibited from taking that preference into account because that would mean taking gender into account. The group realities that make women more in need of alimony are not permitted to matter, because only individual factors, gender-neutrally considered, may matter. So the fact that women will live their lives, as individuals, as members of the group women, with women's chances in a sex discriminatory society, may not count, or else it is sex discrimination. The equality principle in this guise mobilizes the idea that the way to get things for women is to get them for men. Men have gotten them. Have women? We still have not got equal pay, or equal work, far less equal pay for equal work, and we are close to losing separate enclaves like women's schools through this approach.

Here is why. In reality, which this approach is not long on because it is liberal idealism talking to itself, virtually every quality that distinguishes men from women is already affirmatively compensated in this society. Men's physiology defines most sports, their needs define auto and health insurance coverage, their socially designed biographies define workplace expectations and successful career patterns, their perspectives and concerns define quality in scholarship, their experiences and obsessions define merit, their objectification of life defines art, their military service defines citizenship, their presence defines family, their inability to get along with each other—their wars and rulerships—defines history, their image defines god, and their genitals define sex. For each of their differences from women, what amounts to an affirmative action plan is in effect, otherwise known as the structure and values of American society. But whenever women are, by this standard, "different" from men and insist on not having it held against us, whenever a difference is used to keep us second class and we refuse to smile about it, equality law has a paradigm trauma and it's crisis time for the doctrine.

What this doctrine has apparently meant by sex inequality is not what happens to us. The law of sex discrimination that has resulted seems to be looking only for those ways women are kept down that have *not* wrapped themselves up as a difference—whether original, imposed, or imagined. Start with original: what to do about the fact that women actually have an ability men still lack, gestating children in utero. Pregnancy therefore is a difference. Difference doctrine says it is sex discrimination to give women what we need, because only women need it. It is not sex discrimination not to give women what we need because then only women will not get what we need. Move into imposed: what to do about the fact that most women are segregated into low-paying jobs where there are no men. Suspecting that the structure of the marketplace will be entirely subverted if comparable worth is put into effect, difference doctrine says that because there is no man to set a standard from which women's treatment is a deviation, there is no sex discrimination here, only sex difference. Never mind that there is no man to compare with because no man would do that job if he had a choice, and of course he has because he is a man, so he won't.

Now move into the so-called subtle reaches of the imposed category, the de facto area. Most jobs in fact require that the person, gender neutral, who is qualified for them will be someone who is not the primary caretaker of a preschool child. Pointing out that this raises a concern of sex in a society in which women are expected to care for the children is taken as day one of taking gender into account in the structuring of jobs. To do that would violate the rule against not noticing situated differences based on gender, so it never emerges that day one of taking gender into account was the day the job was structured with the expectation that its occupant would have no child care responsibilities. Imaginary sex differences—such as between male and female applicants to administer estates or between males aging and dying and females aging and dying—I will concede, the doctrine can handle.

I will also concede that there are many differences between women and men. I mean, can you imagine elevating one half of a population and denigrating the other half and producing a population in which everyone is the same? What the sameness standard fails to notice is that men's differences from women are equal to women's differences from men. There is an *equality* there. Yet the sexes are not socially equal. The difference approach misses the fact that hierarchy of power produces real as well as fantasied differences, differences that are also inequalities. What is missing in the difference approach is what Aristotle missed in his empiricist notion that equality means treating likes alike and unlikes unlike, and nobody has questioned it since. Why should you have to be the same as a man to get what a man gets simply because he is one? Why does maleness provide an original entitlement, not questioned on the basis of *its* gender, so that it is women—women who want to make a case of unequal treatment in a world men have made in their image (this is really the part Aristotle missed)—who have to show in effect that they are men in every relevant respect, unfortunately mistaken for women on the basis of an accident of birth?

The women that gender neutrality benefits, and there are some, show the suppositions of this approach in highest relief. They are mostly women who have been able to construct a biography that somewhat approximates the male norm, at least on paper. They are the qualified, the least of sex discrimination's victims. When they are denied a man's chance, it looks the most like sex bias. The more unequal society gets, the fewer such women are permitted to exist. Therefore, the more unequal society gets, the *less* likely the difference doctrine is to be able to do anything about it, because unequal power creates both the appearance and the reality of sex differences along the same lines as it creates its sex inequalities.

The special benefits side of the difference approach has not compensated for the differential of being second class. The special benefits rule is the only place in mainstream equality doctrine where you get to identify as a woman and not have that mean giving up all claim to equal treatment—but it comes close. Under its double standard, women who stand to inherit something when their husbands die have gotten the

exclusion of a small percentage of the inheritance tax, to the tune of Justice Douglas waxing eloquent about the difficulties of all women's economic situation. If we're going to be stigmatized as different, it would be nice if the compensation would fit the disparity. Women have also gotten three more years than men get before we have to be advanced or kicked out of the military hierarchy, as compensation for being precluded from combat, the usual way to advance. Women have also gotten excluded from contact jobs in male-only prisons because we might get raped, the Court taking the viewpoint of the reasonable rapist on women's employment opportunities. We also get protected out of jobs because of our fertility. The reason is that the job has health hazards, and somebody who might be a real person some day and therefore could sue—that is, a fetus—might be hurt if women, who apparently are not real persons and therefore can't sue either for the hazard to our health or for the lost employment opportunity, are given jobs that subject our bodies to possible harm. Excluding women is always an option if equality feels in tension with the pursuit itself. They never seem to think of excluding men. Take combat. Somehow it takes the glory out of the foxhole, the buddiness out of the trenches, to imagine us out there. You get the feeling they might rather end the draft, they might even rather not fight wars at all than have to do it with us.

The double standard of these rules doesn't give women the dignity of the single standard; it also does not (as the differences standard does) suppress the gender of its referent, which is, of course, the female gender. I must also confess some affection for this standard. The work of Carol Gilligan on gender differences in moral reasoning gives it a lot of dignity, more than it has ever had, more, frankly, than I thought it ever could have. But she achieves for moral reasoning what the special protection rule achieves in law: the affirmative rather than the negative valuation of that which has accurately distinguished women from men, by making it seem as though those attributes, with their consequences, really are somehow ours, rather than what male supremacy has attributed to us for its own use. For women to affirm difference, when difference means dominance, as it does with gender, means to affirm the qualities and characteristics of powerlessness.

Women have done good things, and it is a good thing to affirm them. I think quilts are art. I think women have a history. I think we create culture. I also know that we have not only been excluded from making what has been considered art; our artifacts have been excluded from setting the standards by which art is art. Women have a history all right, but it is a history both of what was and of what was not allowed to be. So I am critical of affirming what we have been, which necessarily is what we have been permitted, as if it is women's, ours, possessive. As if equality, in spite of everything, already ineluctably exists.

I am getting hard on this and am about to get harder on it. I do not think that the way women reason morally is morality "in a different voice." I think it is morality in a higher register, in the feminine voice.

Women value care because men have valued us according to the care we give them, and we could probably use some. Women think in relational terms because our existence is defined in relation to men. Further, when you are powerless, you don't just speak differently. A lot, you don't speak. Your speech is not just differently articulated, it is silenced. Eliminated, gone. You aren't just deprived of a language with which to articulate your distinctiveness, although you are; you are deprived of a life out of which articulation might come. Not being heard is not just a function of lack of recognition, not just that no one knows how to listen to you, although it is that, it is also silence of the deep kind, the silence of being prevented from having anything to say. Sometimes it is permanent. All I am saying is that the damage of sexism is real, and reifying that into differences is an insult to our possibilities.

So long as these issues are framed this way, demands for equality will always appear to be asking to have it both ways: the same when we are the same, different when we are different. But this is the way men have it: equal and different too. They have it the same as women when they are the same and want it, and different from women when they are different and want to be, which usually they do. Equal and different too would only be parity. But under male supremacy, while being told we get it both ways, both the specialness of the pedestal and an even chance at the race, the ability to be a woman and a person, too, few women get much benefit of either....

There is an alternative approach, one that threads its way through existing law and expresses, I think, the reason equality law exists in the first place. It provides a second answer, a dissident answer in law and philosophy, to both the equality question and the gender question. In this approach, an equality question is a question of the distribution of power. Gender is also a question of power, specifically of male supremacy and female subordination. The question of equality, from the standpoint of what it is going to take to get it, is at root a question of hierarchy, which—as power succeeds in constructing social perception and social reality—derivatively becomes a categorical distinction, a difference. Here, on the first day that matters, dominance was achieved, probably by force. By the second day, division along the same lines had to be relatively firmly in place. On the third day, if not sooner, differences were demarcated, together with social systems to exaggerate them in perception and in fact, *because* the systematically differential delivery of benefits and deprivations required making no mistake about who was who. Comparatively speaking, man has been resting ever since. Gender might not even code as difference, might not mean distinction epistemologically, were it not for its consequences for social power.

I call this the dominance approach, and it is the ground I have been standing on in criticizing mainstream law. The goal of this dissident approach is not to make legal categories trace and trap the way things are. It is not to make rules that fit reality. It is critical of reality. Its task is not to formulate abstract standards that will produce determinate outcomes in particular cases. Its project is more substantive, more jurisprudential than formulaic, which is why it is difficult for the mainstream discourse to dignify it as an approach to doctrine or to imagine it as a rule of law at all. It proposes to expose that which women have had little choice but to be confined to, in order to change it.

The dominance approach centers on the most sex-differential abuses of women as a gender, abuses that sex equality law in its difference garb could not confront. It is based on a reality about which little of a systematic nature was known before 1970, a reality that calls for a new conception of the problem of sex inequality. This new information includes not only the extent and intractability of sex segregation into poverty, which has been known before, but the range of issues termed violence against women, which has not been. It combines women's material desperation, through being relegated to categories of jobs that pay nil, with the massive amount of rape and attempted rape—44 percent of all women—about which virtually nothing is done; the sexual assault of children—38 percent of girls and 10 percent of boys—which is apparently endemic to the patriarchal family; the battery of women that is systematic in one quarter to one third of our homes; prostitution, women's fundamental economic condition, what we do when all else fails, and for many women in this country, all else fails often; and pornography, an industry that traffics in female flesh, making sex inequality into sex to the tune of eight billion dollars a year in profits largely to organized crime.

These experiences have been silenced out of the difference definition of sex equality largely because they happen almost exclusively to women. Understand: for this reason, they are considered *not* to raise sex equality issues. Because this treatment is done almost uniquely to women, it is implicitly treated as a difference, the sex difference, when in fact it is the socially situated subjection of women. The whole point of women's social relegation to inferiority as a gender is that for the most part these things aren't done to men. Men are not paid half of what women are paid for doing the same work on the basis of their equal difference. Everything they touch does not turn valueless because they touched it. When they are hit, a person has been assaulted. When they are sexually violated, it is not simply tolerated or found entertaining or defended as the necessary structure of the family, the price of civilization, or a constitutional right.

Does this differential describe the sex difference? Maybe so. It does describe the systematic relegation of an entire group of people to a condition of inferiority and attribute it to their nature. If this differential were biological, maybe biological intervention would have to be considered. If it were evolutionary, perhaps men would have to evolve differently. Because I think it is political, I think its politics construct the deep structure of society. Men who do not rape women have nothing wrong with their hormones. Men who are made sick by pornography and do not eroticize their revulsion are not under evolved.

This social status in which we can be used and abused and trivialized and humiliated and bought and sold and passed around and patted on the head and put in place and told to smile so that we look as though we're enjoying it all is not what some of us have in mind as sex equality.

This second approach—which is not abstract, which is at odds with socially imposed reality and therefore does not look like a standard according to the standard for standards—became the implicit model for racial justice applied by the courts during the sixties. It has since eroded with the erosion of judicial commitment to racial equality. It was based on the realization that the condition of Blacks in particular was not fundamentally a matter of rational or irrational differentiation on the basis of race but was fundamentally a matter of white supremacy, under which racial differences became invidious as a consequence. To consider gender in this way, observe again that men are as different from women as women are from men, but socially the sexes are not equally powerful. To be on the top of a hierarchy is certainly different from being on the bottom, but that is an obfuscatingly neutralized way of putting it, as a hierarchy is a great deal more than that. If gender were merely a question of difference, sex inequality would be a problem of mere sexism, of mistaken differentiation, of inaccurate categorization of individuals. This is what the difference approach thinks it is and is therefore sensitive to. But if gender is an inequality first, constructed as a socially relevant differentiation in order to keep that inequality in place, then sex inequality questions are questions of systematic dominance, of male supremacy, which is not at all abstract and is anything but a mistake.

If differentiation into classifications, in itself, is discrimination, as it is in difference doctrine, the use of law to change group-based social inequalities becomes problematic, even contradictory. This is because the group whose situation is to be changed must necessarily be legally identified and delineated, yet to do so is considered in fundamental tension with the guarantee against legally sanctioned inequality. If differentiation is discrimination, affirmative action, and any legal change in social inequality, is discrimination—but the existing social differentiations which constitute the inequality are not? This is only to say that, in the view that equates differentiation with discrimination, changing an unequal status quo is discrimination, but allowing it to exist is not.

Looking at the difference approach and the dominance approach from each other's point of view clarifies some otherwise confusing tensions in sex equality debates. From the point of view of the dominance approach, it becomes clear that the difference approach adopts the point of view of male supremacy on the status of the sexes. Simply by treating the status quo as "the standard," it invisibly and uncritically accepts the arrangements under male supremacy. In this sense, the difference approach is masculinist, although it can be expressed in a female voice. The dominance approach, in that it sees the inequalities of the social world from the standpoint of the subordination of women to men, is feminist.

If you look through the lens of the difference approach at the world as the dominance approach imagines it—that is, if you try to see real inequality through a lens that has difficulty seeing an inequality as an inequality if it also appears as a difference—you see demands for change in the distribution of power as demands for special protection. This is because the only tools that the difference paradigm offers to comprehend disparity equate the recognition of a gender line with an admission of lack of entitlement to equality under law. Since equality questions are primarily confronted in this approach as matters of empirical fit—that is, as matters of accurately shaping legal rules (implicitly modeled on the standard men set) to the way the world is (also implicitly modeled on the standard men set)—any existing differences must be negated to merit equal treatment. For ethnicity as well as for gender, it is basic to mainstream discrimination doctrine to preclude any true diversity among equals or true equality within diversity.

To the difference approach, it further follows that any attempt to change the way the world actually is looks like a moral question requiring a separate judgment of how things ought to be. This approach imagines asking the following disinterested question that can be answered neutrally as to groups: against the weight of empirical difference, should we treat some as the equals of others, even when they may not be entitled to it because they are not up to standard? Because this construction of the problem is part of what the dominance approach unmasks, it does not arise with the dominance approach, which therefore does not see its own foundations as moral. If sex inequalities are approached as matters of imposed status, which are in need of change if a legal mandate of equality means anything at all, the question whether women should be treated unequally means simply whether women should be treated as less. When it is exposed as a naked power question, there is no separable question of what ought to be. The only real question is what is and is not a gender question. Once no amount of difference justifies treating women as subhuman, eliminating that is what equality law is for. In this shift of paradigms, equality propositions become no longer propositions of good and evil, but of power and powerlessness, no more disinterested in their origins or neutral in their arrival at conclusions than are the problems they address.

There came a time in Black people's movement for equality in this country when slavery stopped being a question of how it could be justified and became a question of how it could be ended. Racial disparities surely existed, or racism would have been harmless, but at that point—a point not yet reached for issues of sex—no amount of group difference mattered anymore. This is the same point at which a group's characteristics, including empirical attributes, become constitutive of the fully human, rather than being defined as exceptions to or as distinct from the fully human. To one-sidedly measure one group's differences against a standard set by the other incarnates partial standards. The moment when one's particular qualities become part of the standard by which humanity is measured is a millenial moment.

To summarize the argument: seeing sex equality questions as matters of reasonable or unreasonable classification is part of the way male dominance is expressed in law. If you follow my shift in perspective from gender as difference to gender as dominance, gender changes from a distinction that is presumptively valid to a detriment that is presumptively suspect. The difference approach tries to map reality; the dominance approach tries to challenge and change it. In the dominance approach, sex discrimination stops being a question of morality and starts being a question of politics.

You can tell if sameness is your standard for equality if my critique of hierarchy looks like a request for special protection in disguise. It's not. It envisions a change that would make possible a simple equal chance for the first time. To define the reality of sex as difference and the warrant of equality as sameness is wrong on both counts. Sex, in nature, is not a bipolarity; it is a continuum. In society it is made into a bipolarity. Once this is done, to require that one be the same as those who set the standard—those which one is already socially defined as different from—simply means that sex equality is conceptually designed never to be achieved. Those who most need equal treatment will be the least similar, socially, to those whose situation sets the standard as against which one's entitlement to be equally treated is measured. Doctrinally speaking, the deepest problems of sex inequality will not find women "similarly situated" to men. Far less will practices of sex inequality require that acts be intentionally discriminatory. All that is required is that the status quo be maintained. As a strategy for maintaining social power first structure reality unequally, then require that entitlement to alter it be grounded on a lack of distinction in situation; first structure perception so that different equals inferior, then require that discrimination be activated by evil minds who *know* they are treating equals as less.

I say, give women equal power in social life. Let what we say matter, then we will discourse on questions of morality. Take your foot off our necks, then we will hear in what tongue women speak. So long as sex equality is limited by sex difference, whether you like it or don't like it, whether you value it or seek to negate it, whether you stake it out as a grounds for feminism or occupy it as the terrain of misogyny, women will be born, degraded, and die. We would settle for that equal protection of the laws under which one would be born, live, and die, in a country where protection is not a dirty word and equality is not a special privilege.

Notes and Questions

1. Professor MacKinnon argues that there are two approaches to sex discrimination in the law. How does MacKinnon explain the difference approach and the dominance approach to gender in law? Professor Colker has argued for an approach similar to dominance to analyze discrimination and equal protection issues, an approach she labels anti-subordination.

Ruth Colker, *Anti–Subordination Above All: Sex, Race, and Equal Protection,* 61 N.Y.U.L.Rev. 1003 (1986).

2. If equality doctrine inevitably reinstates a male norm and male dominance, what legal concepts can be used instead?

3. If gender is a detriment that is presumptively suspect, does MacKinnon mean law cannot recognize gender at all?

4. Compare MacKinnon's view of gender with the one that Professor Riger develops.

Sex-based differences also involve our sexuality and sexual orientation. Suzanne Pharr demonstrates the links between homophobia, heterosexist privilege, violence against women, economic subordination, and misogyny.

SUZANNE PHARR, HOMOPHOBIA: A WEAPON OF SEXISM

Chapt. 1 (Chardon Press, 1988).

HOMOPHOBIA—the irrational fear and hatred of those who love and sexually desire those of the same sex. Though I intimately knew its meaning, the word homophobia was unknown to me until the late 1970s, and when I first heard it, I was struck by how difficult it is to say, what an ugly word it is, equally as ugly as its meaning. Like racism and anti-Semitism, it is a word that calls up images of loss of freedom, verbal and physical violence, death.

In my life I have experienced the effects of homophobia through rejection by friends, threats of loss of employment, and threats upon my life; and I have witnessed far worse things happening to other lesbian and gay people: loss of children, beatings, rape, death. Its power is great enough to keep ten to twenty percent of the population living lives of fear (if their sexual identity is hidden) or lives of danger (if their sexual identity is visible) or both. And its power is great enough to keep the remaining eighty to ninety percent of the population trapped in their own fears.

Long before I had a word to describe the behavior, I was engaged in a search to discover the source of its power, the power to damage and destroy lives. The most common explanations were that to love the same sex was either abnormal (sick) or immoral (sinful).

My exploration of the sickness theory led me to understand that homosexuality is simply a matter of sexual identity, which, along with heterosexual identity, is formed in ways that no one conclusively understands. The American Psychological Association has said that it is no more abnormal to be homosexual than to be lefthanded. It is simply that a certain percentage of the population *is.* It is not healthier to be heterosexual or righthanded. What is unhealthy—and sometimes a source of stress and sickness so great it can lead to suicide—is homophobia, that societal disease that places such negative messages, condemnation, and violence on gay men and lesbians that we have to struggle throughout our lives for self-esteem.

The sin theory is a particularly curious one because it is expressed so often and with such hateful emotion both from the pulpit and from laypeople who rely heavily upon the Bible for evidence. However, there is significant evidence that the approximately eight references to homosexuality in the Bible are frequently read incorrectly, according to Dr. Virginia Ramey Mollenkott in an essay in *Christianity and Crisis:*

> Much of the discrimination against homosexual persons is justified by a common misreading of the Bible. Many English translations of the Bible contain the word homosexual in extremely negative contexts. But the fact is that the word *homosexual* does not occur anywhere in the Bible. No extant text, no manuscript, neither Hebrew nor Greek, Syriac, nor Aramaic, contains the word. The terms *homosexual* and *heterosexual* were not developed in any language until the 1890's, when for the first time the awareness developed that there are people with a lifelong, constitutional orientation toward their own sex. Therefore the use of the word *homosexuality* by certain English Bible translators is an example of the extreme bias that endangers the human and civil rights of homosexual persons.

Dr. Mollenkott goes on to add that two words in I Corinthians 6:9 and one word in Timothy 1:10 have been used as evidence to damn homosexuals but that well into the 20th century the first of these was understood by everyone to mean masturbation, and the second was known to refer to male prostitutes who were available for hire by either women or men. There are six other Biblical references that are thought by some to refer to homosexuals but each of these is disputed by contemporary scholars. For instance, the sin in the Sodom and Gommorah passage (Genesis 19:1–10) is less about homosexuality than it is about inhospitality and gang rape. The law of hospitality was universally accepted and Lot was struggling to uphold it against what we assume are heterosexual townsmen threatening gang rape to the two male angels in Lot's home. While people dwell on this passage as a condemnation of homosexuality, they bypass what I believe is the central issue or, if you will, *sin:* Lot's offering his two virgin daughters up to the men to be used as they desired for gang rape. Here is a perfectly clear example of devaluing and dehumanizing and violently brutalizing women.

The eight Biblical references (and not a single one by Jesus) to alleged homosexuality are very small indeed when compared to the several hundred references (and many by Jesus) to money and the necessity for justly distributing wealth. Yet few people go on a rampage about the issue of a just economic system, using the Bible as a base.

Finally, I came to understand that homosexuality, heterosexuality, bi-sexuality are *morally neutral*. A particular sexual identity is not an indication of either good or evil. What is important is not the gender of the two people in relationship with each other but the content of that relationship. Does that relationship contain violence, control of one person by the other? Is the relationship a growthful place for the people involved? It is clear that we must hold all relationships, whether opposite sex or same sex, to these standards. . . .

. . . "What will the world be like without homophobia in it—for everyone, female and male, whatever sexual identity?" Simple though the question is, it was at first shocking because those of us who work in the anti-violence movement spend most of our time working with the damaging, negative results of violence and have little time to vision. It is sometimes difficult to create a vision of a world we have never experienced, but without such a vision, we cannot know clearly what we are working toward in our social change work.

Here are some of the answers women have given:

● Kids won't be called tomboys or sissies; they'll just be who they are, able to do what they wish.

● People will be able to love anyone, no matter what sex; the issue will simply be whether or not she/he is a good human being, compatible, and loving.

● Affection will be opened up between women and men, women and women, men and men, and it won't be centered on sex; people won't fear being called names if they show affection to someone who isn't a mate or potential mate.

● If affection is opened up, then isolation will be broken down for all of us, especially for those who generally experience little physical affection, such as unmarried old people.

● Women will be able to work whatever jobs we want without being labeled masculine.

● There will be less violence if men do not feel they have to prove and assert their manhood. Their desire to dominate and control will not spill over from the personal to the level of national and international politics and the use of bigger and better weapons to control other countries.

● People will wear whatever clothes they wish, with the priority being comfort rather than the display of femininity or masculinity.

● There will be no gender roles.

It is at this point in the workshops—having imagined a world without homophobia—that the participants see the analysis begin to fall into place. Someone notes that all the things we have been talking about relate to sexual gender roles. It's rather like the beginning of a course in Sexism 101. The next question is "Imagine the world with no sex roles—sexual identity, which may be in flux, but no sexual gender roles." Further: imagine a world in which opportunity is not determined by gender or race. Just the imagining makes women alive with excitement because it is a vision of freedom, often just glimpsed but always known deep down as truth. Pure joy.

We talk about what it would be like to be born in a world in which there were no expectations or treatment based on gender but instead only the expectation that each child, no matter what race or sex, would be given as many options and possibilities as society could muster. Then we discuss what girls and boys would be like at puberty and beyond if sex role expectations didn't come crashing down on them with girls' achievement levels beginning to decline thereafter; what it would be for women to have the training and options for economic equity with men; what would happen to issues of power and control, and therefore violence, if there were real equality. To have no prescribed sex roles would open the possibility of equality. It is a discussion women find difficult to leave. Freedom calls.

PATRIARCHY—an enforced belief in male dominance and control—is the ideology and sexism the system that holds it in place. The catechism goes like this: Who do gender roles serve? Men and the women who seek power from them. Who suffers from gender roles? Women most completely and men in part. How are gender roles maintained? By the weapons of sexism: economics, violence, homophobia....

Sexism, that system by which women are kept subordinate to men, is kept in place by three powerful weapons designed to cause or threaten women with pain and loss. As stated before, the three are economics, violence, and homophobia....

ECONOMICS must be looked at first because many feminists consider it to be the root cause of sexism. Certainly the United Nations study released at the final conference of the International Decade on Women, held in Nairobi, Kenya, in 1985, supports that belief: of the world's population, women do 75% of the work, receive 10% of the pay and own 1% of the property. In the United States it is also supported by the opposition of the government to the idea of comparable worth and pay equity, as expressed by Ronald Reagan who referred to pay equity as "a joke." Obviously, it is considered a dangerous idea. Men profit not only from women's unpaid work in the home but from our underpaid work within horizontal female segregation such as clerical workers or upwardly mobile tokenism in the workplace where a few affirmative action promotions are expected to take care of all women's economic equality needs. Moreover, they profit from women's bodies through pornography, prostitution, and international female sexual slavery. And white men profit from both the labor of women and of men of color. Forced economic dependency puts women under male control and severely limits women's options for self-determination and self-sufficiency.

This truth is borne out by the fact that according to the National Commission on Working Women, on average, women of all races working year round earn only 64 cents to every one dollar a man makes. Also, the U.S. Census Bureau reports that only 9 percent of working women make over $25,000 a year. There is fierce opposition to women gaining employment in the nontraditional job market, that is, those jobs that traditionally employ less than 25 percent women. After a woman has gained one of these higher paying jobs, she is often faced with sexual harassment, lesbian baiting, and violence. It is clear that in the workplace there is an all-out effort to keep women in traditional roles so that the only jobs we are "qualified" for are the low-paid ones.

Actually, we have to look at economics not only as the root cause of sexism but also as the underlying, driving force that keeps all the oppressions in place. In the United States, our economic system is shaped like a pyramid, with a few people at the top, primarily white males, being supported by large numbers of unpaid or low-paid workers at the bottom. When we look at this pyramid, we begin to understand the major connection between sexism and racism because those groups at the bottom of the pyramid are women and people of color. We then begin to understand why there is such a fervent effort to keep those oppressive systems (racism and sexism and all the ways they are manifested) in place to maintain the unpaid and low-paid labor.

Susan DeMarco and Jim Hightower, writing for *Mother Jones,* report that *Forbes* magazine indicated that.... "By 1983, those at this 1 percent tip of our economy owned 34.3 percent of our wealth.... *Today, the top 1 percent of Americans possesses more net wealth than the bottom 90 percent.*" (My italics.) (*May, 1988, pp. 32–33*)

In order for this top-heavy system of economic inequity to maintain itself, the 90 percent on the bottom must keep supplying cheap labor. A very complex, intricate system of institutionalized oppressions is necessary to maintain the status quo so that the vast majority will not demand its fair share of wealth and resources and bring the system down....

Economics is the great controller in both sexism and racism. If a person can't acquire food, shelter, and clothing and provide them for children, then that person can be forced to do many things in order to survive....

The method is complex: limit educational and training opportunities for women and for people of color and then withhold adequate paying jobs with the excuse that people of color and women are incapable of filling them. Blame the economic victim and keep the victim's self-esteem low through invisibility and distortion within the media and education. Allow a few people of color and women to succeed among the profit-makers so that blaming those who don't "make it" can be intensified. Encourage those few who succeed in gaining power now to turn against those who remain behind rather than to use their resources to make change for all. Maintain the myth of scarcity—that there are not enough jobs, resources, etc., to go around—among the middleclass so that they will not unite with laborers, immigrants, and the unemployed. The method keeps in place a system of control and profit by a few and a constant source of cheap labor to maintain it.

If anyone steps out of line, take her/his job away. Let homelessness and hunger do their work. The economic weapon works. And we end up saying, "I would do this or that—be openly who I am, speak out against injustice, work for civil rights, join a labor union, go to a political march, etc.—if I didn't have this job. I can't afford to lose it." We stay in an abusive situation because we see no other way to survive....

VIOLENCE is the second means of keeping women in line, in a narrowly defined place and role. First, there is the physical violence of battering, rape, and incest....

Violence against women is directly related to the condition of women in a society that refuses us equal pay, equal access to resources, and equal status with males. From this condition comes men's confirmation of their sense of ownership of women, power over women, and assumed right to control women for their own means. Men physically and emotionally abuse women because they *can*, because they live in a world that gives them permission. Male violence is fed by their sense of their *right* to dominate and control, and their sense of superiority over a group of people who, because of gender, they consider inferior to them.

It is not just the violence but the threat of violence that controls our lives. Because the burden of responsibility has been placed so often on the potential victim, as women we have curtailed our freedom in order to protect ourselves from violence. Because of the threat of rapists, we stay on alert, being careful not to walk in isolated places, being careful where we park our cars, adding incredible security measures to our homes—massive locks, lights, alarms, if we can afford them—and we avoid places where we will appear vulnerable or unprotected while the abuser walks with freedom. Fear, often now so commonplace that it is unacknowledged, shapes our lives, reducing our freedom.

As Bernice Reagan of the musical group Sweet Honey in the Rock said at the 1982 National Coalition Against Domestic Violence conference, women seem to carry a genetic memory that women were once burned as witches when we stepped out of line. To this day, mothers pass on to their daughters word of the dangers they face and teach them the ways they must limit their lives in order to survive.

Part of the way sexism stays in place is the societal promise of survival, false and unfulfilled as it is, that women will not suffer violence if we attach ourselves to a man to protect us. A woman without a man is told she is vulnerable to external violence and, worse, that there is something wrong with her. When the male abuser calls a woman a lesbian, he is not so much labeling her a woman who loves women as he is warning her that by resisting him, she is choosing to be outside society's protection from male institutions and therefore from wide-ranging, unspecified, ever-present violence....

Many women say that verbal violence causes more harm than physical violence because it damages self-esteem so deeply. Women have not wanted to hear battered women say that the verbal abuse was as hurtful as the physical abuse: to acknowledge that truth would be tantamount to acknowledging that *virtually every woman is a battered woman.* It is difficult to keep strong against accusations of being a bitch, stupid, inferior, etc., etc. It is especially difficult when these individual assaults are backed up by a society that shows women in textbooks, advertising, TV programs, movies, etc., as debased, silly, inferior, and sexually objectified, and a society that gives tacit approval to pornography. When we internalize these messages, we call the result "low self-esteem," a therapeutic individualized term. It seems to me we should use the more political expression: when we internalize these messages, we experience *internalized sexism,* and we experience it in common with all women living in a sexist world. The violence against us is supported by a society in which woman-hating is deeply imbedded. . . .

HOMOPHOBIA works effectively as a weapon of sexism because it is joined with a powerful arm, heterosexism. Heterosexism creates the climate for homophobia with its assumption that the world is and must be heterosexual and its display of power and privilege as the norm. Heterosexism is the systemic display of homophobia in the institutions of society. Heterosexism and homophobia work together to enforce compulsory heterosexuality and that bastion of patriarchal power, the nuclear family. The central focus of the rightwing attack against women's liberation is that women's equality, women's self-determination, women's control of our own bodies and lives will damage what they see as the crucial societal institution, the nuclear family. The attack has been led by fundamentalist ministers across the country. The two areas they have focused on most consistently are abortion and homosexuality, and their passion has led them to bomb women's clinics and to recommend deprogramming for homosexuals and establishing camps to quarantine people with AIDS. To resist marriage and/or heterosexuality is to risk severe punishment and loss. . . .

There was a time when the two most condemning accusations against a woman meant to ostracize and disempower her were "whore" and "lesbian." The sexual revolution and changing attitudes about heterosexual behavior may have led to some lessening of the power of the word *whore,* though it still has strength as a threat to sexual property and prostitutes are stigmatized and abused. However, the word *lesbian* is still fully charged and carries with it the full threat of loss of power and privilege, the threat of being cut asunder, abandoned, and left outside society's protection.

To be a lesbian is to be *perceived* as someone who has stepped out of line, who has moved out of sexual/economic dependence on a male, who is woman-identified. A lesbian is perceived as someone who can live without a man, and who is therefore (however illogically) against men. . . . Many heterosexual women see her as someone who stands in contradiction to the sacrifices they have made to conform to compulsory heterosexuality. A lesbian is perceived as a threat to the nuclear family, to male dominance and control, to the very heart of sexism.

Gay men are perceived also as a threat to male dominance and control, and the homophobia expressed against them has the same roots in sexism as does homophobia against lesbians. Visible gay men are the objects of extreme hatred and fear by heterosexual men because their breaking ranks with male heterosexual solidarity is seen as a damaging rent in the very fabric of sexism. They are seen as betrayers, as traitors who must be punished and eliminated. In the beating and killing of gay men we see clear evidence of this hatred. When we see the fierce homophobia expressed toward gay men, we can begin to understand the ways sexism also affects males through imposing rigid, dehumanizing gender roles on them. The two circumstances in which it is legitimate for men to be openly physically affectionate with one another are in competitive sports and in the crisis of war. For many men, these two experiences are the highlights of their lives, and they think of them again and again with nostalgia. War and sports offer a cover of all-male safety and dominance to keep away the notion of affectionate openness being identified with homosexuality. When gay men break ranks with male roles through bonding and affection outside the arenas of war and sports, they are perceived as not being "real men," that is, as being identified with women, the weaker sex that must be dominated and that over the centuries has been the object of male hatred and abuse. Misogyny gets transferred to gay men with a vengeance and is increased by the fear that their sexual identity and behavior will bring down the entire system of male dominance and compulsory heterosexuality.

. . . Lesbian baiting is an attempt to control women by labeling us as lesbians because our behavior is not acceptable, that is, when we are being independent, going our own way, living whole lives, fighting for our rights, demanding equal pay, saying no to violence, being self-assertive, bonding with and loving the company of women, assuming the right to our bodies, insisting upon our own authority, making changes that include us in society's decision-making; lesbian baiting occurs when women are called lesbians because we resist male dominance and control. And it has little or nothing to do with one's sexual identity.

To be named as lesbian threatens all women, not just lesbians, with great loss. And any woman who steps out of role risks being called a lesbian. To understand how this is a threat to all women, one must understand that any woman can be called a lesbian and there is no real way she can defend herself: there is no way to credential one's sexuality. ("The Children's Hour," a Lillian Hellman play, makes this point when a student asserts two teachers are lesbians and they have no way to disprove it.) She may be married or divorced, have children, dress in the most feminine manner, have sex with men, be celibate—but there are lesbians who do all those things. *Lesbians look like all women and all women look like lesbians.* There is no guaranteed method of identification, and as we all know, sexual identity can be kept hidden. (The same is true for men. There is no way to prove their sexual identity, though many go to extremes to prove heterosexuality.) Also, women are not necessarily born lesbian. Some seem to be, but others become lesbians later in life after having lived heterosexual lives. Lesbian baiting of heterosexual women would not work if there were a definitive way to identify lesbians (or heterosexuals.)

We have yet to understand clearly how sexual identity develops....

We do know, however, that sexual identity can be in flux, and we know that sexual identity means more than just the gender of people one is attracted to and has sex with. To be a lesbian has as many ramifications as for a woman to be heterosexual. It is more than sex, more than just the bedroom issue many would like to make it: it is a woman-centered life with all the social interconnections that entails. Some lesbians are in long-term relationships, some in short-term ones, some date, some are celibate, some are married to men, some remain as separate as possible from men, some have children by men, some by alternative insemination, some seem "feminine" by societal standards, some "masculine," some are doctors, lawyers and ministers, some laborers, housewives and writers: what all share in common is a sexual/affectional identity that focuses on women in its attractions and social relationships.

... Homophobic people often assert that homosexuals have the choice of not being homosexual; that is, we don't have to act out our sexual identity. In that case, I want to hear heterosexuals talk about their willingness not to act out their sexual identity, including not just sexual activity but heterosexual social interconnections and heterosexual privilege. It is a question of wholeness. It is very difficult for one to be denied the life of a sexual being, whether expressed in sex or in physical affection, and to feel complete, whole. For our loving relationships with humans feed the life of the spirit and enable us to overcome our basic isolation and to be interconnected with humankind.

If, then, any woman can be named a lesbian and be threatened with terrible losses, what is it she fears? Are these fears real? Being vulnerable to a homophobic world can lead to these losses:

● *Employment....*

● *Family.* Their approval, acceptance, love.

● *Children.* Many lesbians and gay men have children, but very, very few gain custody in court challenges, even if the other parent is a known abuser. Other children may be kept away from us as though gays and lesbians are abusers. There are written and unwritten laws prohibiting lesbians and gays from being foster parents or from adopting children. There is an irrational fear that children in contact with lesbians and gays will become homosexual through influence or that they will be sexually abused. Despite our knowing that 95 percent of those who sexually abuse children are heterosexual men, there are no policies keeping heterosexual men from teaching or working with children, yet in almost every school system in America, visible gay men and lesbians are not hired through either written or unwritten law.

• *Heterosexual privilege and protection.* No institutions, other than those created by lesbians and gays . . . affirm homosexuality and offer protection. Affirmation and protection cannot be gained from the criminal justice system, mainline churches, educational institutions, the government.

• *Safety.* There is nowhere to turn for safety from physical and verbal attacks because the norm presently in this country is that it is acceptable to be overtly homophobic. Gay men are beaten on the streets; lesbians are kidnapped and "deprogrammed." The National Gay and Lesbian Task Force, in an extended study, has documented violence against lesbians and gay men and noted the inadequate response of the criminal justice system. . . .

• *Mental health.* An overtly homophobic world in which there is full permission to treat lesbians and gay men with cruelty makes it difficult for lesbians and gay men to maintain a strong sense of well-being and self-esteem. Many lesbians and gay men are beaten, raped, killed, subjected to aversion therapy, or put in mental institutions. The impact of such hatred and negativity can lead one to depression and, in some cases, to suicide. The toll on the gay and lesbian community is devastating.

• *Community.* There is rejection by those who live in homophobic fear, those who are afraid of association with lesbians and gay men. For many in the gay and lesbian community, there is a loss of public acceptance, a loss of allies, a loss of place and belonging.

• *Credibility.* This fear is large for many people: the fear that they will no longer be respected, listened to, honored, believed. They fear they will be social outcasts.

The list goes on and on. But any one of these essential components of a full life is large enough to make one deeply fear its loss. A black woman once said to me in a workshop, "When I fought for Civil Rights, I always had my family and community to fall back on even when they didn't fully understand or accept what I was doing. I don't know if I could have borne losing them. And you people don't have either with you. It takes my breath away." . . .

In the backlash to the gains of the women's liberation movement, there has been an increased effort to keep definitions man-centered. Therefore, to work on behalf of women must mean to work against men. To love women must mean that one hates men. A very effective attack has been made against the word *feminist* to make it a derogatory word. In current backlash usage, *feminist* equals *man-hater* which equals *lesbian*. This formula is created in the hope that women will be frightened away from their work on behalf of women. Consequently, we now have women who believe in the rights of women and work for those rights while from fear deny that they are feminists, or refuse to use the word because it is so "abrasive."

So what does one do in an effort to keep from being called a lesbian? She steps back into line, into the role that is demanded of her, tries to behave in such a way that doesn't threaten the status of men, and if she works for women's rights, she begins modifying that work. When women's organizations begin doing significant social change work, they inevitably are lesbian-baited; that is, funders or institutions or community members tell us that they can't work with us because of our "man-hating attitudes" or the presence of lesbians. We are called too strident, told we are making enemies, not doing good ...

In my view, homophobia has been one of the major causes of the failure of the women's liberation movement to make deep and lasting change. (The other major block has been racism.) We were fierce when we set out but when threatened with the loss of heterosexual privilege, we began putting on brakes. Our best-known nationally distributed women's magazine was reluctant to print articles about lesbians, began putting a man on the cover several times a year, and writing articles about women who succeeded in a man's world. We worried about our image, our being all right, our being "real women" despite our work. Instead of talking about the elimination of sexual gender roles, we stepped back and talked about "sex role stereotyping" as the issue. Change around the edges for middleclass white women began to be talked about as successes. We accepted tokenism and integration, forgetting that equality for all women, for all people—and not just equality of white middleclass women with white men was the goal that we could never put behind us.

But despite backlash and retreats, change is growing from within. The women's liberation movement is beginning to gain strength again because there are women who are talking about liberation for all women. We are examining sexism, racism, homophobia, classism, anti-Semitism, ageism, ableism, and imperialism, and we see everything as connected. This change in point of view represents the third wave of the women's liberation movement, a new direction that does not get mass media coverage and recognition. It has been initiated by women of color and lesbians who were marginalized or rendered invisible by the white heterosexual leaders of earlier efforts.... The third wave of the movement, multi-racial and multi-issued, seeks the transformation of the world for us all. We know that we won't get there until everyone gets there; that we must move forward in a great strong line, hand in hand, not just a few at a time.

Notes and Questions

Professors Mark Fajer and Sylvia Law elaborate on the links between homophobia, gender roles and law. Mark Fajer, *Can Two Real Men Eat Quiche Together? Storytelling, Gender–Role Stereotypes, and Legal Protection for Lesbians and Gay Men*, 46 U.Miami L.Rev. 511, 607–

651 (1992); Sylvia Law, *Homosexuality and the Social Meaning of Gender,* 1988 Wis.L.Rev. 187.

2. *Techniques of Exclusion Based on Sex or Gender*

Ideas that women are inferior and irrational permeate law. Not only were women excluded from power and privilege, they were considered property and controlled as if they were children, incompetents, or mere aspects of their husbands with no independent legal existence, no power to own property or enter contracts or testify in court. *See e.g.,* 1 William Blackstone, Commentaries on the Laws of England §§ 442–445. Even as women gained these rights and laws changed, societal attitudes about women lagged behind and colored outcomes in legal cases by influencing judicial interpretations. In the beginning of Chapter 3, we listed techniques courts use to exclude groups from power and privileges. All those techniques are used with gender, but the principal techniques used in legal opinions to exclude heterosexual women from power and privileges are based on appeals to natural law and nature, history, sex-based stereotyping, and a series of decisions declaring that some form of treatment which disadvantages only women is not sex-based discrimination. Although important language usages and techniques of sex-based exclusion exist in state court and lower federal court cases, the excerpts below are drawn from the U.S. Supreme Court's articulations of the issues.

Legal scholars have recently published wonderful casebooks and materials on gender, women, and law. Katharine Bartlett, Gender and Law: Theory, Doctrine, Commentary (Little, Brown & Co. 1993); Mary Becker, Cynthia Grant Bowman & Morrison Torrey, Feminist Jurisprudence: Taking Women Seriously (West, 1994); Mary Joe Frug, Women and the Law (Foundation Press, 1992); Herma Hill Kay, Sex–Based Discrimination: Text, Cases and Materials (3rd ed., West, 1988); Regina Graycar & Jenny Morgan, The Hidden Gender of Law (The Federation Press, 1990). For some edited collections on feminist legal theories, see D. Kelly Weisberg, ed., Feminist Legal Theory: Foundations (Temple U. Press, 1993); Patricia Smith, ed., Feminist Jurisprudence (Oxford U. Press, 1993); Katharine Bartlett & Roseanne Kennedy, eds., Feminist Legal Theory: Readings in Law and Gender (Westview Press, 1991); Martha A. Fineman & Nancy S. Thomadsen, eds., At the Boundaries of Law: Feminism and Legal Theory (Routledge, 1991); Leslie Friedman Goldstein, ed., Feminist Jurisprudence: The Difference Debate (Rowman & Littlefield, 1992).

a. *Natural Law, History, and Sex Stereotyping*

Justice Bradley's concurrence in *Bradwell v. Illinois* is the classic case of sex-based stereotyping and reference to divine or natural law in a judicial opinion.

BRADWELL v. ILLINOIS

Supreme Court of the United States, 1872.
83 U.S. (16 Wall.) 130, 21 L.Ed. 442.

[After having been denied admission to the Illinois state bar because of her sex, Myra Bradwell sued the State of Illinois arguing that refusal to grant her a license to practice law violated the privileges and immunities clause of the recently enacted Fourteenth Amendment. Neither the Illinois nor United States supreme courts agreed with her. Unwilling to let the case be decided purely on formal grounds about the reach of the Fourteenth Amendment, Justice Bradley, with whom Justices Swayne and Field joined, wrote these infamous paragraphs in his concurrence.]

MR. JUSTICE BRADLEY, concurring.

... The claim of the plaintiff, who is a married woman, to be admitted to practice as an attorney and counsellor-at-law, is based upon the supposed right of every person, man or woman, to engage in any lawful employment for a livelihood. The Supreme Court of Illinois denied the application on the ground that, by the common law, which is the basis of the laws of Illinois, only men were admitted to the bar, and the legislature had not made any change in this respect, but had simply provided that no person should be admitted to practice as attorney or counsellor without having previously obtained a license for that purpose from two justices of the Supreme Court, and that no person should receive a license without first obtaining a certificate from the court of some county of his good moral character. In other respects it was left to the discretion of the court to establish the rules by which admission to the profession should be determined. The court, however, regarded itself as bound by at least two limitations. One was that it should establish such terms of admission as would promote the proper administration of justice, and the other that it should not admit any persons, or class of persons, not intended by the legislature to be admitted, even though not expressly excluded by statute. In view of this latter limitation the court felt compelled to deny the application of females to be admitted as members of the bar. Being contrary to the rules of the common law and the usages of Westminster Hall from time immemorial, it could not be supposed that the legislature had intended to adopt any different rule.

The claim that, under the fourteenth amendment of the Constitution, which declares that no State shall make or enforce any law which shall abridge the privileges and immunities of citizens of the United States, the statute law of Illinois, or the common law prevailing in that State, can no longer be set up as a barrier against the right of females to pursue any lawful employment for a livelihood (the practice of law included), assumes that it is one of the privileges and immunities of women as citizens to engage in any and every profession, occupation, or employment in civil life.

It certainly cannot be affirmed, as an historical fact, that this has ever been established as one of the fundamental privileges and immunities of the sex. On the contrary, the civil law, as well as nature herself, has always recognized a wide difference in the respective spheres and destinies of man and woman. Man is, or should be, woman's protector and defender. The natural and proper timidity and delicacy which belongs to the female sex evidently unfits it for many of the occupations of civil life. The constitution of the family organization, which is founded in the divine ordinance, as well as in the nature of things, indicates the domestic sphere as that which properly belongs to the domain and functions of womanhood. The harmony, not to say identity, of interest and views which belong, or should belong, to the family institution is repugnant to the idea of a woman adopting a distinct and independent career from that of her husband. So firmly fixed was this sentiment in the founders of the common law that it became a maxim of that system of jurisprudence that a woman had no legal existence separate from her husband, who was regarded as her head and representative in the social state; and, notwithstanding some recent modifications of this civil status, many of the special rules of law flowing from and dependent upon this cardinal principle still exist in full force in most States. One of these is, that a married woman is incapable, without her husband's consent, of making contracts which shall be binding on her or him. This very incapacity was one circumstance which the Supreme Court of Illinois deemed important in rendering a married woman incompetent fully to perform the duties and trusts that belong to the office of an attorney and counsellor.

It is true that many women are unmarried and not affected by any of the duties, complications, and incapacities arising out of the married state, but these are exceptions to the general rule. The paramount destiny and mission of woman are to fulfil the noble and benign offices of wife and mother. This is the law of the Creator. And the rules of civil society must be adapted to the general constitution of things, and cannot be based upon exceptional cases.

The humane movements of modern society, which have for their object the multiplication of avenues for woman's advancement, and of occupations adapted to her condition and sex, have my heartiest concurrence. But I am not prepared to say that it is one of her fundamental rights and privileges to be admitted into every office and position, including those which require highly special qualifications and demanding special responsibilities. In the nature of things it is not every citizen of every age, sex, and condition that is qualified for every calling and position. It is the prerogative of the legislator to prescribe regulations founded on nature, reason, and experience for the due admission of qualified persons to professions and callings demanding special skill and confidence. This fairly belongs to the police power of the State; and, in my opinion, in view of the peculiar characteristics, destiny, and mission of woman, it is within the province of the legislature to ordain what offices, positions, and callings shall be filled and discharged by men, and shall receive the benefit of those energies and responsibilities, and that decision and firmness which are presumed to predominate in the sterner sex.

––––––––

Patterns of disadvantaging treatment toward women based on historical discrimination and sex-stereotyping have frequently been upheld by the Supreme Court as consistent with our constitution and laws. This extended note contains some excerpts from classic decisions.

After *Bradwell,* the Supreme Court unanimously decided that the fourteenth amendment also did not prohibit states from denying women the right to vote, *Minor v. Happersett,* 88 U.S. (21 Wall.) 162, 22 L.Ed. 627 (1874). Although the Court did declare that women may be citizens, *Id.* at 165, it unanimously noted that women's citizenship without voting power is consistent with a republican form of government:

> "[I]t is certainly now too late to contend that a government is not republican, within the meaning of this guaranty in the Constitution, because women are not made voters ... Women were excluded from suffrage in nearly all the States by the express provision of their constitutions and laws.... No new State has ever been admitted to the Union which has conferred the right of suffrage upon women, and this has never been considered a valid objection to her admission. On the contrary, as is claimed in the argument, the right of suffrage was withdrawn from women as early as 1807 in the State of New Jersey, without any attempt to obtain the interference of the United States to prevent it. Since then the governments of the insurgent States have been reorganized under a requirement that before their representatives could be admitted to seats in Congress they must have adopted new constitutions, republican in form. In no one of these constitutions was suffrage conferred upon women, and yet the States have all been restored to their original position as States in the Union." *Id.* at 177.

In this excerpt from *Minor* the court uses an additional technique of exclusion that we introduced in an earlier section and saw in the race-based materials as well—relying on past exclusions (history without evaluation) to justify current exclusions. Because we have never let women vote, the Court tells us, we can continue to exclude them. Is this a sound way to make an argument? If our history is laced with practices and laws that excluded groups of people from power and privileges, what constraints should the law put on the use of that history in legal arguments to support further exclusions? This technique of using historical discrimination to justify continued deprivation of rights and privileges occurs frequently in gender cases and reaches its pinnacle in materials on sexual orientation later in this section, particularly in *Bowers v. Hardwick,* 478 U.S. 186, 106 S.Ct. 2841, 92 L.Ed.2d 140 (1986), where Justices White's and Burger's opinions justify denying equal privacy and liberty rights to gays and lesbians because we have historically done so.

Reliance on historical exclusions took a second seat to reliance on stereotypical gender roles in *Hoyt v. Florida,* 368 U.S. 57, 82 S.Ct. 159, 7 L.Ed.2d 118 (1961), where the court decided it was constitutionally permissible to treat women differently with respect to obligations for jury duty. In *Hoyt* a woman criminal defendant accused of killing her husband with a baseball bat argued that her constitutional rights were violated by a Florida law that left her with an all-male jury in what today might be a "battered woman's defense" case, but then was a temporary insanity plea. Under Florida law at that time men were automatically included in the jury rolls, but women would only be included if they came forward and registered. Justice Harlan stated:

> In neither respect can we conclude that Florida's statute is not "based on some reasonable classification," and that it is thus infected with unconstitutionality. Despite the enlightened emancipation of women from the restrictions and protections of bygone years, and their entry into many parts of community life formerly considered to be reserved to men, woman is still regarded as the center of home and family life. We cannot say that it is constitutionally impermissible for a State, acting in pursuit of the general welfare, to conclude that a woman should be relieved from the civic duty of jury service unless she herself determines that such service is consistent with her own special responsibilities.... Florida is not alone in so concluding. Women are now eligible for jury service in all but three States of the Union. Of the forty-seven States where women are eligible, seventeen besides Florida, as well as the District of Columbia, have accorded women an absolute exemption based solely on their sex, exercisable in one form or another. In two of these States, as in Florida, the exemption is automatic, unless a woman volunteers for such service ...

> This case in no way resembles those involving race or color in which the circumstances shown were found by this Court to compel a conclusion of purposeful discriminatory exclusions from jury service. There is present here neither the unfortunate atmosphere of ethnic or racial prejudices which underlay the situations depicted in those cases, nor the long course of discriminatory administrative practice which the statistical showing in each of them evinced.

> In the circumstances here depicted, it indeed "taxes our credulity," Hernandez v. Texas, supra, 347 U.S. at 482, 74 S.Ct. 672 to attribute to these administrative officials a deliberate design to exclude the very class whose eligibility for jury service the state legislature, after many years of contrary policy, had declared only a few years before. It is sufficiently evident from the record that the presence on the jury list of no more than ten or twelve women in the earlier years, and the failure to add in 1957 more women to those already on the list, are attributable not to any discriminatory

motive, but to a purpose to put on the list only those women who might be expected to be qualified for service if actually called. Nor is there the slightest suggestion that the list was the product of any plan to place on it only women of a particular economic or other community or organizational group. *Id.* at 61–69, 82 S.Ct. at 166.

Intentionally treating one group (women) differently from another (men) is not purposeful discrimination to Justice Harlan and the court's majority. Harlan seems to think that discriminations based on "benign" or allegedly "benevolent" purposes are neither purposeful nor violative of equal rights. He also declares the absence of a history of prejudice against women, despite his previous paragraph mentioning "the enlightened emancipation of women from the restrictions and protections of bygone years, and their entry into many parts of community life formerly considered to be reserved to men" and their only recent eligibility for jury service at all. Do his conclusions match your understandings? What understanding or perspective about women would you have to have to write an opinion with the language contained in *Hoyt?* The holding in *Hoyt* did not last long and was overturned in *Taylor v. Louisiana,* 419 U.S. 522, 95 S.Ct. 692, 42 L.Ed.2d 690 (1975), when a man complained about the differential treatment of men and women in the jury pool. In 1994 the Court again faced issues of women and juries when it decided that gender-based peremptory challenges violated the constitution. *J.E.B. v. Alabama ex rel. T.B.,* ___ U.S. ___, 114 S.Ct. 1419, 128 L.Ed.2d 89 (1994).

Justice Frankfurter discussed the legitimacy of states treating women differently from men with respect to bartending, while also approving of treating women under the "control" of men differently from single or independent women with respect to "barmaiding," in *Goesaert v. Cleary,* 335 U.S. 464, 465–67, 69 S.Ct. 198, 199–200, 93 L.Ed. 163 (1948):

> We are, to be sure, dealing with a historic calling. We meet the alewife, sprightly and ribald, in Shakespeare, but centuries before him she played a role in the social life of England. The Fourteenth Amendment did not tear history up by the roots, and the regulation of the liquor traffic is one of the oldest and most untrammeled of legislative powers. Michigan could, beyond question, forbid all women from working behind a bar. This is so despite the vast changes in the social and legal position of women. The fact that women may now have achieved the virtues that men have long claimed as their prerogatives and now indulge in vices that men have long practiced, does not preclude the States from drawing a sharp line between the sexes, certainly, in such matters as the regulation of the liquor traffic. The Constitution does not require legislatures to reflect sociological insight, or shifting social standards, any more than it requires them to keep abreast of the latest scientific standards.

> While Michigan may deny to all women opportunities for bartending, Michigan cannot play favorites among women without

rhyme or reasons. The Constitution in enjoining the equal protection of the laws upon States precludes irrational discrimination as between persons or groups of persons in the incidence of a law. But the Constitution does not require situations "which are different in fact or opinion to be treated in law as though they were the same." Since bartending by women may, in the allowable legislative judgment, give rise to moral and social problems against which it may devise preventive measures, the legislature need not go to the full length of prohibition if it believes that as to a defined group of females other factors are operating which either eliminate or reduce the moral and social problems otherwise calling for prohibition. Michigan evidently believes that the oversight assured through ownership of a bar by a barmaid's husband or father minimizes hazards that may confront a barmaid without such protecting oversight. This Court is certainly not in a position to gainsay such belief by the Michigan legislature. If it is entertainable, as we think it is, Michigan has not violated its duty to afford equal protection of its laws. We cannot cross-examine either actually or argumentatively the mind of Michigan legislators nor question their motives. Since the line they have drawn is not without a basis in reason, we cannot give ear to the suggestion that the real impulse behind this legislation was an unchivalrous desire of male bartenders to try to monopolize the calling.

    ... Nor is it unconstitutional for Michigan to withdraw from women the occupation of bartending because it allows women to serve as waitresses where liquor is dispensed. The District Court has sufficiently indicated the reasons that may have influenced the legislature in allowing women to be waitresses in a liquor establishment over which a man's ownership provides control.

Justice Frankfurter assumes without question that Michigan could treat men and women differently and even exclude all women from certain professions. What about equal protection of the laws, requiring that similarly situated people be treated the same? Is it so obvious or true that men and women are inherently 'different in fact' so that their different treatment could not possibly violate a requirement of formal equality—treating similarly situated persons the same? Apparently Frankfurter and the majority of the Court thought that even minimal explanation or justification of different treatment was unnecessary. The only time reason must intervene to justify different treatment, says Frankfurter, is when addressing differences between how women are treated. And, he concludes, that differences in the treatment of women based on whether they are under the "control" of men are legitimate bases for discrimination. Justice Rutledge, with Justices Douglas and Murphy, dissented, taking issue with Justice Frankfurter's naivite about the rationality of the legislative classification:

    The statute arbitrarily discriminates between male and female owners of liquor establishments. A male owner, although he himself is always absent from his bar, may employ his wife and daughter as barmaids. A female owner may neither work as a barmaid herself nor employ her daughter in that position, even if a man is always present in the establishment to keep order. This inevitable result of the classification belies the assumption that the statute was motivated by a legislative solicitude for the moral and physical well-being of women who, but for the law, would be employed as barmaids. Since there could be no other conceivable justification for such discrimination against women owners of liquor establishments, the statute should be held invalid as a denial of equal protection. *Id.* at 467–68, 69 S.Ct. at 200–201 (Routledge, J. dissenting).

In a fashion similar to opinions already excerpted, Justice Rehnquist upheld the exclusion of women from registration for the military draft based on prior policies excluding them from combat (historical discrimination) and sex-role stereotyping.

> Women as a group, however, unlike men as a group, are not eligible for combat. The restrictions on the participation of women in combat in the Navy and Air Force are statutory. Under 10 U.S.C. § 6015 (1976 ed., Supp. III), "women may not be assigned to duty on vessels or in aircraft that are engaged in combat missions," and under 10 U.S.C. § 8549 female members of the Air Force "may not be assigned to duty in aircraft engaged in combat missions." The Army and Marine Corps preclude the use of women in combat as a matter of established policy. Congress specifically recognized and endorsed the exclusion of women from combat in exempting women from registration. In the words of the Senate Report: "The principle that women should not intentionally and routinely engage in combat is fundamental, and enjoys wide support among our people. It is universally supported by military leaders who have testified before the Committee.... Current law and policy exclude women from being assigned to combat in our military forces, and the Committee reaffirms this policy." ... The reason women are exempt from registration is not because military needs can be met by drafting men. This is not a case of Congress arbitrarily choosing to burden one of two similarly situated groups, such as would be the case with an all-black or all-white, or an all-Catholic or all-Lutheran, or an all-Republican or all-Democratic registration. Men and women, because of the combat restrictions on women, are simply not similarly situated for purposes of a draft or registration for a draft.

Rostker v. Goldberg, 453 U.S. 57, 76–78, 101 S.Ct. 2646, 2658–59, 69 L.Ed.2d 478 (1981). The military had excluded African–Americans from its ranks at times in our history, and we have had segregated armed forces, yet Rehnquist recognizes the illegitimacy of that kind of discrimination justifying exemption from registration for the draft. Why are women different? Is the exclusion of women from combat based on sex-role stereotypes, biological differences, or some other factor? Recent political debate has centered around the role of gays and lesbians in the military. Are the reasons used to justify exclusions of gays and lesbians from the military the same kinds of reasons used to justify the exclusion of women from combat? How is the reasoning the same or different?

Exclusion from combat and military service has a ripple effect in our society, since military service is a valued aspect of a citizen's obligations to his or her country and carries with it other social and economic privileges, like veterans' preferences for employment and veterans' benefits for education, housing and health care. Even after finding that Massachusetts' absolute veterans' preference had "a devastating impact upon the employment opportunities of women," *Personnel Administrator v. Feeney*, 442 U.S. 256, 260, 99 S.Ct. 2282, 2286, 60 L.Ed.2d 870 (1979) ("the statute today benefits an overwhelmingly male class. This is attributable in some measure to the variety of federal statutes, regulations, and policies that have restricted the number of women who could enlist in the United States Armed Forces, and largely to the simple fact that women have never been subjected to a military draft. *Id.* at 269–70, 99 S.Ct. at 2291), Justice Stewart ruled that this did not violate equal protection because it was a gender-neutral law and there was no purpose or intent to discriminate against women as a class. "When the totality of legislative actions establishing and extending the Massachusetts veterans' preference are considered, the law remains what it purports to be: a preference for veterans of either sex over nonveterans of either sex, not for men over women." It did not seem to matter that "[w]hen this litigation was commenced, then, over 98% of the veterans in Massachusetts were male; only 1.8% were female." *Id.* at 270, 99 S.Ct. at 2291.

In *Feeney* the court recognizes that the exclusion of women from combat has decreased the numbers of women who serve in the military and thus decreased the numbers of women eligible for Massachusetts absolute lifetime veterans' preference. Nonetheless, the preference with its unquestionably severe negative impact on women in public employment was upheld. We also saw that Justice Rehnquist in *Rostker* never examines the validity of the exclusion of women from combat, he just accepts it as "natural" and uses it as justification for excluding women from registration. What is there about the exclusion of women from combat that is so fundamental to who women are that it is beyond questioning?

While some women and feminists may not want to engage in combat activities, they claim the rights of citizenship to choose civil disobedience rather than be excluded. Wendy Williams argues that cases like *Rostker* and *Michael M. v. Superior Court* (challenging the sex discrimination in statutory rape laws that punish males but not females for consensual sex with people below a statutorily specified age of consent) feed into cultural images of man as the aggressor in war and sex and woman as the mother of humanity. Wendy Williams, *The Equality Crisis: Some Reflections on Culture, Courts, and Feminism,* 7 Women's Rights L.Rptr. 175 (1982). Christine Littleton makes an interesting argument that the only fair or equal way to deal with veterans' preferences, where most veterans are male, is to employ simultaneously a preference for women's gendered complement to military service and create a mothers' preference. Christine Littleton, *Reconstructing Sexual Equality*, 75 Cal.L.Rev. 1279 (1987).

Sexual stereotyping was the focal issue in *Price Waterhouse v. Hopkins*, 490 U.S. 228, 109 S.Ct. 1775, 104 L.Ed.2d 268 (1989). Finally when sex stereotyping was sufficiently blatant for a majority of the court to see, the court rejected its legitimacy as a motivating factor in employment discrimination. Ann Hopkins sued Price Waterhouse for sex discrimination when it refused her a partnership after many years of successful work for the firm. Among other comments about Hopkins, the record included:

> One partner described her as "macho"; another suggested that she "overcompensated for being a woman"; a third advised her to take "a course at charm school." Several partners criticized her use of profanity; in response, one partner suggested that those partners objected to her swearing only "because it's a lady using foul language." ... But it was the man who ... bore responsibility for explaining to Hopkins the reasons for the Policy Board's decision to place her candidacy on hold who delivered the coup de grace: in order to improve her chances for partnership, Thomas Beyer advised, Hopkins should "walk more femininely, talk more femininely, dress more femininely, wear make-up, have her hair styled, and wear jewelry."

Justice Brennan stated for the majority:

> In saying that gender played a motivating part in an employment decision, we mean that, if we asked the employer at the moment of the decision what its reasons were and if we received a truthful response, one of those reasons would be that the applicant or employee was a woman. In the specific context of sex stereotyping, an employer who acts on the basis of a belief that a woman cannot be aggressive, or that she must not be, has acted on the basis of gender.

> Although the parties do not overtly dispute this last proposition, the placement by Price Waterhouse of "sex stereotyping" in quotation marks throughout its brief seems to us an insinuation either that such stereotyping was not present in this case or that it lacks legal relevance. We reject both possibilities. As to the existence of sex stereotyping in this case, we are not inclined to quarrel with the District Court's conclusion that a number of the partners' comments showed sex stereotyping at work. See infra, at 1793–1794. As for the legal relevance of sex stereotyping, we are beyond the day when an employer could evaluate employees by assuming or insisting that they matched the stereotype associated with their group, for " '[i]n forbidding employers to discriminate against individuals because of their sex, Congress intended to strike at the entire spectrum of disparate treatment of men and women resulting from sex stereotypes.' " An employer who objects to aggressiveness in women but whose positions require this trait places women in an intolerable

and impermissible catch 22: out of a job if they behave aggressively and out of a job if they do not. Title VII lifts women out of this bind. . . .

In finding that some of the partners' comments reflected sex stereotyping, the District Court relied in part on Dr. [Susan] Fiske's expert testimony. . . . Indeed, we are tempted to say that Dr. Fiske's expert testimony was merely icing on Hopkins' cake. It takes no special training to discern sex stereotyping in a description of an aggressive female employee as requiring "a course at charm school." Nor, turning to Thomas Beyer's memorable advice to Hopkins, does it require expertise in psychology to know that, if an employee's flawed "interpersonal skills" can be corrected by a soft-hued suit or a new shade of lipstick, perhaps it is the employee's sex and not her interpersonal skills that has drawn the criticism.

Id., 490 U.S. at 250–256, 109 S.Ct. at 1790–1794.

Notes and Questions

1. This selected sample of Supreme Court case excerpts illustrates how cavalierly the Supreme Court permitted women to be disadvantaged by a history of exclusion and stereotyping of their sex. Not all Supreme Court cases find that differential treatment of men and women based on their sex is legitimate, but ironically, many cases where gender discrimination has been found to violate the constitution were brought by males. E.g., J.E.B. v. Alabama ex rel. T.B., ___ U.S. ___, 114 S.Ct. 1419, 128 L.Ed.2d 89 (1994); Mississippi University for Women v. Hogan, 458 U.S. 718, 102 S.Ct. 3331, 73 L.Ed.2d 1090 (1982) (cases brought by men where exclusion of men was found to be gender discrimination). See also Craig v. Boren, 429 U.S. 190, 97 S.Ct. 451, 50 L.Ed.2d 397 (1976); Orr v. Orr, 440 U.S. 268, 99 S.Ct. 1102, 59 L.Ed.2d 306 (1979); Califano v. Goldfarb, 430 U.S. 199, 97 S.Ct. 1021, 51 L.Ed.2d 270 (1977); Weinberger v. Wiesenfeld, 420 U.S. 636, 95 S.Ct. 1225, 43 L.Ed.2d 514 (1975); Wengler v. Druggists Mut. Ins. Co., 446 U.S. 142, 100 S.Ct. 1540, 64 L.Ed.2d 107 (1980); Taylor v. Louisiana, 419 U.S. 522, 95 S.Ct. 692, 42 L.Ed.2d 690 (1975) (overturning Hoyt v. Florida). But see Kahn v. Shevin, 416 U.S. 351, 94 S.Ct. 1734, 40 L.Ed.2d 189 (1974) and Califano v. Webster, 430 U.S. 313, 97 S.Ct. 1192, 51 L.Ed.2d 360 (1977) (cases brought by men where statutory advantages for women were upheld based on assumptions that they were differently situated because of long-standing disparate treatment). As Margaret Berger notes: "the constant thread through 'women's rights' cases is that most of the winners have been men, and that women have won only when it was not at the expense of a man." M. Berger, Litigation on Behalf of Women: A Review for the Ford Foundation 19 (1980).

2. Notice how Justice Harlan in *Hoyt* argues that the exclusions of women have not been characterized by prejudice and purpose in the way that exclusions of people of color have. Do you agree?

Although he could only get a plurality of the court to agree with him that strict scrutiny ought to apply to gender classifications, Justice Brennan's decision in Frontiero v. Richardson, 411 U.S. 677, 93 S.Ct. 176, 36

L.Ed.2d 583 (1973) contradicts Harlan's assumptions in *Hoyt* about how women have not been subject to disabling prejudices:

> There can be no doubt that our Nation has had a long and unfortunate history of sex discrimination.[13] Traditionally, such discrimination was rationalized by an attitude of "romantic paternalism" which, in practical effect, put women, not on a pedestal, but in a cage. Indeed, this paternalistic attitude became so firmly rooted in our national consciousness that, 100 years ago, a distinguished Member of this Court was able to proclaim: [quotation from Justice Bradley in Bradwell omitted.]
>
> As a result of notions such as these, our statute books gradually became laden with gross, stereotyped distinctions between the sexes and, indeed, throughout much of the 19th century the position of women in our society was, in many respects, comparable to that of blacks under the pre-Civil War slave codes. Neither slaves nor women could hold office, serve on juries, or bring suit in their own names, and married women traditionally were denied the legal capacity to hold or convey property or to serve as legal guardians of their own children. See generally L. Kanowitz, Women and the Law: The Unfinished Revolution 5–6 (1969); G. Myrdal, An American Dilemma 1073 (20th Anniversary ed. 1962). And although blacks were guaranteed the right to vote in 1870, women were denied even that right—which is itself "preservative of other basic civil and political rights"—until adoption of the Nineteenth Amendment half a century later.
>
> It is true, of course, that the position of women in America has improved markedly in recent decades. Nevertheless, it can hardly be doubted that, in part because of the high visibility of the sex characteristic, women still face pervasive, although at times more subtle, discrimination in our educational institutions, in the job market and, perhaps most conspicuously, in the political arena.[17] See generally K. Amundsen, The Silenced Majority: Women and American Democracy (1971); The President's Task Force on Women's Rights and Responsibilities, A Matter of Simple Act of 1964, 84 Harv.L.Rev. 1109 (1971).
>
> Moreover, since sex, like race and national origin, is an immutable characteristic determined solely by the accident of birth, the imposition of special disabilities upon the members of a particular sex because of their sex would seem to violate "the basic concept of our system that legal burdens should bear some relationship to individual responsibili-

13. Indeed, the position of women in this country at its inception is reflected in the view expressed by Thomas Jefferson that women should be neither seen nor heard in society's decisionmaking councils. See M. Gruberg, Women in American Politics 4 (1968). See also 2 A. de Tocqueville, Democracy in America (Reeves trans. 1948).

17. It is true, of course, that when viewed in the abstract, women do not constitute a small and powerless minority. Nevertheless, in part because of past discrimination, women are vastly underrepre-sented in this Nation's decisionmaking councils. There has never been a female President, nor a female member of this Court. Not a single woman presently sits in the United States Senate, and only 14 women hold seats in the House of Representatives. And, as appellants point out, this underrepresentation is present throughout all levels of our State and Federal Government. See Joint Reply Brief of Appellants and American Civil Liberties Union (Amicus Curiae) 9.

ty...." Weber v. Aetna Casualty & Surety Co., 406 U.S. 164, 175, 92 S.Ct. 1400, 1407, 31 L.Ed.2d 768 (1972). And what differentiates sex from such non-suspect statuses as intelligence or physical disability, and aligns it with the recognized suspect criteria, is that the sex characteristic frequently bears no relation to ability to perform or contribute to society. As a result, statutory distinctions between the sexes often have the effect of invidiously relegating the entire class of females to inferior legal status without regard to the actual capabilities of its individual members....

With these considerations in mind, we can only conclude that classifications based upon sex, like classifications based upon race, alienage, or national origin, are inherently suspect, and must therefore be subjected to strict judicial scrutiny.

Id. at 685–87, 93 S.Ct. at 1769–70.

Also, in a case reminiscent of *Goesaert*, the California Supreme Court rejected constraints on women serving as bartenders, finding that sex-based discrimination ought to receive the same strict scrutiny as race-based inequality.

Another characteristic which underlies all suspect classifications is the stigma of inferiority and second class citizenship associated with them. Women, like Negroes, aliens, and the poor have historically labored under severe legal and social disabilities. Like black citizens, they were, for many years, denied the right to vote and, until recently, the right to serve on juries in many states. They are excluded from or discriminated against in employment and educational opportunities. Married women in particular have been treated as inferior persons in numerous laws relating to property and independent business ownership and the right to make contracts.

Laws which disable women from full participation in the political, business and economic arenas are often characterized as "protective" and beneficial. Those same laws applied to racial or ethnic minorities would readily be recognized as invidious and impermissible. The pedestal upon which women have been placed has all too often, upon closer inspection, been revealed as a cage. We conclude that the sexual classifications are properly treated as suspect, particularly when those classifications are made with respect to a fundamental interest such as employment....

The second rationale—that women bartenders would be an "unwholesome influence" on the public—is even weaker than the first. The claim of unwholesomeness is contradicted by statutes which permit women to work as cocktail waitresses, serve beer and wine from behind a bar, or tend bar if they or their husbands hold a liquor license. The objection appears to be based upon notions of what is a "ladylike" or proper pursuit for a woman in our society rather than any ascertainable evil effects of permitting women to labor behind those "permanently affixed fixtures" known as bars. Such notions cannot justify discrimination against women in employment.

Sail'er Inn v. Kirby, 5 Cal.3d 1, 19–20, 95 Cal.Rptr. 329, 340–42, 485 P.2d 529 (1971).

3. Ironically, even though disadvantaging treatment frequently does not seem to violate equality provisions, classifications that seem to benefit women as a group have been held invalid on those grounds. In a case by an "otherwise qualified male" alleging "reverse discrimination," Justice Sandra Day O'Connor, writing for the court's majority, determined that a state-supported all-women's nursing school violated equal protection. *Mississippi University for Women v. Hogan*, 458 U.S. 718, 102 S.Ct. 3331, 73 L.Ed.2d 1090 (1982). She found the underlying gender-based assumptions offensive to the constitution.

MISSISSIPPI UNIVERSITY FOR WOMEN v. HOGAN

Supreme Court of the United States, 1982.
458 U.S. 718, 102 S.Ct. 3331, 73 L.Ed.2d 1090.

JUSTICE O'CONNOR delivered the opinion of the Court.

This case presents the narrow issue of whether a state statute that excludes males from enrolling in a state-supported professional nursing school violates the Equal Protection Clause of the Fourteenth Amendment.

I.

The facts are not in dispute. In 1884, the Mississippi Legislature created the Mississippi Industrial Institute and College for the Education of White Girls of the State of Mississippi, now the oldest state-supported all-female college in the United States. 1884 Miss.Gen.Laws, Ch. 30, § 6. The school, known today as Mississippi University for Women (MUW), has from its inception limited its enrollment to women.

In 1971, MUW established a School of Nursing, initially offering a 2–year associate degree. Three years later, the school instituted a 4–year baccalaureate program in nursing and today also offers a graduate program. The School of Nursing has its own faculty and administrative officers and establishes its own criteria for admission.

Respondent, Joe Hogan, is a registered nurse but does not hold a baccalaureate degree in nursing. Since 1974, he has worked as a nursing supervisor in a medical center in Columbus, the city in which MUW is located. In 1979, Hogan applied for admission to the MUW School of Nursing's baccalaureate program. Although he was otherwise qualified, he was denied admission to the School of Nursing solely because of his sex. School officials informed him that he could audit the courses in which he was interested, but could not enroll for credit.

Hogan filed an action in the United States District Court for the Northern District of Mississippi, claiming the single-sex admissions policy of MUW's School of Nursing violated the Equal Protection Clause of the Fourteenth Amendment. Hogan sought injunctive and declaratory relief, as well as compensatory damages.

Following a hearing, the District Court denied preliminary injunctive relief. The court concluded that maintenance of MUW as a single-sex school bears a rational relationship to the State's legitimate interest "in providing the greatest practical range of educational opportunities for its female student population." Id., at A3. Furthermore, the court stated, the admissions policy is not arbitrary because providing single-sex schools is consistent with a respected, though by no means universally accepted, educational theory that single-sex education affords unique benefits to students. Stating that the case presented no issue of fact, the court informed Hogan that it would enter summary judgment dismissing his claim unless he tendered a factual issue. When Hogan offered no further evidence, the District Court entered summary judgment in favor of the State.

The Court of Appeals for the Fifth Circuit reversed, holding that, because the admissions policy discriminates on the basis of gender, the District Court improperly used a "rational relationship" test to judge the constitutionality of the policy. Instead, the Court of Appeals stated, the proper test is whether the State has carried the heavier burden of showing that the gender-based classification is substantially related to an important governmental objective. Recognizing that the State has a significant interest in providing educational opportunities for all its citizens, the court then found that the State had failed to show that providing a unique educational opportunity for females, but not for males, bears a substantial relationship to that interest. Id., at 1119. Holding that the policy excluding Hogan because of his sex denies him equal protection of the laws, the court vacated the summary judgment entered against Hogan as to his claim for monetary damages, and remanded for entry of a declaratory judgment in conformity with its opinion and for further appropriate proceedings.

On rehearing, the State contended that Congress, in enacting § 901(a)(5) of Title IX of the Education Amendments of 1972, Pub.L. 92–318, 86 Stat. 373, 20 U.S.C. § 1681 et seq., expressly had authorized MUW to continue its single-sex admissions policy by exempting public undergraduate institutions that traditionally have used single-sex admissions policies from the gender discrimination prohibition of Title IX. Through that provision, the State argued, Congress limited the reach of the Fourteenth Amendment by exercising its power under § 5 of the Amendment. The Court of Appeals rejected the argument, holding that § 5 of the Fourteenth Amendment does not grant Congress power to authorize States to maintain practices otherwise violative of the Amendment. ...

We granted certiorari and now affirm the judgment of the Court of Appeals.

II

... That this statutory policy discriminates against males rather than against females does not exempt it from scrutiny or reduce the standard of review....

Although the test for determining the validity of a gender-based classification is straightforward, it must be applied free of fixed notions concerning the roles and abilities of males and females. Care must be taken in ascertaining whether the statutory objective itself reflects archaic and stereotypic notions. Thus, if the statutory objective is to exclude or "protect" members of one gender because they are presumed to suffer from an inherent handicap or to be innately inferior, the objective itself is illegitimate. See Frontiero v. Richardson, 411 U.S. 677 (1973) (plurality opinion).[10]

In limited circumstances, a gender-based classification favoring one sex can be justified if it intentionally and directly assists members of the sex that is disproportionately burdened. However, we consistently have emphasized that "the mere recitation of a benign, compensatory purpose is not an automatic shield which protects against any inquiry into the actual purposes underlying a statutory scheme." The same searching analysis must be made, regardless of whether the State's objective is to eliminate family controversy, to achieve administrative efficiency, or to balance the burdens borne by males and females. . . .

. . . Mississippi has made no showing that women lacked opportunities to obtain training in the field of nursing or to attain positions of leadership in that field when the MUW School of Nursing opened its door or that women currently are deprived of such opportunities. In fact, in 1970, the year before the School of Nursing's first class enrolled, women earned 94 percent of the nursing baccalaureate degrees conferred in Mississippi and 98.6 percent of the degrees earned nationwide. U.S. Dept. of Health, Education, and Welfare, Earned Degrees Conferred: 1969–1970, Institutional Data 388 (1972). That year was not an aberration; one decade earlier, women had earned all the nursing degrees conferred in Mississippi and 98.9 percent of the degrees conferred

---

10. History provides numerous examples of legislative attempts to exclude women from particular areas simply because legislators believed women were less able than men to perform a particular function. In 1873, this Court remained unmoved by Myra Bradwell's argument that the Fourteenth Amendment prohibited a State from classifying her as unfit to practice law simply because she was female. Bradwell v. Illinois, 16 Wall. 130, 21 L.Ed. 442 (1873). In his opinion concurring in the judgment, Justice Bradley described the reasons underlying the State's decision to determine which positions only men could fill: "It is the prerogative of the legislator to prescribe regulations founded on nature, reason, and experience for the due admission of qualified persons to professions and callings demanding special skill and confidence. This fairly belongs to the police power of the State; and, in my opinion, in view of the peculiar characteristics, destiny, and mission of woman, it is within the province of the legislature to ordain what offices, positions, and callings shall be filled and discharged by men, and shall receive the benefit of those energies and responsibilities, and that decision and firmness which are presumed to predominate in the sterner sex." Id., 16 Wall., at 142. In a similar vein, the Court in Goesaert v. Cleary, 335 U.S. 464, 466, 69 S.Ct. 198, 199, 93 L.Ed. 163 (1948), upheld a legislature's right to preclude women from bartending, except under limited circumstances, on the ground that the legislature could devise preventive measures against "moral and social problems" that result when women, but apparently not men, tend bar. Similarly, the many protective labor laws enacted in the late 19th and early 20th centuries often had as their objective the protection of weaker workers, which the laws assumed meant females. See generally B. Brown, A. Freedman, H. Katz, & A. Price, Women's Rights and the Law 209–210 (1977).

nationwide. U.S. Dept. of Health, Education, and Welfare, Earned Degrees Conferred, 1959–1960: Bachelor's and Higher Degrees 135 (1960). As one would expect, the labor force reflects the same predominance of women in nursing. When MUW's School of Nursing began operation, nearly 98 percent of all employed registered nurses were female.

Rather than compensate for discriminatory barriers faced by women, MUW's policy of excluding males from admission to the School of Nursing tends to perpetuate the stereotyped view of nursing as an exclusively woman's job.[15] By assuring that Mississippi allots more openings in its state-supported nursing schools to women than it does to men, MUW's admissions policy lends credibility to the old view that women, not men, should become nurses, and makes the assumption that nursing is a field for women a self-fulfilling prophecy. Thus, we conclude that, although the State recited a "benign, compensatory purpose," it failed to establish that the alleged objective is the actual purpose underlying the discriminatory classification.

... In sum, the record in this case is flatly inconsistent with the claim that excluding men from the School of Nursing is necessary to reach any of MUW's educational goals.

Thus, considering both the asserted interest and the relationship between the interest and the methods used by the State, we conclude that the State has fallen far short of establishing the "exceedingly persuasive justification" needed to sustain the gender-based classification. Accordingly, we hold that MUW's policy of denying males the right to enroll for credit in its School of Nursing violates the Equal Protection Clause of the Fourteenth Amendment. ...

Because we conclude that the State's policy of excluding males from MUW's School of Nursing violates the Equal Protection Clause of the Fourteenth Amendment, we affirm the judgment of the Court of Appeals.

JUSTICE POWELL, with whom JUSTICE REHNQUIST joins, dissenting.

The Court's opinion bows deeply to conformity. Left without honor—indeed, held unconstitutional—is an element of diversity that has characterized much of American education and enriched much of American life. The Court in effect holds today that no State now may provide even a single institution of higher learning open only to women students. It gives no heed to the efforts of the State of Mississippi to provide abundant opportunities for young men and young women to attend coeducational institutions, and none to the preferences of the more than

---

15. Officials of the American Nurses Association have suggested that excluding men from the field has depressed nurses' wages. Hearings before the United States Equal Employment Opportunity Commission on Job Segregation and Wage Discrimination 510–511, 517–518, 523 (Apr. 1980).

To the extent the exclusion of men has that effect, MUW's admissions policy actually penalizes the very class the State purports to benefit. Cf. Weinberger v. Wiesenfeld, 420 U.S. 636, 95 S.Ct. 1225, 43 L.Ed.2d 514 (1975).

40,000 young women who over the years have evidenced their approval of an all-women's college by choosing Mississippi University for Women (MUW) over seven coeducational universities within the State. The Court decides today that the Equal Protection Clause makes it unlawful for the State to provide women with a traditionally popular and respected choice of educational environment. It does so in a case instituted by one man, who represents no class, and whose primary concern is personal convenience. ...

Nor is respondent significantly disadvantaged by MUW's all-female tradition. His constitutional complaint is based upon a single asserted harm: that he must travel to attend the state-supported nursing schools that concededly are available to him. The Court characterizes this injury as one of "inconvenience." Ante, at 3336, n. 8. This description is fair and accurate, though somewhat embarrassed by the fact that there is, of course, no constitutional right to attend a state-supported university in one's home town. Thus the Court, to redress respondent's injury of inconvenience, must rest its invalidation of MUW's single-sex program on a mode of "sexual stereotype" reasoning that has no application whatever to the respondent or to the "wrong" of which he complains. At best this is anomalous. And ultimately the anomaly reveals legal error—that of applying a heightened equal protection standard, developed in cases of genuine sexual stereotyping, to a narrowly utilized state classification that provides an additional choice for women. Moreover, I believe that Mississippi's educational system should be upheld in this case even if this inappropriate method of analysis is applied. ...

The arguable benefits of single-sex colleges also continue to be recognized by students of higher education. The Carnegie Commission on Higher Education has reported that it "favor[s] the continuation of colleges for women. They provide an element of diversity ... and [an environment in which women] generally ... speak up more in their classes, ... hold more positions of leadership on campus, ... and ... have more role models and mentors among women teachers and administrators." Carnegie Report, quoted in K. Davidson, R. Ginsburg, & H. Kay, Sex–Based Discrimination 814 (1975 ed.). A 10–year empirical study by the Cooperative Institutional Research Program of the American Counsel of Education and the University of California, Los Angeles, also has affirmed the distinctive benefits of single-sex colleges and universities. As summarized in A. Astin, Four Critical Years 232 (1977), the data established that "[b]oth [male and female] single-sex colleges facilitate student involvement in several areas: academic, interaction with faculty, and verbal aggressiveness.... Men's and women's colleges also have a positive effect on intellectual self-esteem. Students at single-sex colleges are more satisfied than students at coeducational colleges with virtually all aspects of college life.... The only area where students are less satisfied is social life." ...

The issue in this case is whether a State transgresses the Constitution when—within the context of a public system that offers a diverse range of campuses, curricula, and educational alternatives—it seeks to accommodate the legitimate personal preferences of those desiring the advantages of an all-women's college. In my view, the Court errs seriously by assuming—without argument or discussion—that the equal protection standard generally applicable to sex discrimination is appropriate here. That standard was designed to free women from "archaic and overbroad generalizations...." Schlesinger v. Ballard, 419 U.S. 498, 508. In no previous case have we applied it to invalidate state efforts to expand women's choices. Nor are there prior sex discrimination decisions by this Court in which a male plaintiff, as in this case, had the choice of an equal benefit. ...

By applying heightened equal protection analysis to this case, the Court frustrates the liberating spirit of the Equal Protection Clause. It prohibits the States from providing women with an opportunity to choose the type of university they prefer. And yet it is these women whom the Court regards as the victims of an illegal, stereotyped perception of the role of women in our society. The Court reasons this way in a case in which no woman has complained, and the only complainant is a man who advances no claims on behalf of anyone else. His claim, it should be recalled, is not that he is being denied a substantive educational opportunity, or even the right to attend an all-male or a coeducational college. It is only that the colleges open to him are located at inconvenient distances.

A distinctive feature of America's tradition has been respect for diversity. This has been characteristic of the peoples from numerous lands who have built our country. It is the essence of our democratic system. At stake in this case as I see it is the preservation of a small aspect of this diversity. But that aspect is by no means insignificant, given our heritage of available choice between single-sex and coeducational institutions of higher learning. The Court answers that there is discrimination—not just that which may be tolerable, as for example between those candidates for admission able to contribute most to an educational institution and those able to contribute less—but discrimination of constitutional dimension. But, having found "discrimination," the Court finds it difficult to identify the victims. It hardly can claim that women are discriminated against. A constitutional case is held to exist solely because one man found it inconvenient to travel to any of the other institutions made available to him by the State of Mississippi. In essence he insists that he has a right to attend a college in his home community. This simply is not a sex discrimination case. The Equal Protection Clause was never intended to be applied to this kind of case.

———

In a parallel single-sex school case, United States v. Commonwealth of Virginia, 976 F.2d 890 (4th Cir.1992), cert. denied ___ U.S. ___, 113 S.Ct. 2431, 124 L.Ed.2d 651 (1993), Judge Niemeyer of the Fourth Circuit Court of Appeals ruled that maintenance of Virginia Military

Institute (VMI) as an all-male, single-sex, state-supported institution was permissible under equal protection analysis, so long as Virginia established a comparable, separate, single-sex school for women. The court does not adequately explain how *Hogan* is distinguishable. *Hogan* found a state-supported single-sex nursing school violative of equal protection because it reproduced stereotypical female roles. What could be more stereotypically male than a military school environment, and why is it not offensive to equal protection to reproduce those stereotypes in state-supported institutions? Nor did the court explain why "separate but equal" works for sex but not race. Is there a reason to distinguish between constitutionally permitting all-male or all-white schools and constitutionally permitting all-female or all-black schools? Do the dynamics of privilege and power and historical exclusion alter the ways that equal protection should apply in those circumstances? See Mac-Kinnon, *supra* at 241 and Flagg, *supra* at 196.

There is another follow-up case to the Mississippi University for Women and Virginia Military Institute cases. After reaffirming its reasoning in the VMI case, Judge Niemeyer in a more recent case upheld a district court's issuance of a preliminary injunction requiring the admission of a woman student to The Citadel, a different, state-supported all-male military college in the South. Faulkner v. Jones, 10 F.3d 226 (4th Cir.1993), stay denied, 14 F.3d 3 (1994). The Fourth Circuit found that the district court had not abused its discretion by issuing an injunction forcing the Citadel to accept Shannon Faulkner as a day student until the case is resolved. Ms. Faulkner was "erroneously" admitted to the Citadel because the admissions people thought she was a male, based on her name and her outstanding record of achievement. The Citadel appealed the stay denial to the U.S. Supreme Court and stay was granted in January 1994, pending decision on their petition for a writ of certiorari. ___ U.S. ___, 114 S.Ct. 872, ___ L.Ed.2d ___ (1994).

Justice O'Connor's concerns about the perpetuation of demeaning stereotypes led her to find a constitutional violation in *Hogan*. Perhaps the most interesting permutation of the sex-based stereotyping theme came recently in J.E.B. v. Alabama ex rel. T.B., ___ U.S. ___, 114 S.Ct. 1419, 128 L.Ed.2d 89 (1994) where the U.S. Supreme Court found that uses of peremptory challenges to eliminate jurors from the petit jury on the basis of gender violated the constitution in the same way that race-based exclusions were held to violate the constitution in Batson v. Kentucky, 476 U.S. 79, 106 S.Ct. 1712, 90 L.Ed.2d 69 (1986). Again the court seemed concerned with the effects of stereotyping on women, although the majority's concern in that case seems misplaced. *J.E.B.* was a paternity case in which the putative father objected to the prosecution's removal of men from the petit jury through peremptory challenges. While the case addresses issues of gender inequality and the majority opinion by Justice Blackmun highlights a history of discrimination against women, is this case really about disadvantaging stereotypes being used against women? Although Justice O'Connor agrees with the majority, she wrote an extremely interesting separate concurrence that acknowledged that abstract principles of formal equality, while often required by law, can obscure the facts of people's experiences and understandings. "[T]o say that gender makes no difference as a matter of law is not to say that gender makes no difference as a matter of fact." *Id.* at 4226 (O'Connor, J., concurring). O'Connor would like to limit the majority opinion to preventing gender-based peremptory challenges by the state, but not by private parties or defendants. She clearly worries that this decision which prohibits taking gender into account in peremptory challenges may end up disadvantaging women: "Will we, in the name of fighting gender discrimination, hold that the battered wife—on trial for wounding her abusive husband—is a state actor? Will we preclude her from using her peremptory challenges to ensure that the jury of her peers contains as many women members as possible? I assume we will, but I hope we will not." *Id.*

b. *Pregnancy and Abortion as Not Sex–Based?*

A major difference between men and women is their reproductive organs and the capacity to become pregnant. The law's response to and understanding of this difference teaches us a great deal about power, privilege and perspective. The following two textual cases show ways in which our Supreme Court has understood gender or sex-based inequalities. Pay particular attention to the language the court uses to talk about pregnancy as not sex-related. We have included the dissents to illustrate how arguments within the law could have been made by the court's majority and to show the difference that perspective and norms make.

In 1974 four women who were denied disability coverage during their pregnancies and deliveries challenged the California statute establishing the disability scheme for perpetuating sex-based discrimination in violation of equal protection. Geduldig v. Aiello, 417 U.S. 484, 94 S.Ct. 2485, 41 L.Ed.2d 256 (1974). Justice Stewart, writing for the majority, found that the program withstood constitutional scrutiny because, "There is no risk from which men are protected and women are not. Likewise, there is no risk from which women are protected and men are not." *Id.* at 496, 94 S.Ct. at 2492. Two years later the Court encountered the same kind of scheme in private industry and tested its validity under Title VII of the Civil Rights Act of 1964, 42 U.S.C. § 2000e, instead of under the equal protection clause. Title VII is a congressionally enacted statute that prohibits, among other things, race and sex-based discrimination in private employment. The *General Electric v. Gilbert* decision below includes pertinent language from *Geduldig*.

GENERAL ELECTRIC v. GILBERT

Supreme Court of the United States, 1976.
429 U.S. 125, 97 S.Ct. 401, 50 L.Ed.2d 343.

Mr. Justice Rehnquist delivered the opinion of the Court.

Petitioner, General Electric Co., provides for all of its employees a disability plan which pays weekly nonoccupational sickness and accident benefits. Excluded from the plan's coverage, however, are disabilities arising from pregnancy. Respondents, on behalf of a class of women employees, brought this action seeking, inter alia, a declaration that this exclusion constitutes sex discrimination in violation of Title VII of the Civil Rights Act of 1964, 78 Stat. 253, as amended, 42 U.S.C. § 2000e et seq. The District Court for the Eastern District of Virginia, following a trial on the merits, held that the exclusion of such pregnancy-related disability benefits from General Electric's employee disability plan violated Title VII. The Court of Appeals affirmed, and we granted certiorari. We now reverse. . . .

Section 703(a)(1) provides in relevant part that it shall be an unlawful employment practice for an employer "to discriminate against any individual with respect to his compensation, terms, conditions, or privileges of employment, because of such individual's race, color, religion, sex, or national origin," 42 U.S.C. § 2000e–2(a)(1).

While there is no necessary inference that Congress, in choosing this language, intended to incorporate into Title VII the concepts of discrimination which have evolved from court decisions construing the Equal Protection Clause of the Fourteenth Amendment, the similarities between the congressional language and some of those decisions surely indicate that the latter are a useful starting point in interpreting the former. Particularly in the case of defining the term "discrimination," which Congress has nowhere in Title VII defined, those cases afford an existing body of law analyzing and discussing that term in a legal context not wholly dissimilar to the concerns which Congress manifested in enacting Title VII. We think, therefore, that our decision in Geduldig v. Aiello, supra, dealing with a strikingly similar disability plan, is quite relevant in determining whether or not the pregnancy exclusion did discriminate on the basis of sex. . . .

We rejected appellee's equal protection challenge to this statutory scheme. We first noted: "We cannot agree that the exclusion of this disability from coverage amounts to invidious discrimination under the Equal Protection Clause. California does not discriminate with respect to the persons or groups which are eligible for disability insurance protection under the program. The classification challenged in this case relates to the asserted underinclusiveness of the set of risks that the State has selected to insure." This point was emphasized again, when later in the opinion we noted: "(T)his case is thus a far cry from cases like Reed v. Reed, 404 U.S. 71, 92 S.Ct. 251, 30 L.Ed.2d 225 (1971), and Frontiero v. Richardson, 411 U.S. 677, 93 S.Ct. 1764, 36 L.Ed.2d 583 (1973), involving discrimination based upon gender as such. The California insurance program does not exclude anyone from benefit eligibility because of gender but merely removes one physical condition pregnancy from the list of compensable disabilities. While it is true that only women can become pregnant, it does not follow that every legislative classification concerning pregnancy is a sex-based classification like those considered in Reed, supra, and Frontiero, supra. Normal pregnancy is an objectively identifiable physical condition with unique characteristics. Absent a showing that distinctions involving pregnancy are mere pretexts designed to effect an invidious discrimination against the members of one sex or the other, lawmakers are constitutionally free to include or exclude pregnancy from the coverage of legislation such as this on any reasonable basis, just as with respect to any other physical condition. "The lack of identity between the excluded disability and gender as such under this insurance program becomes clear upon the most cursory analysis. The program divides potential recipients into two groups pregnant women and nonpregnant persons. While the first group is exclusively female, the second includes members of both sexes."

The quoted language from Geduldig leaves no doubt that our reason for rejecting appellee's equal protection claim in that case was that the exclusion of pregnancy from coverage under California's disability-benefits plan was not in itself discrimination based on sex.

We recognized in Geduldig, of course, that the fact that there was no sex-based discrimination as such was not the end of the analysis, should it be shown "that distinctions involving pregnancy are mere pretexts designed to effect an invidious discrimination against the members of one sex or the other," ibid. But we noted that no semblance of such a showing had been made: "There is no evidence in the record that the selection of the risks insured by the program worked to discriminate against any definable group or class in terms of the aggregate risk protection derived by that group or class from the program. There is no risk from which men are protected and women are not. Likewise, there is no risk from which women are protected and men are not."

Since gender-based discrimination had not been shown to exist either by the terms of the plan or by its effect, there was no need to reach the question of what sort of standard would govern our review had there been such a showing.

The Court of Appeals was therefore wrong in concluding that the reasoning of Geduldig was not applicable to an action under Title VII. Since it is a finding of sex-based discrimination that must trigger, in a case such as this, the finding of an unlawful employment practice under § 703(a)(1), Geduldig is precisely in point in its holding that an exclusion of pregnancy from a disability-benefits plan providing general coverage is not a gender-based discrimination at all.

... As we noted in that opinion, a distinction which on its face is not sex related might nonetheless violate the Equal Protection Clause if it were in fact a subterfuge to accomplish a forbidden discrimination. But we have here no question of excluding a disease or disability comparable in all other respects to covered diseases or disabilities and yet confined to the members of one race or sex. Pregnancy is, of course, confined to women, but it is in other ways significantly different from the typical covered disease or disability. The District Court found that it is not a "disease" at all, and is often a voluntarily undertaken and desired condition, 375 F.Supp., at 375, 377. ...

The instant suit was grounded on Title VII rather than the Equal Protection Clause, and our cases recognize that a prima facie violation of Title VII can be established in some circumstances upon proof that the effect of an otherwise facially neutral plan or classification is to discriminate against members of one class or another. See Washington v. Davis, 426 U.S. 229, 246–248, 96 S.Ct. 2040, 2051, 48 L.Ed.2d 597 (1976). For example, in the context of a challenge, under the provisions of § 703(a)(2), to a facially neutral employment test, this Court held that a prima facie case of discrimination would be established if, even absent proof of intent, the consequences of the test were "invidiously to discriminate on the basis of racial or other impermissible classification," Griggs v. Duke Power Co., 401 U.S. 424, 431, 91 S.Ct. 849, 853, 28 L.Ed.2d 158 (1971). Even assuming that it is not necessary in this case to prove intent to establish a prima facie violation of § 703(a)(1), the respondents have not made the requisite showing of gender-based effect. . . .

As in Geduldig, we start from the indisputable baseline that "(t)he fiscal and actuarial benefits of the program . . . accrue to members of both sexes". We need not disturb the findings of the District Court to note that neither is there a finding, nor was there any evidence which would support a finding, that the financial benefits of the Plan "worked to discriminate against any definable group or class in terms of the aggregate risk protection derived by that group or class from the program". The Plan, in effect (and for all that appears), is nothing more than an insurance package, which covers some risks, but excludes others. The "package" going to relevant identifiable groups we are presently concerned with General Electric's male and female employees covers exactly the same categories of risk, and is facially nondiscriminatory in the sense that "(t)here is no risk from which men are protected and women are not. Likewise, there is no risk from which women are protected and men are not." As there is no proof that the package is in fact worth more to men than to women, it is impossible to find any gender-based discriminatory effect in this scheme simply because women disabled as a result of pregnancy do not receive benefits; that is to say, gender-based discrimination does not result simply because an employer's disability-benefits plan is less than all-inclusive. For all that appears, pregnancy-related disabilities constitute an additional risk, unique to women, and the failure to compensate them for this risk does not destroy the presumed parity of the benefits, accruing to men and women alike, which results from the facially evenhanded inclusion of risks. To hold otherwise would endanger the commonsense notion that an employer who has no disability benefits program at all does not violate Title VII even though the "underinclusion" of risks impacts, as a result of pregnancy-related disabilities, more heavily upon one gender than upon the other. Just as there is no facial gender-based discrimination in that case, so, too, there is none here. . . .

[Discussion of EEOC guidelines and Equal Pay Act omitted.]

. . .

Reversed.

MR. JUSTICE BRENNAN, with whom MR. JUSTICE MARSHALL concurs, dissenting. . . .

I

This case is unusual in that it presents a question the resolution of which at first glance turns largely upon the conceptual framework chosen to identify and describe the operational features of the challenged disability program. By directing their focus upon the risks excluded from the otherwise comprehensive program, and upon the purported justifications for such exclusions, the Equal Employment Opportunity Commission, the women plaintiffs, and the lower courts reason that the pregnancy exclusion constitutes a prima facie violation of Title VII. This violation is triggered, they argue, because the omission of pregnancy from the program has the intent and effect of providing that "only women (are subjected) to a substantial risk of total loss of income because of temporary medical disability."

The Court's framework is diametrically different. It views General Electric's plan as representing a gender-free assignment of risks in accordance with normal actuarial techniques. From this perspective the lone exclusion of pregnancy is not a violation of Title VII insofar as all other disabilities are mutually covered for both sexes. This reasoning relies primarily upon the descriptive statement borrowed from Geduldig v. Aiello, 417 U.S. 484, 496–497, 94 S.Ct. 2485, 2491–2492, 41 L.Ed.2d 256 (1974): "There is no risk from which men are protected and women are not. Likewise, there is no risk from which women are protected and men are not." According to the Court, this assertedly neutral sorting process precludes the pregnancy omission from constituting a violation of Title VII.

Presumably, it is not self-evident that either conceptual framework is more appropriate than the other, which can only mean that further inquiry is necessary to select the more accurate and realistic analytical approach. At the outset, the soundness of the Court's underlying assumption that the plan is the untainted product of a gender-neutral risk-assignment process can be examined against the historical backdrop of General Electric's employment practices and the existence or nonexistence of gender-free policies governing the inclusion of compensable risks. Secondly, the resulting pattern of risks insured by General Electric can then be evaluated in terms of the broad social objectives promoted by Title VII. I believe that the first inquiry compels the conclusion that the Court's assumption that General Electric engaged in a gender-neutral risk-assignment process is purely fanciful. The second demonstrates that the EEOC's interpretation that the exclusion of pregnancy from a disability insurance plan is incompatible with the overall objectives of Title VII has been unjustifiably rejected. . . .

Considered most favorably to the Court's view, Geduldig established the proposition that a pregnancy classification standing alone cannot be said to fall into the category of classifications that rest explicitly on "gender as such". Beyond that, Geduldig offers little analysis helpful to decision of this case. Surely it offends common sense to suggest, that a classification revolving around pregnancy is not, at the minimum, strongly "sex related." Indeed, even in the insurance context where neutral actuarial principles were found to have provided a legitimate and independent input into the decisionmaking process, Geduldig's outcome was qualified by the explicit reservation of a case where it could be demonstrated that a pregnancy-centered differentiation is used as a "mere pretext ... designed to effect an invidious discrimination against the members of one sex...."

... [T]he Court simply disregards a history of General Electric practices that have served to undercut the employment opportunities of women who become pregnant while employed.[1] ...

Plainly then, the Court's appraisal of General Electric's policy as a neutral process of sorting risks and "not a gender-based discrimination at all," cannot easily be squared with the historical record in this case. The Court, therefore, proceeds to a discussion of purported neutral criteria that suffice to explain the lone exclusion of pregnancy from the program. The Court argues that pregnancy is not "comparable" to other disabilities since it is a "voluntary" condition rather than a "disease." The fallacy of this argument is that even if "non-voluntariness" and "disease" are to be construed as the operational criteria for inclusion of a disability in General Electric's program, application of these criteria is inconsistent with the Court's gender-neutral interpretation of the company's policy.

For example, the characterization of pregnancy as "voluntary" is not a persuasive factor, for as the Court of Appeals correctly noted, "other than for childbirth disability, (General Electric) had never construed its plan as eliminating all so-called 'voluntary' disabilities," including sport injuries, attempted suicides, venereal disease, disabilities incurred in the commission of a crime or during a fight, and elective cosmetic surgery. Similarly, the label "disease" rather than "disability"

---

1. General Electric's disability program was developed in an earlier era when women openly were presumed to play only a minor and temporary role in the labor force. As originally conceived in 1926, General Electric offered no benefit plan to its female employees because " 'women did not recognize the responsibilities of life, for they probably were hoping to get married soon and leave the company.' " It was not until the 1930's and 1940's that the company made female employees eligible to participate in the disability program. In common with general business practice, however, General Electric continued to pursue a policy of taking pregnancy and other factors into account in order to scale women's wages at two-thirds the level of men's. More recent company policies reflect common stereotypes concerning the potentiali-

ties of pregnant women, and have coupled forced maternity leave with the nonpayment of disability payments. Thus, the District Court found: "In certain instances it appears that the pregnant employee was required to take leave of her position three months prior to birth and not permitted to return until six weeks after the birth. In other instances the periods varied.... In short, of all the employees it is only pregnant women who have been required to cease work regardless of their desire and physical ability to work and only they have been required to remain off their job for an arbitrary period after the birth of their child." In February 1973, approximately coinciding with commencement of this suit, the company abandoned its forced-maternity-leave policy by formal directive.

cannot be deemed determinative since General Electric's pregnancy disqualification also excludes the 10% of pregnancies that end in debilitating miscarriages, the 10% of cases where pregnancies are complicated by "diseases" in the intuitive sense of the word, and cases where women recovering from childbirth are stricken by severe diseases unrelated to pregnancy.

Moreover, even the Court's principal argument for the plan's supposed gender neutrality cannot withstand analysis. The central analytical framework relied upon to demonstrate the absence of discrimination is the principle described in Geduldig: "There is no risk from which men are protected and women are not ... (and) no risk from which women are protected and men are not." In fostering the impression that it is faced with a mere underinclusive assignment of risks in a gender-neutral fashion that is, all other disabilities are insured irrespective of gender the Court's analysis proves to be simplistic and misleading. For although all mutually contractible risks are covered irrespective of gender, the plan also insures risks such as prostatectomies, vasectomies, and circumcisions that are specific to the reproductive system of men and for which there exist no female counterparts covered by the plan. Again, pregnancy affords the only disability, sex-specific or otherwise, that is excluded from coverage.[5] Accordingly, the District Court appropriately remarked "[T]he concern of defendants in reference to pregnancy risks, coupled with the apparent lack of concern regarding the balancing of other statistically sex-linked disabilities, buttresses the Court's conclusion that the discriminatory attitude characterized elsewhere in the Court's findings was in fact a motivating factor in its policy."

If decision of this case, therefore, turns upon acceptance of the Court's view of General Electric's disability plan as a sex-neutral assignment of risks, or plaintiffs' perception of the plan as a sex-conscious process expressive of the secondary status of women in the company's labor force, the history of General Electric's employment practices and the absence of definable gender-neutral sorting criteria under the plan warrant rejection of the Court's view in deference to the plaintiffs'. Indeed, the fact that the Court's frame of reference lends itself to such intentional, sex-laden decisionmaking makes clear the wisdom and propriety of the EEOC's contrary approach to employment disability programs. . . .

III

[A] prima facie violation of Title VII, whether under § 703(a)(1) or § 703(a)(2), also is established by demonstrating that a facially neutral

---

5. Indeed, the shallowness of the Court's "underinclusive" analysis is transparent. Had General Electric assembled a catalogue of all ailments that befall humanity, and then systematically proceeded to exclude from coverage every disability that is female-specific or predominantly afflicts women, the Court could still reason as here that the plan operates equally: Women, like men, would be entitled to draw disability payments for their circumcisions and prostatectomies, and neither sex could claim payment for pregnancies, breast cancer, and the other excluded female-dominated disabilities. Along similar lines, any disability that occurs disproportionately in a particular group sickle-cell anemia, for example could be freely excluded from the plan without troubling the Court's analytical approach.

classification has the effect of discriminating against members of a defined class. ...

General Electric's disability program has three divisible sets of effects. First, the plan covers all disabilities that mutually afflict both sexes. Second, the plan insures against all disabilities that are male-specific or have a predominant impact on males. Finally, all female-specific and female-impacted disabilities are covered, except for the most prevalent, pregnancy. The Court focuses on the first factor the equal inclusion of mutual risks and therefore understandably can identify no discriminatory effect arising from the plan. In contrast, the EEOC and plaintiffs rely upon the unequal exclusion manifested in effects two and three to pinpoint an adverse impact on women. However one defines the profile of risks protected by General Electric, the determinative question must be whether the social policies and aims to be furthered by Title VII and filtered through the phrase "to discriminate" contained in § 703(a)(1) fairly forbid an ultimate pattern of coverage that insures all risks except a commonplace one that is applicable to women but not to men. ...

The Court's belief that the concept of discrimination cannot reach disability policies effecting "an additional risk, unique to women ...," is plainly out of step with the decision three Terms ago in Lau v. Nichols, 414 U.S. 563, 94 S.Ct. 786, 39 L.Ed.2d 1 (1974), interpreting another provision of the Civil Rights Act. There a unanimous Court recognized that discrimination is a social phenomenon encased in a social context and therefore, unavoidably takes its meaning from the desired end products of the relevant legislative enactment, end products that may demand due consideration to the uniqueness of "disadvantaged" individuals. A realistic understanding of conditions found in today's labor environment warrants taking pregnancy into account in fashioning disability policies. Unlike the hypothetical situations conjectured by the Court, contemporary disability programs are not creatures of a social or cultural vacuum devoid of stereotypes and signals concerning the pregnant woman employee. Indeed, no one seriously contends that General Electric or other companies actually conceptualized or developed their comprehensive insurance programs disability-by-disability in a strictly sex-neutral fashion. Instead, the company has devised a policy that, but for pregnancy, offers protection for all risks, even those that are "unique to" men or heavily male dominated. In light of this social experience, the history of General Electric's employment practices, the otherwise all-inclusive design of its disability program, and the burdened role of the contemporary working woman, the EEOC's construction of sex discrimination under § 703(a)(1) is fully consonant with the ultimate objective of Title VII, "to assure equality of employment opportunities and to eliminate those discriminatory practices and devices which have fostered (sexually) stratified job environments to the disadvantage of (women)."

I would affirm the judgment of the Court of Appeals.

Mr. Justice Stevens, dissenting.

... [T]he rule at issue places the risk of absence caused by pregnancy in a class by itself.[5] By definition, such a rule discriminates on account of sex; for it is the capacity to become pregnant which primarily differentiates the female from the male. The analysis is the same whether the rule relates to hiring, promotion, the acceptability of an excuse for absence, or an exclusion from a disability insurance plan. Accordingly, ... I conclude that the language of the statute plainly requires the result which the Courts of Appeals have reached unanimously.

Notes and Questions

1. What understandings about the "normal worker" are being used to decide that coverage of benefits for pregnancy is something "extra"?

2. Do the *Gilbert* and *Geduldig* cases comport with your common sense experience when they conclude that discrimination against "pregnant persons" is not sex-based discrimination?

3. Congress immediately reversed the *Gilbert* decision's interpretation of sex discrimination by enacting the Pregnancy Discrimination Act of 1978, 42 U.S.C. § 2000e(k) (the PDA). That act defines distinctions based pregnancy, childbirth, or related medical conditions as sex discrimination.

About the same time that the PDA passed, some states enacted laws providing job protection and maternity leaves for pregnant employees. California's pregnancy leave statute was challenged by an employer as conflicting with the PDA, because it treated pregnancy differently from other disabilities. California Fed. Sav. & Loan Ass'n v. Guerra, 479 U.S. 272, 107 S.Ct. 683, 93 L.Ed.2d 613 (1987). The employer lost and the California statute providing a maternity leave policy was upheld. Justice Marshall wrote for the court's majority that the PDA and California statute are consistent in their goals of "allow[ing] women, as well as men, to have families without losing their jobs." He also concluded that even if the PDA and California statutes conflicted, employers would not be forced to violate Title VII, because they could extend comparable benefits to other disabled workers.

The Court's recent foray into pregnancy related employment issues was International Union, UAW v. Johnson Controls, Inc., 499 U.S. 187, 111 S.Ct. 1196, 113 L.Ed.2d 158 (1991), in which a battery manufacturer's sex-specific fetal protection policy was found to violate Title VII. Johnson Controls' fetal protection policy prohibited fertile women ("all women except those whose inability to bear children is medically documented") from working in

---

5. It is not accurate to describe the program as dividing " 'potential recipients into two groups pregnant women and nonpregnant persons.' " Insurance programs, company policies, and employment contracts all deal with future risks rather than historic facts. The classification is between persons who face a risk of pregnancy and those who do not. Nor is it accurate to state that under the plan " '(t)here is no risk from which men are protected and women are not.' " If the word "risk" is used narrowly, men are protected against the risks associated with a prostate operation whereas women are not. If the word is used more broadly to describe the risk of uncompensated unemployment caused by physical disability, men receive total protection (subject to the 60% and 26-week limitations) against that risk whereas women receive only partial protection.

the company's higher paying jobs because of potential lead exposure and the consequent risks to unborn children. Justice Blackmun's majority opinion said, "The bias in Johnson Controls' policy is obvious. Fertile men, but not fertile women, are given a choice as to whether they wish to risk their reproductive health for a particular job.... [T]he absence of a malevolent motive does not convert a facially discriminatory policy into a neutral policy with a discriminatory effect.... Concern for a woman's existing or potential offspring historically has been the excuse for denying women equal employment opportunities." According to Title VII, this policy would only be valid if sex was proven to be a bona fide occupational qualification (bfoq). Blackmun concludes that this is not a bfoq for the safe and efficient manufacture of batteries and that the welfare of the next generation does not establish a bfoq of female sterility. While the *Johnson Controls'* holding increases women's employment opportunities, the question is what cost do we all, as members of society, have to incur in order to earn a living wage? That a woman could be made to choose between her reproductive role and economic role in her family does not disturb the court, whose opinion does not challenge the imposition of such a choice on a person, but only suggests that "Congress has left this choice to the woman as hers to make," rather than to the employer or the courts.

As a further response to pregnancy, birth, and child care issues, Congress enacted the Family and Medical Leave Act of 1993, 29 U.S.C.A. §§ 2601, 2612, 107 Stat. 6 (1993), granting "eligible employees," whether male or female, an entitlement to a 12 week unpaid leave for the birth of a child, adoption of a child, to care for a parent, spouse or child with a serious health condition, or for the employee's own illness. This law is gender-neutral, but not neutral as to class or wealth-based differences between employees, because only an employee who can afford to live without her/his income for 12 weeks can take advantage of its guarantees.

4. Sex-based discrimination in employment is too large an area of law to cover here. Workplace discrimination can occur in public or private employment; it can be overt or subtle. Even though a great deal of progress has been made in eliminating overt forms of sex-based discrimination in employment where employers refused to hire women at all, such cases are still occurring. For example, Title VII applies to private employers with over fifteen employees. 42 U.S.C. § 2000e(a). In some jurisdictions this means that employers with less than fifteen employees may still legally discriminate against employees because they are women, as evidenced by an Alabama Supreme Court case, Howard v. Wolff Broadcasting Corp., 611 So.2d 307 (Ala.1992), cert. denied, ___ U.S. ___, 113 S.Ct. 1849, 123 L.Ed.2d 473 (1993). In *Howard* a small radio station owner admittedly fired Ms. Howard from her employment as a disc jockey because she was a woman and the station did not want females on the air. Without Title VII to advance her claim, Howard argued claims of breach of contract, fraud, and public policy wrongful termination for violation of FCC licensing requirements. The Alabama Supreme Court denied her all relief, finding that although they do not condone discharging a person because of her gender, it is up to the legislature to provide people like Ms. Howard relief. The result of their decision is that victims of blatant sex-based discrimination by employers with less than fifteen employees in Alabama are without a remedy.

Sex discrimination employment claims cover a wide range of practices that interfere with women getting jobs, being paid comparably for their work, having legitimate opportunities for advancement and promotion, clothing, appearance, and grooming regulations, height and weight requirements, maternity and childcare provisions, layoffs, seniority, fetal protection policies, and actuarial practices regarding insurance and employment benefits. A new defense in sex discrimination in employment cases claims that women are located in lower paying, dead-end jobs because of their job choices or interests. For example, in E.E.O.C. v. Sears, Roebuck & Co., 839 F.2d 302 (7th Cir.1988) women ran into a roadblock in advancing sex discrimination claims against employers who steer women employees into low-paying jobs within the organization. The EEOC sued Sears, a national retailer, for its sex-based imbalance in employment, where its better-paying commission sales work in big ticket items and appliances were almost uniformly held by men, while women did non-commission sales work in clothing and domestic products. Sears prevailed in the lawsuit, arguing that women chose the less competitive, less aggressive work in non-commission sales jobs because of their natures and lifestyle needs. Judge Cudahy, in his dissent, said that it was like deciding "that women are by nature happier cooking, doing the laundry and chauffeuring the children to softball games than arguing appeals or selling stocks." *Id.* at 361. Fortunately, the *Sears* decision's reasoning has not been persuasive to all judges. Federal District Judge Marilyn Hall Patel rejected Lucky Stores, a large California grocery chain's claim that women were not promoted into management and full-time positions because of their lack of interest. Women argued they were channeled into dead-end jobs working cash registers, in the delicatessens or in the bakeries, rather than in produce, main groceries, or management, where jobs were higher-paid and predicates to advancement. Judge Patel's earlier order led to a landmark settlement of nearly $75 million in damages and an investment of $20 million in affirmative action programs for female employees. If hiring and promotion targets are not met, the settlement calls for an additional $13 million damages. Jane Gross, *Big Grocery Chain Reaches Landmark Sex–Bias Accord,* New York Times, Dec. 17, 1993, A1, col. 1.

Sexual discrimination in employment also includes sexual harassment claims. Meritor Sav. Bank v. Vinson, 477 U.S. 57, 106 S.Ct. 2399, 91 L.Ed.2d 49 (1986). Power, perspectives, and norms play critical roles in determining what constitutes sexual or gender-based harassment. Harris v. Forklift Systems, ___ U.S. ___, 114 S.Ct. 367, 126 L.Ed.2d 295 (1993); Ellison v. Brady, 924 F.2d 872 (9th Cir.1991). Sexual, racial, and class-based power dynamics were foregrounded in the Anita Hill/Clarence Thomas hearings, where Hill's accusations of sexual harassment by Thomas were weighed by the all-male Senate Judiciary Committee who was evaluating Thomas' fitness for the Supreme Court. For a variety of thoughtful reflections on the processes of constructing identities and wielding power in the Hill–Thomas hearings, see Toni Morrison, ed., Race-ing Justice, En-gendering Power: Essays on Anita Hill, Clarence Thomas, and the Construction of Social Reality (1992); *Symposium, Gender, Race, and the Politics of Supreme Court Appointments: The Import of the Anita Hill/Clarence Thomas Hearings,* 65 S.Cal.L.Rev. 1279 (1992); Emma Coleman Jordan, *Race, Gender, and Social Class in the Thomas Sexual Harassment Hearings: The Hidden Fault Line in Political Discourse,* 15 Harv.Women's L.J. 1 (1992).

5. Despite Congress' clear rejection of the Court's *Gilbert* analysis under Title VII when it enacted the PDA (Remember that *Gilbert* relied heavily on the *Geduldig* rationale), the court has reaffirmed its *Geduldig* approach to sex-discrimination under the equal protection clause. In 1993 the court decided a case brought against Operation Rescue abortion protesters for blocking women's entrance into abortion and health care clinics. The plaintiff claimed that the protesters' actions violated 42 U.S.C. § 1985(3), a remaining part of the Civil Rights Act of 1871, which prohibits conspiracies to deprive "any person or class of persons of the equal protection of the laws or equal privileges and immunities under the laws." Following in *Geduldig's* footsteps, Justice Scalia wrote for the court's majority that the animus underlying abortion clinic protesters' interference with women's rights to obtain abortions and health care was not class-based animus against women, and therefore did not fall under the terms of the statute. Note Justices Stevens' and O'Connor's responses in their separate dissents.

BRAY v. ALEXANDRIA WOMEN'S HEALTH CLINIC

Supreme Court of the United States, 1993.
__ U.S. __, 113 S.Ct. 753, 122 L.Ed.2d 34.

JUSTICE SCALIA delivered the opinion of the Court.

This case presents the question whether the first clause of Rev.Stat. § 1980, 42 U.S.C. § 1985(3)—the surviving version of § 2 of the Civil Rights Act of 1871—provides a federal cause of action against persons obstructing access to abortion clinics. Respondents are clinics that perform abortions, and organizations that support legalized abortion and that have members who may wish to use abortion clinics. Petitioners are Operation Rescue, an unincorporated association whose members oppose abortion, and six individuals. Among its activities, Operation Rescue organizes antiabortion demonstrations in which participants trespass on, and obstruct general access to, the premises of abortion clinics. The individual petitioners organize and coordinate these demonstrations.

Respondents sued to enjoin petitioners from conducting demonstrations at abortion clinics in the Washington, D.C., metropolitan area....

I

Our precedents establish that in order to prove a private conspiracy in violation of the first clause of § 1985(3),[1] a plaintiff must show, inter

---

1. Section 1985(3) provides as follows: "If two or more persons in any State or Territory conspire or go in disguise on the highway or on the premises of another, for the purpose of depriving, either directly or indirectly, any person or class of persons of the equal protection of the laws, or of equal privileges and immunities under the laws; or for the purpose of preventing or hindering the constituted authorities of any State or Territory from giving or securing to all persons within such State or Territory the equal protection of the laws; or if two or more persons conspire to prevent by force, intimidation, or threat, any citizen who is lawfully entitled to vote, from giving his

alia, (1) that "some racial, or perhaps otherwise class-based, invidiously discriminatory animus [lay] behind the conspirators' action," and (2) that the conspiracy "aimed at interfering with rights" that are "protected against private, as well as official, encroachment." We think neither showing has been made in the present case.

A

In Griffin [v. Breckenridge, 403 U.S. 88 (1971)] this Court held, reversing a 20–year–old precedent, that § 1985(3) reaches not only conspiracies under color of state law, but also purely private conspiracies. In finding that the text required that expanded scope, however, we recognized the "constitutional shoals that would lie in the path of interpreting § 1985(3) as a general federal tort law." That was to be avoided, we said, "by requiring, as an element of the cause of action, the kind of invidiously discriminatory motivation stressed by the sponsors of the limiting amendment," ibid.—citing specifically Representative Shellabarger's statement that the law was restricted " 'to the prevention of deprivations which shall attack the equality of rights of American citizens; that any violation of the right, the animus and effect of which is to strike down the citizen, to the end that he may not enjoy equality of rights as contrasted with his and other citizens' rights, shall be within the scope of the remedies....' " We said that "[t]he language [of § 1985(3)] requiring intent to deprive of equal protection, or equal privileges and immunities, means that there must be some racial, or perhaps otherwise class-based, invidiously discriminatory animus behind the conspirators' action."

We have not yet had occasion to resolve the "perhaps"; only in Griffin itself have we addressed and upheld a claim under § 1985(3), and that case involved race discrimination. Respondents assert that there qualifies alongside race discrimination, as an "otherwise class-based, invidiously discriminatory animus" covered by the 1871 law, opposition to abortion. Neither common sense nor our precedents support this.

To begin with, we reject the apparent conclusion of the District Court (which respondents make no effort to defend) that opposition to abortion constitutes discrimination against the "class" of "women seeking abortion." Whatever may be the precise meaning of a "class" for purposes of Griffin's speculative extension of § 1985(3) beyond race, the term unquestionably connotes something more than a group of individuals who share a desire to engage in conduct that the § 1985(3) defendant disfavors. Otherwise, innumerable tort plaintiffs would be able to assert

support or advocacy in a legal manner, toward or in favor of the election of any lawfully qualified person as an elector for President or Vice President, or as a Member of Congress of the United States; or to injure any citizen in person or property on account of such support or advocacy; in any case of conspiracy set forth in this section, if one or more persons engaged therein do, or cause to be done, any act in furtherance of the object of such conspiracy, whereby another is injured in his person or property, or deprived of having and exercising any right or privilege of a citizen of the United States, the party so injured or deprived may have an action for the recovery of damages occasioned by such injury or deprivation, against one or more of the conspirators." 42 U.S.C. § 1985(3).

causes of action under § 1985(3) by simply defining the aggrieved class as those seeking to engage in the activity the defendant has interfered with. This definitional ploy would convert the statute into the "general federal tort law" it was the very purpose of the animus requirement to avoid. As Justice Blackmun has cogently put it, the class "cannot be defined simply as the group of victims of the tortious action." "Women seeking abortion" is not a qualifying class.

Respondents' contention, however, is that the alleged class-based discrimination is directed not at "women seeking abortion" but at women in general. We find it unnecessary to decide whether that is a qualifying class under § 1985(3), since the claim that petitioners' opposition to abortion reflects an animus against women in general must be rejected. We do not think that the "animus" requirement can be met only by maliciously motivated, as opposed to assertedly benign (though objectively invidious), discrimination against women. It does demand, however, at least a purpose that focuses upon women by reason of their sex—for example (to use an illustration of assertedly benign discrimination), the purpose of "saving" women because they are women from a combative, aggressive profession such as the practice of law. The record in this case does not indicate that petitioners' demonstrations are motivated by a purpose (malevolent or benign) directed specifically at women as a class; to the contrary, the District Court found that petitioners define their "rescues" not with reference to women, but as physical intervention " 'between abortionists and the innocent victims,' " and that "all [petitioners] share a deep commitment to the goals of stopping the practice of abortion and reversing its legalization." Given this record, respondents' contention that a class-based animus has been established can be true only if one of two suggested propositions is true: (1) that opposition to abortion can reasonably be presumed to reflect a sex-based intent, or (2) that intent is irrelevant, and a class-based animus can be determined solely by effect. Neither proposition is supportable.

As to the first: Some activities may be such an irrational object of disfavor that, if they are targeted, and if they also happen to be engaged in exclusively or predominantly by a particular class of people, an intent to disfavor that class can readily be presumed. A tax on wearing yarmulkes is a tax on Jews. But opposition to voluntary abortion cannot possibly be considered such an irrational surrogate for opposition to (or paternalism towards) women. Whatever one thinks of abortion, it cannot be denied that there are common and respectable reasons for opposing it, other than hatred of or condescension toward (or indeed any view at all concerning) women as a class—as is evident from the fact that men and women are on both sides of the issue, just as men and women are on both sides of petitioners' unlawful demonstrations. . . .

Respondents' case comes down, then, to the proposition that intent is legally irrelevant; that since voluntary abortion is an activity engaged in only by women, to disfavor it is ipso facto to discriminate invidiously against women as a class. Our cases do not support that proposition.

In Geduldig v. Aiello, 417 U.S. 484 (1974), we rejected the claim that a state disability insurance system that denied coverage to certain disabilities resulting from pregnancy discriminated on the basis of sex in violation of the Equal Protection Clause of the Fourteenth Amendment. "While it is true," we said, "that only women can become pregnant, it does not follow that every legislative classification concerning pregnancy is a sex-based classification." Id., at 496, n. 20. We reached a similar conclusion in Personnel Administrator of Mass. v. Feeney, 442 U.S. 256 (1979), sustaining against an Equal Protection Clause challenge a Massachusetts law giving employment preference to military veterans, a class which in Massachusetts was over 98% male, id., at 270. " 'Discriminatory purpose,' " we said, "implies more than intent as volition or intent as awareness of consequences. It implies that the decisionmaker ... selected or reaffirmed a particular course of action at least in part 'because of,' not merely 'in spite of,' its adverse effects upon an identifiable group." Id., at 279 (citation omitted). The same principle applies to the "class-based, invidiously discriminatory animus" requirement of § 1985(3).[4] Moreover, two of our cases deal specifically with the disfavoring of abortion, and establish conclusively that it is not ipso facto sex discrimination. In Maher v. Roe, 432 U.S. 464 (1977), and Harris v. McRae, 448 U.S. 297 (1980), we held that the constitutional test applicable to government abortion-funding restrictions is not the heightened-scrutiny standard that our cases demand for sex-based discrimination, ... but the ordinary rationality standard.

The nature of the "invidiously discriminatory animus" Griffin had in mind is suggested both by the language used in that phrase ("invidious ... [t]ending to excite odium, ill will, or envy; likely to give offense; esp., unjustly and irritatingly discriminating," Webster's Second International Dictionary 1306 (1954)) and by the company in which the phrase is found ("there must be some racial, or perhaps otherwise class-based, invidiously discriminatory animus"). Whether one agrees or disagrees with the goal of preventing abortion, that goal in itself (apart from the use of unlawful means to achieve it, which is not relevant to our discussion of animus) does not remotely qualify for such harsh description, and for such derogatory association with racism. To the contrary, we have said that "a value judgment favoring childbirth over abortion" is proper and reasonable enough to be implemented by the allocation of public funds and Congress itself has, with our approval, discriminated against abortion in its provision of financial support for

---

4. ... In any event, the characteristic that formed the basis of the targeting here was not womanhood, but the seeking of abortion—so that the class the dissenters identify is the one we have rejected earlier: women seeking abortion. The approach of equating opposition to an activity (abortion) that can be engaged in only by a certain class (women) with opposition to that class leads to absurd conclusions. On that analysis, men and women who regard rape with revulsion harbor an invidious antimale animus. Thus, if state law should provide that convicted rapists must be paroled so long as they attend weekly counseling sessions; and if persons opposed to such lenient treatment should demonstrate their opposition by impeding access to the counseling centers; those protesters would, on the dissenters' approach, be liable under § 1985(3) because of their antimale animus.

medical procedures. This is not the stuff out of which a § 1985(3) "invidiously discriminatory animus" is created. ...

JUSTICE STEVENS, with whom JUSTICE BLACKMUN joins, dissenting.

After the Civil War, Congress enacted legislation imposing on the Federal Judiciary the responsibility to remedy both abuses of power by persons acting under color of state law and lawless conduct that state courts are neither fully competent, nor always certain, to prevent. The Ku Klux Act of 1871, 17 Stat. 13, was a response to the massive, organized lawlessness that infected our Southern States during the post-Civil War era. When a question concerning this statute's coverage arises, it is appropriate to consider whether the controversy has a purely local character or the kind of federal dimension that gave rise to the legislation.

Based on detailed, undisputed findings of fact, the District Court concluded that the portion of § 2 of the Ku Klux Act now codified at 42 U.S.C. § 1985(3) provides a federal remedy for petitioners' violent concerted activities on the public streets and private property of law-abiding citizens. The Court of Appeals affirmed. The holdings of the courts below are supported by the text and the legislative history of the statute and are fully consistent with this Court's precedents. Admittedly, important questions concerning the meaning of § 1985(3) have been left open in our prior cases, including whether the statute covers gender-based discrimination and whether it provides a remedy for the kind of interference with a woman's right to travel to another State to obtain an abortion revealed by this record. Like the overwhelming majority of federal judges who have spoken to the issue, I am persuaded that traditional principles of statutory construction readily provide affirmative answers to these questions.

It is unfortunate that the Court has analyzed this case as though it presented an abstract question of logical deduction rather than a question concerning the exercise and allocation of power in our federal system of government. The Court ignores the obvious (and entirely constitutional) congressional intent behind § 1985(3) to protect this Nation's citizens from what amounts to the theft of their constitutional rights by organized and violent mobs across the country. ...

To summarize briefly, the evidence establishes that petitioners engaged in a nationwide conspiracy; to achieve their goal they repeatedly occupied public streets and trespassed on the premises of private citizens in order to prevent or hinder the constituted authorities from protecting access to abortion clinics by women, a substantial number of whom traveled in interstate commerce to reach the destinations blockaded by petitioners. The case involves no ordinary trespass, nor anything remotely resembling the peaceful picketing of a local retailer. It presents a striking contemporary example of the kind of zealous, politically motivated, lawless conduct that led to the enactment of the Ku Klux Act in 1871 and gave it its name. ...

IV

The question left open in Griffin—whether the coverage of § 1985(3) is limited to cases involving racial bias—is easily answered. The text of the statute provides no basis for excluding from its coverage any cognizable class of persons who are entitled to the equal protection of the laws. This Court has repeatedly and consistently held that gender-based classifications are subject to challenge on constitutional grounds, see, e.g., Reed v. Reed, 404 U.S. 71 (1971); Mississippi University for Women v. Hogan, 458 U.S. 718 (1982). A parallel construction of post-Civil War legislation that, in the words of Justice Holmes, "dealt with Federal rights and with all Federal rights, and protected them in the lump," United States v. Mosley, 238 U.S. 383, 387 (1915), is obviously appropriate.

The legislative history of the Act confirms the conclusion that even though it was primarily motivated by the lawless conduct directed at the recently emancipated citizens, its protection extended to "all the thirty-eight millions of the citizens of this nation." Given then prevailing attitudes about the respective roles of males and females in society, it is possible that the enacting legislators did not anticipate protection of women against class-based discrimination. That, however, is not a sufficient reason for refusing to construe the statutory text in accord with its plain meaning, particularly when that construction fulfills the central purpose of the legislation.

The gloss that Justice Stewart placed on the statute in Griffin, then, did not exclude gender-based discrimination from its coverage. But it does require us to resolve the question whether a conspiracy animated by the desire to deprive women of their right to obtain an abortion is "class-based."

V

The terms "animus" and "invidious" are susceptible to different interpretations. The Court today announces that it could find class-based animus in petitioners' mob violence "only if one of two suggested propositions is true: (1) that opposition to abortion can reasonably be presumed to reflect a sex-based intent, or (2) that intent is irrelevant, and a class-based animus can be determined solely by effect." Ante, at 760.

The first proposition appears to describe a malevolent form of hatred or ill-will. When such an animus defends itself as opposition to conduct that a given class engages in exclusively or predominantly, we can readily unmask it as the intent to discriminate against the class itself. See ante, at 759–769. Griffin itself, for instance, involved behavior animated by the desire to keep African–American citizens from exercising their constitutional rights. The defendants were no less guilty of a class-based animus because they also opposed the cause of desegregation or rights of African–American suffrage, and the Court did not require the plaintiffs in Griffin to prove that their beatings were motivated by hatred for African–Americans. Similarly, a decision disfavoring female lawyers,[15] female owners of liquor establishments, or pregnant women may appropriately be characterized as "invidiously discriminatory" even if the decisionmakers have goals other than—or in addition to—discrimination against individual women.[18]

The second proposition deserves more than the Court's disdain. It plausibly describes an assumption that intent lies behind the discriminatory effects from which Congress intended § 1985(3) to protect American citizens. Congress may obviously offer statutory protections against behavior that the Constitution does not forbid, including forms of discrimination that undermine § 1985(3)'s guarantee of equal treatment under the law. Regardless of whether the examples of paternalistic discrimination given above involve a constitutional violation, as a matter of statutory construction it is entirely appropriate to conclude that each would satisfy the class-based animus requirement because none of them poses any danger of converting § 1985(3) into a general tort law or creating concerns about the constitutionality of the statute.

Both forms of class-based animus that the Court proposes are present in this case.

Sex–Based Discrimination

It should be noted that a finding of class-based animus in this case does not require finding that to disfavor abortion is "ipso facto" to discriminate invidiously against women. Respondents do not take that position, and they do not rely on abstract propositions about "opposition to abortion" per se. Instead, they call our attention to a factual record showing a particular lawless conspiracy employing force to prevent women from exercising their constitutional rights. Such a conspiracy, in the terms of the Court's first proposition, may "reasonably be presumed to reflect a sex-based intent."

To satisfy the class-based animus requirement of § 1985(3), the conspirators' conduct need not be motivated by hostility toward individual women. As women are unquestionably a protected class, that requirement—as well as the central purpose of the statute—is satisfied if the conspiracy is aimed at conduct that only members of the protected class have the capacity to perform. It is not necessary that the intended effect upon women be the sole purpose of the conspiracy. It is enough that the conspiracy be motivated "at least in part" by its adverse effects upon women. Cf. Personnel Administrator of Mass. v. Feeney, 442 U.S. 256, 279 (1979). The immediate and intended effect of this conspiracy

---

15. See Bradwell v. Illinois, 16 Wall. 130, 21 L.Ed. 442 (1873). The reasoning of the concurring Justices surely evidenced invidious animus, even though it rested on traditional views about a woman's place in society, rather than on overt hostility toward women.... The Justices who subscribed to those views were certainly not misogynists, but their basic attitude—or animus—toward women is appropriately characterized as "invidiously discriminatory."

18. Last Term in Fort Gratiot Sanitary Landfill, Inc. v. Michigan Dept. of Natural Resources, 504 U.S. __, 112 S.Ct. 2019, 119 L.Ed.2d 139 (1992), we found that Michigan had discriminated against interstate commerce in garbage even though its statutory scheme discriminated against most of the landfill operators in Michigan as well as those located in other States.

was to prevent women from obtaining abortions. Even assuming that the ultimate and indirect consequence of petitioners' blockade was the legitimate and nondiscriminatory goal of saving potential life, it is undeniable that the conspirators' immediate purpose was to affect the conduct of women. Moreover, petitioners target women because of their sex, specifically, because of their capacity to become pregnant and to have an abortion.[20]

It is also obvious that petitioners' conduct was motivated "at least in part" by the invidious belief that individual women are not capable of deciding whether to terminate a pregnancy, or that they should not be allowed to act on such a decision. Petitioners' blanket refusal to allow any women access to an abortion clinic overrides the individual class member's choice, no matter whether she is the victim of rape or incest, whether the abortion may be necessary to save her life, or even whether she is merely seeking advice or information about her options. Petitioners' conduct is designed to deny every woman the opportunity to exercise a constitutional right that only women possess. Petitioners' conspiracy, which combines massive defiance of the law with violent obstruction of the constitutional rights of their fellow citizens, represents a paradigm of the kind of conduct that the statute was intended to cover.

The Court recognizes that the requisite animus may "readily be presumed" on the basis of the relationship between the targeted activity and membership in the targeted class. But the Court insists that opposition to an act engaged in exclusively by members of a protected class does not involve class-based animus unless the act itself is an "irrational object of disfavor." Ibid. The Court's view requires a subjective judicial interpretation inappropriate in the civil rights context,

20. The Court mischaracterizes this analysis by ignoring the distinction between a classification that is sex-based and a classification that constitutes sexual discrimination prohibited by the Constitution or by statute. See ante, at 760–761, n. 3. A classification is sex-based if it classifies on the basis of sex. As the capacity to become pregnant is a characteristic necessarily associated with one sex, a classification based on the capacity to become pregnant is a classification based on sex. See Sunstein, Neutrality in Constitutional Law (With Special Reference to Pornography, Abortion, and Surrogacy), 92 Colum.L.Rev. 1, 32–33 (1992) (footnotes omitted): "The first point is that restrictions on abortion should be seen as a form of sex discrimination. The proper analogy here is to a law that is targeted solely at women, and thus contains a de jure distinction on the basis of sex. A statute that is explicitly addressed to women is of course a form of sex discrimination. A statute that involves a defining characteristic or a biological correlate of being female should be treated in precisely the same way. If a law said that 'no woman' may obtain an abortion, it should readily be seen as a sex-based classification. A law saying that 'no person' may obtain an abortion has the same meaning. "The fact that some men may also be punished by abortion laws—for example, male doctors—does not mean that restrictions on abortion are sex-neutral. Laws calling for racial segregation make it impermissible for whites as well as blacks to desegregate, and this does not make such laws race-neutral. Nor would it be correct to say that restrictions on abortion merely have a discriminatory impact on women, and that they should therefore be treated in the same way as neutral weight and height requirements having disproportionate effects on women. With such requirements, men and women are on both sides of the legal line; but abortion restrictions exclusively target women. A law that prohibited pregnant women, or pregnant people, from appearing on the streets during daylight would readily be seen as a form of de jure sex discrimination. A restriction on abortion has the same sex-based features."

where what seems rational to an oppressor seems equally irrational to a victim. Opposition to desegregation, and opposition to the voting rights of both African–Americans and women, were certainly at one time considered "rational" propositions. But such propositions were never free of the class-based discrimination from which § 1985(3) protects the members of both classes.

The activity of traveling to a clinic to obtain an abortion is, of course, exclusively performed by women. Opposition to that activity may not be "irrational," but violent interference with it is unquestionably "aimed at" women. The Court offers no justification for its newly crafted suggestion that deliberately imposing a burden on an activity exclusively performed by women is not class-based discrimination unless opposition to the activity is also irrational. The Court is apparently willing to presume discrimination only when opposition to the targeted activity is—in its eyes—wholly pretextual: that is, when it thinks that no rational person would oppose the activity, except as a means of achieving a separate and distinct goal.[23] The Court's analysis makes sense only if every member of a protected class exercises all of her constitutional rights, or if no rational excuse remains for otherwise invidious discrimination. Not every member of every protected class chooses to exercise all of his or her constitutional rights; not all of them want to. That many women do not obtain abortions—that many women oppose abortion—does not mean that those who violently prevent the exercise of that right by women who do exercise it are somehow cleansed of their discriminatory intent. In enacting a law such as § 1985(3) for federal courts to enforce, Congress asked us to see through the excuses— the "rational" motives—that will always disguise discrimination. Congress asked us to foresee, and speed, the day when such discrimination, no matter how well disguised, would be unmasked.

Statutory Relief From Discriminatory Effects

As for the second definition of class-based animus, disdainfully proposed by the Court, ante, at 760, there is no reason to insist that a statutory claim under § 1985(3) must satisfy the restrictions we impose on constitutional claims under the Fourteenth Amendment. A congressional statute may offer relief from discriminatory effects even if the Fourteenth Amendment prevents only discriminatory intent.

The Court attempts to refute the finding of class-based animus by relying on our cases holding that the governmental denial of either disability benefits for pregnant women or abortion funding does not violate the Constitution. That reliance is misplaced for several reasons. Cases involving constitutional challenges to governmental plans denying financial benefits to pregnant women, and cases involving Equal Protec-

---

23. The limitations of this analysis are apparent from the example the Court invokes: "A tax on wearing yarmulkes is a tax on Jews." Ante, at 760. The yarmulke tax would not become less of a tax on Jews if the taxing authorities really did wish to burden the wearing of yarmulkes. And the fact that many Jews do not wear yarmulkes—like the fact that many women do not seek abortions—would not prevent a finding that the tax—like petitioners' blockade—targeted a particular class.

tion challenges to facially neutral statutes with discriminatory effects, involve different concerns and reach justifiably different results than a case involving citizens' statutory protection against burdens imposed on their constitutional rights.

In Geduldig v. Aiello, 417 U.S. 484 (1974), we faced the question whether a State's disability insurance system violated the Fourteenth Amendment by excluding benefits for normal pregnancy. A majority of the Court concluded that the system did not constitute discrimination on the basis of sex prohibited by the Equal Protection Clause. Geduldig, of course, did not purport to establish that, as a matter of logic, a classification based on pregnancy is gender-neutral. As an abstract statement, that proposition is simply false; a classification based on pregnancy is a sex-based classification, just as, to use the Court's example, a classification based on the wearing of yarmulkes is a religion-based classification. Nor should Geduldig be understood as holding that, as a matter of law, pregnancy-based classifications never violate the Equal Protection Clause. In fact, as the language of the opinion makes clear, what Geduldig held was that not every legislative classification based on pregnancy was equivalent, for equal protection purposes, to the explicitly gender-based distinctions struck down in Frontiero and Reed. That Geduldig must be understood in these narrower terms is apparent from the sentence which the Court quotes in part: "While it is true that only women can become pregnant, it does not follow that every legislative classification concerning pregnancy is a sex-based classification like those considered in Reed, supra, and Frontiero, supra." Geduldig, 417 U.S., at 496, n. 20 (emphasis added).

Central to the holding in Geduldig was the Court's belief that the disability insurance system before it was a plan that conferred benefits evenly on men and women. Later cases confirmed that the holding in Geduldig depended on an analysis of the insurance plan as a benefit program with an overall nondiscriminatory effect. Nashville Gas Co. v. Satty, 434 U.S. 136 (1977), applied a statute without an intent requirement to an employer's policy denying accumulated seniority to employees returning from pregnancy leave. Notwithstanding Geduldig, the Court found that the policy burdened only women, and therefore constituted discrimination on the basis of sex. The Court stated that "petitioner has not merely refused to extend to women a benefit that men cannot and do not receive, but has imposed on women a substantial burden that men need not suffer. The distinction between benefits and burdens is more than one of semantics." 434 U.S., at 142.[27] The

---

27. The abortion-funding cases cited by the Court similarly turn on the distinction between the denial of monetary benefits and the imposition of a burden. See Maher v. Roe, 432 U.S. 464, 475 (1977) ("There is a basic difference between direct state interference with a protected activity and state encouragement of an alternative activity consonant with legislative policy"); see also Harris v. McRae, 448 U.S. 297, 313–318 (1980). In Harris and Maher, the "suspect classification" that the Court considered was indigency. Relying on San Antonio Independent School Dist. v. Rodriguez, 411 U.S. 1 (1973), and Dandridge v. Williams, 397 U.S. 471 (1970), the Court rejected the argument that "financial need

distinction between those who oppose abortion, and those who physically threaten women and obstruct their access to abortion clinics, is also more than semantic. Petitioners in this case form a mob that seeks to impose a burden on women by forcibly preventing the exercise of a right that only women possess. The discriminatory effect of petitioners' conduct is beyond doubt.

Geduldig is inapplicable for another reason. The issue of class-based animus in this case arises in a statutory, not a constitutional, context. There are powerful reasons for giving § 1985(3) a reading that is broader than the constitutional holdings on which the Court relies. In our constitutional cases, we apply the intent standard to determine whether a constitutional violation has occurred. In cases under § 1985(3), we apply the class-based animus test not to determine whether a constitutional violation has occurred—the violation is independently established—but to determine whether that violation can be remedied. Given the differing roles the intent standard and the class-based animus requirement play in our jurisprudence, there is no justification for applying the same stringent standards in the context of § 1985(3) as in our constitutional cases.

As a matter of statutory interpretation, I have always believed that rules that place special burdens on pregnant women discriminate on the basis of sex, for the capacity to become pregnant is the inherited and immutable characteristic that "primarily differentiates the female from the male." General Electric Co. v. Gilbert, 429 U.S. 125, 162 (1976) (Stevens, J., dissenting). I continue to believe that that view should inform our construction of civil rights legislation.

That view was also the one affirmed by Congress in the Pregnancy Discrimination Act, 92 Stat. 2076, which amended Title VII of the Civil Rights Act of 1964, 42 U.S.C. § 2000e et seq. The Act categorically expressed Congress' view that "discrimination based on a woman's pregnancy is, on its face, discrimination because of her sex." Newport News Shipbuilding & Dry Dock Co. v. EEOC, 462 U.S. 669, 684 (1983). Geduldig had held that a pregnancy-based classification did not constitute forbidden sex discrimination if the classification related to benefits and did not have a discriminatory effect. In the Pregnancy Discrimination Act, Congress rejected Geduldig's focus on benefits and overall impact, instead insisting that discrimination on the basis of pregnancy necessarily constitutes prohibited sex discrimination. See H.R.Rep. No. 95–948, pp. 2–3 (1978). The statements of the bill's proponents demonstrate their disapproval of the Court's reluctance in Gilbert and Geduldig to recognize that discrimination on the basis of pregnancy is always gender-based discrimination. See, e.g., 123 Cong.Rec. 10581 (1977) (remarks of Rep. Hawkins) ("[I]t seems only commonsense, that since only women can become pregnant, discrimination against pregnant people is necessarily discrimination against women ...").

alone identifies a suspect class." Maher, 432 U.S., at 471.

Two Terms ago, in Automobile Workers v. Johnson Controls, 499 U.S. ___, 111 S.Ct. 1196, 113 L.Ed.2d 158 (1991), the Court again faced the question whether a classification based on child-bearing capacity violated a statutory ban on discrimination. That case, arising under Title VII, concerned Johnson Controls' "fetal-protection policy," which excluded all women "capable of bearing children" from jobs requiring exposure to lead. Johnson Controls sought to justify the policy on the basis that maternal exposure to lead created health risks for a fetus. The first question the Court addressed was whether the policy was facially discriminatory or, alternatively, facially neutral with merely a discriminatory effect. The Court concluded that the policy was facially discriminatory. The policy was not neutral, the Court held, "because it does not apply to the reproductive capacity of the company's male employees in the same way as it applies to that of the females." Johnson Controls, I had thought, signaled the Court's recognition that classifications based on ability to become pregnant are necessarily discriminatory. . . .

In the context of a conspiracy that hinders state officials and violates respondents' constitutional rights, class-based animus can be inferred if the conspirators' conduct burdens an activity engaged in predominantly by members of the class. Indeed, it would be faithful both to Griffin and to the text of the state hindrance clause to hold that the clause proscribes conspiracies to prevent local law enforcement authorities from protecting activities that are performed exclusively by members of a protected class, even if the conspirators' animus were directed at the activity rather than at the class members. Thus, even if yarmulkes, rather than Jews, were the object of the conspirators' animus, the statute would prohibit a conspiracy to hinder the constituted authorities from protecting access to a synagogue or other place of worship for persons wearing yarmulkes. Like other civil rights legislation, this statute should be broadly construed to provide federal protection against the kind of disorder and anarchy that the States are unable to control effectively.

With class-based animus understood as I have suggested, the conduct covered by the state hindrance clause would be as follows: a large-scale conspiracy that violates the victims' constitutional rights by overwhelming the local authorities and that, by its nature, victimizes predominantly members of a particular class. I doubt whether it would be possible to describe conduct closer to the core of § 1985(3)'s coverage. This account would perfectly describe the conduct of the Ku Klux Klan, the group whose activities prompted the enactment of the statute. This description also applies to petitioners, who have conspired to deprive women of their constitutional right to choose an abortion by overwhelming the local police and by blockading clinics with the intended effect of preventing women from exercising a right only they possess. The state hindrance clause thus provides an independent ground for affirmance. . . .

VIII

In sum, it is irrelevant whether the Court is correct in its assumption that "opposition to abortion" does not necessarily evidence an intent to disfavor women. Many opponents of abortion respect both the law and the rights of others to make their own decisions on this important matter. Petitioners, however, are not mere opponents of abortion; they are defiant lawbreakers who have engaged in massive concerted conduct that is designed to prevent all women from making up their own minds about not only the issue of abortion in general, but also whether they should (or will) exercise a right that all women—and only women—possess.

Indeed, the error that infects the Court's entire opinion is the unstated and mistaken assumption that this is a case about opposition to abortion. It is not. It is a case about the exercise of Federal power to control an interstate conspiracy to commit illegal acts. I have no doubt that most opponents of abortion, like most members of the citizenry at large, understand why the existence of federal jurisdiction is appropriate in a case of this kind.

The Court concludes its analysis of § 1985(3) by suggesting that a contrary interpretation would have condemned the massive "sit-ins" that were conducted to promote desegregation in the 1960's—a "wildly improbable result." See ante, at 764. This suggestion is profoundly misguided. It assumes that we must totally reject the class-based animus requirement to affirm the District Court, when, in fact, we need only construe that requirement to satisfy its purpose. Moreover, the demonstrations in the 1960's were motivated by a desire to extend the equal protection of the laws to all classes—not to impose burdens on any disadvantaged class. Those who engaged in the nonviolent "sit-ins" to which the Court refers were challenging "a political and economic system that had denied them the basic rights of dignity and equality that this country had fought a Civil War to secure." NAACP v. Claiborne Hardware Co., 458 U.S. 886, 918 (1982). The suggestion that there is an analogy between their struggle to achieve equality and these petitioners' concerted efforts to deny women equal access to a constitutionally protected privilege may have rhetorical appeal, but it is insupportable on the record before us, and does not justify the majority's parsimonious construction of an important federal statute.

JUSTICE O'CONNOR, with whom JUSTICE BLACKMUN joins, dissenting.

... Adhering adamantly to our choice of words in Griffin v. Breckenridge, the Court holds that petitioners did not exhibit a "class-based, invidiously discriminatory animus" against the clinics or the women they serve. I would not parse Griffin so finely as to focus on that phrase to the exclusion of our reasons for adopting it as an element of a § 1985(3) civil action. ...

Griffin's requirement of class-based animus is a reasonable shorthand description of the type of actions the 42d Congress was attempting to address. Beginning with Carpenters v. Scott, 463 U.S. 825, 103 S.Ct.

3352, 77 L.Ed.2d 1049 (1983), however, that shorthand description began to take on a life of its own. . . .

I would find in this case that the statute covers petitioners' conspiracy against the clinics and their clients. Like the Klan conspiracies Congress tried to reach in enacting § 1985(3), "[p]etitioners intended to hinder a particular group in the exercise of their legal rights because of their membership in a specific class." The controversy associated with the exercise of those rights, although legitimate, makes the clinics and the women they serve especially vulnerable to the threat of mob violence. The women seeking the clinics' services are not simply "the group of victims of the tortious action"; as was the case in Carpenters, petitioners' intended targets are clearly identifiable—by virtue of their affiliation and activities—before any tortious action occurs. . . .

I agree with Justice Stevens that "[t]he text of the statute provides no basis for excluding from its coverage any cognizable class of persons who are entitled to the equal protection of the laws." Ante, at 785 (dissenting opinion). At the very least, the classes protected by § 1985(3) must encompass those classifications that we have determined merit a heightened scrutiny of state action under the Equal Protection Clause of the Fourteenth Amendment. Classifications based on gender fall within that narrow category of protected classes. E.g., Mississippi Univ. for Women v. Hogan. Not surprisingly, the seven federal courts of appeals to have addressed the question have all reached the conclusion that the class of "women" falls within the protection of the statute. As Justice White has observed, "[i]t is clear that sex discrimination may be sufficiently invidious to come within the prohibition of § 1985(3)." Great American Fed. Sav. & Loan Assn. v. Novotny, 442 U.S. 366, 389, n. 6 (1979) (dissenting opinion).

If women are a protected class under § 1985(3), and I think they are, then the statute must reach conspiracies whose motivation is directly related to characteristics unique to that class. The victims of petitioners' tortious actions are linked by their ability to become pregnant and by their ability to terminate their pregnancies, characteristics unique to the class of women. Petitioners' activities are directly related to those class characteristics and therefore, I believe, are appropriately described as class based within the meaning of our holding in Griffin.

Petitioners assert that, even if their activities are class based, they are not motivated by any discriminatory animus but only by their profound opposition to the practice of abortion. I do not doubt the sincerity of that opposition. But in assessing the motivation behind petitioners' actions, the sincerity of their opposition cannot surmount the manner in which they have chosen to express it. Petitioners are free to express their views in a variety of ways, including lobbying, counseling, and disseminating information. Instead, they have chosen to target women seeking abortions and to prevent them from exercising their equal rights under law. Even without relying on the federally protected right to abortion, petitioners' activities infringe on a number of state-protected interests, including the state laws that make abortion legal, Va.Code Ann. §§ 18.2–72, 18.2–73 (1988), and the state laws that protect against force, intimidation, and violence, e.g., Va.Code Ann. § 18.2–119 (Supp.1992) (trespassing), § 18.2–120 (1988) (instigating trespass to prevent the rendering of services to persons lawfully on the premises), § 18.2–404 (obstructing free passage of others), § 18.2–499 (conspiring to injure another in his business or profession). It is undeniably petitioners' purpose to target a protected class, on account of their class characteristics, and to prevent them from the equal enjoyment of these personal and property rights under law. The element of class-based discrimination that Griffin read into § 1985(3) should require no further showing.

I cannot agree with the Court that the use of unlawful means to achieve one's goal "is not relevant to [the] discussion of animus." Ante, at 760. To the contrary, the deliberate decision to isolate members of a vulnerable group and physically prevent them from conducting legitimate activities cannot be irrelevant in assessing motivation. Cf. Maher v. Roe (1977) (noting the "basic difference," in constitutional Equal Protection analysis, between "direct ... interference with a protected activity" and "encouragement of an alternative activity"). The clinics at issue are lawful operations; the women who seek their services do so lawfully. In my opinion, petitioners' unlawful conspiracy to prevent the clinics from serving those women, who are targeted by petitioners by virtue of their class characteristics, is a group-based, private deprivation of the "equal protection of the laws" within the reach of § 1985(3).

The Court finds an absence of discriminatory animus by reference to our decisions construing the scope of the Equal Protection Clause, and reinforces its conclusion by recourse to the dictionary definition of the word "invidious." See ante, at 760–761. The first step would be fitting if respondents were challenging state action; they do not. The second would be proper if the word "invidious" appeared in the statute we are construing; it does not. As noted above, Griffin's requirement of "class-based, invidiously discriminatory animus" was a shorthand description of the congressional purpose behind the legislation that became § 1985(3). Microscopic examination of the language we chose in Griffin should not now substitute for giving effect to Congress' intent in enacting the relevant legislative language, i.e., "that any violation of the right, the animus and effect of which is to strike down the citizen, to the end that he [or she] may not enjoy equality of rights as contrasted with ... other citizens' rights, shall be within the scope of the remedies of this section." Cong.Globe, 42d Cong., 1st Sess. 478 (1871) (Rep. Shellabarger).

Because § 1985(3) is a statute that was designed to address deprivations caused by private actors, the Court's invocation of our cases construing the reach of the Equal Protection Clause of the Fourteenth Amendment is misplaced. The Court relies on Geduldig v. Aiello, in which we maintained that, for purposes of the Fourteenth Amendment, "not ... every legislative classification concerning pregnancy is a sex-based classification." Id., at 496, n. 20. But that case construed a constitutional provision governing state action, which is far different than determining the scope of a statute aimed at rectifying harms inflicted by private actors. In fact, in stark contrast to our constitutional holding in Geduldig, Congress has declared that, for purposes of interpreting a more recent antidiscrimination statute, a classification based on pregnancy is considered a classification "on the basis of sex." See Pregnancy Discrimination Act, 42 U.S.C. § 2000e(k). Similarly, although we have determined that a successful constitutional challenge to a regulation that disproportionately affects women must show that the legislature "selected or reaffirmed a particular course of action at least in part 'because of,' not merely 'in spite of,' its adverse effects upon an identifiable group," Personnel Administrator of Mass. v. Feeney, Congress recently has made clear its position that showing subjective intent to discriminate is not always necessary to prove statutory discrimination. See Civil Rights Act of 1991, § 105(a)....

This case is not about abortion. It most assuredly is not about "the disfavoring of abortions" by state legislatures. Ante, at 761. Rather, this case is about whether a private conspiracy to deprive members of a protected class of legally protected interests gives rise to a federal cause of action. In my view, it does, because that is precisely the sort of conduct that the 42d Congress sought to address in the legislation now codified at § 1985(3). Our precedents construing the scope of gender discrimination under the Fourteenth Amendment should not distract us from properly interpreting the scope of the statutory remedy.

Note

Clearly in 1993 the Court is still making arguments that actions directed exclusively at women who are pregnant are not sex-based. If laws or actions affecting pregnancy and childbirth are not sex-based, then what does sex-based mean? While there may be other reasons that one might not want to hold abortion clinic protesters liable for their activities, naming the harm in *Bray* as not class-based seems the most spurious. Male privilege manifests itself in the power to name harms as sex-based or not, regardless of our common sense knowledge and experience. When the law reaches conclusions like *Geduldig, Gilbert,* and *Bray,* does it lose some of its legitimacy?

3. *Techniques of Exclusion Based on Sexual Orientation*

As with discrimination against women, discrimination against gay men, lesbians, and bisexuals appeals to nature, religion, history, family, and crass stereotypes. See if you can identify the kinds of rhetorical patterns we discussed earlier in this chapter in the most infamous U.S. Supreme Court case on this subject.

BOWERS v. HARDWICK

Supreme Court of the United States, 1986.
478 U.S. 186, 106 S.Ct. 2841, 92 L.Ed.2d 140.

JUSTICE WHITE delivered the opinion of the Court.

In August 1982, respondent Hardwick (hereafter respondent) was charged with violating the Georgia statute criminalizing sodomy [1] by committing that act with another adult male in the bedroom of respondent's home. After a preliminary hearing, the District Attorney decided not to present the matter to the grand jury unless further evidence developed.

Respondent then brought suit in the Federal District Court, challenging the constitutionality of the statute insofar as it criminalized consensual sodomy. He asserted that he was a practicing homosexual, that the Georgia sodomy statute, as administered by the defendants, placed him in imminent danger of arrest, and that the statute for several reasons violates the Federal Constitution. The District Court granted the defendants' motion to dismiss for failure to state a claim, relying on Doe v. Commonwealth's Attorney for the City of Richmond, 403 F.Supp. 1199 (ED Va.1975), which this Court summarily affirmed, 425 U.S. 901 (1976).

A divided panel of the Court of Appeals for the Eleventh Circuit reversed.... Relying on our decisions in Griswold v. Connecticut, 381 U.S. 479 (1965); Eisenstadt v. Baird, 405 U.S. 438 (1972); Stanley v. Georgia, 394 U.S. 557 (1969); and Roe v. Wade, 410 U.S. 113 (1973), the court went on to hold that the Georgia statute violated respondent's fundamental rights because his homosexual activity is a private and intimate association that is beyond the reach of state regulation by reason of the Ninth Amendment and the Due Process Clause of the Fourteenth Amendment. The case was remanded for trial, at which, to prevail, the State would have to prove that the statute is supported by a compelling interest and is the most narrowly drawn means of achieving that end....

This case does not require a judgment on whether laws against sodomy between consenting adults in general, or between homosexuals in particular, are wise or desirable. It raises no question about the right or propriety of state legislative decisions to repeal their laws that criminalize homosexual sodomy, or of state-court decisions invalidating those laws on state constitutional grounds. The issue presented is whether the Federal Constitution confers a fundamental right upon homosexuals to engage in sodomy and hence invalidates the laws of the many States that still make such conduct illegal and have done so for a

---

1. Georgia Code Ann. § 16-6-2 (1984) provides, in pertinent part, as follows: "(a) A person commits the offense of sodomy when he performs or submits to any sexual act involving the sex organs of one person and the mouth or anus of another...." "(b) A person convicted of the offense of sodomy shall be punished by imprisonment for not less than one nor more than 20 years...."

very long time. The case also calls for some judgment about the limits of the Court's role in carrying out its constitutional mandate.

We first register our disagreement with the Court of Appeals and with respondent that the Court's prior cases have construed the Constitution to confer a right of privacy that extends to homosexual sodomy and for all intents and purposes have decided this case. The reach of this line of cases was sketched in Carey v. Population Services International, 431 U.S. 678 (1977). Pierce v. Society of Sisters, 268 U.S. 510 (1925), and Meyer v. Nebraska, 262 U.S. 390 (1923), were described as dealing with child rearing and education; Prince v. Massachusetts, 321 U.S. 158 (1944), with family relationships; Skinner v. Oklahoma ex rel. Williamson, 316 U.S. 535 (1942), with procreation; Loving v. Virginia, 388 U.S. 1 (1967), with marriage; Griswold v. Connecticut, supra, and Eisenstadt v. Baird, supra, with contraception; and Roe v. Wade, 410 U.S. 113 (1973), with abortion. The latter three cases were interpreted as construing the Due Process Clause of the Fourteenth Amendment to confer a fundamental individual right to decide whether or not to beget or bear a child. Carey v. Population Services International, supra.

Accepting the decisions in these cases and the above description of them, we think it evident that none of the rights announced in those cases bears any resemblance to the claimed constitutional right of homosexuals to engage in acts of sodomy that is asserted in this case. No connection between family, marriage, or procreation on the one hand and homosexual activity on the other has been demonstrated, either by the Court of Appeals or by respondent. Moreover, any claim that these cases nevertheless stand for the proposition that any kind of private sexual conduct between consenting adults is constitutionally insulated from state proscription is unsupportable. Indeed, the Court's opinion in Carey twice asserted that the privacy right, which the Griswold line of cases found to be one of the protections provided by the Due Process Clause, did not reach so far.

Precedent aside, however, respondent would have us announce, as the Court of Appeals did, a fundamental right to engage in homosexual sodomy. This we are quite unwilling to do. It is true that despite the language of the Due Process Clauses of the Fifth and Fourteenth Amendments, which appears to focus only on the processes by which life, liberty, or property is taken, the cases are legion in which those Clauses have been interpreted to have substantive content, subsuming rights that to a great extent are immune from federal or state regulation or proscription. Among such cases are those recognizing rights that have little or no textual support in the constitutional language. Meyer, Prince, and Pierce fall in this category, as do the privacy cases from Griswold to Carey.

Striving to assure itself and the public that announcing rights not readily identifiable in the Constitution's text involves much more than the imposition of the Justices' own choice of values on the States and the Federal Government, the Court has sought to identify the nature of the

rights qualifying for heightened judicial protection. In Palko v. Connecticut, 302 U.S. 319, 325, 326 (1937), it was said that this category
includes those fundamental liberties that are "implicit in the concept of
ordered liberty," such that "neither liberty nor justice would exist if
[they] were sacrificed." A different description of fundamental liberties
appeared in Moore v. East Cleveland, 431 U.S. 494, 503 (1977) (opinion
of Powell, J.), where they are characterized as those liberties that are
"deeply rooted in this Nation's history and tradition."

It is obvious to us that neither of these formulations would extend a
fundamental right to homosexuals to engage in acts of consensual
sodomy. Proscriptions against that conduct have ancient roots. See
generally, *Survey on the Constitutional Right to Privacy in the Context of
Homosexual Activity*, 40 U.Miami L.Rev. 521, 525 (1986). Sodomy was a
criminal offense at common law and was forbidden by the laws of the
original thirteen States when they ratified the Bill of Rights. In 1868,
when the Fourteenth Amendment was ratified, all but 5 of the 37 States
in the Union had criminal sodomy laws. In fact, until 1961, all 50 States
outlawed sodomy, and today, 24 States and the District of Columbia
continue to provide criminal penalties for sodomy performed in private
and between consenting adults. Against this background, to claim that
a right to engage in such conduct is "deeply rooted in this Nation's
history and tradition" or "implicit in the concept of ordered liberty" is,
at best, facetious.

Nor are we inclined to take a more expansive view of our authority
to discover new fundamental rights imbedded in the Due Process Clause.
The Court is most vulnerable and comes nearest to illegitimacy when it
deals with judge-made constitutional law having little or no cognizable
roots in the language or design of the Constitution. That this is so was
painfully demonstrated by the face-off between the Executive and the
Court in the 1930's, which resulted in the repudiation of much of the
substantive gloss that the Court had placed on the Due Process Clauses
of the Fifth and Fourteenth Amendments. There should be, therefore,
great resistance to expand the substantive reach of those Clauses,
particularly if it requires redefining the category of rights deemed to be
fundamental. Otherwise, the Judiciary necessarily takes to itself further
authority to govern the country without express constitutional authority.
The claimed right pressed on us today falls far short of overcoming this
resistance.

Respondent, however, asserts that the result should be different
where the homosexual conduct occurs in the privacy of the home. He
relies on Stanley v. Georgia, 394 U.S. 557 (1969), where the Court held
that the First Amendment prevents conviction for possessing and reading obscene material in the privacy of one's home: "If the First Amendment means anything, it means that a State has no business telling a
man, sitting alone in his house, what books he may read or what films he
may watch."

Stanley did protect conduct that would not have been protected outside the home, and it partially prevented the enforcement of state obscenity laws; but the decision was firmly grounded in the First Amendment. The right pressed upon us here has no similar support in the text of the Constitution, and it does not qualify for recognition under the prevailing principles for construing the Fourteenth Amendment. Its limits are also difficult to discern. Plainly enough, otherwise illegal conduct is not always immunized whenever it occurs in the home. Victimless crimes, such as the possession and use of illegal drugs, do not escape the law where they are committed at home. Stanley itself recognized that its holding offered no protection for the possession in the home of drugs, firearms, or stolen goods. And if respondent's submission is limited to the voluntary sexual conduct between consenting adults, it would be difficult, except by fiat, to limit the claimed right to homosexual conduct while leaving exposed to prosecution adultery, incest, and other sexual crimes even though they are committed in the home. We are unwilling to start down that road.

Even if the conduct at issue here is not a fundamental right, respondent asserts that there must be a rational basis for the law and that there is none in this case other than the presumed belief of a majority of the electorate in Georgia that homosexual sodomy is immoral and unacceptable. This is said to be an inadequate rationale to support the law. The law, however, is constantly based on notions of morality, and if all laws representing essentially moral choices are to be invalidated under the Due Process Clause, the courts will be very busy indeed. Even respondent makes no such claim, but insists that majority sentiments about the morality of homosexuality should be declared inadequate. We do not agree, and are unpersuaded that the sodomy laws of some 25 States should be invalidated on this basis.

Accordingly, the judgment of the Court of Appeals is

Reversed.

CHIEF JUSTICE BURGER, concurring.

I join the Court's opinion, but I write separately to underscore my view that in constitutional terms there is no such thing as a fundamental right to commit homosexual sodomy.

As the Court notes, the proscriptions against sodomy have very "ancient roots." Decisions of individuals relating to homosexual conduct have been subject to state intervention throughout the history of Western civilization. Condemnation of those practices is firmly rooted in Judeo–Christian moral and ethical standards. Homosexual sodomy was a capital crime under Roman law. During the English Reformation when powers of the ecclesiastical courts were transferred to the King's Courts, the first English statute criminalizing sodomy was passed. Blackstone described "the infamous crime against nature" as an offense of "deeper malignity" than rape, a heinous act "the very mention of which is a disgrace to human nature," and "a crime not fit to be named." The common law of England, including its prohibition of sodomy, became the received law of Georgia and the other Colonies. In 1816 the Georgia Legislature passed the statute at issue here, and that statute has been continuously in force in one form or another since that time. To hold that the act of homosexual sodomy is somehow protected as a fundamental right would be to cast aside millennia of moral teaching.

This is essentially not a question of personal "preferences" but rather of the legislative authority of the State. I find nothing in the Constitution depriving a State of the power to enact the statute challenged here.

JUSTICE POWELL, concurring.

I join the opinion of the Court. I agree with the Court that there is no fundamental right—i.e., no substantive right under the Due Process Clause—such as that claimed by respondent Hardwick, and found to exist by the Court of Appeals. This is not to suggest, however, that respondent may not be protected by the Eighth Amendment of the Constitution. The Georgia statute at issue in this case authorizes a court to imprison a person for up to 20 years for a single private, consensual act of sodomy. In my view, a prison sentence for such conduct—certainly a sentence of long duration—would create a serious Eighth Amendment issue. Under the Georgia statute a single act of sodomy, even in the private setting of a home, is a felony comparable in terms of the possible sentence imposed to serious felonies such as aggravated battery, § 16–5–24, first-degree arson, and robbery.

In this case, however, respondent has not been tried, much less convicted and sentenced.[2] Moreover, respondent has not raised the Eighth Amendment issue below. For these reasons this constitutional argument is not before us.

JUSTICE BLACKMUN, with whom JUSTICE BRENNAN, JUSTICE MARSHALL, and JUSTICE STEVENS join, dissenting.

This case is no more about "a fundamental right to engage in homosexual sodomy," as the Court purports to declare, than Stanley v. Georgia was about a fundamental right to watch obscene movies, or Katz v. United States was about a fundamental right to place interstate bets from a telephone booth. Rather, this case is about "the most comprehensive of rights and the right most valued by civilized men," namely, "the right to be let alone."

2. It was conceded at oral argument that, prior to the complaint against respondent Hardwick, there had been no reported decision involving prosecution for private homosexual sodomy under this statute for several decades. Moreover, the State has declined to present the criminal charge against Hardwick to a grand jury, and this is a suit for declaratory judgment brought by respondents challenging the validity of the statute. The history of nonenforce-ment suggests the moribund character today of laws criminalizing this type of private, consensual conduct. Some 26 States have repealed similar statutes. But the constitutional validity of the Georgia statute was put in issue by respondents, and for the reasons stated by the Court, I cannot say that conduct condemned for hundreds of years has now become a fundamental right.

The statute at issue denies individuals the right to decide for themselves whether to engage in particular forms of private, consensual sexual activity. The Court concludes that § 16–6–2 is valid essentially because "the laws of ... many States ... still make such conduct illegal and have done so for a very long time." But the fact that the moral judgments expressed by statutes like § 16–6–2 may be " 'natural and familiar ... ought not to conclude our judgment upon the question whether statutes embodying them conflict with the Constitution of the United States.' " Like Justice Holmes, I believe that "[i]t is revolting to have no better reason for a rule of law than that so it was laid down in the time of Henry IV. It is still more revolting if the grounds upon which it was laid down have vanished long since, and the rule simply persists from blind imitation of the past." I believe we must analyze Hardwick's claim in the light of the values that underlie the constitutional right to privacy. If that right means anything, it means that, before Georgia can prosecute its citizens for making choices about the most intimate aspects of their lives, it must do more than assert that the choice they have made is an " 'abominable crime not fit to be named among Christians.' " ...

I

... [T]he Court's almost obsessive focus on homosexual activity is particularly hard to justify in light of the broad language Georgia has used. Unlike the Court, the Georgia Legislature has not proceeded on the assumption that homosexuals are so different from other citizens that their lives may be controlled in a way that would not be tolerated if it limited the choices of those other citizens. Rather, Georgia has provided that "[a] person commits the offense of sodomy when he performs or submits to any sexual act involving the sex organs of one person and the mouth or anus of another." The sex or status of the persons who engage in the act is irrelevant as a matter of state law. In fact, to the extent I can discern a legislative purpose for Georgia's 1968 enactment of § 16–6–2, that purpose seems to have been to broaden the coverage of the law to reach heterosexual as well as homosexual activity. I therefore see no basis for the Court's decision to treat this case as an "as applied" challenge to § 16–6–2, or for Georgia's attempt, both in its brief and at oral argument, to defend § 16–6–2 solely on the grounds that it prohibits homosexual activity. Michael Hardwick's standing may rest in significant part on Georgia's apparent willingness to enforce against homosexuals a law it seems not to have any desire to enforce against heterosexuals. But his claim that § 16–6–2 involves an unconstitutional intrusion into his privacy and his right of intimate association does not depend in any way on his sexual orientation....

II

"Our cases long have recognized that the Constitution embodies a promise that a certain private sphere of individual liberty will be kept largely beyond the reach of government." In construing the right to privacy, the Court has proceeded along two somewhat distinct, albeit complementary, lines. First, it has recognized a privacy interest with reference to certain decisions that are properly for the individual to make. Second, it has recognized a privacy interest with reference to certain places without regard for the particular activities in which the individuals who occupy them are engaged. The case before us implicates both the decisional and the spatial aspects of the right to privacy.

A

The Court concludes today that none of our prior cases dealing with various decisions that individuals are entitled to make free of governmental interference "bears any resemblance to the claimed constitutional right of homosexuals to engage in acts of sodomy that is asserted in this case." While it is true that these cases may be characterized by their connection to protection of the family, the Court's conclusion that they extend no further than this boundary ignores the warning in Moore v. East Cleveland, against "clos[ing] our eyes to the basic reasons why certain rights associated with the family have been accorded shelter under the Fourteenth Amendment's Due Process Clause." We protect those rights not because they contribute, in some direct and material way, to the general public welfare, but because they form so central a part of an individual's life. "[T]he concept of privacy embodies the 'moral fact that a person belongs to himself and not others nor to society as a whole.'" And so we protect the decision whether to marry precisely because marriage "is an association that promotes a way of life, not causes; a harmony in living, not political faiths; a bilateral loyalty, not commercial or social projects." We protect the decision whether to have a child because parenthood alters so dramatically an individual's self-definition, not because of demographic considerations or the Bible's command to be fruitful and multiply. And we protect the family because it contributes so powerfully to the happiness of individuals, not because of a preference for stereotypical households. The Court recognized in Roberts, that the "ability independently to define one's identity that is central to any concept of liberty" cannot truly be exercised in a vacuum; we all depend on the "emotional enrichment from close ties with others."

Only the most willful blindness could obscure the fact that sexual intimacy is "a sensitive, key relationship of human existence, central to family life, community welfare, and the development of human personality." The fact that individuals define themselves in a significant way through their intimate sexual relationships with others suggests, in a Nation as diverse as ours, that there may be many "right" ways of conducting those relationships, and that much of the richness of a relationship will come from the freedom an individual has to choose the form and nature of these intensely personal bonds.

In a variety of circumstances we have recognized that a necessary corollary of giving individuals freedom to choose how to conduct their lives is acceptance of the fact that different individuals will make different choices. For example, in holding that the clearly important state interest in public education should give way to a competing claim by the Amish to the effect that extended formal schooling threatened their way of life, the Court declared: "There can be no assumption that today's majority is 'right' and the Amish and others like them are 'wrong.' A way of life that is odd or even erratic but interferes with no rights or interests of others is not to be condemned because it is different." Wisconsin v. Yoder, 406 U.S. 205 (1972). The Court claims that its decision today merely refuses to recognize a fundamental right to engage in homosexual sodomy; what the Court really has refused to recognize is the fundamental interest all individuals have in controlling the nature of their intimate associations with others.

B

The behavior for which Hardwick faces prosecution occurred in his own home, a place to which the Fourth Amendment attaches special significance. The Court's treatment of this aspect of the case is symptomatic of its overall refusal to consider the broad principles that have informed our treatment of privacy in specific cases. Just as the right to privacy is more than the mere aggregation of a number of entitlements to engage in specific behavior, so too, protecting the physical integrity of the home is more than merely a means of protecting specific activities that often take place there. Even when our understanding of the contours of the right to privacy depends on "reference to a 'place,'" Katz v. United States (Harlan, J., concurring), "the essence of a Fourth Amendment violation is 'not the breaking of [a person's] doors, and the rummaging of his drawers,' but rather is 'the invasion of his indefeasible right of personal security, personal liberty and private property.'"

The Court's interpretation of the pivotal case of Stanley v. Georgia is entirely unconvincing. Stanley held that Georgia's undoubted power to punish the public distribution of constitutionally unprotected, obscene material did not permit the State to punish the private possession of such material. According to the majority here, Stanley relied entirely on the First Amendment, and thus, it is claimed, sheds no light on cases not involving printed materials. But that is not what Stanley said. Rather, the Stanley Court anchored its holding in the Fourth Amendment's special protection for the individual in his home: "'The makers of our Constitution undertook to secure conditions favorable to the pursuit of happiness. They recognized the significance of man's spiritual nature, of his feelings and of his intellect. They knew that only a part of the pain, pleasure and satisfactions of life are to be found in material things. They sought to protect Americans in their beliefs, their thoughts, their emotions and their sensations.'

. . .

"These are the rights that appellant is asserting in the case before us. He is asserting the right to read or observe what he pleases—the right to satisfy his intellectual and emotional needs in the privacy of his own home." ... "The right of the people to be secure in their ... houses," expressly guaranteed by the Fourth Amendment, is perhaps the most "textual" of the various constitutional provisions that inform our understanding of the right to privacy, and thus I cannot agree with the Court's statement that "[t]he right pressed upon us here has no ... support in the text of the Constitution." Indeed, the right of an individual to conduct intimate relationships in the intimacy of his or her own home seems to me to be the heart of the Constitution's protection of privacy.

III

... Essentially, petitioner argues, and the Court agrees, that the fact that the acts described in § 16–6–2 "for hundreds of years, if not thousands, have been uniformly condemned as immoral" is a sufficient reason to permit a State to ban them today.

I cannot agree that either the length of time a majority has held its convictions or the passions with which it defends them can withdraw legislation from this Court's scrutiny.[5] As Justice Jackson wrote so eloquently for the Court in West Virginia Board of Education v. Barnette, "we apply the limitations of the Constitution with no fear that freedom to be intellectually and spiritually diverse or even contrary will disintegrate the social organization.... [F]reedom to differ is not limited to things that do not matter much. That would be a mere shadow of freedom. The test of its substance is the right to differ as to things that touch the heart of the existing order." It is precisely because the issue raised by this case touches the heart of what makes individuals what they are that we should be especially sensitive to the rights of those whose choices upset the majority.

The assertion that "traditional Judeo–Christian values proscribe" the conduct involved cannot provide an adequate justification for § 16–6–2. That certain, but by no means all, religious groups condemn the behavior at issue gives the State no license to impose their judgments on the entire citizenry.... A State can no more punish private behavior because of religious intolerance than it can punish such behavior because of racial animus. "The Constitution cannot control such prejudices, but

---

5. The parallel between Loving and this case is almost uncanny. There, too, the State relied on a religious justification for its law. Compare 388 U.S., at 3, (quoting trial court's statement that "Almighty God created the races white, black, yellow, malay and red, and he placed them on separate continents.... The fact that he separated the races shows that he did not intend for the races to mix"), with Brief for Petitioner 20–21 (relying on the Old and New Testaments and the writings of St. Thomas Aquinas to show that "traditional Judeo–Christian values proscribe such conduct"). There, too, defenders of the challenged statute relied heavily on the fact that when the Fourteenth Amendment was ratified, most of the States had similar prohibitions. Compare Brief for Appellee in Loving v.

Virginia, O.T.1966, No. 395, pp. 28–29, with ante, at 2844–2845, and n. 6. There, too, at the time the case came before the Court, many of the States still had criminal statutes concerning the conduct at issue. Compare 388 U.S., at 6, n. 5 (noting that 16 States still outlawed interracial marriage), with [section] (noting that 24 States and the District of Columbia have sodomy statutes). Yet the Court held, not only that the invidious racism of Virginia's law violated the Equal Protection Clause, see 388 U.S., at 7–12, but also that the law deprived the Lovings of due process by denying them the "freedom of choice to marry" that had "long been recognized as one of the vital personal rights essential to the orderly pursuit of happiness by free men." Id., at 12.

neither can it tolerate them. Private biases may be outside the reach of the law, but the law cannot, directly or indirectly, give them effect." Palmore v. Sidoti, 466 U.S. 429, 433 (1984). No matter how uncomfortable a certain group may make the majority of this Court, we have held that "[m]ere public intolerance or animosity cannot constitutionally justify the deprivation of a person's physical liberty.". . .

IV

. . . I can only hope that here the Court soon will reconsider its analysis and conclude that depriving individuals of the right to choose for themselves how to conduct their intimate relationships poses a far greater threat to the values most deeply rooted in our Nation's history than tolerance of nonconformity could ever do. Because I think the Court today betrays those values, I dissent.

The *Hardwick* opinion leaves out information about how Michael Hardwick ended up being arrested for a private, consensual sexual encounter in his own bedroom. Peter Irons relates the story in Hardwick's own voice.

PETER IRONS, THE COURAGE OF THEIR CONVICTIONS
392–397 (Free Press, 1988).

I was born in Miami in 1954 and raised in Miami. My mother is a very wonderful and intelligent and sensitive woman. My father was a very intelligent and crafty-type man. He was a fireman and worked during the Cuban missile crisis with fallout shelters and radiation. My parents divorced when I was twelve years old and I lived with my mom until I was seventeen. I went to high school here and it was pretty normal, just like high school anywhere.

I have two sisters and a brother that are all older than me. My older sister is forty and she is a lesbian. She has a daughter who is sixteen and she's been a strong influence on me all my life. I have an older brother who is straight and married and has children.

I wanted to be a landscape architect, and I went to school in botany and horticulture at Florida State University in Gainesville. I spent three years up there, pretty much as a spiritual recluse. I was seriously considering becoming a Buddhist monk, and I was into a very spiritual frame, as far as Karma and all of that.

From Gainesville, I went up to Atlanta and met this man that I fell in love with. When I met this guy it seemed like a perfectly normal thing and that was that. Things didn't work out between me and this man in Atlanta. He had a lover, which I didn't know, so I left and went to Knoxville, Tennessee. . . .

Then I left and went back down to Miami and told my mother and my sister I was gay, and they were very supportive. I was twenty-one years old at the time. And I've been out since then. My mother was very accepting. . . .

[Years later I returned to Atlanta] which is how this whole case started. I had been working for about a year, in a gay bar that was getting ready to open up a discothèque. I was there one night until seven o'clock in the morning, helping them put in insulation. When I left, I went up to the bar and they gave me a beer. I was kind of debating whether I wanted to leave, because I was pretty exhausted, or stay and finish the beer. I decided to leave, and I opened the door and threw the beer bottle into this trash can by the front door of the bar. I wasn't really in the mood for the beer.

Just as I did that I saw a cop drive by. I walked about a block, and he turned around and came back and asked me where the beer was. I told him I had thrown it in the trash can in front of the bar. He insisted I had thrown the beer bottle right as he pulled up. He made me get in the car and asked me what I was doing. I told him that I worked there, which immediately identified me as a homosexual, because he knew it was a homosexual bar. He was enjoying *his* position as opposed to *my* position.

After about twenty minutes of bickering he drove me back so I could show him where the beer bottle was. There was no way of getting out of the back of a cop car. I told him it was in the trash can and he said he couldn't see it from the car. I said fine, just give me a ticket for drinking in public. He was just busting my chops because he knew I was gay.

Anyway, the ticket had a court date on the top and a date in the center and they didn't coincide; they were one day apart. Tuesday was the court date, and the officer had written Wednesday on top of the ticket. So Tuesday, two hours after my court date, he was at my house with a warrant for my arrest. This was Officer Torick. This was unheard of, because it takes forty-eight hours to process a warrant. What I didn't realize, and didn't find out until later, was that he had personally processed a warrant for the first time in ten years. So I think there is reason to believe that he had it out for me.

I wasn't there when he came with the warrant. I got home that afternoon and my roommate said there was a cop here with a warrant. I said, That's impossible; my court date isn't until tomorrow. I went and got my ticket and realized the court date was Tuesday, not Wednesday. I asked my roommate if he'd seen the warrant and he said he hadn't. So I went down to the county clerk and showed him the discrepancy on the ticket. He brought it before the judge, and he fined me $50. I told the county clerk the cop had already been at my house with a warrant and he said that was impossible. He said it takes forty-eight hours to process a warrant. He wrote me a receipt just in case I had any problems with it further down the road. That was that, and I thought I had taken care of it and everything was finished and I didn't give it much thought.

Three weeks went by, and my mom had come up to visit me. I came home one morning after work at 6:30 and there were three guys standing in front of my house. I cannot say for *sure* that they had anything to do with this, but they were very straight, middle thirties, civilian clothes. I got out of the car, turned around, and they said 'Michael' and I said yes, and they proceeded to beat the hell out of me. Tore all the cartilage out of my nose, kicked me in the face, cracked about six of my ribs. I passed out. I don't know how long I was unconscious. When I came to, all I could think of was, God, I don't want my *mom* to see me like this!

I managed to crawl up the stairs into the house, into the back bedroom. What I didn't realize was that I'd left a trail of blood all the way back. My mom woke up, found this trail of blood, found me passed out, and just freaked out. I assured her that everything was okay, that it was like a fluke accident, these guys were drunk or whatever. They weren't drunk, they weren't ruffians, and they knew who I was. I convinced her everything was okay and she left to go visit a friend in Pennsylvania.

I had a friend come in a few days later who was from out of town, in Atlanta to apply for a government job. He waited for me to get off work, we went home, and then my roommate left for work. That night at work, another friend of mine had gotten really drunk, and I took his car keys, put him in a cab, and sent him to my house, so he was passed out on the couch in the living room. He did not hear me and my friend come in. I retired with my friend. He had left the front door open, and Officer Torick came into my house about 8:30 in the morning. He had a warrant that had not been valid for three weeks and that he didn't bother to call in and check on. Officer Torick came in and woke up the guy who was passed out on my couch, who didn't know I was there and had a friend with me.

Officer Torick then came to my bedroom. The door was cracked, and the door opened up and I looked up and there was nobody there. I just blew it off as the wind and went back to what I was involved in, which was mutual oral sex. About thirty-five seconds went by and I heard another noise and I looked up, and this officer is standing in my bedroom. He identified himself when he realized I had seen him. He said, My name is Officer Torick. Michael Hardwick, you are under arrest. I said, For what? What are you doing in my bedroom? He said, I have a warrant for your arrest. I told him the warrant isn't any good. He said, It doesn't matter, because I was acting under good faith.

I asked Torick if he would leave the room so we could get dressed and he said, There's no reason for that, because I have already seen you in your most intimate aspect. He stood there and watched us get dressed, and then he brought us over to a substation. We waited in the car for about twenty-five minutes, handcuffed to the back floor. Then he brought us downtown; brought us in and made sure everyone in the holding cells and guards and people who were processing us knew I was in there for 'cocksucking' and that I should be able to get what I was looking for. The guards were having a *real* good time with that.

There was somebody there to get me out of jail within an hour, but it took them twelve hours to get me out. In the meantime, after they processed me and kept me in a holding cell for about four hours, they brought me up to the third floor, where there was convicted criminals. I had no business being up there. They again told all the people in the cells what I was in there for. It was not a pleasant experience. My friend was freaking out, and when I got out of jail I came back within an hour and got him out. He decided because of his government position he could not go on with the case.

I was contacted about three days later by a man named Clint Sumrall who was working in and out of the ACLU. For the last five years, he would go to the courts every day and find sodomy cases and try to get a test case. By this time, my mom had come back into town and found out what had happened. We had a typical mother conversation— she was saying, I *knew* I shouldn't have left! So she went with me to meet with Sumrall and this team of ten lawyers. I asked them what was the worst that could happen, what was the best that could happen? They explained to me that the judge could make an example out of me and give me twenty years in jail. My mom was saying, Do you realize I'll be *dead* before I see you again? So they said, Just think about it for two or three days.

I realized that if there was anything I could do, even if it was just laying the foundation to change this horrendous law, that I would feel pretty bad about myself if I just walked away from it. One thing that influenced me was that they'd been trying for five years to get a perfect case. Most of the arrests that are made for sodomy in Atlanta are of people who are having sex outside in public; or an adult and a minor; or two consenting adults, but their families don't know they are gay; or they went through seven years of college to teach and they'd be jeopardizing their teaching position. There's a lot of different reasons why people would not want to go on with it. I was fortunate enough to have a supportive family who knew I was gay. I'm a bartender, so I can always work in a gay bar. And I was arrested in my own house. So I was a perfect test case.

Notes and Questions

1. How do the analytical techniques we developed in other cases help you evaluate the *Hardwick* opinions? How a court frames and articulates the issue can often determine the outcome of a case and the shape of the law. One of the interesting things the majority opinion did in this case was reframe the question as one about whether there is a constitutionally-based "fundamental right of homosexuals to engage in sodomy." The case, in fact, was an "on its face", not "as applied," challenge to the Georgia sodomy law which said nothing about same-sex or homosexual acts. Hardwick's lawyers

framed the case as one about the scope of the existing right of privacy for consensual sexual acts in one's own bedroom.

2. *Hardwick* concludes that state laws can punish consensual same-sex intercourse without violating the federal constitution or due process concepts. Would it make more sense for the constitutionality of the law to depend upon a distinction between punishing consensual sodomy and punishing forcible sodomy, as clearly a law punishing consensual heterosexual intercourse would violate due process and privacy rights, whereas punishment for forcible rape does not? Or should the constitutionality of punishment here turn entirely on the presence of consent without requiring any evidence of force? For a study of sodomy laws and their relationship to rape, see Larry Cata Backer, *Raping Sodomy and Sodomizing Rape: A Moral Tale About the Transformation of Modern Sodomy Jurisprudence,* 21 Am. J.Crim.L. 37 (1993).

3. Many scholars have written about *Bowers v. Hardwick* over the years, so there is a rich library of resources to draw upon for critiques. To mention just a few: Patricia Cain has written a brilliant and comprehensive legal history of gay rights litigation that is a "must read" for studying law and sexual orientation, in which she strategizes about how to get around *Hardwick*. Patricia A. Cain, *Litigating for Lesbian and Gay Rights: A Legal History,* 79 Va.L.Rev. 1551 (1993). Sylvia Law explored how the heterosexism of the majority and concurring opinions in *Bowers v. Hardwick* is strongly related to traditional concepts of masculinity, femininity, and gender roles in our society. Sylvia Law, *Homosexuality and the Social Meaning of Gender,* 1988 Wis.L.Rev. 187. Additionally, Justice White's majority opinion has been criticized for its inaccurate history of sodomy, including its errors in defining sodomy to exclude heterosexual encounters, despite the sex-neutrality of the Georgia sodomy statute, Anne B. Goldstein, *History, Homosexuality, and Political Values: Searching for the Hidden Determinants of Bowers v. Hardwick,* 97 Yale.L.J. 1073 (1988) and for its conflation of the sexual *act* (sodomy) with the *identity* of the person (homosexual), Janet Halley, *Reasoning About Sodomy: Act and Identity in and after Bowers v. Hardwick,* 79 Va.L.Rev. 1721 (1993). Not all homosexuals commit sodomy and not all sodomy is committed by homosexuals. Kendall Thomas has taken Halley's rhetorical and textual analysis one step further by developing a biting psychoanalytic, Freudian-based, deconstructive analysis of White's opinion. Kendall Thomas, *The Eclipse of Reason: A Rhetorical Reading of Bowers v. Hardwick,* 79 Va.L.Rev. 1805 (1993).

An excellent collection of materials that covers all aspects of gay and lesbian life as they intersect with law has been edited by William B. Rubenstein entitled Lesbians, Gay Men, and the Law (New Press "Law in Context" Series Reader, 1993). See also Ruthann Robson, Lesbian (Out)law (Firebrand, 1992).

4. After he retired from the Court, Justice Lewis F. Powell admitted to making an error in signing on to the majority position in Bowers v. Hardwick. Anand Agneshwar, *Ex–Justice Says He May Have Been Wrong: Powell on Sodomy,* The National Law Journal, Nov. 5, 1990, p. 3. His vote created the majority in the 5–4 decision. Despite Powell's admission of error, *Bowers v. Hardwick* continues to be cited as authority to sustain the

constitutionality of sodomy and "unnatural intercourse" statutes as applied to consenting adults, see e.g., Miller v. State, 636 So.2d 391, 1994 WL 125291 (Miss.1994), although other courts have finally overturned their state statutes. Commonwealth v. Wasson, 842 S.W.2d 487 (Ky.1992); State v. Morales, 826 S.W.2d 201 (Tex.App.1992), reversed, 869 S.W.2d 941 (Tex.1994) (on jurisdictional grounds).

5.   Some legal theorists seeking to empower lesbians and gay men have rejected the use of a privacy rights argument, even in its eloquent enunciation in Justice Blackmun's dissent in *Hardwick*. Kendall Thomas argues for a less abstract, corporeal "body-based" approach rooted in the Eighth Amendment's concept of cruel and unusual punishment which recognizes the link between body pain, violence against gay men and lesbians, and the existence of state laws against sodomy. Kendall Thomas, *Beyond the Privacy Principle,* 92 Colum.L.Rev. 1431 (1992). Rhonda Copelon offers the following provocative critique of the use of a privacy rationale for lesbian and gay rights.

RHONDA COPELON, A CRIME NOT FIT TO BE NAMED: SEX, LIES, AND THE CONSTITUTION

in The Politics of Law 177 (D. Kairys, ed., rev. ed., 1990).

A STORY

Although he entered the overwhelming world of law school wanting, like everyone else, not to be scrutinized, Rob was—almost immediately. It began with appearance: he wore glasses with rather bold black frames, and earrings; he didn't dress jock. There was his manner: he was a bit too aloof from the carousing of some of the younger men. After a while, there were his words: in class discussion about discrimination, Rob risked noting the failure to mention lesbians and gays. Then the questions began: "Why do you wear earrings? Does that signal you're available for sex? Are you gay? Do you like gay bars? Why won't you answer our questions?" Their own motives and unease unacknowledged, some claimed that the questions were an attempt to make Rob feel comfortable. One student, purporting to reassure, told him, "I don't like gays, but I don't let it affect the way I treat them."

The discomfort was unbearable. Rob exchanged his bold black frames for ordinary wire rims. But he was isolated. A faculty member to whom Rob turned told him, "Unpopularity is the price we pay for our politics." To Rob, the price he was paying for his life was hate. He tried to take it on. He put up a sign—"Heterosexism Can Be Cured." It was torn down. To some, this confirmed he had only gotten what he deserved; he had insulted heterosexuality. Nobody was responsible, except Rob. In lawyerly fashion, some began to defend: the First Amendment protects even offensive speech. But they missed the point. The harassment—the hate—was largely unseen and uncriticized. Few defended his right to respect, or to peace.

The semester ended, and, shaken, Rob traveled home. One night someone never to be known or confronted trashed Rob's desk. Half the student body met to protest, while others blamed Rob for disrupting their studies. Doubt was expressed that this was a homophobic act. A few people suggested that maybe Rob did it.

Rob's story is a stigma contest which pits the power of the stigmatizer against the resistance of the stigmatized. It typifies the dynamic of deviance creation, and particularly, of homophobic harassment. Gay men, lesbians, and bisexuals may choose to be "out," or they may wish not to self-identify and yet will not or cannot bury their self sufficiently to escape notice. Attention is drawn to culturally determined indicators of "otherness"—dress, joviality, manner, and the mention of gay and lesbian concerns. By violating the "norm," the gay person threatens the conventions of gender identity, the boundaries of gendered sexuality, and heterosexuality itself. One becomes an object of curiosity and of derision, the cause, rather than the victim, of division and distraction. Harassment helps to consolidate the righteousness of the threatened majority; their prejudice is exalted, but never examined. The homophobia that underlies feelings, reactions, words, and even assault is trivialized and denied. The harassers draw power from the discomfort and, ultimately, the silent complicity of others, the very fear of the word. The only alternatives are retreat or resistance; the only safety rests in support.

Lawsuits, too, are stigma contests, and the judicial opinions they generate are stories. Civil rights suits challenge exclusion and stigmatization, both practically and symbolically. Lesbian and gay rights advocates challenge homophobia and heterosexism and the multitude of harms these processes wreak. Judges bring to the resolution of these claims a deep and often unrecognized homophobia that leads to a similar, albeit more subtle, process by which norms are reinforced and variety is stigmatized.

This essay is about the way the judiciary resolves the stigma contest over sexual orientation, and, in so doing, reveals the societal tension between bigotry, tolerance, and affirmation. The focus here is on several leading privacy decisions both because they provide an essential text on homophobia and because they demonstrate some of the pitfalls of seeking liberation through the liberal concept of negative rights.

> ... the question is more akin to whether those suffering from measles have a constitutional right, in violation of quarantine regulations, to associate together and with others who do not presently have measles ...
>
> —Chief Justice William Rehnquist

To compare homosexuality and contagious disease, as the Chief Justice did in a 1978 opinion, is quintessential homophobia. If a "disease," homosexuality is, according to the dictionary, an "impairment of the normal state of the living animal," a "disorder or derangement," an "alteration that impairs the quality of a product." To be labeled diseased is to be inferior and to evoke revulsion, avoidance, anger, and pity. But the notion that homosexuality might be "contagious"—"communicable by contact," "spreading," "catching," and, tellingly, "exciting similar emotions or conduct in others"—challenges the norm of dichotomized gender identity and the superiority of heterosexuality itself, and calls for the sternest measures. First to contain sin, then to contain sickness, Western society has, at different times, branded and hanged sodomites, burned witches, jailed "deviants," and tortured gays and lesbians with shock treatment and behavior modification. The imposition of such punishments does not aim to rout out all the "wrongdoers," however; draconian measures create stigma, stereotypes, marginalization, invisibility, and denial.

Whether caught in the sting of church, state, or medical enforcement, or in the oppressive but also subversive refuge of secrecy and dissemblance, gay women and men have braved enormous odds simply to love, to share pleasure, to survive, and to resist. In the last twenty years this resistance has burst into the open. Nurtured by the underground societies of the 1950s, the experience of the civil rights movement, and the courage of thousands of "comings-out," the lesbian and gay movement of our time embraces open, collective, and multifaceted resistance to antigay measures and practices as well as to the invisibility and degradation they [entail].

In the courts, the movement launched a multifaceted attack, a centerpiece of which was the challenge to the criminal sodomy laws, for the criminalization of gay sexuality is a cornerstone of the legal and societal oppression of gay people. With the caution that judicial confrontations are but a small part of broader conflict over homophobia in everyday life, the focus here is primarily on the 1986 decision of the Supreme Court in *Bowers v. Hardwick,* the case in which the Court answered, for the nonce, the fundamental question whether gay people have a protected right or a contagious disease. A majority of five ruled that the constitutional right of privacy provided no protection, and, in doing so, upheld the criminalization of sodomy, the symbolic quarantine of gays and lesbians. Some lesbians and gay men are likely to be jailed as a result of the *Hardwick* decision. But even more terrible is the fact that it gives constitutional approval to the criminalization of gay love and sex; brands lesbian, gay, and bisexual people as evil or sick; threatens their right to hold on to their children and jobs, and to obtain housing and benefits; legitimizes violence and degradation; and denies the very right to be.

The majority position in *Hardwick* operates as "law," but it was the product of a deeply divided Court. Four justices joined in a landmark dissent recognizing that the right to choose one's intimate relationships is central to authenticity and self-realization. Justice Blackmun, who only eight years earlier had wondered with Chief Justice Rehnquist whether homosexuality was a contagious disease, wrote that dissent. *Hardwick* reflects not only the power of the majoritarian norm of heterosexuality but also the strength of the lesbian/gay movement both in the fear that threads the majority decisions approving criminalization and in the sharp split on the Court for which the movement can claim substantial credit. The only question before the Supreme Court in the *Hardwick* case was whether gay sex should be protected within the right of privacy.

There were many ways for the Court to have recognized a right of privacy in this case. It could have emphasized the geographical location of Hardwick's arrest as a paradigmatic example of privacy, compatible at least to the use of obscenity in the home which drew constitutional protection in *Stanley v. Georgia*. It could have used the facts of this case to deplore the horrors of invading the bedroom, as it did in *Griswold v. Connecticut,* which invalidated prohibitions on contraceptive use as an invasion of marital intimacy. It could have recognized that sheltered sexual activity and the intimacy of association involved is akin to the values underlying the recognition of privacy in the contraception and abortion cases. To do this, however, the Court would have had to acknowledge something it consistently avoided in those cases—that the protection of procreative choice is inextricable from recognition of the right to sexual pleasure independent of reproduction or marriage.

The majority refused all these routes. And while it claimed to do so as an exercise of judicial restraint, its reasoning is an example of homophobic excess. The majority decision, written by Justice White, explicitly disclaims at the outset to have any position on the wisdom of criminal sodomy laws or the propriety of legislative repeal. White argues that he is only declining to recognize rights for which there is no explicit textual support and, thereby, preserving the proper relationship between the Court and the legislatures. But White does not usually subscribe to the originalist school of interpretation which sacralizes the Founding Fathers and the text of the Constitution as the fount of wisdom. Although some form of originalism, which would resurrect the patriarchal value system that dominated the eighteenth and nineteenth centuries, is nearly dominant on the Court with the addition of Justices Scalia and Kennedy, *Hardwick* is not simply a product of its growing ascendance. Because White supports the contraception decisions and abhors the abortion decisions, and because Justice Powell, the swing vote in *Hardwick,* supported them both, the task of the majority was to draw lines. The invocation of judicial restraint is but a thin veil for the condemnation of gay and lesbian sexuality; it is homophobia, not jurisprudence, that drives the majority's analysis.

This implicit equation of gay sexuality with evil and danger underpins White's rejection of Hardwick's argument that the protection previously recognized by the Court for marriage, procreation, and family relationships logically extends to sexual intimacy. To deny this claim would seem to require some explanation. Instead, White baldly asserts that there is no "resemblance" or "connection between family, marriage, or procreation on the one hand and homosexual activity on the other." The gay person is served up as a creature apart, and gay intimacy is treated as unrelated to heterosexual intimacy whether it be a one-night stand or a lasting relationship.

The danger of gay sexuality is also underscored by the Court's rejection of the claim that gay sex, like obscenity, should at least be protected in the home. Although obscenity is sexually explicit material which is unprotected by the First Amendment, and, therefore, subject to criminal sanction, *Stanley v. Georgia* protected it because it was found in the home. Nonetheless, the *Hardwick* majority reinterpreted *Stanley* as a First Amendment decision, distinguishing sexual speech from sexual conduct (and ignoring that sexual conduct often accompanies the use of sexually explicit materials in the home). It emphasized that the home does not confer immunity for criminal conduct, comparing gay sex first to drugs, firearms, and stolen goods and then to adultery, incest, and bigamy. In so doing, the Court evoked images of dissolution, fear, seizure, and instability.

The confusion between consensual sodomy and nonconsensual, exploitative sexuality such as incest echoes the stereotypical fear of gay men as predators and child molesters, even though the incidence of child molestation and sexual harassment is disproportionately committed by heterosexual males. The analogy to adultery reflects fears that gay sexuality challenges the traditional monogamous heterosexual family. By contrast, Justice Blackmun excoriates the majority's choice of analogies and its failure to explain why it did not use nonthreatening analogies such as private, consensual heterosexual activity or even sodomy within marriage for comparison. While for feminists the notion of privacy in the home has been fraught with danger, as is the ambiguity of consent in the domestic or sexual sphere, the kind of privacy claimed in *Hardwick*—the right of sexual self-determination—is precisely that which has been legally denied to women and gay people.

Thus in rejecting Michael Hardwick's claim that his constitutional right of privacy was infringed, the majority advances, mostly by implication, its view of gay sexuality as unrelated to recognized forms of sexual activity or intimate relationship, and as exploitative, predatory, threatening to personal and social stability. In so doing, it echoes the stereotypes at the heart of homophobia—the portrayal of gay people as dangerous as well as subhuman "others."

The Limits of Privacy

It is astonishing that, in 1986, the Court would not see fit to protect voluntary sexual activity in the bedroom. From the perspective of the liberal theory of rights, Michael Hardwick was not asking for much—only that the state not punish cloistered private choices. Under this view, private choices are tolerable because they are of great import to the individual, but of little consequence to society. By protecting these private choices, the law is saved from the embarrassment of widespread disrespect and unenforceability. The trade-off is small because recognition of a negative right of privacy does not require that society renounce its prejudices. The liberal view of privacy is perfectly consistent with the view that homosexuality is "deviant" and "disgusting," but "OK so long as it doesn't show."

Rob's story, however, illustrates the illusiveness of this notion of privacy. Just as he could not conceal the possibility of his different sexuality without denuding his identity, so sexual self-definition must cross the bounds of privacy. While privacy implies secrecy and shame, the choice of sexual partners of the same sex is no more intrinsically private than the identity of one's spouse. Nor is this choice easily confined to the private realm of the bed or the closet. It involves not only sexual, but also social and familial identity—who one is in public as well as in private and what the legal norms are. To accept mere tolerance of hidden sexual difference is not only degrading; it is ultimately self-defeating.

Beyond the inefficacy of secrecy, the liberal notion of privacy reinforces the hierarchy embodied in heterosexism. To protect sexual "difference" reminds us that heterosexuality is the norm, the preferred and privileged status, while a same-sex or bisexual orientation is aberrant, inferior, tolerated at best. The protection of sexual "difference" does not protect the expression of variety in everyday life. It carves out an exception to the norm; it preserves deviance by the very act of permitting it limited scope.

To critique the liberal notion of privacy does not mean that the loss of such protection in *Hardwick* is not of enormous significance. In the realm of sexuality—fraught as it is with taboo—the notion of a sphere of noninterference with consensual activity is a necessary, albeit insufficient, condition for self-determination. The terrible penalties imposed on gays and lesbians in the past are warning enough of the dangers of sexual repression. Beyond that, there is no doubt that even the recognition of a narrow right of privacy in *Hardwick* would have had broad social impact. No longer could the criminal law be invoked as a source of stigma or as a basis for denying people their children or their wherewithal to live. While discrimination and certainly prejudice would not magically be eradicated, the protection of privacy would inevitably spill over into greater safety in everyday life, greater legitimacy in public.

Herein lies the paradox that privacy authorizes too little and challenges too much. Although the notion of privacy parades as a value-free basis for decision, *Hardwick* demonstrates that the agnostic stance of liberal privacy as to the value of the protected activity does not survive where prejudice and fear are deep. It is doubtful that any of the students harassing Rob or standing by in silence would have argued that he had no right to choose his sexual partners. But their actions indicate, as do all opinions of the majority Justices in *Hardwick,* that privacy is not tolerable when it suggests a proud alternative to social norms.

Without underestimating the raw threat of sexuality, it is important to underscore the relationship between the stigmatization of gays and the preservation of the differentiation between men and women. As both stories demonstrate, same-sex intimacy is threatening to gender identity, gendered sexual boundaries, the expectation of heterosexuality, and the power relations it embodies. A heterosexist culture goes to elaborate lengths to construct distinct gender identities as well as the propensity toward heterosexuality. It may be that the very fragility of the channeled sexual self heightens the danger presented by crossing the line; that precisely because sexual identity and heterosexuality are not preordained but encultured and even chosen, those who deviate from the heterosexual norm must be stigmatized and excluded.

To acknowledge the flaws in the liberal concept of privacy not only refuses the legal closet and reveals the sources of prejudice; it also suggests alternative strategies more consonant with the original goals of the movements for sexual and women's liberation. It requires insistence on the right of expression rather than of privacy. And it requires a demand—suggested by Justice Blackmun's dissent—that people's sexual and intimate choices be equally honored and supported by the society. It means talking straight about sex as well as dismantling the complex social apparatus that channels sexuality into preferred forms. As Adrienne Rich has written:

> Heterosexuality as an institution has also drowned in silence the erotic feelings between women. I myself lived half a lifetime in the lie of that denial. That silence makes us all to some degree, into liars ... The possibilities that exist between two people ... are ... the most interesting things in life. The liar is someone who keeps losing sight of these possibilities.

Challenging the dynamic of homophobia and the systemization of heterosexual privilege thus contains the possibility of not only undoing stereotypes and oppression but also fostering more authentic and ultimately more secure sexual choices—whether gay, straight, or bisexual—for everyone. Privacy provides but a small and dangerously limited step in the much larger project of liberation, and its ultimate success will depend more on the progress of the larger project than on the effort to closet its potential.

TRANSCENDING *HARDWICK*

Though the 5–4 decision in *Hardwick* appears to have resolved the stigma contest, it is far from the last word. In one sense, *Hardwick* can be seen as a desperate attempt to maintain the status quo in the face of new claims of human rights, and, as such, it is one in a line of infamous decisions rejecting claims to full citizenship on the part of different groups. In *Dred Scott v. Sandford* a former slave sought recognition as a free citizen. Relying on the constitutional framers' view and hoping to defuse the burgeoning abolition movement, the Court rejected his claim and pronounced the constitutional inferiority of African–American people, fixing "a stigma, of the deepest degradation, ... upon the whole race." Twenty years later, in *Bradwell v. Illinois* the Court heard the first claim of women to the rights of citizenship, a claim that came on the heels of the defeat of the first wave of the feminist movement. While the majority ruled on grounds fairly applicable to both men and women, a concurring opinion which appears to have influenced the law for almost a hundred years, declared that by virtue of divine ordinance and natural law, women could have no rights inconsistent with their "paramount destiny" as wives and mothers. And less than twenty-five years later, after the radicalism of post-Civil War Reconstruction had been systematically dismantled, the Court, in *Plessy v. Ferguson,* interred the promise of the Civil War by declaring that racial segregation, premised again on the inferiority of African–Americans, would survive under the ruse of "separate but equal." It took almost a hundred years to begin to undo the premises of each of these latter decisions.

Hardwick, like *Dred Scott,* was decided not after a movement had peaked, but at a point when it was on the rise. Obviously, the status of gay people will not be determined by a civil war, but rather through a process of gradual emancipation. Despite the set-back dealt and intended by the Court majority, *Hardwick* has not dampened the ardor of nor decimated participation in the lesbian and gay rights movement. Paradoxically, it may have radicalized segments of the gay movement who were economically comfortable and less cognizant of their vulnerability. While *Hardwick* surely drove many people into deeper secrecy, it has also been a catalyst for others to come out. The "safety" of the closet and the false security of material comfort have been shattered by AIDS and by the homophobic action and inaction that it produced. It is a testimony to the strength of this movement that in this new panic over contagion, draconian proposals for mandatory testing and quarantine have made slow progress. And it is a testimony to the need of lesbians and gays to both live and die with honor that recognition of familial rights traditionally the preserve of heterosexuals—to procreate, keep custody of one's children, enjoy partnership benefits, exercise guardianship, and perhaps even marry—proceeds in state courts and legislative bodies. Just as *Hardwick* was in part the product of organizing a movement which refused to be maligned, so its consequence and longevity, will be determined by the courage of lesbians and gay men and their demand that everyone acknowledge and transcend homophobia and heterosexism, sexual lies, gendered straightjackets, and ultimately, perhaps, sexual classification itself.

———

Bowers v. Hardwick has also been used to justify the lack of protection from discrimination afforded gay men, lesbians and bisexuals under the equal protection clause, particularly in the context of evaluating government and military employment policies. A fairly typical early argument is found in Padula v. Webster, 822 F.2d 97 (D.C.Cir.1987), a case about the FBI's denial of Temple University law student, Margaret Padula's application as a special agent, where she was denied equal protection heightened review.

PADULA v. WEBSTER

United States Court of Appeals, District of Columbia Circuit, 1987.
822 F.2d 97, 99, 101–104.

In the summer of 1982, Padula applied for a position as a special agent with the FBI. On the basis of a written examination and an interview, the FBI ranked her 39th out of 303 qualified female applicants and 279th out of 1273 male and female applicants. Following these screening tests, the FBI conducted a routine background check. In addition to revealing favorable information about the applicant's abilities and character, the background investigation disclosed that appellant is a practicing homosexual. At a follow-up interview, Padula confirmed that she is a homosexual—explaining that although she does not flaunt her sexual orientation, she is unembarrassed and open about it and it is a fact well known to her family, friends and co-workers.

On October 19, 1983, the Bureau notified Padula that it was unable to offer her a position; her subsequent attempt to obtain reconsideration of the decision was denied. It was explained to her that her application had been evaluated in the same manner as all others, but had been rejected due to intense competition. Seventeen months later, Padula filed suit in the United States District Court for the District of Columbia. She alleged the FBI's decision not to hire her was based solely on the fact that she was a homosexual and that this decision violated the Bureau's "stated policy" not to discriminate on the basis of an applicant's sexual orientation. She also charged that the decision violated her constitutional rights to privacy, equal protection and due process under the first, fourth, fifth and ninth amendments to the Constitution.

· · ·

III.

... Padula alleges that the FBI refused to hire her solely because of her homosexuality and that this action denied her the equal protection of the law guaranteed by the fourteenth amendment. She urges us to recognize homosexuality as a suspect or quasi-suspect classification. A suspect classification is subjected to strict scrutiny and will be sustained only if "suitably tailored to serve a compelling state interest." City of Cleburne v. Cleburne Living Center, 473 U.S. 432 (1985), whereas under heightened scrutiny given to a quasi-suspect class, the challenged classification must be "substantially related to a legitimate state interest." Mills v. Habluetzel, 456 U.S. 91, 99 (1982).

We perceive ostensible disagreement between the parties as to the description of the class in question. The government insists the FBI's hiring policy focuses only on homosexual conduct, not homosexual status. By that, we understand the government to be saying that it would not consider relevant for employment purposes homosexual orientation that did not result in homosexual conduct. Plaintiff rejects that distinction, suggesting that "homosexual status is accorded to people who engage in homosexual conduct, and people who engage in homosexual conduct are accorded homosexual status." But whether or not homosexual status attaches to someone who does not—for whatever reason—engage in homosexual conduct, appellant does not claim those circumstances apply to her. The parties' definitional disagreement is therefore irrelevant to this case. The issue presented us is only whether homosexuals, when defined as persons who engage in homosexual conduct, constitute a suspect or quasi-suspect classification and accordingly whether the FBI's hiring decision is subject to strict or heightened scrutiny.

The Supreme Court has used several explicit criteria to identify suspect and quasi-suspect classifications.... Appellant, asserting that homosexuals meet all the requisite criteria, would have us add homosexuality to that list [of suspect or quasi-suspect classes]. Appellees, on the other hand, contend that two recent cases, Bowers v. Hardwick, 106 S.Ct. 2841 (1986) and Dronenburg v. Zech, 741 F.2d 1388 (D.C.Cir.1984), are insurmountable barriers to appellant's claim. We agree.

In Dronenburg, a naval petty officer claimed violation of his constitutional rights to privacy and to equal protection of the laws because he was discharged from the Navy for engaging in homosexual conduct. A panel of this court rejected the claim, holding that "we can find no constitutional right to engage in homosexual conduct and, ... as judges, we have no warrant to create one." Id. at 1397. Although the court's opinion focused primarily on whether the constitutional right to privacy protected homosexual conduct, the court reasoned that if the right to privacy did not provide protection "then appellant's right to equal protection is not infringed unless the Navy's policy is not rationally related to a permissible end." Id. at 1391. The unique needs of the military, the court concluded, justified discharge for homosexual conduct. Id. at 1398.

Dronenburg anticipated by two years the Supreme Court's decision in Hardwick, in which the Court upheld a Georgia law criminalizing sodomy against a challenge that it violated the due process clause. In Hardwick, the Court explained that the right to privacy as defined in its previous decisions inheres only in family relationships, marriage and procreation and does not extend more broadly to all kinds of private sexual conduct between consenting adults. 106 S.Ct. at 2844. Putting the privacy precedent aside, the Court further concluded that a right to engage in consensual sodomy is not constitutionally protected as a fundamental right since it is neither "implicit in the concept of ordered liberty," id. at 2844 (quoting Palko v. Connecticut, 302 U.S. 319, 325–26 (1937)), nor "deeply rooted in this Nation's history and tradition." Id. (quoting Moore v. East Cleveland, 431 U.S. 494, 503 (1977) (opinion of Powell, J.)). Accordingly, the Court's review of the Georgia statute inquired only whether a rational basis for the law existed. And the Court determined that the presumed beliefs of the Georgia electorate that sodomy is immoral provide an adequate rationale for criminalizing such conduct. Id. at 2846.

Padula argues that both Dronenburg and Hardwick are inapposite because they addressed only the scope of the privacy right, not what level of scrutiny is appropriate under equal protection analysis. But as we have noted, Dronenburg did involve an equal protection claim. Although the court did not explicitly consider whether homosexuals should be treated as a suspect class, it seemed to regard that question settled by its conclusion that the Constitution does not afford a privacy right to engage in homosexual conduct. In Hardwick, to be sure, plaintiffs did not rely on the equal protection clause, but after the Court rejected an extension of the right to privacy, it responded to plaintiffs' alternate argument that the Georgia law should be struck down as without rational basis (under the due process clause) since it was predicated merely on the moral judgment of a majority of the Georgia electorate. The Court summarily rejected that position, refusing to declare the Georgian majoritarian view "inadequate" to meet a rational basis test. Hardwick, 106 S.Ct. at 2846. We therefore think the courts' reasoning in Hardwick and Dronenburg forecloses appellant's efforts to gain suspect class status for practicing homosexuals. It would be quite anomalous, on its face, to declare status defined by conduct that states may constitutionally criminalize as deserving of strict scrutiny under the equal protection clause. More importantly, in all those cases in which the Supreme Court has accorded suspect or quasi-suspect status to a class, the Court's holding was predicated on an unarticulated, but necessarily implicit, notion that it is plainly unjustifiable (in accordance with standards not altogether clear to us) to discriminate invidiously against the particular class. E.g. compare Frontiero v. Richardson, 411 U.S. 677, 686–87 (1973) (statutory distinctions between the sexes often invidiously relegate women to inferior positions); with Massachusetts Board of Retirement v. Murgia, 427 U.S. 307, 313 (1976) (aged have not been subject to invidious discrimination justifying extra protection from the political process). If the Court was unwilling to object to state laws that criminalize the behavior that defines the class, it is hardly open to a lower court to conclude that state sponsored discrimination against the class is invidious. After all, there can hardly be more palpable discrimination against a class than making the conduct that defines the class criminal. Accord Baker v. Wade, 769 F.2d 289, 292 (5th Cir.1985); Rich v. Secretary of the Army, 735 F.2d 1220, 1229 (10th Cir.1984).

That does not mean, however, that any kind of negative state action against homosexuals would be constitutionally authorized. Laws or government practices must still, if challenged, pass the rational basis test of the equal protection clause. A governmental agency that discriminates against homosexuals must justify that discrimination in terms of some government purpose. Appellants did not specifically argue that the FBI's practices challenged here failed that lesser examination— perhaps because the Supreme Court in Hardwick rejected a similar rational basis argument under the due process clause. But assuming the argument is implicit in their equal protection challenge, we think it was squarely rejected in Dronenburg. In Dronenburg, the court held that it was rational for the Navy to conclude that homosexual conduct was detrimental to the maintenance of morale and discipline. 741 F.2d at 1398. The court observed that homosexuality "generate[s] dislike and disapproval among many ... who find it morally offensive," and, moreover, is criminalized in many states. Id.

The FBI, as the Bureau points out, is a national law enforcement agency whose agents must be able to work in all the states of the nation. To have agents who engage in conduct criminalized in roughly one-half of the states would undermine the law enforcement credibility of the Bureau. Perhaps more important, FBI agents perform counterintelligence duties that involve highly classified matters relating to national security. It is not irrational for the Bureau to conclude that the criminalization of homosexual conduct coupled with the general public opprobrium toward homosexuality exposes many homosexuals, even "open" homosexuals, to the risk of possible blackmail to protect their partners, if not themselves. We therefore conclude the Bureau's specialized functions, like the Navy's in Dronenburg, rationally justify consideration of homosexual conduct that could adversely affect that agency's responsibilities. The judgment of the district court is hereby Affirmed.

————

Margaret Padula is denied relief based directly on *Hardwick* and *Dronenberg*. It is interesting to see a Court's analysis that tests the idea of homosexuality as a suspect class more closely, but still uses *Hardwick* as a major authority.

HIGH TECH GAYS v. DEFENSE INDUSTRIAL SEC. CLEARANCE OFFICE

United States Court of Appeals, Ninth Circuit, 1990.
895 F.2d 563, 565–567, 571–574, rehearing denied 909 F.2d 375 (9th Cir.1990).

BRUNETTI, CIRCUIT JUDGE:

The plaintiffs-appellees challenge ... whether the alleged DoD policy and practice of refusing to grant security clearances to known or suspected gay applicants, violates the equal protection component of the Fifth Amendment's Due Process Clause and the rights of free association guaranteed by the First Amendment.

In analyzing the equal protection challenge, the district court concluded that "gay people are a 'quasi-suspect class' entitled to heightened scrutiny," High Tech Gays v. Defense Industrial Security Clearance Office, 668 F.Supp. 1361, 1368 (N.D.Cal.1987), and that the DoD security clearance regulations "must withstand strict scrutiny because they impinge upon the right of lesbians and gay men to engage in any homosexual activity, not merely sodomy, and thus impinge upon their exercise of a fundamental right." Id. at 1370.... The district court therefore concluded that the DoD policy violates the Constitution and granted summary judgment to the plaintiffs. We reverse the part of the district court's order granting summary judgment to the plaintiffs, vacate the part denying summary judgment to the DoD, and remand to enter summary judgment in favor of the DoD.

BACKGROUND

This appeal involves a class action challenging the mandatory investigation of all homosexual applicants seeking a Secret or Top Secret clearance. The clearance process begins when the defense contractor forwards an individual's name to the DoD for Secret or Top Secret clearance. 32 C.F.R. §§ 154.30, .31 (1987). For a Secret clearance, the Defense Industrial Security Clearance Organization (DISCO) conducts a National Agency Check (NAC), which consists at a minimum of a record check of the Federal Bureau of Investigation and the Defense Central Intelligence Index, but may also include a record check of the Office of Personnel Management, the Immigration and Naturalization Service, the State Department, and the Central Intelligence Agency. 32 C.F.R. § 154.3(m); DoD 5200.2-R, app. B (1979). For Top Secret clearance, the Defense Investigative Service (DIS) completes a Background Investigation (BI) for each applicant, which consists of a NAC, local records check, and interviews with personal sources.

DISCO will grant a Secret clearance if no adverse or questionable information is developed by the NAC.... For both Secret and Top Secret clearances, if DISCO cannot find that granting the security clearance would be clearly consistent with the national interest, the case is referred to the Directorate for Industrial Security Clearance Review (DISCR) for review and adjudication. DISCR evaluates the application under the standards and criteria set forth in the DoD directives and determines whether or not to grant a clearance....

Section 154.7 provides a list of criteria for determining eligibility for a clearance under this standard.[4] These criteria are further explained in 32 C.F.R. pt. 154, appendices D and H. In appendix D, number 2, acts of sexual misconduct under 32 C.F.R. § 154.7(q) are defined to include "all indications of moral turpitude, heterosexual promiscuity, aberrant, deviant or bizarre sexual conduct or behavior, transvestitism [sic], transsexualism, indecent exposure, rape, contributing to the delinquency of a minor, child molestation, wife-swapping, window peeping, and similar situations from whatever source." 32 C.F.R. pt. 154, app. D, no. 2....

III.

... It is well established that there are three standards we may apply in reviewing the plaintiffs' equal protection challenge to the DoD Security Clearance Regulations: strict scrutiny, heightened scrutiny, and

---

4. 32 C.F.R § 154.7 provides in pertinent part: The criteria for determining eligibility for a clearance under the security standard shall include, but not be limited to the following: (a) Commission of any act of sabotage, espionage, treason, terrorism, anarchy, sedition, or attempts threat or preparation therefor ... (q) Acts of sexual misconduct or perversion indicative of moral turpitude, poor judgment, or lack of regard for the laws of society.

rational basis review. See Cleburne, 473 U.S. at 440–41. The plaintiffs assert that homosexuality should be added to the list of suspect or quasi-suspect classifications requiring strict or heightened scrutiny. We disagree and hold that the district court erred in applying heightened scrutiny to the regulations at issue and that the proper standard is rational basis review. Accord Ben–Shalom v. Marsh, 881 F.2d 454, 464 (7th Cir.1989), cert. denied, (U.S.1990); Woodward v. United States, 871 F.2d 1068, 1076 (Fed.Cir.1989), cert. denied, (U.S.1990); Padula v. Webster, 822 F.2d 97, 103 (D.C.Cir.1987).

The Supreme Court has ruled that homosexual activity is not a fundamental right protected by substantive due process and that the proper standard of review under the Fifth Amendment is rational basis review. Bowers v. Hardwick, 478 U.S. 186, 194–96 (1986). The Court explained that the right to privacy inheres only in family relationships, marriage and procreation, and does not extend to all private sexual conduct between consenting adults. Id. at 190–91....

... If for federal analysis we must reach equal protection of the Fourteenth Amendment by the Due Process Clause of the Fifth Amendment, and if there is no fundamental right to engage in homosexual sodomy under the Due Process Clause of the Fifth Amendment, see Hardwick, it would be incongruous to expand the reach of equal protection to find a fundamental right of homosexual conduct under the equal protection component of the Due Process Clause of the Fifth Amendment.

Other circuits are in accord and have held that although the Court in Hardwick analyzed the constitutionality of the sodomy statute on a due process rather than equal protection basis, by the Hardwick majority holding that the Constitution confers no fundamental right upon homosexuals to engage in sodomy, and because homosexual conduct can thus be criminalized, homosexuals cannot constitute a suspect or quasi-suspect class entitled to greater than rational basis review for equal protection purposes. See Ben–Shalom, 881 F.2d at 464–65; Woodward, 871 F.2d at 1076; Padula, 822 F.2d at 103.[6]

... Further, the majority [of this court] in our recent Watkins en banc case did not rule that homosexuality is subject to heightened scrutiny. See Watkins v. United States Army, 875 F.2d 699, 705 (9th Cir.1989) (en banc) (Watkins II).[9]

---

6. "The Constitution, in light of Hardwick, cannot otherwise be rationally applied, lest an unjustified and indefensible inconsistency result." Ben–Shalom, 881 F.2d at 464–65. "After Hardwick it cannot logically be asserted that discrimination against homosexuals is constitutionally infirm." Woodward, 871 F.2d at 1076. "It would be quite anomalous, on its face, to declare status defined by conduct that states may constitutionally criminalize as deserving of strict [or heightened] scrutiny under the equal protection clause.... If the Court was unwilling to object to state laws that criminalize the behavior that defines the class, it is hardly open to a lower court to conclude that state sponsored discrimination against the class is invidious. After all, there can hardly be more palpable discrimination against a class than making conduct that defines the class criminal." Padula, 822 F.2d at 103 (citations omitted).

9. In Watkins II, the majority specifically declined to reach the constitutional equal

. . . .

It is apparent that while the Supreme Court has identified that legislative classifications based on race, alienage, or national origin are subject to strict scrutiny and that classifications based upon gender or illegitimacy call for a heightened standard, the Court has never held homosexuality to a heightened standard of review.

To be a "suspect" or "quasi-suspect" class, homosexuals must 1) have suffered a history of discrimination; 2) exhibit obvious, immutable, or distinguishing characteristics that define them as a discrete group; and 3) show that they are a minority or politically powerless, or alternatively show that the statutory classification at issue burdens a fundamental right. Bowen v. Gilliard, 483 U.S. 587, 602–03 (1987) (due to a lack of these characteristics, the statutory classifications of the Federal Aid to Families with Dependent Children Program were subject to only a rational basis review) (citing Lyng v. Castillo, 477 U.S. 635, 638 (1986) (due to a lack of these characteristics, the statutory classifications of the Federal Food Stamp Program were subject to only a rational basis review)).

While we do agree that homosexuals have suffered a history of discrimination, we do not believe that they meet the other criteria. Homosexuality is not an immutable characteristic; it is behavioral and hence is fundamentally different from traits such as race, gender, or alienage, which define already existing suspect and quasi-suspect classes. Accord Woodward, 871 F.2d at 1076. The behavior or conduct of such already recognized classes is irrelevant to their identification. Id.

Moreover, legislatures have addressed and continue to address the discrimination suffered by homosexuals on account of their sexual orientation through the passage of anti-discrimination legislation.[10] Thus,

protection issues concerning homosexuality raised by the panel opinion. Watkins II, 875 F.2d at 705. We instead relied upon equitable estoppel, holding that the Army was estopped from refusing to reenlist Watkins on the basis of his homosexuality. Id. at 711. Judge Norris' concurrence in Watkins II, joined by Judge Canby, expresses the opinion that homosexuals constitute a suspect class, arguing that the Hardwick Court's concerns about substantive due process have little or no relevance to equal protection doctrine. See id. at 716–28 (Norris, J., concurring). We disagree. . . . The Watkins II concurring opinion's conclusion that homosexuals constitute a suspect class is also based in part on an analysis distinguishing Hardwick as a "conduct" rather than an "orientation" case. However, this differentiation is not relevant to this case, as the DoD regulations challenged by the plaintiffs all relate to conduct. See DIS 20–1–M (1985).

10. For example: Wisconsin has a comprehensive statute barring employment discrimination on the basis of sexual orientation, Wis.Stat.Ann. §§ 111.31–.395 (West 1988); California has barred violence against persons or property based on sexual orientation, Cal.Civ.Code § 51.7 (West 1984); and Michigan has barred the denial of care in health facilities on the basis of sexual orientation, Mich.Comp.Laws Ann. § 333.20201(2)(a) (West 1984). Executive Orders in the other states prohibit such discrimination. See e.g., N.Y.Comp.Codes R. & Regs. tit. 4, § 28 (1983) (barring discrimination in state employment or in the provision of state services and benefits on the basis of sexual orientation). Many cities and counties have also enacted anti-discrimination regulations, including New York, Los Angeles, Chicago, Washington D.C., Atlanta, Boston, Philadelphia, Seattle, and San Francisco. Developments in the Law, Sexual Orientation and the Law, 102

homosexuals are not without political power; they have the ability to and do "attract the attention of the lawmakers," as evidenced by such legislation. See Cleburne, 473 U.S. at 445. Accord Ben–Shalom, 881 F.2d at 466. Lastly, as previously noted, homosexual conduct is not a fundamental right. Hardwick, 478 U.S. at 194.

Our review compels us to agree with the other circuits that have ruled on this issue and to hold that homosexuals do not constitute a suspect or quasi-suspect class entitled to greater than rational basis scrutiny under the equal protection component of the Due Process Clause of the Fifth Amendment.

Notes and Questions

1. **More on Equal Protection.** For an analysis similar to High Tech Gays, see Ben–Shalom v. Marsh, 881 F.2d 454 (7th Cir.1989), cert. denied sub nom. Ben–Shalom v. Stone, 494 U.S. 1004, 110 S.Ct. 1296, 108 L.Ed.2d 473 (1990). No appellate court to date has granted gay men and lesbians suspect status under equal protection, particularly because of their alleged political power as the court held in High Tech Gays. See e.g., Jantz v. Muci, 759 F.Supp. 1543 (D.Kan.1991), reversed 976 F.2d 623 (10th Cir.1992), cert. denied ___ U.S. ___, 113 S.Ct. 2445, 124 L.Ed.2d 662 (1993); Dahl v. Secretary of the United States Navy, 830 F.Supp. 1319 (E.D.Cal.1993). One wonders how much political power a group has when anti-gay initiatives can be adopted by municipalities and states, see note 2 below.

The Ninth Circuit had granted suspect class status to homosexuals in Watkins v. U.S. Army, 847 F.2d 1329 (9th Cir.1988), but that opinion was withdrawn a year later. Watkins v. U.S. Army, 875 F.2d 699 (9th Cir.1989) (en banc), cert. denied 498 U.S. 957, 111 S.Ct. 384, 112 L.Ed.2d 395 (1990). Most recently the Ninth Circuit decided that an "active" rational basis approach is required in these cases, even if suspect classification does not apply. Pruitt v. Cheney, 963 F.2d 1160 (9th Cir.1991), cert. denied ___ U.S. ___, 113 S.Ct. 655, 121 L.Ed.2d 581 (1992).

Using rational basis and other rationales, but not suspect class, courts lately have preliminarily enjoined enforcement of government regulations discriminating against homosexuals. E.g., Able v. United States, 847 F.Supp. 1038 (E.D.N.Y.1994) (enjoins enforcement of Section 571 of the National Defense Authorization Act for the Fiscal Year 1994, 10 USC 654, because although it says it only imposes punitive rules on gay men and lesbians for homosexual conduct, it unlawfully includes in the definition of conduct a statement of homosexual identity); Steffan v. Aspin, 8 F.3d 57 (D.C.Cir.1993), vacated for rehearing in banc (1994) (the court refused to decide whether even homosexual orientation (without any evidence of conduct) was to be accorded suspect or quasi-suspect class, because it found that the Department of Defense Directives could not even survive a rationality review); Meinhold v. U.S. Department of Defense, 808 F.Supp. 1455 (C.D.Cal.1993), amended 1993 WL 513209 (C.D.Cal.1993), stay granted in part, denied in part pending appeal to Ninth Circuit, ___ U.S. ___, 114 S.Ct. 374, 126 L.Ed.2d 344 (1993); Dahl, supra.

Harv.L.Rev. 1509, 1667–68, n. 49–51 (citations omitted).

Several prominent scholars have consistently argued that homosexuality ought to be a suspect class. See e.g., Janet E. Halley, *The Politics of the Closet: Towards Equal Protection for Gay, Lesbian, and Bisexual Identity,* 36 U.C.L.A.L.Rev. 915 (1989); Nan D. Hunter, *Life After Hardwick,* 27 Harv. C.R.–C.L. L.Rev. 531 (1992); Cass R. Sunstein, *Sexual Orientation and the Constitution: A Note on the Relationship Between Due Process and Equal Protection,* 55 U.Chi.L.Rev. 1161 (1988).

2. No "special protections" amendments. Possibly in response to the license given them by *Bowers v. Hardwick,* several states, cities and communities have enacted homophobic provisions as amendments to their constitutions, charters or local ordinances. A notorious example is Colorado's Amendment 2 to its Constitution, adopted by the voters on November 3, 1992, which states:

> No Protected Status Based on Homosexual, Lesbian, or Bisexual Orientation. Neither the State of Colorado, through any of its branches or departments, nor any of its agencies, political subdivisions, municipalities or school districts, shall enact, adopt or enforce any statute, regulation, ordinance or policy whereby homosexual, lesbian or bisexual orientation, conduct, practice or relationships shall constitute or otherwise be the basis of or entitle any person or class of persons to have or claim any minority status quota preferences, protected status or claim of discrimination. This Section of the Constitution shall be in all respects self-executing.

In a challenge to the constitutionality of this amendment, the Colorado Supreme Court refused to find that lesbians, gay men or bisexuals were a suspect class so that legislation discriminating against them would be strictly or more closely scrutinized, but did find that this amendment was invalid because it violated fundamental rights to participate equally in the political process. Evans v. Romer, 854 P.2d 1270 (Colo.1993), cert. denied ___ U.S. ___, 114 S.Ct. 419, 126 L.Ed.2d 365 (1993), on remand 1993 WL 518586 (Colo.Dist.Ct.1993) (deciding on remand that the amendment is unconstitutional, but refusing to find that homosexuals constituted a suspect or quasi-suspect class). Accord, Equality Foundation of Greater Cincinnati v. The City of Cincinnati, 838 F.Supp. 1235 (S.D.Ohio 1993) (issuing preliminary injunction against similar city charter amendment in Cincinnati based on *Evans* rationale). A California appeals court found an anti-gay initiative requiring a majority vote to enact any prohibition on sexual orientation discrimination to lack a rational basis. Citizens for Responsible Behavior v. Superior Court, 1 Cal.App. 4th 1013, 2 Cal.Rptr.2d 648 (1991).

Oregon's proposed constitutional amendment, Measure No. 9, was defeated on the same day that Colorado's was passed, but it received 44% of the vote:

> Section 41(1) This state shall not recognize any categorical provision such as "sexual orientation," "sexual preference," and similar phrases that includes homosexuality, pedophilia, sadism or masochism. Quotas, minority status, affirmative action, or any similar concepts, shall not apply to these forms of conduct, nor shall government promote these behaviors.

(2) State, regional and local governments and their properties and monies shall not be used to promote, encourage, or facilitate homosexuality, pedophilia, sadism or masochism.

(3) State, regional and local governments and their departments, agencies and other entities, including specifically the State Department of Higher Education and the public schools, shall assist in setting a standard for Oregon's youth that recognizes homosexuality, pedophilia, sadism and masochism as abnormal, wrong, unnatural, and perverse and that these behaviors are to be discouraged and avoided.

Timothy Egan, *Oregon Measure Asks State to Repress Homosexuality,* N.Y. Times, Aug. 16, 1992, § 1 at 1, 34. One of the primary arguments against granting gays and lesbians suspect class status is that they have adequate political power and are not a discrete and insular minority. Although evidence of the defeat of the Oregon measure may be used to support that hypothesis, it is questionable how much political power a group could have if the community at large felt it could draft and try to enact a constitutional amendment that named that group as "abnormal, wrong, unnatural and perverse." Do you think similar legislation directed at other groups in America could be proposed and get through the entire process of coming to a vote? What groups if any?

3. Anti-gay violence. Gay men accounted for 27% of the 783 hate crimes logged by local law enforcement and community groups in Los Angeles County in 1993, exceeding for the first time hate crimes based on race and antisemitism. Denise Hamilton & Julie Tamaki, *Gay Men are leading target of hate crime violence: County report shows overall incidents rose 6.4% in 1993,* Los Angeles Times, Valley Edition, May 10, 1994, Metro, B1, col. 2.

The National Gay and Lesbian Task Force has collected statistics about reported incidents of anti-gay violence, sometimes called gay bashing, for years. After five years of steady increases, 1993 showed a decline of 14% in reported anti-gay incidents in five major cities. The sixth city, Denver, where Amendment 2 was passed, saw an increase of 12 percent. Reuter, *Survey Shows Decline in Anti-Gay Incidents,* Washington Post, March 9, 1994, at A02. Additionally, D.C. suffered from increased incidents of anti-gay harassment and physical violence in 1993, 440 incidents as opposed to 283 in 1992, according to a Gay Men & Lesbians Opposing Violence (GLOV) report. Santiago O'Donnell, *District Plans First Report on Hate Crimes,* The Washington Post, March 9, 1994, at B01. For an argument that the state is responsible for much of this violence against gay men and lesbians, see Kendall Thomas, *Beyond the Privacy Principle,* 92 Colum.L.Rev. 1431, 1462–70 (1992).

Harassment of a lesbian couple who run a women's camp on 120 acres in Ovett, Mississippi was so dangerous that Attorney General Janet Reno had to order in civil rights mediators from the Justice Department. *Reno orders mediators in lesbian harassment,* Detroit Free Press, Feb. 19, 1994, News, at 4A.

4. Anti-discrimination provisions. A Harvard Law Review note provides an elaborate appendix indicating the 139 jurisdictions in the United States that have enacted legislation protecting lesbians, gay men, and

bisexuals from discrimination. Note, *Constitutional Limits on Anti–Gay Rights Initiatives,* 106 Harv.L.Rev. 1905, appendix (1993) (also citing National Gay and Lesbian Task Force Policy Institute, Lesbian and Gay Civil Rights in the U.S. 1–4 (1993)). Several states, including Wisconsin, Connecticut, New Jersey, Vermont, California, Minnesota, Massachusetts and Hawaii, and cities, including New York, Los Angeles, Washington, D.C., San Francisco, Boston, Atlanta, Detroit, Philadelphia, Houston, Denver and Baltimore, have enacted laws forbidding discrimination based upon sexual orientation. See Marie Elena Peluso, Note, Tempering Title VII's Straight Arrow Approach: Recognizing and Protecting Gay Victims of Employment Discrimination, 46 Vand.L.Rev. 1533, 1558, n. 207 (1993); See also, Developments in the Law—Sexual Orientation and the Law, 102 Harv.L.Rev. 1508 (1989).

Many traditional civil rights avenues for redress have failed to adequately protect lesbians, gay men, and bisexuals as currently written or interpreted. Title VII, 42 USC 2000–e, which protects against sexual discrimination in employment, has been interpreted as not prohibiting discrimination on the basis of homosexuality, sexual orientation, or effeminacy. Dillon v. Frank, 952 F.2d 403 (6th Cir.1992); Williamson v. A.G. Edwards and Sons, 876 F.2d 69 (8th Cir.1989), cert. denied 493 U.S. 1089, 110 S.Ct. 1158, 107 L.Ed.2d 1061 (1990); DeSantis v. Pacific Telephone & Telegraph Co., 608 F.2d 327 (9th Cir.1979); Smith v. Liberty Mutual Ins. Co., 569 F.2d 325 (5th Cir.1978).

The Unruh Act, Cal.Civil Code section 51, prohibits discrimination in "business establishments" and has been read to include prohibitions against discrimination on the basis of sex by organizations such as the Boys' Clubs. Isbister v. Boys' Club of Santa Cruz, 40 Cal.3d 72, 219 Cal.Rptr. 150, 707 P.2d 212 (1985). Nonetheless, the California Court of Appeals ruled that the Boy Scouts of America's refusal to hire an "out" gay man as a scout leader did not violate the Unruh Act, because Boy Scouts was not a business establishment, contrary to *Boys' Clubs* holding, and because this case was not about discrimination in the privilege of membership, but in the Boy Scouts' "freedom of expressive association and its right to preserve the basic tenets of the scouts as expressed in its charter." Curran v. Mount Diablo Council of the Boy Scouts of America, 23 Cal.App. 4th 1307, 29 Cal.Rptr.2d 580 (1994). The Appeals Court finds that the Boy Scouts' expressive association exists to instill values and help young people make ethical choices, and since the Scouts view homosexuality as immoral behavior inconsistent with the Scout Oath, forcing them to hire an openly gay man would infringe on their expressive association rights. One wonders whether the California Supreme Court will agree. Can an expressive association exist to further any goals or are some discriminations violative of our basic principles of equality? See The Invisible Empire of the Knights of the Ku Klux Klan v. Mayor of Thurmont, 700 F.Supp. 281 (D.Md.1988) (district court found that application of nondiscrimination principles to the Klan, requiring them to permit blacks and nonchristians to march with them, would undermine their expressive association rights and therefore they could not be required to act nondiscriminatorily). Would California Courts decide the Boy Scouts case differently under the Unruh Act if instead the Boy Scouts believed that interracial marriage was immoral and refused to hire a man who had married a woman of a different race and who had spoken publicly denying the immorality of interracial unions?

In a progressive decision providing a kind of remedy for workplace discrimination based on sexual orientation, the Minnesota Court of Appeals recently ruled that an openly gay employee who quit his job because of sexual orientation harassment was entitled to unemployment compensation benefits. Hanke v. Safari Hair Adventure, 512 N.W.2d 614 (Minn.App. 1994).

5. Just as we saw with race and gender, debates have raged about whether sexual orientation is biologically–based or culturally–constructed. This constructivism/essentialism debate has taken on renewed importance with the recent studies of Simon LeVay and others that claim to have found biological differences in the brains or genetic structures of gay men. See e.g., Simon LeVay, *A Difference in Hypothalamic Structure Between Heterosexual and Homosexual Men*, 253 Science 1034 (1991); Dean H. Hamer, Stella Hu, Victoria L. Magnuson, Nan Hu & Angela M.L. Pattatucci, *A Linkage Between DNA Markers on the X Chromosome and Male Sexual Orientation*, 261 Science 321 (1993); Michael Bailey and Richard C. Pillard, *A Genetic Study of Male Sexual Orientation*, 40 Archives Gen. Psychiatry 1089 (1991). For an analysis deciding that this debate is not really about the causes of sexual orientation but about the politics of gay identity, see Daniel R. Ortiz, *Creating Controversy: Essentialism and Constructivism and the Politics of Gay Identity*, 79 Va.L.Rev. 1833 (1993) and Janet E. Halley, *Sexual Orientation and the Politics of Biology: A Critique of the Argument from Immutability*, 46 Stanford L.Rev. 503 (1994). For more insight on gay identity issues, see also Ruthann Robson, *The Specter of a Lesbian Supreme Court Justice: Problems of Identity in Lesbian Legal Theorizing*, 5 St. Thomas L.Rev. 433 (1993) and Mark A. Fajer, *Can Two Real Men Eat Quiche Together? Storytelling, Gender–Role Stereotypes, and Legal Protection for Lesbians and Gay Men*, 46 U.Miami L.Rev. 511 (1992).

6. Family life. Another principal area of subordination of lesbians, gay men, and bisexuals is family life. Despite serious debate about the value and meaning of marriage, lesbian and gay couples seeking to marry have been denied that "fundamental right" in most states. *See e.g.,* Dean v. District of Columbia, No. 90–13892, slip op. (D.C.Super.Ct. Dec. 30, 1991); Singer v. Hara, 11 Wash.App. 247, 522 P.2d 1187 (1974), rev. denied 84 Wash.2d 1008 (1974); Suzanne Sherman, ed., Lesbian and Gay Marriage (Temple v. Press, 1992); Nan D. Hunter, *Marriage, Law and Gender: A Feminist Inquiry*, 1 Law & Sexuality 9 (1991); William N. Eskridge, Jr., A History of Same–Sex Marriage, 79 Va.L.Rev. 1419 (1993). For a passionate plea to gay men and lesbians to spend their political currency and energies in different places than pushing for a right to marriage, which will merely reproduce hierarchical gendered roles, see Nancy D. Polikoff, *We Will Get What We Ask For: Why Legalizing Gay and Lesbian Marriage Will not "Dismantle the Legal Structure of Gender in Every Marriage,"* 79 Va.L.Rev. 1535 (1993). While the Hawaii Supreme Court did not find that its constitution contained a fundamental right of persons of the same sex to marry, it did decide that restriction of marital relations to a male or a female establishes a sex-based classification subject to strict scrutiny, and hence remanded to a lower court a case challenging the refusal to grant marriage

licenses to gay and lesbian couples. Baehr v. Lewin, 74 Hawaii 530, 852 P.2d 44 (1993).

Lesbian mothers and gay fathers have been deprived of custody and visitation of their biological children, DiStefano v. DiStefano, 60 A.D.2d 976, 401 N.Y.S.2d 636 (App.Div.1978); Gottlieb v. Gottlieb, 108 A.D.2d 120, 488 N.Y.S.2d 180 (1985), but more recently some appellate courts have concluded that a parent's sexual orientation is not grounds to limit visitation. In re Marriage of Pleasant, 256 Ill.App.3d 742, 195 Ill.Dec. 169, 628 N.E.2d 633 (1993); Stroman v. Williams, 291 S.C. 376, 353 S.E.2d 704 (App.1987); In re Marriage of Ashling, 42 Or.App. 47, 599 P.2d 475 (1979), review denied 288 Or. 113; In re Marriage of Cabalquinto, 43 Wash.App. 518, 718 P.2d 7 (1986); In re Marriage of Birdsall, 197 Cal.App.3d 1024, 243 Cal.Rptr. 287 (1988); Conkel v. Conkel, 509 N.E.2d 983 (Ohio App.1987). Nancy Polikoff, *This Child Does Have Two Mothers: Redefining Parenthood to Meet the Needs of Children in Lesbian–Mother and Other Nontraditional Families*, 78 Geo.L.J. 459 (1990). Two states still specifically prohibit gay and lesbian adoption by statute. Fla.Stat.Ann. § 63.042(3) (West 1985) (One appeals court in Florida found this statute unconstitutional, but that holding is not binding on the other judicial districts, Seebol v. Farie, No. 90–923–CA–18 (Fla. 16th Judicial Circuit, 1991)); N.H.Rev.Stat.Ann. § 170–B:4 (1988) (N.H. statute found constitutional in In re Opinion of the Justices, 129 N.H. 290, 530 A.2d 21 (1987)).

Lesbians, involved in the birth of a child to their relationship, but who are not the biological mothers, have been denied parental rights to visitation and custody. *E.g.,* Matter of Alison D. v. Virginia M., 77 N.Y. 651, 569 N.Y.S.2d 586, 572 N.E.2d 27 (1991). Gay and lesbian parents also have been prohibited from adoption and foster parenting. State, Dept. of Health and Rehabilitative Services v. Cox, 627 So.2d 1210 (Fla.App. 2d Dist.1993); But some recent cases have permitted second parent and other adoption by lesbians and gay men: Adoption of Tammy, 416 Mass. 205, 619 N.E.2d 315 (1993) (adoption statute did not preclude same-sex cohabitants from jointly adopting child); Adoptions of B.L.V.B. and E.L.V.B., 628 A.2d 1271 (Vt. 1993) (non-biological parent able to adopt while leaving natural mother's parental rights intact); In re Petition of L.S. and V.L. for the Adoption of Minors (T.) and (M.), 1991 WL 219598 (D.C.Super.1991); In the Matter of Adoption of Caitlin & Emily, 1994 WL 149728 (N.Y.Fam.Ct.1994); In re Adoption of Evan, 153 Misc.2d 844, 583 N.Y.S.2d 997 (Sur.Ct.1992); In Matter of Adoption of Child by J.M.G., 267 N.J.Super. 622, 632 A.2d 550 (Ch.Div.1993); Nancy S. v. Michele G., 228 Cal.App.3d 831, 279 Cal.Rptr. 212 (1991).

Without legally recognized family structures, gay and lesbian couples are often unable to get health care and other benefits for their life partners, Phillips v. Wisconsin Personnel Commission, 167 Wis.2d 205, 482 N.W.2d 121 (App.1992); have been unable to elect against a will as surviving spouse, In the Matter of Cooper, 187 A.D.2d 128, 592 N.Y.S.2d 797 (1993), *appeal dismissed* 82 N.Y.2d 801, 604 N.Y.S.2d 558, 624 N.E.2d 696; are unable to take by intestacy as a spouse would, unable to receive death insurance spousal benefits, denied unemployment or workers' compensation dependent benefits, Ross v. Denver Dept. of Health and Hospitals, ___ P.2d ___, 1994 WL 115870 (Colo.App.1994); and are unauthorized to serve as guardians or health care proxies, In re Guardianship of Kowalski, 478 N.W.2d 790 (Minn.App.1991). *See generally* Nan Hunter et al., The Rights of Lesbians and Gay Men (3d ed. 1992); Anne Goldstein, *Representing Lesbians,* 1 Texas J. of Women & L. 301 (1992); *Developments in the Law—Sexual Orientation and the Law,* 102 Harv.L.Rev. 1508 (1989). Since the IRS does not recognize same-sex couples, there are also tax and property transfer consequences to same sex life partnerships that differ from heterosexual marriages. *See* Patricia Cain, *Same–Sex Couples and the Federal Tax Laws,* 1 Law & Sexuality 97 (1991).

E. THE POOR

1. *Who Are the "Poor"?*

In the 1960s, the federal government established an official standard for measuring poverty. That standard judges each member of a family as poor if the family has a pretax income less than three times the cost of a nutritionally adequate diet. In 1991, for example, the poverty level for a four person family was $13,924. The standard does not make adjustments for differences in cost of living and is not adjusted when the overall standard of living changes. Under this standard, the "poor" are easily defined as those who live in families earning below the poverty level.

A definition of poverty based solely on annual income, however, provides an incomplete and rather inadequate picture of the poor. "Defining a poverty line strictly on the basis of annual income is convenient and plausible to researchers, but it misses much of what stirs the heart and mind in any discussion of the poor." David Ellwood, Poor Support 82 (Basic Books 1988). We begin this section, therefore, with excerpts that provide various perspectives on "who are the poor."

DAAN BRAVEMAN, CHILDREN, POVERTY AND STATE CONSTITUTIONS

38 Emory L.J. 577, 577–85 (1989).

The face of poverty in our country has changed. In the early 1970's, the elderly constituted the largest age group of poor people. Today, children hold that terrible distinction, having displaced the aged as the poorest group. Most disturbing is that in the past decade child poverty has continued to grow deeper and more widespread. . . .

Shamal Jackson was eight months old when he died from complications created by poverty: low birthweight, poor nutrition, and viral infection. During his brief life he never had a home; indeed, he had never slept in a house or an apartment. Instead, he lived in shelters with strangers, in hospitals, in welfare offices, and in the subways of New York City. Shamal was among the millions of children living in poverty, and one of the "human tragedies" behind the statistics described in this section. . . .

An extensive study conducted in 1984 by the Congressional Research Service (CRS) and the Congressional Budget Office (CBO) found that the number of children living below the poverty level rose sharply from 1979 to 1983. It found such an increase regardless of whether poverty is measured before or after government transfer payments (e.g., welfare and social security) and whether the income includes non-cash benefits (e.g., food stamps, school meals, medical care) and money paid as taxes....

[I]n 1983 one child in four was poor if only market income is considered. Even after cash benefits are added to market income, more than two out of every nine children were living in poverty. Factoring in non-cash benefits reduced the poverty rate, depending on how the non-cash benefits were valued. However, the rate climbed when income and payroll taxes (which reduce income available for consumption) were deducted from family income.

The level of poverty among children has not changed dramatically since the CRS/CBO study. A report ... by the Children's Defense Fund puts the official child poverty rate at twenty-one percent for 1984 and a little over twenty percent for each year from 1985 to 1987. Thus, one out of every five of our children is living in poverty.

The data on child poverty further reveal that race and family composition have a significant impact on poverty rates. A black child was almost three times as likely as a white child to be poor in 1983; an Hispanic child was more than twice as likely as a white child to be poor. Similarly, household composition has a profound impact on the poverty rate. In 1983, more than half of poor children were in female-headed single parent families. Of all poor children, thirty-two percent lived with mothers who had separated or divorced; fifteen percent with mothers who had never married; and five percent with mothers who were widowed.

Various reasons have been suggested for the high rate of child poverty. First, because of the eroding value of the minimum wage, a large number of people work while remaining below the poverty level. The minimum wage has been $3.35 since 1981, although the cost of living has increased thirty-five percent since then. Second, although unemployment has dropped in the past few years, high unemployment persists in inner cities, in certain regions, and particularly among minorities and young workers. Moreover, unemployment rates do not reflect the fact that a growing number of employed people cannot find full-time jobs and thus work only part-time. Third, female-headed single parent families face additional burdens in combating poverty. In 1987, women's hourly wages were only seventy-one percent of men's. Additionally, child care costs consume a large share of the mother's income. In major cities, the typical annual cost of center-based child care is around $3000. This amount is about half of the median income of single mothers who are raising one or more children under six years old. Finally, the high child poverty rate exists because government welfare programs are inadequate and fail to raise very many families out of poverty.

The failure of welfare programs was the subject of a recent nation-wide study by the Center on Budget and Policy Priorities. Its findings exposed the gaping holes in the supposed safety nets.... [I]n 32 states the maximum grant for a family of three under the Aid to Families with Dependent Children (AFDC) program—the single largest welfare program for children—is below fifty percent of the poverty line.... [I]n no state, except Alaska, does the combined maximum AFDC grant and food stamp benefit lift above the poverty line a family of three without other income....

Finally, the study found that states do not fill the gaps in the safety net through operation of their own programs for impoverished children. Eight states have general cash assistance programs for single people and childless couples. Thirteen states operate their own programs for disabled or elderly people. Sixteen have county-based programs, but these are often limited in scope. Only three states operate their own emergency assistance program.

The rather distressing conclusion derived from this material is that millions of our children are condemned to a life of poverty. Unless action is taken child poverty will continue to increase. It is estimated that if we continue on the present course, one out of every four children—sixteen million in total—will be suffering the hardships of poverty in the year 2000.

These numbers should not obscure the real hardship to children like Shamal Jackson. A recent book by Jonathan Kozol exposes much better than these statistics the devastating impact and legacy of poverty. Kozol visited the New York City welfare hotels that house homeless families with children and listened to the stories of the residents. Rachel was one of these residents. She was without a home and was forced to live in welfare hotels with her young children. While in the depths of poverty, she raised questions that cannot be ignored:

> My children, they be treated like chess pieces. Send all of that money off to Africa? You hear that song? They're not thinkin' about people starvin' here in the United States. I was thinkin': Get my kids and all the other children here to sing, 'We are the world. We live here too.' How come do you care so much for people you can't see? Ain't we the world? Ain't we a piece of it? We are so close they be afraid to see. Give us a shot at something. We are something! Ain't we something? I'm depressed. But we are something! People in America don't want to see.

AUDREY ROWE, THE FEMINIZATION OF POVERTY: AN ISSUE FOR THE 90'S

4 Yale J.L. & Feminism 73, 73–76 (1991).

... During the past decade, foundations and federal, state and city governments have focused a lot of attention on the increase in poverty, particularly the increase among woman-maintained households. (I prefer that term to "female heads of households.") Researchers have coined the phrase "feminization of poverty" to describe this trend. Diana Pearce, a feminist researcher who is now the director of the Women in Poverty Center in Washington, D.C., first introduced that concept in 1978, based on her research, which clearly demonstrated a correlation between gender and poverty and the importance of gender in understanding poverty.

I think in order to talk about poverty, we should start by talking about how we measure poverty. The Census Bureau's way of measuring poverty, as I'm sure many of you are well aware, is to decide what resources a family of a particular size requires to meet its basic needs, and to compare that figure to a family's income to determine whether the family is able to meet those needs or falls short. If the family falls short, then it falls out in the poverty statistics. However, those statistics don't give a very clear picture of poverty in general, and especially not the trend toward the feminization of poverty.

Look, for example, at how woman-maintained families are slipping into poverty compared to families in general. During the last quarter of a century, the number of woman-maintained families who are living in poverty has more than doubled, while the number of families overall who are in poverty has decreased slightly. In 1989, there were 3.6 million woman-maintained households living below the poverty level.

When we take a closer look at these numbers, we find that the proportion of poverty-level households that are maintained by women has risen in all racial and ethnic groups. For example, in 1959, 20% of white families living in poverty were headed by women; in 1987, 42% of poor white families were woman-maintained. During the same period, the proportion of African–American households maintained by women rose from 46% to 74%. Data on Hispanic families was not collected until 1973, so we can only compare 1973 to 1987, and the increase in woman-maintained households during that period was from 45% to 47%.

This data, though sobering, still does not reflect an accurate count of poverty among woman-maintained households. To understand why, I must take a moment to explain the use of the term "households in poverty." The Census Bureau has chosen to measure poverty by households rather than by individuals. When we count individuals, we find the greatest number of individuals in poverty are children, and so you're constantly hearing people talk about the increased number of children in poverty. But children are not isolated entities; they are parts of households and so you also have to look at households in poverty.

One reason households in poverty are undercounted is the new phenomenon of doubling up and tripling up that is being seen particularly in urban centers throughout the country—that is, two and three families living together in living quarters designed for one family. The Census Bureau counts as separate households only those "subfamilies" who are unrelated to the renters or the owners of the housing unit. Now it's clear that if you have a grandmother, and her daughter, and now her granddaughter who are all parents living in one household, you have three individual families. If each of these women has an income below the poverty level, there are three families living in poverty. The Census Bureau, however, counts them all as one household. The Bureau does this because it assumes that related subfamilies pool their resources to meet their basic needs, and in some situations, this method of counting households in poverty might be accurate. However, when no one in the household is earning enough money to raise the others out of poverty, this method of counting means we are not able to get a clear count of the number of families who are living below the poverty level. We can only talk about the numbers of households living in poverty.

Recent studies reported by Diana Pearce suggest the extent of this undercounting problem: in 1986, half of the 1.4 million members of unrelated subfamilies living in doubled-up households were poor. If half the unrelated subfamilies are poor, it is very likely that a disproportionate number of related subfamilies are poor. Since most subfamilies are headed by women, not counting impoverished subfamilies in their own right means that the extent of poverty among women is underestimated.

Another indicator of potential poverty among woman-maintained households that is too easily ignored relates to homelessness. The fastest-growing segment of the homeless population is families with children, the majority of whom are headed by women. I have seen estimates of the increase between 1986 and 1989 in the number of homeless families seeking emergency shelter ranging from as low as 40% to as high as 90%. Many of these families one would consider to be among the "new poor" that we hear about. A "new poor" family is one that had a source of income until its primary breadwinner—usually a woman—was laid off. The family has lost its benefits, and now finds itself coming in for emergency housing and being a part of our welfare program.

If one adds to the doubling up phenomenon the potential for homelessness among woman-maintained households, the problem of poverty in these households becomes even more staggering. This is especially true because poverty among woman-maintained households is greater and more persistent than poverty among other poor families. According to researchers, about half of female-headed households have incomes that are less than 50% of the poverty level, compared to fewer than one-third of other poor families; and 60% of people who live in sustained poverty—at least eight out of ten years—are in woman-maintained households.

There is a new study that is about to be released by the Joint Center for Political and Economic Studies (a Black think tank in Washington), which has been looking at African–American children and families in poverty. The figure in that study that probably concerned me most as I read it is the projection that the average African–American child born in 1990 to a single mother in a major urban center will spend fifteen years of childhood living in poverty. The likelihood that they will ever have the income to maintain their families above the poverty level is extremely slim. So what this means is that the concentration and persistence of poverty in our country is getting worse.

For minority groups, particularly African–Americans and Hispanics, gender is but one significant factor in understanding the higher rates of poverty. Indeed, race and gender interact to drive up the proportion of minority female-headed households.

Racial discrimination continues to keep African–American and Hispanic women at the lower end of the salary scale. The decrease in service industry jobs and the lack of training opportunities limit the earning ability of these women. So if you are a minority woman, if you're an African–American or a Hispanic, not only do you have to deal consistently with the gender question, you also have to deal with the race question, and the two are very much interrelated. . . .

DAVID ELLWOOD, POVERTY IN TWO–PARENT FAMILIES

in Poor Support 81–89, 96–97 (Basic Books 1988).

The poverty of two-parent families is the poverty of the working poor. The fortunes of these families are closely linked to the performance of the economy. Good times help, but bad times may be devastating. By some measures, these two-parent families are the least secure members of society, for they get little in the way of income or medical supports despite their vulnerability to swings in the economy. If we are really serious about reinforcing the values of autonomy, work, family, and community, then we must find a way to improve the economic security of this group without putting them into a welfare system. . . .

How Bad Is the Poverty of Two-Parent Families?

The poverty of single parents gets all the attention. It is easy to see why. If we exclude all governmental transfers from income, single-parent families with children had a "pretransfer" poverty rate of roughly 50 percent in 1984. (A pretransfer poor family is one whose income, *not counting any governmental transfers* such as welfare, Social Security and the like, is below the poverty line for its family size.) By contrast, the rate was 15 percent for two-parent families with children.

Moreover, poverty usually lasts a shorter time in two-parent families than in single-parent families. . . . [I]f we look at the first ten years of life for children who grew up in the 1970s, those who lived entirely in two-parent families in the 1970s were far more likely to escape poverty, particularly long-term poverty, than those who spent at least some time in single-parent homes. . . . [S]ome 80 percent of the children who were growing up in stable two-parent homes escaped poverty, and just 2 percent were long-term poor. By contrast, only 27 percent of those who spent at least some time in single-parent homes avoided poverty, and over 20 percent literally grew up poor.

If poverty is relatively uncommon in stable two-parent homes and if it is often short lived, perhaps two-parent poverty deserves its uncelebrated status. Not so. Since so many more children live in two-parent families than in single-parent ones, half the poor children in America are living in two-parent homes—and they live in families that are suffering genuine economic hardship. Furthermore, the poverty rate for children in two-parent homes is not so low. It still exceeds the poverty rate among persons over age 65 (after governmental transfers).

Moreover, if we are really interested in supporting and promoting two-parent families, concentrating exclusively on single-parent families is not only uncaring but counterproductive. Most of the children shown in figure 4.1 who did not live entirely in two-parent families started out life in them, but the families split apart. Poverty may have been a contributing factor to the breakup of these families. In chapter 3, I made clear that one of the most appealing ways to try and influence the changing structure of families in America is to seek ways to strengthen two-parent families—ways that help poor families and reinforce our values.

Why Are Two-Parent Families Poor?

Unfortunately, there are few clear answers to the question of why a family is poor. Two people who observe the same family in the same situation can reach different conclusions. Suppose, for example, we observe a poor two-parent family in which the husband works full time all year and the mother stays at home with the children. What is the cause of the family's poverty?

One answer would be that low wages are to blame. The father is already working full time and the mother is taking care of the children. What more should it take to escape poverty? For some reason, the husband is not being paid enough to support himself and his family. This looks like a societal problem in the marketplace or in the educational system.

Another answer could be that the mother is not working outside the home to help support the family. After all, the majority of mothers now work at least part time. Surely, we can expect this mother to do so as well. A variation on this theme would be that the mother may not be able to work because affordable day care is not available.

Yet another answer could be that these people should not have become parents in the first place if they could not support their children. One might be particularly concerned if this was a large family that would be poor even with the earnings from a fairly good job.

If we could talk to the family in person, we might be able to decide which of these explanations seemed most fair. If it turned out that the wife had tried to work but quit when she found that her low earnings simply did not compensate enough for the high cost of day care combined with the stress that working placed on the family, then we would be less inclined to suggest that she was not doing enough. If she was alone at home while the children were in school, we might feel differently.

The case I just described is one of the easy ones. What about a family in which the husband and wife say they are unemployed? How could we tell if they really could not find work? What if one had lost a high-paying job but had recently turned down a low-paying one? What if one of the adults was not looking for work because of "child care responsibilities" even while the other was unemployed?

There is no way to look at every poor family and make a decision about the "true" cause of their low income. And we certainly could not expect the government to make such determinations on a case-by-case basis. It is precisely this ambiguity that leads academics and advocates alike to turn quickly to a welfare model of support. Welfare does not try to decide why people are poor; it only guarantees some minimal income.

But adopting a policy that recognizes no causes leads to no solutions. A great deal of the ambiguity comes from our unwillingness to decide what is reasonable to expect of families. If we are willing to decide on some minimal standards of responsibility for citizens and society, then we can go a long way toward determining the causes of poverty. From that determination, we can often find nonwelfare alternatives that support and reinforce people's efforts to support themselves.

Reasonable Responsibility

We might start by asking, "How much work should it take for a healthy two-parent family to achieve the *minimum* standard of living (as defined by the government's poverty standard)?" Whatever the answer, it simultaneously defines the expectations of citizens and of society. Society's responsibility is to ensure that everyone has the opportunity to fulfill the standard of work it sets and that wages are sufficient to achieve a minimum standard of living. If society meets that responsibility, then healthy citizens can reasonably be expected to provide for themselves by working at that level.

I believe that in a two-parent family, the earnings of one person working full year, full time (or the equivalent number of hours of combined work by a husband and wife) ought to be sufficient for a family to reach the poverty line. Consider the hypothetical couple already described in which the husband is working full time and the wife is at home taking care of the children. It is hard to expect more from the husband, although he could perhaps find a second job. We do not know whether the wife has tried to find work, but, without more information, it is hard to fault her chosen role of raising the children, especially since we cannot be sure that day care is available. This family already seems to be doing a lot to help themselves. The father is probably working at an unpleasant low-paying job to pay the bills. The mother is trying to run the household on too little money. They appear to be the "value rich" but "money poor" people described in a 1986 Reagan administration report on the family.

If we accept this initial guidepost, we can break families into two obvious categories, those who are meeting the standard and those who are not. One reason why people may not be working fully is illness or disability. Such families ought to be considered in a different light. Thus, there seem to be three classifications with which we can start to examine the causes of poverty among two-parent families: full-time working families (defined as a case where one adult works fully or the combined effort of both adults is equivalent), families in which one adult is aged or disabled, and families in which the adults are partially employed or unemployed. . . .

It should surprise no one to learn that work and poverty are closely related. The poverty rate among fully working families before governmental transfers is just .06; for the others, it is ten times that level. Fortunately, the vast majority of two-parent families are full-time working families. Only 6 percent fall into the partially employed or unemployed category (and work is common even in that group). It turns out that only 1 percent of families have two healthy parents who both report no work at all during the year.

But, rather startlingly, even though the poverty rate among full-time working families is low, such families still make up 44 percent of the poor two-parent families. Thus, work does not always guarantee a route out of poverty. A full-time minimum-wage job (that pays $3.35 per hour) does not even come close to supporting a family of three at the poverty line. Even one full-time job and one half-time job at the minimum wage will not bring a family of four up to the poverty line. Therefore, even though most full-time working families escape poverty, the ones who do not represent a large share of the poor. . . .

The image that emerges of poor two-parent families is surprising. It is largely a picture of families who are struggling to provide for themselves and who are sharply affected by the availability of jobs and the wages being paid. This image is different from the one portrayed in recent conservative books on poverty that have emphasized the ghetto underclass and the television specials and newscasts that show the poor being isolated economically, socially, geographically, and culturally from the rest of society. Some of these isolated people may be found among poor two-parent families, but they are outnumbered by others who are not isolated. Remember that ghetto poverty probably represents less than 10 percent of the poverty in America. It is an even smaller part of the poverty of two-parent families.

Aside from the group that is disabled or retired, poor two-parent families really are the working poor. Perhaps the best proof of this lies in a test of an old conservative proposition: trickle-down. I have argued that there are three basic causes of poverty for these families: low wages, unemployment, and disability. Disability should be roughly constant from year to year. But wages and unemployment rates vary considerably over time. If those were the driving forces affecting the poverty of two-parent families, then we ought to be able to predict fluctuations in poverty for two-parent families by using only a measure of aggregate wages in the economy and a measure of unemployment. In short, the poverty of two-parent families ought to mimic economic conditions.

So I looked to see if I could predict poverty rates strictly on the basis of overall wage rates and unemployment. I plotted the actual poverty rate and the one I would have predicted on the basis of just two measures of economic conditions: median income of full-year full-time workers (a measure of wages for full-time workers) and unemployment.... [T]he startling results—a perfect match. In the 1960s, when real wages were rising fast and unemployment dropped, poverty fell precipitously. In the 1970s, when earnings were largely unchanged (after adjusting for inflation), poverty changed little. And in the 1980s, when the economy turned sour, the poverty rate jumped up.

... [T]here is nothing mysterious or suggestive about the lack of progress in eliminating poverty among two-parent families in the 1970s and 1980s. This is the group for whom trickle-down works well. When the economy booms and wages grow while unemployment falls, this group is carried with the tide. That is just what happened in the 1960s. If economic growth was strong over an extended period, the number of poor two-parent families would rapidly diminish and eventually those who were still poor would be the disabled and a much smaller pool of families with an unemployed adult who had just lost a job, who was just starting out, or who was living in an area where the local economy was weak.

The poverty line is not changed by growth, but the incomes of most two-parent families are. Growth may not reduce the difference in the incomes of the highest and lowest families (it may not narrow the distribution of income), but it will push more and more low-income families over the fixed poverty line. Indeed, in Massachusetts in 1984, when the unemployment rate was under 4 percent and growth had been strong for several years, the pretransfer poverty rate for two-parent families with children was under 6 percent—less than half the national figure of 12 percent.

So a couple of decades of strong growth would be just what the doctor ordered for most poor two-parent families. But no one knows how to recapture the dramatic growth of the 1960s. Instead, we seem locked in a period of slow growth. And trickle-down has its obverse side as well: when the economy stumbles, the working poor fall....

————

Recently, considerable attention has shifted to examination of poverty among the "urban underclass." Before offering descriptions of that group, it should be noted that the term itself has generated debate. Some have used it in conjunction with the notion of a "culture of poverty," a phrase which is loaded with a "victim-blaming" explanation for poverty. *See* Donald Judges, *Bayonets for the Wounded: Constitutional Paradigms and Disadvantaged Neighborhoods,* 19 Hastings Con. L.Q. 599, 683 n. 348 (1992). Others have suggested that the term "underclass" is one that " 'can be used by conservatives, liberals, and radicals alike' " and that accurately conveys "the image of marginalization relevant to the group it describes, is not inherently pejorative, and finds general currency in the social science literature." *Id.* (quoting Paul Peterson, "The Urban Underclass and the Poverty Paradox", in The Urban Underclass 3 (Christopher Jencks & Paul Peterson eds., 1991). See also, The Underclass Question (Bill E. Lawson, ed., Temple U.Press, 1992). We have suggested throughout these materials that how we choose to talk about issues does matter. You should consider, therefore, the various images conveyed by the word "underclass" and the implications that might flow from its use.

It is important to note that the underclass "is not merely poor. Its members face an overwhelming combination of socioeconomic problems—including long-term unemployment, street crime and other antisocial behavior, drug dependency, residential segregation, broken families, chronic poverty, and welfare dependency...." *Id.* at 683. William Julius Wilson offered his theory of the underclass in his book, The Truly Disadvantaged: The Inner City, The Underclass, and Public Policy (U. Chicago Press 1988), and later summarized his arguments as follows:

WILLIAM JULIUS WILSON, PUBLIC POLICY RESEARCH AND *THE TRULY DISADVANTAGED*

in The Urban Underclass 461–479 (Christopher Jencks
& Paul Peterson eds., Brookings 1991).

I argue in *The Truly Disadvantaged* that historical discrimination and a migration to large metropolises that kept the urban minority population relatively young created a problem of weak labor force attachment among urban blacks and, especially since 1970, made them particularly vulnerable to the industrial and geographic changes in the economy. The shift from goods-producing to service-producing industries, the increasing polarization of the labor market into low-wage and high-wage sectors, innovations in technology, the relocation of manufacturing industries out of central cities, and periodic recessions have forced up the rate of black joblessness (unemployment and nonparticipation in the labor market), despite the passage of antidiscrimination legislation and the creation of affirmative action programs. The rise in joblessness has in turn helped trigger an increase in the concentrations of poor people, a growing number of poor single-parent families, and an increase in welfare dependency. These problems have been especially evident in the ghetto neighborhoods of large cities, not only because the most impoverished minority populations live there but also because the neighborhoods have become less diversified in a way that has severely worsened the impact of the continuing economic changes.

Especially since 1970, inner-city neighborhoods have experienced an outmigration of working- and middle-class families previously confined to them by the restrictive covenants of higher-status city neighborhoods and suburbs. Combined with the increase in the number of poor caused by rising joblessness, this outmigration has sharply concentrated the poverty in inner-city neighborhoods. The number with poverty rates that exceed 40 percent—a threshold definition of "extreme poverty" neighborhoods—has risen precipitously. And the dwindling presence of middle- and working-class households has also removed an important social buffer that once deflected the full impact of the kind of prolonged high levels of joblessness in these neighborhoods that has stemmed from uneven economic growth and periodic recessions.

In earlier decades, not only were most of the adults in ghetto neighborhoods employed, but black working and middle classes brought stability. They invested economic and social resources in the neighborhoods, patronized the churches, stores, banks, and community organizations, sent their children to the local schools, reinforced societal norms and values, and made it meaningful for lower-class blacks in these segregated enclaves to envision the possibility of some upward mobility.

However, today the ghetto features a population, the underclass, whose primary predicament is joblessness reinforced by growing social isolation. Outmigration has decreased the contact between groups of different class and racial backgrounds and thereby concentrated the adverse effects of living in impoverished neighborhoods. These concentration effects, reflected, for example, in the residents' self-limiting social dispositions, are created by inadequate access to jobs and job networks, the lack of involvement in quality schools, the unavailability of suitable marriage partners, and the lack of exposure to informal mainstream social networks and conventional role models.

Accordingly, *The Truly Disadvantaged* argued that the factors associated with the recent increases in social dislocation in the ghetto are complex. They cannot be reduced to the easy explanations of a "culture of poverty" that have been advanced by those on the right, or of racism, posited by those on the left. Although the ghetto is a product of historical discrimination and although present-day discrimination has undoubtedly contributed to the deepening social and economic woes of its residents, to understand the sharp increase in these problems requires the specification of a complex web of other factors, including shifts in the American economy.

THE FORMAL STRUCTURE OF THE THEORETICAL FRAMEWORK

This summary of *The Truly Disadvantaged* does not make explicit the fact that social-structural, social-psychological, and cultural variables are integrated into my theoretical framework. A more formal statement of this framework is that a structure of inequality has evolved which is linked to contemporary behavior in the inner city by a combination of constraints, opportunities, and social psychology.

The exogenous factors, representing the sources of the racial concentration of urban poverty, include racial discrimination, changes in the economy that have relocated industries and restructured occupations, and political processes (antibias legislation and affirmative action programs) that have had the unanticipated consequence of widening class divisions among urban blacks. The endogenous determinants created by these exogenous factors include such demographic variables as urban migration, age structures, and the pool of marriageable men, and economic factors such as the distribution of employment and income. These variables are important for understanding the experiences of all low-income urban groups, not just the ghetto underclass.

The endogenous determinants further include social isolation, which is unique to the social environment of the underclass. Social isolation deprives residents of inner-city neighborhoods not only of resources and conventional role models, whose former presence buffered the effects of neighborhood joblessness, but also of the kind of cultural learning from mainstream social networks that facilitates social and economic advancement in modern industrial society. The lack of neighborhood material resources, the relative absence of conventional role models, and the circumscribed cultural learning produce outcomes, or concentration effects, that restrict social mobility. Some of these outcomes are structural (lack of labor force attachment and access to informal job networks), and some are social-psychological (negative social dispositions, limited aspirations, and casual work habits). . . .

THE ECONOMY AND WEAK LABOR FORCE ATTACHMENT IN THE INNER CITY

In my attempt in *The Truly Disadvantaged* to examine empirically the problem of the growing concentration of poverty, I used census tracts as proxies for nonpoverty and inner-city areas. The latter was divided into poverty, high-poverty, and extreme poverty neighborhoods. Most of my analysis of concentrated poverty focused on areas of extreme poverty, that is, those in which at least 40 percent of the people are poor. More recent studies have followed this lead by defining ghettos as those areas with poverty rates of at least 40 percent. The ghetto poor are therefore identified as those among the poor in the inner city who reside in these neighborhoods of extreme poverty.

. . . [T]he proportion of the poor who reside in ghetto neighborhoods varies dramatically by race. Whereas only 2 percent of the non-Hispanic white poor lived in ghettos in 1980, some 21 percent of black poor and 16 percent of Hispanic poor resided there. And almost a third of all metropolitan blacks lived in a ghetto in 1980. Sixty-five percent of the 2.4 million ghetto poor in the United States are black, 22 percent Hispanic, and 13 percent non-Hispanic and other races. Thus to speak of the ghetto poor in the United States is to refer primarily to blacks and Hispanics. This has both descriptive and theoretical significance.

. . . [T]he increase of ghetto poverty occurred mainly in only two regions of the country: the Midwest and the Northeast. Moreover, ten cities accounted for three-fourths of the total rise of ghetto poverty during the 1970s. One-third of the increase was accounted for solely by New York City, and one-half by New York and Chicago together. By adding Philadelphia, Newark, and Detroit, two-thirds of the total increase is accounted for. The others in the top ten were Columbus, Ohio, Atlanta, Baltimore, Buffalo, and Paterson, New Jersey. Of the 195 standard metropolitan areas in 1970 that recorded some ghetto poverty, 88 experienced decreases in the number of ghetto poor by 1980. Those with the largest decreases were Texas cities with significant declines in Hispanic ghetto poverty and southern cities with sharp drops in black ghetto poverty.

The focus of *The Truly Disadvantaged,* however, was on the increase in ghetto poverty. The questions are why did this increase occur and why was most of it confined to the large industrial metropolises of the Northeast and Midwest? Because these two regions experienced massive industrial restructuring and loss of blue-collar jobs. Cities of the frost-belt suffered overall employment decline because "growth in their predominantly information-processing industries could not numerically compensate for substantial losses in their more traditional industrial sectors, especially manufacturing." Cities in the sunbelt experienced job growth in all major sectors of the economy (manufacturing, retail and wholesale, white-collar services, and blue-collar services) between 1970 and 1986.

In *The Truly Disadvantaged* I maintained that one result of these changes for many urban blacks has been a growing mismatch between the location of employment and residence in the inner city.... Recent research conducted mainly by urban and labor economists strongly shows that the decentralization of employment is continuing and that employment in manufacturing, most of which is already suburbanized, has decreased in central cities, particularly in the Northeast and Midwest. Blacks living in central cities have less access to employment, as measured by the ratio of jobs to people and the average travel time to and from work, than do central-city whites. Unlike most other groups of workers, less educated central-city blacks receive lower wages in the central city than less educated suburban blacks. And the decline in earnings of central-city blacks is positively associated with the extent of metropolitan job decentralization....

The occupational advancement of the more disadvantaged urban minority members has also been severely curtailed by industrial restructuring. John Kasarda's research demonstrates that "the bottom fell out in urban industrial demand for poorly educated blacks," particularly in the goods-producing industries, in northeastern and midwestern cities. And data collected from the Chicago Urban Poverty and Family Life Survey show that efforts by out-of-school inner-city black men to obtain blue-collar jobs in the industries in which their fathers had been employed have been hampered by industrial restructuring. "The most common occupation reported by the cohort of respondents at ages 19 to 28 changed from operative and assembler jobs among the oldest cohorts to service jobs (waiters and janitors) among the youngest cohort." ...

As I pointed out in *The Truly Disadvantaged,* manufacturing industries have been a major source of black employment in the twentieth century. Unfortunately, these industries are particularly sensitive to a slack economy, and blacks lost a considerable number of jobs during the recession-plagued decade of the 1970s.... Although jobless rates remain high among disadvantaged minority youths, dramatic progress occurred during the economic recovery of the late 1980s in the metropolitan areas with the tightest labor markets.

If a tight labor market reduces joblessness among the disadvantaged, it also effectively reduces poverty.... Changes in employment and poverty are likely to appear much sooner following changes in the economy than changes in family formation because the latter not only represent a more indirect relationship to the economy but a more complex and subtle process of human experience as well....

The data that would be most relevant for understanding the relationship between employment and marriage among the underclass are those collected from inner cities. Since the publication of *The Truly Disadvantaged,* this relationship has been examined more closely with data from the inner-city neighborhoods of Chicago as a part of the Urban Poverty and Family Life Study. A recent paper by Mark Testa based on these data shows that black men in inner-city Chicago who have stable work are twice as likely to marry as black men who are jobless and are not in school or in the military.

However, Testa's study also shows that the decline in marriage among inner-city blacks is not simply a function of the proportion of jobless men. Because the disparity in marriage rates between employed and jobless black men was smaller for older cohorts, it is reasonable to consider the effects of weaker social strictures against out-of-wedlock births. "In earlier years," he comments, "the social stigma of illegitimacy counterbalanced economic considerations in the decision to marry. As the norms of legitimacy weakened, marriage rates dropped precipitously among chronically jobless men as couples no longer felt obliged to legitimate the birth of a child for social reasons."

In *The Truly Disadvantaged* I related the increasing jobless rate among black men to geographic, industrial, and other shifts in the economy. This hypothesis has drawn criticism because some observers believed that the focus on impersonal economic forces overlooked willful acts of employment discrimination against racial minorities. Although empirical research on such discrimination is scarce, data from the Chicago Urban Poverty and Family Life Study's survey of employers, as reported in the paper by Joleen Kirschenman and Kathryn Neckerman, suggest that inner-city blacks, particularly black men, do indeed face negative attitudes from employers. They report that many employers consider inner-city workers, especially young black men, to be uneducated, uncooperative, and unstable. Accordingly, employers may practice what economists call statistical discrimination, making judgments about an applicant's productivity, which are often too difficult or too expensive to measure, on the basis of his or her race, ethnic, or class background. Although only a few employers explicitly expressed racist attitudes or a categorical loathing of blacks, many did in fact practice statistical discrimination by screening out black job applicants because of their social class, public school education, and inner-city residence. These factors also served as proxies for judgments about productivity.

As the research of Richard Freeman suggests, however, the practice of statistical discrimination will vary according to the tightness of the labor market. It therefore ought not be analyzed without reference to the overall state of the local or national economy. In a tight labor market, job vacancies are more prevalent, unemployment is of shorter duration, and wages are higher. The pool of potential workers expands because an increase in job opportunities not only lowers unemployment but also draws into the labor force those workers who respond to fading job prospects in slack markets by dropping out of the labor force altogether. Accordingly, the status of disadvantaged minorities improves in a tight labor market because unemployment is reduced, better jobs are available, and wages are higher. In contrast, in a slack labor market employers are—indeed, can afford to be—more selective in recruiting and in granting promotions. They inflate job prerequisites and the importance of experience. In such an economic climate, the level of employer discrimination rises and disadvantaged minorities suffer disproportionately.

Although basic economic transformations and changes in labor markets are important for understanding the life experiences of the urban minority poor, *The Truly Disadvantaged* also argued that the out-migration of higher-income residents from certain parts of the inner city resulted in a higher concentration of residents in ghetto neighborhoods. This contention has been controversial. Douglas Massey and Mitchell Eggers, for instance, have found that the increase of segregation among black social classes during the 1970s was not sufficient to account for the rise in concentrated urban black poverty. They argue that because of persisting segregation, higher-income blacks have been less able than the privileged of other groups to separate themselves from the poor. Accordingly, an increase in the poverty rate of a highly segregated group will be automatically accompanied by an increase in the concentration of poverty. Reynolds Farley reaches the same conclusion ...: "Wilson's conclusion that poor blacks in Chicago lived in proportionally more impoverished neighborhoods in 1980 than in 1970 ... is accurate ... but the situation occurred because of overall increases in black poverty rather than because of higher levels of social class residential segregation or a new outmigration of prosperous blacks." ...

SOCIAL ENVIRONMENT AND LABOR FORCE ATTACHMENT IN THE INNER CITY

The exodus of higher-income blacks was not only a factor in the growth of ghetto poverty. It also deprived these neighborhoods of structural resources, such as social buffers to minimize the effects of growing joblessness, and cultural resources, such as conventional role models for neighborhood children, therefore further contributing to the economic marginality of the underclass.

In *The Truly Disadvantaged* I argued that the central problem of the underclass is joblessness reinforced by increasing social isolation in impoverished neighborhoods, as reflected, for example, in the residents' declining access to job information network systems. Martha Van Haitsma, in an important conceptual paper, has more sharply delineated the relationship between the social environment and experiences in the labor market by distinguishing those persons with weak attachment to the labor force whose social context "tends to maintain or further weaken this attachment." I would like to include this more explicit notion in my framework by equating the social context with the neighborhood....

To understand the unique position of the underclass, it is important to understand the association between attachment to the labor force and the neighborhood context.... Poor people who reside in neighborhoods that foster or support strong labor force attachment are in a much different social context than those with similar educations and occupational skills living in neighborhoods that promote or reinforce weak labor force attachment. Thus neighborhoods that have few legitimate employment opportunities, inadequate job information networks, and poor schools not only give rise to weak labor force attachment but also raise the likelihood that people will turn to illegal or deviant activities for income, thereby further weakening their attachment to the legitimate labor market. A jobless family in such a neighborhood is influenced by the behavior, beliefs, orientations, and social perceptions of other disadvantaged families disproportionately concentrated in the neighborhood. To capture this process I used the term "concentration effects," that is, the effects of living in an overwhelmingly impoverished environment....

SOCIAL THEORY AND THE CONCEPT OF THE UNDERCLASS

In my formulation the concept of underclass derives its meaning from a theoretical framework that links structural, social-psychological, and cultural arguments....

In early studies of the inner city, some observers argued that ghetto-specific behaviors were unique adaptations to the restricted opportunities of the disadvantaged in American society, not a different system of values. Although they discussed the influence of culture—that is, the extent to which people follow their inclinations as they have been developed by learning from other members of the community—they did not argue that the influence takes on a life of its own or is autonomous in the ghetto. In other words, these authors demonstrated the possibility of seeing the importance of macrostructural constraints (that is, of avoiding the extreme assumption of a culture of poverty) while still recognizing the value of a more subtle cultural analysis of life in poverty.... Is there a fundamental difference between "a person who is alone in being exposed to certain macrostructural constraints" and a person "who is influenced both by these constraints and by the behavior of others who are affected by them"?

What distinguishes members of the underclass from those of other economically disadvantaged groups is that their marginal economic position or weak attachment to the labor force is uniquely reinforced by the neighborhood or social milieu. . . .

THE UNDERCLASS AND PUBLIC POLICY

The growing concentration of poverty and social isolation of the inner cities has implications not only for the quality of life and patterns of social interaction in impoverished urban neighborhoods, but for the larger urban environment as well. None of these cities can escape the deleterious consequences of the social transformation of the inner city and the growth of an underclass.

The problem is not simply the fiscal burden created by the sharp deterioration of aggregate family income or the erosion of the municipal tax base caused by the growth in the number of "high-cost" citizens at the very time that large and increasing numbers of higher-income families have abandoned the cities. The deterioration of ghetto neighborhoods has also sapped the vitality of local businesses and other institutions, and it has led to fewer and shabbier movie theaters, bowling alleys, restaurants, public parks and playgrounds, and other recreational facilities. Residents of inner-city neighborhoods are therefore often compelled to seek leisure activity in other areas of the city, where they come into brief contact with citizens of different racial, ethnic, or class backgrounds. Sharp differences in cultural style and patterns of interaction that reflect the social isolation of neighborhood networks often lead to clashes. Both the white and minority classes have complained bitterly about how certain conveniently located areas of the central city have deteriorated following the influx of inner-city residents. The complaints have inevitably come to be directed at the underclass itself.

Meanwhile, racial tensions between poor blacks and working-class whites reflect an even more serious consequence of the social transformation of the inner city. Working-class whites, like inner-city minorities, have felt the full impact of the urban fiscal crisis in the United States. Unlike middle-class whites, they have been forced by financial exigencies to remain in the poorer parts of the cities and suffer the strains of crime, poorer services, and higher taxes. Unlike the more affluent whites who choose to remain in the wealthier sections of the cities, they cannot easily escape the problems of deteriorating public schools by sending their children to private schools, a problem made worse by the sharp decrease in the numbers of urban parochial schools. Thus, in recent years, the racial struggle for power and privilege in the cities has been essentially a struggle between the have-nots over access to and control of decent housing and decent neighborhoods.

Working-class whites are more likely than middle-class whites to express their hostility in blatantly racist terms and behavior, sometimes manifested in acts of violence such as the recent killing of a young black man in the white ethnic neighborhood of Bensonhurst in New York City, and they are less likely to distinguish between middle-class and disadvantaged minorities. Middle-class whites are more subtle in their expressions of hostility and are more likely to direct their racial antagonisms specifically toward poor minorities.

The increasing antagonism has been further aggravated by a conservative political atmosphere, particularly during the Reagan presidency, that has not only reinforced the dominant American belief system that poverty is a reflection of individual inadequacy but has discouraged efforts for new and stronger social programs to address the growing problems of urban inequality.

These changes in the racial and political climate in America have profound implications for the way we will address the problems of race and class in the inner cities. I am therefore reminded of the words of the late black economist, Vivian Henderson, who wrote, "The economic future of blacks in the United States is bound up with that of the rest of the nation. Policies, programs, and politics designed in the future to cope with the problems of the poor and victimized will also yield benefits to blacks. In contrast, any efforts to treat blacks separately from the rest of the nation are likely to lead to frustration, heightened racial animosities, and a waste of the country's resources and the precious resources of black people."

I agree with Henderson. In the coming years the best political strategy for those committed to racial justice is to place more emphasis on race-neutral programs that would not only address the plight of the disadvantaged among minorities but would apply to all groups in America. After all, Americans across racial and class lines continue to be concerned about increased unemployment, decreased job security, deteriorating real wages, poorer public education, escalating medical and hospital costs, the lack of good child care, and more crime and drug trafficking in their neighborhoods. Because these problems are more highly concentrated in the inner cities as a result of cumulative effects of decades of racial subjugation, programs that aggressively address them will disproportionately benefit the underclass.

... The issue is not simply the degree to which universal or targeted programs can sustain political support. The important question is whether costly programs perceived to be targeted to minorities can be generated and adequately supported in the present climate of budgetary constraint and racial antagonism. Although many social programs did indeed survive the Reagan budget cuts, they are hardly sufficient to address the manifold problems gripping the ghettos. We must generate new initiatives if we are indeed to move significant numbers of American citizens out of the underclass....

This was my concern when I wrote *The Truly Disadvantaged* and argued for improving the life chances of truly disadvantaged groups such as the ghetto underclass by emphasizing programs to which the more advantaged groups of all races and class backgrounds can positively relate. I now believe that this is best achieved not simply through a combination of targeted and universal initiatives, but through targeted and universal initiatives that are clearly race neutral.

————

In the following excerpt, Christopher Jencks questions the usefulness of the underclass concept.

CHRISTOPHER JENCKS, RETHINKING SOCIAL POLICY

143–45, 198–203 (Harvard U. Press 1992).

The ambiguity of phrases like "middle class" and "underclass" derives from the fact that Americans use a multitude of different criteria to rank one another, including how much income they have, where they get it, whether they have mastered the cultural skills most Americans value, and whether people conform to American ideals about social behavior. Because we all use different criteria to rank one another, we end up assigning different people to the social elite, to the middle class, and to the underclass. If you rank people primarily according to how much income they have, while I rank people according to where they get their money, we will put different people in the underclass. Likewise, if you think the underclass is composed of men who mug their neighbors or women who have babies out of wedlock, while I think of the underclass as composed of people who lack the social and cultural skills required to deal with mainstream American institutions, we will often disagree about whether specific individuals belong to the underclass or not. In this chapter I consider four ranking schemes, each of which implies a different definition of the underclass.

Income level. Some social scientists equate membership in the underclass with persistent poverty. In everyday usage, however, the underclass does not include the elderly poor, the working poor, or others who are poor through no fault of their own. The underclass includes only those families whose poverty is attributable to a violation of one or more widely shared social norms, such as the family head's failure to work regularly or to marry before having children. I will call this group the "impoverished underclass."

Income sources. Sociologists have traditionally assigned people to classes primarily on the basis of where they get their money rather than how much money they have. They assume that the upper class get its income from capital, the middle and working classes get their money from regular jobs (or job-related pensions), and the lower class gets its money from irregular work, crime, public assistance, and handouts. I will call this last group the "jobless underclass."

Cultural skills. Many Americans assign people to classes primarily on the basis of how they talk, how much they know, and how they deal with other people. From this perspective the middle class is composed of people who think, talk, and act like those who manage America's major institutions. The underclass is composed of people who lack the basic skills required to deal with these institutions. For lack of a better term I will call this group "the educational underclass."

Moral norms. Americans also talk a lot about middle-class "values," and some social critics use the term "underclass" to describe people who seem indifferent to these values. Three middle-class values (or as I would prefer to say, ideals) are especially salient in discussions of this kind:

- Working-age men should have a steady job. Those who violate this norm constitute the jobless underclass.

- Women should postpone childbearing until they are married. Those who violate this norm constitute what I will call the reproductive underclass.

- Everyone should refrain from violence. Those who violate this norm constitute what I will call the violent underclass.

Whether you conclude that the underclass is growing depends on which of these ranking schemes you adopt.

Many Americans also think of the underclass as almost exclusively nonwhite. This perception may be partly due to racism, but it derives primarily from our habit of equating people's class position with their address. Using most of the ranking schemes described above, the underclass includes considerably more whites than nonwhites. But the underclass constitutes only a small fraction of the white population, and American neighborhoods are only moderately segregated along economic lines. As a result, underclass whites are seldom a majority in any neighborhood. This means that if you equate membership in the underclass with living in an underclass neighborhood, not many whites will qualify.

Nonwhites are far more likely than whites to have underclass characteristics, and they almost always live in racially segregated neighborhoods. Because the underclass constitutes a relatively large fraction of the nonwhite population, it is a majority or near majority in some nonwhite neighborhoods. Those who equate membership in the underclass with living in an underclass neighborhood therefore see the underclass as nonwhite....

Americans started talking about the underclass during the 1980s because they sensed that their society was becoming more unequal. The rich were getting richer, but the poor were as numerous as ever. Skilled professionals and business executives commanded ever higher salaries, but a growing fraction of working-age men had no job at all. At the same time, the fabric of lower-class society seemed to be unraveling. Poor couples were having more of their babies without marrying, and millions of single mothers were trying to live on welfare checks that paid less than the rich spent every year on vacations. Crime was rampant in many poor neighborhoods. Inner-city schools seemed unable to teach most of their students even basic skills. As a result, poor children no longer seemed to have much chance of escaping from poverty, as earlier generations had.

If all these problems had arisen more or less simultaneously, the claim that shrinking economic opportunities were creating a new underclass would be hard to resist. In reality, however, while economic conditions began to deteriorate for less skilled workers in the 1970s, most of the other problems that led Americans to start talking about an underclass followed different trajectories. Some had been getting worse for a long time. Some had gotten worse between 1965 and 1975 but then leveled off. Some never got worse. Some were actually getting better. Thus, when we try to link changes in family structure, welfare use, school enrollment, academic achievement, or criminal violence to changes in economic opportunity, the connections prove elusive. To see why, it is helpful to compare the timing of changes in different areas.

Which problems have gotten steadily worse? Long-term joblessness is somewhat sensitive to the business cycle, but the underlying rate among twenty-five to fifty-four-year-old men rose during both the 1970s and the 1980s.

The number of babies born to unmarried women did not rise much from 1960 to 1975, but the number of babies born to married women fell a lot, so the proportion of babies born out of wedlock rose. After 1975, the number of babies born to women while they were unmarried began to rise. Since divorce has also become more common, the fraction of women raising children without male help has risen steadily.

Which problems have stopped getting worse? While single motherhood increased steadily after 1960, the proportion of single mothers collecting welfare rose only between 1964 and 1974. After that, it began to decline again. As a result, the proportion of all mothers collecting welfare rose dramatically between 1964 and 1974 but then leveled off.

Violent crime doubled between 1964 and 1974, remained roughly constant during the late 1970s, declined significantly in the early 1980s, and edged up in the late 1980s. As a result, violence was somewhat less common in the late 1980s than in 1980 or 1970. This was especially true among blacks.

Which problems have gotten steadily better? Both non-Hispanic whites and blacks were more likely to earn a high-school diploma or GED certificate in the late 1980s than at any time in the past. The disparity between blacks and whites was also smaller. Improvements on these indices were, however, somewhat slower in the 1980s than in the 1960s or 1970s.

The proportion of seventeen-year-olds with basic reading skills rose steadily during the 1970s and 1980s, especially among blacks. The increase among whites was much smaller. Disparities between the best and worst readers, while still huge, diminished significantly. The proportion of seventeen-year-old blacks with basic math skills also rose during the 1980s.

Among blacks, educational attainment became less dependent on family background between 1940 and 1980. As a result, black children from disadvantaged backgrounds had better educational prospects in the 1980s than in 1970. Among whites, there was little change after 1970. I found no evidence on whether disadvantaged children's chances of growing up to be poor, jobless, or dependent on welfare have changed over time.

Which problems have stopped getting better? Teenage motherhood declined during the 1960s and 1970s. There was no clear trend during the 1980s. Teenage fatherhood rose during the 1960s, declined during the 1970s, and was roughly constant during the 1980s.

The proportion of individuals with family incomes below the poverty line, which had fallen steadily from 1940 to 1970, has not changed much since 1970. Only the character of poverty has changed. It has become less common among the elderly and more common among children. Poverty has also become more concentrated among families in which the head does not work regularly.

Which problems have I ignored? Drug use is a persistent problem, especially among the underclass. I have not discussed it because I have not been able to find any convincing quantitative evidence about the prevalence or severity of the problem. Surveys of high-school students show dramatic declines in almost all forms of drug use during the 1980s. Yet people who spend time in poor communities are convinced that drugs became a more serious problem during the 1980s. Both claims may be correct.

The trends I have described do not fit together in any simple or obvious way. Those who think that everything has gotten worse for people at the bottom of the social pyramid since 1970 are clearly wrong. Economic conditions have deteriorated for workers without higher education, and two-parent families have become scarcer, but welfare dependency has not increased since the early 1970s, and illiteracy, teenage motherhood, and violence have declined somewhat.

So far as I can see, the claim that America has a growing underclass does not help us understand complex changes of the kind I have described. On the contrary, arguments that use class as their central explanatory idea obscure what is going on. The reasons for this deserve brief discussion.

We use terms such as "middle class" and "underclass" because we know that occupation, income, educational credentials, cognitive skills, a criminal record, out-of-wedlock childbearing, and other personal characteristics are somewhat correlated with one another. Class labels provide a short-hand device for describing people who differ along many of these dimensions simultaneously. The term "middle class," for example, evokes someone who has attended college, holds a steady job, earns an adequate income, got married before having children, and has never murdered, raped, robbed, or assaulted anyone. The term "underclass," in contrast, conjures up a chronically jobless high-school dropout who has had two or three children out of wedlock, has very little money to support them, and probably has either a criminal record or a history of welfare dependence.

Relatively few people fit either of these stereotypes perfectly. Many people are middle class in some respects, working class in others, and underclass in still others. But those who use class labels always assume that everyone is a member of some class or other. In order to assign everyone to a class, they allow their classes to be internally heterogeneous. If they assign people to classes on the basis of how they make their living, they allow the members of these classes to differ with regard to income, educational credentials, cognitive skills, family structure, and arrest record. Everyone who stops to think recognizes that the world is untidy in this sense. We use class labels precisely because we want to make the world seem tidier than it is. The purpose of labels is to draw attention to the differences between classes. But by emphasizing differences between classes, such labels inevitably encourage us to forget about the much larger differences that exist *within* classes.

The illusion of class homogeneity does no harm in some contexts, but it encourages two kinds of logical error when we try to describe social change. First, whenever we observe an increase in behavior that has traditionally been correlated with membership in a particular class, we tend to assume that the class in question must be getting bigger. If more working-age men are jobless, we assume that the underclass must be getting bigger, without stopping to ask whether the men who have become jobless have other attributes that might make them part of the underclass. The second error is a mirror image of the first. Once we decide that a class is growing, we tend to assume that every form of behavior associated with membership in that class is becoming more common. Having concluded that the underclass is getting bigger, we assume that dropout rates, crime, and teenage parenthood must also be rising. The underlying logic here is that if one correlate of membership in the underclass is rising, all must be rising.

If we want to understand what is happening to those at the bottom of American society, we need to examine their problems one at a time, asking how each has changed and what has caused the change. Instead of assuming that the problems are closely linked to one another, we need to treat their interrelationships as a matter for empirical investigation. When we do that, the relationships are seldom as strong as class stereotypes lead us to expect. As a result, some problems can become more common while others become less so.

Exaggerating the correlations among social problems can have political costs as well. Portraying poverty, joblessness, illiteracy, violence, unwed motherhood, and drug abuse as symptoms of a larger metaproblem, such as the underclass, encourages people to look for metasolutions.

We are frequently told, for example, that piecemeal reform is pointless and that we need a comprehensive approach to the problems of the underclass. Some even believe we need a revolutionary change, although revolutions are so out of favor at the moment that few favor them publicly.

Our most pressing need, it seems to me, is for schools, employers, police forces, churches, health maintenance organizations, and welfare offices that can deal with poor people's problems in more realistic ways— ways that build on people's strengths without ignoring their weaknesses. Changes of this kind require an immense amount of trial and error. Unfortunately, America has never been very good at learning from its mistakes. Instead of looking for ways of improving our institutions, we tend to blame some politician for every failure and look for a replacement. Politicians therefore become specialists in avoiding blame, not in solving problems. This may be unavoidable in a large, diverse society. But if we cannot manage piecemeal reforms, looking for metasolutions is almost certain to be time wasted so far as the American underclass is concerned. If we want to reduce poverty, joblessness, illiteracy, violence, or despair, we will surely need to change our institutions and attitudes in hundreds of small ways, not in one big way.

2. *Exclusion of the Poor*

THOMAS ROSS, THE RHETORIC OF POVERTY: THEIR IMMORALITY, OUR HELPLESSNESS

79 Georgetown L.J. 1499, 1499–1515, 1539–46 (1991).

I. INTRODUCTION

Poor people are different from us. Most of them are morally weak and undeserving. And, in any event, we are helpless to solve the complex and daunting problem of poverty. This is the rhetoric of poverty.

The United States Supreme Court has addressed the constitutional claims of poor people in a range of contemporary cases. The rhetoric of poverty runs through these opinions. Poor people, it is said or implied, are unwilling to work and especially likely to commit fraud or child abuse, or to violate other legal and moral norms. They have bad attitudes and are the cause of their own poverty. At the same time, the problem of poverty is, in the Court's rhetoric, a problem of daunting complexity that is virtually beyond solution. Hard choices, suffering, even "Kafkaesque" results are simply unavoidable.

The purposes of this article are to reveal the presence of these rhetorical themes in the Supreme Court's opinions and to argue that the Court's choices are disturbing. These themes, seen in the context of the individual cases, are either shamefully inapt or, at the very least, problematic. When we see that the Court's decisions are shored up by this rhetorical structure, we have good reason to question those decisions.

The first rhetorical step, the creation of the abstraction the "poor," is an easily overlooked yet powerful part of the rhetoric of poverty. We are so used to speaking of the poor as a distinct class that we overlook the rhetorical significance of speaking this way. By focusing on the single variable of economic wealth and then drawing a line on the wealth continuum, we create a class of people who are them, not us. Creating this abstraction is, in one sense, merely a way of speaking. We do this because to speak of the world in sensible ways we must resort to categories and abstractions. There are meaningful differences between the circumstances of people below the poverty line and the circumstances of middle class people, and to ignore these real differences can lead to injustice. Thus, to speak of the "poor" is a sensible way to talk. In the rhetorical context, however, it is also much more.

The creation of the category of the "poor", also makes possible the assertion of their moral weakness. To assert their moral weakness, "they" must exist as a conceptually distinct group. There is a long history of speaking of the poor as morally weak, or even degenerate. Thus, when we hear legal rhetoric about the poor, we often hear an underlying message of deviance: we are normal, they are deviant. Our feelings about their deviance range from empathy to violent hatred. Still, even in the most benevolent view, they are not normal. Their deviance is a product of a single aspect of their lives, their relative wealth position. All other aspects of their lives are either distorted by the label of deviance or ignored. By creating this class of people, we are able at once to distinguish us from them and to appropriate normalcy to our lives and circumstances.

The rhetorical assertion of judicial helplessness is also connected to widely shared and long-standing cultural assumptions about the nature of poverty. This rhetoric depends on the assumption that poverty is somehow built into the basic structure of our society and system of law. We assume that the eradication of poverty, even if possible in theory, would require the radical transformation of our society. The causes of poverty, we assume, are a product of a complex set of factors tied to politics, culture, history, psychology, and philosophy. Thus, only in a radically different world might poverty cease to exist. And, whatever the extent of the powers of the Court, radically remaking the world is not one of them.

The dual themes of moral deviance and judicial helplessness at first seem to be inconsistent. The premise of moral weakness suggests that the problem is really quite simple. If poor people simply chose to "straighten up and fly right," all would be well. If they would accept and commit to the moral norms of those of us not in poverty, they would cease to be poor, albeit only after a long time and much hard work. In this vision of poverty, the problem is uni-dimensional and is intractable only to the extent that poor people resist the personal, individual reform of their moral lives. The judicial helplessness theme depends, on the other hand, on the complexity of the problem and on the existence of multiple, intertwined causes. Despite this apparent inconsistency, the Justices-rhetoricians use both themes, often in tandem, throughout their opinions.

This apparent inconsistency in the Court's rhetoric of poverty may be related to yet another enduring cultural assumption, the division of the poor into classes of the deserving and the undeserving poor. These classes have been drawn somewhat differently throughout history. The contemporary division of the poor distinguishes between able-bodied adults and the children, the aged, and the disabled. This distinction is premised on the ability of the former class to perform work. For this able-bodied class, the moral weakness rhetoric is especially potent—I work, they don't, they could. This argument does not fit members of the second group because we assume that work is not readily available to them. For this class, the judicial helplessness plea is the perfect response. The rhetoric of helplessness allows the expression of sympathy for the deserving poor while avoiding the burden of intervention.

The dual rhetoric of moral weakness and judicial helplessness fits the needs of a Court that has chosen to minimize the constitutional basis for intervention on behalf of the poor. Under this rhetoric, either the poor do not deserve our intervention or, if they do have a claim to our sense of justice, we are functionally helpless to do justice. . . .

II.   THE RHETORIC OF POVERTY

Rhetoric is built from the cultural assumptions and attitudes available to its creator. The contemporary legal rhetoric of poverty is built on premises that have both a validity in the contemporary culture and a history of their own. The premise of the moral weakness of the poor has been around in various forms throughout our history. Likewise, the argument that we are all helpless to change the harsh reality of the poor has a long lineage in American public discourse. And the particular argument of judicial helplessness has served as the rhetorical linchpin for important legal issues throughout our history. To understand the nature and power of the contemporary legal rhetoric of poverty requires some understanding of the history and cultural standing of its basic premises.

A.   The Immorality of the Poor

The separation and stigmatization of people in poverty is not new. In various manifestations, it has been a constant feature of our culture. In fact, the cultural separation and stigmatization of the poor has been a feature of most Western cultures throughout modern history. In one fashion or another the poor have always been separated by class distinctions and labels. They have been labeled ''paupers,'' ''peasants,'' and ''strangers.'' They have been cast as different, deviant, and morally weak. These assumptions make coherent the physical separation of the poor from the affluent.

Just as the separation and stigmatization of the poor is a recurring cultural assumption, the intensified suffering of those in poverty in times of natural or man-made disaster has been a recurring societal reality. During the great plagues of Europe, for example, the poor were left in what became ghettos of disease and death while the affluent left for enclaves outside the cities. As a result, the plagues took the lives of a much larger percentage of the poor. Famine, wars, and natural disasters have followed a similar pattern, with the burdens falling disproportionately on the poor. The cultural assumptions and the societal realities cannot be disconnected. The assumptions make the disproportionate suffering coherent.

The particular assumptions made about the poor have varied greatly across cultures and time. Still, the recurrent expression of their immorality in world history makes this assumption one that cannot be easily sloughed off by those who live today. We would like to think that our assumptions about poor people are not anything like the assumptions of our European ancestors who walled the poor into plague-ridden urban ghettos. Yet, throughout this country's history the poor have been distinguished from those not in poverty and have been, in one fashion or another, the subject of moral censure.

In eighteenth century America, laws typically imposed some responsibility on communities to assist poor members. Poor people found within the boundaries of the community who were not members of the community were forced to leave. Communities expended many resources shunting poor people out and resisting the claims of the outsiders.

Many American communities in the late eighteenth and early nineteenth centuries concluded that even the burden of providing assistance to members of the community had become too great. The problem, they concluded, was the able-bodied, and hence undeserving, recipient of public assistance. The solution was to purge undeserving poor from the system of public assistance. To do so required that the community make a distinction that to this day remains etched in our cultural and legal conceptions of poverty—the distinction between the deserving and the undeserving poor. The distinction created a line running through the poor, putting the aged, infant, and disabled on one side of the line, and the able-bodied on the other side.

In the nineteenth century the label for the able-bodied poor was "paupers." The Reverend Charles Burroughs, preaching at the opening of a chapel in a New Hampshire poorhouse in 1834, spoke of the distinction between "poverty" and "pauperism:"

> In speaking of poverty, let us never forget that there is a distinction
> between this and pauperism. The former is an unavoidable evil....
> It is the result, not of our faults, but of our misfortunes....
> Pauperism is the consequence of wilful error, of shameful indolence,
> of vicious habits. It is a misery of human creation, the pernicious

work of man, the lamentable consequence of bad principles and morals.

This moral censure of the able-bodied recipient of public assistance has never left us.

The Depression, as with all great social dislocations, changed somewhat the way we thought about things. The commonly held assumptions regarding the able-bodied man, unemployed and poor, were obviously affected by the experience of the Depression. Nonetheless, the social stigma attached to the receipt of public assistance remained. Even during times of catastrophic levels of unemployment, we could not shake the idea that there was something wrong about an able-bodied man receiving public assistance.

A special and enduring legacy of the Depression and the New Deal was yet another line drawn through the ranks of the poor—the distinction between those receiving "public assistance" and "social insurance." Social insurance, exemplified by the Social Security benefit programs for the aged and the disabled, was thought of as a form of insurance against the "natural" events that impose financial hardships on all of us. People who were merely poor, on the other hand, depended instead on "public assistance." This distinction ignored the fortuities that might have forced the poor person into her current status, and did not bother with the fact that the benefits paid out to the aged and the disabled under Social Security may exceed the value of the private contributions made. These new categories served to underscore the undeserved quality of the benefits extended to recipients of public assistance.

Societal line drawing and moral censure took a brief detour in the 1960s. The "War on Poverty" was the product of a period of unrelenting growth in the gross national product and unbounded optimism about society's ability to abolish poverty without any real sacrifice. During this time, people spoke of the cruel error of assuming a correlation between poverty and moral weakness. As more Americans focused on the eradication of poverty, there was less interest in separating and stigmatizing the poor. Yet, as the "War on Poverty" came unraveled in the wash of blood, here and in Southeast Asia, and as people came to see the actual sacrifice entailed in eliminating poverty, the public discourse soon drifted back to the theme of moral weakness.

The rhetoric of poverty in the 1980s was exemplified by the myth of the welfare mother with a Cadillac and by the rise of yet another category of the poor, the "underclass." This new category of the poor included:

(a) the *passive poor,* usually long-term welfare recipients; (b) the *hostile* street criminals who terrorize most cities, and who are often school drop-outs and drug addicts; (c) the *hustlers,* who, like street criminals, may not be poor and who earn their livelihood in an underground economy, but rarely commit violent crimes; (d) the *traumatized* drunks, drifters, homeless shopping-bag ladies and released mental patients who frequently roam or collapse on city streets.

Membership in the underclass was determined by behavior which was either patently immoral or socially deviant. The concept of the underclass etched deeper the division between us and them. It also connected perfectly with the rhetorical theme of moral weakness. Except for some examples of the "traumatized" members of the underclass, the behavior that characterized the underclass was criminal, deviant, or that of a person without hope or dignity. The idea of the "passive" poor, people beyond hope and without any sense of initiative, expressed the pervasive notion that poor people were unwilling to pull themselves up by their bootstraps and were instead happy to feed at the public trough.

The "underclass" thus was a late twentieth century form of the historically persistent category, the undeserving poor. And like its historical antecedents, the idea of the "underclass" seemed to be driven more by ideology than by any attempt accurately to generalize about the circumstances and nature of poverty in America. Michael Katz contrasted the idea of the underclass and the reality:

> [A]s a metaphor, the underclass obscures more than it reveals. It glosses over differences in condition that require varied forms of help, and it passes lightly over two salient features of poverty and welfare in America: their widespread and transient character. In the Michigan study, which followed a large sample of American families for 10 years, ... [b]oth poverty and welfare use ... lasted relatively briefly, and children whose parents relied on welfare were no more likely to need public assistance as adults than were others in the sample. What the study shows, in short, is that poverty is more accurately perceived now, as before in American history, as a point on a continuum rather than a sharp, clearly demarcated category of social experience. In truth, the forces that push individuals and families into poverty originate in the structure of America's political economy. Some of us are lucky, not different.

As a metaphor, the underclass is the perfect expression of the rhetorical themes of difference and deviance. Perhaps because it so perfectly expresses these persistent historical themes, it has remained as part of the public discourse on poverty notwithstanding its metaphoric and distorting quality.

The precise content of the commonly held assumptions about the poor has changed throughout American history. The idea of the nineteenth century "pauper" is different from the idea of the late twentieth century "underclass." Still, the basic premises of the rhetoric of poverty run through history, drawing lines between groups of people and labeling categories as deviant and undeserving. There has always been an "us/them" conception of people in poverty. We have always found ways to make their suffering intellectually coherent.

B. Our Helplessness

The other central theme of the rhetoric of poverty is helplessness. This theme is expressed in two related ways. First, poverty is said to be an inescapable societal tragedy that we are helpless to remedy. Second, in the legal rhetoric of poverty, judges profess to be helpless in their judicial role. Their helplessness places the particular legal problems related to poverty beyond the perimeters of their power and jurisdiction. Using this rhetoric of helplessness, judges sometimes concede that the problem of poverty may be capable of solution, and then assert that they, however, are not empowered to solve it. They identify someone else, typically the legislature, as the body empowered to address the problem.

In cases dealing with poverty, the rhetoric of judicial helplessness sometimes incorporates the idea that poverty is an intractable, if not inevitable, social problem. In this sense of helplessness, the judges are helpless both as individuals (poverty is a complex and intractable problem) and as judges (in any event, we are without the power to deal with this particular issue relating to poverty). This sense of helplessness of both judges and the public in the face of poverty has a history that accounts in part for its contemporary presence and rhetorical power.

1. The Helplessness of Those Not in Poverty

The idea that poverty in America is inherent or practically irremediable is commonly held today. Expressions like "there have always been poor people; there always will be poor people" are abundant in our discourse. We bemoan the complex and intractable nature of the problem.

Observers often interweave the premise of moral weakness with the argument for the intractable nature of poverty. After all, if poverty is essentially a problem of moral weakness, if poor people must undergo a personal transformation, what can we do to effect such a change? Historically, we have often encouraged such a change on the part of the poor by making the conditions of poverty so appalling that we imagine poor people will do whatever it takes to avoid them. We are disappointed when so many poor people seem to insist on not mending their ways and, to our surprise, seem willing to go on living in the horrific conditions of poverty. This disappointment feeds the argument of helplessness. If poor people are unwilling to change their behavior and values in response to the strongest of incentives, the horror of life in poverty, what else can we do?

Another version of the argument for helplessness is the characterization of poverty as a product of a mix of abstract forces and ideas, beyond our practical control. Poverty is built into the basic structure of our society, it is a product of our history, traditions, philosophies, political structures, and economic structures. Observers who espouse this view of the origins of poverty either see no realistic solution or else see a solution that entails the loss of our most basic social structures.

This particular profession of helplessness is problematic because poverty arises out of the "politics of distribution." Poverty is not a matter of scarcity. We have more than enough to meet the basic needs of everyone in our society, yet we continue to speak about poverty as though it were a problem beyond the reach of our material resources. Perhaps the persistence of poverty leads to the idea that it is inherent in the structure of our society. But all that has ever been required to eliminate poverty is a redistribution of wealth. Although the complex mix of history, traditions, and political structures may help to explain why Americans have chosen not to abolish poverty, it does not explain how that choice is a product of helplessness.

2. *The Helplessness of Judges*

There is another version of the argument for helplessness that exists in the legal rhetoric of poverty. It is the special plea of judicial helplessness. This argument asserts that judges do not possess the power to act. It is the most powerful form of legal rhetoric. When a court acts, the judge's argument is about the wisdom and coherence of the action taken. This form of argument invites the reader's consideration and acceptance. The argument of judicial helplessness, on the other hand, purports to shut off the debate. The court has no power to act; therefore, considerations of the wisdom and utility of the actions that might have been taken are beside the point. Normative debate is not invited.

The falsity of this argument is found in the "irony of jurisdiction." The extent of the court's power is determined by the court. In a governmental structure premised on multiple sources of power, each source must have some limits, and someone must draw the boundaries. In our federal system, the Supreme Court defines the limits of power of each branch of government. The Court sometimes chooses wisely and sometimes tragically, but the choices are always made. Thus, judges are rendered helpless by their own choice....

III. THE CONTEMPORARY LEGAL RHETORIC OF POVERTY

Legal rhetoric embodies dominant cultural assumptions. When judges construct their arguments, they must depend on assumptions widely shared by their audience. Judges depend on these assumptions both because they give their arguments power and the potential for influence, and because the judges, as members of the culture, are likely to believe them. For example, during the nineteenth century, when the dominant and explicit cultural assumption was that blacks were inferior, the legal rhetoric was explicitly racist in its premises both because arguments built on racist premises had the potential for influence, and because the judges typically believed the premise of racism. Similarly, because the dominant nineteenth century cultural assumption was that the poor were morally degenerate, the premise of moral degeneracy of poor people was part of the legal rhetoric of the period.

The embodiment of cultural assumptions in legal rhetoric occurs in two ways: judges state the assumptions explicitly, and they implicitly incorporate the assumptions by making arguments that invite the reader to supply them. For example, Justice Henry Brown, writing for the majority in *Plessy v. Ferguson,* utilized explicit and implicit assumptions of racism. On an explicit level, in an effort to justify the court's conclusion that de jure racial segregation was constitutional, Brown spoke unselfconsciously of "the reputation of belonging to the dominant race" as the "property" of the white man. He also implicitly invited his reader to supply the assumption of racism when he conjured up the specter of the "enforced commingling of the two races."

Discerning legal rhetoric's "invitation" to the reader is difficult. Each act of reading a judicial opinion brings an individual reader in a particular setting to the text. The meaning each person takes from the opinion is partly individual in nature, a product of her own experiences and purposes. The meaning is also a product of the cultural influences that affect each person's reading of the opinion. The nineteenth century reader of Brown's *Plessy* opinion brought the pervasive cultural assumption of the racial inferiority of African Americans to the opinion. Some nineteenth century readers consciously rejected this assumption. Yet, many more either consciously accepted the premise or assimilated it on some unconscious level. Thus, for most nineteenth century readers, Brown's invocation of "enforced commingling" was a disturbing specter. The readers were disturbed without the need for an explicit reminder of why living together with African Americans would be disturbing. The culture had taught the lesson so well that there was no need to say it out loud.

Our legal rhetoric is littered with similar examples of the explicit and implicit invocation of the assumptions of the rhetoric of poverty.... The cultural stereotype of the female-headed household receiving public assistance has evolved from the image of the white widow to the image of the black welfare mother. The rediscovery of those in poverty and the short-lived War on Poverty affected an entire generation's assumptions about the poor. Today, our cultural attitudes about those in poverty are complex and varied. Still, the idea that poor people are different and morally weak persists, in one form or another, for most contemporary Americans....

IV. The Power of Rhetoric—The Responsibility of the Reader

The contemporary Court, in a range of cases dealing with the rights and interests of the poor, has adopted a non-interventionist approach. The Court has left the law's treatment of people in poverty largely to the political processes, acknowledging only the narrowest constitutional grounds for addressing their interests. The Justices have put forth opinions abundant with both explicit and, more often, implicit assumptions of the difference and moral weakness of the poor. Repeatedly, the Justices have stressed their own helplessness to correct the problems of poverty.

This pattern of choice and rhetoric provides a structure for understanding the power of rhetoric. Out of an understanding of the nature of the rhetoric of poverty emerges a responsibility, an ethic, incumbent on the reader. As we read the Court's opinions embodying the rhetoric of poverty we are engaged in an activity with moral connotations. Once we have read the opinions, there is no morally neutral position available—we must act as critics. Here, even silence is a morally charged position. We, as readers, have a responsibility to resist the rhetorician's magic and to see the subject of our inquiry as clearly and fully as possible....

A.   The Power of Rhetoric

The analysis of judicial rhetoric is an exploration of the human activity of reading. This activity is at once both simple to describe and difficult to understand. How the reader derives meaning from text is hard to say, and how that meaning influences the reader in her understanding of the constitutional issues of poverty is unclear.

Surely, many who read the judicial rhetoric of poverty are influenced by it. Although rhetoric rarely changes the reader's mind, it often subtly influences people by either creating doubt or strengthening resolve. When the Justices repeat the argument of judicial helplessness in case after case, the reader may begin to wonder whether there truly is any choice in the matter. When the reader is repeatedly confronted with the conceptual segregation of the poor, she is more likely to accept some version of the us/them idea embedded in this rhetoric. Our own experiences of reading judicial rhetoric tell us that these sorts of effects do occur. What we need to understand is *how* this happens to us.

1.   Conceptual Segregation and Moral Weakness

The Court's rhetoric of poverty has conceptually segregated the poor in various ways. When Justice Stewart, in *Dandridge,* demanded an "equitable balance" between the "families on welfare and those supported by an employed breadwinner," he conceptually separated those families in poverty and receiving public assistance from other families. In his validation of the Texas AFDC scheme in *Jefferson,* Justice Rehnquist separated AFDC recipients into the undeserving, able-bodied poor, and the deserving, disabled and aged poor. Running through the cases ... particularly those dealing with disability benefits and food stamps, is the specter of fraud, which in turn depends on the segregation of recipients of public assistance into a group especially likely to deceive.

The very act of conceptual segregation has rhetorical power. When the members of the segregated group are defined by their difference from those in a dominant position in society, the very act of segregation suggests not simply difference but also deviance. The norm is defined by the dominant group; the segregated group is defined by deviance from that norm. The power of this segregation is vividly revealed in the rhetoric of poverty....

In its assertion or suggestion of the difference and deviance of the poor, the rhetoric of poverty is both revealing and obscuring. The rhetoric reveals the reality of criminal and immoral behavior among the poor. The rich are not the only ones who defraud the government and abuse their children. At the same time, the rhetoric of poverty obscures the aspects of poverty that reflect our own lives. The lives of the poor have always mirrored the lives of the rest of society. Many of us struggle to raise children and to find and do work. We all feel humiliation and have aspirations. We all face desperate moral choices of one sort or another; we all succumb to temptation or despair at one time or another; we all, at the end, have good reason to question the strength of our individual will.

The Court's arguments in the poverty cases are much more than rhetorical forms. They are a lens through which we see poverty. Once we accept the rhetoric's depiction of poverty, we are done, the answer to the legal issue is ordained. For example, if we see the AFDC mother as different, prone to child abuse, and an ungrateful recipient of public largesse, the legal issue of whether the government can demand home visits to protect the welfare of the child as a condition of that largesse seems easily answered. By contrast, if we see Mrs. James as like us, a mother struggling to hold her family together and keep a sense of personal dignity through it all, the legal issue becomes more problematic.

The rhetoric of poverty invites the reader to provide a part of the picture, to bring to the reading culturally taught, stereotypical assumptions about the poor. This invitation is the most powerful aspect of the rhetoric...

Some readers will resist the vision of poverty suggested by the rhetoric, and no individual reader will follow exactly the path suggested above. The assumptions and experiences of the individual, the purpose and context of the reading, and other variables will affect the nature of any particular reading of these opinions. Still, for all readers drawn from a culture that teaches the difference and deviance of the poor, the assertion or suggestion of those cultural themes is not simply and easily ignored. Thus, the judicial rhetoric of poverty draws power from the explicit and implicit depiction of poverty. In the hands of the most skillful of the Court's rhetoricians, it is used to craft a picture that, if accepted, leaves the reader with no other choice but the Court's.

The rhetoric of poverty also works in a more general way to influence our understanding of the poor. The experience of reading this rhetoric may diminish the possibility for empathy. So long as we think of those in poverty as "them" and not "us," we are less likely to share in their pain and humiliation. We can imagine that they do not suffer as we would, or that their suffering, unlike ours, is inevitable or even deserved.

Our inability to imagine the poor as strong, successful, ambitious, and responsible people who win the battles of life prevents us from feeling empathy for them. The persistent idea of the "passive poor" in the "underclass" keeps blocking our imagination. Yet, the story of people in poverty in this country has been a story of strength and success. Against all odds, facing social stigma and working through maddening systems of public assistance, the poor have survived. Many poor women and men have kept their families together and maintained safe and decent lives in the midst of conditions that would seem to make family disintegration inescapable. The rhetoric of poverty highlights only the stories of failure and obscures the stories of success.

2. *Helplessness*

The contemporary Court's rhetoric of helplessness seeks to move the reader to a position beyond choice. The problem of poverty is presented either as a matter of personal transformation for which we cannot be responsible, or as a matter of such daunting complexity that we cannot solve it . . . .

This profession of helplessness in the rhetoric of poverty is both revealing and obscuring. The "personal transformation" argument reveals the problem of individual responsibility in the matter of poverty. Some people do remain poor, in part, because they lack the will to change. The "too many forces" argument reveals the power of history and tradition. When generations of Americans have grown up with poverty as an enduring feature of the cultural landscape, the assumption that poverty is built into our society becomes difficult to change . . . .

The argument for judicial helplessness does not rely on the assumption that the problem of poverty is intractable. Although the assertion of the complexity and intractability of poverty is typically woven into the Court's rhetoric, the plea of judicial helplessness requires only the assertion that the Court is not the proper institution to act.

The plea of judicial helplessness is an especially strong rhetorical move because it eliminates the question of the wisdom or justice of the outcome. It diverts the reader's attention to the abstract issues of separation of powers and the appropriate role of the judiciary, and obscures the inescapable element of choice. The plea of judicial helplessness directs the debate toward the bloodless ground of the separation of powers doctrine and away from the particular suffering of those who inhabit the Kafkaesque world of contemporary poverty . . . .

B. *The Responsibility of the Reader*

When we read an opinion dealing with the constitutional status of poverty we are engaged in an activity with moral connotations. After reading the opinion, no morally neutral position is available to us. If we speak about the case, we take on the role and responsibility of the critic. The discourse of the critic is the discourse of normative analysis. In one way or another, we speak of what ought to be. Our membership within the community of law makes even silence a morally charged position . . . .

What, then, is the ethic of reader responsibility? It is to read with the largest measure of care, imagination, and knowledge we can muster. We should recognize the nature and consequences of the choices set forth in the text. We should seek to listen to the arguments of the text, yet break past the confines of those arguments, using our imagination and our knowledge of the world in which these decisions will be played out. We must become the most skillful readers we can be, because the process of reading is always followed by the necessity of our own choice in the matter....

... We bring to the reading some idea of poverty. The rhetoric not only seeks to reveal and obscure, it also invites. The reader is invited to supply cultural stereotypes of poverty. It is as though the reader is looking through an etched glass at a night sky that she in part creates by the process of looking. Thus, the reader must not merely see the pieces obscured by the Court's rhetoric, she must realize also that what she sees is in part shaped by the assumptions she brings to the reading. If, for example, she brings the assumption of the moral weakness of the poor to the reading, she must struggle to see that assumption in her reading. She must struggle to bring that assumption out of the murky place of the unstated and assumed into the light of the explicit assertion, where she can judge its truth for herself....

SAN ANTONIO INDEPENDENT SCHOOL DISTRICT v. RODRIGUEZ

Supreme Court of the United States, 1973.
411 U.S. 1, 93 S.Ct. 1278, 36 L.Ed.2d 16.

MR. JUSTICE POWELL delivered the opinion of the Court.

This suit attacking the Texas system of financing public education was initiated by Mexican–American parents whose children attend the elementary and secondary schools in the Edgewood Independent School District, an urban school district in San Antonio, Texas. They brought a class action on behalf of schoolchildren throughout the State who are members of minority groups or who are poor and reside in school districts having a low property tax base....

The school district in which appellees reside, the Edgewood Independent School District, has been compared throughout this litigation with the Alamo Heights Independent School District. This comparison between the least and most affluent districts in the San Antonio area serves to illustrate the manner in which the dual system of finance operates and to indicate the extent to which substantial disparities exist despite the State's impressive progress in recent years. Edgewood is one of seven public school districts in the metropolitan area. Approximately 22,000 students are enrolled in its 25 elementary and secondary schools. The district is situated in the core-city sector of San Antonio in a residential neighborhood that has little commercial or industrial property. The residents are predominantly of Mexican–American descent: approximately 90% of the student population is Mexican–American and over 6% is Negro. The average assessed property value per pupil is $5,960—the lowest in the metropolitan area—and the median family income ($4,686) is also the lowest. At an equalized tax rate of $1.05 per $100 of assessed property—the highest in the metropolitan area—the district contributed $26 to the education of each child for the 1967–1968 school year above its Local Fund Assignment for the Minimum Foundation Program. The Foundation Program contributed $222 per pupil for a state-local total of $248. Federal funds added another $108 for a total of $356 per pupil.

Alamo Heights is the most affluent school district in San Antonio. Its six schools, housing approximately 5,000 students, are situated in a residential community quite unlike the Edgewood District. The school population is predominantly "Anglo," having only 18% Mexican–Americans and less than 1% Negroes. The assessed property value per pupil exceeds $49,000, and the median family income is $8,001. In 1967–1968 the local tax rate of $.85 per $100 of valuation yielded $333 per pupil over and above its contribution to the Foundation Program. Coupled with the $225 provided from that Program, the district was able to supply $558 per student. Supplemented by a $36 per-pupil grant from federal sources, Alamo Heights spent $594 per pupil. . . .

. . . [S]ubstantial interdistrict disparities in school expenditures found by the District Court to prevail in San Antonio and in varying degrees throughout the State still exist. And it was these disparities, largely attributable to differences in the amounts of money collected through local property taxation, that led the District Court to conclude that Texas' dual system of public school financing violated the Equal Protection Clause. The District Court held that the Texas system discriminates on the basis of wealth in the manner in which education is provided for its people. Finding that wealth is a "suspect" classification and that education is a "fundamental" interest, the District Court held that the Texas system could be sustained only if the State could show that it was premised upon some compelling state interest. On this issue the court concluded that "[n]ot only are defendants unable to demonstrate compelling state interests . . . they fail even to establish a reasonable basis for these classifications." . . .

II

The District Court's opinion does not reflect the novelty and complexity of the constitutional questions posed by appellees' challenge to Texas' system of school financing. In concluding that strict judicial scrutiny was required, that court relied on decisions dealing with the rights of indigents to equal treatment in the criminal trial and appellate processes, and on cases disapproving wealth restrictions on the right to vote. Those cases, the District Court concluded, established wealth as a suspect classification. Finding that the local property tax system discriminated on the basis of wealth, it regarded those precedents as controlling. It then reasoned, based on decisions of this Court affirming the undeniable importance of education, that there is a fundamental right to education and that, absent some compelling state justification, the Texas system could not stand.

We are unable to agree that this case, which in significant aspects is *sui generis,* may be so neatly fitted into the conventional mosaic of constitutional analysis under the Equal Protection Clause. Indeed, for the several reasons that follow, we find neither the suspect-classification nor the fundamental-interest analysis persuasive.

A

The wealth discrimination discovered by the District Court in this case, and by several other courts that have recently struck down school-financing laws in other States, is quite unlike any of the forms of wealth discrimination heretofore reviewed by this Court. Rather than focusing on the unique features of the alleged discrimination, the courts in these cases have virtually assumed their findings of a suspect classification through a simplistic process of analysis: since, under the traditional systems of financing public schools, some poorer people receive less expensive educations than other more affluent people, these systems discriminate on the basis of wealth. This approach largely ignores the hard threshold questions, including whether it makes a difference for purposes of consideration under the Constitution that the class of disadvantaged "poor" cannot be identified or defined in customary equal protection terms, and whether the relative—rather than absolute—nature of the asserted deprivation is of significant consequence. Before a State's laws and the justifications for the classifications they create are subjected to strict judicial scrutiny, we think these threshold considerations must be analyzed more closely than they were in the court below.

The case comes to us with no definitive description of the classifying facts or delineation of the disfavored class. Examination of the District Court's opinion and of appellees' complaint, briefs, and contentions at oral argument suggests, however, at least three ways in which the discrimination claimed here might be described. The Texas system of school financing might be regarded as discriminating (1) against "poor" persons whose incomes fall below some identifiable level of poverty or who might be characterized as functionally "indigent," or (2) against those who are relatively poorer than others, or (3) against all those who, irrespective of their personal incomes, happen to reside in relatively poorer school districts. Our task must be to ascertain whether, in fact, the Texas system has been shown to discriminate on any of these possible bases and, if so, whether the resulting classification may be regarded as suspect.

The precedents of this Court provide the proper starting point. The individuals, or groups of individuals, who constituted the class discriminated against in our prior cases shared two distinguishing characteristics: because of their impecunity they were completely unable to pay for some desired benefit, and as a consequence, they sustained an absolute deprivation of a meaningful opportunity to enjoy that benefit. . . .

Only appellees' first possible basis for describing the class disadvantaged by the Texas school-financing system—discrimination against a class of definably "poor" persons—might arguably meet the criteria established in these prior cases. Even a cursory examination, however, demonstrates that neither of the two distinguishing characteristics of wealth classifications can be found here. First, in support of their charge that the system discriminates against the "poor," appellees have made no effort to demonstrate that it operates to the peculiar disadvantage of any class fairly definable as indigent, or as composed of persons whose incomes are beneath any designated poverty level. Indeed, there is reason to believe that the poorest families are not necessarily clustered in the poorest property districts. A recent and exhaustive study of school districts in Connecticut concluded that ... the poor were clustered around commercial and industrial areas—those same areas that provide the most attractive sources of property tax income for school districts. Whether a similar pattern would be discovered in Texas is not known, but there is no basis on the record in this case for assuming that the poorest people—defined by reference to any level of absolute impecunity—are concentrated in the poorest districts.

Second, neither appellees nor the District Court addressed the fact that, unlike each of the foregoing cases, lack of personal resources has not occasioned an absolute deprivation of the desired benefit. The argument here is not that the children in districts having relatively low assessable property values are receiving no public education; rather, it is that they are receiving a poorer quality education than that available to children in districts having more assessable wealth. Apart from the unsettled and disputed question whether the quality of education may be determined by the amount of money expended for it, a sufficient answer to appellees' argument is that, at least where wealth is involved, the Equal Protection Clause does not require absolute equality or precisely equal advantages. Nor indeed, in view of the infinite variables affecting the educational process, can any system assure equal quality of education except in the most relative sense....

As suggested above, appellees and the District Court may have embraced a second or third approach, the second of which might be characterized as a theory of relative or comparative discrimination based on family income. Appellees sought to prove that a direct correlation exists between the wealth of families within each district and the expenditures therein for education. That is, along a continuum, the poorer the family the lower the dollar amount of education received by the family's children....

If, in fact, these correlations could be sustained, then it might be argued that expenditures on education—equated by appellees to the quality of education—are dependent on personal wealth. Appellees' comparative-discrimination theory would still face serious unanswered questions, including whether a bare positive correlation or some higher degree of correlation is necessary to provide a basis for concluding that the financing system is designed to operate to the peculiar disadvantage of the comparatively poor, and whether a class of this size and diversity could ever claim the special protection accorded "suspect" classes. These questions need not be addressed in this case, however, since appellees' proof fails to support their allegations or the District Court's conclusions....

... It is evident that, even if the conceptual questions were answered favorably to appellees, no factual basis exists upon which to found a claim of comparative wealth discrimination.

This brings us, then, to the third way in which the classification scheme might be defined—*district* wealth discrimination. Since the only correlation indicated by the evidence is between district property wealth and expenditures, it may be argued that discrimination might be found without regard to the individual income characteristics of district residents. Assuming a perfect correlation between district property wealth and expenditures from top to bottom, the disadvantaged class might be viewed as encompassing every child in every district except the district that has the most assessable wealth and spends the most on education. Alternatively, as suggested in Mr. Justice Marshall's dissenting opinion, the class might be defined more restrictively to include children in districts with assessable property which falls below the statewide average, or median, or below some other artificially defined level.

However described, it is clear that appellees' suit asks this Court to extend its most exacting scrutiny to review a system that allegedly discriminates against a large, diverse, and amorphous class, unified only by the common factor of residence in districts that happen to have less taxable wealth than other districts. The system of alleged discrimination and the class it defines have none of the traditional indicia of suspectness: the class is not saddled with such disabilities, or subjected to such a history of purposeful unequal treatment, or relegated to such a position of political powerlessness as to command extraordinary protection from the majoritarian political process.

We thus conclude that the Texas system does not operate to the peculiar disadvantage of any suspect class. But in recognition of the fact that this Court has never heretofore held that wealth discrimination alone provides an adequate basis for invoking strict scrutiny, appellees have not relied solely on this contention. They also assert that the State's system impermissibly interferes with the exercise of a "fundamental" right and that accordingly the prior decisions of this Court require the application of the strict standard of judicial review.... It is this question—whether education is a fundamental right, in the sense that it is among the rights and liberties protected by the Constitution—which has so consumed the attention of courts and commentators in recent years.

B

In Brown v. Board of Education, 347 U.S. 483 (1954), a unanimous Court recognized that "education is perhaps the most important function of state and local governments." What was said there in the context of racial discrimination has lost none of its vitality with the passage of time:

"Compulsory school attendance laws and the great expenditures for education both demonstrate our recognition of the importance of education to our democratic society. It is required in the performance of our most basic public responsibilities, even service in the armed forces. It is the very foundation of good citizenship. Today it is a principal instrument in awakening the child to cultural values, in preparing him for later professional training, and in helping him to adjust normally to his environment. In these days, it is doubtful that any child may reasonably be expected to succeed in life if he is denied the opportunity of an education. Such an opportunity, where the state has undertaken to provide it, is a right which must be made available to all on equal terms."

This theme, expressing an abiding respect for the vital role of education in a free society, may be found in numerous opinions of Justices of this Court writing both before and after *Brown* was decided.

Nothing this Court holds today in any way detracts from our historic dedication to public education. We are in complete agreement with the conclusion of the three-judge panel below that "the grave significance of education both to the individual and to our society" cannot be doubted. But the importance of a service performed by the State does not determine whether it must be regarded as fundamental for purposes of examination under the Equal Protection Clause....

The lesson of these cases in addressing the question now before the Court is plain. It is not the province of this Court to create substantive constitutional rights in the name of guaranteeing equal protection of the laws. Thus, the key to discovering whether education is "fundamental" is not to be found in comparisons of the relative societal significance of education as opposed to subsistence or housing. Nor is it to be found by weighing whether education is as important as the right to travel. Rather, the answer lies in assessing whether there is a right to education explicitly or implicitly guaranteed by the Constitution....

Education, of course, is not among the rights afforded explicit protection under our Federal Constitution. Nor do we find any basis for saying it is implicitly so protected. As we have said, the undisputed importance of education will not alone cause this Court to depart from the usual standard for reviewing a State's social and economic legislation. It is appellees' contention, however, that education is distinguishable from other services and benefits provided by the State because it bears a peculiarly close relationship to other rights and liberties accorded protection under the Constitution. Specifically, they insist that education is itself a fundamental personal right because it is essential to the effective exercise of First Amendment freedoms and to intelligent utilization of the right to vote. In asserting a nexus between speech and education, appellees urge that the right to speak is meaningless unless the speaker is capable of articulating his thoughts intelligently and persuasively. The "marketplace of ideas" is an empty forum for those lacking basic communicative tools. Likewise, they argue that the corollary right to receive information becomes little more than a hollow privilege when the recipient has not been taught to read, assimilate, and utilize available knowledge.

A similar line of reasoning is pursued with respect to the right to vote. Exercise of the franchise, it is contended, cannot be divorced from the educational foundation of the voter. The electoral process, if reality is to conform to the democratic ideal, depends on an informed electorate: a voter cannot cast his ballot intelligently unless his reading skills and thought processes have been adequately developed.

We need not dispute any of these propositions. The Court has long afforded zealous protection against unjustifiable governmental interference with the individual's rights to speak and to vote. Yet we have never presumed to possess either the ability or the authority to guarantee to the citizenry the most *effective* speech or the most *informed* electoral choice. That these may be desirable goals of a system of freedom of expression and of a representative form of government is not to be doubted. These are indeed goals to be pursued by a people whose thoughts and beliefs are freed from governmental interference. But they are not values to be implemented by judicial intrusion into otherwise legitimate state activities.

Even if it were conceded that some identifiable quantum of education is a constitutionally protected prerequisite to the meaningful exercise of either right, we have no indication that the present levels of educational expenditures in Texas provide an education that falls short. Whatever merit appellees' argument might have if a State's financing system occasioned an absolute denial of educational opportunities to any of its children, that argument provides no basis for finding an interference with fundamental rights where only relative differences in spending levels are involved and where—as is true in the present case—no charge fairly could be made that the system fails to provide each child with an opportunity to acquire the basic minimal skills necessary for the enjoyment of the rights of speech and of full participation in the political process.

Furthermore, the logical limitations on appellees' nexus theory are difficult to perceive. How, for instance, is education to be distinguished from the significant personal interests in the basics of decent food and shelter? Empirical examination might well buttress an assumption that the ill-fed, ill-clothed, and ill-housed are among the most ineffective participants in the political process, and that they derive the least enjoyment from the benefits of the First Amendment....

We have carefully considered each of the arguments supportive of the District Court's finding that education is a fundamental right or liberty and have found those arguments unpersuasive. In one further respect we find this a particularly inappropriate case in which to subject state action to strict judicial scrutiny. The present case, in another basic sense, is significantly different from any of the cases in which the Court has applied strict scrutiny to state or federal legislation touching upon constitutionally protected rights. Each of our prior cases involved legislation which "deprived," "infringed," or "interfered" with the free exercise of some such fundamental personal right or liberty. A critical distinction between those cases and the one now before us lies in what Texas is endeavoring to do with respect to education. . . .

. . . Every step leading to the establishment of the system Texas utilizes today—including the decisions permitting localities to tax and expend locally, and creating and continuously expanding the state aid— was implemented in an effort to *extend* public education and to improve its quality. Of course, every reform that benefits some more than others may be criticized for what it fails to accomplish. But we think it plain that, in substance, the thrust of the Texas system is affirmative and reformatory and, therefore, should be scrutinized under judicial principles sensitive to the nature of the State's efforts and to the rights reserved to the States under the Constitution.

C

It should be clear, for the reasons stated above and in accord with the prior decisions of this Court, that this is not a case in which the challenged state action must be subjected to the searching judicial scrutiny reserved for laws that create suspect classifications or impinge upon constitutionally protected rights.

We need not rest our decision, however, solely on the inappropriateness of the strict-scrutiny test. A century of Supreme Court adjudication under the Equal Protection Clause affirmatively supports the application of the traditional standard of review, which requires only that the State's system be shown to bear some rational relationship to legitimate state purposes. This case represents far more than a challenge to the manner in which Texas provides for the education of its children. We have here nothing less than a direct attack on the way in which Texas has chosen to raise and disburse state and local tax revenues. We are asked to condemn the State's judgment in conferring on political subdivisions the power to tax local property to supply revenues for local interests. In so doing, appellees would have the Court intrude in an area in which it has traditionally deferred to state legislatures. . . .

Thus, we stand on familiar grounds when we continue to acknowledge that the Justices of this Court lack both the expertise and the familiarity with local problems so necessary to the making of wise decisions with respect to the raising and disposition of public revenues. Yet, we are urged to direct the States either to alter drastically the present system or to throw out the property tax altogether in favor of some other form of taxation. No scheme of taxation, whether the tax is imposed on property, income, or purchases of goods and services, has yet been devised which is free of all discriminatory impact. In such a complex arena in which no perfect alternatives exist, the Court does well not to impose too rigorous a standard of scrutiny lest all local fiscal schemes become subjects of criticism under the Equal Protection Clause.

In addition to matters of fiscal policy, this case also involves the most persistent and difficult questions of educational policy, another area in which this Court's lack of specialized knowledge and experience counsels against premature interference with the informed judgments made at the state and local levels. Education, perhaps even more than welfare assistance, presents a myriad of "intractable economic, social, and even philosophical problems." The very complexity of the problems of financing and managing a statewide public school system suggests that "there will be more than one constitutionally permissible method of solving them," and that, within the limits of rationality, "the legislature's efforts to tackle the problems" should be entitled to respect. On even the most basic questions in this area the scholars and educational experts are divided. Indeed, one of the major sources of controversy concerns the extent to which there is a demonstrable correlation between educational expenditures and the quality of education—an assumed correlation underlying virtually every legal conclusion drawn by the District Court in this case. Related to the questioned relationship between cost and quality is the equally unsettled controversy as to the proper goals of a system of public education. And the question regarding the most effective relationship between state boards of education and local school boards, in terms of their respective responsibilities and degrees of control, is now undergoing searching re-examination. The ultimate wisdom as to these and related problems of education is not likely to be divined for all time even by the scholars who now so earnestly debate the issues. In such circumstances, the judiciary is well advised to refrain from imposing on the States inflexible constitutional restraints that could circumscribe or handicap the continued research and experimentation so vital to finding even partial solutions to educational problems and to keeping abreast of ever-changing conditions.

It must be remembered, also, that every claim arising under the Equal Protection Clause has implications for the relationship between national and state power under our federal system. Questions of federalism are always inherent in the process of determining whether a State's laws are to be accorded the traditional presumption of constitutionality, or are to be subjected instead to rigorous judicial scrutiny. While "[t]he maintenance of the principles of federalism is a foremost consideration in interpreting any of the pertinent constitutional provisions under which this Court examines state action," it would be difficult to imagine a case having a greater potential impact on our federal system than the one now before us, in which we are urged to abrogate systems of financing public education presently in existence in virtually every State.

The foregoing considerations buttress our conclusion that Texas' system of public school finance is an inappropriate candidate for strict judicial scrutiny. These same considerations are relevant to the determination whether that system, with its conceded imperfections, nevertheless bears some rational relationship to a legitimate state purpose. It is to this question that we next turn our attention.

III

... While assuring a basic education for every child in the State, [the Texas system] permits and encourages a large measure of participation in and control of each district's schools at the local level. In an era that has witnessed a consistent trend toward centralization of the functions of government, local sharing of responsibility for public education has survived. . . .

The persistence of attachment to government at the lowest level where education is concerned reflects the depth of commitment of its supporters. In part, local control means. . . . the freedom to devote more money to the education of one's children. Equally important, however, is the opportunity it offers for participation in the decisionmaking process that determines how those local tax dollars will be spent. Each locality is free to tailor local programs to local needs. Pluralism also affords some opportunity for experimentation, innovation, and a healthy competition for educational excellence. . . .

Appellees do not question the propriety of Texas' dedication to local control of education. To the contrary, they attack the school-financing system precisely because, in their view, it does not provide the same level of local control and fiscal flexibility in all districts. Appellees suggest that local control could be preserved and promoted under other financing systems that resulted in more equality in educational expenditures. While it is no doubt true that reliance on local property taxation for school revenues provides less freedom of choice with respect to expenditures for some districts than for others, the existence of "some inequality" in the manner in which the State's rationale is achieved is not alone a sufficient basis for striking down the entire system. It may not be condemned simply because it imperfectly effectuates the State's goals. Nor must the financing system fail because, as appellees suggest, other methods of satisfying the State's interest, which occasion "less drastic" disparities in expenditures, might be conceived. Only where state action impinges on the exercise of fundamental constitutional rights or liberties must it be found to have chosen the least restrictive alternative. It is also well to remember that even those districts that have reduced ability to make free decisions with respect to how much they spend on education still retain under the present system a large measure of authority as to how available funds will be allocated. They further enjoy the power to make numerous other decisions with respect to the operation of the schools. The people of Texas may be justified in believing that other systems of school financing, which place more of the financial responsibility in the hands of the State, will result in a comparable lessening of desired local autonomy. That is, they may believe that along with increased control of the purse strings at the state level will go increased control over local policies.

Appellees further urge that the Texas system is unconstitutionally arbitrary because it allows the availability of local taxable resources to turn on "happenstance." They see no justification for a system that allows, as they contend, the quality of education to fluctuate on the basis of the fortuitous positioning of the boundary lines of political subdivisions and the location of valuable commercial and industrial property. But any scheme of local taxation—indeed the very existence of identifiable local governmental units—require the establishment of jurisdictional boundaries that are inevitably arbitrary. It is equally inevitable that some localities are going to be blessed with more taxable assets than others. Nor is local wealth a static quantity. Changes in the level of taxable wealth within any district may result from any number of events, some of which local residents can and do influence. For instance, commercial and industrial enterprises may be encouraged to locate within a district by various actions—public and private.

Moreover, if local taxation for local expenditures were an unconstitutional method of providing for education then it might be an equally impermissible means of providing other necessary services customarily financed largely from local property taxes, including local police and fire protection, public health and hospitals, and public utility facilities of various kinds. We perceive no justification for such a severe denigration of local property taxation and control as would follow from appellees' contentions. It has simply never been within the constitutional prerogative of this Court to nullify statewide measures for financing public services merely because the burdens or benefits thereof fall unevenly depending upon the relative wealth of the political subdivisions in which citizens live....

MR. JUSTICE WHITE, with whom MR. JUSTICE DOUGLAS and MR. JUSTICE BRENNAN join, dissenting....

I cannot disagree with the proposition that local control and local decisionmaking play an important part in our democratic system of government. Much may be left to local option, and this case would be quite different if it were true that the Texas system, while insuring minimum educational expenditures in every district through state funding, extended a meaningful option to all local districts to increase their per-pupil expenditures and so to improve their children's education to the extent that increased funding would achieve that goal. The system would then arguably provide a rational and sensible method of achieving the stated aim of preserving an area for local initiative and decision.

The difficulty with the Texas system, however, is that it provides a meaningful option to Alamo Heights and like school districts but almost none to Edgewood and those other districts with a low per-pupil real estate tax base. In these latter districts, no matter how desirous parents are of supporting their schools with greater revenues, it is impossible to do so through the use of the real estate property tax. In these districts, the Texas system utterly fails to extend a realistic choice to parents because the property tax, which is the only revenue-raising mechanism extended to school districts, is practically and legally unavailable....

... If the State aims at maximizing local initiative and local choice, by permitting school districts to resort to the real property tax if they choose to do so, it utterly fails in achieving its purpose in districts with property tax bases so low that there is little if any opportunity for interested parents, rich or poor, to augment school district revenues. Requiring the State to establish only that unequal treatment is in furtherance of a permissible goal, without also requiring the State to show that the means chosen to effectuate that goal are rationally related to its achievement, makes equal protection analysis no more than an empty gesture. In my view, the parents and children in Edgewood, and in like districts, suffer from an invidious discrimination violative of the Equal Protection Clause.

This does not, of course, mean that local control may not be a legitimate goal of a school-financing system. Nor does it mean that the State must guarantee each district an equal per-pupil revenue from the state school-financing system. Nor does it mean, as the majority appears to believe, that, by affirming the decision below, this Court would be "imposing on the States inflexible constitutional restraints that could circumscribe or handicap the continued research and experimentation so vital to finding even partial solutions to educational problems and to keeping abreast of ever-changing conditions." On the contrary, it would merely mean that the State must fashion a financing scheme which provides a rational basis for the maximization of local control, if local control is to remain a goal of the system. . . .

Perhaps the majority believes that the major disparity in revenues provided and permitted by the Texas system is inconsequential. I cannot agree, however, that the difference of the magnitude appearing in this case can sensibly be ignored, particularly since the State itself considers it so important to provide opportunities to exceed the minimum state educational expenditures.

There is no difficulty in identifying the class that is subject to the alleged discrimination and that is entitled to the benefits of the Equal Protection Clause. I need go no farther than the parents and children in the Edgewood district, who are plaintiffs here and who assert that they are entitled to the same choice as Alamo Heights to augment local expenditures for schools but are denied that choice by state law. This group constitutes a class sufficiently definite to invoke the protection of the Constitution. . . . [W]e would blink reality to ignore the fact that school districts, and students in the end, are differentially affected by the Texas school-financing scheme with respect to their capability to supplement the Minimum Foundation School Program. At the very least, the law discriminates against those children and their parents who live in districts where the per-pupil tax base is sufficiently low to make impossible the provision of comparable school revenues by resort to the real property tax which is the only device the State extends for this purpose.

MR. JUSTICE MARSHALL, with whom MR. JUSTICE DOUGLAS concurs, dissenting. . . .

In my judgment, the right of every American to an equal start in life, so far as the provision of a state service as important as education is concerned, is far too vital to permit state discrimination on grounds as tenuous as those presented by this record. Nor can I accept the notion that it is sufficient to remit these appellees to the vagaries of the political process which, contrary to the majority's suggestion, has proved singularly unsuited to the task of providing a remedy for this discrimination. I, for one, am unsatisfied with the hope of an ultimate "political" solution sometime in the indefinite future while, in the meantime, countless children unjustifiably receive inferior educations that "may affect their hearts and minds in a way unlikely ever to be undone." ...

Funds to support public education in Texas are derived from three sources: local ad valorem property taxes; the Federal Government; and the state government. It is enlightening to consider these in order.

Under Texas law, the only mechanism provided the local school district for raising new, unencumbered revenues is the power to tax property located within its boundaries. At the same time, the Texas financing scheme effectively restricts the use of monies raised by local property taxation to the support of public education within the boundaries of the district in which they are raised, since any such taxes must be approved by a majority of the property-taxpaying voters of the district.

The significance of the local property tax element of the Texas financing scheme is apparent from the fact that it provides the funds to meet some 40% of the cost of public education for Texas as a whole. Yet the amount of revenue that any particular Texas district can raise is dependent on two factors—its tax rate and its amount of taxable property. The first factor is determined by the property-taxpaying voters of the district. But, regardless of the enthusiasm of the local voters for public education, the second factor—the taxable property wealth of the district—necessarily restricts the district's ability to raise funds to support public education. Thus, even though the voters of two Texas districts may be willing to make the same tax effort, the results for the districts will be substantially different if one is property rich while the other is property poor. The necessary effect of the Texas local property tax is, in short, to favor property-rich districts and to disfavor property-poor ones....

The appellants do not deny the disparities in educational funding caused by variations in taxable district property wealth. They do contend, however, that whatever the differences in per-pupil spending among Texas districts, there are no discriminatory consequences for the children of the disadvantaged districts. They recognize that what is at stake in this case is the quality of the public education provided Texas children in the districts in which they live. But appellants reject the suggestion that the quality of education in any particular district is determined by money—beyond some minimal level of funding which they believe to be assured every Texas district by the Minimum Foundation School Program. In their view, there is simply no denial of equal educational opportunity to any Texas school children as a result of the widely varying per-pupil spending power provided districts under the current financing scheme.

In my view, though, even an unadorned restatement of this contention is sufficient to reveal its absurdity. Authorities concerned with educational quality no doubt disagree as to the significance of variations in per-pupil spending. Indeed, conflicting expert testimony was presented to the District Court in this case concerning the effect of spending variations on educational achievement. We sit, however, not to resolve disputes over educational theory but to enforce our Constitution. It is an inescapable fact that if one district has more funds available per pupil than another district, the former will have greater choice in educational planning than will the latter. In this regard, I believe the question of discrimination in educational quality must be deemed to be an objective one that looks to what the State provides its children, not to what the children are able to do with what they receive. That a child forced to attend an underfunded school with poorer physical facilities, less experienced teachers, larger classes, and a narrower range of courses than a school with substantially more funds—and thus with greater choice in educational planning—may nevertheless excel is to the credit of the child, not the State. Indeed, who can ever measure for such a child the opportunities lost and the talents wasted for want of a broader, more enriched education? Discrimination in the opportunity to learn that is afforded a child must be our standard....

Despite the evident discriminatory effect of the Texas financing scheme, both the appellants and the majority raise substantial questions concerning the precise character of the disadvantaged class in this case....

I believe it is sufficient that the overarching form of discrimination in this case is between the schoolchildren of Texas on the basis of the taxable property wealth of the districts in which they happen to live.... [T]he children of a district are excessively advantaged if that district has more taxable property per pupil than the average amount of taxable property per pupil considering the State as a whole. By contrast, the children of a district are disadvantaged if that district has less taxable property per pupil than the state average.... Whether this discrimination, against the schoolchildren of property-poor districts, inherent in the Texas financing scheme, is violative of the Equal Protection Clause is the question to which we must now turn....

... I must once more voice my disagreement with the Court's rigidified approach to equal protection analysis. The Court apparently seeks to establish today that equal protection cases fall into one of two neat categories which dictate the appropriate standard of review—strict scrutiny or mere rationality. But this Court's decisions in the field of equal protection defy such easy categorization. A principled reading of what this Court has done reveals that it has applied a spectrum of standards in reviewing discrimination allegedly violative of the Equal Protection Clause. This spectrum clearly comprehends variations in the degree of care with which the Court will scrutinize particular classifications, depending, I believe, on the constitutional and societal importance of the interest adversely affected and the recognized invidiousness of the basis upon which the particular classification is drawn....

Nevertheless, the majority today attempts to force this case into the same category for purposes of equal protection analysis as decisions involving discrimination affecting commercial interests. By so doing, the majority singles this case out for analytic treatment at odds with what seems to me to be the clear trend of recent decisions in this Court, and thereby ignores the constitutional importance of the interest at stake and the invidiousness of the particular classification, factors that call for far more than the lenient scrutiny of the Texas financing scheme which the majority pursues. Yet if the discrimination inherent in the Texas scheme is scrutinized with the care demanded by the interest and classification present in this case, the unconstitutionality of that scheme is unmistakable. . . .

. . . [T]he fundamental importance of education is amply indicated by the prior decisions of this Court, by the unique status accorded public education by our society, and by the close relationship between education and some of our most basic constitutional values.

The special concern of this Court with the educational process of our country is a matter of common knowledge. Undoubtedly, this Court's most famous statement on the subject is that contained in Brown v. Board of Education.

> "Today, education is perhaps the most important function of state and local governments. Compulsory school attendance laws and the great expenditures for education both demonstrate our recognition of the importance of education to our democratic society. It is required in the performance of our most basic public responsibilities, even service in the armed forces. It is the very foundation of good citizenship. Today it is a principal instrument in awakening the child to cultural values, in preparing him for later professional training, and in helping him to adjust normally to his environment."
>
> . . .

Education directly affects the ability of a child to exercise his First Amendment rights, both as a source and as a receiver of information and ideas, whatever interests he may pursue in life. . . .

Of particular importance is the relationship between education and the political process. Education serves the essential function of instilling in our young an understanding of and appreciation for the principles and operation of our governmental processes. Education may instill the interest and provide the tools necessary for political discourse and debate. Indeed, it has frequently been suggested that education is the dominant factor affecting political consciousness and participation. . . . But of most immediate and direct concern must be the demonstrated effect of education on the exercise of the franchise by the electorate. . . .

While ultimately disputing little of this, the majority seeks refuge in the fact that the Court has "never presumed to possess either the ability or the authority to guarantee to the citizenry the most *effective* speech or the most *informed* electoral choice." *Ante* at 1298. This serves only to blur what is in fact at stake. With due respect, the issue is neither provision of the most *effective* speech nor of the most *informed* vote. Appellees do not now seek the best education Texas might provide. They do seek, however, an end to state discrimination resulting from the unequal distribution of taxable district property wealth that directly impairs the ability of some districts to provide the same educational opportunity that other districts can provide with the same or even substantially less tax effort. . . .

The District Court found that in discriminating between Texas schoolchildren on the basis of the amount of taxable property wealth located in the district in which they live, the Texas financing scheme created a form of wealth discrimination. This Court has frequently recognized that discrimination on the basis of wealth may create a classification of a suspect character and thereby call for exacting judicial scrutiny. The majority, however, considers any wealth classification in this case to lack certain essential characteristics which it contends are common to the instances of wealth discrimination that this Court has heretofore recognized. We are told that in every prior case involving a wealth classification, the members of the disadvantaged class have "shared two distinguishing characteristics: because of their impecunity they were completely unable to pay for some desired benefit, and as a consequence, they sustained an absolute deprivation of a meaningful opportunity to enjoy that benefit." I cannot agree. . . .

This is not to say that the form of wealth classification in this case does not differ significantly from those recognized in the previous decisions of this Court. Our prior cases have dealt essentially with discrimination on the basis of personal wealth. Here, by contrast, the children of the disadvantaged Texas school districts are being discriminated against not necessarily because of their personal wealth or the wealth of their families, but because of the taxable property wealth of the residents of the district in which they happen to live. The appropriate question, then, is whether the same degree of judicial solicitude and scrutiny that has previously been afforded wealth classifications is warranted here.

As the Court points out, no previous decision has deemed the presence of just a wealth classification to be sufficient basis to call forth rigorous judicial scrutiny of allegedly discriminatory state action. That wealth classifications alone have not necessarily been considered to bear the same high degree of suspectness as have classifications based on, for instance, race or alienage may be explainable on a number of grounds. The "poor" may not be seen as politically powerless as certain discrete and insular minority groups. Personal poverty may entail much the same social stigma as historically attached to certain racial or ethnic groups. But personal poverty is not a permanent disability; its shackles may be escaped. Perhaps most importantly, though, personal wealth may not necessarily share the general irrelevance as a basis for legislative action that race or nationality is recognized to have. While the "poor" have frequently been a legally disadvantaged group, it cannot be ignored that social legislation must frequently take cognizance of the economic status of our citizens. Thus, we have generally gauged the invidiousness of wealth classifications with an awareness of the importance of the interests being affected and the relevance of personal wealth to those interests.

When evaluated with these considerations in mind, it seems to me that discrimination on the basis of group wealth in this case likewise calls for careful judicial scrutiny. First, it must be recognized that while local district wealth may serve other interests, it bears no relationship whatsoever to the interest of Texas schoolchildren in the educational opportunity afforded them by the State of Texas. Given the importance of that interest, we must be particularly sensitive to the invidious characteristics of any form of discrimination that is not clearly intended to serve it, as opposed to some other distinct state interest. Discrimination on the basis of group wealth may not, to be sure, reflect the social stigma frequently attached to personal poverty. Nevertheless, insofar as group wealth discrimination involves wealth over which the disadvantaged individual has no significant control, it represents in fact a more serious basis of discrimination than does personal wealth. For such discrimination is no reflection of the individual's characteristics or his abilities....

The disability of the disadvantaged class in this case extends as well into the political processes upon which we ordinarily rely as adequate for the protection and promotion of all interests. Here legislative reallocation of the State's property wealth must be sought in the face of inevitable opposition from significantly advantaged districts that have a strong vested interest in the preservation of the status quo....

Nor can we ignore the extent to which, in contrast to our prior decisions, the State is responsible for the wealth discrimination in this instance.... [W]e have no such simple *de facto* wealth discrimination here. The means for financing public education in Texas are selected and specified by the State. It is the State that has created local school districts, and tied educational funding to the local property tax and thereby to local district wealth....

In the final analysis, then, the invidious characteristics of the group wealth classification present in this case merely serve to emphasize the need for careful judicial scrutiny of the State's justifications for the resulting interdistrict discrimination in the educational opportunity afforded to the schoolchildren of Texas....

The only justification offered by appellants to sustain the discrimination in educational opportunity caused by the Texas financing scheme is local educational control....

At the outset, I do not question that local control of public education, as an abstract matter, constitutes a very substantial state interest.... But I need not now decide how I might ultimately strike the balance were we confronted with a situation where the State's sincere concern for local control inevitably produced educational inequality. For, on this record, it is apparent that the State's purported concern with local control is offered primarily as an excuse rather than as a justification for interdistrict inequality.

In Texas, statewide laws regulate in fact the most minute details of local public education. For example, the State prescribes required courses. All textbooks must be submitted for state approval, and only approved textbooks may be used. The State has established the qualifications necessary for teaching in Texas public schools and the procedures for obtaining certification. The State has even legislated on the length of the school day....

Moreover, even if we accept Texas' general dedication to local control in educational matters, it is difficult to find any evidence of such dedication with respect to fiscal matters. It ignores reality to suggest— as the Court does—that the local property tax element of the Texas financing scheme reflects a conscious legislative effort to provide school districts with local fiscal control. If Texas had a system truly dedicated to local fiscal control, one would expect the quality of the educational opportunity provided in each district to vary with the decision of the voters in that district as to the level of sacrifice they wish to make for public education. In fact, the Texas scheme produces precisely the opposite result. Local school districts cannot choose to have the best education in the State by imposing the highest tax rate. Instead, the quality of the educational opportunity offered by any particular district is largely determined by the amount of taxable property located in the district—a factor over which local voters can exercise no control....

The Court seeks solace for its action today in the possibility of legislative reform. The Court's suggestions of legislative redress and experimentation will doubtless be of great comfort to the schoolchildren of Texas' disadvantaged districts, but considering the vested interests of wealthy school districts in the preservation of the status quo, they are worth little more. The possibility of legislative action is, in all events, no answer to this Court's duty under the Constitution to eliminate unjustified state discrimination. In this case we have been presented with an instance of such discrimination, in a particularly invidious form, against an individual interest of large constitutional and practical importance. To support the demonstrated discrimination in the provision of educational opportunity the State has offered a justification which, on analysis, takes on at best an ephemeral character. Thus, I believe that the wide disparities in taxable district property wealth inherent in the local property tax element of the Texas financing scheme render that scheme violative of the Equal Protection Clause....

Notes and Questions

1. *Rodriguez* has been described as the "*Dred Scott* decision for the underclass." Donald Judges, *Bayonets for the Wounded: Constitutional Paradigms and Disadvantaged Neighborhoods*, 19 Hastings Con.L.Q. 599, 604–05 (1992). Is this a fair description? In what ways are the two cases similar?

2. Can you find examples of the kinds of techniques and assumptions used in the cases in the other sections?

3. Does the Court describe the disadvantaged group in ways similar to *Hernandez* (supra at 225) and *Gilbert* (supra at 283)?

4. How does the result in *Rodriguez* help to perpetuate existing patterns of privilege and power?

5. Because of *Rodriguez*, those seeking to challenge school financing schemes have been forced to rely on state courts and state constitutions, which often contain clauses directly related to education. *See, e.g.,* Molly McUsic, *The Use of Education Clauses in School Finance Reform Litigation,* 28 Harv.J.Legis. 307 (1991).

6. In his book, Savage Inequalities, Jonathan Kozol examines the tragic inequalities in today's educational system. In the following excerpt, he discusses the significance of the *Rodriguez* decision and describes the San Antonio School system 23 years after that decision.

JONATHAN KOZOL, SAVAGE INEQUALITIES

213–214, 223–229 (Crown Publishers, 1991).

In surveying the continuing tensions that exist between the claims of local liberty and those of equity in public education, historians have noted three distinguishable trends within this century. From the turn of the century until the 1950s, equity concerns were muted and the courts did not intrude much upon local governance. From 1954 (the year in which *Brown v. Board of Education* was decided) up to the early 1970s, equity concerns were more pronounced, although the emphasis was less on economic than on racial factors. From the early 1970s to the present, local control and the efficiency agenda have once again prevailed. The decisive date that scholars generally pinpoint as the start of the most recent era is March 21 of 1973: the day on which the high court overruled the judgment of a district court in Texas that had found the local funding scheme unconstitutional—and in this way halted in its tracks the drive to equalize the public education system through the federal courts. . . .

. . . It is 23 years now since Demetrio Rodriguez went to court. Things have not changed very much in the poor neighborhoods of Texas. After 23 years of court disputes and numerous state formula revisions, per-pupil spending ranges from $2,000 in the poorest districts to some $19,000 in the richest. The minimum foundation that the state allows the children in the poorest districts—that is to say, the funds that guarantee the minimal basic education—is $1,477. Texas, moreover, is one of the ten states that gives no financial aid for school construction to the local districts.

In San Antonio, where Demetrio Rodriguez brought his suit against the state in 1968, the children of the poor still go to separate and unequal schools.

"The poor live by the water ditches here," said O.Z. White as we were driving through the crowded streets on a hot day in 1989. "The water is stagnant in the ditches now but, when the rains come, it will rise quite fast—it flows south into the San Antonio River. . . .

"The rich live on the high ground to the north. The higher ground in San Antonio is Monte Vista. But the very rich—the families with old money—live in the section known as Alamo Heights."

Alamo Heights, he told me, is a part of San Antonio. "It's enclosed by San Antonio but operated as a separate system. Dallas has a similar white enclave known as Highland Park, enclosed on four sides by the Dallas schools but operated as a separate district. We call these places 'parasite districts' since they give no tax support to the low-income sections.

"Alamo Heights is like a different world. The air is fresher. The grass is greener. The homes are larger. And the schools are richer."

Seven minutes from Alamo Heights, at the corner of Hamilton and Guadalupe, is Cassiano—a low-income housing project. Across the street from Cassiano, tiny buildings resembling shacks, some of them painted pastel shades, house many of the children who attend the Cooper Middle School, where 96 percent of children qualify by poverty for subsidized hot lunches and where 99.3 percent are of Hispanic origin. At Cooper, $2,800 is devoted to each child's education and 72 percent of children read below grade level. Class size ranges from 28 to 30. Average teacher salary is $27,000.

In Alamo Heights, where teachers average $31,000, virtually all students graduate and 88 percent of graduates go on to college. Classes are small and $4,600 is expended yearly on each child.

Fully 10 percent of children at the Cooper Middle School drop out in seventh and eighth grades. Of the survivors, 51 percent drop out of high school.

In 1988, Alamo Heights spent an average of $46 per pupil for its "gifted" program. The San Antonio Independent District, which includes the Cooper Middle School, spent only $2 for each child for its "gifted" program. In the Edgewood District, only $1 was spent per child for the "gifted" program.

Although the property tax in Alamo Heights yielded $3,600 for each pupil, compared to $924 per pupil in the San Antonio district and only $128 in Edgewood, Alamo Heights also received a share of state and federal funds—almost $8,000 yearly for a class of 20 children. Most of this extra money, quite remarkably, came to Alamo Heights under the "equalizing" formula.

Some hope of change was briefly awakened in the fall of 1989 when front-page headlines in the *New York Times* and other leading papers heralded the news that the school funding system in the state of Texas had been found unconstitutional under state law. In a nine-to-zero decision, the state supreme court, citing what it termed "glaring dispari- ·

ties" in spending between wealthy and poor districts, said that the funding system was in violation of the passage in the Texas constitution that required Texas to maintain an education system for "the general diffusion of knowledge" in the state. The court's decision summarized some of the most extreme inequities: District spending ranged from $2,112 to $19,333. The richest district drew on property wealth of $14 million for each student while the poorest district drew on property worth only $20,000 for each student. The 100 wealthiest districts taxed their local property, on the average, at 47 cents for each $100 of assessed worth but spent over $7,000 for each student. The 100 poorest districts had an average tax rate more than 50 percent higher but spent less than $3,000 for each student. Speaking of the "evident intention" of "the framers of our [Texas] Constitution to provide equal educational advantages for all," the court said, "Let there be no misunderstanding. A remedy is long overdue." There was no reference this time to the U.S. Constitution.

Stories related to the finding dominated the front page and the inside pages of the *San Antonio Express–News*. "Students cheered and superintendents hugged lawyers in an emotional display of joy," the paper said. In the library of John F. Kennedy High School in the Edgewood district, Demetrio Rodriguez put his hand on his chest to fight back tears as students, teachers and community leaders cheered his vindication and their victory. As the crowd rose to applaud the 64–year-old man, Rodriguez spoke in halting words: "I cried this morning because this is something that has been in my heart.... My children will not benefit from it.... Twenty-one years is a long time to wait." Rodriguez, a sheet-metal worker at a nearby U.S. Air Force base, had lived in San Antonio for 30 years. "My children got caught in this web. It wasn't fair ... but there is nothing I can do about it now." The problem, he said to a reporter, should have been corrected 20 years before.

In an editorial that day, the paper said that what the court had found "should have been obvious to anyone" from the beginning.

The Edgewood superintendent, who had been the leader in the latest round of litigation, spoke of the attacks that he had weathered in the course of years. He had been a high school principal in 1974 when the original *Rodriguez* finding had been overruled by the U.S. Supreme Court. "It was like somebody had died ...," he said. In the years since, he had gone repeatedly to the state capital in Austin, where he was met by promises from legislators that they would "take care of it," he said. "More and more task forces studied education," he recalled, while another generation of poor children entered and passed through the Edgewood schools. At length, in 1984, Edgewood joined with seven other poor school districts and brought suit against the state and 48 rich districts. The suit was seen by some as a class war, he said. He was accused of wanting to take away the "swimming pools," the "tennis courts" and "carpeted football fields" from wealthy districts. "They'd say I was being Robin Hood ...," he said. The district, he assured reporters, was not looking to be given swimming pools. All the district wanted was "to get us up to the average...." Children in Edgewood, he said, had suffered most from being forced to lower their horizons. "Some of the students don't ... know how to dream.... They have accepted [this]," he said, as if it were "the way [that] things should be."

The governor of Texas, who had opposed the suit and often stated he was confident the court would find against the claims of the poor districts, told the press of his relief that the Supreme Court hadn't mandated an immediate solution. "I am extremely pleased," he said, "that this is back in the hands of the legislature...."

The chairman of the Texas Railroad Commission, who was running for governor as a Republican, voiced his concern that people might use this court decision to impose an income tax on Texas.

The U.S. Secretary of Education, Lauro Cavazos, came to Texas and provided fuel for those who sought to slow down implementation of the court's decision. "First," he said, "money is clearly not the answer...." Furthermore, he said, "there is a wide body of research" to support that view and, he added, in apparent disregard of the conclusions of the court, "the evidence here in Texas corroborates those findings." He then went on to castigate Hispanic parents for not caring about education.

Meanwhile, the press observed that what it termed "the demagoguery" of "anti-tax vigilantes" posed another threat. "Legions of tax protestors" had been mobilized, a local columnist said. It was believed that they would do their best to slow down or obstruct the needed legislative action. Others focused on the likelihood that wealthy people would begin to look outside the public schools. There were already several famous private schools in Texas. Might there soon be several more?

Predictions were heard that, after legislative red tape and political delays, a revised state formula would be developed. The court would look it over, voice some doubts, but finally accept it as a reasonable effort. A few years later, O.Z. White surmised, "we'll discover that they didn't do the formula 'exactly' right. Edgewood probably will be okay. It's been in the news so it will have to be a showpiece of improvement. What of the children in those other districts where the poor Hispanic families have no leaders, where there isn't a Rodriguez? Those are the ones where children will continue to be cheated and ignored.

"There's lots of celebration now because of the decision. Wait a year. Watch and see the clever things that people will contrive. You can bet that lots of folks are thinking hard about this 'Robin Hood' idea. Up in Alamo Heights I would expect that folks have plenty on their minds tonight. I don't blame them. If I lived in Alamo Heights, I guess I'd be doing some hard thinking too....

"We're not talking about some abstraction here. These things are serious. If all of these poor kids in Cassiano get to go to real good schools—I mean, so they're educated *well* and so they're smart enough to go to colleges and universities—you have got to ask who there will be to trim the lawns and scrub the kitchen floors in Alamo Heights. Look at the lights up there. The air is nice and clean when you're up high like that in Texas. It's a different world from Guadalupe. Let me tell you something. Folks can hope, and folks can try, and folks can dream. But those two worlds are never going to meet. Not in my life. Not in yours. Not while any of these little kids in Cassiano are alive. Maybe it will happen someday. I'm not going to be counting."

Around us in the streets, the voices of children filled the heavy air. Teen-age girls stood in the doorways of the pastel houses along Guadalupe while the younger children played out in the street. Mexican music drifted from the houses and, as evening came to San Antonio, the heat subsided and there was a sense of order and serenity as people went about their evening tasks, the task of children beginning [sic] play and of their older sisters to go in and help their mothers to make dinner.

"Everything is acceptance," said O.Z. "People get used to what they have. They figure it's the way it's supposed to be and they don't think it's going to change. All those court decisions are so far away. And Alamo Heights seems far away, so people don't compare. And that's important. If you don't know what you're missing, you're not going to get angry. How can you desire what you cannot dream of?" But this may not really be the case; for many of the women in this neighborhood do get to see the richer neighborhoods because they work in wealthy people's homes.

According to the principal of Cooper Middle School, crack addiction isn't a real problem yet for younger children. "Here it's mainly chemical inhalants. It can blind you, I've been told. They get it mainly out of spray-paint cans and liquid paper," he says wearily.

But a social worker tells me there's a crack house right on Guadalupe. "There is a lot of prostitution here as well," she says. "Many of these teen-age girls helping their mothers to make supper will be pregnant soon. They will have children and leave school. Many will then begin the daily trip to Alamo Heights. They'll do domestic work and bring up other people's kids. By the time they know what they were missing, it's too late."

It is now the spring of 1991. A year and a half has passed since these events took place. The Texas legislature has at last, and with much rhetoric about what many legislators call "a Robin Hood approach," enacted a new equalizing formula but left a number of loopholes that perpetuate the fiscal edge enjoyed by very wealthy districts. Plaintiffs' attorneys are guarded in their expectations. If the experience of other states holds true in Texas, there will be a series of delays and challenges and, doubtless, further litigation. The implementation of the newest plan, in any case, will not be immediate. Twenty-three years after Demetrio Rodriguez went to court, the children of the poorest people in the state of Texas still are waiting for an equal chance at education....

... Surely there is enough for everyone within this country. It is a tragedy that these good things are not more widely shared. All our children ought to be allowed a stake in the enormous richness of America. Whether they were born to poor white Appalachians or to wealthy Texans, to poor black people in the Bronx or to rich people in Manhasset or Winnetka, they are all quite wonderful and innocent when they are small. We soil them needlessly.

WYMAN v. JAMES

Supreme Court of the United States, 1971.
400 U.S. 309, 91 S.Ct. 381, 27 L.Ed.2d 408.

MR. JUSTICE BLACKMUN delivered the opinion of the Court.

This appeal presents the issue whether a beneficiary of the program for Aid to Families with Dependent Children (AFDC) may refuse a home visit by the caseworker without risking the termination of benefits....

Plaintiff Barbara James is the mother of a son, Maurice, who was born in May 1967. They reside in New York City. Mrs. James first applied for AFDC assistance shortly before Maurice's birth. A caseworker made a visit to her apartment at that time without objection. The assistance was authorized.

Two years later, on May 8, 1969, a caseworker wrote Mrs. James that she would visit her home on May 14. Upon receipt of this advice, Mrs. James telephoned the worker that, although she was willing to supply information "reasonable and relevant" to her need for public assistance, any discussion was not to take place at her home. The worker told Mrs. James that she was required by law to visit in her home and that refusal to permit the visit would result in the termination of assistance. Permission was still denied.

On May 13 the City Department of Social Services sent Mrs. James a notice of intent to discontinue assistance because of the visitation refusal. The notice advised the beneficiary of her right to a hearing before a review officer. The hearing was requested and was held on May 27. Mrs. James appeared with an attorney at that hearing. They continued to refuse permission for a worker to visit the James home, but again expressed willingness to cooperate and to permit visits elsewhere. The review officer ruled that the refusal was a proper ground for the termination of assistance. His written decision stated:

> "The home visit which Mrs. James refuses to permit is for the purpose of determining if there are any changes in her situation that might affect her eligibility to continue to receive Public Assistance, or that might affect the amount of such assistance, and to see if there are any social services which the Department of Social Services can provide to the family."

A notice of termination issued on June 2....

When a case involves a home and some type of official intrusion into that home, as this case appears to do, an immediate and natural reaction is one of concern about Fourth Amendment rights and the protection which that Amendment is intended to afford. Its emphasis indeed is upon one of the most precious aspects of personal security in the home: "The right of the people to be secure in their persons, houses, papers, and effects * * *." This Court has characterized that right as "basic to a free society." And over the years the Court consistently has been most protective of the privacy of the dwelling. . . .

This natural and quite proper protective attitude, however, is not a factor in this case, for the seemingly obvious and simple reason that we are not concerned here with any search by the New York social service agency in the Fourth Amendment meaning of that term. It is true that the governing statute and regulations appear to make mandatory the initial home visit and the subsequent periodic "contacts" (which may include home visits) for the inception and continuance of aid. It is also true that the caseworker's posture in the home visit is perhaps, in a sense, both rehabilitative and investigative. But this latter aspect, we think, is given too broad a character and far more emphasis than it deserves if it is equated with a search in the traditional criminal law context. We note, too, that the visitation in itself is not forced or compelled, and that the beneficiary's denial of permission is not a criminal act. If consent to the visitation is withheld, no visitation takes place. The aid then never begins or merely ceases, as the case may be. There is no entry of the home and there is no search.

If however, we were to assume that a caseworker's home visit, before or subsequent to the beneficiary's initial qualification for benefits, somehow (perhaps because the average beneficiary might feel she is in no position to refuse consent to the visit), and despite its interview nature, does possess some of the characteristics of a search in the traditional sense, we nevertheless conclude that the visit does not fall within the Fourth Amendment's proscription. This is because it does not descend to the level of unreasonableness. It is unreasonableness which is the Fourth Amendment's standard. . . .

There are a number of factors that compel us to conclude that the home visit proposed for Mrs. James is not unreasonable:

1. The public's interest in this particular segment of the area of assistance to the unfortunate is protection and aid for the dependent child whose family requires such aid for that child. The focus is on the *child* and, further, it is on the child who is *dependent*. There is no more worthy object of the public's concern. The dependent child's needs are paramount, and only with hesitancy would we relegate those needs, in the scale of comparative values, to a position secondary to what the mother claims as her rights.

2. The agency, with tax funds provided from federal as well as from state sources, is fulfilling a public trust. The State, working through its qualified welfare agency, has appropriate and paramount interest and

concern in seeing and assuring that the intended and proper objects of that tax-produced assistance are the ones who benefit from the aid it dispenses. Surely it is not unreasonable, in the Fourth Amendment sense or in any other sense of that term, that the State have at its command a gentle means, of limited extent and of practical and considerate application, of achieving that assurance.

3. One who dispenses purely private charity naturally has an interest in and expects to know how his charitable funds are utilized and put to work. The public, when it is the provider, rightly expects the same. It might well expect more, because of the trust aspect of public funds, and the recipient, as well as the caseworker, has not only an interest but an obligation.

4. The emphasis of the New York statutes and regulations is upon the home, upon "close contact" with the beneficiary, upon restoring the aid recipient "to a condition of self-support," and upon the relief of his distress. The federal emphasis is no different. It is upon "assistance and rehabilitation," upon maintaining and strengthening family life, and upon "maximum self-support and personal independence consistent with the maintenance of continuing parental care and protection, * * *" ... It requires cooperation from the state agency upon specified standards and in specified ways. And it is concerned about any possible exploitation of the child.

5. The home visit, it is true, is not required by federal statute or regulation. But it has been noted that the visit is "the heart of welfare administration"; that it affords "a personal, rehabilitative orientation, unlike that of most federal programs"; and that the "more pronounced service orientation" effected by Congress with the 1956 amendments to the Social Security Act "gave redoubled importance to the practice of home visiting." ... The home visit is an established routine in States besides New York.

6. The means employed by the New York agency are significant. Mrs. James received written notice several days in advance of the intended home visit. The date was specified.... Privacy is emphasized. The applicant-recipient is made the primary source of information as to eligibility. Outside informational sources, other than public records, are to be consulted only with the beneficiary's consent. Forcible entry or entry under false pretenses or visitation outside working hours or snooping in the home are forbidden.... All this minimizes any "burden" upon the homeowner's right against unreasonable intrusion.

7. Mrs. James, in fact, on this record presents no specific complaint of any unreasonable intrusion of her home and nothing that supports an inference that the desired home visit had as its purpose the obtaining of information as to criminal activity. She complains of no proposed visitation at an awkward or retirement hour. She suggests no forcible entry. She refers to no snooping. She describes no impolite or reprehensible conduct of any kind. She alleges only, in general and nonspecific terms, that on previous visits and, on information and belief, on

visitation at the home of other aid recipients, "questions concerning personal relationships, beliefs and behavior are raised and pressed which are unnecessary for a determination of continuing eligibility." Paradoxically, this same complaint could be made of a conference held elsewhere than in the home, and yet this is what is sought by Mrs. James. The same complaint could be made of the census taker's questions. What Mrs. James appears to want from the agency that provides her and her infant son with the necessities for life is the right to receive those necessities upon her own informational terms, to utilize the Fourth Amendment as a wedge for imposing those terms, and to avoid questions of any kind.[9]

8. We are not persuaded, as Mrs. James would have us be, that all information pertinent to the issue of eligibility can be obtained by the agency through an interview at a place other than the home, or, as the District Court majority suggested, by examining a lease or a birth certificate, or by periodic medical examinations, or by interviews with school personnel. Although these secondary sources might be helpful, they would not always assure verification of actual residence or of actual physical presence in the home, which are requisites for AFDC benefits, or of impending medical needs. And, of course, little children, such as Maurice James, are not yet registered in school.

9. The visit is not one by police or uniformed authority. It is made by a caseworker of some training whose primary objective is, or should be, the welfare, not the prosecution, of the aid recipient for whom the worker has profound responsibility. As has already been stressed, the program concerns dependent children and the needy families of those children. It does not deal with crime or with the actual or suspected perpetrators of crime. The caseworker is not a sleuth but rather, we trust, is a friend to one in need.

10. The home visit is not a criminal investigation, does not equate with a criminal investigation, and despite the announced fears of Mrs. James and those who would join her, is not in aid of any criminal proceeding. If the visitation serves to discourage misrepresentation or fraud, such a byproduct of that visit does not impress upon the visit itself a dominant criminal investigative aspect. And if the visit should, by chance, lead to the discovery of fraud and a criminal prosecution should follow,[12] then, even assuming that the evidence discovered upon the home visitation is admissible, an issue upon which we express no opinion, that is a routine and expected fact of life and a consequence no

9. We have examined Mrs. James' case record with the New York City Department of Social Services, which, as an exhibit, accompanied defendant Wyman's answer. It discloses numerous interviews from the time of the initial one on April 27, 1967, until the attempted termination in June 1969. The record is revealing as to Mrs. James' failure ever really to satisfy the requirements for eligibility; as to constant and repeated demands; as to attitude to-ward the caseworker; as to reluctance to cooperate; as to evasiveness; and as to occasional belligerency. There are indications that all was not always well with the infant Maurice (skull fracture, a dent in the head, a possible rat bite). The picture is a sad and unhappy one.

12. See, for example, New York Social Services Law § 145.

greater than that which necessarily ensues upon any other discovery by a citizen of criminal conduct.

11. The warrant procedure, which the plaintiff appears to claim to be so precious to her, even if civil in nature, is not without its seriously objectionable features in the welfare context. If a warrant could be obtained (the plaintiff affords us little help as to how it would be obtained), it presumably could be applied for *ex parte,* its execution would require no notice, it would justify entry by force, and its hours for execution [13] would not be so limited as those prescribed for home visitation. The warrant necessarily would imply conduct either criminal or out of compliance with an asserted governing standard. Of course, the force behind the warrant argument, welcome to the one asserting it, is the fact that it would have to rest upon probable cause, and probable cause in the welfare context, as Mrs. James concedes, requires more than the mere need of the caseworker to see the child in the home and to have assurance that the child is there and is receiving the benefit of the aid that has been authorized for it. In this setting the warrant argument is out of place.

It seems to us that the situation is akin to that where an Internal Revenue Service agent, in making a routine civil audit of a taxpayer's income tax return, asks that the taxpayer produce for the agent's review some proof of a deduction the taxpayer has asserted to his benefit in the computation of his tax. If the taxpayer refuses, there is, absent fraud, only a disallowance of the claimed deduction and a consequent additional tax. The taxpayer is fully within his "rights" in refusing to produce the proof, but in maintaining and asserting those rights a tax detriment results and it is a detriment of the taxpayer's own making. So here Mrs. James has the "right" to refuse the home visit, but a consequence in the form of cessation of aid, similar to the taxpayer's resultant additional tax, flows from that refusal. The choice is entirely hers, and nothing of constitutional magnitude is involved. ...

We therefore conclude that the home visitation as structured by the New York statutes and regulations is a reasonable administrative tool; that it serves a valid and proper administrative purpose for the dispensation of the AFDC program; that it is not an unwarranted invasion of personal privacy; and that it violates no right guaranteed by the Fourth Amendment....

Mr. Justice Douglas, dissenting.

We are living in a society where one of the most important forms of property is government largesse which some call the "new property." The payrolls of government are but one aspect of that "new property." Defense contracts, highway contracts, and the other multifarious forms of contracts are another part. So are subsidies to air, rail, and other carriers. So are disbursements by government for scientific research. So are TV and radio licenses to use the air space which of course is part

---

13. New York Code Crim.Proc. § 801.

of the public domain. Our concern here is not with those subsidies but with grants that directly or indirectly implicate the *home life* of the recipients.

In 1969 roughly 127 billion dollars were spent by the federal, state, and local governments on "social welfare." To farmers alone almost four billion dollars were paid, in part, for not growing certain crops. Almost 129,000 farmers received $5,000 or more, their total benefits exceeding $1,450,000,000. Those payments were in some instances very large, a few running a million or more a year. But the majority were payments under $5,000 each.

Yet almost every beneficiary whether rich or poor, rural or urban, has a "house"—one of the places protected by the Fourth Amendment against "unreasonable searches and seizures." The question in this case is whether receipt of largesse from the government makes the *home* of the beneficiary subject to access by an inspector of the agency of oversight, even though the beneficiary objects to the intrusion and even though the Fourth Amendment's procedure for access to one's *house* or *home* is not followed. The penalty here is not, of course, invasion of the privacy of Barbara James, only her loss of federal or state largesse. That, however, is merely rephrasing the problem. Whatever the semantics, the central question is whether the government by force of its largesse has the power to "buy up" rights guaranteed by the Constitution. But for the assertion of her constitutional right, Barbara James in this case would have received the welfare benefit....

Is a search of her home without a warrant made "reasonable" merely because she is dependent on government largesse?

Judge Skelly Wright has stated the problem succinctly:

> "Welfare has long been considered the equivalent of charity and its recipients have been subjected to all kinds of dehumanizing experiences in the government's effort to police its welfare payments. In fact, over half a billion dollars are expended annually for administration and policing in connection with the Aid to Families with Dependent Children program. Why such large sums are necessary for administration and policing has never been adequately explained. No such sums are spent policing the government subsidies granted to farmers, airlines, steamship companies, and junk mail dealers, to name but a few. The truth is that in this subsidy area society has simply adopted a double standard, one for aid to business and the farmer and a different one for welfare." Poverty, Minorities, and Respect For Law, 1970 Duke L.J. 425, 437–438.

If the welfare recipient was not Barbara James but a prominent, affluent cotton or wheat farmer receiving benefit payments for not growing crops, would not the approach be different? Welfare in aid of dependent children, like social security and unemployment benefits, has an aura of suspicion. There doubtless are frauds in every sector of public welfare whether the recipient be a Barbara James or someone who is prominent or influential. But constitutional rights—here the privacy of the *home*—are obviously not dependent on the poverty or on the affluence of the beneficiary. It is the precincts of the *home* that the Fourth Amendment protects; and their privacy is as important to the lowly as to the mighty. . . .

I would place the same restrictions on inspectors entering the *homes* of welfare beneficiaries as are on inspectors entering the *homes* of those on the payroll of government, or the *homes* of those who contract with the government, or the *homes* of those who work for those having government contracts. The values of the *home* protected by the Fourth Amendment are not peculiar to capitalism as we have known it; they are equally relevant to the new form of socialism which we are entering. Moreover, as the numbers of functionaries and inspectors multiply, the need for protection of the individual becomes indeed more essential if the values of a free society are to remain. . . .

MR. JUSTICE MARSHALL, whom MR. JUSTICE BRENNAN joins, dissenting.

Although I substantially agree with its initial statement of the issue in this case, the Court's opinion goes on to imply that the appellee has refused to provide information germane to a determination of her eligibility for AFDC benefits. The record plainly shows, however, that Mrs. James offered to furnish any information that the appellants desired and to be interviewed at any place other than her home. Appellants rejected her offers and terminated her benefits solely on the ground that she refused to permit a home visit. In addition, appellants make no contention that any sort of probable cause exists to suspect appellee of welfare fraud or child abuse.

Simply stated, the issue in this case is whether a state welfare agency can require all recipients of AFDC benefits to submit to warrantless "visitations" of their homes. In answering that question, the majority dodges between constitutional issues to reach a result clearly inconsistent with the decisions of this Court. We are told that there is no search involved in this case; that even if there were a search, it would not be unreasonable; and that even if this were an unreasonable search, a welfare recipient waives her right to object by accepting benefits. I emphatically disagree with all three conclusions. Furthermore, I believe that binding regulations of the Department of Health, Education, and Welfare prohibit appellants from requiring the home visit.

II

The Court's assertion that this case concerns no search "in the Fourth Amendment meaning of that term" is neither "obvious" nor "simple." I should have thought that the Fourth Amendment governs all intrusions by agents of the public upon personal security. . . . This Court has rejected as "anomalous" the contention that only suspected criminals are protected by the Fourth Amendment, Camara v. Municipal Court, 387 U.S. 523, 530 (1967). In an era of rapidly burgeoning governmental activities and their concomitant inspectors, caseworkers, and researchers, a restriction of the Fourth Amendment to "the traditional criminal law context" tramples the ancient concept that a man's home is his castle....

Even if the Fourth Amendment does not apply to each and every governmental entry into the home, the welfare visit is not some sort of purely benevolent inspection. No one questions the motives of the dedicated welfare caseworker. Of course, caseworkers seek to be friends, but the point is that they are also required to be sleuths. The majority concedes that the "visitation" is partially investigative, but claims that this investigative aspect has been given too much emphasis. Emphasis has indeed been given. Time and again, in briefs and at oral argument, appellants emphasized the need to enter AFDC homes to guard against welfare fraud and child abuse, both of which are felonies. The New York statutes provide emphasis by requiring all caseworkers to report any evidence of fraud that a home visit uncovers. And appellants have strenuously emphasized the importance of the visit to provide evidence leading to civil forfeitures including elimination of benefits and loss of child custody....

Conceding for the sake of argument that someone might view the "visitation" as a search, the majority nonetheless concludes that such a search is not unreasonable. However, its mode of reaching that conclusion departs from the entire history of Fourth Amendment case law. Of course, the Fourth Amendment test is reasonableness, but in determining whether a search is reasonable, this Court is not free merely to balance, in a totally ad hoc fashion, any number of subjective factors. An unbroken line of cases holds that, subject to a few narrowly drawn exceptions, any search without a warrant is constitutionally unreasonable....

First, it is argued that the home visit is justified to protect dependent children from "abuse" and "exploitation." These are heinous crimes, but they are not confined to indigent households. Would the majority sanction, in the absence of probable cause, compulsory visits to all American homes for the purpose of discovering child abuse? Or is this Court prepared to hold as a matter of constitutional law that a mother, merely because she is poor, is substantially more likely to injure or exploit her children? Such a categorical approach to an entire class of citizens would be dangerously at odds with the tenets of our democracy.

Second, the Court contends that caseworkers must enter the homes of AFDC beneficiaries to determine eligibility. Interestingly, federal regulations do not require the home visit. In fact, the regulations specify the recipient himself as the primary source of eligibility information thereby rendering an inspection of the home only one of several alternative secondary sources. The majority's implication that a biannual home visit somehow assures the verification of actual residence or actual physical presence in the home strains credulity in the context of urban poverty. Despite the caseworker's responsibility for dependent children, he is not even required to see the children as a part of the home visit. Appellants offer scant explanation for their refusal even to attempt to utilize public records, expenditure receipts, documents such as leases, non-home interviews, personal financial records, sworn declarations, etc.—all sources that governmental agencies regularly accept as adequate to establish eligibility for other public benefits. In this setting, it ill behooves appellants to refuse to utilize informational sources less drastic than an invasion of the privacy of the home.

We are told that the plight of Mrs. James is no different from that of a taxpayer who is required to document his right to a tax deduction, but this analogy is seriously flawed. The record shows that Mrs. James has offered to be interviewed anywhere other than her home, to answer any questions, and to provide any documentation that the welfare agency desires. The agency curtly refused all these offers and insisted on its "right" to pry into appellee's home. Tax exemptions are also governmental "bounty." A true analogy would be an Internal Revenue Service requirement that in order to claim a dependency exemption, a taxpayer *must* allow a specially trained IRS agent to invade the home for the purpose of questioning the occupants and looking for evidence that the exemption is being properly utilized for the benefit of the dependent. If such a system were even proposed, the cries of constitutional outrage would be unanimous.

Appellants offer a third state interest that the Court seems to accept as partial justification for this search. We are told that the visit is designed to rehabilitate, to provide aid. This is strange doctrine indeed. A paternalistic notion that a complaining citizen's constitutional rights can be violated so long as the State is somehow helping him is alien to our Nation's philosophy. . . .

Throughout its opinion, the majority alternates between two views of the State's interest in requiring the home visit. First we are told that the State's purpose is benevolent so that no search is involved. Next we are told [sic] that the State's need to prevent child abuse and to avoid the misappropriation of welfare funds justifies dispensing with the warrant requirement. But when all the State's purposes are considered at one time, I can only conclude that the home visit is a search and that, absent a warrant, that search is unreasonable.

Although the Court does not agree with my conclusion that the home visit is an unreasonable search, its opinion suggests that even if the visit were unreasonable, appellee has somehow waived her right to object. Surely the majority cannot believe that valid Fourth Amendment consent can be given under the threat of the loss of one's sole means of support. Nor has Mrs. James waived her rights. Had the Court squarely faced the question of whether the State can condition welfare payments on the waiver of clear constitutional rights, the answer would be plain. The decisions of this Court do not support the notion that a State can use welfare benefits as a wedge to coerce "waiver" of Fourth Amendment rights. . . .

In deciding that the homes of AFDC recipients are not entitled to protection from warrantless searches by welfare caseworkers, the Court

declines to follow prior case law and employs a rationale that, if applied
to the claims of all citizens, would threaten the vitality of the Fourth
Amendment. This Court has occasionally pushed beyond established
constitutional contours to protect the vulnerable and to further basic
human values. I find no little irony in the fact that the burden of
today's departure from principled adjudication is placed upon the lowly
poor. Perhaps the majority has explained why a commercial warehouse
deserves more protection than does this poor woman's home. I am not
convinced; and, therefore, I must respectfully dissent.

BOWEN v. GILLIARD

Supreme Court of the United States, 1987.
483 U.S. 587, 107 S.Ct. 3008, 97 L.Ed.2d 485.

JUSTICE STEVENS delivered the opinion of the Court.

As part of its major effort to reduce the federal deficit through the
Deficit Reduction Act of 1984, 98 Stat. 494, Congress amended the
statute authorizing Federal Aid to Families with Dependent Children
(AFDC) to require that a family's eligibility for benefits must take into
account, with certain specified exceptions, the income of all parents,
brothers, and sisters living in the same home. The principal question
presented in this litigation is whether that requirement violates the
Fifth Amendment to the United States Constitution when it is applied to
require a family wishing to receive AFDC benefits to include within its
unit a child for whom child support payments are being made by a
noncustodial parent. . . .

[T]he 1984 amendment forced families to include in the filing unit
children for whom support payments were being received, the practical
effect was that many families' total income was reduced. The burden of
the change was mitigated somewhat by a separate amendment providing
that the first $50 of child support collected by the State must be
remitted to the family and not counted as income for the purpose of
determining its benefit level. Thus, the net effect of the 1984 amendments for a family comparable to Gilliard's would include three changes:
(1) the addition of the child receiving support would enlarge the filing
unit and entitle the family to a somewhat larger benefit; (2) child
support would be treated as family income and would be assigned to the
State, thereby reducing the AFDC benefits by that amount; and (3) the
reduction would be offset by $50 if that amount was collected from an
absent parent. In sum, if the assigned support exceeded $50 plus the
difference in the benefit level caused by adding the child or children
receiving support, the family would suffer; if less than $50 and the
difference in the benefit level was collected as support, it would not. . . .

The District Court was undoubtedly correct in its perception that a
number of needy families have suffered, and will suffer, as a result of the
implementation of the DEFRA amendments to the AFDC program.
Such suffering is frequently the tragic byproduct of a decision to reduce
or to modify benefits to a class of needy recipients. Under our structure

of government, however, it is the function of Congress—not the courts—to determine whether the savings realized, and presumably used for other critical governmental functions, are significant enough to justify the costs to the individuals affected by such reductions. The Fifth Amendment "gives the federal courts no power to impose upon [Congress] their views of what constitutes wise economic or social policy," by telling it how "to reconcile the demands of ... needy citizens with the finite resources available to meet those demands." *Dandridge v. Williams,* 397 U.S. 471, 486 (1970). Unless the Legislative Branch's decisions run afoul of some constitutional edict, any inequities created by such decisions must be remedied by the democratic processes....

The precepts that govern our review of appellees' due process and equal protection challenges to this program are similar to those we have applied in reviewing challenges to other parts of the Social Security Act:

> "[O]ur review is deferential. 'Governmental decisions to spend money to improve the general public welfare in one way and not another are "not confided to the courts. The discretion belongs to Congress unless the choice is clearly wrong, a display of arbitrary power, not an exercise of judgment.' "

... The District Court had before it evidence that the DEFRA amendment was severely impacting some families. For example, some noncustodial parents stopped making their support payments because they believed that their payments were helping only the State, and not their children. It is clear, however, that in the administration of a fund that is large enough to have a significant impact on the Nation's deficit, general rules must be examined in light of the broad purposes they are intended to serve. The challenged amendment unquestionably serves Congress' goal of decreasing federal expenditures.... The evidence that a few noncustodial parents were willing to violate the law by not making court-ordered support payments does not alter the fact that the entire program has resulted in saving huge sums of money.

The rationality of the amendment denying a family the right to exclude a supported child from the filing unit is also supported by the Government's separate interest in distributing benefits among competing needy families in a fair way. Given its perceived need to make cuts in the AFDC budget, Congress obviously sought to identify a group that would suffer less than others as a result of a reduction in benefits. When considering the plight of two five-person families, one of which receives no income at all while the other receives regular support payments for some of the minor children, it is surely reasonable for Congress to conclude that the former is in greater need than the latter. This conclusion is amply supported by Congress' assumption that child support payments received are generally beneficial to the entire family unit, and by "the common sense proposition that individuals living with others usually have reduced per capita costs because many of their expenses are shared."

It was therefore rational for Congress to adjust the AFDC program to reflect the fact that support money generally provides significant benefits for entire family units. This conclusion is not undermined by the fact that there are no doubt many families in which some—or perhaps all—of the support money is spent in a way that does not benefit the rest of the family. In determining how best to allocate limited funds among the extremely large class of needy families eligible for AFDC benefits, Congress is entitled to rely on a classwide presumption that custodial parents have used, and may legitimately use, support funds in a way that is beneficial to entire family units. . . .

Appellees argue (and the District Court ruled), however, that finding that Congress acted rationally is not enough to sustain this legislation. Rather, they claim that some form of "heightened scrutiny" is appropriate because the amendment interferes with a family's fundamental right to live in the type of family unit it chooses. We conclude that the District Court erred in subjecting the DEFRA amendment to any form of heightened scrutiny. That some families may decide to modify their living arrangements in order to avoid the effect of the amendment, does not transform the amendment into an act whose design and direct effect are to "intrud[e] on choices concerning family living arrangements." . . .

Last Term we rejected a constitutional challenge to a provision in the Federal Food Stamp Program, which determines eligibility and benefit levels on a "household" rather than an individual basis. *Lyng v. Castillo,* 477 U.S. 635 (1986). We held that the guarantee of equal treatment in the Due Process Clause of the Fifth Amendment was not violated by the statutory requirement that generally treated parents, children, and siblings who lived together as a single household, and explained:

"The disadvantaged class is that comprised by parents, children, and siblings. Close relatives are not a 'suspect' or 'quasi-suspect' class. As a historical matter, they have not been subjected to discrimination; they do not exhibit obvious, immutable, or distinguishing characteristics that define them as a discrete group; and they are not a minority or politically powerless. In fact, quite the contrary is true.

"Nor does the statutory classification 'directly and substantially' interfere with family living arrangements and thereby burden a fundamental right."

. . . And as in *Lyng,* "the justification for the statutory classification is obvious." The provisions at issue do not violate the Due Process Clause.

Aside from holding that the amendment violated the Due Process Clause of the Fifth Amendment and its equal protection component, the District Court invalidated the DEFRA amendments as a taking of private property without just compensation. The court based this holding on the premise that a child for whom support payments are made has a right to have the support money used exclusively in his or her "best interest." Yet, the court reasoned, the requirements (1) that a custodial parent who applies for AFDC must include a child's support money in computing family income, and (2) that the support must be assigned to the State, effectively converts the support funds that were once to be used exclusively for the child's best interests into an AFDC check which, under federal law, must be used for the benefit of all the children. Therefore, the District Court held that the State was "taking" that child's right to exclusive use of the support money. In addressing this issue, it is helpful to look first at whether the State "takes" the child's property when it considers the support payments as part of the family's income in computing AFDC eligibility. We will then consider whether the requirement that support payments be assigned to the State requires a finding that the amendments violate the taking prohibition.

Some perspective on the issue is helpful here. Had no AFDC program ever existed until 1984, and had Congress then instituted a program that took into account support payments that a family receives, it is hard to believe that we would seriously entertain an argument that the new benefit program constituted a taking. Yet, somehow, once benefits are in place and Congress sees a need to reduce them in order to save money and to distribute limited resources more fairly, the "takings" label seems to have a bit more plausibility. For legal purposes though, the two situations are identical. Congress is not, by virtue of having instituted a social welfare program, bound to continue it at all, much less at the same benefit level. Thus, notwithstanding the technical legal arguments that have been advanced, it is imperative to recognize that the amendments at issue merely incorporate a definitional element into an entitlement program. It would be quite strange indeed if, by virtue of an offer to *provide* benefits to needy families through the entirely voluntary AFDC program, Congress or the States were deemed to have *taken* some of those very family members' property.

The basic requirement that the AFDC filing unit must include all family members living in the home, and therefore that support payments made on behalf of a member of the family must be considered in determining that family's level of benefits, does not even arguably take anyone's property. The family members other than the child for whom the support is being paid certainly have no takings claim, since it is clear that they have no protected property rights to continued benefits at the same level. Nor does the simple inclusion of the support income in the benefit calculation have any legal effect on the child's right to have it used for his or her benefit. To the extent that a child has the right to have the support payments used in his or her "best interest," he or she fully retains that right. Of course, the effect of counting the support payments as part of the filing unit's income often reduces the family's resources, and hence increases the chances that sharing of the support money will be appropriate. But given the unquestioned premise that the Government has a right to reduce AFDC benefits generally, that result does not constitute a taking of private property without just compensation.

The only possible legal basis for appellees' takings claim, therefore, is the requirement that an applicant for AFDC benefits must assign the support payments to the State, which then will remit the amount collected to the custodial parent to be used for the benefit of the entire family. This legal transformation in the status of the funds, the argument goes, modifies the child's interest in the use of the money so dramatically that it constitutes a taking of the child's property. As a practical matter, this argument places form over substance, and labels over reality. Although it is true that money which was earmarked for a specific child's or children's "best interest" becomes a part of a larger fund available for all of the children, the difference between these concepts is, as we have discussed, more theoretical than practical. . . .

First, in evaluating the economic impact of the assignment, it is important to remember that it is the impact on the child, not on the entire family unit, that is relevant. Thus, the fact that the entire family's net income may be reduced does not necessarily mean that the amount of money spent for the benefit of a supported child will be any less than the amount of the noncustodial parent's support payments. The reality is that the money will usually continue to be used in the same manner that it was previously since the typical AFDC parent will have used the support money as part of the general family fund even without its being transferred through AFDC. Moreover, any diminution in the value of the support payments for the child is mitigated by the extra $50 that the family receives as a result of the assignment, by the extra AFDC benefits that are received by the inclusion of an additional family member in the unit, and by the fact that the State is using its own enforcement power to collect the support payments, and is bearing the risk of nonpayment in any given month. Whatever the diminution in value of the child's right to have support funds used for his or her "exclusive" benefit may be, it is not so substantial as to constitute a taking under our precedents.

Second, the child receiving support payments holds no vested protectable expectation that his or her parent will continue to receive identical support payments on the child's behalf, and that the child will enjoy the same rights with respect to them. . . .

Finally, the character of the governmental action here militates against a finding that the States or Federal Government unconstitutionally take property through the AFDC program. It is obviously necessary for the Government to make hard choices and to balance various incentives in deciding how to allocate benefits in this type of program. But a decision to include child support as part of the family income certainly does not implicate the type of concerns that the Takings Clause protects. This is by no means an enactment that forces "some people alone to bear public burdens which, in all fairness and justice, should be borne by the public as a whole."

The law does not require any custodial parent to apply for AFDC benefits. Surely it is reasonable to presume that a parent who does make such an application does so because she or he is convinced that the family as a whole—as well as *each* child committed to her or his custody—will be better off with the benefits than without. In making such a decision, the parent is not taking a child's property without just compensation; nor is the State doing so when it responds to that decision by supplementing the collections of support money with additional AFDC benefits....

The judgment of the District Court is *Reversed*.

JUSTICE BRENNAN, with whom JUSTICE MARSHALL joins, dissenting.

Government in the modern age has assumed increasing responsibility for the welfare of its citizens. This expansion of responsibility has been accompanied by an increase in the scale and complexity of the activities that government conducts. Respect for the enormity of the administrative task that confronts the modern welfare state, as well as for the scarcity of government resources, counsels that public officials enjoy discretion in determining the most effective means of fulfilling their responsibilities.

The very pervasiveness of modern government, however, creates an unparalleled opportunity for intrusion on personal life. In a society in which most persons receive some form of government benefit, government has considerable leverage in shaping individual behavior. In most cases, we acknowledge that government may wield its power even when its actions likely influence choices involving personal behavior. On certain occasions, however, government intrusion into private life is so direct and substantial that we must deem it intolerable if we are to be true to our belief that there is a boundary between the public citizen and the private person.

This is such a case. The Government has told a child who lives with a mother receiving public assistance that it cannot both live with its mother and be supported by its father. The child must either leave the care and custody of the mother, or forgo the support of the father and become a Government client. The child is put to this choice not because it seeks Government benefits for itself, but because of a fact over which it has no control: the need of *other* household members for public assistance. A child who lives with one parent has, under the best of circumstances, a difficult time sustaining a relationship with both its parents. A crucial bond between a child and its parent outside the home, usually the father, is the father's commitment to care for the material needs of the child, and the expectation of the child that it may look to its father for such care. The Government has thus decreed that a condition of welfare eligibility for a mother is that her child surrender a vital connection with either the father or the mother.

The Court holds that the Government need only show a rational basis for such action. This standard of review has regularly been used in evaluating the claims of applicants for Government benefits, since "a noncontractual claim to receive funds from the public treasury enjoys no constitutionally protected status." *Weinberger v. Salfi*, 422 U.S. 749,

772, 95 S.Ct. 2457, 2470, 45 L.Ed.2d 522 (1975). Plaintiff child support recipients in this case, however, are children who wish *not* to receive public assistance, but to continue to be supported by their noncustodial parent. Their claim is *not* that the Government has unfairly denied them benefits, but that it has intruded deeply into their relationship with their parents. More than a mere rational basis is required to withstand this challenge, and, . . . the Government can offer no adequate justification for doing such damage to the parent-child relationship. . . .

Increasing numbers of children in this country thus reside only with their mother, in a household whose financial condition is precarious. These children have a fundamental interest in sustaining a relationship with their mother, since she is their primary source of daily emotional support. They also have a fundamental interest, of course, in sustaining a relationship with their father, whose absence from the household does not diminish the protection that must be afforded this parent-child relationship. . . . Research indicates that maintenance of a relationship with both parents is particularly important for children whose parents have divorced. . . .

The Government's insistence that a child living with an AFDC mother relinquish its child support deeply intrudes on the father-child relationship, for child support is a crucial means of sustaining the bond between a child and its father outside the home. A father's support represents a way in which the father can make an important contribution to raising the child, and the benefits to the child are both financial and emotional.

Financially, child support makes available resources to help meet the child's daily material needs—resources especially important because of the financial difficulties that confront many households headed by women. Child support is also integrally related to the father's ongoing involvement in raising the child. The father is not there on a daily basis to wake the child in the morning, bring him or her to school, answer innumerable questions, offer guidance with personal problems, put the child to bed, and provide the countless doses of encouragement and consolation that daily life requires. Nonetheless, by helping to meet the child's daily material needs, the father can let the child know that the father is committed to participating in the child's upbringing. Meals, clothes, toys, and other things made possible by this support represent this commitment even when the father cannot be there to affirm it himself.

The provision of support by a father outside the home therefore constitutes a parent-child relationship founded upon the pledge of the father to provide support that is responsive to the particular needs of the unique child that is the father's own. Braces, special shoes, lessons—a father may not be able to provide all these things for his child, but he is entitled to try. . . .

Through child support, then, children in the increasing number of one-parent families in this country have a means of sustaining a relationship with both parents. The bond with the custodial parent, usually the mother, is forged through daily contact and care. The bond with the parent outside the home, usually the father, is maintained to a significant degree through provision for the child's material needs. In these ways, the family sustains the involvement of both parents in the upbringing of the child as best as the fragmentation of their lives will permit....

The intrusion on the fundamental interest in family life ... should be apparent to us all....

Diane Thomas, for instance, has two children, Crystal, aged 9, and Sherrod, aged 7. Although she has sought gainful employment, she has been unable to find work. Crystal's father has almost never complied with a court order requiring him to contribute to Crystal's support. Sherrod's father, however, has voluntarily paid $200 a month on a regular basis toward Sherrod's support. Prior to October 1984, Ms. Thomas received $194 a month in AFDC for the support of herself and Crystal. In October, she received a notice that if she did not file an AFDC application for Sherrod and assign his child support to the State her assistance would be terminated. She then applied for benefits for herself and both her children, assigning Sherrod's child support rights to the State. Because the child support is now regarded as the income of the whole household, the AFDC grant has been reduced to $73 a month. Whereas Sherrod formerly had been entitled to $200 a month in support, he is now entitled to one-third of the $273 total income attributed to the household, or $91, and to $50 of his father's monthly support check assigned to the State, for a total of $141. The financial cost to Sherrod of staying with his mother is thus $59 a month.

Sherrod has paid an emotional price for continuing to live with his mother as well. Two months after the household began receiving welfare, Sherrod's father began to withhold support payments. Ms. Thomas stated: "He informed me that as long as I was going to use Sherrod's support money to keep up my daughter Crystal, he would continue to withhold the support." Furthermore, he has not visited Sherrod since beginning to withhold support payments. As Ms. Thomas stated, "[Sherrod's father] is extremely opposed to his son being on welfare benefits, and has told me that he stopped seeing his son because I now receive AFDC for Sherrod." Sherrod, of course, has no control over any of this, but nonetheless must suffer the loss of his father's care:

> "Sherrod is very upset that his father no longer visits him. He frequently asks me why his daddy does not come to see him anymore. Since the time his father has stopped visitation, Sherrod has begun to wet his bed on a frequent basis. Also since the visitation stopped, Sherrod has become much more disruptive, especially in school. Furthermore, his performance in school seems to have declined."

... The reaction of Sherrod's father may be misguided. It may be that he should overcome the obstacles the Government has placed in his way, and still maintain some form of involvement in Sherrod's life. The point, however, is that he should not have to try.

The financial and emotional cost of losing this connection with the father may be too much for the child to bear. If so, the only way to avoid it is for the child to leave the custody of the mother. This price for continuing to receive support from the father also is not speculative. At least one of the families in this case has chosen this course. Mary Medlin has four children, one of whom, Karen, receives $200 in child support from her father, and another of whom, Jermaine, receives $50 in support. Ms. Medlin originally received $223 in AFDC for herself and her two other children. When, as required, she added Karen and Jermaine to the welfare rolls, her entire family became ineligible for AFDC. In order to obtain assistance for her family, she agreed to relinquish custody of Karen to her father.

Karen may now keep her $200 in child support, and her mother may now obtain AFDC for herself and her other children. They may no longer, however, live in the same household. The burden of their choice hardly requires elaboration. . . .

It is thus clear that in these cases the Government " 'directly and substantially' interfere[s] with family living arrangements and thereby burden[s] a fundamental right." . . .

The nature of the interest asserted in these cases, as well as the direct disruption produced by the Government, distinguishes this litigation from typical challenges to the operation of Government benefit programs.

First, unlike those cases on which the Court relies, plaintiff children receiving child support do *not* assert that they have been unfairly denied a Government benefit. Rather, they claim that the Government has deeply intruded on their relationships with their parents. . . .

. . . [T]he burden placed on the child is not the result of his or her voluntary application for AFDC benefits. Indeed, participants in this litigation are children who do *not* wish to receive AFDC. Rather, the child must choose between the father and mother solely because *other* household members are indigent and desire public assistance. It is the presence of *these* persons in the household, not the child's voluntary application for public assistance, that triggers the requirement that it choose which parental relationship to maintain.

The Government has thus placed a burden on the child's fundamental interest in a relationship with both parents on the basis of a factor over which the child has no control. . . .

. . . Contemporary life offers countless ways in which family life can be fractured and families made unhappy. The children who increasingly live in these families are entitled to the chance to sustain a special relationship with both their fathers and their mothers, regardless of how difficult that may be. Parents are entitled to provide both daily emotional solace and to meet their child's material needs; the fact that in some families a different parent may take on each role does not diminish the child's right to the care of both parents. The Government could not prohibit parents from performing these duties, and what it cannot do by direct fiat it should not be able to do by economic force. The Government has decreed that the only way a child can live with its mother and be supported by its father is if the mother is wealthy enough not to require public assistance. A child cannot be held responsible for the indigency of its mother, and should not be forced to choose between parents because of something so clearly out of its control. No society can assure its children that there will be no unhappy families. It *can* tell them, however, that their Government will not be allowed to contribute to the pain.

I dissent.

Notes and Questions

1. In *Wyman* and *Bowen,* did the Court use some of the techniques and assumptions that were used in the race and gender cases?

2. In these two opinions, can you find examples of the immorality and judicial helplessness themes developed by Professor Ross (369, *supra*)?

3. In Dandridge v. Williams, 397 U.S. 471, 90 S.Ct. 1153, 25 L.Ed.2d 491 (1970), the Court adopted a deferential standard for evaluating social welfare classifications. In so doing, it relied on cases involving state regulation of business or industry. The Court recognized the "dramatically real factual differences" between business regulation and administration of social welfare programs. The latter, as the Court said, "involves the most basic needs of impoverished human beings." *Id.* at 485, 90 S.Ct. at 1161. Nevertheless, the Court could find "no basis for applying a different constitutional standard." *Id.*

This conclusion provoked the following response by Justice Marshall: "This case, involving the literally vital interests of a powerless minority— poor families without breadwinners—is far removed from the area of business regulation, as the Court concedes. Why then is the standard used in those cases imposed here? We are told no more than this case falls in the 'area of economics and social welfare,' with the implication that from there the answer is obvious.... It is the individual interests here at stake that ... most distinguish this case from the 'business regulation' equal protection cases. AFDC support to needy children provides the stuff that sustains those children's lives: food, clothing, shelter." *Id.* at 520, 522, 90 S.Ct. at 1179, 1180.

4. Can the poor adequately protect their interests through the political process? On the one hand, it might be argued that the existence of various social welfare programs is evidence of the adequacy of the political process. On the other hand, some have maintained that such programs are used to regulate the poor, rather than benefit them. *See* Frances Fox Piven & Richard Cloward, Regulating the Poor (Pantheon Books 1971). Consider also the following excerpt from Stephen Loffredo, *Poverty, Democracy and Constitutional Law,* 141 U.Pa.L.Rev. 1277, 1388–89 (1993).

The Court's poverty discourse ignores the power that money wields in the political sphere and mistakenly ascribes to the poor a political potency that those without economic resources simply lack.... [T]he myth of democratic legitimacy ... stands at the core of the poverty cases and their use of rationality review.

This myth of democratic legitimacy is harmful in at least two interconnected respects. First, the Court's use of rationality review, despite the political marginalization of the poor, facilitates a politics of scapegoating and sensationalism in which stereotype masquerades as fact and stigma displaces deliberation. This lack of reasoned decision-making is an extreme example of a broader democratic defect that the courts must correct through heightened review. But the damage wrought by the democratic myth in the Court's poverty discourse is more personal and more tragic. When the poor and homeless bring their constitutional claims to court, the stakes are very high if concern and empathy are denied.... [T]he court's deliberative indifference may mean the difference between life and death itself.... [T]he Court's broad deference to majoritarian outcomes that condemn poor people to starvation or worse cannot be justified where the political order is "distorted and corroded" by economic inequalities.

The Court abdicates its fundamental responsibility to dispense justice when it stands passively in the face of democratic failure caused by disparities of wealth in the political sphere. Twenty years ago, the Court was unable to find any distinction between laws that affect the most basic of human wants and mere commercial restrictions. It found nothing troubling about having "the starving man or woman accept the majority's vote on whether he or she shall live or not." ... [T]he relation between democracy and wealth compels the Court to reassess its treatment of a politically powerless minority and to offer protection against a polity that claims to possess a government of and for the community, and yet would allow its members to perish when there are resources available to provide for them. Extending some kind of heightened protection to the poor may not seem like much where hardship is so great. But the modest hope is that it will reorient social policies in a more humane and caring direction.

F. PEOPLE WITH DISABILITIES

1. *The Hidden Minority*

As Stephen Percy observes in the following excerpt, people with disabilities have been a neglected and hidden minority.

STEPHEN PERCY, DISABILITY, CIVIL RIGHTS AND PUBLIC POLICY

1–11 (U. of Alabama Press, 1989).

Citizens who experience mental or physical disability have traditionally represented a hidden minority in American society. Literally through institutionalization, and subtly through negative attitudes and treatment, persons with disabilities have been isolated from the social mainstream and denied the benefits and opportunities available to nondisabled persons. This exclusion results, in part, from limitations in mobility, dexterity, and communication imposed by disabling conditions. But even greater barriers to the opportunities of modern society have been imposed by nonhandicapped persons, who have feared disabled people and have been preoccupied with that group's *inabilities* and problems rather than their *capabilities*. America's citizens and institutions—both public and private—have systematically ignored the needs of disabled persons when designing facilities, employment practices, educational programs, and the delivery of public services....

Disabilities result from a large variety of sources, including birth defects; occupational, traffic, and other accidents; drug abuse; military action; mental illness; and even the natural process of aging. When one reviews the extent and types of disabling conditions, it becomes apparent that this minority, while often hidden, is not small. Statistics to determine the number of disabled Americans demonstrate substantial range, depending upon the definition of disability used and the validity of measurement techniques.

Figures from several sources document the extent and costs of disability in America. The White House Conference on Handicapped Individuals (1977) estimated that as many as thirty-five million Americans experience some form of physical or mental disability. From the perspective of employment, a 1978 survey estimated that, of 127 million adults of working age, 21.9 million (17.2 percent) considered themselves as having work limitations resulting from health problems, and 11 million reported severe disabilities. And from the perspective of disability costs, the Institute for Rehabilitation and Disability Management reported that in 1981 the cost of disability payments and health care services for handicapped Americans totaled over $184 billion—$114 billion for health care and $70.6 billion for wage replacement.

These figures suggest that disability is not an isolated phenomenon but instead is prevalent throughout society. With a broad definition, one can estimate that as much as twenty to twenty-five percent of Americans experience some form of mental or physical handicap. These data also indicate substantial diversity in the nature and source of disability. Handicapped people are by no means a homogeneous group; they differ markedly in extent of impairment and range of potential abilities. This point is often missed by nondisabled persons, who tend to lump most types of disability into a single "handicapped" category. This tendency is not only frustrating to disabled people's sense of individuality but is also an impediment to development of enlightened policies to expand the opportunities afforded to handicapped persons.

The Hidden Minority

Persons with disabilities have been a neglected minority in American society, isolated from the mainstream. Those who have been able to succeed have generally been able to do so only by masking their disability....

Disability has often been viewed as a form of social stigma, generating reactions of pity, helplessness, distrust, uneasiness, and even fear:

> The attitudes we normals have toward a person with a stigma, and the actions we take in regard to him, are well known, since these responses are what benevolent social action is designed to soften and ameliorate. By definition, of course, we believe the person with a stigma is not quite human. On this assumption, we exercise varieties of discrimination, through which we effectively, if often unthinkingly, reduce his life chances.

Nonhandicapped people generally do not understand the problems and realities in the lives of persons with mental and physical disabilities. Instead, they tend to have views of handicapped persons that are unrealistic, negative, and paternalistic. Americans often desire to help handicapped persons yet, at the same time, see those persons as "different" and not equal to others in society.

Certain classes of disability, including drug abuse, alcoholism, and mental retardation, have frequently been misunderstood and viewed in a negative light. Until the past few decades, institutionalization was the primary form of treatment for mental illness. Once placed in institutions, mentally disabled persons were often sterilized against their own will, a practice that continued well into this century. Only recently have noninstitutional forms of treatment, such as halfway houses and sheltered workshops, been made available to those with serious mental disabilities.

Many analysts contend that discrimination is rooted in inaccurate and limited conceptions, or paradigms, of disability and the needs and potentialities of disabled individuals:

> For many generations mainstream society's attempts to deal humanely with the disabled and the professional's vision of the nature of disability have been shaped by a host of mutually reinforcing paradigms. Starting from different intellectual premises, these frameworks have converged to produce a set of flawed assessments of the disabled person's needs and the place of disabled in American society. Indeed, despite their condemnations of prejudice toward the disabled, these models share far more with longstanding myths and stereotypes about handicaps than has generally been recognized.

Breaking down these paradigmatic conceptions has been one of the most difficult tasks of handicapped rights advocates.

Researchers have examined the origins of social attitudes about disability and handicapped persons and have found that negative and inaccurate perceptions arise from many sources. One source has been literary and media depictions of disabled people.... [L]iterary characters with disabilities, from Captain Hook to the Hunchback of Notre Dame to Captain Ahab, have been depicted as evil, vengeful, and freakish. [A] review of other research studies ... reach[es] a similar conclusion about the negative images of disabled persons as portrayed in literature and television. One analyst sums up the literary depiction of handicapped persons as narrow and typical of society's purposeful neglect of and distaste for disability: "Handicapped people are not especially important to writers.... In the area of the handicapped it turns out that writers have not so much led as reflected what they have found around them, and what they have found around them, of course, has been general neglect".

The development of negative and unrealistic attitudes toward persons with handicaps is attributed to other sources besides literature and the media.... Among the sources of negative attitudes ... are social customs and norms, child-rearing practices, and psychological fears and anxieties.... [T]hese attitudes are "learned and conditioned over many years," and ... efforts to change them require substantial effort.

... [N]egative views lead to discriminating attitudes against handicapped persons, or "handicapism," similar in nature to racism or sexism.... "The condition of the Negro is imposed from outside. Obviously, this is not altogether true of the cripple. But while his physical condition is not imposed from outside, the way in which he exists in the world is. His relationship to the community is, by and large, dependent upon the special sufferance the community accords him."

... [N]egative views of handicapped persons result from fears and anxieties of nonhandicapped individuals about their own vulnerability to disability: "Such anxieties may well reflect the distressing thought that we too are vulnerable, a need to avoid identification with the disabled, an inability to tolerate helplessness, discomfort with the ambiguities which are often associated with disability, and even the embarrassment that many people feel because they do not know what to say or do in the presence of those whose condition makes them feel anxious." These fears and anxieties about interaction with disabled persons are commonplace, often magnified by unrealistic portrayals and by social and physical barriers that reduce the frequency of interpersonal contacts between disabled and unimpaired persons.

Researchers have considered the extent as well as the source of public attitudes toward handicapped people.... "[T]he attitudes of the general public toward physically disabled persons in general suggest that nearly half of the non-disabled public have primarily negative attitudes toward physically disabled persons." Other research shows these negative attitudes to extend to many aspects of the lives of disabled persons.... For example, a study of college students ... showed that otherwise sexually liberated college students had disapproving attitudes about the sexual activity of disabled persons.

Public attitudes about and perceptions of disabled individuals arise, then, from many sources, ranging from personal fears and anxieties to inaccurate media and literary portrayals. These attitudes appear to be deeply based and difficult to change. *Their impact cannot be overstated, for it is clear that these attitudes have generated behaviors and decisions that have limited the opportunities and life-styles of disabled persons.*

Often the most damaging effects have arisen from prejudices against disabled persons and misunderstandings about their plights and potential *abilities*....

> We have created an image of disabled people that is perhaps the greatest barrier they face. We see the disability—the chrome and the leather, the guide dog, the hearing aid, the crutches—and look the other way. Just as we cannot seem to see the man in the policeman, so imposing are the uniform and the cultural expectations that go with it, so we cannot see the woman in the wheelchair. We do not see, nor do we look to find, her abilities, interests, and desires.

Because of these perceptions and attitudes, society as a whole has not been open to the idea that disabled individuals can meaningfully participate in most life activities.... "Society invariably perceives the disabled in terms of their disabilities, for what they cannot do, not for what they can do. This almost universal view is far more handicapping than any particular disability." Because of its blindness to those potentialities, society has erected many barriers, tangible and intangible, which impede the ability of disabled persons to participate in many facets of contemporary life. It is against this background that disabled citizens have struggled to change society so as to increase their opportunities and end their segregated status.

A Profile of Disabled Individuals

A survey of disabled individuals conducted by Louis Harris and Associates for the International Center for the Disabled in late 1985 presents data that profile the current status and perceptions of persons with physical and mental handicaps....

The portrait provided by the study shows that forty-four percent of those interviewed experienced some form of physical disability; thirteen percent suffered sensory impairment (e.g., blindness, deafness); six percent reported mental disability; five percent had respiratory ailments; and sixteen percent suffered from other disabling diseases (e.g., heart and blood diseases). Compared to nondisabled persons, handicapped individuals received much less education, were far more likely to be unemployed, and earned less income when employed.

The impact of disability on the lives of handicapped persons is clear from survey questions about social interactions and ability to reach personal potential. Over half of the respondents reported that their disabilities prevented them from achieving full potential in life, and fifty-six percent said that their handicaps prevented movement in the community, attending cultural and sports events, and socializing with friends outside of the home.

Respondents were asked about barriers that prevented them from entering the mainstream of society. The most frequently cited impediment was fear that their disabilities might cause them to get hurt, sick, or victimized by crime if they left home more frequently. In addition to

health and safety concerns, respondents also pointed to physical obstacles to their mobility. Forty-nine percent of those interviewed said that
they were not able to use public transportation or gain access to
specialized transportation services; forty percent said mobility was limited by buildings that were inaccessible or unequipped with restrooms
they could use; and forty-seven percent of working-age respondents
stated that employers would not recognize that they were capable of
performing full-time work. While those interviewed indicated that significant progress had been made since the 1960s to improve the position
of disabled persons, these persistent barriers were identified.

Public Policy and Disability

With the exception of schools for handicapped children, particularly
those serving hearing- and sight-impaired students, and the creation of
public institutions providing custodial care, public policy efforts on
behalf of persons with disabilities have largely taken place during this
century. Policy initiatives can be categorized into at least three types:
rehabilitative services, income supports, and civil rights protections.
One set of policies centers on services to help disabled persons deal with
and overcome their disabling conditions. Vocational rehabilitation programs originated in the United States immediately following the First
World War, largely in response to the number of veterans who returned
home with combat injuries. Programs were expanded to all physically
disabled persons, with the expectation that vocational rehabilitation
would return them to the work force and remove them from public
assistance programs. Later, mental disabilities came to be included
within the set of conditions that made individuals eligible for rehabilitative services.

Next came a series of public programs to provide income supports to
persons whose disabilities prevent gainful employment. Relevant here
are Social Security Disability Insurance and Supplemental Security
Income. These programs, which were begun in the mid-1950s and were
expanded in scope and eligibility during the 1970s, were designed to
ensure that disabled citizens and their families receive financial support.

The third policy initiative has centered on efforts to legislate and
enforce legal protections for those who experience mental or physical
handicaps. Disability rights legislation includes sections 501 through
504 of the Rehabilitation Act of 1973, the Education for All Handicapped
Children Act (1975), and the Architectural Barriers Act (1968). These
laws, following a half century of federal programs to provide rehabilitation services and income supports to citizens with handicaps, represent a
new and bold direction in public policy for disabled citizens. With these
laws, emphasis shifted from "treating" and "supporting" disabled individuals to creating legally protected opportunities and rights. The
advocates of these policies recognized that most handicapped people can
adapt to their disabilities and pursue meaningful and productive lives, if
social and governmental barriers to their participation in society are
removed.

With passage of this legislation, the move to ensure the rights of persons with disabilities shifted to the implementation arena. Getting rights protections stated in public laws is one thing; having them effectively and regularly enforced is another. The disability rights legislation was significant in symbolic value, committing the public sector to protecting and aiding mentally and physically handicapped citizens. At the same time, these laws did not provide clear direction as to the appropriate mechanisms or strategies for implementation. In the period since the passage of disabled rights laws, much of the implementation effort has centered on interpreting laws and developing guidelines for administrative action.

Without question, significant gains have been made as the result of the new rights-oriented laws. Some changes, including the provision of specially designated handicapped parking spaces proximate to commercial enterprises and public buildings, have been smoothly implemented with little uproar. The American public, which seldom has paid much attention to the needs of its disabled citizens, has become accustomed to handicapped parking spaces, as well as to special entry ramps and door entrances, curb cuts, elevators with braille floor designations, and specially designed restroom facilities. These modifications, so important to the mobility and access of disabled citizens, have become commonplace, and many have been achieved at relatively small cost.

Yet advancing the opportunities of disabled citizens involves more than "toilets and ramps." It requires systematic review of social practices and public policies in order that discriminatory actions can be identified and eliminated. . . .

The Americans with Disabilities Act of 1990, 42 U.S.C. 12101 represents the most significant attempt by the federal government to address the widespread discrimination against people with disabilities. The need for the comprehensive legislation is detailed in the following excerpt from the Report of the Committee on Education and Labor.

HOUSE REPORT NO. 101–485 (II)

1990 U.S. Code Cong. & Ad. News 310–332.

NATURE AND EXTENT OF DISCRIMINATION ON
THE BASIS OF DISABILITY IN GENERAL

Testimony presented to the Subcommittees on Select Education and Employment Opportunities, two recent reports by the National Council on Disability (*Toward Independence* (1986) and *On the Threshold of Independence* (1988)), a report by the U.S. Civil Rights Commission (*Accommodating the Spectrum of Individual Abilities* (1983)), polls taken by Louis Harris and Associates (*The ICD Survey of Disabled Americans: Bringing Disabled Americans into the Mainstream* (March, 1986) and

The ICD Survey II: Employing Disabled Americans (1987)), a report of the Presidential Commission on the Human Immunodeficiency Virus Epidemic (1988), and the report by the Task Force on the Rights and Empowerment of Americans with Disabilities all reach the same fundamental conclusions:

(1) historically, individuals with disabilities have been isolated and subjected to discrimination and such isolation and discrimination is still pervasive in our society;

(2) discrimination still persists in such critical areas as employment in the private sector, public accommodations, public services, transportation, and telecommunications;

(3) current Federal and State laws are inadequate to address the discrimination faced by people with disabilities in these critical areas;

(4) people with disabilities as a group occupy an inferior status socially, economically, vocationally, and educationally; and

(5) discrimination denies people with disabilities the opportunity to compete on an equal basis with others and costs the United States, State and local governments, and the private sector billions of dollars in unnecessary expenses resulting from dependency and non-productivity.

Discrimination against people with disabilities includes segregation, exclusion, or other denial of benefits, services, or opportunities to people with disabilities that are as effective and meaningful as those provided to others.

Discrimination against people with disabilities results from actions or inactions that discriminate by effect as well as by intent or design. Discrimination also includes harms resulting from the construction of transportation, architectural, and communication barriers or the adoption or application of standards, criteria, practices or procedures that are based on thoughtlessness or indifference—that discrimination resulting from benign neglect.

The testimony presented by Judith Heumann, World Institute on Disability, illustrates several of these forms of discrimination:

When I was 5 my mother proudly pushed my wheelchair to our local public school, where I was promptly refused admission because the principal ruled that I was a fire hazard. I was forced to go into home instruction, receiving one hour of education twice a week for 3½ years. My entrance into mainstream society was blocked by discrimination and segregation. Segregation was not only on an institutional level but also acted as an obstruction to social integration. As a teenager, I could not travel with my friends on the bus because it was not accessible. At my graduation from high school, the principal attempted to prevent me from accepting an award in a ceremony on stage simply because I was in a wheelchair.

When I was 19, the house mother of my college dormitory refused me admission into the dorm because I was in a wheelchair and needed assistance. When I was 21 years old, I was denied an elementary school teaching credential because of "paralysis of both lower extremities sequelae of poliomyelitis." At the time, I did not know what sequelae meant. I went to the dictionary and looked it up and found out that it was "because of." So it was obviously because of my disability that I was discriminated against.

At the age of 25, I was told to leave a plane on my return trip to my job here in the U.S. Senate because I was flying without an attendant. In 1981, an attempt was made to forcibly remove me and another disabled friend from an auction house because we were "disgusting to look at." In 1983, a manager at a movie theater attempted to keep my disabled friend and myself out of his theater because we could not transfer out of our wheelchair.

These are only a few examples of discrimination I have faced in my 40-year life. I successfully fought all of these attempted actions of discrimination through immediate aggressive confrontation or litigation. But this stigma scars for life.

Discrimination against people with disabilities also includes adverse actions taken against individuals with histories of a disability, and adverse actions taken against those regarded by others as having a disability. It also includes discrimination against persons associated with individuals with disabilities. Such discrimination often results from false presumptions, generalizations, misperceptions, patronizing attitudes, ignorance, irrational fears, and pernicious mythologies....

The Committee heard testimony about a woman from Kentucky who was fired from the job she had held for a number of years because the employer found out that her son, who had become ill with AIDS, had moved into her house so she could care for him. In that case, the woman was discriminated against simply because of her association with a person with a disability....

The U.S. Commission on Civil Rights recently concluded, with respect to people with disabilities, that:

> Despite some improvements ... [discrimination] persists in such critical areas as education, employment, institutionalization, medical treatment, involuntary sterilization, architectural barriers, and transportation.

... The Louis Harris polls found that:

> By almost any definition, Americans with disabilities are uniquely underprivileged and disadvantaged. They are much poorer, much less well educated and have much less social life, have fewer amenities and have a lower level of self-satisfaction than other Americans.

EMPLOYMENT

Individuals with disabilities experience staggering levels of unemployment and poverty. According to a recent Louis Harris poll "not working" is perhaps the truest definition of what it means to be disabled in America. Two-thirds of all disabled Americans between the age of 16 and 64 are not working at all; yet, a large majority of those not working say that they want to work. Sixty-six percent of working-age disabled persons, who are not working, say that they would like to have a job. Translated into absolute terms, this means that about 8.2 million people with disabilities want to work but cannot find a job.

Despite the enactment of Federal legislation such as the Education for all Handicapped Children Act of 1975 and the Rehabilitation Act of 1973, a U.S. Census Bureau Report issued in July, 1989 reported the following findings:

(A) The percentage of men with a work disability working full time fell 7 percent from 20 percent in 1981 to 23 percent in 1988.

(B) The income of workers with disabilities dropped sharply compared to other workers. In 1980, men with disabilities earned 23 percent less than men with no work disability, and by 1988 this had dropped to 36 percent less than their counterparts. In 1980, women with disabilities earned 30 percent less than women with no disabilities, and by 1988 this had dropped to 38 percent less than their counterparts.

Forty percent of all adults with disabilities did not finish high school—three times more than non-disabled individuals. In 1984, fifty percent of all adults with disabilities had household incomes of $15,000 or less. Among non-disabled persons, only twenty-five percent had household incomes in this wage bracket. . . .

Louis Harris' poll also found that large majorities of top managers (72 percent), equal opportunity officers (76 percent), and department heads/line managers (80 percent) believe that individuals with disabilities often encounter job discrimination from employers and that discrimination by employers remains an inexcusable barrier to increased employment of disabled people.

According to testimony presented to the Subcommittees by Arlene Mayerson of the Disabilities Rights Education and Defense Fund, the major categories of job discrimination faced by people with disabilities include: use of standards and criteria that have the effect of denying such individuals equal job opportunities; failure to provide or make available reasonable accommodations; refusal to hire based on presumptions, stereotypes and myths about job performance, safety, insurance costs, absenteeism, and acceptance by others; placement into dead-end jobs; under-employment and lack of promotion opportunities; and use of application forms and other pre-employment inquiries that inquire about the existence of a disability rather than about the ability to perform the essential functions of a job. . . .

In sum, testimony indicates that the provision of various types of reasonable accommodations for individuals with various types of disabilities is essential to accomplishing the critical goal of this legislation—to allow individuals with disabilities to be part of the economic mainstream of our society.

Public Accommodations

Based on testimony presented at the hearings and recent national surveys and reports, it is clear that an overwhelming majority of individuals with disabilities lead isolated lives and do not frequent places of public accommodation.

The National Council on Disability summarized the findings of a recent Louis Harris poll:

> The survey results dealing with social life and leisure experiences paint a sobering picture of an isolated and secluded population of individuals with disabilities. The large majority of people with disabilities do not go to movies, do not go to the theater, do not go to see musical performances, and do not go to sports events. A substantial minority of persons with disabilities never go to a restaurant, never go to a grocery store, and never go to a church or synagogue ... The extent of non-participation of individuals with disabilities in social and recreational activities is alarming.

Several witnesses addressed the obvious question: "Why don't people with disabilities frequent places of public accommodations and stores as often as other Americans?" Three major reasons were given by witnesses.

The first reason is that people with disabilities do not feel that they are welcome and can participate safely in places of public accommodation because of discriminatory actions that have occurred in the past. The second reason is fear and self-consciousness about their disabilities—also stemming from degrading and discriminatory experiences that they or their friends with disabilities have experienced in the past. The third reason is architectural, communication, and transportation barriers....

Public Services

Currently, Title V of the Rehabilitation Act of 1973 prohibits recipients of Federal assistance from discriminating against individuals with disabilities. Many agencies of State and local government receive Federal aid and thus are currently prohibited from engaging in discrimination on the basis of disability. However, where there is no state law prohibiting discriminatory practices, two programs that are exactly alike, except for funding sources, can treat people with disabilities completely differently than others who don't have disabilities. The resulting inconsistent treatment of people with disabilities by different State or local government agencies is both inequitable and illogical for a society committed to full access for people with disabilities.

TRANSPORTATION

Transportation is the linchpin which enables people with disabilities to be integrated and mainstreamed into society. The National Council on Disability has declared that "accessible transportation is a critical component of a national policy that promotes the self-reliance and self-sufficiency of people with disabilities. People who cannot get to work or to the voting place cannot exercise their rights and obligations as citizens. Accessible transportation will become increasingly important in coming decades as the baby-boom population grows older and experiences the increased transportation handicaps associated with aging."
. . .

For some people with disabilities who lead or would like to lead spontaneous, independent lives integrated into the community, paratransit is often inadequate or inappropriate for the following reasons, among others: the need to make reservations in advance often conflicts with one's work schedule or interests in going out to restaurants and the like; the cost of rides when used frequently is often exorbitant; limitations on time of day and the number of days that the paratransit operates; waiting time; restrictions on use by guests and nondisabled companions who are excluded from accompanying the person with a disability; the expense to the public agency; and restrictions on eligibility placed on use by social service agencies. . . .

However, witnesses also stressed that there are some people with disabilities who are so severely disabled that they cannot use accessible mainline transit and thus there is a need to have a paratransit system for these people. . . .

TELECOMMUNICATIONS

Gregory Hlibok, President of the Student Body Government at Gallaudet University, described some of the obstacles to daily living faced by hearing impaired people:

> Many of us confront discrimination every day. We have experienced the disappointment of being turned down for a job or promotion because we were told the communication barriers were too great. My own deaf brother was told he had to pay for his own interpreter on his job. We have tried to call the police for help using our telecommunications devices for the deaf, but the police hang up on us, because they had no TDD's. I remember when I was fifteen I left school without money to take the bus home. I had no way to call my parents or the police. I had to walk the 3 miles home in the snow.

Mr. Hlibok concluded that accessible communications systems are necessary for deaf and hearing impaired people to participate equally and effectively in society.

Currently, 19 States have intrastate TDD relay systems in place which enable hearing impaired and communication impaired persons who use telecommunication devices for the deaf (TDD's) to make calls to and receive calls from individuals using voice telephones. Ten more states are scheduled to begin intrastate service within the next year. The requirement for nationwide intrastate and interstate relay services will enable deaf and hearing impaired people who use TDD's to make calls to and receive calls from individuals using voice telephones in any part of the United States, which enhance both their personal lives and employment opportunities.

ENFORCEMENT

Several witnesses emphasized that the rights guaranteed by the ADA are meaningless without effective enforcement provisions. Elmer Bartels, Commissioner of the Massachusetts Rehabilitation Commission, stated "We know that any law is not self enforcing and that continued efforts to educate and press for policy implementation and support will be necessary."

Sandy Parrino related her personal experiences as the mother of two disabled children in lamenting the poor enforcement of existing federal disability rights legislation requiring school buildings to be accessible:

> There is not enough compliance. The village I live in, in Westchester County (N.Y.), Briar Cliff Manor ... could not see fit to put a ramp in until just this year. Therefore ... physically disabled people were never able to get into that town hall. That is just one example that has certainly irritated me for many years ... There has not been enough compliance with the 504 regulations ... It is not enough to just have it down on the books ... Many schools do not have the elevators or the accessibilities, to this day, 13 years after the bill was enacted. They still are not accessible and the classrooms are not accessible.

Howard Wolf, Chairman of the Board of The Institute of Rehabilitation and Research and a practicing attorney in Houston, Texas, stated that successful attempts to weaken the remedies available under the ADA would make the ADA an "empty promise of equality." ...

SUMMARY

As the summary of the testimony before the Committee demonstrates, the unfortunate truth is that individuals with disabilities are a discrete, specific minority who have been insulated in many respects from the general public. Such individuals have been faced with a range of restrictions and limitations in their lives. Further, they have been subjected to unequal and discriminatory treatment in a range of areas, based on characteristics that are beyond the control of such individuals and resulting from stereotypical assumptions, fears and myths not truly indicative of the ability of such individuals to participate in and contribute to society. Finally, such individuals have often not had the political power and muscle to demand the protections that are rightfully theirs. The simple fact that this Act has taken this long to pass Congress, twenty-five years after other civil rights legislation has been passed, is a testament to that fact. This Act will finally set in place the necessary civil rights protections for people with disabilities.

The Effects of Discrimination on Individuals With Disabilities

Discrimination has many different effects on individuals with disabilities. Arlene Mayerson of the Disability Rights Education and Defense Fund testified about the nature of discrimination against people with disabilities:

> The discriminatory nature of policies and practices that exclude and segregate disabled people has been obscured by the unchallenged equation of disability with incapacity and by the gloss of "good intentions." The innate biological and physical "inferiority" of disabled people is considered self-evident. This "self-evident" proposition has served to justify the exclusion and segregation of disabled people from all aspects of life. The social consequences that have attached to being disabled often bear no relationship to the physical or mental limitations imposed by the disability. For example, being paralyzed has meant far more than being unable to walk—it has meant being excluded from public schools, being denied employment opportunities, and being deemed an "unfit parent." These injustices coexist with an atmosphere of charity and concern for disabled people.

Sandy Parrino, Chairperson of the National Council on Disability explained that:

> Disability does not mean incompetence. The perception that persons with disabilities are dependent by nature is the result of discriminatory attitudes, not the result of disability.

Charles Crawford, Commissioner of the Massachusetts Commission for the Blind, explained that:

> For far too long and far too many centuries, disabled people have felt the pain of discrimination, of being held separate, at being looked at as different, as somehow being viewed as lesser ... I personally have felt the discrimination, the isolation, the sense of helplessness and the sense of no ability to relate to other people because they have shut me out.

Charles Sabatier stated:

> Sometimes we get robbed of our dignity, our self-respect, we swallow insults on a daily basis to continue to get along in our society.

Emeka Nwojke made the same point when he said:

> It is the elimination of dignity associated with being a human being that I am talking about.

Judith Heumann explained that:

> In the past disability has been a cause of shame. This forced acceptance of second-class citizenship has stripped us as disabled people of pride and dignity ... This stigma scars for life.

Larry Espling stated:

> At the ethnic festival in Waltham in 1986, I wanted to buy a book on Lithuania at one of the booths. The person sitting there said, "Why do you want this book? You can't read." Another misconception is that if a person with cerebral palsy marries, any children will have C.P. I know of two C.P. couples with normal children. It's not hereditary ... People say things sometimes as if you can't hear them. I was on a bus and two men near me said, "He'll be put away." I've had things like that happen before.

Virginia Domini explained:

> You know the general public doesn't want to see you doing your laundry, being a case worker, a shopper, or a Mom. It is difficult to see yourself as a valuable member of society, and sometimes it is hard to see yourself as a person worthy of so much more respect than you get from the general public.

Discrimination produces fear and reluctance to participate on the part of people with disabilities. Fear of mistreatment and discrimination, and the existence of architectural, transportation, and communication barriers, are critical reasons why individuals with disabilities do not participate to the same extent as nondisabled people in public accommodations and transportation.

Ruth Long, Peer Advocate Counselor for the Vermont Center for Independent Living testified about the factors that isolate people with disabilities, and how they are amplified by the rural factor. "Nobody believes that there is really a disabled community in the State of Vermont because they are invisible," she stated.

Discrimination results in social isolation and in some cases suicide.

Justin Dart testified before the Committee about how his brother and two other family members had committed suicide because of their disabilities and about a California woman, a mother and a TV director before becoming disabled, who said to him:

> We can go just so long constantly reaching dead ends. I am broke, degraded, and angry, have attempted suicide three times. I know hundreds. Most of us try but which way and where can we go? What and who can we be? If I were understood, I would have something to live for.

The frustration experienced by many Americans with disabilities was expressed by Cindy Miller:

> I am tired of being tired, fighting angry, and depressed every day fighting for my rights ... I do not want to be Rosa Parks, I just want to be Cindy Miller.

THE EFFECTS OF DISCRIMINATION ON SOCIETY

The Committee also heard testimony and reviewed reports concluding that discrimination results in dependency on social welfare programs that cost the taxpayers unnecessary billions of dollars each year....

Justin Dart testified that it is discrimination and segregation that are preventing persons with disabilities from becoming self-reliant:

> ... and that are driving us inevitably towards an economic and moral disaster of giant, paternalistic welfare bureaucracies. We are [sic] already paying unaffordable and rapidly escalating billions in public and private funds to maintain ever-increasing millions of potentially productive Americans in unjust, unwanted dependency.

Thus, discrimination makes people with disabilities dependent on social welfare programs rather than allowing them to be taxpayers and consumers.

Discrimination also deprives our nation of a critically needed source of labor in a period where demographic and other changes in our society are creating shortages of qualified applicants in many jobs.

In the increasingly competitive international economy, our nation must adopt policies which result in a bridging of the vast gulf separating the actual from the potential contributions of people with disabilities to the health of our economy. To remove the unnecessary barriers shackling people with disabilities is to avail our society of the full range of their talents and abilities....

Discrimination also negates the billions of dollars we invest each year to educate our children and youth with disabilities and train and rehabilitate adults with disabilities....

Apart from the economic benefits to individuals with disabilities and to the nation that this legislation is expected to bring about, its non-economic improvements in the quality of life of millions of Americans are no less important. The deaf person who can, because of the mandated nationwide TDD hookup, now spontaneously communicate with hearing friends in or out of their state; the woman who uses a wheelchair who can now accompany her children to the newly accessible museum using an accessible bus, or visit her sick mother in another state using a newly accessible intercity bus, or enter the supermarket; the blind individual who can, using newly marked elevator buttons, conveniently get to her sixth floor office appointment; the woman with cerebral palsy now allowed to enter the movie theater—the value of such benefits to individuals who seek to live a full life, free from arbitrary, confining, and humiliating treatment, cannot be calculated. The commitment to promote greater dignity and an improved quality of life for people with disabilities evinced in the provisions of the Act provide further powerful justification for its enactment.

CURRENT FEDERAL AND STATE LAWS ARE INADEQUATE;
NEED FOR COMPREHENSIVE FEDERAL LEGISLATION

State laws are inadequate to address the pervasive problems of discrimination that people with disabilities are facing....

The fifty State Governor's Committees, with whom the President's Committee on Employment of People with Disabilities works, report that existing state laws do not adequately counter acts of discrimination against people with disabilities.

Current Federal law is also inadequate. Currently, Federal anti-discrimination laws only address discrimination by Federal agencies, entities that have contracts with the Federal government, and recipients of Federal financial assistance. Last year, Congress amended the Fair Housing Act to prohibit discrimination against people with disabilities in the sale and rental of private housing. However, there are still no protections against discrimination by employers in the private sector, by places of public accommodation, by State and local government agencies that do not receive Federal aid, and with respect to the provision of telecommunication services. With respect to the provisions of accessible transportation services, there have been misinterpretations by executive agencies and some courts regarding the prohibition against discrimination by public entities under the Rehabilitation Act and there has been no protection from discrimination by private transportation companies not otherwise covered under federal laws....

VISION FOR THE FUTURE

Many of the witnesses described the vision of the Americans With Disabilities Act.

Sandy Parrino testified that:

Martin Luther King had a dream. We have a vision. Dr. King dreamed of an America "where a person is judged not by the color of his skin, but by the content of his character." ADA's vision is of an America where persons are judged by their abilities and not on the basis of their disabilities.

Tony Coelho shared the following observation with the Committee:

While the charity model once represented a step forward in the treatment of persons with handicaps, in today's society it is irrelevant, inappropriate and a great disservice. Our model must change. Disabled people are sometimes impatient, and sometimes angry, for good reason—they are fed up with discrimination and exclusion, tired of denial, and are eager to seize the challenges and opportunities as quickly as the rest of us....

CONCLUSION

In conclusion, there is a compelling need to provide a clear and comprehensive national mandate for the elimination of discrimination against individuals with disabilities and for the integration of persons with disabilities into the economic and social mainstream of American life. Further, there is a need to provide clear, strong, consistent, enforceable standards addressing discrimination against individuals with disabilities. Finally, there is a need to ensure that the Federal Government plays a central role in enforcing these standards on behalf of individuals with disabilities.

The difficult task before the Committee and, indeed, before the Congress, is to establish standards that fulfill this mandate in a clear, balanced, and reasonable manner. The Committee believes that this legislation has done that. This report explains in detail how that balance has been struck....

Notes and Questions

1. The ADA was enacted in 1990, and the various sections became effective in stages over the following four years.

2. The Act defines the term "disability" to mean:

(A) a physical or mental impairment that substantially limits one or more of the major life activities of such individual;

(B) a record of such an impairment; or

(C) being regarded as having such an impairment.

42 U.S.C. § 12102(2). It excludes from the definition the following:

(a) Homosexuality and bisexuality

For purposes of the definition of "disability" in section 12102(2) of this title, homosexuality and bisexuality are not impairments and as such are not disabilities under this chapter.

(b) Certain conditions

Under this chapter, the term "disability" shall not include—

(1) transvestism, transsexualism, pedophilia, exhibitionism, voyeurism, gender identity disorders not resulting from physical impairments, or other sexual behavior disorders;

(2) compulsive gambling, kleptomania, or pyromania; or

(3) psychoactive substance use disorders resulting from current illegal use of drugs.

42 U.S.C. § 12211.

3. It is significant that the Act includes in the definition those who are perceived to have an impairment, whether or not they in fact have one. 42 U.S.C. § 12102(2)(C). Could such a standard that relies on perception be used in other areas you have been studying?

4. Generally, the Act prohibits discrimination in employment, public services, public accomodations, and telecommunications services.

5. To what extent is our understanding of physical and emotional disabilities socially constructed? Consider the following explanation of discussion of the "social construction" approach and how it relates to our understanding of the behavior of children with emotional disabilities.

THERESA GLENNON, DISABLING AMBIGUITIES: CONFRONTING BARRIERS TO THE EDUCATION OF STUDENTS WITH EMOTIONAL DISABILITIES

60 Tenn.L.Rev. 295, 313–19, 364 (1993).

The basis for the "social construction" approach lies in an insight shared by many sociologists, anthropologists, literary theorists, legal scholars, and others. According to this notion, much of what we accept as fact and view as immutable is actually an interpretation of phenomena. No specific interpretation of a phenomenon is inherent or given. Rather, there are patterns of thought in society that lead individuals to interpret phenomena in specific ways. Thus, human understanding is "socially constructed."

Peter Berger describes the process through which individual members of a society share the same interpretations of events:

> Every society has its specific way of defining and perceiving reality—its world, its universe, its overarching organization of symbols. This is already given in the language that forms the symbolic base of the society. Erected over this base, and by means of it, is a system of ready-made typifications, through which the innumerable experiences of reality come to be ordered. These typifications and their order are held in common by the members of society, thus acquiring not only the character of objectivity, but being taken for granted as the world *tout court,* the only world of which normal men can conceive.

We are each born into a society in which a web of social meanings already exists. These meanings predate our arrival, and we are each socialized to them. Through this socialization, we come to view these meanings as necessary, as immutable facts. The relative nature of meaning becomes evident, however, when one moves to a different cultural setting. For example, in the United States, it is an expression of affection for an adult to pat a child on the head. In Thailand, this same act is considered rude and unacceptable. We also learn many of these social meanings as applicable to particular social contexts. Stanley Fish tells the story of listing the names of several linguists on the board as part of a reading assignment for one class. When the next class of literature students entered, he told them that the list of names constituted a "religious poem" and the students immediately began to provide sophisticated interpretations of the "poem" presented to them. In the context of a college-level literature class, the students saw what they expected to see.

Within the larger society are powerful social institutions in which common meanings also develop and become taken-for-granted. While most meanings developed in these institutions are part of the social meanings of the larger society, institutions may also develop their own understandings. These social institutions, such as prisons, corporations, and schools, shape the understandings of individuals within them. Schools function as one of these powerful communities, for they are usually close-knit collections of faculty, staff, and students. Schools are worlds in which to raise one's hand is to ask for recognition and permission to speak; to walk down a hallway without a pass is to risk punishment; and to visit the principal is itself a form of punishment.

Whether an individual shares a social meaning may depend on the perspective the individual brings to the occurrence. This can be true at the societal level as well as in social institutions such as schools. The approach I employ here requires looking not only for the perspectives that are dominant, but searching out and, if necessary, imagining the perspectives that have been silenced.

Some sharing of meanings is essential to our everyday functioning. If some of us failed to believe that red lights require us to stop and green lights permit us to proceed, we could not safely drive to work in the morning. It is the ability to share many such beliefs that makes it possible for us to negotiate our way through the day without questioning each phenomenon that appears before us. Yet, while people can and do take most of their inherited understandings of the world for granted, it is also possible for new meanings to be imagined and to become part of the inheritance of the next generation. Through this process, American society has undergone radical transformations in its understanding both of the position of women in our society and of childhood.

The idea that meaning is socially constructed has been applied widely in the community of legal scholars. ... In particular, a number of scholars have seen this perspective as especially useful in understanding the sociology of education and societal responses to individuals with disabilities....

B. *Interpreting the Behavior of Children with Emotional Disabilities*

Nine-year-old Bruce:

engaged in the following ... activities while on school property: climbing on the furniture; talking back to his teacher; distracting the other students; poking other students; kicking other students; spitting upon other students; leaving his seat without permission; making belching noises; speaking at improper times; forging his father's signature on a note sent to his home; sticking his tongue out and making faces to the other students; attacking other children with sufficient force to knock them off of their feet; moving furniture in the classroom; intentionally running into other children; eating meals without employing his utensils; and licking the food off of his tray in the lunchroom.

Seventeen-year-old A.N.:

[exhibits] episodes of loss of control of aggressive impulses resulting in serious assaultive acts or destruction of property....

... During the Easter weekend in April 1987, he went to visit a female friend. He was told she was away on vacation. As he left her home he broke the aerial on a car in the driveway and damaged the paint on the car. There was a pitchfork in the area. He used the pitchfork to damage a second car in the driveway.

His behavior was manipulative and also an expression of severe frustration....

... [H]e has an engaging friendly manner, however the relationships he forms are superficial. And he is a master at "making deals," but rarely keeps his end of the bargain. He tends to be a loner and does not interact with peers.

These descriptions of Bruce's and A.N.'s behavior, while not devoid of evaluative wording, do not tell us much about how to interpret their behavior. We can easily imagine the discomfort or shock we would feel when confronted by a nine-year-old child attacking his peers or licking the food off of his tray, or a seventeen-year-old boy bashing a car with a pitchfork. This discomfort, however, does not compel a particular interpretation of their behaviors.

Rather, these behaviors could evoke several quite different interpretations. One possible interpretation is that A.N. and Bruce are bad, undisciplined children who require punishment in order to learn that they must control their behavior. A second interpretation is that they are suffering from a psychiatric illness and require medical attention, such as hospitalization or medication. A third interpretation is that Bruce and A.N. do not understand the reasons for their behavior, and therefor they need to learn to understand the causes of their feelings and to develop more socially appropriate ways of expressing those feelings. A fourth interpretation is that the institutional structure within which Bruce and A.N. function is, to some degree, a *cause* of their behaviors.

Each of these interpretations is possible, as is holding more than one at the same time. The first two interpretations "come naturally." That is, they are the dominant interpretations available in this society— "unreflective actions that follow from being embedded in a context of practice." The notion that children who exhibit the above described behaviors—or many of the other behaviors that we see in children labeled emotionally disabled—are either bad or sick has a long and unfortunate history. This history explains why these interpretations are the easiest and clearest responses to the unsettling behaviors of children with emotional disabilities.

Both interpretations—bad and sick—excuse educators from continuing to interact with a child. If an educator believes a child is bad, the child may be sent to the principal's office, expelled, or, in the more extreme cases, referred to the police and juvenile court. If an educator believes a child is sick, the child may be sent to the nurse's office, sent home or to a doctor, or, in the more extreme cases, sent to a psychiatric hospital. When either of these interpretations predominates, educators are not viewing the child primarily as a learner and are therefore excused from teaching.

The third interpretation, which emphasizes a "learning paradigm," requires a radically different response and does not excuse educators who are unsettled by the described behaviors from continuing to interact with their students. It also requires a broader frame of reference. When a child makes belching noises or kicks his peers, educators are presented with a learning opportunity. Educators informed about the child's history can explore with that child the feelings that led up to the behaviors, the consequences of such inappropriate behaviors, and ideas for more socially appropriate and helpful responses to those feelings. This response requires educators to listen to the children's perspectives in order to begin to understand how they experience what is happening.

The third interpretation also leads educators to the fourth interpretation—a reflection on the structure of the classroom or schooling experience. For example, a classroom structure that requires students to remain quiet and in their seats for long periods of time may be unbearable to hyperactive students, who may then overreact and cause trouble in class. While teachers may interpret this behavior as "they'd rather roam the halls than sit in class," physically uncomfortable students may paradoxically prefer walking to the principal's office in disgrace to remaining in their seats. Both the third and fourth interpretations are in accord with the learning paradigm. They do not, however, "come naturally." While there are researchers and educators who espouse a combined learning-reflective approach, they are seeking to change beliefs that are deeply embedded in the structure of our schools....

The assumption that children with emotional disabilities are either bad children who need to be punished or sick children who need medical treatment has impeded the development of effective special education and related services for this group of children. Advocates, parents, educators, and public officials must work together to change these attitudes and to see children with emotional disabilities as *learners*. They must redefine the sphere of education to include the behavioral, social, and emotional skills needed by these children and consider the ways schools can change to become supportive environments in which all children will grow and develop. Little by little, we must reconstruct our views of our most troublesome children in order to put their learning first.

SCHOOL BOARD OF NASSAU COUNTY v. ARLINE

Supreme Court of the United States, 1987.
480 U.S. 273, 107 S.Ct. 1123, 94 L.Ed.2d 307.

JUSTICE BRENNAN delivered the opinion of the Court.

Section 504 of the Rehabilitation Act of 1973, 87 Stat. 394, as amended, 29 U.S.C. § 794 (Act), prohibits a federally funded state program from discriminating against a handicapped individual solely by reason of his or her handicap. This case presents the questions whether a person afflicted with tuberculosis, a contagious disease, may be considered a "handicapped individual" within the meaning of § 504 of the Act, and, if so, whether such an individual is "otherwise qualified" to teach elementary school.

I

From 1966 until 1979, respondent Gene Arline taught elementary school in Nassau County, Florida. She was discharged in 1979 after suffering a third relapse of tuberculosis within two years. After she was denied relief in state administrative proceedings, she brought suit in federal court, alleging that the school board's decision to dismiss her because of her tuberculosis violated § 504 of the Act.

A trial was held in the District Court, at which the principal medical evidence was provided by Marianne McEuen, M.D., an assistant director of the Community Tuberculosis Control Service of the Florida Department of Health and Rehabilitative Services. According to the medical records reviewed by Dr. McEuen, Arline was hospitalized for tuberculosis in 1957. For the next 20 years, Arline's disease was in remission. Then, in 1977, a culture revealed that tuberculosis was again active in her system; cultures taken in March 1978 and in November 1978 were also positive.

The superintendent of schools for Nassau County, Craig Marsh, then testified as to the school board's response to Arline's medical reports. After both her second relapse, in the spring of 1978, and her third relapse in November 1978, the school board suspended Arline with pay for the remainder of the school year. At the end of the 1978–1979 school year, the school board held a hearing, after which it discharged Arline, "not because she had done anything wrong," but because of the "continued reoccurence [sic] of tuberculosis." . . .

II

In enacting and amending the Act, Congress enlisted all programs receiving federal funds in an effort "to share with handicapped Americans the opportunities for an education, transportation, housing, health care, and jobs that other Americans take for granted." . . . To that end, Congress not only increased federal support for vocational rehabilitation, but also addressed the broader problem of discrimination against the handicapped by including § 504, . . . [which] reads in pertinent part:

"No otherwise qualified handicapped individual in the United States, as defined in section 706(7) of this title, shall, solely by reason of his handicap, be excluded from participation in, be denied the benefits of, or be subjected to discrimination under any program or activity receiving Federal financial assistance. . . ." 29 U.S.C. § 794. In 1974 Congress expanded the definition of "handicapped individual" for use in § 504 to read as follows:

"[A]ny person who (i) has a physical or mental impairment which substantially limits one or more of such person's major life activities, (ii) has a record of such an impairment, or (iii) is regarded as having such an impairment." 29 U.S.C. § 706(7)(B). The amended definition reflected Congress' concern with protecting the handicapped against discrimination stemming not only from simple prejudice, but also from "archaic attitudes and laws" and from "the fact that the American people are simply unfamiliar with and insensitive to the difficulties confront[ing] individuals with handicaps." To combat the effects of erroneous but nevertheless prevalent perceptions about the handicapped, Congress expanded the definition of "handicapped individual" so as to preclude discrimination against "[a] person who has a record of, or is regarded as having, an impairment [but who] may at present have no actual incapacity at all."

In determining whether a particular individual is handicapped as defined by the Act, the regulations promulgated by the Department of Health and Human Services are of significant assistance.... The regulations are particularly significant here because they define two critical terms used in the statutory definition of handicapped individual. "Physical impairment" is defined as follows:

"[A]ny physiological disorder or condition, cosmetic disfigurement, or anatomical loss affecting one or more of the following body systems: neurological; musculoskeletal; special sense organs; respiratory, including speech organs; cardiovascular; reproductive, digestive, genito-urinary; hemic and lymphatic; skin; and endocrine." 45 CFR § 84.-3(j)(2)(i) (1985). In addition, the regulations define "major life activities" as "functions such as caring for one's self, performing manual tasks, walking, seeing, hearing, speaking, breathing, learning, and working." § 84.3(j)(2)(ii).

III

Within this statutory and regulatory framework, then, we must consider whether Arline can be considered a handicapped individual. According to the testimony of Dr. McEuen, Arline suffered tuberculosis "in an acute form in such a degree that it affected her respiratory system," and was hospitalized for this condition. Arline thus had a physical impairment as that term is defined by the regulations, since she had a "physiological disorder or condition ... affecting [her] ... respiratory [system]." 45 CFR § 84.3(j)(2)(i) (1985). This impairment was serious enough to require hospitalization, a fact more than sufficient to establish that one or more of her major life activities were substantially limited by her impairment. Thus, Arline's hospitalization for tuberculosis in 1957 suffices to establish that she has a "record of ... impairment" within the meaning of 29 U.S.C. § 706(7)(B)(ii), and is therefore a handicapped individual.

Petitioners concede that a contagious disease may constitute a handicapping condition to the extent that it leaves a person with "diminished physical or mental capabilities," and concede that Arline's hospitalization for tuberculosis in 1957 demonstrates that she has a record of a physical impairment. Petitioners maintain, however, that Arline's record of impairment is irrelevant in this case, since the school board dismissed Arline not because of her diminished physical capabilities, but because of the threat that her relapses of tuberculosis posed to the health of others.

We do not agree with petitioners that, in defining a handicapped individual under § 504, the contagious effects of a disease can be meaningfully distinguished from the disease's physical effects on a claimant in a case such as this. Arline's contagiousness and her physical impairment each resulted from the same underlying condition, tuberculosis. It would be unfair to allow an employer to seize upon the distinction between the effects of a disease on others and the effects of a disease on a patient and use that distinction to justify discriminatory treatment.

Nothing in the legislative history of § 504 suggests that Congress intended such a result. That history demonstrates that Congress was as concerned about the effect of an impairment on others as it was about its effect on the individual. Congress extended coverage, in 29 U.S.C. § 706(7)(B)(iii), to those individuals who are simply "regarded as having" a physical or mental impairment. The Senate Report provides as an example of a person who would be covered under this subsection "a person with some kind of visible physical impairment which in fact does not substantially limit that person's functioning." Such an impairment might not diminish a person's physical or mental capabilities, but could nevertheless substantially limit that person's ability to work as a result of the negative reactions of others to the impairment.

Allowing discrimination based on the contagious effects of a physical impairment would be inconsistent with the basic purpose of § 504, which is to ensure that handicapped individuals are not denied jobs or other benefits because of the prejudiced attitudes or the ignorance of others. By amending the definition of "handicapped individual" to include not only those who are actually physically impaired, but also those who are regarded as impaired and who, as a result, are substantially limited in a major life activity, Congress acknowledged that society's accumulated myths and fears about disability and disease are as handicapping as are the physical limitations that flow from actual impairment. Few aspects of a handicap give rise to the same level of public fear and misapprehension as contagiousness. Even those who suffer or have recovered from such noninfectious diseases as epilepsy or cancer have faced discrimination based on the irrational fear that they might be contagious. The Act is carefully structured to replace such reflexive reactions to actual or perceived handicaps with actions based on reasoned and medically sound judgments: the definition of "handicapped individual" is broad, but only those individuals who are both handicapped and otherwise qualified are eligible for relief. The fact that some persons who have contagious diseases may pose a serious health threat to others under certain circumstances does not justify excluding from the coverage of the Act all persons with actual or perceived contagious diseases. Such exclusion would mean that those accused of being contagious would never have the opportunity to have their condition evaluated in light of medical evidence and a determination made as to whether they were "otherwise qualified." Rather, they would be vulnerable to discrimination on the basis of mythology—precisely the type of injury Congress sought to prevent. We conclude that the fact that a person with a record of a physical impairment is also contagious does not suffice to remove that person from coverage under § 504.

The remaining question is whether Arline is otherwise qualified for the job of elementary schoolteacher. To answer this question in most cases, the district court will need to conduct an individualized inquiry and make appropriate findings of fact. Such an inquiry is essential if § 504 is to achieve its goal of protecting handicapped individuals from deprivations based on prejudice, stereotypes, or unfounded fear, while giving appropriate weight to such legitimate concerns of grantees as avoiding exposing others to significant health and safety risks. The basic factors to be considered in conducting this inquiry are well established. In the context of the employment of a person handicapped with a contagious disease, we agree with amicus American Medical Association that this inquiry should include

"[findings of] facts, based on reasonable medical judgments given the state of medical knowledge, about (a) the nature of the risk (how the disease is transmitted), (b) the duration of the risk (how long is the carrier infectious), (c) the severity of the risk (what is the potential harm to third parties) and (d) the probabilities the disease will be transmitted and will cause varying degrees of harm." In making these findings, courts normally should defer to the reasonable medical judgments of public health officials. The next step in the "otherwise-qualified" inquiry is for the court to evaluate, in light of these medical findings, whether the employer could reasonably accommodate the employee under the established standards for that inquiry.

Because of the paucity of factual findings by the District Court, we, like the Court of Appeals, are unable at this stage of the proceedings to resolve whether Arline is "otherwise qualified" for her job. The District Court made no findings as to the duration and severity of Arline's condition, nor as to the probability that she would transmit the disease. Nor did the court determine whether Arline was contagious at the time she was discharged, or whether the School Board could have reasonably accommodated her. Accordingly, the resolution of whether Arline was otherwise qualified requires further findings of fact.

We hold that a person suffering from the contagious disease of tuberculosis can be a handicapped person within the meaning of § 504 of the Rehabilitation Act of 1973, and that respondent Arline is such a person. We remand the case to the District Court to determine whether Arline is otherwise qualified for her position. The judgment of the Court of Appeals is

Affirmed.

CHIEF JUSTICE REHNQUIST, with whom JUSTICE SCALIA joins, dissenting. . . .

. . . [T]he Court never questions that Arline was discharged because of the threat her condition posed to others. Instead, it posits that the contagious effects of a disease cannot be "meaningfully" distinguished from the disease's effect on a claimant under the Act. To support this position, the Court observes that Congress intended to extend the Act's protections to individuals who have a condition that does not impair their mental and physical capabilities, but limits their major life activities because of the adverse reactions of others. This congressional recognition of a handicap resulting from the reactions of others, we are told, reveals that Congress intended the Rehabilitation Act to regulate discrimination on the basis of contagiousness.

This analysis misses the mark in several respects. To begin with, Congress' recognition that an individual may be handicapped under the Act solely by reason of the reactions of others in no way demonstrates that, for the purposes of interpreting the Act, the reactions of others to the condition cannot be considered separately from the effect of the condition on the claimant. In addition, the Court provides no basis for extending the Act's generalized coverage of individuals suffering discrimination as a result of the reactions of others to coverage of individuals with contagious diseases. Although citing examples of handicapped individuals described in the regulations and legislative history, the Court points to nothing in these materials suggesting that Congress contemplated that a person with a condition posing a threat to the health of others may be considered handicapped under the Act. . . .

Notes and Questions

1. What is the basis for the Court's determination that Gene Arline is a handicapped individual for purposes of the Rehabilitation Act? Does it rely on the effect of tuberculosis on Arline? Does it rely on the reactions of others to Arline?

2. How does the dissent differ from the majority on the question of who is a handicapped person under the Act?

3. Could a federally funded program refuse to hire an applicant who is a carrier of the Acquired Immune Deficiency Syndrome (AIDS) virus?

4. Does the Court use a social construction approach in determining who is protected by the Act? Should it?

2. Exclusion of People With Disabilities

BOARD OF EDUCATION v. ROWLEY
Supreme Court of the United States, 1982.
458 U.S. 176, 102 S.Ct. 3034, 73 L.Ed.2d 690.

JUSTICE REHNQUIST delivered the opinion of the Court.

This case presents a question of statutory interpretation. Petitioners contend that the Court of Appeals and the District Court misconstrued the requirements imposed by Congress upon States which receive federal funds under the Education of the Handicapped Act. We agree and reverse the judgment of the Court of Appeals.

I

The Education of the Handicapped Act (Act), 84 Stat. 175, as amended, 20 U.S.C. § 1401 et seq. (1976 ed. and Supp. IV), provides federal money to assist state and local agencies in educating handicapped children, and conditions such funding upon a State's compliance with extensive goals and procedures. The Act represents an ambitious federal effort to promote the education of handicapped children, and was passed in response to Congress' perception that a majority of handicapped children in the United States "were either totally excluded from schools or [were] sitting idly in regular classrooms awaiting the time when they were old enough to 'drop out.'" The Act's evolution and major provisions shed light on the question of statutory interpretation which is at the heart of this case.

Congress first addressed the problem of educating the handicapped in 1966 when it amended the Elementary and Secondary Education Act of 1965 to establish a grant program "for the purpose of assisting the States in the initiation, expansion, and improvement of programs and projects ... for the education of handicapped children." That program was repealed in 1970 by the Education of the Handicapped Act, Pub.L. 91–230, 84 Stat. 175, Part B of which established a grant program similar in purpose to the repealed legislation. Neither the 1966 nor the 1970 legislation contained specific guidelines for state use of the grant money; both were aimed primarily at stimulating the States to develop educational resources and to train personnel for educating the handicapped.

Dissatisfied with the progress being made under these earlier enactments, and spurred by two District Court decisions holding that handicapped children should be given access to a public education, Congress in 1974 greatly increased federal funding for education of the handicapped and for the first time required recipient States to adopt "a goal of providing full educational opportunities to all handicapped children." The 1974 statute was recognized as an interim measure only, adopted "in order to give the Congress an additional year in which to study what if any additional Federal assistance [was] required to enable the States to meet the needs of handicapped children." The ensuing year of study produced the Education for All Handicapped Children Act of 1975.

In order to qualify for federal financial assistance under the Act, a State must demonstrate that it "has in effect a policy that assures all handicapped children the right to a free appropriate public education." That policy must be reflected in a state plan submitted to and approved by the Secretary of Education, § 1413, which describes in detail the goals, programs, and timetables under which the State intends to educate handicapped children within its borders. States receiving money under the Act must provide education to the handicapped by priority, first "to handicapped children who are not receiving an education" and second "to handicapped children ... with the most severe handicaps who are receiving an inadequate education," and "to the maximum extent appropriate" must educate handicapped children "with children who are not handicapped." The Act broadly defines "handicapped children" to include "mentally retarded, hard of hearing, deaf, speech impaired, visually handicapped, seriously emotionally disturbed, orthopedically impaired, [and] other health impaired children, [and] children with specific learning disabilities."

The "free appropriate public education" required by the Act is tailored to the unique needs of the handicapped child by means of an "individualized educational program" (IEP). The IEP, which is prepared at a meeting between a qualified representative of the local educational agency, the child's teacher, the child's parents or guardian, and, where appropriate, the child, consists of a written document containing "(A) a statement of the present levels of educational performance of such child, (B) a statement of annual goals, including short-term instructional objectives, (C) a statement of the specific educational services to be provided to such child, and the extent to which such child will be able to participate in regular educational programs, (D) the projected date for initiation and anticipated duration of such services, and (E) appropriate objective criteria and evaluation procedures and schedules for determining, on at least an annual basis, whether instructional objectives are being achieved." Local or regional educational agencies must review, and where appropriate revise, each child's IEP at least annually.

In addition to the state plan and the IEP already described, the Act imposes extensive procedural requirements upon States receiving federal funds under its provisions. Parents or guardians of handicapped children must be notified of any proposed change in "the identification, evaluation, or educational placement of the child or the provision of a free appropriate public education to such child," and must be permitted to bring a complaint about "any matter relating to" such evaluation and education. Complaints brought by parents or guardians must be resolved at "an impartial due process hearing," and appeal to the state educational agency must be provided if the initial hearing is held at the local or regional level. Thereafter, "[a]ny party aggrieved by the findings and decision" of the state administrative hearing has "the right to bring a civil action with respect to the complaint . . . in any State court of competent jurisdiction or in a district court of the United States without regard to the amount in controversy."

Thus, although the Act leaves to the States the primary responsibility for developing and executing educational programs for handicapped children, it imposes significant requirements to be followed in the discharge of that responsibility. Compliance is assured by provisions permitting the withholding of federal funds upon determination that a participating state or local agency has failed to satisfy the requirements of the Act, and by the provision for judicial review. At present, all States except New Mexico receive federal funds under the portions of the Act at issue today.

II

This case arose in connection with the education of Amy Rowley, a deaf student at the Furnace Woods School in the Hendrick Hudson Central School District, Peekskill, N.Y. Amy has minimal residual hearing and is an excellent lipreader. During the year before she began attending Furnace Woods, a meeting between her parents and school administrators resulted in a decision to place her in a regular kindergarten class in order to determine what supplemental services would be necessary to her education. Several members of the school administration prepared for Amy's arrival by attending a course in sign-language interpretation, and a teletype machine was installed in the principal's office to facilitate communication with her parents who are also deaf. At the end of the trial period it was determined that Amy should remain in the kindergarten class, but that she should be provided with an FM hearing aid which would amplify words spoken into a wireless receiver by the teacher or fellow students during certain classroom activities. Amy successfully completed her kindergarten year.

As required by the Act, an IEP was prepared for Amy during the fall of her first-grade year. The IEP provided that Amy should be educated in a regular classroom at Furnace Woods, should continue to use the FM hearing aid, and should receive instruction from a tutor for the deaf for one hour each day and from a speech therapist for three hours each week. The Rowleys agreed with parts of the IEP, but insisted that Amy also be provided a qualified sign-language interpreter in all her academic classes in lieu of the assistance proposed in other parts of the IEP. Such an interpreter had been placed in Amy's kindergarten class for a 2–week experimental period, but the interpreter had reported that Amy did not need his services at that time. The school administrators likewise concluded that Amy did not need such an interpreter in her first-grade classroom. They reached this conclusion after consulting the school district's Committee on the Handicapped, which had received expert evidence from Amy's parents on the importance of a sign-language interpreter, received testimony from Amy's teacher and other persons familiar with her academic and social progress, and visited a class for the deaf.

When their request for an interpreter was denied, the Rowleys demanded and received a hearing before an independent examiner. After receiving evidence from both sides, the examiner agreed with the administrators' determination that an interpreter was not necessary because "Amy was achieving educationally, academically, and socially" without such assistance. The examiner's decision was affirmed on appeal by the New York Commissioner of Education on the basis of substantial evidence in the record. Pursuant to the Act's provision for judicial review, the Rowleys then brought an action in the United States District Court for the Southern District of New York, claiming that the administrators' denial of the sign-language interpreter constituted a denial of the "free appropriate public education" guaranteed by the Act.

The District Court found that Amy "is a remarkably well-adjusted child" who interacts and communicates well with her classmates and has "developed an extraordinary rapport" with her teachers. It also found that "she performs better than the average child in her class and is advancing easily from grade to grade," but "that she understands considerably less of what goes on in class than she could if she were not deaf" and thus "is not learning as much, or performing as well academically, as she would without her handicap." This disparity between Amy's achievement and her potential led the court to decide that she was not receiving a "free appropriate public education," which the court defined as "an opportunity to achieve [her] full potential commensurate with the opportunity provided to other children." According to the District Court, such a standard "requires that the potential of the handicapped child be measured and compared to his or her performance, and that the resulting differential or 'shortfall' be compared to the shortfall experienced by nonhandicapped children." The District Court's definition arose from its assumption that the responsibility for "giv[ing] content to the requirement of an 'appropriate education'" had "been left entirely to the [federal] courts and the hearing officers."

A divided panel of the United States Court of Appeals for the Second Circuit affirmed. . . .

We granted certiorari to review the lower courts' interpretation of the Act. Such review requires us to consider two questions: What is meant by the Act's requirement of a "free appropriate public education"? And what is the role of state and federal courts in exercising the review granted by 20 U.S.C. § 1415? We consider these questions separately.

III

A

. . . [T]he Act does expressly define "free appropriate public education": "The term 'free appropriate public education' means special education and related services which (A) have been provided at public expense, under public supervision and direction, and without charge, (B) meet the standards of the State educational agency, (C) include an appropriate preschool, elementary, or secondary school education in the State involved, and (D) are provided in conformity with the individualized education program required under section 1414(a)(5) of this title." "Special education," as referred to in this definition, means "specially designed instruction, at no cost to parents or guardians, to meet the unique needs of a handicapped child, including classroom instruction, instruction in physical education, home instruction, and instruction in hospitals and institutions." "Related services" are defined as "transportation, and such developmental, corrective, and other supportive services . . . as may be required to assist a handicapped child to benefit from special education." . . .

According to the definitions contained in the Act, a "free appropriate public education" consists of educational instruction specially designed to meet the unique needs of the handicapped child, supported by such services as are necessary to permit the child "to benefit" from the instruction. Almost as a checklist for adequacy under the Act, the definition also requires that such instruction and services be provided at public expense and under public supervision, meet the State's educational standards, approximate the grade levels used in the State's regular education, and comport with the child's IEP. Thus, if personalized instruction is being provided with sufficient supportive services to permit the child to benefit from the instruction, and the other items on the definitional checklist are satisfied, the child is receiving a "free appropriate public education" as defined by the Act.

Other portions of the statute also shed light upon congressional intent. Congress found that of the roughly eight million handicapped children in the United States at the time of enactment, one million were "excluded entirely from the public school system" and more than half were receiving an inappropriate education. In addition, as mentioned in Part I, the Act requires States to extend educational services first to those children who are receiving no education and second to those children who are receiving an "inadequate education." When these express statutory findings and priorities are read together with the Act's extensive procedural requirements and its definition of "free appropriate public education," the face of the statute evinces a congressional intent to bring previously excluded handicapped children into the public education systems of the States and to require the States to adopt procedures which would result in individualized consideration of and instruction for each child.

Noticeably absent from the language of the statute is any substantive standard prescribing the level of education to be accorded handicapped children. Certainly the language of the statute contains no requirement like the one imposed by the lower courts—that States maximize the potential of handicapped children "commensurate with the opportunity provided to other children." That standard was expounded by the District Court without reference to the statutory definitions or even to the legislative history of the Act. Although we find the statutory definition of "free appropriate public education" to be helpful in our interpretation of the Act, there remains the question of whether the legislative history indicates a congressional intent that such education meet some additional substantive standard. For an answer, we turn to that history.

B

(i)

As suggested in Part I, federal support for education of the handicapped is a fairly recent development. Before passage of the Act some States had passed laws to improve the educational services afforded handicapped children, but many of these children were excluded completely from any form of public education or were left to fend for themselves in classrooms designed for education of their nonhandicapped peers. As previously noted, the House Report begins by emphasizing this exclusion and misplacement, noting that millions of handicapped children "were either totally excluded from schools or [were] sitting idly in regular classrooms awaiting the time when they were old enough to 'drop out.'" ...

This concern, stressed repeatedly throughout the legislative history, confirms the impression conveyed by the language of the statute: By passing the Act, Congress sought primarily to make public education available to handicapped children. But in seeking to provide such access to public education, Congress did not impose upon the States any greater substantive educational standard than would be necessary to make such access meaningful. Indeed, Congress expressly "recognize[d] that in many instances the process of providing special education and related services to handicapped children is not guaranteed to produce any particular outcome." Thus, the intent of the Act was more to open the door of public education to handicapped children on appropriate terms than to guarantee any particular level of education once inside. ...

That the Act imposes no clear obligation upon recipient States beyond the requirement that handicapped children receive some form of specialized education is perhaps best demonstrated by the fact that Congress, in explaining the need for the Act, equated an "appropriate education" to the receipt of some specialized educational services. The Senate Report states: "[T]he most recent statistics provided by the Bureau of Education for the Handicapped estimate that of the more than 8 million children ... with handicapping conditions requiring special education and related services, only 3.9 million such children are receiving an appropriate education." This statement, which reveals Congress' view that 3.9 million handicapped children were "receiving an appropriate education" in 1975, is followed immediately in the Senate Report by a table showing that 3.9 million handicapped children were "served" in 1975 and a slightly larger number were "unserved." A similar statement and table appear in the House Report.

It is evident from the legislative history that the characterization of handicapped children as "served" referred to children who were receiving some form of specialized educational services from the States, and that the characterization of children as "unserved" referred to those who were receiving no specialized educational services.... By characterizing the 3.9 million handicapped children who were "served" as children who were "receiving an appropriate education," the Senate and House Reports unmistakably disclose Congress' perception of the type of education required by the Act: an "appropriate education" is provided when personalized educational services are provided.

(ii)

Respondents contend that "the goal of the Act is to provide each handicapped child with an equal educational opportunity." We think, however, that the requirement that a State provide specialized educational services to handicapped children generates no additional requirement that the services so provided be sufficient to maximize each child's potential "commensurate with the opportunity provided other children." Respondents and the United States correctly note that Congress sought "to provide assistance to the States in carrying out their responsibilities under ... the Constitution of the United States to provide equal protection of the laws." But we do not think that such statements imply a congressional intent to achieve strict equality of opportunity or services.

The educational opportunities provided by our public school systems undoubtedly differ from student to student, depending upon a myriad of factors that might affect a particular student's ability to assimilate information presented in the classroom. The requirement that States provide "equal" educational opportunities would thus seem to present an entirely unworkable standard requiring impossible measurements and comparisons. Similarly, furnishing handicapped children with only such services as are available to nonhandicapped children would in all probability fall short of the statutory requirement of "free appropriate public education"; to require, on the other hand, the furnishing of every special service necessary to maximize each handicapped child's potential is, we think, further than Congress intended to go. Thus to speak in terms of "equal" services in one instance gives less than what is required by the Act and in another instance more. The theme of the Act is "free appropriate public education," a phrase which is too complex to be captured by the word "equal" whether one is speaking of opportunities or services. . . .

In explaining the need for federal legislation, the House Report noted that "no congressional legislation has required a precise guarantee for handicapped children, i.e. a basic floor of opportunity that would bring into compliance all school districts with the constitutional right of equal protection with respect to handicapped children." Assuming that the Act was designed to fill the need identified in the House Report— that is, to provide a "basic floor of opportunity" consistent with equal protection—neither the Act nor its history persuasively demonstrates that Congress thought that equal protection required anything more than equal access. Therefore, Congress' desire to provide specialized educational services, even in furtherance of "equality," cannot be read as imposing any particular substantive educational standard upon the States.

The District Court and the Court of Appeals thus erred when they held that the Act requires New York to maximize the potential of each handicapped child commensurate with the opportunity provided nonhandicapped children. Desirable though that goal might be, it is not the standard that Congress imposed upon States which receive funding under the Act. Rather, Congress sought primarily to identify and evaluate handicapped children, and to provide them with access to a free public education.

(iii)

Implicit in the congressional purpose of providing access to a "free appropriate public education" is the requirement that the education to which access is provided be sufficient to confer some educational benefit upon the handicapped child. It would do little good for Congress to spend millions of dollars in providing access to a public education only to have the handicapped child receive no benefit from that education. The statutory definition of "free appropriate public education," in addition to requiring that States provide each child with "specially designed instruction," expressly requires the provision of "such . . . supportive services . . . as may be required to assist a handicapped child to benefit from special education." We therefore conclude that the "basic floor of opportunity" provided by the Act consists of access to specialized instruction and related services which are individually designed to provide educational benefit to the handicapped child.

The determination of when handicapped children are receiving sufficient educational benefits to satisfy the requirements of the Act presents a more difficult problem. The Act requires participating States to educate a wide spectrum of handicapped children, from the marginally hearing-impaired to the profoundly retarded and palsied. It is clear that the benefits obtainable by children at one end of the spectrum will differ dramatically from those obtainable by children at the other end, with infinite variations in between. One child may have little difficulty competing successfully in an academic setting with nonhandicapped children while another child may encounter great difficulty in acquiring even the most basic of self-maintenance skills. We do not attempt today to establish any one test for determining the adequacy of educational benefits conferred upon all children covered by the Act. Because in this case we are presented with a handicapped child who is receiving substantial specialized instruction and related services, and who is performing above average in the regular classrooms of a public school system, we confine our analysis to that situation.

The Act requires participating States to educate handicapped children with nonhandicapped children whenever possible. When that "mainstreaming" preference of the Act has been met and a child is being educated in the regular classrooms of a public school system, the system itself monitors the educational progress of the child. Regular examinations are administered, grades are awarded, and yearly advancement to higher grade levels is permitted for those children who attain an adequate knowledge of the course material. The grading and advancement system thus constitutes an important factor in determining educational benefit. Children who graduate from our public school systems are considered by our society to have been "educated" at least to the grade level they have completed, and access to an "education" for handicapped children is precisely what Congress sought to provide in the Act.

C

When the language of the Act and its legislative history are considered together, the requirements imposed by Congress become tolerably clear. Insofar as a State is required to provide a handicapped child with a "free appropriate public education," we hold that it satisfies this requirement by providing personalized instruction with sufficient support services to permit the child to benefit educationally from that instruction. Such instruction and services must be provided at public expense, must meet the State's educational standards, must approximate the grade levels used in the State's regular education, and must comport with the child's IEP. In addition, the IEP, and therefore the personalized instruction, should be formulated in accordance with the requirements of the Act and, if the child is being educated in the regular classrooms of the public education system, should be reasonably calculated to enable the child to achieve passing marks and advance from grade to grade.[26]

IV

A

... As mentioned in Part I, the Act permits "[a]ny party aggrieved by the findings and decision" of the state administrative hearings "to bring a civil action" in "any State court of competent jurisdiction or in a district court of the United States without regard to the amount in controversy." § 1415(e)(2)....

[A] court's inquiry in suits brought under § 1415(e)(2) is twofold. First, has the State complied with the procedures set forth in the Act? And second, is the individualized educational program developed through the Act's procedures reasonably calculated to enable the child to receive educational benefits? If these requirements are met, the State has complied with the obligations imposed by Congress and the courts can require no more.

B

In assuring that the requirements of the Act have been met, courts must be careful to avoid imposing their view of preferable educational methods upon the States. The primary responsibility for formulating the education to be accorded a handicapped child, and for choosing the

---

26. In defending the decisions of the District Court and the Court of Appeals, respondents and the United States rely upon isolated statements in the legislative history concerning the achievement of maximum potential as support for their contention that Congress intended to impose greater substantive requirements than we have found. These statements, however, are too thin a reed on which to base an interpretation of the Act which disregards both its language and the balance of its legislative history.... Moreover, even were we to agree that these statements evince a congressional intent to maximize each child's potential, we could not hold that Congress had successfully imposed that burden upon the States. "[L]egisla-tion enacted pursuant to the spending power is much in the nature of a contract: in return for federal funds, the States agree to comply with federally imposed conditions. The legitimacy of Congress' power to legislate under the spending power thus rests on whether the State voluntarily and knowingly accepts the terms of the 'contract.' ... Accordingly, if Congress intends to impose a condition on the grant of federal moneys, it must do so unambiguously." As already demonstrated, the Act and its history impose no requirements on the States like those imposed by the District Court and the Court of Appeals. A fortiori Congress has not done so unambiguously, as required in the valid exercise of its spending power.

educational method most suitable to the child's needs, was left by the Act to state and local educational agencies in cooperation with the parents or guardian of the child. . . .

We previously have cautioned that courts lack the "specialized knowledge and experience" necessary to resolve "persistent and difficult questions of educational policy." We think that Congress shared that view when it passed the Act. As already demonstrated, Congress' intention was not that the Act displace the primacy of States in the field of education, but that States receive funds to assist them in extending their educational systems to the handicapped. Therefore, once a court determines that the requirements of the Act have been met, questions of methodology are for resolution by the States.

V

Entrusting a child's education to state and local agencies does not leave the child without protection. Congress sought to protect individual children by providing for parental involvement in the development of state plans and policies, and in the formulation of the child's individual educational program. . . .

VI

Applying these principles to the facts of this case, we conclude that the Court of Appeals erred in affirming the decision of the District Court. Neither the District Court nor the Court of Appeals found that petitioners had failed to comply with the procedures of the Act, and the findings of neither court would support a conclusion that Amy's educational program failed to comply with the substantive requirements of the Act. On the contrary, the District Court found that the "evidence firmly establishes that Amy is receiving an 'adequate' education, since she performs better than the average child in her class and is advancing easily from grade to grade." In light of this finding, and of the fact that Amy was receiving personalized instruction and related services calculated by the Furnace Woods school administrators to meet her educational needs, the lower courts should not have concluded that the Act requires the provision of a sign-language interpreter. Accordingly, the decision of the Court of Appeals is reversed, and the case is remanded for further proceedings consistent with this opinion.

So ordered.

JUSTICE BLACKMUN, concurring in the judgment.

. . . The clarity of the legislative intent convinces me that the relevant question here is not, as the Court says, whether Amy Rowley's individualized education program was "reasonably calculated to enable [her] to receive educational benefits," measured in part by whether or not she "achieve[s] passing marks and advance[s] from grade to grade." Rather, the question is whether Amy's program, viewed as a whole, offered her an opportunity to understand and participate in the classroom that was substantially equal to that given her nonhandicapped classmates. This is a standard predicated on equal educational opportunity and equal access to the educational process, rather than upon Amy's achievement of any particular educational outcome.

In answering this question, I believe that the District Court and the Court of Appeals should have given greater deference than they did to the findings of the School District's impartial hearing officer and the State's Commissioner of Education, both of whom sustained petitioners' refusal to add a sign-language interpreter to Amy's individualized education program....

JUSTICE WHITE, with whom JUSTICE BRENNAN and JUSTICE MARSHALL join, dissenting....

I agree that the language of the Act does not contain a substantive standard beyond requiring that the education offered must be "appropriate." However, if there are limits not evident from the face of the statute on what may be considered an "appropriate education," they must be found in the purpose of the statute or its legislative history. The Act itself announces it will provide a "full educational opportunity to all handicapped children." ... This goal is repeated throughout the legislative history. ... Indeed, at times the purpose of the Act was described as tailoring each handicapped child's educational plan to enable the child "to achieve his or her maximum potential." ... The legislative history thus directly supports the conclusion that the Act intends to give handicapped children an educational opportunity commensurate with that given other children.

The majority opinion announces a different substantive standard, that "Congress did not impose upon the States any greater substantive educational standard than would be necessary to make such access meaningful." While "meaningful" is no more enlightening than "appropriate," the Court purports to clarify itself. Because Amy was provided with some specialized instruction from which she obtained some benefit and because she passed from grade to grade, she was receiving a meaningful and therefore appropriate education.

This falls far short of what the Act intended. The Act details as specifically as possible the kind of specialized education each handicapped child must receive. It would apparently satisfy the Court's standard of "access to specialized instruction and related services which are individually designed to provide educational benefit to the handicapped child," for a deaf child such as Amy to be given a teacher with a loud voice, for she would benefit from that service. The Act requires more. It defines "special education" to mean "specifically designed instruction, at no cost to parents or guardians, to meet the unique needs of a handicapped child...." Providing a teacher with a loud voice would not meet Amy's needs and would not satisfy the Act; the basic floor of opportunity is instead, as the courts below recognized, intended to eliminate the effects of the handicap, at least to the extent that the child will be given an equal opportunity to learn if that is reasonably possible. Amy Rowley, without a sign-language interpreter, comprehends less than half of what is said in the classroom—less than half of what normal children comprehend. This is hardly an equal opportunity to learn, even if Amy makes passing grades. . . .

The Court's discussion of the standard for judicial review is as flawed as its discussion of a "free appropriate public education." According to the Court, a court can ask only whether the State has "complied with the procedures set forth in the Act" and whether the individualized education program is "reasonably calculated to enable the child to receive educational benefits." Both the language of the Act and the legislative history, however, demonstrate that Congress intended the courts to conduct a far more searching inquiry. . . .

The legislative history shows that judicial review is not limited to procedural matters and that the state educational agencies are given first, but not final, responsibility for the content of a handicapped child's education. . . .

[T]he Court's limitations on judicial review have no support in either the language of the Act or the legislative history. Congress did not envision that inquiry would end if a showing is made that the child is receiving passing marks and is advancing from grade to grade. Instead, it intended to permit a full and searching inquiry into any aspect of a handicapped child's education. . . .

Notes and Questions

1. Which techniques were used in *Rowley*?

2. Do you see any similarities between *Rowley* and *Rodriguez* (supra at 381)? In this regard, consider the Court's observation that the Act was intended "more to open the door of public education to handicapped children on appropriate terms than to guarantee any particular level of education once inside."

3. Review Martha Minow's discussion of the unstated assumptions underlying the difference dilemma (supra at 91). Are those assumptions present in *Rowley*?

4. In the following excerpt, Martha Minow suggests an alternative way to construct our view of the choices in *Rowley*.

MARTHA MINOW, MAKING ALL THE DIFFERENCE

82–86 (Cornell U. Press 1990).

In many ways, the two sides of the argument agreed more than they differed. Both sides assumed that the problem was Amy's: because she was different from other students, the solution must focus on her. Both sides deployed the unstated norm of the hearing student who receives educational input from a teacher, rather than imagining a different norm around which the entire classroom might be constructed. To some extent the school system and the Rowleys differed in perspective: the school officials understandably assumed the perspective of the school's needs as a whole, while the Rowleys, also understandably, focused on their daughter's special needs. But even this apparent contrast in perspective rested on a shared assumption that the classroom and the school as they already existed set the boundaries for any solution. Only minor modifications, leaving the rest of the school the same, were contemplated by either side.

But there were other possibilities besides those raised by the parties and considered by the Court. One obvious alternative would have been to enroll Amy in a school or class designed entirely for hearing-impaired students. Advocated by some educators and some hearing-impaired adults, specialized schooling may produce better social experiences and more sensitivity to individual student needs. To no small degree, special schools have the opportunity to regard the disabled student as the norm and to design an entire educational and social program taking that student's needs into account. Amy would have been the same as other students in a classroom consisting entirely of hearing-impaired students. There, sign-language instruction could be employed for all of them. Even if the school included students with different handicaps, all the students would need and obtain special assistance responsive to their particular disabilities.

The choice between segregated and integrated education for a deaf child presents the difference dilemma in stark form. In separate schooling the child may feel less different in the classroom but more different in society, while in a mainstream classroom the hearing-impaired child may be treated as different from the other students even while sharing their educational experience. Congress, however, had already selected an alternative: the Education for All Handicapped Children Act directs participating states to mainstream handicapped students, "to the maximum extent appropriate," in regular public school programs. The drafters of the act, in waging a campaign against the legacies of isolation and misunderstanding of disabled people, embraced an overarching legislative commitment to place students in the least restrictive situation that would still meet the individual student's needs. Thus, because the choice between segregated and mainstreamed education had already been curbed by the legislative preference for integrating disabled students, Amy's proven ability to learn in the mainstream classroom would defeat any objection to keeping her there.

Yet there did remain another alternative for Amy, one never discussed in the litigation. To glimpse it, we need first to return to the assumptions behind the choices that were addressed. The lawful choices considered by the Court were to include Amy in regular classroom instruction, supplemented by some separate instruction during part of the week, or else to provide a full-time sign-language interpreter to translate for Amy in the mainstream classroom. Both alternatives assume that the problem of difference is located in the hearing-impaired child. Both conceive of equal treatment as treating this child the same as other children, while making unimpaired students—and the classroom designed for them—the norm used in this comparison. The school and the Rowleys simply disagreed about what the "same" treatment would mean under these circumstances: the school reasoned that essentially it meant including Amy in the same educational program as her class-mates; her parents argued that the "same" treatment would make available to her the same educational input—100 percent of the oral communication—as her classmates were receiving. Both approaches, in different ways, single her out and assign the difference to Amy.

A difference stance would treat the problem of difference as embed-ded in the relationships among all the students, making all of them part of the problem. The individual teacher would need to use an approach that would work to the educational benefit of every student in the classroom, resisting the temptation to treat the problem as belonging to the "different" child. Similarly, this different stance would challenge the perspective of any observer who assumed the existing classroom instructional mode to be natural and necessary. Some alternatives to the status quo in the very processes of communication in the classroom would need consideration.

In this light, what if the teacher instructed all the students in sign language and ran the class in both spoken and sign language simulta-neously? This approach conceives of the problem as a problem for all the students. After all, if Amy cannot communicate with her class-mates, they cannot communicate with her, and all lose the benefit of exchange. Moreover, conducting the class in sign language would en-gage all the students in the difficult and instructive experience of communicating across traditional lines of difference. All the students could learn to struggle with problems of translation and learn to empath-ize by experiencing firsthand discomfort with an unfamiliar mode of expression. It would be educational for all of them to discover that all languages are arrangements of signs and to use group action to improve the situation of an individual. Involving classmates in the solution affords a different stance toward the dilemma of difference: it no longer makes the trait of hearing impairment signify stigma or isolation but responds to that trait as an issue for the entire community.

The idea that more people could learn and use sign language, thereby ending the barriers in communication between hearing-impaired and hearing people, has historical support. In her book *Everyone Here Spoke Sign Language,* cultural anthropologist Nora Groce described how an unusually high rate of profound hereditary deafness in Martha's Vineyard from the seventeenth through the early twentieth century created a setting where the cultural meaning of deafness was quite different than it has been elsewhere in the United States. Deaf people were completely integrated into the Martha's Vineyard society, and everyone spoke sign language. Even people who were not hearing impaired sometimes communicated with one another in sign language. The sharp contrast between attitudes toward hearing-impaired people in that community and attitudes elsewhere suggests the considerable con-tribution of social constructions to the meanings of a "disability" or particular trait of difference among people. Understanding the relation-ships between people within which differences are constructed and given meaning can offer new alternatives and perhaps some ways out of the difference dilemma.

This solution is not itself the answer for all communities or all classrooms. There is no promise that all non-hearing-impaired students would happily respond to such an approach or that their parents would accept it. Nor does it bear obvious fruit for educational decisions about other kinds of disabled students. And an analogous approach to bilingual education, such as instructing each child in the languages used by classmates at home, could be unwieldy, especially if the class includes students with many different primary languages. But conducting Amy's class in sign language offers a glimpse of what it would mean to relocate the problem in the relationships within which difference arises. This marks a new approach to the dilemma of difference. Taking the students' relationships as the point of departure makes the "problem" one for the whole class, whose members are deprived of communicating fully with the "different" student just as she is deprived of communicating fully with them. If her classmates learned to communicate with Amy, they could also learn how much of their understanding of disability rests on social practices that they themselves can change. They could discover that differences are features of relationships rather than traits residing in the "different" person. This insight would be helpful as they encountered differences in others and in themselves during the rest of their lives. A relational understanding of difference can replace debates over similar or different treatment with analysis of the ways in which institutions construct and utilize differences to justify and enforce exclusions—and the ways in which such institutional practices can be changed.

A class of students all fluent in sign language would not be an option reached through an individualized special education plan. Planning for an individual, by its very focus on the particular child, tends to ignore the child's relationships with others and the construction of difference in those relationships. At the same time, the individualized plans leave in place the existing classroom methods. Mainstreaming the disabled child means producing expectations that this child will adjust to the existing educational structure, with modifications focused on her through individualized instruction at limited times. It preserves the unstated norm of the nonhandicapped student and continues to make difference seem the handicapped student's problem. As a result the social attitudes about disability which may be the largest obstacle to integrating a disabled person fully would remain barely challenged. Teaching all the students sign language, on the other hand, would involve every member of the class in altering the classroom structure that has disabled one student's participation....

Chapter Four

IDENTITY

A. INTRODUCTION

A study of privilege, power and law would be incomplete if it focused only on such characteristics as race, gender, class, sexuality and disability in isolation from each other. To be sure, the law may reflect this kind of compartmentalization. Civil rights statutes, for example, prohibit discrimination on the basis of several specified characteristics, but treat them as separate and distinct. This single-issue approach fails to recognize the potential harm to those who fall within more than one of the subordinated categories, and, as the following excerpt contends, may lead to further marginalization of people within disadvantaged groups.

KIMBERLÉ CRENSHAW, DEMARGINALIZING THE INTERSECTION OF RACE AND SEX: A BLACK FEMINIST CRITIQUE OF ANTIDISCRIMINATION DOCTRINE, FEMINIST THEORY AND ANTIRACIST POLITICS

1989 U.Chi.Legal Forum 139, 141–51.

I. THE ANTIDISCRIMINATION FRAMEWORK

A. *The Experience of Intersectionality and the Doctrinal Response*

One way to approach the problem of intersectionality is to examine how courts frame and interpret the stories of Black women plaintiffs. While I cannot claim to know the circumstances underlying the cases that I will discuss, I nevertheless believe that the way courts interpret claims made by Black women is itself part of Black women's experience and, consequently, a cursory review of cases involving Black female plaintiffs is quite revealing. To illustrate the difficulties inherent in judicial treatment of intersectionality, I will consider three Title VII cases: *DeGraffenreid v. General Motors, Moore v. Hughes Helicopter* and *Payne v. Travenol.*

1. *DeGraffenreid v. General Motors.*

In *DeGraffenreid,* five Black women brought suit against General Motors, alleging that the employer's seniority system perpetuated the

465

effects of past discrimination against Black women. Evidence adduced
at trial revealed that General Motors simply did not hire Black women
prior to 1964 and that all of the Black women hired after 1970 lost their
jobs in a seniority-based layoff during a subsequent recession. The
district court granted summary judgment for the defendant, rejecting
the plaintiffs' attempt to bring a suit not on behalf of Blacks or women,
but specifically on behalf of Black women. The court stated:

> [P]laintiffs have failed to cite any decisions which have stated that
> Black women are a special class to be protected from discrimination.
> The Court's own research has failed to disclose such a decision. The
> plaintiffs are clearly entitled to a remedy if they have been discrimi-
> nated against. However, they should not be allowed to combine
> statutory remedies to create a new 'super-remedy' which would give
> them relief beyond what the drafters of the relevant statutes intend-
> ed. Thus, this lawsuit must be examined to see if it states a cause
> of action for race discrimination, sex discrimination, or alternatively
> either, but not a combination of both.

Although General Motors did not hire Black women prior to 1964,
the court noted that "General Motors has hired ... female employees for
a number of years prior to the enactment of the Civil Rights Act of
1964." Because General Motors did hire women—albeit *white women*—
during the period that no Black women were hired, there was, in the
court's view, no sex discrimination that the seniority system could
conceivably have perpetuated.

After refusing to consider the plaintiffs' sex discrimination claim,
the court dismissed the race discrimination complaint and recommended
its consolidation with another case alleging race discrimination against
the same employer. The plaintiffs responded that such consolidation
would defeat the purpose of their suit since theirs was not purely a race
claim, but an action brought specifically on behalf of Black women
alleging race *and* sex discrimination. The court, however, reasoned:

> The legislative history surrounding Title VII does not indicate that
> the goal of the statute was to create a new classification of 'black
> women' who would have greater standing than, for example, a black
> male. The prospect of the creation of new classes of protected
> minorities, governed only by the mathematical principles of permu-
> tation and combination, clearly raises the prospect of opening the
> hackneyed Pandora's box.

Thus, the court apparently concluded that Congress either did not
contemplate that Black women could be discriminated against as "Black
women" or did not intend to protect them when such discrimination
occurred. The court's refusal in *DeGraffenreid* to acknowledge that
Black women encounter combined race and sex discrimination implies
that the boundaries of sex and race discrimination doctrine are defined
respectively by white women's and Black men's experiences. Under this
view, Black women are protected only to the extent that their experiences coincide with those of either of the two groups. Where their

experiences are distinct, Black women can expect little protection as long as approaches, such as that in *DeGraffenreid,* which completely obscure problems of intersectionality prevail.

2. *Moore v Hughes Helicopter, Inc.*.

Moore v Hughes Helicopters, Inc. presents a different way in which courts fail to understand or recognize Black women's claims. *Moore* is typical of a number of cases in which courts refused to certify Black females as class representatives in race *and* sex discrimination actions. In *Moore,* the plaintiff alleged that the employer, Hughes Helicopter, practiced race and sex discrimination in promotions to upper-level craft positions and to supervisory jobs. Moore introduced statistical evidence establishing a significant disparity between men and women, and somewhat less of a disparity between Black and white men in supervisory jobs.

Affirming the district court's refusal to certify Moore as the class representative in the sex discrimination complaint on behalf of all women at Hughes, the Ninth Circuit noted approvingly:

> . . . Moore had never claimed before the EEOC that she was discriminated against as a female, *but only* as a Black female. . . . [T]his raised serious doubts as to Moore's ability to adequately represent white female employees.

The curious logic in *Moore* reveals not only the narrow scope of antidiscrimination doctrine and its failure to embrace intersectionality, but also the centrality of white female experiences in the conceptualization of gender discrimination. One inference that could be drawn from the court's statement that Moore's complaint did not entail a claim of discrimination "against females" is that discrimination against Black females is something less than discrimination against females. More than likely, however, the court meant to imply that Moore did not claim that *all* females were discriminated against *but only* Black females. But even thus recast, the court's rationale is problematic for Black women. The court rejected Moore's bid to represent all females apparently because her attempt to specify her race was seen as being at odds with the standard allegation that the employer simply discriminated "against females."

The court failed to see that the absence of a racial referent does not necessarily mean that the claim being made is a more inclusive one. A white woman claiming discrimination against females may be in no better position to represent all women than a Black woman who claims discrimination as a Black female and wants to represent all females. The court's preferred articulation of "against females" is not necessarily more inclusive—it just appears to be so because the racial contours of the claim are not specified.

The court's preference for "against females" rather than "against Black females" reveals the implicit grounding of white female experiences in the doctrinal conceptualization of sex discrimination. For white women, claiming sex discrimination is simply a statement that but for gender, they would not have been disadvantaged. For them there is no need to specify discrimination as *white* females because their race does not contribute to the disadvantage for which they seek redress. The view of discrimination that is derived from this grounding takes race privilege as a given.

Discrimination against a white female is thus the standard sex discrimination claim; claims that diverge from this standard appear to present some sort of hybrid claim. More significantly, because Black females' claims are seen as hybrid, they sometimes cannot represent those who may have "pure" claims of sex discrimination. The effect of this approach is that even though a challenged policy or practice may clearly discriminate against all females, the fact that it has particularly harsh consequences for Black females places Black female plaintiffs at odds with white females.

Moore illustrates one of the limitations of antidiscrimination law's remedial scope and normative vision. The refusal to allow a multiply-disadvantaged class to represent others who may be singularly-disadvantaged defeats efforts to restructure the distribution of opportunity and limits remedial relief to minor adjustments within an established hierarchy. Consequently, "bottom-up" approaches, those which combine all discriminatees in order to challenge an entire employment system, are foreclosed by the limited view of the wrong and the narrow scope of the available remedy. If such "bottom-up" intersectional representation were routinely permitted, employees might accept the possibility that there is more to gain by collectively challenging the hierarchy rather than by each discriminatee individually seeking to protect her source of privilege within the hierarchy. But as long as antidiscrimination doctrine proceeds from the premise that employment systems need only minor adjustments, opportunities for advancement by disadvantaged employees will be limited. Relatively privileged employees probably are better off guarding their advantage while jockeying against others to gain more. As a result, Black women—the class of employees which, because of its intersectionality, is best able to challenge all forms of discrimination—are essentially isolated and often required to fend for themselves.

In *Moore,* the court's denial of the plaintiff's bid to represent all Blacks and females left Moore with the task of supporting her race and sex discrimination claims with statistical evidence of discrimination against Black females alone. Because she was unable to represent white women or Black men, she could not use overall statistics on sex disparity at Hughes, nor could she use statistics on race. Proving her claim using statistics on Black women alone was no small task, due to the fact that she was bringing the suit under a disparate impact theory of discrimination.

The court further limited the relevant statistical pool to include only Black women who it determined were qualified to fill the openings in upper-level labor jobs and in supervisory positions. According to the court, Moore had not demonstrated that there were any qualified Black women within her bargaining unit or the general labor pool for either category of jobs. Finally, the court stated that even if it accepted Moore's contention that the percentage of Black females in supervisory positions should equal the percentage of Black females in the employee pool, it still would not find discriminatory impact. Because the promotion of only two Black women into supervisory positions would have achieved the expected mean distribution of Black women within that job category, the court was "unwilling to agree that a prima facie case of disparate impact ha[d] been proven."

The court's rulings on Moore's sex and race claim left her with such a small statistical sample that even if she had proved that there were qualified Black women, she could not have shown discrimination under a disparate impact theory. *Moore* illustrates yet another way that antidiscrimination doctrine essentially erases Black women's distinct experiences and, as a result, deems their discrimination complaints groundless.

   3. *Payne v. Travenol.*

Black female plaintiffs have also encountered difficulty in their efforts to win certification as class representatives in some race discrimination actions. This problem typically arises in cases where statistics suggest significant disparities between Black and white workers and further disparities between Black men and Black women. Courts in some cases have denied certification based on logic that mirrors the rationale in *Moore:* The sex disparities between Black men and Black women created such conflicting interests that Black women could not possibly represent Black men adequately. In one such case, *Payne v. Travenol,* two Black female plaintiffs alleging race discrimination brought a class action suit on behalf of all Black employees at a pharmaceutical plant. The court refused, however, to allow the plaintiffs to represent Black males and granted the defendant's request to narrow the class to Black women only. Ultimately, the district court found that there had been extensive racial discrimination at the plant and awarded back pay and constructive seniority to the class of Black female employees. But, despite its finding of general race discrimination, the court refused to extend the remedy to Black men for fear that their conflicting interests would not be adequately addressed; the Fifth Circuit affirmed.

Notably, the plaintiffs in *Travenol* fared better than the similarly-situated plaintiff in *Moore:* They were not denied use of meaningful statistics showing an overall pattern of race discrimination simply because there were no men in their class. The plaintiffs' bid to represent all Black employees, however, like Moore's attempt to represent all women employees, failed as a consequence of the court's narrow view of class interest.

Even though *Travenol* was a partial victory for Black women, the case specifically illustrates how antidiscrimination doctrine generally creates a dilemma for Black women. It forces them to choose between specifically articulating the intersectional aspects of their subordination, thereby risking their ability to represent Black men, or ignoring intersectionality in order to state a claim that would not lead to the exclusion of Black men. When one considers the political consequences of this dilemma, there is little wonder that many people within the Black community view the specific articulation of Black women's interests as dangerously divisive.

In sum, several courts have proved unable to deal with intersectionality, although for contrasting reasons. In *DeGraffenreid,* the court refused to recognize the possibility of compound discrimination against Black women and analyzed their claim using the employment of white women as the historical base. As a consequence, the employment experiences of white women obscured the distinct discrimination that Black women experienced.

Conversely, in *Moore,* the court held that a Black woman could not use statistics reflecting the overall sex disparity in supervisory and upper-level labor jobs because she had not claimed discrimination as a woman, but "only" as a Black woman. The court would not entertain the notion that discrimination experienced by Black women is indeed sex discrimination—provable through disparate impact statistics on women.

Finally, courts, such as the one in *Travenol,* have held that Black women cannot represent an entire class of Blacks due to presumed class conflicts in cases where sex additionally disadvantaged Black women. As a result, in the few cases where Black women are allowed to use overall statistics indicating racially disparate treatment Black men may not be able to share in the remedy.

Perhaps it appears to some that I have offered inconsistent criticisms of how Black women are treated in antidiscrimination law: I seem to be saying that in one case, Black women's claims were rejected and their experiences obscured because the court refused to acknowledge that the employment experience of Black women can be distinct from that of white women, while in other cases, the interests of Black women were harmed because Black women's claims were viewed as so distinct from the claims of either white women or Black men that the court denied to Black females representation of the larger class. It seems that I have to say that Black women are the same and harmed by being treated differently, or that they are different and harmed by being treated the same. But I cannot say both.

This apparent contradiction is but another manifestation of the conceptual limitations of the single-issue analyses that intersectionality challenges. The point is that Black women can experience discrimination in any number of ways and that the contradiction arises from our assumptions that their claims of exclusion must be unidirectional. Consider an analogy to traffic in an intersection, coming and going in all four directions. Discrimination, like traffic through an intersection, may flow in one direction, and it may flow in another. If an accident happens in an intersection, it can be caused by cars traveling from any number of directions and, sometimes, from all of them. Similarly, if a Black woman is harmed because she is in the intersection, her injury could result from sex discrimination or race discrimination.

Judicial decisions which premise intersectional relief on a showing that Black women are specifically recognized as a class are analogous to a doctor's decision at the scene of an accident to treat an accident victim only if the injury is recognized by medical insurance. Similarly, providing legal relief only when Black women show that their claims are based on race or on sex is analogous to calling an ambulance for the victim only after the driver responsible for the injuries is identified. But it is not always easy to reconstruct an accident: Sometimes the skid marks and the injuries simply indicate that they occurred simultaneously, frustrating efforts to determine which driver caused the harm. In these cases the tendency seems to be that no driver is held responsible, no treatment is administered, and the involved parties simply get back in their cars and zoom away.

To bring this back to a non-metaphorical level, I am suggesting that Black women can experience discrimination in ways that are both similar to and different from those experienced by white women and Black men. Black women sometimes experience discrimination in ways similar to white women's experiences; sometimes they share very similar experiences with Black men. Yet often they experience double-discrimination—the combined effects of practices which discriminate on the basis of race, and on the basis of sex. And sometimes, they experience discrimination as Black women—not the sum of race and sex discrimination, but as Black women.

Black women's experiences are much broader than the general categories that discrimination discourse provides. Yet the continued insistence that Black women's demands and needs be filtered through categorical analyses that completely obscure their experiences guarantees that their needs will seldom be addressed.

B. *The Significance of Doctrinal Treatment of Intersectionality*

DeGraffenreid, Moore and *Travenol* are doctrinal manifestations of a common political and theoretical approach to discrimination which operates to marginalize Black women. Unable to grasp the importance of Black women's intersectional experiences, not only courts, but feminist and civil rights thinkers as well have treated Black women in ways that deny both the unique compoundedness of their situation and the centrality of their experiences to the larger classes of women and Blacks. Black women are regarded either as too much like women or Blacks and the compounded nature of their experience is absorbed into the collective experiences of either group or as too different, in which case Black women's Blackness or femaleness sometimes has placed their needs and perspectives at the margin of the feminist and Black liberationist agendas.

While it could be argued that this failure represents an absence of political will to include Black women, I believe that it reflects an uncritical and disturbing acceptance of dominant ways of thinking about discrimination. Consider first the definition of discrimination that seems to be operative in antidiscrimination law: Discrimination which is wrongful proceeds from the identification of a specific class or category; either a discriminator intentionally identifies this category, or a process is adopted which somehow disadvantages all members of this category. According to the dominant view, a discriminator treats all people within a race or sex category similarly. Any significant experiential or statistical variation within this group suggests either that the group is not being discriminated against or that conflicting interests exist which defeat any attempts to bring a common claim. Consequently, one generally cannot combine these categories. Race and sex, moreover, become significant only when they operate to explicitly *disadvantage* the victims; because the *privileging* of whiteness or maleness is implicit, it is generally not perceived at all.

Underlying this conception of discrimination is a view that the wrong which antidiscrimination law addresses is the use of race or gender factors to interfere with decisions that would otherwise be fair or neutral. This process-based definition is not grounded in a bottom-up commitment to improve the substantive conditions for those who are victimized by the interplay of numerous factors. Instead, the dominant message of antidiscrimination law is that it will regulate only the limited extent to which race or sex interferes with the process of determining outcomes. This narrow objective is facilitated by the top-down strategy of using a singular "but for" analysis to ascertain the effects of race or sex. Because the scope of antidiscrimination law is so limited, sex and race discrimination have come to be defined in terms of the experiences of those who are privileged *but for* their racial or sexual characteristics. Put differently, the paradigm of sex discrimination tends to be based on the experiences of white women; the model of race discrimination tends to be based on the experiences of the most privileged Blacks. Notions of what constitutes race and sex discrimination are, as a result, narrowly tailored to embrace only a small set of circumstances, none of which include discrimination against Black women. . . .

In Section B of this Chapter, we provide various perspectives on identity. How do we define and describe ourselves? How do we describe others? What are the multiple aspects of our identities? To what extent does context influence which aspects are significant at any one moment?

In the following part we examine the kinds of questions raised by Kimberlé Crenshaw regarding intersectionality. Does the failure to recognize the significance of intersectionality reinforce existing patterns of power and privilege? On the other hand, does an emphasis on intersectionality and differences create the potential of further dividing traditionally excluded groups?

In the final section, we look for commonalities and possibilities of crossing the various identity boundaries. Can we truly recognize and understand the subordination of those in groups other than our own? How might coalitions be built across the boundaries?

B. IDENTITY

ELIZABETH SPELMAN, INESSENTIAL WOMAN

1–3 (Beacon Press, 1988).

In one of the typically theory-drenched chapters of Iris Murdoch's novel *The Nice and the Good,* an elderly gentleman, Uncle Theo, sits with his twin niece and nephew while they play on the seashore. The beach is a source of acute discomfort to Uncle Theo. While the children's noise and exuberance bother him, what really seems to make him most anxious is the multiplicity of *things.* As if twinness weren't already enough of an ontological disturbance, there are on the beach all those pebbles, each clamoring in its particularity, the totality of them threatening the intelligibility, the tractability, the manageability of the world. Theo is a man who can only negotiate the possibility of plurality if the many can be reduced to a few or, best of all, to one. The horror of the manyness of the pebbles could then be stilled by the awareness that they are all instances of a single thing, pebblehood.

In describing this man's preoccupation with perceptual and conceptual tidiness, Murdoch presents, with a twist of existential angst, the throes of a problem that appeared in Western philosophical literature long before Plato: what is the world *really* made of? Do we get closer to an answer to this question by noting the manyness of the pebbles, or by reflecting on the fact that though there are *many* pebbles, there is only *one* kind of thing, the kind of thing that they all are, namely, a pebble? Does their significance stem from their distinctness from one another, despite the fact that all are pebbles, or does it reside in what they share in common as pebbles, despite the fact that in other ways they are distinct from one another?

How one answers all these questions depends of course on one's scheme for ranking things according to some "reality" scale and some "significance" scale. To the extent that the Murdoch character echoes Plato, he might answer these questions in the following way: The pebbles that we see and touch aren't really "real"; as material things, they are mere appearances of the Form "pebblehood," which is singular and "real." The pebbles, in their multiplicity, physicality, and changeability, are significant only insofar as they are instantiations of the single, nonphysical, and unchanging Form of pebblehood. At least, according to Plato, this is what the true *philosopher* would say, even though the man in the street, and surely almost any woman anywhere, will most likely be drawn to the pebbles they can see and touch, and will think that what they can see and touch is what is most real. Uncle Theo exhibits not merely a Platonic disdain for the physical things of the world, but a plethoraphobic distaste for and discomfort with their manyness; the twins, on the other hand, display a childlike delight in multiplicity and physicality, which Plato would regard as antithetical to philosophical inquiry. Real philosophers, Plato tells us, don't "lose themselves and wander amid the multiplicities of multifarious things" (*Republic* 454b). Uncle Theo is thus overwhelmed by the multitude of colors, shapes, and sizes that confront him:

> Uncle Theo ... fingered the mauve and white pebbles on the beach. These stones, which brought such pleasure to the twins, were a nightmare to Theo. Their multiplicity and randomness appalled him.... The pebbles ... looked at closely ... exhibited almost every intermediate colour and also varied considerably in size and shape. All were rounded, but some were flattish, some oblong, some spherical; some were almost transparent, others more or less copiously speckled, others close-textured and nearly black, a few of a brownish-red, some of a pale grey, others of a purple which was almost blue.

> ... If I'm studying pebbles, and want to learn the truth about them, I want to focus on what can be said about any and all pebbles, not just about some. I want to focus on what can be said about pebbles as pebbles, and not about, say, pebbles as found art objects or pebbles as slingshot ammunition.... After all, if I am interested in pebbles as pebbles, then I best not be distracted by the flatness of some or the roundness of others, the beige of one or the rosiness of another. For it is their pebbleness I said I was interested in, not their shape or their color.

> On the other hand, if I am interested in knowing about all the pebbles, how can I disregard those features of each pebble that may distinguish it from others?

Does the pebble analogy present a paradox? Elizabeth Spelman observed that it indeed leads to the paradox that is "at the heart of feminism: Any attempt to talk about all women in terms of something we have in common undermines attempts to talk about the differences among us, and vice versa. Is it possible to give the things women have in common their full significance without thereby implying that the differences among us are less important? How can we describe those things that differentiate women without eclipsing what we share in common?" *Id.* at 3. But then she noted that the analogy may be misleading because it "suggests that for feminism the problem has been how we weigh what we have in common against what differentiates us. But the real problem has been how feminist theory has confused the condition of one group of women with the condition of all." *Id.* at 4.

Is Spelman raising concerns similar to those discussed by Crenshaw? Do these concerns apply not only to feminist theory but more generally to all kinds of intersectionality problems?

MARTINEZ v. SANTA CLARA PUEBLO

United States Court of Appeals, Tenth Circuit, 1976.
540 F.2d 1039, reversed, 436 U.S. 49 (1978).

DOYLE, CIRCUIT JUDGE.

This case draws into question the validity of a membership ordinance of the Santa Clara Pueblo in New Mexico. The challenge is by appellants, on behalf of themselves and others similarly situated. This appellant class is composed of female members of the Pueblo, who are married to non-members, together with their children. Appellees, on the other hand, are the Pueblo and Lucario Padilla, individually and as governor of the Pueblo. The ordinance grants membership in the Pueblo to "(a)ll children born of marriages between male members of the Santa Clara Pueblo and non-members...." It precludes membership for "(c)hildren born of marriages between female members of the Santa Clara Pueblo and non-members...." Appellants have alleged that the ordinance contravenes the equal protection and due process provisions of the Indian Civil Rights Act of 1968, 25 U.S.C. Section 1302(8). In a trial to the court the decision was in favor of defendants.

The subject membership ordinance was enacted on December 15, 1939, in response to a marked increase in marriages between Pueblo members and non-members. Prior to 1930 these had been rare. Prior to the enactment, membership in the Pueblo for children of mixed marriages had been determined on an individual basis. In addition, witnesses for the Pueblo testified that there had been several instances, prior to 1939, in which the offspring of female line mixed marriages had been granted membership. The increase in mixed marriages produced concern about the enlarged demands for allocation of land and other tribal resources. The Pueblo's elders were apprehensive that the population increase resulting from intermarriage would strain the Pueblo's finite resources. It was, then, in response to the economic consequences of mixed marriages that the Pueblo Council determined that the offspring of female line mixed marriages would be denied membership while the offspring of male line mixed marriages would be admitted to membership.

Appellant Julia Martinez, whose parents were Santa Clarans, is a member of the Pueblo. Her husband is a full-blooded Navajo and is not a member of the Pueblo. Their eight living children, including appellant Audrey Martinez, are as a result of the ordinance barred from membership in the Pueblo. The Martinezes have lived at the Pueblo continuously since their marriage in 1941. All of the Martinez children were reared at the Pueblo; all speak Tewa, the traditional and official language of the Pueblo; all are allowed to practice the traditional religion. In effect, the Martinez children are, culturally, members of the Pueblo.

Since 1946, Ms. Martinez has attempted to enroll her children in the Pueblo through all of the procedures available under the Pueblo government. When her resort to Pueblo remedies proved unavailing, she brought this action.

Appellants have alleged that the ordinance deprives the non-member children of various rights, including residence at the Pueblo as a matter of right; certain political rights, such as voting, holding secular office, bringing matters before the Pueblo Council; sharing in the material benefits of Pueblo membership, such as using the land, hunting and fishing. Appellants also contended that the ordinance prevents Ms. Martinez from passing her possessory interest in land on to her children.

The trial court ruled for the Tribe, holding that the ordinance did not violate the Indian Civil Rights Act. Judge Mechem recognized the Pueblo's interest in membership policies generally and in the 1939 ordinance specifically and noted that if the Pueblo's ability to define who is a Santa Claran is limited or restricted, the Pueblo's culture would be changed. He recognized also the legitimacy of the Pueblo's interest in its economic survival and that economic survival and cultural autonomy are interrelated, i.e., economics affects the Pueblo's ability to maintain its cultural autonomy and identity. While Judge Mechem found that the ordinance had no bearing on Pueblo religion, he did find that the male-female distinction was "rooted in certain traditional values," the Pueblo's patrilineal and patrilocal traditions. In assessing the scope of the Indian Civil Rights Act, Judge Mechem found that the scope of the Act's equal protection provision was not coterminous with the constitutional guarantee of equal protection. "... (T)he Act and its equal protection guarantee must be read against the background of tribal sovereignty and interpreted within the context of tribal law and custom." He concluded "that 25 U.S.C. Section 1302(8) should not be construed in a manner that would invalidate a tribal membership ordinance when the classification attacked is one based on criteria that have been traditionally employed by the tribe in considering membership questions." And that, thus, the ordinance did not deny appellants equal protection within the meaning of the Indian Civil Rights Act....

The Act of Congress in question which is found at 25 U.S.C. Section 1302, undertakes to single out the more important civil rights contained in the Constitution and to render those applicable to tribal members who reside on the reservation....

It is conceded that if the validity of the instant ordinance were to be measured by the Fourteenth Amendment alone, it would have to be held violative because it draws its classification lines solely on the basis of sex. The offspring of a mixed marriage in which the woman is a Santa Claran are, by the terms of the ordinance, disqualified from membership in the Pueblo. Where, however, the man is a member of the Santa Clara Pueblo, the offspring of this mixed marriage suffer no such disability.

An enactment which works this kind of discrimination violates the equal protection clause of the United States Constitution.

The Fourteenth Amendment standards do not, however, apply with full force. They do, nevertheless, serve as a persuasive guide to the decision. The history and decisions teach us that the Indian Bill of Rights is modeled after the Constitution of the United States and is to be interpreted in the light of constitutional law decisions.

But we must still ask: is the Tribe justified in deviating from the Fourteenth Amendment standard on the basis that tribal, cultural and ethnic survival would suffer from full-scale enforcement of subsection (8) to these facts? We must hold that the facts do not support a decision that the Tribe's interest is compelling. The children of Julia and Myles Martinez are 100 percent Indian and 50 percent Santa Claran. They speak the language of the Santa Clara Pueblo, namely, Tewa. They practice the customs of the Tribe and are accepted into the Tribe's religion; nevertheless, they are denied membership and face exclusion with attendant loss of rights of inheritance, residency and voting, together with ability to pass tribal membership to their offspring, solely because their mother rather than their father is a Santa Claran. Compare this with the rights that are accorded the male member of the Santa Clara Pueblo. Even if he marries outside the Pueblo one who is not an Indian, and even though his family resides outside the territory of the Tribe, the offspring are entitled to tribal membership. The Tribe has not shown how such an incongruous and unreasonable result fosters and promotes cultural survival.

The contention is that the culture is patrilineal, patrilocal or patricultural. These, however, are conclusory characterizations. What is the history? The ordinance was passed in 1939 to deal with an unprecedented phenomenon, namely, mixed marriages on a relatively wide scale which resulted from Indians of different tribes meeting and encountering one another in Indian schools. An added element was Indians becoming acquainted while employed off the reservation. They met not only Indians from other tribes, but Anglos as well. Traditionally the Santa Clara female moved to the house of the Santa Clara husband and undoubtedly the Santa Clara male played a large role in educating the children in the Pueblo's traditions. This is the strongest argument in favor of the Tribe, but it falls short of justifying sex discrimination since there could have been a solution without discrimination. It is important to note also that prior to the adoption of this ordinance the mixed marriage problem was dealt with on an individual case basis. The evidence shows that under this policy there were situations in which the offspring of a Santa Clara woman were admitted to the Pueblo and so historically the 1939 ordinance cannot be said to represent the Santa Clara tradition.

There is evidence that the ordinance was the product of economics and pragmatics. It appeared to the governing body of the Tribe that the offspring of mixed marriages threatened to swell the population of the

Pueblo and diminished individual shares of the property. If this were the pressing problem it could have been solved without resorting to discrimination by simply excluding the offspring of both sexes where the parent, either male or female, married outside the Pueblo.

We do not deny that the power to control and define tribal membership is important in preserving the Tribe's culture and ethnic identity. Also of great importance is the interest of the individual Indian in tribal membership. His interest extends to living in a particular cultural setting in close relationship with fellow members, inheriting tribal rights, and enjoying federal and other incidental benefits. But if the equal protection clause of the ICRA is to have any consequence, it must operate to ban invidious discrimination of the kind present in this case.

The effect of the ordinance under attack is not to exclude cultural outsiders from the Santa Clara Pueblo. The Martinez children and many others of the class "have been brought up on the Pueblo, speak the Tewa language, participate in its life, and are, culturally, for all practical purposes, Santa Clara Indians." They are persons within the cultural group who have been allowed to develop a substantial stake in the life of the Tribe.

The express terms and conditions of subsection (8) purport to guarantee equal justice. Congress could have couched this provision in different terms if it had not intended to enact an effective provision. It did not do so. It is not for us to say that the meaning is unclear or that some other effect was intended. We must conclude that subsection (8) means what it says and that the ordinance is out of harmony with it. The instant tribe policy is of relatively recent origin and so it does not merit the force that would be attributable to a venerable tradition. Also, inasmuch as it originates from practical economic considerations, it becomes an arbitrary and expedient solution to the problem which was then confronting the Tribe. In sum, if we were to approve their ordinance and in turn approve this plain discrimination, it would be tantamount to saying that the Indian Bill of Rights is merely an abstract statement of principle.

The judgment of the district court is reversed and the cause is remanded for further proceedings.

Notes and Questions

1. The Supreme Court reversed the judgment of the Court of Appeals but did not address the merits of whether the policy violated the ICRA. 436 U.S. 49, 98 S.Ct. 1670, 56 L.Ed.2d 106 (1978). Instead, the Court ruled that the ICRA does not authorize a private action in federal court for declaratory or injunctive relief. The Court stated that its reluctance to imply a remedy was reinforced by the legislative history of the ICRA which revealed a congressional desire to avoid unnecessary intrusions on tribal government. The decision leaves the policy intact, subject to challenge, if at all, in the tribal courts.

2. How should the merits be resolved? Do you agree with the District Court or the Court of Appeals? What are the tensions created by the multiple aspects of Martinez' identity?

3. In what ways does the case raise the questions addressed by Kimberlé Crenshaw and illustrate the paradox described by Elizabeth Spelman? Consider the following perspectives on the case.

CATHARINE MacKINNON, FEMINISM UNMODIFIED

65–69 (Harvard University Press, 1987).

In this context, I want to raise and consider, far from resolve, some of the issues from the case of Julia Martinez against the Santa Clara Pueblo, a lawsuit a Native American woman brought against her tribe. This case is important not because the most pressing inequalities involve discriminations against Native women by Native tribes. Genocide in all its forms is a massive imposition of inequality on Native peoples and Native cultures by white people and white culture. I raise this case because its poses difficult tensions, even conflicts, between equality of the sexes, on the one hand, and the need to approach those questions within their particular cultural meanings, in an awareness of history and out of respect for cultural diversity and the need for cultural survival, on the other. If questions of sex and sexism are not to be separated from questions of race and racism under the specific cultural and historical conditions in which both arise, as I think they cannot be, we need to ask: who will define what equality means? White man's equality law has largely defined it the way I have sketched. The issue I want to raise, which the *Martinez* case in the end leaves open, is how Native people will define it. . . .

Whatever you think of the reasons, the result is that the tribes will define what equality of the sexes is going to mean, at least on the question of who is an Indian.

I find *Martinez* a difficult case on a lot of levels, and I don't usually find cases difficult. Missing from the Supreme Court's account of the case is the history of the tribal rule. I am told that the rule was made in 1939 after the General Allotment Act divided up communal lands into individually held parcels, in something like an attempt to make Indians into proper agrarians. Although this law did not apply to the Pueblos, they recognized that Congress could apply it to them at any time. In the experience of tribes it did apply to, lands were being taken away by white men marrying Native women. The Santa Clara rule was passed to prevent women who married out from passing land out, in an attempt to secure the survival of a culture for which land is life. Without knowing this, which I have by word of mouth, it is hard to understand what the Supreme Court meant when it said that this rule was " 'no more or less than a mechanism of social ... self-definition,' and as such [was] basic to the tribes' survival as a cultural and economic entity." The rule was seen as basic to survival because it discouraged Native women from marrying white men—or white men from marrying Native women, depending on how you see who does what—because that was taking away Native land. When Native men married white women, the experience apparently had been that white women more often integrated with the tribe.

Given this history, which the tribe did not choose or make, I imagine the tribe saying, we need this rule. I imagine Julia Martinez replying: I understand that history, it is also my history, but this is a male supremacist solution to a problem male supremacy created. The rule keeps Indian women for Indian men at the price of loss of tribal rights, from a time when Native women did not have formal power in rule-making. What would be wrong with preventing *any* child from inheriting land from parents who were not both tribal members? Whose system is it that ties ownership of land to ownership of women? Is that *our* tradition? Why is it seen as a matter of cultural survival when men guarantee exclusive access to Indian women as a requirement of tribal membership, but when an Indian woman attempts to claim that her family is an Indian family, to choose who to make a family with, it's called a *threat* to cultural survival? Whose culture is this culture? Is male supremacy sacred because it has become a tribal tradition? Under what conditions?

The tribe says: how can you apply the white cultural idea of equality to take us into this foreign court that has historically justified the atrocities that have subjected our people? Julia Martinez responds, how can you say that my desire for equality is not an Indian idea? When I say I am the equal of an Indian man, why do you say that I do not speak as an Indian woman? Why do you make me choose between my equality as woman and my cultural identity? The tribe says: because of the white man's history of racism and genocide, this is not an issue of sex discrimination. Your claim cannot be separated from either our history or your forum. How can you go to them for justice? Julia Martinez replies, how could the tribe make this rule? Why have you made me go to them for justice? Directly to me, I hear her say: since when is the way a woman is treated *anywhere* strictly an internal or national matter for you? If your country treated *you* this way, wouldn't you want somewhere else to go for justice?

As I said, the Supreme Court decided to stay out of this. I want to suggest that cultural survival is as contingent upon equality between women and men as it is upon equality among peoples. The sex division in this case undermined the ability of Native Americans to survive as autonomous cultures. It was certainly not a means of promoting that survival. This is not the case because Julia Martinez fought over it, and not because she fought it in the white man's court, but because the tribe was willing to sacrifice *her tribal connection,* her full membership in the tribal community, in the face of a white male supremacist threat. Their rule did nothing to address or counteract the reasons why Native women were vulnerable to white male land imperialism through marriage—it gave in to them, by punishing the *woman,* the Native person. Sex inequality, looked at close up, may threaten the cultural survival of

Native peoples just as going outside the culture to resolve it threatens tribal sovereignty. But this only appears if one recognizes that the systematic vulnerability of Native women to marriages that can destroy the tribe indicates the *tribe* has a problem—and not a problem to be solved by punishing Native women through their children to provide a disincentive. Why is excluding women always an option for solving problems men create between men? Maybe women's loyalty would be more reliable if their communities were more equitable.

In the *Martinez* case, the Supreme Court allowed the tribe to make its own rules, allowing—even if for some reasons I might criticize—that the most important meanings of equality are the meanings communities make for themselves. The question now is, what will the tribes make equality mean, and whose voice will speak for them? When I discuss this issue, I find that some people consider equality to be a white idea. If you think equality means what the white man has made it mean— being the same as him—it definitely is a white idea. But the aspiration of women to be no less than men—not to be punished where a man is glorified, not to be considered damaged or disloyal where a man is rewarded or left in peace, not to lead a derivative life, but to do everything and be anybody at all—is an aspiration indigenous to women across place and across time. I think the tribal rule in the *Martinez* case is male supremacist, not just sex differentiated. Since when is male supremacy a tribal tradition? For at least some tribes, since *contact* with European whites. At that point, it looks more like *in*equality is the white idea. And what women like Julia Martinez might make equality mean, no white man invented.

JUDITH RESNIK, DEPENDENT SOVEREIGNS: INDIAN TRIBES, STATES AND THE FEDERAL COURTS

56 U.Chi.L.Rev. 671, 722–26 (1989).

The Santa Clara Pueblo choose to link membership with gender and to limit membership to those who could claim that their fathers were Santa Claran. I do not know the genesis of this rule. Some suggest that the rule reflects the gendered hierarchy of the Pueblo, that the male members of the Pueblo wanted to deter women from marrying non-Santa Claran men. But questions need to be asked about how the Pueblo's gendered hierarchy came into being; the United States often singled out men to be designated as leaders of Indian tribes. Santa Claran men might have held the power to make rules at least in part because the United States assumed men and only men could be rulemakers.

The 1939 Santa Clara membership rules are also congruent with United States' traditions of subordination of women. United States common law rules were that the husband conferred status upon the wife and the father conferred status on the child. As one nineteenth century lawyer explained, "[t]he rule is a very old one, both by the Roman civil

law and the English common law, too elementary to require authorities
. . . that the offspring of married parents takes the status of the father.''
In contrast, some nineteenth century writers described the interests of
Indian women in tribal property to be great, and sometimes greater
than, the interests of men. The writers also stated that such treatment
of women was further proof of Indian tribes' lack of "civilized" ways.

When considering the genesis of the Santa Clara membership rules,
I wonder whether federal statutes, existing since the late 1880s and
linking gender, lineage, and property rights, played any role. In 1888,
Congress enacted a statute (still on the books) that provided that an
"Indian woman" who married a citizen of the United States gained
United States citizenship but retained her interest in tribal property. In
1897, Congress legislated that the children of an "Indian woman" and a
"white man" married prior to the enactment of that legislation would
have the same rights and privileges as did other members of the
mothers' tribe. This legislation altered the United States' common law
rule that the "condition of the father prevails in determining the status
of the offspring." Some federal officials explained the 1888 legislation
as aimed at encouraging assimilation of Indians. The thesis was that
women would follow men and that male heads of households would
provide the cultural framework for the household. It was hoped and
assumed that if "white men" could not by virtue of marriage assert title
over tribal property, white men would not live with the Indian women to
whom they were married on the reservation. When the women followed
the men, they would then live and raise their children in a white culture.
Federal administrative regulations have also distinguished between "Indian men" and "Indian women"; for example, the BIA provided families
of Indian men, married to non-Indian women, with general assistance
more readily than when Indian women married non-Indian men.

The 1939 codification of female subordination seems to have been
supported, if not influenced and encouraged, by the traditions of the
United States, a country in which women have long been expected to
"follow their men," a country in which home, name, income and status
are for many women defined by the home, name, income and status of
the men to whom they are related as wives and daughters. . . .

. . . I cannot share the ease with which the Supreme Court in Santa
Clara Pueblo assumed the 1939 Ordinance to be an artifact of Santa
Clara sovereignty. The emergence of a codified, written, non-discretion-
ary, gender-based membership rule is linked to the Pueblo's decision to
organize under guidance of the Department of the Interior, is linked to
the Pueblo as a recipient of federal funds, and is linked to the Pueblo as
situated in a United States culture that has made patrilineal and
patriarchal rules so familiar that, to some, they seem uncontroversial.

These interdependencies do not leap out from the pages of the
Supreme Court opinion in Santa Clara Pueblo. Rather, the Court's
construction of the legal issues submerges the traces of the federal role
in the Santa Clara decision to exclude the children of some of its women

members. The Court cast the statutory interpretation question as pitting a group's decision about how to describe its membership against the rights of one of that group's members. As the Court stated: "[E]fforts by the federal judiciary to apply ... [the Indian Civil Rights Act] ... may substantially interfere with a tribe's ability to maintain itself as a culturally and politically distinct entity." Under that framework, the case has considerable poignancy; decisions about membership, about inclusion and exclusion, are at the core of self description. If the federal government were serious about Indian tribes' rights of self constitution, how could a federal court or even Congress intrude? Given the current federal policy of support of tribal sovereignty, given some members of the Supreme Court's ambivalence about women's rights, and given some members of that Court's unease about any "new" implied federal causes of action, the Court's construction of the problem is understandable.

But the majority's description is too simple, too easy, and ultimately deceptive. The "Santa Clara Rule" is intertwined with United States' rules and culture. James Clifford has said it well: "Modern Indian lives—lived within and against the dominant culture and state—are not captured by categories like tribe or identity." Implicit in the Court's opinion, in its references to Santa Clara Pueblo as a distinct political entity, is what Clifford calls the erroneous "idea of cultural wholeness." The restrictive, gender-discriminatory membership rule "of" the Santa Clara Pueblo is generated out of conditions of adversity, conditions imposed by centuries of United States policy towards Indian tribes. The rule is written in the light of limited federal benefits to be divided amongst those who bear the label "Santa Claran." The rule is comprehensible to the "dominant culture" because it too accepts subordination of women.

Many commentators sympathetic to tribal sovereignty have heralded the Santa Clara Pueblo case as an important marker in federal Indian law. From the perspective of tribes, the Indian Civil Rights Act of 1968 is an example of federal intrusion; Santa Clara Pueblo is, to some extent, a buffer. I have not explored the Santa Clara Pueblo case to offer a "better" answer on the tribal sovereignty/federal intrusion issue than that given by the Court, nor am I claiming that the role the United States played in creating tribal rules justifies further intrusion. Rather, my purpose is to demonstrate that the case tells more about United States' norms than it does about tribal norms. I am skeptical about how much of a safe haven Santa Clara Pueblo provides for those seeking tribal sovereignty. Because federal norms about the treatment of women were not really threatened by the Santa Clara Pueblo membership rule, the case was an "easy" one for the Court to proclaim its commitment to tribal sovereignty. For those of us who believe in women's rights and are also concerned about federal government imperialism, the case becomes hard....

ANGELA HARRIS, RACE AND ESSENTIALISM
IN FEMINIST LEGAL THEORY
42 Stan.L.Rev. 581, 593–94 (1990).

MacKinnon repeatedly seems to recognize the inadequacy of theories that deal with gender while ignoring race, but having recognized the problem, she repeatedly shies away from its implications. Thus, she at times justifies her essentialism by pointing to the essentialism of the dominant discourse: "My suggestion is that what we have in common is not that our conditions have no particularity in ways that matter. But we are all measured by a male standard for women, a standard that is not ours." At other times she deals with the challenge of black women by placing it in footnotes. For example, she places in a footnote without further comment the suggestive, if cryptic, observation that a definition of feminism "of coalesced interest and resistance" has tended both to exclude and to make invisible "the diverse ways that many women—notably Blacks and working-class women—have *moved* against their determinants." In another footnote generally addressed to the problem of relating Marxism to issues of gender and race, she notes that "[a]ny relationship *between* sex and race tends to be left entirely out of account, since they are considered parallel 'strata,'" but this thought simply trails off into a string cite to black feminist and social feminist writings.

Finally, MacKinnon postpones the demand of black women until the arrival of a "general theory of social inequality"; recognizing that "gender in this country appears partly to comprise the meaning of, as well as bisect, race and class, even as race and class specificities make up, as well as cross-cut, gender," she nevertheless is prepared to maintain her "colorblind" approach to women's experience until that general theory arrives (presumably that is someone else's work).

The results of MacKinnon's refusal to move beyond essentialism are apparent in the most tentative essay in *Whose Culture? A Case Note on Martinez v. Santa Clara Pueblo....*

MacKinnon starts her discussion with an admission: "I find *Martinez* a difficult case on a lot of levels, and I don't usually find cases difficult." She concludes that the Pueblo ordinance was wrong, because it "did nothing to address or counteract the reasons why Native women were vulnerable to white male land imperialism through marriage—it gave in to them, by punishing the *woman*, the Native person." Yet she reaches her conclusion, as she admits, without knowledge other than "word of mouth" of the history of the ordinance and its place in Santa Clara Pueblo culture.

MacKinnon has Julia Martinez ask her tribe, "Why do you make me choose between my equality as woman and my cultural identity?" But she, no less than the tribe, eventually requires Martinez to choose; and the correct choice is, of course, that Martinez's female identity is more important than her tribal identity. MacKinnon states,

[T]he aspiration of women to be no less than men—not to be punished where a man is glorified, not to be considered damaged or disloyal where a man is rewarded or left in peace, not to lead a derivative life, but to do everything and be anybody at all—is an aspiration indigenous to women across place and across time.

What MacKinnon does not recognize, however, is that though the aspiration may be everywhere the same, its expression must depend on the social historical circumstances. In this case, should Julia Martinez be content with struggling for change from within, or should the white government have stepped in "on her behalf"? What was the meaning of the ordinance within Pueblo discourse, as opposed to a transhistorical and transcultural feminist discourse? How did it come about and under what circumstances? What was the status of women within the tribe, both historically and at the time of the ordinance and at the present time, and was Martinez's claim heard and understood by the tribal authorities or simply ignored or derided? What were the Pueblo traditions about children of mixed parentage, and how were those traditions changing? In a jurisprudence based on multiple consciousness, rather than the unitary consciousness of MacKinnon's dominance theory, these questions would have to be answered before the ordinance could be considered on its merits and even before the Court's decision to stay out could be evaluated. MacKinnon does not answer these questions, but leaves the essay hanging with the idea that the male supremacist ideology of some Native American tribes may be adopted from white culture and therefore invalid. MacKinnon's tentativeness may be due to not wanting to appear a white cultural imperialist, speaking for a Native American tribe, but to take up Julia Martinez's claim at all is to take that risk. Without a theory that can shift focus from gender to race and other facets of identity and back again, MacKinnon's essay is ultimately crippled. Martinez is made to choose her gender over her race, and her experience is distorted in the process.

———

The *Martinez* case and the discussion it generated lead us to more general questions about identity. How can we give full significance to those facets of identity that are in common, while recognizing the importance of those aspects that differentiate us? Questions about identity, as one observer recently wrote, "are some of the most ancient in Western philosophical tradition." Dale Jamieson, *The Poverty of Postmodern Theory*, 62 Colorado L.Rev. 577, 584 (1991). We do not intend to explore in depth the traditions of philosophical debate about identity. Rather, we hope to raise some questions about how law constructs, and should construct, identity. The following excerpts examine contemporary concepts of identity and their implications for the legal subject.

ALLAN HUTCHINSON, IDENTITY CRISIS: THE POLITICS OF INTERPRETATION

26 New England L.Rev. 1173, 1191–93, 1197–98 (1992).

In modernist discourse, an identity is something that each person has by virtue of their existence as unique individuals. At its most extreme and historical, there still seems to persist the idea that each subject is born normatively full-grown, like Zeus' children, with a raw set of values, preferences and characteristics that can be more or less given expression to in the historical act of living and socializing. For instance, women are marked by their biology and it is for society to organize affairs in such a way that they can be truly women and express the essence of their female being. Under this view, freedom is the successful resolution of both the search for that true intrinsic identity that lies within and the struggle to live one's life in accordance with its dictates. In both its vulgar libertarian and Marxist guise, justice is reached when people attain an unimpeded sense of themselves: false consciousness is so much old clothing to be discarded in the unveiling of the true self. On a more enlightened modernist version of identity, society plays a more formative role, but is still secondary to the givenness of a particular identity. Either way, the identity is a given quality that must be perceived and preserved.

By contrast, postmodernism rejects the notion of an abiding, fixed or essential identity. Identity is relative, not intrinsic; fluid, not fixed; perspectival, not neutral; and protean, not perfected. The subject is a cultural creation, not a biological given. Nevertheless, while people are not fundamentally fixed by their experience of race, gender and class, they are distinctively marked by such social categorizations: "Identity is in the etched details of mediated lives and struggle." Like history, identity cannot be completely got out of or into: its presence is never entirely self-present to itself so that it can be summarily embraced or evaded. Always shifting and often self-contradictory, identity is part of history, not a ground or precondition for attempts to resist or reinforce history's meaning.

If there is no Knowledge or Truth, there is also no Identity that is unchangeable or beyond re-interpretation. Of course, there are lots of identities, but not one Identity. At any particular time or place, individuals will feel acutely the pushes and pulls of their identity. Being contingent and in flux, the experience is no less real or limiting. To think or postulate otherwise would be to deny and invalidate the racial and gendered oppression of many. But accepting the experiences of racism and sexism as true and real does not deliver a fatal blow to the anti-essentialist project. Postmodernism does not denigrate or dismiss the value and truth of experience—that would be nonsensical. Instead, what it does do is avoid essentializing its value or truth. That experience is given historical force by interrogating it and resisting the modernist temptation to reduce it to a new authoritative source of epistemological knowledge. In this way, the subject becomes a site for the constant and continuing struggle to take on an identity that is conducive to a truly egalitarian society. Notions like subjectivity, false consciousness, experience and personal destiny need not be jettisoned as so much excessive baggage in the postmodern portmanteau, but are retained in a fresh and revitalized shape and substance. In particular, postmodernists suggest that the traditional notion of authenticity—"to thine own self be true"—is an immediate patient for postmodern surgery.

The political implications of this interpretive retooling are wide-ranging, but themselves are never beyond contestation or interpretation. However, the challenge to the conventional idea of autonomy as a negatively defined zone of non-interference and self-realization is especially strong. It gives the theoretical lie to the practical understanding that freedom is an individual state of mind and passive virtue which aspires to transcend social constraints. Instead, a postmodern insight reconfigures individual freedom more as a public project than a private undertaking: it is as much a social state of affairs as anything else. In short, postmodernism is devoted to "deconstructing the self who could embody that freedom." Accordingly, the achievement of freedom comes to look less like a session of personal therapy and more like a social project to multiply the opportunities to transform oneself. . . .

But this does not mean that identity does not matter. It matters majorly: it simply does not do so in the essentialist or metaphysical manner that is traditionally thought. Identity's significance is political and all the more significant for that. The relation between persons and their contexts is like that between writers and texts—*nothing necessarily follows*. Context is not the author of the person in the sense of inhibiting, binding, or constraining its identity. It is relevant, but not determinative. Similarly, while it is never possible to pin down context in any fixed or finished way, so it is not possible to isolate authorial identity and, therefore, the meaning of the text from that author.

By divesting identity of its spurious claim to metaphysical authority, it is released to play a more important and less confined role in textual, sexual, racial and any other politics. Identity becomes a site that, while guaranteeing nothing, makes everything possible. By moving beyond the debilitating politics of abstraction and ahistoricality, postmodernism looks to create meaning and knowledge in the situated particulars of embedded experience. The ambition is not to fix an all-encompassing Truth in a distant metaphysical realm, but to pay constant attention to the multiple truths and contextual details of engaged living in the here-and-now. Of course, being political, that process will always be open and fluid; meaning will always be provisional and revisable. Moreover, by using rich accounts and critical readings of historical experience to promote political knowledge and action, that politics will always be contestable: politics itself can never be a privileged ground for anything. . . .

JOAN WILLIAMS, DISSOLVING THE SAME-NESS/DIFFERENCE DEBATE: A POST–MODERN PATH BEYOND ESSENTIALISM IN FEMINIST AND CRITICAL RACE THEORY

1991 Duke L.J. 296, 306–310, 322–23.

... I was having lunch with a friend at the faculty club of my university. At the time, he and his wife had two children under three years of age, an experience that struck both of us as miserable. Yet the more he talked, the more I felt how "male" his reaction was. I am not sure why anymore, but it had something to do with his attitudes towards work and family. Then the topic shifted to birth control; his reaction struck me as shockingly Catholic. We proceeded through the lunch line and he bantered with the cashier—and I recognized a mixture of tension and camaraderie that I attributed to the complex dynamic between privileged and working-class blacks, complicated by a sexual flirtation that I had never seen before, though I had often been through the line with white male colleagues. (There was probably more camaraderie and less tension in the reaction I saw because my friend is handsome and personable.) Then we sat down, talked about scholarship for a while and he struck me as just another upper-middle-class academic like myself.

For me, that lunch dissolved the sameness/difference debate. On the one hand, it dramatized the truth of anti-essentialism. My friend does not have "a" minority perspective, he has many different perspectives: male, Catholic, upper-middle-class black, upper-middle-class generic, upper-middle-class academic. Which one is relevant depends on the situation: what he is discussing or doing, and with whom. To reify his viewpoint as "black" (or "male") is to make a set of extremely troubling value choices by silencing all the ways in which his life is shaped by forces other than his race (or sex). Now, at some level, one can interpret every other category in terms of his race and say he reacted as a black Catholic, a black academic, etc. And sometimes I do feel that he is reacting as a black Catholic, but not always. Note that the only context in which I felt the need to use what I think of as "junction categories" was to describe his interaction with a fellow African–American of lower status. This is a concrete way to illustrate my rejection of a single African–American voice, much less one minority voice, because the interaction of two Hispanics or two Asian–Americans would have been unutterably different.

Yet if my analysis dramatizes the contingency of categories, and warns against reifying any one category as being always of interpretive importance, it also expresses certain value judgments about what are the most useful categories for interpreting this sequence of events. The categories that I chose do not strike me as controversial (though I am not the best judge of this; I chose them because they seemed "obvious" to me). But it is useful to note that I focused on race, class, and gender—the traditional troika of American social commentary—with religion added, an overlooked but vital engine of American life. The traditional troika reflects the realities of power in American life, and thus dramatizes Foucault's insistence on the links between knowledge and power. My choice of those categories suggests a new way to interpret difference. Claims of difference simply mean that *in some contexts* gender or race may shape (or even determine) one's outlook. This reformulation of difference, which we could call post-modern difference, avoids essentialism because it refuses to concede that race, gender—or, indeed, *any* given category—will always be determinative. It allows us to argue that, although race and gender may prove determinative *in some particular context,* this is a far cry from a reified "minority perspective" or "women's voice" that determines how a given individual will react in every situation.

This post-modern approach starts from the notion of a fragmented and shifting self. Sometimes I feel like a white, sometimes a heterosexual, sometimes a Jew, sometimes a lawyer, sometimes an Episcopalian. Often I feel simply like my mother's daughter. A post-modern approach to difference highlights that each person is embedded in a matrix of social and psychological factors that interact in different contexts. Essentialism dissolves before the notion of a shifting, constantly reconfigured self, shaped but not determined by membership in sets of social categories that crystallize power relations in America.

A. Reformulating Sameness

The basic problem with sameness arguments is the claim that people who are as "obviously" different as men and women or blacks and whites are actually the same. This embarrassment is easy to solve if we stress not sameness but equal dignity. The basic claim ("I'm just as good as you!") need not entail a claim that I am the *same* as you. One only needs to say that "I will fulfill the conventional requirements for excellence in my own way—which, after all, is all anyone can ever do."

Once reformulated in this way, "sameness" entails not a claim that A and B are the same; instead, it entails the assertion that the differences that exist should be irrelevant in this particular context. This approach links equality with questions of policy rather than biology. Ultimately, one is left with disagreements not about who is similar to whom, but about which differences should matter in which contexts.

This approach to sameness reflects a post-modern sensitivity to the constructedness of categories. After all, no two people are truly "the same." Thus, when we call Person A the same as Person B we are constructing a category of "sameness" that ignores a whole series of differences for strategic reasons. The assertion that A and B are "the same" is not merely an assertion of *fact*. Instead, it is an argument that the characteristics that A and B share are more important for the purpose at issue than the ones they do not share.

Post-modern sameness makes it easier to see that, where women or minorities are not "the same," their failure often reflects their inability to measure up to a standard stacked against them. The "ideal worker" standard is stacked against women; elite schools' standards for law professors are stacked against those who lack access to cultural and class privileges that shape the usual path to academic "merit." This approach links sameness with power: We as outsiders are not the same because we are disinherited by our own tradition. Post-modern sameness cannot be reversed for use against outsiders because it does not make misleading claims that people as "obviously" different as blacks and whites, women and men, are the same. Neither is it content to leave intact supposedly neutral standards such as that of the ideal worker. Post-modern sameness makes explicit outsiders' demand not to be disadvantaged by physical (or social) characteristics that should be irrelevant when it comes to distributing societal benefits.

B.   REFORMULATING DIFFERENCE

Because sameness feminism has been under siege for nearly a decade, the leading sameness advocate has reformulated sameness along post-modern lines. Difference feminists have generally not done the same with difference, despite the growing anti-essentialist critique. Thus far, the leading anti-essentialists have generally focused on the fact that descriptions of women's "difference" tend to describe white women.

Beyond critiquing existing descriptions of difference, how can we reformulate difference in ways that are true to outsiders' experience while avoiding essentialism? We begin once again with a post-modern sensitivity to the constructedness of categories. Traditional epistemology assumed the existence of a firm foundation, a "God's eye point of view," a truth not dependent upon human strivings. Non-foundationalists since the late nineteenth century have stressed the inevitability of different perspectives and different truths, starting from the axiom that things look different from different points of view. Non-foundationalists argue that because every interpretation entails a viewpoint, no interpretation is final or objective. Different interpretations serve different purposes.

This outlook offers a way to dissolve difference in much the same way that it dissolved sameness. Post-modern sameness translated arguments about physical or cultural *similarity* into arguments about which differences are relevant in which contexts. Post-modern difference dissolves claims about *difference* into arguments about which differences should matter in which contexts. Once reformulated, difference dissolves into sameness and vice versa. . . .

. . . One can believe that gender or race is not the operative category in a range of contexts without claiming that gender or race is *never* determinative. This is an important point because of the widespread sense that sameness feminism has been discredited because "women and men obviously aren't the same."

A second advantage of a post-modern reformulation of sameness and difference is that it suggests that sameness advocates acknowledge differences and that difference advocates acknowledge sameness. The basic claim of post-modern sameness feminism is not that men and women (or whites and blacks) are *identical,* but that the importance of gender is at times overshadowed by race, class, personality, or any of a number of other factors. This is a position with which, I suspect, most difference advocates would agree....

A post-modern approach to the debate ultimately dissolves the traditional dichotomy between sameness and difference. Sameness claims are best viewed as policy arguments about which categories applicable to a given individual ought to matter in a specific context. This revamping of the sameness argument makes it easier to link assertions about sameness with the need for transformation. If I cannot be "the same" in a context in which equality depends on sameness, this means that the "neutral" standard that I cannot live up to is not, in fact, neutral.

Post-modern difference also begins from the notion that a myriad of possible categories are applicable to any individual. Assertions about difference are arguments that a given category—sex, race, class, etc.—is likely to yield powerful interpretive results in a particular context. The categories that crystallize power relations in America (race, sex, class) will often prove indispensable to analysis of sameness. This is not to say, though, that any category will always prove important, or even relevant. Women do not *always* react as women; sometimes they react as Democrats, lesbians, bigots, or blacks. This formulation of difference shows that any assertion of a unified outlook entails an interpretive decision to reify gender, or race, or some other characteristic, to assert that the particular characteristic *always* overrides all other possible characteristics in importance. Without a biological link to render such an interpretive decision "objective," this approach will normally prove repressive of the complex and changing forces that shape individuals.

This analysis helps us to understand that sameness and difference are not arguments about the essential nature of human beings. Instead, they are questions that stem from the fact that "neutral" standards systematically disadvantage outsiders: The "ideal worker" standard disadvantages women; conventional notions of merit disadvantage African–Americans; and both institutions and physical structures disadvantage the disabled.

If we insist on changing these standards, the need for outsiders to claim sameness or difference will disappear. Once the standard is designed with them in mind, they will simply meet it. Unfortunately, this solution is tidy in theory but difficult in practice....

Although we will not soon escape the difference dilemma, we can try to avoid diverting our energy into arguments amongst ourselves over whether outsiders are "really" the same or "really" different. Reformulating sameness and difference along post-modern lines largely dissolves the divergence between these two positions. Such reformulations can help refocus our attention onto two topics of abiding concern. The first is how to describe differences between outsiders and the mainstream in ways that do not reinforce stereotypes. The second is to forge working agreements on the most effective strategies to pursue in the face of the supposedly "neutral" standards of a tradition that disinherits us.

JENNIFER WICKE, POSTMODERN IDENTITY AND THE LEGAL SUBJECT

62 Colorado L.Rev. 455, 465–468 (1991).

In the Native American struggles for self-determination and acknowledgment of their distinct cultural identity, these contradictions of postmodern identity and the legal subject are writ large, since the postmodern insistence on heterogeneity as opposed to identity and on the passe nature of a discourse of rights and nationalism as belonging to the discredited "narrative" mode comes into focus in these struggles. Here, too, one would wish that postmodernism's optic would cast a revivified look at the law, in particular at the decrepit legal formulations that make up the ongoing history of the Native American presence in American courts of law. The ebullient heterogeneity ... does not accord well, as it happens, with the need to deploy a language of the legal subject, in other words, a language of rights and a language of cultural identity, in securing cultural justice.... [A] reading of the case of the Mashpee Indians ... highlights this gap in postmodern identity.

The trial of Mashpee versus the New Seabury Corporation took place in 1976 as the Mashpee Indians of Cape Code sought to establish their claims to land bought up by the corporation; in order to do so it was incumbent on them to prove they were a tribe, in other words, to get recognition for themselves in court as a tribe while their request to the Federal government for such legal recognition was still in limbo. "Tribe" as an identity had to be proven in relation to the legal definition proffered by the 1901 Supreme Court decision, containing an antiquated (by any anthropological or disciplinary measure) and actively hostile and ignorant (by any Indian measure whatever) definition of what constituted a "tribe." Thus the legal identity of a tribe was by no means an innocent or innate one, but nonetheless the legal standard was what needed to be demonstrated by the Mashpee, and this they were unable to do. An all-white jury from the Boston area found, in a rather spectacular decision, that the Mashpee had indeed constituted a tribe in 1834 and 1842, but not in the all-important year of 1790, the date when the Indian Non–Intercourse Act was passed, on which many land claims are based, nor in the subsequent years of 1869, 1870, and, most relevantly, 1976. The phantom status of tribal identity, waxing and waning over the years, efflorescing at one juncture and then ebbing forever, itself has a liminal quality—but one that served to deny the Mashpee any grounds as legal subjects. Their identity in this case was entirely predicated on their establishing the legal subject-category of "member of the Mashpee tribe." To be an Indian is a pre-existent cultural identity, of course, but in this instance and many others what was needed to bring about the desired result—the return of their land and thus their land-based cultural identity—revolved around a legal definition of their identity as tribal Indians and required their officially becoming Mashpee Indian legal subjects. To achieve this result an acceptance of the discourse of rights and national identity is not just strategic, but necessary.

This postmodern political dilemma connects with problems in Critical Legal Studies, where that discourse also seeks to "deconstruct" or dissolve the language of rights, scrutinizing rights as innately unstable and indeterminant, and replacing the rights vocabulary with one of "needs." Among the many resulting difficulties is the status of "needs," as identity-groups come under a protectionist shield of "need" where they remain victims in need of help. Critical Legal Studies has also implied that a rights discourse like that of Native American demands for the upholding of treaties succumbs to a self-defeating legitimation of government power in the first place. Along these lines we can think of the current upheavals in Wisconsin surrounding the spearfishing rights of the Lac du Flambeau-area Indians, who are fighting for an enhanced and protected fishing domain on the terms of the government's initial dealings with their tribe, on promises made in original treaties, and on the definition of their cultural identity as land-based. The symbolic gestures of the Mexican–American movement of the 1960s and 70s, coalescing in New Mexico in the Tierra Amarilla area and dedicated to the return of property traced back to land-grants honored by the Treaty of the Mexican–American war, had a similar thrust; the battle in the courts revolved around the honoring of these claims as the treaty promised to uphold them, despite the dubious historical circumstances under which the treaty was signed. To seek to dissolve these "rights" away under the acid bath of postmodern multiplicity simply erases the grounds for self-determination, which can only be coded as an identity (collective or individual) possessing rights. Self-determination would seem to entail the embrace of legal subject-hood, as the vocabulary of rights may still be the only viable means to secure that selfhood. A postmodernism that ignores or deplores this necessity reveals its supposition that "rights" are already adequately secured and that the legal arena cannot be bent to a variety of discursive purposes. A related struggle is ensuing in those localities where gay rights activists are applying pressure for the right to marry. Marriage can be subjected to a withering critique as a transparently ideological institution, but in this case too the importance of reserving a vocabulary of "rights" as a legal subject transcends those objections since the political objectives of securing gay marriage rights outweigh any hesitance about the identities presupposed by marriage.

A paradox of the postmodern, which any teacher of the humanities can detail, is the coincident and vociferous rise of an identity-based politics hard on the heels of a postmodernist or at least poststructuralist consensus which would seem to question identity at large as an essentialist category. Even where there is some circumspection about making the "mistake" of essentialism (and here I will admit I concur with the assessment that it is a mistake), a separatist identity politics is coming to the fore. With it a kind of "serial identity" politics, along the lines of serial monogamy, is especially often antagonistic and rampant. In this mode identities are seen as additive or cumulative, with smaller and smaller subdivisions to mark more and more specialized identity formations. Part of the impetus for this discursive and political phenomenon arises out of cultural and historical roots in the United States, where an individualizing rhetoric permeates all our major social forms. The community identity models itself on individual identity and coheres around shared attributes which are seen as defining, while the extent to which these community identities arise in relation to a social dominant becomes obscured. Onto this atomizing and even sentimentalizing identity politics a postmodernism of local determination gets grafted, with powerful but often mixed results.... The one-note song of an irreducible identity is hard to fuse with the dissolving logic of identity, the insistence on internal differences. The laudable goal of opening up social space to a multiplicity of approaches, a postmodern postMarxism, ends up depending on the mobilization of *singular* identities. As long as the postmodern in practice involves such contradictions, the relation between postmodern identity and the legal subject will be in question, too—these confusions in practice will infect the transferring over of postmodern elements to the legal sphere....

Notes and Questions

1. What is the "postmodern" notion of identity? How does it contrast with a modernist notion?

2. How might we design civil rights laws to protect individuals and groups if identity is fluid, culturally created and inessential? Should we abandon the single issue categories that now serve as the basis for civil rights laws? With what would we replace them? How might law protect against gender discrimination and at the same time preserve the separate cultural identity of the Santa Clara Pueblo Indians?

3. What is the "postmodern political dilemma" described by Jennifer Wicke? Does Joan Williams offer any way out of the dilemma?

C. MULTIPLE IDENTITIES AND PATTERNS OF POWER AND PRIVILEGE

ELIZABETH SPELMAN, INESSENTIAL WOMAN

115–132 (Beacon Press, 1988).

It is not easy to think about gender, race, and class in ways that don't obscure or underplay their effects on one another. The crucial question is how the links between them are conceived ...

[W]e shall examine in more detail how additive analyses of identity and of oppression can work against an understanding of the relations between gender and other elements of identity, between sexism and other forms of oppression. In particular we will see how some very interesting and important attempts to link sexism and racism themselves reflect and perpetuate racism. Ironically, the categories and methods we may find most natural and straightforward to use as we explore the connections between sex and race, sexism and racism, confuse those connections rather than clarify them.

As has often been pointed out, what have been called the first and second waves of the women's movement in the United States followed closely on the heels of women's involvement in the nineteenth-century abolitionist movement and the twentieth-century civil rights movement. In both centuries, challenges to North American racism served as an impetus to, and model for, the feminist attack on sexist institutions, practices, and ideology. But this is not to say that all antiracists were antisexists, or that all antisexists were antiracists. Indeed, many abolitionists of the nineteenth century and civil rights workers of the twentieth did not take sexism seriously, and we continue to learn about the sad, bitter, and confusing history of women who in fighting hard for feminist ends did not take racism seriously.

Recent feminist theory has not totally ignored white racism, though white feminists have paid much less attention to it than have Black feminists. Much of feminist theory has reflected and contributed to what Adrienne Rich has called "white solipsism": the tendency "to think, imagine, and speak as if whiteness described the world." While solipsism is "not the consciously held belief that one race is inherently superior to all others, but a tunnel-vision which simply does not see nonwhite experience or existence as precious or significant, unless in spasmodic, impotent guilt-reflexes, which have little or no long-term, continuing momentum or political usefulness." . . .

I shall not explicitly be examining class and classism, though at a number of points I suggest ways in which considerations of class and classism affect the topic at hand. Many of the questions I raise about comparisons between sexism and racism could also be raised about comparison between sexism and classism or racism and classism. . . .

First of all, sexism and racism do not have different "objects" in the case of Black women. It is highly misleading to say, without further explanation, that Black women experience "sexism and racism." For to say merely that suggests that Black women experience one form of oppression, as Blacks (the same thing Black men experience) and that they experience another form of oppression, as women (the same thing white women experience). While it is true that images and institutions that are described as sexist affect both Black and white women, they are affected in different ways, depending upon the extent to which they are affected by other forms of oppression. Thus, as noted earlier, it will not do to say that women are oppressed by the image of the "feminine" woman as fair, delicate, and in need of support and protection by men. As Linda Brent succinctly puts it, "That which commands admiration in the white woman only hastens the degradation of the female slave." More specifically, as Angela Davis reminds us, "the alleged benefits of the ideology of femininity did not accrue" to the Black female slave—she was expected to toil in the fields for just as long and hard as the Black male was.

Reflection on the experience of Black women also shows that it is not as if one form of oppression is merely piled upon another. As Barbara Smith has remarked, the effect of multiple oppression "is not merely arithmetic." This additive method informs Gerda Lerner's analysis of the oppression of Black women under slavery: "Their work and duties were the same as that of the men, while childbearing and rearing fell upon them as an added burden." But as Angela Davis has pointed out, the mother/housewife role (even the words seem inappropriate) doesn't have the same meaning for women who experience racism as it does for those who are not so oppressed:

> In the infinite anguish of ministering to the needs of the men and children around her (who were not necessarily members of her immediate family), she was performing the only labor of the slave community which could not be directly and immediately claimed by the oppressor.

The meaning and the oppressive nature of the "housewife" role has to be understood in relation to the roles against which it is contrasted. The work of mate/mother/nurturer has a different meaning depending on whether it is contrasted to work that has high social value and ensures economic independence or to labor that is forced, degrading, and unpaid. All of these factors are left out in a simple additive analysis. How one form of oppression is experienced is influenced by and influences how another form is experienced. An additive analysis treats the oppression of a Black woman in a society that is racist as well as sexist as if it were a further burden when, in fact, it is a different burden. As the work of Davis, among others, shows, to ignore the difference is to deny the particular reality of the Black woman's experience.

If sexism and racism must be seen as interlocking, and not as piled upon each other, serious problems arise for the claim that one of them is more fundamental than the other. As we saw, one meaning of the claim that sexism is more fundamental than racism is that sexism causes racism: racism would not exist if sexism did not, while sexism could and would continue to exist even in the absence of racism. In this connection, racism is sometimes seen as something that is both derivative from sexism and in the service of it: racism keeps women from uniting in alliance against sexism....

This view not only ignores the role women play in racism and classism, but it seems to deny the positive aspects of racial identities. It ignores the fact that being Black is a source of pride, as well as an occasion for being oppressed. It suggests that once racism is eliminated, Black women no longer need be concerned about or interested in their Blackness—as if the only reason for paying attention to one's Blackness is that it is the source of pain and sorrow and agony. The assumption that there is nothing positive about having a Black history and identity is racism pure and simple. Recall the lines of Nikki Giovanni:

and I really hope no white person ever has cause

to write about me

because they never understand Black love is

Black wealth and they'll

probably talk about my hard childhood

and never understand that

all the while I was quite happy.

Or recall the chagrin of the central character in Paule Marshall's story "Reena," when she discovered that her white boyfriend could only see her Blackness in terms of her suffering and not as something compatible with taking joy and pleasure in life. I think it is helpful too in this connection to remember the opening lines of Pat Parker's "For the white person who wants to know how to be my friend":

The first thing you do is to forget that i'm Black.

Second, you must never forget that i'm Black.

Perhaps it does not occur to feminists who are white that celebrating being white has anything to do with our celebrating being women. But that may be so because celebrating being white is already taken care of by the predominantly white culture in which we live in North America. . . .

In sum, according to an additive analysis of sexism and racism, all women are oppressed by sexism; some women are further oppressed by racism. Such an analysis distorts Black women's experiences of oppression by failing to note important differences between the contexts in which Black women and white women experience sexism. The additive analysis also suggests that a woman's racial identity can be "subtracted" from her combined sexual and racial identity: "We are all women." But this does not leave room for the fact that different women may look to different forms of liberation just because they are white or Black women, rich or poor women, Catholic or Jewish women. . . .

I have been discussing the ways in which some aspects of feminist theory exhibit what Adrienne Rich has called "white solipsism." In particular, I have been examining ways in which some prominent claims about the relation between sexism and racism ignore the realities of racism. I have also suggested that there are ways of thinking about women's oppression and about women's liberation that reflect and encourage white solipsism, but that thinking differently about women and about sexism might lead to thinking differently about Blackness and about racism.

First, we have to continue to reexamine the traditions which reinforce sexism and racism. Though feminist theory has recognized the connection between somatophobia and misogyny/gynephobia, it has tended to challenge the misogyny without challenging the somatophobia, and without fully appreciating the connection between somatophobia and racism.

Second, we have to keep a cautious eye on discussions of racism versus sexism. They keep us from seeing ways in which what sexism means and how it works is modulated by racism, and ways in which what racism means is modulated by sexism. Most important, discussions of sexism versus racism tend to proceed as if Black women—to take one example—do not exist. None of this is to say that sexism and racism are thoroughly and in every context indistinguishable.... But as long as Black women and other women of color are at the bottom of the economic heap (which clearly we cannot fully understand in the absence of a class analysis), and as long as our descriptions of sexism and racism themselves reveal racist and sexist perspectives, it seems both empirically and conceptually premature to make grand claims about whether sexism or racism is "more fundamental." For many reasons, then, it seems wise to proceed very cautiously in this inquiry.

Third, it is crucial to sustain a lively regard for the variety of women's experiences. On the one hand, what unifies women and justifies us in talking about the oppression of women is the overwhelming evidence of the worldwide and historical subordination of women to men. On the other, while it may be possible for us to speak about women in a general way, it also is inevitable that any statement we make about women in some particular place at some particular time is bound to suffer from ethnocentrism if we try to claim for it more generality than it has. So, for example, to say that the image of woman as frail and dependent is oppressive is certainly true. But it is oppressive to white women in the United States in quite a different way than it is oppressive to Black women, for the sexism Black women experience is in the context of their experience of racism. In Toni Morrison's *The Bluest Eye*, the causes and consequences of Pecola's longing to have blue eyes are surely quite different from the causes and consequences of a white girl with brown eyes having a similar desire. More to the point, the consequences of *not* having blue eyes are quite different for the two. Similarly, the family may be the locus of oppression for white middle-class women, but to claim that it is the locus of oppression for all women is to ignore the fact that for Blacks in America the family has been a source of resistance against white oppression.

In short, the claim that all women are oppressed is fully compatible with, and needs to be explicated in terms of, the many varieties of oppression that different populations of women have been subject to. After all, why should oppressors settle for uniform kinds of oppression, when to oppress their victims in many different ways—consciously or unconsciously—makes it more likely that the oppressed groups will not perceive it to be in their interest to work together?

Finally, it is crucial not to see Blackness only as the occasion for oppression—any more than one sees being a woman only as the occasion for oppression. No one ought to expect the forms of our liberation to be any less various than the forms of our oppression. We need to be at least as generous in imagining what women's liberation will be like as our oppressors have been in devising what women's oppression has been.

Notes and Questions

1. What does Elizabeth Spelman mean when she observes that sexism and racism must be seen as interlocking and not as piled on each other?

2. How do essentialist notions perpetuate patterns of power and privilege?

3. Will inessentialism arguments prevent traditionally excluded groups from working together? Or, is Spelman arguing that it is the failure to recognize differences that prevents such coalitions?

4. The following excerpts explore the interlocking effects of gender, race and sexual preference (Patricia Cain); class, race, and gender (Audre Lorde and Emma Coleman Jordan); gender, race, and American Indian culture (Robert Williams); and gender and poverty (Valerie Polakow). In each instance, consider how the interlocking of the characteristics works to perpetuate exclusion.

PATRICIA CAIN, FEMINIST JURISPRUDENCE: GROUNDING THE THEORIES

4 Berkeley Women's L.J. 191, 205–214 (1988–89).

I believe that current feminist legal theory is deficient and impoverished because it has not paid sufficient attention to the real life experiences of women who do not speak the "dominant discourse." Elsewhere I have urged that feminist law teaching ought to include "listening to difference" and "making connections." Here I urge the same for feminist legal scholarship.

Most feminist legal theorists, by focusing on sameness and difference, have fallen into either the assimilationist trap (all women are the same as men/all women are the same) or the essentialist trap (all women are different from men in one essential way/all women are different, but what counts is their essential commonality). The only difference between assimilationists and essentialists is that the former ignore the reality of differences whereas the latter say that differences generally do not matter. The two concepts, assimilationism and essentialism, collapse into each other to the extent they treat women as a single class that is essentially the same.

Elizabeth Spelman describes the essentialist's solution to the "differences" problem in feminist theory: "The way to give proper significance to differences among women is to say that such differences simply are less significant than what women have in common. This solution is very neat, for it acknowledges differences among women only enough to bury them." The difficulty arises when an individual essentialist theorist must determine the content of this commonality which is so significant that it trumps differences. When white, straight, economically-privileged feminists name the commonality, and ignore differences, the result may be that all women are assimilated into a single class of white, straight, middle-class women.

It is not enough to name the differences of race, class, and sexuality. The differences need to be understood. Much recent feminist legal scholarship includes the perfunctory footnote, dropped the first time the essential category "woman" is mentioned, which acknowledges the differences of race and class, and sometimes of sexual preference. Such politically correct footnotes name the differences, but I see no evidence in the accompanying texts that the differences matter. Scholarship that nominally recognizes differences, but still categorizes "woman" from a single perspective is stuck in the assimilationist/essentialist trap.

I do not mean to ignore the importance of our commonalities. It is valuable to identify the similarities among all women. When we identify what we have in common, we begin to build bridges and connections. Yet if we ignore the differences, we risk distorting those connections, because any connection that fails to recognize differences is not a connection to the *whole* of the other self. A normative principle that honors only what I have in common with each of you fails to respect each of you for the individual woman that you are. To respect you, despite your difference, is an insult. Such respect is not respect for your difference, but only for our sameness. Such respect belittles your difference and says it does not matter. Such "respect" falls into the assimilationist/essentialist trap.

Let me give you an example. A white law professor says to her Black female colleague: "Sometimes I forget that you are Black. Sometimes I think of you as white." The comment is meant as a compliment, but it denies the real life experience of the Black woman to whom it is addressed. It says, ultimately, "what I respect in you is only what you have in common with me."

Now let me give you an example out of lesbian experience. A lesbian college teacher proposes a course entitled "The Outsider in Twentieth–Century American Literature." The course is to include writings of lesbians and gay men, as well as other outsiders, such as persons who have been in mental institutions or prisons. In discussing the potential course, the teacher's (presumably) heterosexual colleagues dismiss the notion that an author's sexuality might be an important aspect of her or his writing, claiming that sexuality is no different from "a thousand other things" that might influence the writer. None of the teacher's colleagues considers "having to live as a 'different' person in a heterosexist culture" as a factor important to one's writing.

Adrienne Rich, a lesbian poet, echoes the same theme in the following story:

Two friends of mine, both artists, wrote me about reading the "Twenty–One Love Poems" with their male lovers, assuring me how "universal" the poems were. I found myself angered, and when I asked myself why, I realized that it was anger at having my work essentially assimilated and stripped of its meaning, "integrated" into heterosexual romance. That kind of "acceptance" of the book seems to me a refusal of its deepest implications. The longing to simplify ... to assimilate lesbian experience by saying that "relationship" is really all the same, love is always difficult—I see that as a denial, a kind of resistance, a refusal to read and hear what I've actually written, to acknowledge what I am.

There is a commonality between Adrienne Rich and her heterosexual artist friends. They all experience love and relationship. Yet even if some portion of the love experience is universal, the heterosexual world will never understand the gay and lesbian world if we all focus on the commonality, the universal. To claim that lesbians are the same as heterosexual women or that Black women are the same as white women is to fall into the assimilationist/essentialist trap. Such claims deny the reality of our differences by ignoring or discounting them. Yet it is not enough to recognize and name the differences among us as women. We must also understand those differences.

I ask those of you in the audience who are heterosexual to focus on an important love relationship in your life. This could be a present relationship or a past one, or even the relationship you hope to have. I ask you: how would you feel about this relationship if it had to be kept utterly secret? Would you feel "at one with the world" if a slight mistake in language ("we" instead of "I") could lead to alienation from your friends and family, loss of your job? Would you feel at one with your lover if the only time you could touch or look into each other's eyes was in your own home—with the curtains drawn? What would such self-consciousness do to your relationship? ...

... Because of the pervasive influences of sexism, racism, and heterosexism, white, heterosexual women think of gender as something that sets them apart, as something that defines them, whereas neither race nor sexuality seems to matter much. Yet if neither race nor sexuality matters much to a white, heterosexual woman, how can she begin to understand the ways in which it matters to others who are different from her in these dimensions?

I wonder sometimes whether heterosexual women really understand the role that heterosexuality plays in the maintenance of patriarchy. Indeed, I sometimes wonder whether lesbians really understand. And yet, if feminist legal theory is to provide meaningful guidance for the abolition of patriarchy, feminist theorists must understand heterosexuality as an institution and not merely as the dominant form of sexuality....

The most consistent feminist claim, at least since the publication of Simone de Beauvoir's *The Second Sex,* is that knowledge of reality has been constructed from a male-centered standpoint. From their position as outsider, women have questioned that reality, because women's life experiences differ—often dramatically—from those of men. The most cohesive and challenging critiques of male-centered reality have been made by women from standpoints that are exactly opposite, experientially, from those of men. One such critique is made by cultural feminists from the "woman as mother" standpoint. Another is made by other radical feminists from the "woman as sexual subordinate" standpoint.

The fact that so many women can identify common life experiences that are ignored by the male version of reality makes any critique based on such common experiences compelling and powerful. But theorists ought to resist transforming a critical standpoint into a new all-encompassing version of reality. Indeed, my fear is that what started as a useful critique of one privileged (male) view of reality may become a substitute claim for a different privileged (female) view of reality.

Catharine MacKinnon, for example, critiques the patriarchy from a "woman as sexual subordinate" standpoint. As compelling as her critique is, it should not be viewed as the one and only existential reality for women. And yet MacKinnon herself is so committed to this standpoint that she sometimes seems to claim it as the only reality for women.

MacKinnon's theory is that woman's subordination is universal and constant, but not necessarily inevitable. She cautions against building theory on the basis of Carol Gilligan's discovery of woman's "different voice" because the women Gilligan listened to were all victims of the patriarchy. Thus, MacKinnon is wary of assigning value to their moral voice. As she explains,

> [b]y establishing that women reason differently from men on moral questions, [Gilligan] revalues that which has accurately distinguished women from men by making it seem as though women's moral reasoning is somehow women's, rather than what male supremacy has attributed to women for its own use. When difference means dominance as it does with gender, for women to affirm differences is to affirm the qualities and characteristics of powerlessness.... To the extent materialism means anything at all, it means that what women have been and thought is what they have been permitted to be and think. Whatever this is, it is not women's, possessive.

When MacKinnon espoused these beliefs regarding women's subordination and inauthenticity in a dialogue with Gilligan at the now somewhat infamous "Mitchell Lecture" at Buffalo, Mary Dunlap (a lesbian), who was also a speaker at the event, interrupted. Dunlap said:

> I am speaking out of turn. I am also standing, which I am told by some is a male thing to do. But I am still a woman—standing.

> I am not subordinate to any man! I find myself very often contesting efforts at my subordination—both standing and lying down and sitting and in various other positions—but I am not subordinate to any man! And I have been told by Kitty MacKinnon that women have never not been subordinate to men. So I stand here an exception and invite all other women here to be an exception and stand.

MacKinnon has subsequently described this event as "a stunning example of the denial of gender," claiming that Dunlap was saying, "all women who are exempt from the condition of women, all women who are not women, stand with me." I believe MacKinnon misinterpreted Dunlap's reaction. Dunlap's claim that her experiential reality is often free of male domination was not a denial of the existence of male power, nor a statement that she had risen above other women. It was merely a statement of fact about her reality, a statement she felt compelled to make because MacKinnon's description of "what is" had continued to exclude Dunlap's reality.

Dunlap's reality is not irrelevant to feminist theory. Mary Dunlap, and I, and other lesbians who live our private lives removed from the intimate presence of men do indeed experience time free from male domination. When we leave the male-dominated public sphere, we come home to a woman-identified private sphere. That does not mean that the patriarchy as an institution does not exist for us or that the patriarchy does not exist during the time that we experience freedom from male domination. It means simply that we experience significant periods of nonsubordination, during which we, as women, are free to develop a sense of self that is our own and not a mere construct of the patriarchy.

Nor do we work at this experience of nonsubordination and creation of authentic self to set ourselves apart from other women. We are not asserting a "proud disidentification from the rest of [our] sex and proud denial of the rest of [our] life." The struggle is to make nonsubordination a reality for all women, and the reality of nonsubordination in some women's lives is relevant to this struggle. The reality of nonsubordination in lesbian lives offers the "lesbian possibility" as a solution.

At the same time, I believe MacKinnon's claim that all women are subordinate to men all the time is a fair claim upon which to critique the male version of reality, because subordination is such a pervasive experience for women. Her claim gives her a valid standpoint for her critique even though it is not experientially true for all women. Similarly, I believe Robin West's claim that all women are "connected" to life is a fair claim upon which to critique the male version of the "separation thesis." But I do not believe that the "connection thesis" is true of all women. Feminist legal theorists must be careful not to confuse "standpoint critiques" with existential reality. And the theorist who has not confused the two must also be careful to prevent her readers from making the confusion.

The problem with current feminist theory is that the more abstract and universal it is, the more it fails to relate to the lived reality of many women. One problem with much feminist legal theory is that it has abstracted and universalized from the experience of heterosexual women. Consider again Marilyn Frye's challenge to heterosexual academic feminists: "I wish you would notice that you are heterosexual. I wish you would grow to the understanding that you choose heterosexuality

... that you are and choose to be a member of a privileged and dominant class, one of your privileges being not to notice." ...

My "lesbian standpoint" enables me to see two versions of reality. The dominant reality, which I experience as "theirs," includes the following: lesbians are not mothers, all women are dominated by men, male relationships are valuable and female relationships are not, lesbian is a dirty word, lesbians are sick, women who live alone desire men, women who live together desire men, no one knows a lesbian, lesbians don't have families, all feminist legal theorists are heterosexual, all women in this room are heterosexual, lesbians are sex, most women are heterosexual and not lesbian.

By contrast, the reality that I live, the reality I call "mine," includes the following: some mothers are lesbian, many women are lesbian, many lesbian women are not dominated by men, many women do not desire men, lesbian is a beautiful word, lesbians are love, love is intimacy, the heterosexual/lesbian dichotomy is false, all lesbians are born into families, lesbians are family, some feminist legal theorists are lesbian, lesbians are brave.

Why is the lesbian so invisible in feminist legal theory? Why is "my reality" so different from "their reality?" And which reality is true? For the postmodernist, the last question is meaningless. But the first two are not.

AUDRE LORDE, AGE, RACE, CLASS, AND SEX: WOMEN REDEFINING DIFFERENCE

in Sister Outsider 114–123 (Crossing Press, 1984).

Much of Western European history conditions us to see human differences in simplistic opposition to each other: dominant/subordinate, good/bad, up/down, superior/inferior. In a society where the good is defined in terms of profit rather than in terms of human need, there must always be some group of people who, through systematized oppression, can be made to feel surplus, to occupy the place of the dehumanized inferior. Within this society, that group is made up of Black and Third World people, working-class people, older people, and women.

As a forty-nine-year-old Black lesbian feminist socialist mother of two, including one boy, and a member of an inter-racial couple, I usually find myself a part of some group defined as other, deviant, inferior, or just plain wrong. Traditionally, in american society, it is the members of oppressed, objectified groups who are expected to stretch out and bridge the gap between the actualities of our lives and the consciousness of our oppressor. For in order to survive, those of us for whom oppression is as american as apple pie have always had to be watchers, to become familiar with the language and manners of the oppressor, even sometimes adopting them for some illusion of protection. Whenever the need for some pretense of communication arises, those who profit from our oppression call upon us to share our knowledge with them. In other words, it is the responsibility of the oppressed to teach the oppressors their mistakes. I am responsible for educating teachers who dismiss my children's culture in school. Black and Third World people are expected to educate white people as to our humanity. Women are expected to educate men. Lesbians and gay men are expected to educate the heterosexual world. The oppressors maintain their position and evade responsibility for their own actions. There is a constant drain of energy which might be better used in redefining ourselves and devising realistic scenarios for altering the present and constructing the future.

Institutionalized rejection of difference is an absolute necessity in a profit economy which needs outsiders as surplus people. As members of such an economy, we have *all* been programmed to respond to the human differences between us with fear and loathing and to handle that difference in one of three ways: ignore it, and if that is not possible, copy it if we think it is dominant, or destroy it if we think it is subordinate. But we have no patterns for relating across our human differences as equals. As a result, those differences have been misnamed and misused in the service of separation and confusion.

Certainly there are very real differences between us of race, age, and sex. But it is not those differences between us that are separating us. It is rather our refusal to recognize those differences, and to examine the distortions which result from our misnaming them and their effects upon human behavior and expectation.

Racism, the belief in the inherent superiority of one race over all others and thereby the right to dominance. Sexism, the belief in the inherent superiority of one sex over the other and thereby the right to dominance. Ageism. Heterosexism. Elitism. Classism.

It is a lifetime pursuit for each one of us to extract these distortions from our living at the same time as we recognize, reclaim, and define those differences upon which they are imposed. For we have all been raised in a society where those distortions were endemic within our living. Too often, we pour the energy needed for recognizing and exploring difference into pretending those differences are insurmountable barriers, or that they do not exist at all. This results in a voluntary isolation, or false and treacherous connections. Either way, we do not develop tools for using human difference as a springboard for creative change within our lives. We speak not of human difference, but of human deviance.

Somewhere, on the edge of consciousness, there is what I call a *mythical norm*, which each one of us within our hearts knows "that is not me." In america, this norm is usually defined as white, thin, male, young, heterosexual, christian, and financially secure. It is with this mythical norm that the trappings of power reside within this society. Those of us who stand outside that power often identify one way in which we are different, and we assume that to be the primary cause of all oppression, forgetting other distortions around difference, some of which we ourselves may be practising. By and large within the women's movement today, white women focus upon their oppression as women and ignore differences of race, sexual preference, class, and age. There is a pretense to a homogeneity of experience covered by the word *sisterhood* that does not in fact exist.

Unacknowledged class differences rob women of each others' energy and creative insight. Recently a women's magazine collective made the decision for one issue to print only prose, saying poetry was a less "rigorous" or "serious" art form. Yet even the form our creativity takes is often a class issue. Of all the art forms, poetry is the most economical. It is the one which is the most secret, which requires the least physical labor, the least material, and the one which can be done between shifts, in the hospital pantry, on the subway, and on scraps of surplus paper. Over the last few years, writing a novel on tight finances, I came to appreciate the enormous differences in the material demands between poetry and prose. As we reclaim our literature, poetry has been the major voice of poor, working class, and Colored women. A room of one's own may be a necessity for writing prose, but so are reams of paper, a typewriter, and plenty of time. The actual requirements to produce the visual arts also help determine, along class lines, whose art is whose. In this day of inflated prices for material, who are our sculptors, our painters, our photographers? When we speak of a broadly based women's culture, we need to be aware of the effect of class and economic differences on the supplies available for producing art.

As we move toward creating a society within which we can each flourish, ageism is another distortion of relationship which interferes without vision. By ignoring the past, we are encouraged to repeat its mistakes. The "generation gap" is an important social tool for any repressive society. If the younger members of a community view the older members as contemptible or suspect or excess, they will never be able to join hands and examine the living memories of the community, nor ask the all important question, "Why?" This gives rise to a historical amnesia that keeps us working to invent the wheel every time we have to go to the store for bread.

We find ourselves having to repeat and relearn the same old lessons over and over that our mothers did because we do not pass on what we have learned, or because we are unable to listen. For instance, how many times has this all been said before? For another, who would have believed that once again our daughters are allowing their bodies to be hampered and purgatoried by girdles and high heels and hobble skirts?

Ignoring the differences of race between women and the implications of those differences presents the most serious threat to the mobilization of women's joint power.

As white women ignore their built-in privilege of whiteness and define *woman* in terms of their own experience alone, then women of Color become "other," the outsider whose experience and tradition is too "alien" to comprehend. An example of this is the signal absence of the experience of women of Color as a resource for women's studies courses.

The literature of women of Color is seldom included in women's literature courses and almost never in other literature courses, nor in women's studies as a whole. All too often, the excuse given is that the literatures of women of Color can only be taught by Colored women, or that they are too difficult to understand, or that classes cannot "get into" them because they come out of experiences that are "too different." I have heard this argument presented by white women of otherwise quite clear intelligence, women who seem to have no trouble at all teaching and reviewing work that comes out of the vastly different experiences of Shakespeare, Molière, Dostoyefsky, and Aristophanes. Surely there must be some other explanation.

This is a very complex question, but I believe one of the reasons white women have such difficulty reading Black women's work is because of their reluctance to see Black women as women and different from themselves. To examine Black women's literature effectively requires that we be seen as whole people in our actual complexities—as individuals, as women, as human—rather than as one of those problematic but familiar stereotypes provided in this society in place of genuine images of Black women. And I believe this holds true for the literatures of other women of Color who are not Black.

The literatures of all women of Color recreate the textures of our lives, and many white women are heavily invested in ignoring the real differences. For as long as any difference between us means one of us must be inferior, then the recognition of any difference must be fraught with guilt. To allow women of Color to step out of stereotypes is too guilt provoking, for it threatens the complacency of those women who view oppression only in terms of sex.

Refusing to recognize difference makes it impossible to see the different problems and pitfalls facing us as women.

Thus, in a patriarchal power system where whiteskin privilege is a major prop, the entrapments used to neutralize Black women and white women are not the same. For example, it is easy for Black women to be used by the power structure against Black men, not because they are men, but because they are Black. Therefore, for Black women, it is necessary at all times to separate the needs of the oppressor from our own legitimate conflicts within our communities. This same problem does not exist for white women. Black women and men have shared racist oppression and still share it, although in different ways. Out of that shared oppression we have developed joint defenses and joint vulnerabilities to each other that are not duplicated in the white community, with the exception of the relationship between Jewish women and Jewish men.

On the other hand, white women face the pitfall of being seduced into joining the oppressor under the pretense of sharing power. This possibility does not exist in the same way for women of Color. The tokenism that is sometimes extended to us is not an invitation to join power; our racial "otherness" is a visible reality that makes that quite clear. For white women there is a wider range of pretended choices and rewards for identifying with patriarchal power and its tools.

Today, with the defeat of ERA, the tightening economy, and increased conservatism, it is easier once again for white women to believe the dangerous fantasy that if you are good enough, pretty enough, sweet enough, quiet enough, teach the children to behave, hate the right people, and marry the right men, then you will be allowed to co-exist with patriarchy in relative peace, at least until a man needs your job or the neighborhood rapist happens along. And true, unless one lives and loves in the trenches it is difficult to remember that the war against dehumanization is ceaseless.

But Black women and our children know the fabric of our lives is stitched with violence and with hatred, that there is no rest. We do not deal with it only on the picket lines, or in dark midnight alleys, or in the places where we dare to verbalize our resistance. For us, increasingly, violence weaves through the daily tissues of our living—in the supermarket, in the classroom, in the elevator, in the clinic and the schoolyard, from the plumber, the baker, the saleswoman, the bus driver, the bank teller, the waitress who does not serve us.

Some problems we share as women, some we do not. You fear your children will grow up to join the patriarchy and testify against you, we fear our children will be dragged from a car and shot down in the street, and you will turn your backs upon the reasons they are dying.

The threat of difference has been no less blinding to people of Color. Those of us who are Black must see that the reality of our lives and our struggle does not make us immune to the errors of ignoring and misnaming difference. Within Black communities where racism is a living reality, differences among us often seem dangerous and suspect. The need for unity is often misnamed as a need for homogeneity, and a Black feminist vision mistaken for betrayal of our common interests as a people. Because of the continuous battle against racial erasure that Black women and Black men share, some Black women still refuse to recognize that we are also oppressed as women, and that sexual hostility against Black women is practiced not only by the white racist society, but implemented within our Black communities as well. It is a disease striking the heart of Black nationhood, and silence will not make it disappear. Exacerbated by racism and the pressures of powerlessness, violence against Black women and children often becomes a standard within our communities, one by which manliness can be measured. But these woman-hating acts are rarely discussed as crimes against Black women.

As a group, women of Color are the lowest paid wage earners in america. We are the primary targets of abortion and sterilization abuse, here and abroad. In certain parts of Africa, small girls are still being sewed shut between their legs to keep them docile and for men's pleasure. This is known as female circumcision, and it is not a cultural affair as the late Jomo Kenyatta insisted, it is a crime against Black women.

Black women's literature is full of the pain of frequent assault, not only by a racist patriarchy, but also by Black men. Yet the necessity for and history of shared battle have made us, Black women, particularly vulnerable to the false accusation that anti-sexist is anti-Black. Meanwhile, womanhating as a recourse of the powerless is sapping strength from Black communities, and our very lives. Rape is on the increase, reported and unreported, and rape is not aggressive sexuality, it is sexualized aggression. As Kalamu ya Salaam, a Black male writer points out, "As long as male domination exists, rape will exist. Only women revolting and men made conscious of their responsibility to fight sexism can collectively stop rape."

Differences between ourselves as Black women are also being misnamed and used to separate us from one another. As a Black lesbian feminist comfortable with the many different ingredients of my identity, and a woman committed to racial and sexual freedom from oppression, I find I am constantly being encouraged to pluck out some one aspect of myself and present this as the meaningful whole, eclipsing or denying the other parts of self. But this is a destructive and fragmenting way to live. My fullest concentration of energy is available to me only when I integrate all the parts of who I am, openly, allowing power from particular sources of my living to flow back and forth freely through all my different selves, without the restrictions of externally imposed definition. Only then can I bring myself and my energies as a whole to the service of those struggles which I embrace as part of my living.

A fear of lesbians, or of being accused of being a lesbian, has led many Black women into testifying against themselves. It has led some of us into destructive alliances, and others into despair and isolation. In the white women's communities, heterosexism is sometimes a result of identifying with the white patriarchy, a rejection of that interdependence between women-identified women which allows the self to be, rather than to be used in the service of men. Sometimes it reflects a die-hard belief in the protective coloration of heterosexual relationships, sometimes a self-hate which all women have to fight against, taught us from birth.

Although elements of these attitudes exist for all women, there are particular resonances of heterosexism and homophobia among Black women. Despite the fact that woman-bonding has a long and honorable history in the African and African-american communities, and despite the knowledge and accomplishments of many strong and creative women-identified Black women in the political, social and cultural fields, heterosexual Black women often tend to ignore or discount the existence and work of Black lesbians. Part of this attitude has come from an understandable terror of Black male attack within the close confines of Black society, where the punishment for any female self-assertion is still to be accused of being a lesbian and therefore unworthy of the attention or support of the scarce Black male. But part of this need to misname and ignore Black lesbians comes from a very real fear that openly women-identified Black women who are no longer dependent upon men for their self-definition may well reorder our whole concept of social relationships.

Black women who once insisted that lesbianism was a white woman's problem now insist that Black lesbians are a threat to Black nationhood, are consorting with the enemy, are basically un-Black. These accusations, coming from the very women to whom we look for deep and real understanding, have served to keep many Black lesbians in hiding, caught between the racism of white women and the homophobia of their sisters. Often, their work has been ignored, trivialized, or misnamed, as with the work of Angelina Grimke, Alice Dunbar–Nelson, Lorraine Hansberry. Yet women-bonded women have always been some part of the power of Black communities, from our unmarried aunts to the amazons of Dahomey.

And it is certainly not Black lesbians who are assaulting women and raping children and grandmothers on the streets of our communities.

Across this country, as in Boston during the spring of 1979 following the unsolved murders of twelve Black women, Black lesbians are spearheading movements against violence against Black women.

What are the particular details within each of our lives that can be scrutinized and altered to help bring about change? How do we redefine difference for all women? It is not our differences which separate women, but our reluctance to recognize those differences and to deal effectively with the distortions which have resulted from the ignoring and misnaming of those differences.

As a tool of social control, women have been encouraged to recognize only one area of human difference as legitimate, those differences which exist between women and men. And we have learned to deal across those differences with the urgency of all oppressed subordinates. All of us have had to learn to live or work or coexist with men, from our fathers on. We have recognized and negotiated these differences, even when this recognition only continued the old dominant/subordinate mode of human relationship, where the oppressed must recognize the masters' difference in order to survive.

But our future survival is predicated upon our ability to relate within equality. As women, we must root out internalized patterns of oppression within ourselves if we are to move beyond the most superficial aspects of social change. Now we must recognize differences among women who are our equals, neither inferior nor superior, and devise ways to use each others' difference to enrich our visions and our joint struggles.

The future of our earth may depend upon the ability of all women to identify and develop new definitions of power and new patterns of relating across difference. The old definitions have not served us, nor the earth that supports us. The old patterns, no matter how cleverly rearranged to imitate progress, still condemn us to cosmetically altered repetitions of the same old exchanges, the same old guilt, hatred, recrimination, lamentation, and suspicion.

For we have, built into all of us, old blueprints of expectation and response, old structures of oppression, and these must be altered at the same time as we alter the living conditions which are a result of those structures. For the master's tools will never dismantle the master's house.

As Paulo Freire shows so well in *The Pedagogy of the Oppressed,* the true focus of revolutionary change is never merely the oppressive situations which we seek to escape, but that piece of the oppressor which is planted deep within each of us, and which knows only the oppressors' tactics, the oppressors' relationships.

Change means growth, and growth can be painful. But we sharpen self-definition by exposing the self in work and struggle together with those whom we define as different from ourselves, although sharing the same goals. For Black and white, old and young, lesbian and heterosexual women alike, this can mean new paths to our survival.

> *We have chosen each other*
> *and the edge of each others battles*
> *the war is the same*
> *if we lose*
> *someday women's blood will congeal*
> *upon a dead planet*
> *if we win*
> *there is no telling*
> *we seek beyond history*
> *for a new and more possible meeting.*

EMMA COLEMAN JORDAN, RACE, GENDER, AND SOCIAL CLASS IN THE THOMAS SEXUAL HARASSMENT HEARINGS: THE HIDDEN FAULT LINES IN POLITICAL DISCOURSE

15 Harv. Women's L.J. 1–21 (1992).

The Thomas sexual harassment hearings were a Rorschach test of race, gender, and social class. A powerful swirl of visual and rhetorical images spilled into our living rooms like ink on a bone-dry blotter. What you saw depended on who you were. The fact that the central figures of this deadly linguistic duel, Judge Clarence Thomas and Professor Anita Hill, were both black was lost on no one. ...

III. The Influence of Social Class, Race, and Gender

The cues to race, gender, and social class were oddly distorted in that super-heated weekend under the intensity of the klieg lights. Many pre-existing racial and sexual stereotypes undercut Professor Hill's credibility: a man does not commit sexual harassment unless the woman encouraged his sexual interests in some way; a charge of sexual harassment made against a man of high status by a woman of lesser status is to be viewed with suspicion because the woman has something to gain from publicity, no matter how unflattering; sexual harassment charges are frequently concocted and therefore there must be independent corroboration of the events alleged; black women are unchaste; black women who report sexual misconduct by black men are traitors to the race and do not deserve community support. Professor Hill found herself burdened by all of these stereotypes.

A. Social Class

Professor Anita Hill emerged from the hearings as a national figure of enormous stature, widely admired for her courage and willingness to absorb the brutal innuendo of the Simpson–Specter–Hatch trio of Senatorial attackers. Her account of sexual harassment by a male supervisor rang true for many women, particularly those in the professions. ...

Analyzing the social class variables that were at work during the hearings is difficult, because explicit discussions about socio-economic status are virtually taboo in polite conversation in America. We all cherish the myth of our classless society. However, drawing subtle class distinctions between Hill and other women was an apparent part of the Thomas strategy to search and destroy his accuser.

This strategy exploited a complicated irony of women's upward mobility—the undercurrent of competition between women in jobs traditionally reserved for women, such as secretaries and administrative assistants, and women who aspire to break the glass ceiling by joining the executive ranks. While virtually all women acknowledge that sexual harassment in the workplace exists, a sharp division among women regarding Professor Hill's allegations emerged based on socio-economic status.

The first four "character" witnesses for Judge Thomas—all women of color—sought to separate Professor Hill from the national audience of middle and working class women. These Thomas witnesses attempted to strip Professor Hill of her racial and working class identity, to sever her from her black, Baptist, farm-family origins. Her strengths were portrayed as faults. Her upward mobility from National Merit Scholar and class valedictorian in tiny, rural Morris, Oklahoma to Yale Law School and beyond became a basis for criticism.

J.C. Alvarez, a former Thomas special assistant, openly displayed her animosity toward Professor Hill's achievements. Alvarez's testimony is a classic example of the subtle warfare that takes place in many offices across the nation. Alvarez testified that Hill was a "relentless debater ... [who] always acted as if she was a little bit superior to everyone, a little holier than thou ... mostly kept to herself ... [and] only occasionally participate[d] in some of the girl talk among the women at the office...."

For some women, "Hill's ambitiousness was a liability that shifted the burden of proof to her." The fact that "she was using him, as he was using her" led some to diminish the importance of her complaint. From this perspective she did not need the job to "put food on the table" and therefore was expected to quit at the first sign of trouble. This provides one explanation for poll results that showed that women of lower socio-economic status disbelieved Hill's allegations.

Hill's ten-year delay in reporting, and her decision to follow Thomas from the Department of Education to the EEOC, are understandable to a narrow band of women for whom ambition is a virtue, not a vice. The choices such women make are driven by recognition that in the highest levels of management and government service, a small group of highly influential mentors may enjoy a lifetime of input into one's career advancement. These "women who have ambition to get ahead, women who are not just looking for money, those who are looking for personal fulfillment, power, and influence in their line of work are especially vulnerable to a sexual harasser." Professor Hill guessed correctly that Clarence Thomas's star would continue to rise and that he would therefore be one of a painfully small number of influential blacks in the Reagan and Bush administrations whose opinion of her could undo her hard won academic and professional achievements.

B. Reckoning With the Racial Realities

In the Hill–Thomas dispute, the fact that the central figures of this high-stakes dispute are both black was at once supremely important, and of no particular importance. For Judge Thomas, the process by which he had risen in the ranks of black conservatives required him to carve a deep ravine between his own views and the social and political preferences of a majority of black citizens.

Thomas was introduced to the American public by a President who was willing to assert boldly that Judge Thomas's race had nothing to do with his selection. Two profoundly contradictory messages soon became apparent. On the one hand, he was a black man from Pin Point, Georgia, whose dramatic rise from poverty and the crushing limitations of racial segregation made him an icon of neo-conservatism, whose success could be cited as proof of the viability of self-help economics and the racial fairness of white conservatives who supported him. On the other hand, it was argued that because Judge Thomas's successes were achieved despite traumatic incidents of racism, he would bring a deep personal sensitivity to the resolution of the racial conflicts that often form the basis of Supreme Court litigation.

Professor Hill's racial identity also rested on a foundation of ambiguous characterization. Thomas and his supporters sought to portray her as a "white" feminist who happened to be black, a tool of abortion-rights supporters who sought to bring down Thomas with a last-minute claim of sexual harassment.

This characterization was plausible because of the inflexibility of our models for race and gender debates. In the shorthand of public policy discourse about gender conflicts, we assume that all women are white and that all blacks are men. When a black woman appears to speak for herself, these unspoken assumptions force her to shed one identity or the other. Moreover, when there are conflicts between a black man and a black woman, racism "trumps" sexism. The hierarchy of interests within the black community assigns a priority to protecting the entire community against the assaultive forces of racism. This conceptualization of the relationship between the entire community and the interests of its female members creates a powerful dynamic in which black women must subordinate matters of vital concern in order to continue to participate in community life. Women who break the expectation of silence may be made to feel disloyal, shunned, or vilified.

A new organization of black women, "African American Women in Defense of Ourselves," has sought to project a zone of political and cultural self-defense for black women by refusing to honor the expectation of silence regarding black male sexual misconduct. They note that "[m]any have erroneously portrayed [the hearings] as [addressing] an issue of either gender or race. As women of African descent, we understand sexual harassment as both.... This country has never taken the sexual abuse of Black women seriously. [B]lack women have been sexually stereotyped as immoral, insatiable, [and] perverse...."

Complex racial and cultural arguments are now being developed, in a series of highly publicized controversies, in defense of black men who use obscene, often violent language and imagery in communicating with and about black women. One such argument is that obscenity is part of the black vernacular and should be understood by both black men and women as harmless, situationally appropriate repartee between the sexes....

1. The Lynching Metaphor

The single most intriguing aspect of the Hill–Thomas hearings was Thomas's complete abandonment of his earlier plea to be judged by the content of his character, not by the color of his skin.... Thomas in his writings and speeches prior to nomination subscribed to the view that black people have developed a "victim-focused" identity which leads "us ... to claim more racial victimization than we have actually endured." Judge Thomas frowned on this "whining" from civil rights leaders. Yet, in his opening statement he charged the Senate Judiciary Committee with conducting a "high-tech lynching." He told the Committee that stereotypes existed in the "language about the sexual prowess of black men, language about the sex organs of black men, ... and these are charges that play into racist, bigoted, stereotypes, and these are the kind of charges that are impossible to wash off." He went on to say that: "I wasn't harmed by the Klan. I wasn't harmed by the Knights of Camellia. I wasn't harmed by the Ar[y]an race. I wasn't harmed by a racist group. I was harmed by this process."

Because no one on the Committee responded to his lynching charge, the country was left with a distorted image of a racial victim. No one pointed out that it was a black woman who claimed he had victimized her. No one pointed out the terrible harms and stereotypes to which black women have been subjected. Although the sexual stereotypes of all black people are damaging, "[t]he institutionalized rape of black women has never been as powerful a symbol of black oppression [within the black community] as the spectacle of lynching."

2. *Historical Resistance to Sexual Predation*

Black women, like black men, have labored under corrosive myths of paranormal sexuality. Stripped of cultural and legal protection from sexual predation, black women have had to construct a network of self-defense. Even after slavery, black women were "[r]egarded as immoral and loose.... [They] spent an inordinate amount of time ... in attempts to establish themselves as virtuous women, as a rebuke to the rash of hypersexual images that flooded contemporary consciousness in those days, images that rationalized the routine sexual abuse of black women ... by white men."

Historian Darlene Clark Hine asserts that during slavery, black women, vulnerable to rape and domestic violence, "resisted the misappropriation and [sought] to maintain the integrity of their own sexuality." The history of the struggle of black women has always contained an element of resistance to sexual predation. The most vivid illustrations of such self-defense are those of slave women who forcefully resisted the rape of slavemasters.

The story of Celia, a young slave woman who murdered her master, is one example. John Newsom purchased Celia at age fourteen and raped her repeatedly. She had two children by him, but subsequently developed a stable relationship with a fellow slave named George. Celia then attempted, unsuccessfully, to terminate the abusive relationship with Newsom. She warned her master not to come to her private cabin, and when he disregarded her wishes, she struck him with a club, killing him. Celia was tried for murder. However, she was not permitted to testify on her own behalf, because a slave could not legally testify against a white person. Nor did the law recognize the crime of rape against a slave. However, a statute did make it a crime "to take any woman against her will." Celia's lawyer introduced evidence of the ongoing rapes and made the innovative argument that "even a slave woman could resist sexual advances with deadly force." Although the statute applied to "any woman," the court rejected the argument that it included slave women, because it would "threaten the very foundations of the institution of slavery ... [to allow a slave woman legal entitlement] to use deadly force to protect her honor." Since white women were barred from jury service, the "trial" was held before a jury of all white males. Under these circumstances, it should come as no surprise that Celia was found guilty and hanged.

Slave women were sexual property. The world they inhabited was bereft of legal protection for their sexual autonomy. Today, black women seek to claim that vital core of individual dignity, the right to determine one's sexual interactions. These efforts present complex challenges to the definitions of acceptable interaction between the genders. The slave legacy stands as a reminder that black women can successfully resist sexual imposition despite disabling legal doctrine.

3. The Power of Racial Memory

Judge Thomas's use of powerful racial imagery transformed him from sexual harasser to racial victim, perhaps the single most important element leading to his confirmation. His use of race worked to his advantage because "the critical segment of public opinion was the opinion of black voters in the black belt of the South. Thomas reminded black people that he was a black man who was in danger of being oppressed for being uppity, by going beyond his assigned station in life."

This perception tapped the widely shared belief among large segments of the black community that black politicians and other prominent leaders are subject to a double standard of morality....

C. A Gendered Understanding

Those who sought to discredit Professor Hill made use of a treacherous combination of stereotypes and myths about black and white women. The Freudian notion of women's hysterical fabrication of claims of sexual abuse merged with the politico-psychiatric diagnosis of erotomania, to provide a formidable tool with which to shape public opinion and diminish Professor Hill's powerful presentation....

Because Professor Hill is a black woman, she was portrayed not only as delusional, but also as Sapphire: the black, gonad-grinding woman "out of control." The Sapphire image with all of its connotations of black male emasculation resonated within the black community. Hill's status as a black woman multiplied the possible lines of attack by making available additional stereotypes that could be used against her....

ROBERT WILLIAMS, JR., GENDERED CHECKS AND BALANCES: UNDERSTANDING THE LEGACY OF WHITE PATRIARCHY IN AN AMERICAN INDIAN CULTURAL CONTEXT

24 Georgia L.Rev. 1019, 1022–44 (1990).

Advocates of outsider jurisprudential perspectives recognize that our individual ways of seeing the world can distort our understanding of another culture's sense of reality. Without ever realizing that we may harbor certain prejudices or stereotypes, our understanding of a situation becomes disabled by the same faults we identify and critique in the dominant, essentialist discourses of our society. Certainly, sexism and prejudice exist in traditional Indian communities. Looking for such faults, however, in the usual places one finds them in a system based on the values of white patriarchy can lead to fundamental misunderstandings about Indian cultures.

As I will attempt to show, the very legacy of white patriarchy stands as a principle barrier encumbering our ability to meaningfully comprehend most, if not all, of the distinctive aspects of Indian cultures. The problem for those who would practice outsider jurisprudence is to understand an Indian cultural context according to its own terms—terms that possess meaning for Indian people—instead of terms derived from a much different cultural perspective grounded in the legacy of white patriarchy. . . .

II. Developing Outsider Perspectives: Understanding Traditional Indian Communities

A. *Giant Steps*

Keeping this problem of perspective and interpretation in mind, I would like to extend the inquiry one step further, into an aspect of Indian culture that is likely not very familiar to most non-Indians at all: relations of gender and power in a traditional North American Indian community.

First, briefly catalog in your own mind *what,* if anything, you know, or think you know, about gender roles in traditional Indian cultures. My experience has been that most non-Indians know very little about this complex and multifaceted topic. And absent some specialized knowledge in cultural anthropology, what most non-Indians usually think they know is largely distorted by the dominant value systems of white patriarchy.

Gauge your reaction, for instance, to the following gendered example of Indian humor. I recently confronted this gendered text while at an Indian crafts show in Arizona Indian Country. On a bumper sticker, prominently placed on a booth run by an Indian couple, was a stereotyped cartoon of an Indian brave. The bare-chested brave was wearing a feather in his hair and sitting under a tree not doing much of anything. The caption on the sticker read as follows:

> Ugh! Before White Man come to this country—no taxes, no deficit, and women did all the work. Ugh! White Man thought he had better system.

My experience has been that many, if not most, non-Indian readers of that bumper sticker interpret some sense of ridicule at work in that joke. They usually try to understand the bumper sticker by connecting a large part of that apparent ridicule to their own suppositions about the role of women in traditional Indian cultures. Those suppositions, I have found, are often tied to various familiar aspects of the legacy of white patriarchy they clearly understand.

Most non-Indians, for example, understand that women's work is often ridiculed in the social systems most familiar to them. In fact, the social systems most familiar to most non-Indians are usually dominated by widespread affirmation of white patriarchal values throughout their social reward structures. Thus, non-Indians can feel safe in assuming that women's work must also be ridiculed in Indian cultures. Therefore, the joke must mean the same thing in an Indian context as it does in a non-Indian context.

But must white patriarchal values affect the complex social systems of all peoples in identical ways? Might not the cluster system of values associated with white patriarchy sustain a plurality of effects, engender a thousand discourses throughout the multifaceted cultural processes it encounters on its path as knowledge *and* power? These are questions central to the theory and practice of outsider jurisprudence.

I want to suggest several interpretations of this bumper sticker that might not be immediately accessible to many non-Indians. Importantly, I am emphatically *not* purporting to describe the only plausible Indian interpretations of the bumper sticker. I am simply trying to offer some possible alternative interpretations of the bumper sticker that I have found are not readily available to most non-Indians who lack specialized knowledge about gender roles in Indian tribal cultures.

Primarily, I want to show how placing this joke in an Indian cultural context might liberate a much larger space for cross-cultural understandings of the many destructive meanings of white patriarchy in all of our lives. The lessons about sexism and cultural stereotyping that can be taught by use of the bumper sticker have meanings that can be significantly enriched by considering the plurality of interpretative contexts engendered by the bumper sticker.

B. Next Big Step

Consider for a moment the degree to which your own understanding of gender roles in Indian cultures might be distorted by the legacy of white patriarchy itself. First, while Indian men and women might differ widely in their assessments of its significance in and for their own lives, most contemporary Indian people have some general level of historical awareness of a deeply entrenched racial stereotype of their cultures held by the dominant society. The stereotype of the "lazy Indian," always implicitly understood as the lazy Indian *male,* has been propounded by white society since the era of the first cultural encounters between the peoples of the Old World and New World. The stereotype of the lazy Indian male populates numerous texts of white scholars, government officials, missionaries, traders and gentlemen-travellers through the late nineteenth century. The stereotype's legacy has survived into our own century.

Whites have utilized the stereotype of the lazy Indian male for many purposes, but it has primarily served to explain the traditional gendered division of labor in many North American tribal communities. Whites early on saw the need to interpret the distinctive and unique patterns they thought they saw at work in many tribal cultures. From their perspective as outsiders, whites generally understood life in many American Indian tribes to be comprised primarily of men engaging in hunting, fishing and warfare and women controlling the children, the household and agricultural subsistence production. To whites, what stood out in this stereotype of American Indian tribalism was the degree of control Indian women seemed to exercise over tribal crop agriculture.

Whites generally understood this distinctive cultural pattern which seemed to prevail in so many Indian cultures to mean that as a race, Indian men were generally lazy, doing no work of real value in the tribe. According to the value structures of white patriarchy brought to the New World by Europeans, hunting and fishing were sport. War (like politics in many ways) was conceived of as just another, more serious variation of sport. Raising children and controlling the household did not count for much in the reward structure of classical white patriarchy, but according to these same white patriarchal values, crop agricultural production was work. Therefore, concluded generations of whites, women did all the work in Indian communities.

Many Indian people, even today, are very much aware of this stereotype; in fact, my own experience has been that Indian men and women can sometimes be quite sensitive about its legacy. Any identifiable traces of this legacy in Indian humor, therefore, ought to be approached with some degree of rigor and scholarly openness to the plausibility of multiple interpretations about its meanings for Indian people.

It is possible that a person raised in a traditional Indian community may understand the bumper sticker as somehow intended to ridicule women in the same way that women and the work they do are often ridiculed in a social system dominated by the values of white patriarchy. But it is also possible that in cultures that teach the individual to think independently and act for others, the work that women do might be differently valued than in a culture ordered according to the more individualistic values of white patriarchy.

Given the widely diffused white stereotype of the lazy Indian male, itself a reflection of white patriarchal values, an Indian person might also plausibly interpret the bumper sticker as ridiculing the history of white ignorance and arrogance about Indian cultures that engendered and continues to sustain the stereotype. In this context, Indians who understand the bumper sticker as reaffirming some deeper, more positive communal understanding of Indian values, realize how ridiculous the White Man can be. He has never really understood anything about Indian people, and so will never quite get the joke.

Alternatively, an Indian person may interpret the bumper sticker as ridiculing Indian cultural values. Such an interpretation accepts the stereotype as capturing a large degree of truth about Indian cultures: Indian men have always been lazy; women have always done all the work. After all, the Indian male in the bumper sticker is sitting under a tree, not doing much of anything. No matter what "system" rules his life, the typical Indian male will always be lazy and will always avoid doing real work.

Such an interpretation is not at all implausible, given my own experience that some Indian people hold very negative views about aspects of their own cultures. Despite the self-critical nature of such views, this possible interpretation may itself be subject to the hegemonical functioning [18] of white patriarchy's value structures in contemporary Indian life. The bumper sticker in such a context can then be understood in a more profound and even disturbing manner. Its image of self-hate can be understood as the Indian equivalent of the traveling minstrel show, confirming the dominant society's worst stereotypes of Indian people.

What I am arguing for in each of these varying and admittedly over-simplified, contextualized accounts is simply acceptance of the initial plausibility of multiple interpretations of the bumper sticker. Particularly given the context of a dominant culture's deeply entrenched racial stereotypes of the lazy Indian male, the bumper sticker may well be meant to convey a series of humorous meditations on the values of white patriarchy and their meanings in the lives of Indian people, men as well as women....

III. Gender, Power and Property in One Traditional North American Indian Tribe: The Iroquois

As I seek to suggest, the legacy of white patriarchy might be plausibly understood to function quite differently in different cultural contexts. The possibility that gender roles in some Indian cultures might be understood differently and in ways unfamiliar to white patriarchal values certainly merits closer investigation by anyone interested in the perspectives that can be engendered by outsider jurisprudence.

There are, of course, many Indian tribes and communities, and therefore many different Indian cultural contexts. Gender roles differ radically among various Indian tribes; even within a particular tribe, the position of women may be perceived differently by different tribal members. Such variability across the broad spectrum of traditional and contemporary American Indian cultural patterns makes any effort at generalizations about the positions of women in Indian societies difficult, if not impossible, to sustain beyond just a few instances.

But even an interpretation of the bumper sticker developed from within one particular tribal perspective—for example, the unique perspective of traditional Iroquois tribal culture—can prove useful to outsider jurisprudence. It can help an outsider develop a deeper understanding of the ways peoples of a different culture contextualize the distinctive meanings of the legacy of white patriarchy in and for their own lives. That understanding, in and of itself, is valuable knowledge to possess, and can be put to use for many liberating purposes....

The Iroquois are actually a confederacy of five tribes: the Mohawks, Seneca, Cayuga, Oneida and Onondaga. They are governed by a Council of fifty chiefs distributed among the five tribes. A distinctive feature of

---

18. By hegemonical functioning, I mean the social processes whereby the values of the dominant culture are accepted as true and inevitable conclusions about social life in general by outsider groups, even though such acceptance might be contrary to group interests....

Iroquois society (from a non-Indian perspective at least) is that, like many North American tribal societies, they are organized culturally, socially and politically by a matrilineal clan system. Eight different clans are distributed throughout the five tribes. An Iroquois can marry anyone from the five Iroquois tribes, including a member of his or her own tribe, so long as he or she is not a member of the same clan. A child's clan affiliation is determined at birth by his or her mother's clan. If your mother, for example, is a member of the Seneca Bear Clan and your father of the Mohawk Wolf Clan, you would be a Seneca Bear Clan member, regardless of your sex.

The matrilineal clan system of the Iroquois differs markedly from the patriarchy models brought to North America by white society. For our purposes, the most important differences relate to the gendered distributions of political and economic power in the tribe. The Iroquois *did not* believe in formal equalities between the sexes as a principle of political or economic organization of the tribe.

Under Iroquois law, the transmission of all titles, rights and property descended through the female clan line to the exclusion of the male. *Culturally,* this meant that the women owned and controlled the giving of names in the clan. In many ways, this was one of their most powerful roles in a culture that relied (and continues to rely) largely on oral transmission of its many forms of knowledge. *Politically,* this power of naming held consequences in nearly all aspects of tribal life, including the tribal individual's life. This gendered power to name extended all the way to the naming of chiefs on the tribal council.

All of the fifty chieftainships, by tribal tradition, were held by male members of the tribe. But most importantly, the chieftainships were the property of individual clans. There was no right of primogeniture in the male line. The father could not be succeeded by his wife's son, because the son belonged to the mother's clan, not the father's.

In Iroquois culture, therefore, the clan chieftainships were controlled as the property of the matrilineal clan mothers. When the Seneca Bear Clan chief died, for example, his name and title reverted back to the head clan mother. According to tribal tradition, the head clan mother, in consultation with the other women in the clan, selected a new chief from among the clan males. A favored son or a nephew born of a sister might often be preferred, but the clan women would be guided primarily in their decision upon a chief on the basis of leadership qualities valued in Iroquois culture and a sense of that person's likely standing in the community. Leaders should show generosity, courage, patience, temperance and, importantly, a good sense of Indian humor.

Not only did the women of the clan name the Chief, but they had the power to take away the name of a chief deemed unfit to serve. If the clan women became displeased with a chief's performance or service, he was literally "dehorned," that is impeached. The chief's head dress, made of the horns from a deer, would be removed by the clan mother.

This power of naming and removing chiefs was further enhanced by the fact that tribal policy could be set by the Tribal Council only when there was a clear consensus among all fifty chiefs and when all other tribal members, men and women alike, agreed with the Council's consensus. The Iroquois constitutional system of gendered checks and balances sought to insure, at least in theory, that women's voices could always be heard and respected on all issues of tribal policy.

In practice, this gendered distribution of political power in Iroquois society was reinforced by a gendered division of labor in the tribe. In Iroquois culture, men's domain was the forest; women owned and controlled the village. This meant that women owned and controlled the clan longhouses where extended families, usually a grandmother, her daughters, their husbands and the children lived, ate and slept. Women also owned and worked the clan's subsistence agricultural fields on the outskirts of the village. These fields provided the primary, reliable source of food for the clan longhouse. "Women's work" provided the bulk of the clan's regularly relied-on subsistence needs. Men hunted, fished and protected the tribe in war.

It was this gendered division of labor that whites most always focused on when they remarked that women did all the work in Indian cultures such as those of the Iroquois. What white observers did not recognize was that hunting and fishing on a rigorous and daily basis provided regular supplements to the Indian diet. And because whites were, if at all, usually only casual *outside* observers of Indian village life, they also did not see that Indian men did do some useful things around the house and village. The men, for example, performed the rather strenuous tasks of actually building the longhouses. They also cleared the forests for new agricultural fields.

Within an Iroquois cultural context, therefore, both men and women did their share of hard labor in the tribe. Whites, however, generally failed to understand this fact of tribal life. As outside observers, they were unwilling and, therefore, unable to understand Iroquois culture on its own terms as a society functioning according to a widely diffused system of gendered checks and balances throughout the tribe. Instead, they focused on what they understood, from their white patriarchal perspective, as the distinctive feature of the Iroquois—the gendered division of labor in the tribe. On this narrow basis, they concluded that Iroquois women did all the work in the tribe.

By relying on the certitude of the categories shaped by their own white patriarchal ways of seeing the world, whites also failed to recognize another important cluster of facts about gender roles in Iroquois culture. Iroquois notions of property, which also seemed distinctive and unusual from a white patriarchal perspective, played a crucial role in sustaining the Iroquois system of gendered checks and balances.

In Iroquois culture, for example, women's work was highly valued because Iroquois notions of property focused on what whites would call usufructuary rights: in most traditional tribal societies like the Iroquois, you owned what you used. There were no wage or market economies. In Iroquois culture, women literally owned everything worth owning from a white perspective. The clan women owned the longhouses and everything in them. The agricultural fields and the produce and any surplus from those fields were owned by the women. Men, in fact, owned very little. Personal effects such as knives and guns measured the extent of their recognized property interests in the tribe. Even the food which men killed belonged to the wife's clan.

Given these recognized ownership rights which stemmed from a system of gendered property rights distributed according to the principle of "what you use, you own," it is possible to develop a better sense of the position of women and the scope of power they effectively exercised in Iroquois tribal life. Women could literally call off a war by refusing to provide the necessary food provisions to the warriors in the field. Women were also responsible for determining the distribution of the clan's food supply within the longhouse, and to other clan longhouses if there was a surplus. Sustaining the complex network of clan relations that provided vital political and social cohesion between widely dispersed tribal communities was one of the most important roles assumed by women in Iroquois life. In Iroquois diplomatic discourse, for example, the term "Woman" was synonymous with the term "Peacemaker."

Like most tribal societies, the Iroquois valued highly the actions of individuals done for others. It is not surprising, therefore, that women's work was highly valued in the delicate system of gendered checks and balances which distributed power, property and influence throughout the many vectors of traditional Iroquois life. Given such facts, is it implausible to suggest that developing a better understanding of gender roles in an Iroquois cultural context might well engender some valuable insights and strategies relevant to the outsider jurisprudential project of dismantling white patriarchy in our own society? . . .

This brief introduction to some of the distinctive aspects of Iroquois gender roles reveals a number of plausible interpretations for this bumper sticker from an Iroquois cultural context. Relations of gender, power and property in at least one traditional Indian community, the Iroquois, initially appear to be organized according to an entirely different set of values than those characterizing systems of white patriarchy familiar to most non-Indians.

An Iroquois cross-cultural perspective of the bumper sticker might, therefore, recognize that women did not do all the work in the Iroquois system; rather, white outsiders tended to interpret these unfamiliar Indian cultural patterns in this way. In fact, the work Iroquois women did was highly valued, as suggested by a property system in which women owned all the property they used and made productive. Significantly, there was no need for taxes in that system, because women enforced the clan scheme of redistribution of wealth. There was no deficit, because if a tribal policy proved too costly to pursue (such as war), women (the peacemakers in the tribe) could demand that it be terminated. In an Iroquois cultural context, therefore, this bumper sticker might be understood not only as ridiculing white patriarchy's misinformed stereotypes of Indian cultures but also as ridiculing white patriarchy's whole system of values which generations of whites have regarded as somehow superior to the Iroquois system of distributing power and property based on principles of gendered checks and balances.

Before we could ever hope to have access to the many complex meanings of the bumper sticker in an Iroquois cultural context, we would need to know a great deal more about the stories and experiences of oppression belonging to both Iroquois men and women. These experiences may be engendered and sustained by systems of white patriarchal values, or they may be integral to cultural patterns specific to the Iroquois. I wish only to suggest the initial plausibility of a plurality of interpretations of the bumper sticker from an Iroquois cultural perspective. Other plausible accounts are certainly possible, given the vast complexities of Iroquois culture and the heterogeneity of experiences we all bring to our individual ways of seeing the world.

The Iroquois, like many other American Indian tribes, are a multi-faceted and still vital traditional people, with a great deal to teach anyone interested in developing outsider jurisprudential perspectives. Understanding the complexities of their culture and different ways of life may well lead to a deeper understanding of the legacy of white patriarchy on all of our ways of seeing the world. Treating one's own perspective as just one of many possible points of view affected by white patriarchal systems of racism, colonialism, sexism and homophobia is just one critical part of a method that must be continually developed and refined by the emerging legal voices of outsider jurisprudence. This distinctive way of seeing the world expresses a vision of a scholarly community dedicated to intensifying the struggle for human rights on all fronts of our shared social life.

VALERIE POLAKOW, THE OTHER MOTHERHOOD: THE LANDSCAPE OF SINGLE MOTHERS IN POVERTY

in Lives on the Edge 43–44, 46–48, 51–53, 60–62 (U. Chicago, 1993).

UNPACKING POVERTY DISCOURSE

The way in which we choose to talk about poverty—as a social problem, an urgent issue in need of attention, a dilemma, a menace, a threat to the society, a cost to the taxpayer, or, as one of my colleagues once stated, just "another variable of development"—creates a noise, followed by echoes that locate the invisible lives of poor women and their children. They, living out there in the unnamed landscapes, periodically swell into visibility as the poverty *issue* is targeted for public attention by competing political agendas. Poverty talk, however, is always a discourse about *them*. As they get closer and their proximity makes us uncomfortable, we clamor for laws to contain them, to regulate their space in relation to ours, to keep the most destitute and homeless away from our homes, our walking and jogging routes, our subway stations, our parking lots, our libraries. When we turn and look at *their children,* we feel concern about this future citizenry, this growing young population "at risk," whom we call "at risk" less out of outrage and compassion than because their condition threatens our security and comfort, our children, our schools, our neighborhoods, our property values. Their *otherness* places *us* "at risk"; yet it is we who have named them. We have both invented and named poverty.

Calling poverty a "disease" implies a fatalistic perspective: poverty hits those who are less healthy than us; the unchecked virus that afflicts them must be contained, and it may be possible to effect a cure if they take the medicine we have prescribed for them. Or there is the "poverty as enemy" talk, necessitating a war on poverty, which, we are now told, has been fought and lost at taxpayer expense. Another discourse entangles poverty with immorality and depravity and draws the boundaries of poverty in family pathology. Still another creates a geography of poverty as an embedded culture from which there is no psychological exit. But, there is one common theme that unites the different forms of poverty discourse—the silence about class, about a political economy that creates poverty by its very economic structure. For as Michel Foucault has pointed out, poverty is always an essential ingredient of wealth. Yet the language of poverty continues to contaminate our sensibilities, to frame our ways of seeing and not seeing. Why, we might ask, is it so difficult to see that children do not catch poverty but are made poor by state neglect; that single mothers need not be destined to fall into poverty but are made poor by a state-constructed policy. ...

Not much has shifted in our public sensibilities from the religious moralism of the eighteen hundreds pointing to the depravity of the undeserving poor, to contemporary conservative commentaries on the "politics of conduct" of the nonworking poor. Poverty is a private affair—its causes are rooted in failed individuals, failed families, and moral degeneration rather than in a failed public economy and a discriminatory public policy. It is an individual or underclass or ethnic problem in need of redress, not a structural one requiring a fundamental shift in our ways of seeing the politics of distribution.

This perception of poverty as a private affair, argue Grubb and Lazerson, is rooted in a basic nineteenth-century American dilemma—public or private responsibility and the role of the state, "whether poverty should be considered a public problem requiring expanded state involvement, or a private and individual problem for which the state should accept minimal responsibility." As the ideal of family as a domestic island, and the cult of motherhood, emerged during the mid-nineteenth century, the doctrine of *parens patriae* permitted public intervention, when parenting was judged inadequate, by legitimating surveillance and regulation of "defective" families in order to protect children. This intervention targeted poor and vulnerable families, such as those headed by a woman, even though the doctrine legally applied to

all families. As public responsibility for children received major attention during the Progressive Era, the assumption that families would
remain private persisted, as did the assumption that the economy would
remain private. If public money was to be spent, it should always be
less than what the individual would gain in the private market. The
consequence was that poor families should have poor children, whose
lives should have fewer perceived advantages than those of other children. Thus public action becomes "a second-best resort, aiding those
who are often considered second-class citizens." This instrumental view
of children, which in contemporary form represents a more sophisticated
view of the non-deserving poor, also continues to rationalize a minimalist
public responsibility where anticipated payoffs are supposed to justify
the interventions. The success of both Head Start and High/Scope early
intervention programs is demonstrated by their outcomes in terms of
later payoffs for society. High/Scope has shown a 7.01 percent rate of
return for one year of compensatory preschool, which is widely touted as
the rationale for continued funding. It is argued that these results
demonstrate among targeted participants, that there is less crime, less
drain on state resources, less adolescent pregnancy, and a decreased high
school dropout rate.

        None of these arguments is premised on compassion for children or
concern for their existential well-being. Strangely absent for poor
children is the democratic expectation that all young children are entitled to a decent life and to an equal educational opportunity. Rather,
because their parents are poor, they too are punished. This construct of
poverty as a private affair continues to mask the causes of poverty,
which lie in structural inequalities of access and opportunity. In turn
this has effectively limited public responsibility which has "reinforced
the tendency towards private wealth and public squalor." As long as the
notion of poverty as a private affair dominates our public discourse, the
dominant focus will be the "politics of conduct" of the poor. This
discourse serves to conceal the continuing mean-spirited treatment of
poor people and legitimates the minimalist and degrading support policies for single mothers and their children, who suffer the snowball
effects of class and race as well as gender discrimination. Their poverty
is viewed not as state-constructed but as their due, a condition into
which they are born or fall and, most importantly, which they perpetuate. Poverty is regarded as a deserved condition. We see how pervasive
the ideology of "blaming the victim" has been, and how it continues
when those of us who are both privileged and non-poor attempt to
understand the condition of otherness. When otherness is imputed to
those with least power—poor women and their children—a viable childhood and motherhood are dramatically eroded. But do incomplete
mothers who have made incomplete families deserve decent lives? ...

        The gendered nature of the welfare state has often concealed the
roots of poverty for women and children. It is an economy of inequitable distribution and production that creates the need for women's
welfare programs in the first place. The relationship of women to the

welfare state has always been one of contingency and subordination to the ideal of domesticity. Mothers' Pensions, the forerunner of Aid to Families with Dependent Children (AFDC), was expressly designed to keep woman at home when a male breadwinner was absent, thereby defining her dependent status and relegating her to a regulated life. Welfare expenditure funneled to AFDC has not transcended the norm of a stay-at-home, unskilled, untrained mother, to be supported by her husband. But those norms represent an ideology of domesticity and motherhood which are themselves the product of a gendered system. This ideology continues to see women as citizen-mothers, not citizen-workers, thereby perpetuating low-wage temporary employment, low-status pink-collar jobs, and the unavailability of public child care and maternity leave provisions, all of which leave poor single women with few options other than welfare when they have young children.

To pursue this long-standing public perception of women as mothers rather than citizen-workers, let us shift our attention back to France, where, as we have seen, a cult of the "new mother" had dominated bourgeois sensibilities. By the end of the nineteenth century, the French perceived working women quite differently than did the Americans. In France, women were seen as citizen-workers whose necessary participation in the labor force required state policies for their protection in their dual roles of worker and mother. It followed that both working mothers and their babies were entitled to state protection, and while women still lacked political rights, they were accorded civil rights in recognition of their productive and reproductive functions. As France continued to debate its "social question," single mothers, *femmes isolées*, were viewed as the representation of misery, the potential producers of the "dangerous classes"; hence French social policy began to take a radically different turn. Because high infant mortality rates were linked to deprivation of breastfeeding in the first months after birth, paid pre- and postnatal maternity leave was instituted and written into labor legislation at the turn of the century. Factory creches, state-provided child care, and the regulation of hours for women working in factories all served as protective legislation for working women, where state policy recognized and supported women's needs as workers and mothers. Ironically, while such workplace rights were guaranteed, female suffrage was opposed; for France affirmed the social-economic identity of woman as citizen-worker but denied her identity as political actor.

In the United States, however, maternity leave, paid or unpaid, was never entrenched as state policy. In 1916, the American Association for Labor Legislation lobbied to introduce maternity legislation modeled on that of northern Europe; but it was opposed as unnecessary by employers who did not think women should work after marriage. Once again, the implicit moral assumption was that only married women needed consideration and that these were best taken care of by husband-breadwinners; single mothers were excluded from the discourse. Hence the ideology of separate spheres, of dependence and self-sufficiency, of private and public realms, haunted the working women of the first decade of the twentieth century and continues to do so in the 1990s. The United States stands together with South Africa as the only Western postindustrial society with no maternity policies for working mothers. American working women thus became "invisible as workers for everyone but those who argued for their 'exceptional' needs. Women's citizenship rights were claimed almost exclusively because of their supposed maternal qualities. Absent was an identity for working women or for women unencumbered by nurturing responsibilities." ...

Attempts at welfare reform during the past years have failed to confront the gender base of the welfare system and the issues of private, public, and corporate responsibility. The Family Support Act of 1988, which the states began to implement in 1990, was a small and mean-spirited attempt to reform welfare, but along *workfare* lines. The act, written by Senator Moynihan, passed with bipartisan support on the assumption that paid employment leads women off the welfare rolls. The states are permitted to require mothers of children over one year of age to participate in welfare-to-work programs. Both the training and child care benefits built into the act, however, are woefully inadequate; the latter do not meet the costs of enrolling a child in a quality child care center. States are allowed to receive federal matching funds for child care only at the 75th percentile of the local market rate, condemning the vast majority of young poor children to substandard care. Given the current crisis in child care availability, the Children's Defense Fund estimates that in the majority of states, only a fraction of AFDC children find child care slots. While the Family Support Act does provide federal support for education and training through the new Job Opportunities and Basic Skills Program (JOBS), there is pressure to operate very short-term low-cost programs. As states lay off workers and attempt to trim budgets, such pressures increase, and the first programs targeted are the welfare programs.

The conviction that AFDC women should have to work went counter to a pervasive set of ideological assumptions about domesticity. Yet the assumptions correlative to welfare reform—that women are entitled to public child care, maternity leaves, and child allowances, as is the case in all western European countries—are seldom voiced in American legislatures. The current reform package reflects "a strange and novel combination of conservative motives (tax cutting, hostility to single mothers and to women's sexual and reproductive independence, racism) with an acceptance of women's employment." Both conservative and liberal views are injurious to women, argues Diana Pearce, as both perspectives are grounded *either* in the assumption that women should be male-dependent, *or* in the assumption that women are second-class workers.

Many women are poor for the same reasons men are poor—because they lack education or skills, or live in a poor job area, or are minorities who suffer the long-term continuing effects of discrimination. But women are also poor because they are both nurturers of and providers for their children, and because they are disadvantaged in the labor market. The median income for a woman worker in 1989 was only 68 percent of the median income for a male worker. The average woman college graduate working full time, earned less than the average male high school graduate. Women are far less able to obtain full-time, year-round work. Many mothers who attempt to support their families can find only part-time or seasonal work, and encounter severe child care problems if their children are young. Women often become casual, secondary-sector workers, ineligible for unemployment and health insurance benefits by virtue of their low wages and part-time work. For women, particularly mothers, a job is no certain route out of poverty, precisely because there is no job security and few fringe benefits. In contrast, workers in the primary sector receive higher pay as well as fringe benefits, and if they lose their jobs they are entitled to unemployment compensation. As Pearce points out, disproportionate numbers of women and minorities occupy the secondary sector: 87 percent of the recipients of primary benefits are in white families headed by men or married couples; only 3 percent are headed by black single mothers. The difference in poverty incidence between those who receive social insurance and those who receive welfare is dramatic: only 8 percent of the families of primary-sector beneficiaries as against almost 75 percent of the families of secondary-sector beneficiaries are living in poverty. Women, especially minority women, are disproportionately represented in the latter category. Pearce concludes that "the secondary welfare sector destroys not only one's incentives but also one's prospect of ever working one's way out of poverty." While public myths implicate welfare mothers as nonworkers, recent studies indicate that 90 percent of welfare mothers have worked, many recently, and that they apply for public assistance only when men and the labor market fail to provide income support for family maintenance. The tragedy is that AFDC fails dismally as a back-up support and serves to disempower and humiliate such mothers further, as the welfare bureaucracy creates modern-day paupers of them and their children.

Yet there are stories to be told that float between the coarse pages of welfare statistics, there are voices that speak not a language of otherness, but a language of ours—of mothers and children who confront the dailiness of lives in poverty. It is time to listen to their stories.

D. COMMONALITIES

The essays in this final section examine the possibilities of transcending identity boundaries, seeing commonalities, and perhaps making coalitions with those who are different from you. In attempting to understand and cross these boundaries, we often attempt to make comparisons between various forms of exclusion. The Supreme Court used this precise technique in *J.E.B. v. Alabama ex rel. T.B.,* ___ U.S. ___, 114 S.Ct. 1419, 120 L.Ed.2d 89 (1994). There, the Court considered the constitutionality of peremptory jury challenges based on gender. In striking down such use of peremptory challenges, the Court compared race discrimination and gender discrimination. Justice Blackmun wrote for the majority:

J.E.B. v. ALABAMA EX REL. T.B.

United States Supreme Court, 1994.
___ U.S. ___, 114 S.Ct. 1419, 120 L.Ed.2d 89.

JUSTICE BLACKMUN delivered the opinion of the Court.

While the prejudicial attitudes toward women in this country have not been identical to those held toward racial minorities, the similarities between the experiences of racial minorities and women, in some contexts, "overpower those differences." ... As a plurality of this Court observed in *Frontiero v. Richardson,* 411 U.S. 677, 685 (1973):

> "[T]hroughout much of the 19th century the position of women in our society was, in many respects, comparable to that of blacks under the pre-Civil War slave codes. Neither slaves nor women could hold office, serve on juries, or bring suit in their own names, and married women traditionally were denied the legal capacity to hold or convey property or to serve as legal guardians of their own children.... And although blacks were guaranteed the right to vote in 1870, women were denied even that right—which is itself 'preservative of other basic civil and political rights'—until adoption of the Nineteenth Amendment half a century later." (Footnotes omitted.)

Certainly, with respect to jury service, African–Americans and women share a history of total exclusion, a history which came to an end for women many years after the embarrassing chapter in our history came to an end for African–Americans.

We need not determine, however, whether women or racial minorities have suffered more at the hands of discriminatory state actors during the decades of our Nation's history. It is necessary only to acknowledge that "our Nation has had a long and unfortunate history of sex discrimination," a history which warrants the heightened scrutiny we afford all gender-based classifications today. Under our equal protection jurisprudence, gender-based classifications require "an exceedingly persuasive justification" in order to survive constitutional scrutiny. See *Personnel Administrator of Mass. v. Feeney,* 442 U.S. 256, 273 (1979). See also *Mississippi University for Women v. Hogan,* 458 U.S. 718, 724 (1982); *Kirchberg v. Feenstra,* 450 U.S. 455, 461 (1981). Thus, the only question is whether discrimination on the basis of gender in jury selection substantially furthers the State's legitimate interest in achieving a fair and impartial trial. In making this assessment, we do not weigh the value of peremptory challenges as an institution against our asserted commitment to eradicate invidious discrimination from the courtroom. Instead, we consider whether peremptory challenges based on gender stereotypes provide substantial aid to a litigant's effort to secure a fair and impartial jury.

Far from proffering an exceptionally persuasive justification for its gender-based peremptory challenges, respondent maintains that its decision to strike virtually all the males from the jury in this case "may reasonably have been based upon the perception, supported by history, that men otherwise totally qualified to serve upon a jury might be more sympathetic and receptive to the arguments of a man alleged in a paternity action to be the father of an out-of-wedlock child, while women equally qualified to serve upon a jury might be more sympathetic and receptive to the arguments of the complaining witness who bore the child."

We shall not accept as a defense to gender-based peremptory challenges "the very stereotype the law condemns." Respondent's rationale, not unlike those regularly expressed for gender-based strikes, is reminiscent of the arguments advanced to justify the total exclusion of women from juries. Respondent offers virtually no support for the conclusion that gender alone is an accurate predictor of juror's attitudes; yet it urges this Court to condone the same stereotypes that justified the wholesale exclusion of women from juries and the ballot box. Respondent seems to assume that gross generalizations that would be deemed impermisssible if made on the basis of race are somehow permissible when made on the basis of gender.

Discrimination in jury selection, whether based on race or on gender, causes harm to the litigants, the community, and the individual jurors who are wrongfully excluded from participation in the judicial process. The litigants are harmed by the risk that the prejudice which motivated the discriminatory selection of the jury will infect the entire proceedings. ... The community is harmed by the State's participation in the perpetuation of invidious group stereotypes and the inevitable loss of confidence in our judicial system that state-sanctioned discrimination in the courtroom engenders.

When state actors exercise peremptory challenges in reliance on gender stereotypes, they ratify and reinforce prejudicial views of the relative abilities of men and women. Because these stereotypes have wreaked injustice in so many other spheres of our country's public life, active discrimination by litigants on the basis of gender during jury selection "invites cynicism respecting the jury's neutrality and its obligation to adhere to the law." The potential for cynicism is particularly acute in cases where gender-related issues are prominent, such as cases involving rape, sexual harassment, or paternity. Discriminatory use of peremptory challenges may create the impression that the judicial system has acquiesced in suppressing full participation by one gender or that the "deck has been stacked" in favor of one side....

How helpful is the use of such comparisons and analogies? Consider the following.

TRINA GRILLO & STEPHANIE WILDMAN, OBSCURING THE IMPORTANCE OF RACE: THE IMPLICATION OF MAKING COMPARISONS BETWEEN RACISM AND SEXISM (OR OTHER–ISMS)

1991 Duke L.J. 397, 397–411.

PROLOGUE

Between the time when the *Duke Law Journal* first solicited this Essay and the present, one of the authors, Trina Grillo, who is of Afro–Cuban and Italian descent, was diagnosed as having Hodgkin's Disease (a form of cancer) and has undergone radiation therapy. In talking about this experience she said that "cancer has become the first filter through which I see the world. It used to be race, but now it is cancer. My neighbor just became pregnant, and all I could think was 'How could she get pregnant? What if she gets cancer?' "

Stephanie Wildman, the co-author, who is Jewish and white, heard this remark and thought, "I understand how she feels; I worry about getting cancer too. I probably worry about it more than most people, because I am such a worrier."

But Stephanie's worry is not the same as Trina's. Someone with cancer can think of nothing else. She cannot watch the World Series without wondering which players have had cancer or who in the players' families might have cancer. This world-view with cancer as a filter is different from just thinking or even worrying often about cancer. The worrier has the privilege of forgetting the worry sometimes, even much of the time. The worry can be turned off. The cancer patient does not have the privilege of truly forgetting about her cancer; even when it is not in the forefront of her thoughts, it remains in the background, coloring her world.

This dialogue about cancer illustrates a principal problem with comparing one's situation to another's. The "analogizer" often believes that her situation is the same as another's. Nothing in the comparison process challenges this belief, and the analogizer may think that she understands the other's situation in its fullness. The analogy makes the analogizer forget the difference and allows her to stay focused on her own situation without grappling with the other person's reality.

Yet analogies are necessary tools to teach and to explain, so that we can better understand each others' experiences and realities. We have no other way to understand each others' lives, except by making analogies to events in our own experience. Thus, the use of analogies provides both the key to greater comprehension and the danger of false understanding.

I. Introduction

Like cancer, racism/white supremacy is a societal illness. To people of color, who are the victims of racism/white supremacy, race is a filter through which they see the world. Whites do not look at the world through this filter of racial awareness, even though they also comprise a race. This privilege to ignore their race gives whites a societal advantage distinct from any advantage received from the existence of discriminatory racism. Throughout this Essay we use the term racism/white supremacy to emphasize the link between the privilege held by whites to ignore their own race and discriminatory racism. . . .

This Essay originated when the authors noticed that several identifiable phenomena occurred without fail, in any racially mixed group, whenever sex discrimination was analogized (implicitly or explicitly) to race discrimination. Repeatedly, at the annual meeting of the Association of American Law Schools (AALS), at meetings of feminist legal scholars, in classes on Sex Discrimination and the Law, and in law school women's caucus meetings, the pattern was the same. In each setting, although the analogy was made for the purpose of illumination, to explain sexism and sex discrimination, another unintended result ensued—the perpetuation of racism/white supremacy.

When a speaker compared sexism and racism, the significance of race was marginalized and obscured, and the different role that race plays in the lives of people of color and of whites was overlooked. The concerns of whites became the focus of discussion, even when the conversation had been supposedly centered on race discrimination. Essentialist presumptions became implicit in the discussion; it would be assumed, for example, that all women are white and all African-Americans are men. Finally, people with little experience in thinking about racism/white supremacy, but who had a hard-won understanding of the allegedly analogous oppression (sexism or some other -ism), assumed that they comprehended the experience of people of color and thus had standing to speak on their behalf.

No matter how carefully a setting was structured to address the question of racism/white supremacy, these problems always arose. Each of the authors has unwittingly participated in creating these problems on many occasions, yet when we have tried to avoid them, we have found ourselves accused of making others uncomfortable. Even after we had identified these patterns, we found ourselves watching in amazement as they appeared again and again, and we were unable to keep ourselves from contributing to them.

We began to question why this pattern persisted. We concluded that these phenomena have much to do with the dangers inherent in what had previously seemed to us to be a creative and solidarity-producing process—analogizing sex discrimination to race discrimination. These dangers were obscured by the promise that to discuss and compare oppressions might lead to coalition-building and understanding. On an individual psychological level, the way we empathize with and understand others is by comparing their situations with some aspects of our own. As Lynn Henderson explains:

> Analogizing, or drawing upon one's own experience to understand another's feelings or experiences, is a part of relating to another, if for no other reason than that no one has exactly the same experiences as anyone else. But this is an obvious point. The less obvious point is that it is possible to draw on one's own similar experiences to understand another. One could otherwise not empathize with another's grief at losing a parent at all if one could not draw on one's own experiences of loss....

Roberto Unger describes the importance of analogy in the human thought process as follows:

> We compare the issues about which we have the greatest certainty with those that baffle us more. The decision to liken one instance to another, or to distinguish them, turns on a judgment of what differences and similarities are most significant to the moral beliefs at stake.

Thus, analogies deepen our consciousness and permit us to progress in our thinking. Analogies are an important, perhaps indispensable, tool in individual moral reasoning.

This Essay is our effort to begin to understand how the process of comparing oppressions creates the phenomena that consolidate racism/white supremacy. We believe that the participants in the meetings we have described, who used analogies between sexism and racism, were well-intentioned. They were people with anti-racist politics and no desire to perpetuate racism/white supremacy. But even well-intentioned people may act unwittingly to maintain racism/white supremacy.

Although the central focus of this Essay is the analogy between sexism and racism, we also discuss comparisons with other "-isms," including anti-Semitism, heterosexism, and the treatment of the physically-challenged. The use of these comparisons further illuminates the analogy problem because the issues surrounding the use of analogies exist for these -isms as well.

II. How The Sex/Race Analogy Perpetuates Patterns of Racial Domination

Comparing sexism to racism perpetuates patterns of racial domination by marginalizing and obscuring the different roles that race plays in the lives of people of color and of whites. The comparison minimizes the impact of racism, rendering it an insignificant phenomenon—one of a laundry list of -isms or oppressions that society must suffer. This marginalization and obfuscation is evident in three recognizable patterns: (1) the taking back of center-stage from people of color, even in discussions of racism, so that white issues remain or become central in the dialogue; (2) the fostering of essentialism, so that women and people of color are implicitly viewed as belonging to mutually exclusive categories, rendering women of color invisible; and (3) the appropriation of pain or the denial of its existence that results when whites who have compared other oppressions to race discrimination believe that they understand the experience of racism.

A. *Taking Back the Center*

White supremacy creates in whites the expectation that issues of concern to them will be central in every discourse. Analogies serve to perpetuate this expectation of centrality. The center-stage problem occurs because dominant group members are already accustomed to being on center-stage. They have been treated that way by society; it feels natural, comfortable, and in the order of things. ...

Because whiteness is the norm, it is easy to forget that it is not the only perspective. Thus, members of dominant groups assume that their perceptions are the pertinent perceptions, that their problems are the problems that need to be addressed, and that in discourse they should be the speaker rather than the listener. Part of being a member of a privileged group is being the center and the subject of all inquiry in which people of color or other non-privileged groups are the objects....

The problem of taking back the center exists apart from the issue of analogies; it will be with us as long as any group expects, and is led to expect, to be constantly the center of attention. But the use of analogies exacerbates this problem, for once an analogy is taken to heart, it seems to the center-stealer that she is not stealing the center, but rather is continuing the discussion on the same topic, and one that she knows well. So when the format of the program implicitly analogized gender and sexual preference to race, the center-stealer was encouraged to think "why not go further to another perceived oppression?"

When socially-subordinated groups are lumped together, oppression begins to look like a uniform problem and one may neglect the varying and complex contexts of the different groups being addressed. If oppression is all the same, then we are all equally able to discuss each oppression, and there is no felt need for us to listen to and learn from other socially-subordinated groups.

B. *Fostering Essentialism*

Essentialism is implicit in analogies between sex and race. Angela Harris explains gender essentialism as "[t]he notion that there is a monolithic 'women's experience' that can be described independent of other facets of experience like race, class, and sexual orientation...." She continues: "A corollary to gender essentialism is 'racial essentialism'—the belief that there is a monolithic 'Black Experience,' or 'Chicano Experience.'"

To analogize gender to race, one must assume that each is a distinct category; the impact of which can be neatly separated, one from the other. The essentialist critique shows that this division is not possible. Whenever it is attempted, the experience of women of color, who are at the intersection of these categories and cannot divide themselves to compare their own experiences, is rendered invisible. Analogizing sex discrimination to race discrimination makes it seem that all the women are white and all the men are African–American. The experiential reality of women of color disappears....

C. The Appropriation of Pain or the Rejection of Its Existence

Part of the privilege of whiteness is the freedom not to think about race. Whites need to reject this privilege and to recognize and speak about their role in the racial hierarchy. Yet whites cannot speak validly for people of color, but only about their own experiences as whites. Comparing other oppressions to race gives whites a false sense that they fully understand the experience of people of color. Sometimes the profession of understanding by members of a privileged group may even be a guise for a rejection of the existence of the pain of the unprivileged. For people of color, listening to whites who purport to represent the experience of racism feels like an appropriation of the pain of living in a world of racism/white supremacy....

Not all people who learn about others' oppressions through analogy are blessed with an increased commitment to listening. White people who grasp an analogy between an oppression they have suffered and race discrimination may think that they understand the phenomenon of racism/white supremacy in all its aspects. They may believe that their opinions and judgments about race are as cogent as those of victims of racism. In this circumstance, something approximating a lack of standing to speak exists because the insight gained by personal experience cannot easily be duplicated—certainly not without careful study of the oppression under scrutiny. The power of comparisons undermines this lack of standing, because by emphasizing similarity and obscuring difference, it permits the speaker implicitly to demonstrate authority about both forms of oppression. If we are members of the privileged halves of the social pairs, then what we say about the dichotomy will be listened to by the dominant culture. Thus, when we employ analogies to teach and to show oppression in a particular situation, we should be careful that in borrowing the acknowledged and clear oppression, we do not neutralize it, or make it appear fungible with the oppression under discussion.

The use of analogies by whites allows them to focus on their own experience and to avoid working on understanding racism/white supremacy. Even whites who wish to end discrimination want people of color to teach them about race and are often unwilling to use their personal resources to explore this dangerous subject. As bell hooks has written:

> In talking about race and gender recently, the question most often asked by white women has to do with white women's response to black women or women of color insisting that they are not willing to teach them about their racism—to show the way. They want to know: What should a white person do who is attempting to resist racism? It is problematic to assert that black people and other people of color who are sincerely committed to struggling against white supremacy should be unwilling to help or teach white people.

She says that many people of color have responded with an unwillingness to teach whites about combatting racism/white supremacy because it often seems that white people are asking people of color to do all the work. She concludes, however, that "[i]t is our collective responsibility as people of color and as white people who are committed to ending white supremacy to help one another."

Author hooks encourages people of color to continue to struggle with whites about racism. To whites, the need for such encouragement may seem surprising, because many whites might ask, "How can we work on racism by ourselves, without people of color?" Listening to the reality of people of color is very important for learning about the oppression of racism/white supremacy. But whites need to examine their (our) own role in benefiting from that social construct. When white women analogize sexism to racism to emphasize the disadvantages imposed by the culture upon women, they (we) must also remember the privileging granted by that same society to whites.

Trying to educate whites about race is a great risk for people of color. They risk not only that whites will not care and will prefer to perpetuate the status quo, but also that even caring whites will not hear or understand the pain of racism. Talking about racism/white supremacy is painful for whites as well, but in a different way. Whites must confront their role as oppressors, or at least as beneficiaries of the racial oppression of others, in a race-based hierarchy. The pain of oppression must be communicated to the dominant group if there is to be any understanding of racism/white supremacy. This act of sharing, however, contains the risk that the pain of oppression will be appropriated by the dominant group for its own purpose....

III. CONCLUSION

Given the problems that analogies create and perpetuate, should we ever use them? Analogies can be helpful. They are part of legal discourse, as well as common conversation. Consciousness raising may be the beginning of knowledge. Starting with ourselves is important, and analogies may enable us to understand the oppression of another in a way we could not without making the comparison. Instead of drawing false inferences of similarities from analogies, it is important for whites to talk about white supremacy, rather than leaving all the work for people of color. Questions remain regarding whether analogies to race can be used, particularly in legal argument, without reinforcing racism/white supremacy. There are no simple answers to this thorny problem. We will have to continue to struggle with it, and accept that our progress will be slow and tentative. We offer two preliminary suggestions, each with its own pitfalls, to illustrate the sort of changes we might make in daily discourse to guide the use of comparisons: recognition time and coalition work.

Recognition time is time devoted exclusively to examining one oppression. It may mitigate one problem created by making analogies to race—the marginalizing and obscuring of racism/white supremacy. Recognition time acknowledges both the need to honor the pain of those oppressed by other -isms, each in their turn, and the need to allow the oppression being focused upon to remain center-stage.

Creating recognition time may not be an easy process, and raises problems of its own. An African–American woman law professor who teaches a seminar on women of color and the law has said that she finds it difficult to focus the students on gender issues; they want to stay with race. Why might this happen? If the first filter through which one looks at the world is not acknowledged, one cannot move on to other, perhaps even equally important, filters. When we combine several socially-subordinated groups into one discussion (as analogies implicitly do) and do not identify a distinct time to recognize one specific oppression or another, other than to use them as reference points for an analogy, we create an inability to focus on any one of them. This does not mean that the oppressions are unrelated, but rather, that they must be studied separately as well as together. To allow these separate and focused recognition times might relax people.

The danger of recognition time, if defined too narrowly, is that it would encourage essentialism. Essentialism could be avoided if each oppression were examined in its fullness. In discussing sexism, for example, we need to recognize that every woman is affected by racism/white supremacy in one way or another. Within the context of a full discussion of sexual oppression, one would necessarily talk about the effect of race.

For people facing oppression, working together or coalition building is also critically important. In a racism class at one law school, I [Stephanie] was asked to team-teach a class on Jewish Racism and African–American Anti–Semitism. The Jewish students felt that anti-semitic remarks had been made throughout the semester and that neither the law school's curriculum nor its culture addressed issues of anti-semitism. The students of color felt that during the one course in the curriculum designed to address their issues, the white students once again had taken the airwaves from the students of color for their own purpose. Both groups were correct. Coalition work is essential to make sure that each group gets access to the airwaves.

A fundamental tension exists whenever analogies are used to compare other oppressions to racism. The comparison perpetuates racism/white supremacy, but is also a necessary tool to teach about the oppression being compared. Any analogy to race must be used ethically and with care. We must always consider if we are perpetuating or deconstructing societal racism at the conclusion of any analogy discussion. . . .

————

The final two excerpts in this chapter discuss ways in which we might begin to recognize commonalities without ignoring differences.

ANGELA HARRIS, RACE AND ESSENTIALISM IN LEGAL THEORY

42 Stan.L.Rev. 581, 584, 608–15 (1990).

... It is a premise of this article that we are not born with a "self," but rather are composed of a welter of partial, sometimes contradictory, or even antithetical "selves." A unified identity, if such can ever exist, is a product of will, not a common destiny or natural birthright. Thus, consciousness is "never fixed, never attained once and for all"; it is not a final outcome or a biological given, but a process, a constant contradictory state of becoming, in which both social institutions and individual wills are deeply implicated. A multiple consciousness is home both to the first and the second voices, and all the voices in between.

As I use the phrase, "multiple consciousness" as reflected in legal or literary discourse is not a golden mean or static equilibrium between two extremes, but rather a process in which propositions are constantly put forth, challenged, and subverted....

Black women experience not a single inner self (much less one that is essentially gendered), but many selves. This sense of multiplicitous self is not unique to black women, but black women have expressed this sense in ways that are striking, poignant, and potentially useful to feminist theory. bell hooks describes her experience in a creative writing program at a predominantly white college, where she was encouraged to find "her voice," as frustrating to her sense of multiplicity.

> It seemed that many black students found our situations problematic precisely because our sense of self, and by definition our voice, was not unilateral, monologist, or static but rather multi-dimensional. We were as at home in dialect as we were in standard English. Individuals who speak languages other than English, who speak patois as well as standard English, find it a necessary aspect of self-affirmation not to feel compelled to choose one voice over another, not to claim one as more authentic, but rather to construct social realities that celebrate, acknowledge, and affirm differences, variety.

This experience of multiplicity is also a sense of self-contradiction, of containing the oppressor within oneself. In her article On Being the Object of Property, Patricia Williams writes about herself writing about her great-great-grandmother, "picking through the ruins for my roots." What she finds is a paradox: She must claim for herself "a heritage the weft of whose genesis is [her] own disinheritance." Williams's great-great-grandmother, Sophie, was a slave, and at the age of about eleven was impregnated by her owner, a white lawyer named Austin Miller. Their daughter Mary, Williams's great-grandmother, was taken away from Sophie and raised as a house servant.

When Williams went to law school, her mother told her, "The Millers were lawyers, so you have it in your blood." Williams analyzes this statement as asking her to acknowledge contradictory selves:

[S]he meant that no one should make me feel inferior because someone else's father was a judge. She wanted me to reclaim that part of my heritage from which I had been disinherited, and she wanted me to use it as a source of strength and self-confidence. At the same time, she was asking me to claim a part of myself that was the dispossessor of another part of myself; she was asking me to deny that disenfranchised little black girl of myself that felt powerless, vulnerable and, moreover, rightly felt so.

The theory of black slavery, Williams notes, was based on the notion that black people are beings without will or personality, defined by "irrationality, lack of control, and ugliness." In contrast, "wisdom, control, and aesthetic beauty signify the whole white personality in slave law." In accepting her white self, her lawyer self, Williams must accept a legacy of not only a disinheritance but a negation of her black self: To the Millers, her forebears, the Williamses, her forebears, did not even have selves as such.

Williams's choice ultimately is not to deny either self, but to recognize them both, and in so doing to acknowledge guilt as well as innocence. She ends the piece by invoking "the presence of polar bears;" bears that mauled a child to death at the Brooklyn Zoo and were subsequently killed themselves, bears judged in public debate as simultaneously "innocent, naturally territorial, unfairly imprisoned, and guilty."

This complex resolution rejects the easy innocence of supposing oneself to be an essential black self with a legacy of oppression by the guilty white Other. With such multilayered analyses, black women can bring to feminist theory stories of how it is to have multiple and contradictory selves, selves that contain the oppressor as well as the oppressed.

B. Strategic Identities and "Difference"

A post-essentialist feminism can benefit not only from the abandonment of the quest for a unitary self, but also from Martha Minow's realization that difference—and therefore identity—is always relational, not inherent. Zora Neale Hurston's work is a good illustration of this notion.

In an essay written for a white audience, How It Feels to Be Colored Me, Hurston argues that her color is not an inherent part of her being, but a response to her surroundings. She recalls the day she "became colored"—the day she left her home in an all-black community to go to school: "I left Eatonville, the town of the oleanders, as Zora. When I disembarked from the river-boat at Jacksonville, she was no more. It seemed that I had suffered a sea change. I was not Zora of Orange County any more, I was now a little colored girl." But even as an adult, Hurston insists, her colored self is always situational: "I do not always feel colored. Even now I often achieve the unconscious Zora of Eatonville before the Hegira. I feel most colored when I am thrown against a sharp white background."

As an example, Hurston describes the experience of listening to music in a jazz club with a white male friend:

> My pulse is throbbing like a war drum. I want to slaughter something—give pain, give death to what, I do not know. But the piece ends. The men of the orchestra wipe their lips and rest their fingers. I creep back slowly to the veneer we call civilization with the last tone and find the white friend sitting motionless in his seat, smoking calmly.

> "Good music they have here," he remarks, drumming the table with his fingertips.

> Music. The great blobs of purple and red emotion have not touched him. He has only heard what I felt. He is far away and I see him but dimly across the ocean and the continent that have fallen between us. He is so pale with his whiteness then and I am so colored.

In reaction to the presence of whites—both her white companion and the white readers of her essay—Hurston invokes and uses the traditional stereotype of black people as tied to the jungle, "living in the jungle way." Yet in a later essay for a black audience, "What White Publishers Won't Print," she criticizes the white "folklore of 'reversion to type' ":

> This curious doctrine has such wide acceptance that it is tragic. One has only to examine the huge literature on it to be convinced. No matter how high we may seem to climb, put us under strain and we revert to type, that is, to the bush. Under a superficial layer of western culture, the jungle drums throb in our veins.

The difference between the first essay, in which Hurston revels in the trope of black person as primitive, and the second essay, in which she deplores it, lies in the distinction between an identity that is contingent, temporary, and relational, and an identity that is fixed, inherent, and essential. Zora as jungle woman is fine as an argument, a reaction to her white friend's experience; what is abhorrent is the notion that Zora can always and only be a jungle woman. One image is in flux, "inspired" by a relationship with another; the other is static, unchanging, and ultimately reductive and sterile rather than creative.

Thus, "how it feels to be colored Zora" depends on the answer to these questions: " 'Compared to what? As of when? Who is asking? In what context? For what purpose? With what interests and presuppositions?' What Hurston rigorously shows is that questions of difference and identity are always functions of a specific interlocutionary situation—and the answers, matters of strategy rather than truth." Any "essential self" is always an invention; the evil is in denying its artificiality.

To be compatible with this conception of the self, feminist theorizing about "women" must similarly be strategic and contingent, focusing on relationships, not essences. One result will be that men will cease to be a faceless Other and reappear as potential allies in political struggle. Another will be that women will be able to acknowledge their differences without threatening feminism itself. In the process, as feminists begin to attack racism and classism and homophobia, feminism will change from being only about "women as women" (modified women need not apply), to being about all kinds of oppression based on seemingly inherent and unalterable characteristics. We need not wait for a unified theory of oppression; that theory can be feminism....

Finally, black women can help feminist movement move beyond its fascination with essentialism through the recognition that wholeness of the self and commonality with others are asserted (if never completely achieved) through creative action, not realized in shared victimization. Feminist theory at present, especially feminist legal theory, tends to focus on women as passive victims....

This story of woman as victim is meant to encourage solidarity by emphasizing women's shared oppression, thus denying or minimizing difference, and to further the notion of an essential woman—she who is victimized. But as bell hooks has succinctly noted, the notion that women's commonality lies in their shared victimization by men "directly reflects male supremacist thinking. Sexist ideology teaches women that to be female is to be a victim." Moreover, the story of woman as passive victim denies the ability of women to shape their own lives, whether for better or worse. It also may thwart their abilities.... [W]omen who rely on their victimization to define themselves may be reluctant to let it go and create their own self-definitions.

At the individual level, black women have had to learn to construct themselves in a society that denied them full selves. Again, Zora Neale Hurston's writings are suggestive. Though Hurston plays with being her "colored self" and again with being "the eternal feminine with its string of beads," she ends How It Feels to Be Colored Me with an image of herself as neither essentially black nor essentially female, but simply

> a brown bag of miscellany propped against a wall. Against a wall in company with other bags, white, red and yellow. Pour out the contents, and there is discovered a jumble of small things priceless and worthless. A first-water diamond, an empty spool, bits of broken glass, lengths of string, a key to a door long since crumbled away, a rusty knife-blade, old shoes saved for a road that never was and never will be, a nail bent under the weight of things too heavy for any nail, a dried flower or two still fragrant. In your hand is the brown bag. On the ground before you is the jumble it held—so much like the jumble in the bags, could they be emptied, that all might be dumped in a single heap and the bags refilled without altering the content of any greatly. A bit of colored glass more or less would not matter. Perhaps that is how the Great Stuffer of Bags filled them in the first place—who knows?

Hurston thus insists on a conception of identity as a construction, not an essence—something made of fragments of experience, not discovered in one's body or unveiled after male domination is eliminated.

This insistence on the importance of will and creativity seems to threaten feminism at one level, because it gives strength back to the concept of autonomy, making possible the recognition of the element of consent in relations of domination, and attributes to women the power that makes culpable the many ways in which white women have actively used their race privilege against their sisters of color. Although feminists are correct to recognize the powerful force of sheer physical coercion in ensuring compliance with patriarchal hegemony, we must also "come to terms with the ways in which women's culture has served to enlist women's support in perpetuating existing power relations."

However, at another level, the recognition of the role of creativity and will in shaping our lives is liberating, for it allows us to acknowledge and celebrate the creativity and joy with which many women have survived and turned existing relations of domination to their own ends. Works of black literature like Beloved, The Color Purple, and Song of Solomon, among others, do not linger on black women's victimization and misery; though they recognize our pain, they ultimately celebrate our transcendence.

Finally, on a collective level this emphasis on will and creativity reminds us that bridges between women are built, not found. The discovery of shared suffering is a connection more illusory than real; what will truly bring and keep us together is the use of effort and imagination to root out and examine our differences, for only the recognition of women's differences can ultimately bring feminist movement to strength. This is hard work, and painful work; but it is also radical work, real work. As Barbara Smith has said, "What I really feel is radical is trying to make coalitions with people who are different from you. I feel it is radical to be dealing with race and sex and class and sexual identity all at one time. I think that is really radical because it has never been done before." ...

JUDY SCALES–TRENT, COMMONALITIES: ON BEING BLACK AND WHITE, DIFFERENT, AND THE SAME

2 Yale J. Law and Feminism 305, 322–24 (1990).

Many in my family are various shades of brown, as is common in most black families. Many others of us, however, look white. I wrote these journal notes, and this essay, as a way of coming to terms with the dilemma of being black and looking white in a society which does not handle anomalies very well.

It is only recently that I have realized that the work that I do is deeply connected with my struggle to live within this dilemma. I am a lawyer and a professor of law. I write about the intersection of race and sex in American law, focusing on the status of black women in the law, that is, on the group which stands at the intersection of the race category and the sex category. I used to define my work in that way. Now that I have written this essay, I see my work differently. In this essay, I struggle to combine two statuses which our society says cannot be combined: black cannot be white, and white cannot be black. In my earlier work on race and sex, I argued that it did not make sense to try to maintain two distinct categories of race and sex in the law, when that separation ignored the very real existence of black women. There again, I argued that the categories seen as so pure, were not pure; that the boundaries thought impermeable were not impermeable. Looking at all of my work, I now understand that I have been working at the intersection of race and sex because I exist at the intersection of race and color, and because I understand, in a very profound way, that in order for me to exist, I must transgress boundaries.

I think this makes people profoundly uncomfortable. Categories make the world appear understandable and safe. Nonetheless, in this essay I ask you to experience my vision of the world—a world where the categories do not clarify, but confuse; a world where one must question the very existence of those categories in order to survive....

... Let me tell you about Dianna. We worked at the appellate division together. And one of the strange things about that office is that it was comprised of about twenty attorneys all in various stages of avoiding writing a brief. One day, when I was in the "walk-the-hall" stage of avoidance, I dropped into Dianna's office and started complaining about the general run of men about town, and the general level of confusion and poverty in my life. "What I need," I said to her, "is to find a prosperous, slightly boring dentist to settle down with." "Oh, I know just what you mean," she declared emphatically. "And if you find one, ask him if he has a sister!" We burst out laughing. And that's how I learned that Dianna was a lesbian.

It wasn't until years later that I realized that gay people, like me, are faced with the problem of "coming out" to people. Dianna has to decide when she should come out to someone, and how. She has to worry about how that person will respond. And as long as she keeps meeting new people, she will have to keep dealing with those issues of self-identification and exposure. These are issues I deal with also: when do I tell someone that I am black? and how? and how will they respond? And if I don't tell people (the apartment rental agent, the cab driver), aren't I "passing"? But Lord knows there's no reason for me to get into self-revelation with someone who's paid to drive me from home to the car shop.

"And why?" I think. "Why should my lesbian sisters have to come out to people? why are they not allowed to keep their sexual life private? why do they have to say: 'this is who I am. I hope you can deal with it. Even if you can't, I need for you to know who I am. I am a member of a despised group. If we are to know each other, you must know this.'"

As I write the words, I know why they must come out. They must be clear about who they are, and one way to do this is to force other people to see who they are. As I do. This is also why I "come out." And, with them, I brace myself for the flinch, the startled look, the anxious intake of breath, the wary eye. I come out to white people to say to them: "Beware. I am Other. Proceed with caution." And I come out to black people (how painful it is to have to do it ...) to say: "I am family. You are safe with me. I am you." But, of course, if you have to *say* that you are black, if your skin doesn't say it for you, then how safe are you, really? how can you be family? And again, I brace myself for not so much the startled look (black people are used to white black people), but for the wary eye. For I am still Other. Coming out only proclaims how I am different, not that I am the same.

I think sometimes how similar are the problems my lesbian sisters and I pose when we come out. Does the person who hears me come out have to confront the notion of black being white? Does the person who hears my lesbian sister come out have to confront the notion of female being male (that is, if one who loves women is a male)? How unsettling it must be to have someone announce to you that black is white, that female is male. We are talking about "transgressed boundaries, potent fusions and dangerous possibilities."

My lesbian sisters have shown me that I am not the only one who has to struggle with coming out. Their courage gives me courage. . . .

The last story I want to tell you is one that I am really not proud of. I like to think it would not have happened if we hadn't been so tired and jet-lagged. But we were. There were eighteen of us coming from all parts of the country for a two day board meeting in Oakland. We were a group of feminist lawyers and activists, a group very self-consciously created to represent as many different kinds of women as possible. In general, we enjoyed getting together enough to travel thousands of miles for a grueling two day session. It was a group of women who are smart, considerate, funny, and committed to women's issues. Our first meeting was scheduled for Friday night at eight o'clock. We decided to hold the meeting at a restaurant near the hotel.

Now you must remember that for some of us, meeting at eight in the evening was in reality meeting at eleven in the evening, after an exhausting day of travel. Nonetheless, we were all energized by being together, and off we went to search for a restaurant with a table large enough to accommodate us. What a relief it was to find one, only a few blocks away. There were about a dozen of us there, and we were seated around a large round table. Menus came out, along with pots of tea and cups for sipping tea. We started to relax, to look with relish at the menu, to talk about what we would order and how we would share the food. And it was then that Dai broke into the over-tired, energetic talking and said, with a flat voice, "I think we should all consider leaving this restaurant." Dai travels through the world in a wheelchair. And it appeared that this restaurant *was* wheelchair-accessible, but only if you didn't mind going through the back door, past bags of smelly garbage, and through a dirty corridor. Dai was visibly wounded by that process, and although she was by now seated at the table with us, she thought we should leave in protest. There was a long silence. And I don't remember exactly what happened next. But what I do remember is that, at first, no one wanted to leave. There was the suggestion that perhaps we could go ahead and eat, and write a letter of complaint to the management later. Dai was bitter, and angry at us. "You wouldn't stay here if there were an entrance for blacks only." I remember being torn by her analogy. Was she right? But surely not: the only reason she couldn't come in the front door was because she couldn't maneuver her wheelchair up the stairs, a physical, not political, problem. Not a problem of status and degradation. But what I remember most clearly was being angry at her for having to deal with her anger when all I wanted to do was to enjoy my all-too-late dinner after an all-too-long day.

Eventually, of course, we left the restaurant. Two of the group stayed behind to explain to the manager why we left. Another was given the task of writing the owner about his non-compliance with relevant regulations on accessibility. We decided to check the restaurant for compliance before including it in our material for conference attendees that spring. But what struck me the most was that instant when I recalled a conversation with another black woman academic returning from a conference composed predominantly of white feminists, one of whom stated that she was tired of dealing with the anger of black women. We were outraged by their "fatigue." But that evening in Oakland, I saw that I could be, no, *was,* like those white women who were tired of dealing with my anger. For I did not want to deal with Dai's anger. And because I was not in the wheelchair, I was the one who was empowered. I was the one who could listen or not, pay attention to her anger or not, understand or refuse to understand, let my hunger for my own comfort get in the way of recognizing her pain. Dai showed me that in some ways, and to some people, anybody who is not in a wheelchair, be they black, Chinese, Indian, gay, is the insider. And she is the outsider, beating on the door, crying for inclusion. Wanting to be seen, wanting to be known.

I have learned many things from my sisters about being different and being the same. Sometimes, like that time, I did not want to learn the lesson. But it was an important lesson. I learned that sometimes I am the one who gets to wave "the magic wand ... of exclusion and inclusion." I am like Dai, who feels her difference and her exclusion so keenly. But I am also the non-disabled one. And thus, I am the insider. I am like my white sister too. ...

There are many more stories I could tell, for once I was able to see the commonalities I see them everywhere. And yet there are more questions, so many more unanswered questions.

I have been wondering why difference is so hard to accept. I have been wondering why difference makes us all so anxious that we create categories, and then expend enormous amounts of energy to make sure people fit in them, and stay in them. And I have been wondering why the system of dualism is so important: what is there about a continuum that is unsatisfying? frightening? Why must life—and we—be seen in either "black" or "white," with no shades in between? For it is this system of rigid dualism that fosters so much anxiety when people don't fit into the categories neatly, when people "transgress boundaries."

And why is it that we look so hard for sameness, when we are, each and every one of us, so different from each other?

And why is it that we find it so hard to find sameness, when we are, in so many ways, so much the same?

But this is the work of another paper. For now, it must suffice that I have come a little way along this path. I have been engaged in my own struggle with being different, and I have found, along the way, the sameness, the connectedness I needed. I have been able to see the commonalities. And have found a home.

Chapter Five

VISIONS OF JUSTICE

If knowledge is power, then what power can be gained from our developing knowledge about the ways in which law both produces and reproduces patterns of power and privilege? How can lawyers use these understandings of the relationships between power, privilege, and law to move us closer towards goals of equality and justice? As we have collated, edited and commented upon these materials, as we teach and write and practice law, we continue to struggle with these questions each day. We believe that one of the most important ways to bring about change is through education and consciousness-raising. Just as we continually learn to think differently as we learn from others, so each of us can share what we have learned with others in our lives. We can help educate others in all the spaces that we live and work.

Part of lawyering is the constant quest for justice, however we come to define it in our lives. If we can continue to learn better ways to see how law is used to subordinate others, we can build our arguments for justice and equality from different premises and in different fashions. Perhaps we can avoid some of the pitfalls that have trapped some attorneys, judges and social activists in the past. Perhaps our insights about identity, rhetoric, groups, hierarchy, rights, and politics can help us construct new paradigms for problem-solving in and through law as well as new ways to interact with people in legal arenas.

We recognize that our concentrated focus on the harsh realities of oppression, subordination, injustice, and inequalities in law may be depressing and enervating for students. But it need not be. It can empower you to be a more effective attorney or advocate for justice. It can also impress upon you how much and how urgently your work is needed. As future lawyers and social activists, so long as there is injustice, you will always have work to do.

This last chapter is intended to re-energize you. We have designed the readings and commentaries to expose you to some of the insights that contemporary legal scholars and practitioners have cultivated to challenge existing structures of power and privilege. We all can learn from their efforts to rethink legal paradigms. We hope you will feel inspired, so that when we update this book, we can include stories about the work you are doing or excerpts from things you have written.

A. RIGHTS CRITIQUES AND ALTERNATIVES

One traditional way that lawyers have attempted to achieve justice for their clients and for oppressed groups is to argue in terms of rights violations and to seek appropriate remedies to vindicate those rights. Several critical legal studies (CLS) scholars have argued that rights-based strategies are ill-conceived.

MARK TUSHNET, THE CRITIQUE OF RIGHTS

47 SMU L.Rev. 23, (1993).

. . . In its weakest version the critique of rights argues that there is no necessary connection between winning legal victories and advancing political goals; in a somewhat stronger version it argues that, more frequently than most lawyers think, winning legal victories either does not advance political goals or actually impedes them. In the strongest and most implausible version the critique of rights argues that winning legal victories almost never advances political goals.

I. WINNING AND LOSING

The critique of rights distinguishes between winning legal victories and winning political ones. Sometimes this is simply a distinction between short-term effects and long-term ones. Merely getting a judgment from the Supreme Court that constitutional rights have been violated may not have much meaning unless that judgment is enforced. The history of school desegregation litigation, one of the prime examples for the critique of rights, illustrates this difficulty. The Supreme Court held school segregation unconstitutional in 1954, but its judgment was so widely disregarded in the deep South that only a tiny number of schools there were desegregated by 1964. In this sense Brown v. Board of Education was a short-term victory (the short term being the days following the Court's decision) and a long-term irrelevancy (the long term being the ensuing decade). . . .

Another way to think about the relation between legal victories and political ones is to distinguish between ideological effects and material ones. The Court's statement that segregation was unconstitutional could be an ideological victory in court even if it had no material effects on schools in the deep South. And, ideological victories can have material effects over the long run; the principle the Court articulated in Brown may have become embedded in the nation's self-understanding in ways that affect race relations much more generally.

These distinctions help in explaining the critique of rights. If we start with the simple distinction between legal outcomes and political outcomes, there are four possibilities: winning a legal victory and winning politically (Category I); losing in court but winning politically (Category II); winning a legal victory but losing politically (Category

III); and losing in court and in politics, too (Category IV). The abortion case press conferences show people trying to put their causes in Category III. The weak version of the critique of rights claims that there are interesting and important examples in all four categories. . . .

Sometimes winning a legal victory can actually impede further progressive change. This argument comes in a narrow and a broad version. The narrow version points out that some ways of articulating rights have ideological implications that work against progressive change. The earliest presentations of this narrow argument used the experience of the U.S. labor movement and the Wagner Act of 1937. Critics argued that the Wagner Act embedded a vision of labor-management relations in law that, in the immediate circumstances of 1937, advanced labor's interests but that, in the longer run, provided a strong ideological defense for the exercise of management prerogatives over a wide domain. Another version of the narrow argument is Catherine MacKinnon's controversial claim that the Supreme Court, in protecting a woman's right to choose to have or not have a child as an aspect of her right of privacy, helped define a sphere of private life into which the government could not intrude. According to MacKinnon, this way of approaching the abortion issue helped immunize the "private" sphere of domestic relations from government regulation even though women are severely disadvantaged within that sphere, as when they are beaten by men they live with, or are coerced into having sex with those men.

This narrow argument is, once again, a caution: Progressive lawyers ought to be careful in articulating their legal claims, so that if the courts adopt their arguments the long-term prospects for progressive change will not be impaired by the ideological implications of the way in which the legal claims were made. So, for example, perhaps it would be better to defend the right to choose as an aspect of women's equality, as essential to their full participation in social life in all its aspects, rather than as an aspect of privacy.

The broader version of this argument asserts that these cautions almost certainly cannot succeed. In part this is because advocates lose control over the arguments they make once courts accept them; after that, what privacy means, or what equality means, is substantially determined by courts, which are almost certainly not going to be as progressive as the progressive advocates would like.

More important in the broad version of the argument, though, is the claim that legal rights are essentially individualistic, at least in the U.S. constitutional and legal culture, and that progressive change requires undermining the individualism that vindicating legal rights reinforces. The argument's conclusion is that the long-term ideological consequences of winning victories in courts are almost certainly going to be adverse to progressive change.

Why, though, are rights-claims so essentially individualistic? After all, we can easily define rights that attach to groups; contemporary international human rights law, for example, recognizes rights of cultural minorities for preservation of their cultures, or of linguistic minorities for preservation of their languages. Yet, these group rights have two characteristics: Recognizing them as rights is quite controversial, and their recognition has been quite recent. These characteristics actually support the broader version of the argument that rights are ideologically troublesome because they are almost necessarily individualistic. They show that, in the modern world, rights-claims really do have a strong individualist spin, which advocates of group rights must work to overcome. . . .

III.   Losing by Winning, Winning by Losing

The critique of rights is most controversial among lawyers when it is applied to Category III (losing by winning). In that category, groups that win legal victories nonetheless are worse off because they lost politically. By insisting that Category III situations sometimes arise, the critique of rights threatens the self-understanding of lawyers who believe that the legal work they do contributes to progressive social change. For political scientists, less directly involved in legal work, the critique of rights is less troublesome.

The basic dynamic in Category III (and, in a related way, in Category II—winning by losing) is simple. Consider how proponents and opponents of social change can respond to a legal victory. (The argument is clearest when the legal victory involves constitutional law, but the underlying political dynamics remain the same if the legal victory involves development of the common law or statutory interpretation.) Having won the legal victory, the proponents can turn their attention to another part of their political agenda. They will invest less than they had before in securing or protecting this particular claim. Meanwhile, their opponents may continue to invest as before. Facing constant pressure from the opponents and reduced pressure from supporters, the courts may whittle away at the prior legal victory. Further, having won in court, supporters of change may think that they no longer have to be as worried, and can turn their attention from political and legal matters to other things, such as raising children or making money. On the other side, their opponents may have been outraged by the legal victory, and they may devote even more energy than before to opposing social change. When supporters become complacent and opponents mobilize, the result of winning the legal victory can be losing the political battle.

To make the argument somewhat more concrete, consider the following version of the history of abortion litigation in the United States. The Supreme Court struck down most states' abortion laws in 1973. Its decision provided some opportunities for anti-choice forces to try to enact restrictive legislation. Pro-choice activists, though, believed—correctly, for a decade or so—that the courts would strike down restrictive abortion laws. Sensibly enough, they devoted their political energies to other issues, relying on the low-cost courts for protection against restrictive abortion laws. Meanwhile, their opponents mobilized around the abortion issue, but their political concerns were broader. In the short to medium term, their efforts to enact restrictive abortion laws were unavailing, but they had real influence over other issues. That is, pro-choice forces found themselves facing stronger forces on issues other than abortion than they had faced before their legal victory in the abortion cases.

Pro-choice forces prevailed, again for a decade or so, on abortion issues, but lost on the other issues they hoped to advance. And, among those other issues was the overall composition of the federal judiciary. That is, the pro-choice legal victories contributed to the right-wing transformation of the federal courts. With that transformation, the pro-choice victories themselves eroded. Perhaps on balance the benefits for pro-choice forces, measured by what happened on the abortion issue over the years since 1973 (including the erosion, but not the overruling, of the initial victory), exceeded their losses on other issues. The critique of rights argues that that is the relevant issue for advocates of progressive legal change to consider.

Although the political dynamic of demobilization after a legal victory is the largest component of the critique of rights in Category III, it has other elements. As I have argued, the critique of rights acknowledges that legal victories can be ideologically or culturally significant, particularly in offering support from important social institutions to claims that no such institution had taken seriously before. Like the victories themselves, however, the ideological significance may erode.

When a court recognizes a claim as a legal right, and particularly as a constitutional right, it treats the claim as really important: Rights outweigh ordinary policy concerns, for example. People on the other side of the issue then have to respond. They can say, as they often do, that the court made a mistake. But, at least in the short run, that may not be a promising strategy. Instead, they can argue that, although the court found a right on the other side (and so overrode mere policy objections), it did not consider whether that right was countered by some other right. That is, the rhetoric of rights generates a rhetoric of counter-rights. Against the right to choose, the right to life is deployed; against affirmative action, the language of discrimination against white men begins to be used.

Proponents of progressive social change tend to treat the rhetoric of counter-rights as phony; for them it is a distortion of the language of rights to say that white men have rights infringed by affirmative action. Counter-rights are invoked so often, though, that they should be understood as systematically bound up with the rights themselves.

Once counter-rights come into play, two things happen. First, and less significant, the framework of legal analysis changes. Rights may outweigh mere policies, but the outcome when a right is arrayed against a counter-right is far less clear. The rhetoric of counter-rights, that is, may assist the courts if they want to whittle away at the initial legal victory.

Second, and more important, at the outset rights seem to be particularly powerful claims on society. Such powerful claims are needed because they are asserted on behalf of those previously excluded from serious consideration; having been excluded before, these groups not only should be allowed to take part in ordinary politics, they should receive special consideration because of their prior exclusion. As rights proliferate and generate counter-rights, the special force attached to the language of rights dissipates. The distinction between rights and mere policies weakens, and proponents of rights-claims become just another interest group in the ordinary play of politics. Of course, to the extent that the real benefit of recognizing their rights was ideological, in validating their participation in politics, this transformation should be expected. It is likely to be experienced, however, as a betrayal of the promises made when rights, those especially powerful claims on society, were recognized.

The dialectic of rights and counter-rights has another effect. Because rights seem to be especially powerful claims, discussions of rights and counter-rights tend to get particularly heated. When rights are involved, really fundamental matters seem to be at stake. Losing then seems tremendously damaging, something to be avoided at almost all cost. And, because something fundamental is involved, compromises may seem unacceptable in principle: How could pro-choice (or anti-choice) activists compromise to accept a legal regime in which women's access to abortions was impeded (restricting the fundamental right to choose), but not made impossible (contrary to the fetus's fundamental right to life)? Yet, if compromise is ruled out, either one side will face a permanent defeat on an issue it regards as fundamental (which could have bad effects on social stability), or policy will swing wildly from protecting one right and denying the counter-right to protecting the counter-right and denying the initial one.

Of course, if progressives could be assured that they would end up on the winning side in this dialectic, if they knew that they would win a permanent victory, the prospect would hardly trouble them. In the long run, though, the chance of wild swings may be great enough that progressives ought to be willing to accept compromises that are, from their point of view, favorable on balance; the losses during the periods when their opponents are in control may be large enough to outnumber the losses that happen under the permanent compromise regime.

IV. THE CRITIQUE OF RIGHTS AND THE INDETERMINACY THESIS

The critique of rights is connected to the indeterminacy thesis. The most straight-forward connection is this: According to the indeterminacy thesis, nothing whatever follows from a court's adoption of some legal rule (except insofar as the very fact that a court has adopted the rule has some social impact—the ideological dimension with which the critique of rights is concerned). Progressive legal victories occur, according to the indeterminacy thesis, because of the surrounding social circumstances. If those circumstances support material as well as ideological gains, well and good. And, of course, as long as those circumstances are stable, the legal victory will be so as well. But, if circumstances change, the "rule" could be eroded or, more interestingly, interpreted to support anti-progressive change.

Another connection between the critique of rights and the indeterminacy thesis results from the combination of the individualism of rights in our legal culture with the dialectic of rights and counter-rights. Sometimes progressive lawyers propose changes that, their critics say, infringe on constitutional rights. Recent controversies over regulating hate speech and pornography illustrate the issue (although those proposals have been controversial within progressive ranks as well). Conservatives who in other contexts would not blink at suppressing speech, particularly sexually explicit speech, suddenly become ardent (in the case of hate speech regulation) or ambivalent (in the case of pornography) defenders of the First Amendment.

The indeterminacy thesis provides the conceptual tool for those who want to support these proposals. It detaches them from a deep First Amendment absolutism and allows them to develop legal theories that explain why free speech principles to which they remain committed nonetheless are not violated by their proposals. (Of course, the indeterminacy thesis by itself does not tell lawyers what those theories are; it does, however, assure them that it is possible to develop such theories, and thereby encourages a search that might not otherwise occur.) The critique of rights, though, cautions against expecting too much of these sorts of changes. By identifying the possibility of losing by winning, the critique directs attention to questions about the political forces supporting the changes and whether those same forces are likely to interpret and apply the new rules in a progressive manner. (Are minorities more likely to be prosecuted under hate speech regulations than those who abuse minorities, for example?)

The critique of rights also points out that the rhetoric of rights is available to anti-progressives. This has two aspects worth noting. First, if the rhetoric of rights in our culture is individualistic (and if that sort of individualism is anti-progressive in today's circumstances), conservatives are more likely than progressives to find the rhetoric of rights helpful. For example, conservatives have used the rhetoric of rights to obstruct progressive regulation of property and—in a directly related field—to challenge campaign finance regulation on the ground that it violates free speech rights. On this view, progressive victories are likely to be short-term only; in the longer run the individualism of rights-rhetoric will stabilize existing social relations rather than transform them.

Second, when conservatives use the rhetoric of rights, the dialectic of counter-rights occurs. Here, progressives must characterize their proposals as themselves vindications of rights: Hate speech and pornography regulations must be said to protect the constitutional rights of African–Americans and women to full participation in social life, for example. The indeterminacy thesis establishes, of course, that these characterizations are possible, and scholars have provided the relevant arguments. Still, it remains true that defending these proposals as required by the Constitution—in order to overcome the conservative rights-claim that they are prohibited by the Constitution—is more difficult than defending them as good policy.

V. Conclusion

Nothing in the critique of rights ought to be particularly surprising to political activists or political scientists. They know that a legal victory has complicated relations to ideological and material change, in both the short and the long term—and similarly with legal defeats. The critique of rights is directed primarily at progressive lawyers who, inspired by what turned out to be the brief, perhaps aberrational, and sometimes overstated role of the Supreme Court in advancing progressive goals in the 1960s, overestimate the importance of the work they do. And, even there, it hardly undermines that work. Unless the resources the lawyers use would be used in some other, more productive way (which is quite unlikely), the critique of rights says primarily that lawyers should not expect too much from what they do, and that they should not be surprised if things turn out rather differently from what they expected when they urged courts to adopt some progressive formulation of the rights we have.

Notes and Questions

1. Does Professor Tushnet's critique of rights change the way you understand rights-based arguments? Will you think about things differently before you make rights-based arguments for your clients or to advance progressive causes?

For a fascinating combination of the rights critique with feminist theory in an examination of Michael M. v. Superior Court, 450 U.S. 464, 101 S.Ct. 1200, 67 L.Ed.2d 437 (1981), statutory rape laws and public policies about male and female exercises of sexuality, *see* Frances Olsen, *Statutory Rape: A Feminist Critique of Rights Analysis*, 63 Tex.L.Rev. 387 (1984).

2. Professor Derrick Bell has a different skepticism about rights. He argues that rights will only be granted to oppressed groups by the state or the majority when it is in the majority's interest, not because they are just claims or morally required. Derrick A. Bell, Jr., *Brown v. Board of Education and the Interest–Convergence Dilemma*, 93 Harv.L.Rev. 518 (1980). Bell has carried this thesis through his two remarkable books of chronicles about racism and law, which should be read by all Americans. Derrick Bell, And We Are Not Saved: The Elusive Quest for Racial Justice (Basic Books, 1987); Derrick Bell, Faces at the Bottom of the Well: The Permanence of Racism (Basic Books, 1992). See also Derrick Bell, Race, Racism and American Law (3d.ed., Little Brown & Co., 1992). Following in Bell's footsteps, Richard Delgado has produced a compelling set of chronicles examining race and law through conversations between a fictional law professor and his mentee/protegee, Rodrigo. Richard Delgado, *Rodrigo's Sixth Chronicle: Intersections, Essences, and the Dilemma of Social Reform,*

68 N.Y.U.L.Rev. 639 (1993); *Rodrigo's Fifth Chronicle: Civitas, Civil Wrongs, and the Politics of Denial,* 45 Stan.L.Rev. 1581 (1993); *Rodrigo's Fourth Chronicle: Neutrality and Stasis in Antidiscrimination Law,* 45 Stan.L.Rev. 1133 (1993); *Rodrigo's Third Chronicle: Care, Competition, and the Redemptive Tragedy of Race,* 81 Cal.L.Rev. 387 (1993); *Rodrigo's Second Chronicle: The Economics and Politics of Race,* 91 Mich.L.Rev. 1183 (1993); *Rodrigo's Chronicle,* 101 Yale L.J. 1357 (1992).

3. Professor Tushnet argues that the use of rights rhetoric in the abortion context ended up both galvanizing forces who were opposed to abortion and arming anti-abortion forces with counter-rights arguments that have ultimately enabled them to whittle away at *Roe v. Wade.* Michael Klarman does a similar analysis of the way that *Brown v. Board of Education* galvanized forces in opposition to racial integration in schools, but comes up with a completely different assessment. Michael J. Klarman, *Brown, Racial Change, and the Civil Rights Movement,* 80 Va.L.Rev. 7 (1994). He says that the Court's granting to African–American children equality rights to a racially integrated education caused southern racist forces to mount a vigorous and often violent response, but the violence and aggression then served to motivate northern white liberals and civil rights advocates to discard their apathy and work for the passage of the Civil Rights Act of 1964. Is the difference between the responses to *Brown* and *Roe* that the Southern response to *Brown* was not an argument from rights?

Is the appropriate response to the counter-rights arguments against *Roe v. Wade* the enactment of "civil rights legislation" as was done after *Brown?* Although pro-choice activists' attempts to use traditional civil rights statutes to protect themselves from violence and interference with women's exercises of their rights have failed, Bray v. Alexandria Women's Health Clinic, ___ U.S. ___, 113 S.Ct. 753, 122 L.Ed.2d 34 (1993), supra Chapter 3, they rallied legislative support in the Congress with the passage and presidential signing of the Freedom of Access to Clinic Entrances Act in May, 1994, 18 U.S.C.A. § 248, 108 Stat. 694. This act makes it a federal crime to blockade, commit violence against, or intimidate women trying to obtain abortions or clinic workers trying to provide abortion services and also provides a private cause of action for compensatory and punitive damages against protesters violating the act.

4. *Brown's* 40th anniversary. The fortieth anniversary of the *Brown* decision was celebrated in May 1994. Since *Brown,* African–Americans have graduated from high school and college at historically high rates, but 66% of the nation's African–American children attend schools with mostly minority students. Juan Williams, Roger Wilkins, & Kristen Hays, *Integration turns 40,* 37 Modern Maturity 24 (1994). Despite the "rights" granted in *Brown* and the Civil Rights Act of 1964 and all the subsequent legislation attempting to end segregation, race-based segregation in schools, particularly in the north, remains the norm. Gary Orfield, principal author of a study for the National School Board Association by the Harvard Project on School Desegregation, found that half of the black students in the northeast (CT, ME, MA, NH, NJ, NY, PA, RI & VT) are enrolled in schools that are overwhelmingly black—10% or fewer whites. Illinois tops the list where 59% of black students attend overwhelmingly black schools. Ron Grossman, Joseph Kir-

by, Charles Leroux & Jerry Thomas, *In North, Desegregation Still Unfinished Business,* Chicago Tribune, May 17, 1994, News, p. 1. The study reports that in the large cities, 15 of every 16 African–American and Latino students are in schools where most of the students are non-white. Nearly two-thirds of black and three-fourths of Hispanic students in the country as a whole attend schools where fewer than half the students are white. In addition, almost 60% of Asian–American students in the West attend schools that are mainly non-white. But, the NSBA study shows, that in California 44% of Asian students "attend school with 'advantaged' white students, while most black and Hispanic children go to school with economically 'disadvantaged' students." Williams, et al., *supra.* Orfield concludes that Hispanics are now the most racially isolated group.

In New York City schools in 1992, black students typically attended schools with only 8.4% whites. Margaret L. Usdansky, *Segregated schools are once again the norm,* USA Today, May 12, 1994, News, 8A. Reporting on schools on Long Island in New York, Peggy Brown notes that in 1992–3, "blacks made up less than 5 percent of the students in nearly 63 percent of the schools districts in Suffolk and almost 70 percent of the districts in Nassau. On the other side, there are a number of districts that are nearly all black." Peggy Brown, *On LI, Race Looms Large,* Newsday, May 20, 1994, at A06. Orfield's study shows that schools where children of color predominate are often poor schools with fewer resources and more poverty. He urges us to recognize and finally discuss openly the connection between race and poverty/class. Dorothy Gilliam, *Turning the Tide on School Segregation,* Washington Post, May 21, 1994, at B1 (interviewing Orfield).

Almost 50% of black children are being raised in poverty. Segregation of the urban poor from economically stable community members has increased by 13 percent nationally between 1970 and 1990, and in some regions like Chicago, the increase is up to 20 percent. Patrick T. Reardon, *Needy Become More and More Isolated,* Chicago Tribune, May 22, 1994, Chicagoland, at p. 1. Douglas Massey and Nancy Denton attribute segregated schools, high rates of unemployment, and minority crime rates to these patterns of residential segregation. They urge the dismantling of the black ghetto to ameliorate racial inequality in America. Douglas Massey & Nancy Denton, American Apartheid: Segregation and the Making of the Underclass (Harvard U. Press, 1993).

How does this statistical information about continued racial segregation in schools and housing affect your thinking about strategies for change, justice, rights and the law? Does it make sense for lawyers attempting to use law to remedy these problems to argue about race without class or schools without housing? What parts of these arguments ought to be rights-based?

5. In an earlier and fuller exposition about rights, Tushnet argued that rights rhetoric lacked utility, which led him to conclude that a needs-based discourse might be preferable. Mark Tushnet, *An Essay on Rights,* 62 Tex.L.Rev. 1386 (1982). See also Alan Freeman, *Legitimizing Racial Discrimination Through Anti–Discrimination Law: A Critical Review of Supreme Court Doctrine,* 62 Minn.L.Rev. 1049 (1978) (illustrating how rights discourse and anti-discrimination law have not necessarily been progressive

or consistent); Peter Gabel, *The Phenomenology of Rights–Consciousness and the Pact of the Withdrawn Selves,* 62 Tex.L.Rev. 1563 (1984).

Some feminist and critical race legal theorists challenged the CLS critique of rights as missing important aspects of rights discourse that empower groups of people and force the state and others to listen to them. E.g. Elizabeth Schneider, *The Dialectic of Rights and Politics: Perspectives from the Women's Movement,* 61 N.Y.U.L.Rev. 589 (1986). In 1987, the Harvard Civil Rights–Civil Liberties Law Review published a series of essays in response to the CLS critique of rights, entitled *Minority Critiques of the Critical Legal Studies Movement,* 22 Harv.C.R.–C.L.L.Rev. (1987) (articles by Delgado, Williams, Matsuda, Bracamonte, and Dalton). Since that first collection, proponents of these minority perspectives have renamed their enterprise as "outsider jurisprudence," "race critical" and/or "critical race" theories. Mari Matsuda, *Public Response to Racist Speech: Considering the Victim's Story,* 87 Mich.L.Rev. 2320 (1989); Robert Williams, Jr., *Gendered Checks and Balances: Understanding the Legacy of White Patriarchy in an American Indian Cultural Context,* 24 Ga.L.Rev. 1019 (1990). For an incredibly useful and comprehensive bibliography of critical race theory scholarship, see Richard Delgado and Jean Stefancic, *Critical Race Theory: An Annotated Bibliography,* 79 Va.L.Rev. 461 (1993).

Professors Kimberlé Crenshaw and Richard Delgado, for example, argue that despite its flaws, rights discourse "gives pause" to the oppressors and at least provides some option for subordinated people in their struggles for justice. Kimberlé Crenshaw, *Race, Reform, and Retrenchment: Transformation and Legitimation in Antidiscrimination Law,* 101 Harv.L.Rev. 1331, 1384–5 (1988); Richard Delgado, *The Ethereal Scholar: Does Critical Legal Studies Have What Minorities Want?,* 22 Harv.C.R.–C.L.L.Rev. 301, 305 (1987). The next excerpt, from Patricia Williams' thoughtful book, was originally published as part of the "minority" critiques challenging the CLS critique of rights.

PATRICIA J. WILLIAMS, THE ALCHEMY OF RACE AND RIGHTS: DIARY OF A LAW PROFESSOR

148–165 (Harvard U. Press, 1991).

The unifying theme of Peter's and my discussions [see Williams excerpt about discussion with Gabel, chapter 2, p. 35] is that one's sense of empowerment defines one's relation to the law, in terms of trust/distrust, formality/informality, or rights/no-rights ("needs"). In saying this I am acknowledging points that are central in most CLS literature—that rights may be unstable and indeterminate. Despite this recognition, however, and despite a mutual struggle to reconcile freedom with alienation, and solidarity with oppression, Peter and I found the expression of our social disillusionment lodged on opposite sides of the rights/needs dichotomy.

On a semantic level, Peter's language of circumstantially defined need, of informality, solidarity, overcoming distance, sounded dangerously like the language of oppression to someone like me who was looking for freedom through the establishment of identity, the formulation of an autonomous social self. To Peter, I am sure, my insistence on the protective distance that rights provide seemed abstract and alienated.

Similarly, while the goals of CLS and of the direct victims of racism may be much the same, what is too often missing is acknowledgment that our experiences of the same circumstances may be very different; the same symbol may mean different things to each of us. At this level, the insistence of certain scholars that the "needs" of the oppressed should be emphasized rather than their "rights" amounts to no more than a word game. The choice has merely been made to put needs in the mouth of a rights discourse—thus transforming need into a new form of right. "Need" then joins "right" in the pantheon of reified representations of what it is that you, I, and we want from ourselves and society.

Although rights may not be ends in themselves, rights rhetoric has been and continues to be an effective form of discourse for blacks. The vocabulary of rights speaks to an establishment that values the guise of stability, and from whom social change for the better must come (whether it is given, taken, or smuggled). Change argued for in the sheep's clothing of stability ("rights") can be effective, even as it destabilizes certain other establishment values (segregation). The subtlety of rights' real instability thus does not render unusable their persona of stability.

What is needed, therefore, is not the abandonment of rights language for all purposes, but an attempt to become multilingual in the semantics of evaluating rights. One summer when I was about six, my family drove to Maine. The highway was straight and hot and shimmered darkly in the sun. My sister and I sat in the back seat of the Studebaker and argued about what color the road was. I said black, she said purple. After I had harangued her into admitting that it was indeed black, my father gently pointed out that my sister still saw it as purple. I was unimpressed with the relevance of that at the time; but with the passage of years, and much more observation, I have come to see endless overheated highways as slightly more purple than black. My sister and I will probably argue about the hue of life's roads forever. But the lesson I learned from listening to her wild perceptions is that it really is possible to see things—even the most concrete things—simultaneously yet differently; and that seeing simultaneously yet differently is more easily done by two people than one, but that one person can get the hang of it with time and effort. ...

... If it took years for me to understand my own sister, probably the best that Peter and I can do—as friends and colleagues, but very different people—is to listen intently to each other so that maybe our children can bridge the experiential distance. Bridging such gaps requires listening at a very deep level, to the uncensored voices of others. To me, therefore, one of the most troubling positions advanced by some in CLS is that of rights' *disutility* in political advancement. The CLS disutility argument is premised on the assumption that rights' rigid systematizing may keep one at a permanent distance from situations that could profit from closeness and informality: "It is not just that rights-talk does not do much good. In the contemporary United States it is positively harmful." Furthermore, any marginal utility to be derived from rights discourse is perceived as being had at the expense of larger issues, rights being pitted against, rather than asserted on behalf of, agendas of social reform. This line of reasoning underlies much of the rationale for CLS' abandonment of rights discourse and for its preference for informality—for restyling, for example, arguments about rights to shelter for the homeless into arguments about the needs of the homeless.

Such statements, however, about the relative utility of needs over rights discourse overlook that blacks have been describing their needs for generations. They overlook a long history of legislation *against* the self-described needs of black people. While it is no longer against the law to teach black people to read, there is still within the national psyche a deep, self-replicating strain of denial of the urgent need for a literate black population. ("*They're* not intellectual," "*They* can't ...") In housing, in employment, in public and private life, it is the same story: the undesired needs of black people transform them into those-without-desire. ("*They're* lazy," "*They* don't want to ...")

For blacks, describing needs has been a dismal failure as political activity. It has succeeded only as a literary achievement. The history of our need is certainly moving enough to have been called poetry, oratory, epic entertainment—but it has never been treated by white institutions as the statement of a political priority. (I don't mean to undervalue the liberating power for blacks of such poetry, oratory, and epic; my concern is the degree to which it has been compartmentalized by the larger culture as something other than political expression.) Some of our greatest politicians have been forced to become ministers or blues singers. Even white descriptions of "the blues" tend to remove the daily hunger and hurt from need and abstract it into a mood. And whoever would legislate against depression? Particularly something as rich, soulful, and sonorously productive as black depression.

It may be different when someone white is describing need. Shorn of the hypnotic rhythmicity that blacks are said to bring to their woe, white statements of black needs suddenly acquire the sort of stark statistical authority that lawmakers can listen to and politicians hear. But from blacks, stark statistical statements of need are heard as strident, discordant, and unharmonious. Heard not as political but only against the backdrop of their erstwhile musicality, they are again abstracted to mood and angry sounds. (Mythologically speaking, black anger inspires white fear and fear is the one mood to which legislators have responded, but that story has nothing to do with black need.)

For blacks, then, the battle is not deconstructing rights, in a world of no rights; nor of constructing statements of need, in a world of abundantly apparent need. Rather the goal is to find a political mechanism that can confront the *denial* of need. The argument that rights are disutile, even harmful, trivializes this aspect of black experience specifically, as well as that of any person or group whose vulnerability has been truly protected by rights.

This difference of experience from whites is not, I think, solely attributable to such divisions as positive/negative, bourgeois/proletariat; given our history, it is a difference rooted in race and in the unconsciousness of racism. It is only in acknowledging this difference, however, that one can fully appreciate the underlying common ground of the radical left and the historically oppressed: the desire to heal a profound existential disillusionment. Wholesale rejection of rights does not allow for the expression of such difference.

... For others, ... slaves, sharecroppers, prisoners, mental patients—the experience of poverty and need is fraught with the terrible realization that they are dependent "on the uncertain and fitful protection of a world conscience," which has forgotten them as individuals. For the historically disempowered, the conferring of rights is symbolic of all the denied aspects of their humanity: rights imply a respect that places one in the referential range of self and others, that elevates one's status from human body to social being. For blacks, then, the attainment of rights signifies the respectful behavior, the collective responsibility, properly owed by a society to one of its own.

Another way of describing the dissonance between blacks and CLS is in terms of the degree of moral utopianism with which blacks regard rights. For blacks, the prospect of attaining full rights under law has been a fiercely motivational, almost religious, source of hope ever since arrival on these shores. It is an oversimplification to describe that hope as merely a "compensation for ... feelings of loss," rights being a way to "conceal those feelings." Black loss is not of the sort that can be compensated for or concealed by rights assertion. It must be remembered that *from the experiential perspective of blacks*, there was no such thing as "slave law." The legal system did not provide blacks, even freed blacks, with structured expectations, promises, or reasonable reliances of any sort. If one views rights as emanating from either slave "legal" history or from that of modern bourgeois legal structures, then of course rights would mean nothing because blacks have had virtually nothing under either. And if one envisions rights as economic advantages over others, one might well conclude that "because this sense of illegitimacy [of incomplete social relations] is always threatening to erupt into awareness, there is a need for 'the law.' "

But where one's experience is rooted not just in a sense of illegitimacy but in *being* illegitimate, in being raped, and in the fear of being murdered, then the black adherence to a scheme of both positive and negative rights—to the self, to the sanctity of one's own personal boundaries—makes sense.

The individual unifying cultural memory of black people is the helplessness of living under slavery or in its shadow. I grew up living in the past: the future, some versions of which had only the vaguest possibility of happening, was treated with the respect of the already-happened, seen through the prismatic lenses of what had already occurred. Thus, when I decided to go to law school, my mother told me that "the Millers were lawyers so you have it in your blood." (Of course Mother did not mean that law was literally part of my genetic makeup; she meant that law was an intimate part of the socially constructed reality into which I had been born. She meant that dealing with law and lawyers was something with which my ancestors were all too familiar.) Now the Millers were the slaveholders of my maternal grandmother's clan. The Millers were also my great-great-grandparents and great-aunts and who knows what else. My great-great-grandfather Austin Miller, a thirty-five-year-old lawyer, impregnated my eleven-year-old great-great-grandmother Sophie, making her the mother of Mary, my great-grandmother, by the time she was twelve.

In ironic, perverse obeisance to the rationalizations of this bitter ancestral mix, the image of this self-centered child molester became the fuel for my survival in the dispossessed limbo of my years at Harvard, the *Bakke* years, when everyone was running around telling black people that they were very happy to have us there but, after all, they did have to lower the standards and readjust the grading system. (I do not mean this as a criticism of affirmative action, but of those who tried to devalue the presence and contributions of us, the affirmatively active.) And it worked. I got through law school, quietly driven by the false idol of white-man-within-me, and absorbed much of the knowledge and values that had enslaved my foremothers.

I learned about images of power in the strong, sure-footed arm's-length transactor. I learned about unique power-enhancing lands called Whiteacre and Blackacre, and the mystical fairy rings encircling them, called restrictive covenants. I learned that excessive power overlaps generously with what is seen as successful, good, efficient, and desirable in our society.

I learned to undo images of power with images of powerlessness; to clothe the victims of excessive power in utter, bereft, naiveté; to cast them as defenseless supplicants pleading defenses of duress, undue influence, and fraud. A quick review of almost any contracts text will show that most successful defenses feature women, particularly if they are old and widowed; illiterates; blacks and other minorities; the abjectly poor; and the old and infirm. A white male student of mine once remarked that he couldn't imagine "reconfiguring his manhood" to live up to the "publicly craven defenselessness" of defenses like duress and undue influence.

I learned that the best way to give voice to those whose voice had been suppressed was to argue that they had no voice.

· · ·

To say that blacks never fully believed in rights is true. Yet it is also true that blacks believed in them so much and so hard that we gave them life where there was none before; we held onto them, put the hope of them into our wombs, mothered them and not the notion of them. And this was not the dry process of reification, from which life is drained and reality fades as the cement of conceptual determinism hardens round—but its opposite. This was the resurrection of life from ashes four hundred years old. The making of something out of nothing took immense alchemical fire—the fusion of a whole nation and the kindling of several generations. The illusion became real for only a few of us; it is still elusive for most. But if it took this long to breathe life into a form whose shape had already been forged by society, and which is therefore idealistically if not ideologically accessible, imagine how long the struggle would be without even that sense of definition, without the power of that familiar vision. What hope would there be if the assignment were to pour hope into a timeless, formless futurism? The desperate psychological and physical oppression suffered by black people in this society makes such a prospect either unrealistic (experienced as unattainable) or other-worldly (as in the false hopes held out by many religions of the oppressed.)

It is true that the constitutional foreground of rights was shaped by whites, parceled out to blacks in pieces, ordained from on high in small favors, random insulting gratuities. Perhaps the predominance of that imbalance obscures the fact that the recursive insistence of those rights is also defined by black desire for them—desire fueled not by the sop of minor enforcement of major statutory schemes like the Civil Rights Act, but by knowledge of, and generations of existing in, a world without any meaningful boundaries—and "without boundary" for blacks has meant not untrammeled vistas of possibility but the crushing weight of total—bodily and spiritual—*intrusion*. "Rights" feels new in the mouths of most black people. It is still deliciously empowering to say. It is the magic wand of visibility and invisibility, of inclusion and exclusion, of power and no power. The concept of rights, both positive and negative, is the marker of our citizenship, our relation to others.

In many mythologies, the mask of the sorcerer is also the source of power. To unmask the sorcerer is to depower. So CLS's unmasking of rights mythology in liberal America is to reveal the source of much powerlessness masquerading as strength; it reveals a universalism of need and oppression among whites as well as blacks. In those ancient mythologies, however, unmasking the sorcerer was only part of the job. It was impossible to destroy the mask without destroying the balance of things, without destroying empowerment itself. The mask had to be donned by the acquiring shaman and put to good ends.

The task for Critical Legal Studies, then, is not to discard rights but to see through or past them so that they reflect a larger definition of privacy and property: so that privacy is turned from exclusion based on self-regard into regard for another's fragile, mysterious autonomy; and so that property regains its ancient connotation of being a reflection of the universal self. The task is to expand private property rights into a conception of civil rights, into the right to expect civility from others. In discarding rights altogether, one discards a symbol too deeply enmeshed in the psyche of the oppressed to lose without trauma and much resistance. Instead, society must *give* them away. Unlock them from reification by giving them to slaves. Give them to trees. Give them to cows. Give them to history. Give them to rivers and rocks. Give to all of society's objects and untouchables the rights of privacy, integrity, and self-assertion; give them distance and respect. Flood them with the animating spirit that rights mythology fires in this country's most oppressed psyches, and wash away the shrouds of inanimate-object status, so that we may say not that we own gold but that a luminous golden spirit owns us.

Notes and Questions

1. Can Patricia Williams' understanding of rights be reconciled with Mark Tushnet's? How do experience and perspective influence their different understandings?

2. Professor Monica Evans takes a slightly different approach from both the CLS critique of rights and the traditional race-critical response. Monica J. Evans, *Stealing Away: Black Women, Outlaw Culture and the Rhetoric of Rights,* 28 Harv.C.R.–C.L.L.Rev. 263 (1993). She argues that both strategies err in defining rights as rooted in a kind of individualism that is opposed to and separate from a discourse about relationships. Rights are not located in individuals alone or in groups alone. Using African–American women's experiences in churches and clubs as a model, Evans describes an understanding of rights which is entirely consistent with and built upon relationships:

> Clubwomen can teach us alternative ways to think about rights. Stepping out of binary thinking can free us to imagine paradigms other than the rights/autonomy paradigm or the ethics of care/relationships paradigm. While clubwomen engaged in a struggle for rights, their concept of the self and the rights to which the self is entitled was not conflated with the idea of atomistic individualism. They did not define their mission in terms of a self-interested utility maximization as an autonomy-based rights discourse might. Rather, as their motto indicates, they lived out the relationship between rights and responsibilities by "lifting as we climb." For clubwomen, the struggle for rights was incoherent unless it simultaneously nurtured communal relationships that were predicated on a responsibility for uplifting the race.

Id. at 295–6.

3. Social relations approach. Martha Minow, in her path-breaking book, Making All the Difference: Inclusion, Exclusion and American Law (Cornell U. Press, 1990), has an entire chapter devoted to rights theories and their critiques, Id. at 146, concluding that "rights analysis provides incremental reforms but leaves the larger sources of the problem in place." Id. at 215. She proposes the adoption of a social relations approach which questions either/or constructions of problems, urges decision makers to attend to the process of categorization, acknowledges the interdependence of people and alternative solutions, and recognizes the dilemma of difference. Minow

sets out the following instructions for changing our paradigm from a rights-based approach to a social relations approach:

> For legal analysis, relational approaches may best be articulated as imperatives to engage an observer—a judge, a legislator, or a citizen—in the problems of difference: *Notice* the mutual dependence of people. *Investigate* the construction of difference in light of the norms and patterns of interpersonal and institutional relationships which make some traits matter. *Question* the relationship between the observer and the observed in order to situate judgments in the perspective of the actual judge. *Seek out and consider* competing perspectives, especially those of people defined as the problem. *Locate* theory within context; *criticize* practice in light of theoretical commitments; and *challenge* abstract theories in light of their practical effects. *Connect* the parts and the whole of a situation; *see* how the frame of analysis influences what is assumed to be given.

Id. at 213.

B.   LAWYERING FOR SOCIAL CHANGE AND JUSTICE

1.   *Shifts in the practice and teaching of law*

Using narratives, careful attention to traditionally excluded voices, and insights about the ways in which power and privilege function in lawyering practice, prominent legal theorists have articulated a new "theoretics" of legal practice (particularly, but not exclusively poverty law practice). A marvelous collections of readings can open up this world for law students: *Theoretics of Practice: The Integration of Progressive Thought and Action,* 43 Hastings L.J. 717–1257 (1992). *See also* Symposium, *Poverty Law and Policy,* 81 Geo.L.J. (1993). Professor Lucie White is a pre-eminent scholar working to alter the ways we practice and think about law as it functions at the intersections of race, gender and class subordination. The following excerpt sharing her experiences representing and learning from Mrs. G. is one of the finest examples of this scholarship.

LUCIE E. WHITE, SUBORDINATION, RHETORICAL SURVIVAL SKILLS, AND SUNDAY SHOES: NOTES ON THE HEARING OF MRS. G.

38 Buffalo L.Rev. 1 (1990).

The profound political intervention of feminism has been ... to redefine the very nature of what is deemed political.... The literary ramifications of this shift involve the discovery of the rhetorical survival skills of the formerly unvoiced. Lies, secrets, silences, and deflections of all sorts are routes taken by voices or messages not granted full legitimacy in order not to be altogether lost.

In 1970 the Supreme Court decided *Goldberg v. Kelly.* The case, which held that welfare recipients are entitled to an oral hearing prior to having their benefits reduced or terminated, opened up a far-reaching conversation among legal scholars over the meaning of procedural justice. All voices in this conversation endorse a normative floor that would guarantee all persons the same formal opportunities to be heard in adjudicatory proceedings, regardless of such factors as race, gender, or class identity. Beyond this minimal normative consensus, however, two groups of scholars have very different visions of what procedural justice would entail. One group, seeing procedure as an *instrument* of just government, seeks devices that will most efficiently generate legitimate outcomes in a complex society. Other scholars, however, by taking the perspective of society's marginalized groups, give voice to a very different—I will call it a "humanist"—vision. According to this vision, "procedural justice" is a normative *horizon* rather than a technical problem. This horizon challenges us to realize the promise of formal procedural equality in the real world. But this horizon may beckon us even farther than equality of access to current adjudicatory rituals. It may invite us to create new legal and political institutions that will frame "stronger," more meaningful opportunities for participation than we can imagine within a bureaucratic state. *Goldberg* can be read to pre-figure this humanist vision of procedural justice. The Court's decision to mandate prior oral hearings for welfare recipients suggests "the Nation's basic commitment" to both substantive equality and institutional innovation in participation opportunities, in order to "foster the dignity and well-being of *all* persons within its borders."

I begin this essay by assuming that the meaningful participation by all citizens in the governmental decisions that affect their lives—that is, the humanist vision—reflects a normatively compelling and widely shared intuition about procedural justice in our political culture. The essay explores a disjuncture between this vision and the conditions in our society in which procedural rituals are actually played out. Familiar cultural images and long-established legal norms construct the subjectivity and speech of socially subordinated persons as inherently inferior to the speech and personhood of dominant groups. Social subordination itself can lead disfavored groups to deploy verbal strategies that mark their speech as deviant when measured against dominant stylistic norms. These conditions—the web of subterranean speech norms and coerced speech practices that accompany race, gender, and class domination—undermine the capacity of many persons in our society to use the procedural rituals that are formally available to them. Furthermore, bureaucratic institutions disable *all* citizens—especially those from subordinated social groups—from meaningful participation in their own political lives.

This disjuncture between the norm of at least *equal*—if not also *meaningful*—participation opportunities for all citizens and a deeply stratified social reality reveals itself when subordinated speakers attempt to use the procedures that the system affords them. The essay tells the story of such an attempt—a story of enforced silence, rhetorical survival, and chance, as a poor woman engages in an administrative hearing at a welfare office. I tell the story more as a meditation than an argument—a meditation on the conditions that undermine the humanist project of procedural justice in our present society and the changes that might bring us closer to realizing that vision in the future. ...

A. THE STORY

Mrs. G. is thirty-five years old, Black, and on her own. She has five girls, ranging in age from four to fourteen. She has never told me anything about their fathers; all I know is that she isn't getting formal child support payments from anyone. She lives on an AFDC grant of just over three hundred dollars a month and a small monthly allotment of Food Stamps. She probably gets a little extra money from occasional jobs as a field hand or a maid, but she doesn't share this information with me and I don't ask. She has a very coveted unit of public housing, so she doesn't have to pay rent. She is taking an adult basic education class at the local community action center, which is in the same building as my own office. I often notice her in the classroom as I pass by.

The first thing that struck me about Mrs. G., when she finally came to my office for help one day, was the way she talked. She brought her two oldest daughters with her. She would get very excited when she spoke, breathing hard and waving her hands and straining, like she was searching for the right words to say what was on her mind. Her daughters would circle her, like two young mothers themselves, keeping the air calm as her hands swept through it. I haven't talked with them much, but they strike me as quite self-possessed for their years.

At the time I met Mrs. G., I was a legal aid lawyer working in a small community in south central North Carolina. I had grown up in the state, but had been away for ten years, and felt like an outsider when I started working there. I worked out of two small rooms in the back of the local community action center. The building was run-down, but it was a store front directly across from the Civil War Memorial on the courthouse lawn, so it was easy for poor people to find.

There were two of us in the office, myself and a local woman who had spent a few years in Los Angeles, working as a secretary and feeling free, before coming back to the town to care for her aging parents. Her family had lived in the town for generations. Not too long ago they, and most of the other Black families I worked with, had been the property of our adversaries—the local landowners, businessmen, bureaucrats, and lawyers. Everyone seemed to have a strong sense of family, and of history, in the town.

In the late 1960s, the town had erupted into violence when a local youth who had read some Karl Marx and Malcolm X led some five thousand people down the local highway in an effort to integrate the county swimming pool. He had been charged with kidnapping as a result of the incident and had fled to Cuba, China, and ultimately Detroit. My colleague would talk to me about him in secretive tones. Her father was one of those who sheltered him from justice on the evening of his escape. I think she expected that one day he would come back to take up the project that was abandoned when he fled.

Since World War II, the town had been a real backwater for Black people. People told me that it was a place that was there to be gotten out of, if you could figure out how. Only gradually, in the 1980s, were a few African American families moving back into the area, to take up skilled jobs in chemicals and electronics. But the lives of most Blacks in the county in the early 1980s could be summed up by its two claims to fame. It was the county where the state's arch-conservative senior Senator had grown up. Locals claimed that the Senator's father, the chief of police at one time, was known for the boots he wore and the success he had at keeping Black people in their place. It was also the county where Steven Spielberg filmed *The Color Purple*. By the time Spielberg discovered the county, the dust from the 1960s had long since settled, and the town where I worked had the look of a sleepy Jim Crow village that time had quite entirely passed by.

Mrs. G. and two daughters first appeared at our office one Friday morning at about ten, without an appointment. I was booked for the whole day; the chairs in the tiny waiting room were already filled. But I called her in between two scheduled clients. Mrs. G. looked frightened. She showed me a letter from the welfare office that said she had received an "overpayment" of AFDC benefits. Though she couldn't read very well, she knew that the word "overpayment" meant fraud. Reagan's newly appointed United States attorney, with the enthusiastic backing of Senator Jesse Helms, had just announced plans to prosecute "welfare cheats" to the full extent of the law. Following this lead, a grand jury had indicted several local women on federal charges of welfare fraud. Therefore, Mrs. G. had some reason to believe that "fraud" carried the threat of jail.

The "letter" was actually a standardized notice that I had seen many times before. Whenever the welfare department's computer showed that a client had received an overpayment, it would kick out this form, which stated the amount at issue and advised the client to pay it back. The notice did not say why the agency had concluded that a payment error had been made. Nor did it inform the client that she might contest the county's determination. Rather, the notice assigned the client a time to meet with the county's fraud investigator to sign a repayment contract and warned that if the client chose not to show up at this meeting further action would be taken. Mrs. G.'s meeting with the fraud investigator was set for the following Monday.

At the time, I was negotiating with the county over the routine at these meetings and the wording on the overpayment form. Therefore, I knew what Mrs. G. could expect at the meeting. The fraud worker would scold her and then ask her to sign a statement conceding the overpayment, consenting to a 10 percent reduction of her AFDC benefits until the full amount was paid back, and advising that the government could still press criminal charges against her.

I explained to Mrs. G. that she did not have to go to the meeting on Monday, or to sign any forms. She seemed relieved and asked if I could help her get the overpayment straightened out. I signed her on as a client and, aware of the other people waiting to see me, sped through my canned explanation of how I could help her. Then I called the fraud investigator, canceled Monday's meeting, and told him I was representing her. Thinking that the emergency had been dealt with, I scheduled an appointment for Mrs. G. for the following Tuesday and told her not to sign anything or talk to anyone at the welfare office until I saw her again.

The following Tuesday Mrs. G. arrived at my office looking upset. She said she had gone to her fraud appointment because she had been "afraid not to." She had signed a paper admitting she owed the county about six hundred dollars, and agreeing to have her benefits reduced by thirty dollars a month for the year and a half it would take to repay the amount. She remembered I had told her not to sign anything; she looked like she was waiting for me to yell at her or tell her to leave. I suddenly saw a woman caught between two bullies, both of us ordering her what to do.

I hadn't spent enough time with Mrs. G. the previous Friday. For me, it had been one more emergency—a quick fix, an appointment, out the door. It suddenly seemed pointless to process so many clients, in such haste, without any time to listen, to challenge, to think together. But what to do, with so many people waiting at the door? I mused on these thoughts for a moment, but what I finally said was simpler. I was furious. Why had she gone to the fraud appointment and signed the repayment contract? Why hadn't she done as *we* had agreed? Now it would be so much harder to contest the county's claim: we would have to attack *both* the repayment contract *and* the underlying overpayment claim. Why hadn't she listened to me?

Mrs. G. just looked at me in silence. She finally stammered that she knew she had been "wrong" to go to the meeting when I had told her not to and she was "sorry."

After we both calmed down I mumbled my own apology and turned to the business at hand. She told me that a few months before she had received a cash settlement for injuries she and her oldest daughter had suffered in a minor car accident. After medical bills had been paid and her lawyer had taken his fees, her award came to $592. Before Mrs. G. cashed the insurance check, she took it to her AFDC worker to report it and ask if it was all right for her to spend it. The system had trained her to tell her worker about every change in her life. With a few exceptions, any "income" she reported would be subtracted, dollar for dollar, from her AFDC stipend.

The worker was not sure how to classify the insurance award. After talking to a supervisor, however, she told Mrs. G. that the check would not affect her AFDC budget and she could spend it however she wanted.

Mrs. G. cashed her check that same afternoon and took her five girls on what she described to me as a "shopping trip." They bought Kotex, which they were always running short on at the end of the month. They also bought shoes, dresses for school, and some frozen food. Then she made two payments on her furniture bill. After a couple of wonderful days, the money was gone.

Two months passed. Mrs. G. received and spent two AFDC checks. Then she got the overpayment notice, asking her to repay to the county an amount equal to her insurance award.

When she got to this point, I could see Mrs. G. getting upset again. She had told her worker everything, but nobody had explained to her what she was supposed to do. She hadn't meant to do anything wrong. I said I thought the welfare office had done something wrong in this case, not Mrs. G. I thought we could get the mess straightened out, but we'd need more information. I asked if she could put together a list of all the things she had bought with the insurance money. If she still had any of the receipts, she should bring them to me. I would look at her case file at the welfare office and see her again in a couple of days.

The file had a note from the caseworker confirming that Mrs. G. had reported the insurance payment when she received it. The note also showed that the worker did not include the amount in calculating her stipend. The "overpayment" got flagged two months later when a supervisor, doing a random "quality control" check on her file, discovered the worker's note. Under AFDC law, the insurance award was considered a "lump sum payment." Aware that the law regarding such payments had recently changed, the supervisor decided to check out the case with the state quality control office.

He learned that the insurance award did count as income for AFDC purposes under the state's regulations; indeed, the county should have cut Mrs. G. off of welfare entirely for almost two months on the theory that her family could live for that time off of the insurance award. The lump sum rule was a Reagan Administration innovation designed to teach poor people the virtues of saving money and planning for the future. Nothing in the new provision required that clients be warned in advance about the rule change, however. Only in limited circumstances was a state free to waive the rule. Without a waiver, Mrs. G. would have to pay back $592 to the welfare office. If the county didn't try to collect the sum from Mrs. G., it would be sanctioned for an administrative error.

I met again with Mrs. G. the following Friday. When I told her what I had pieced together from her file, she insisted that she had asked her worker's permission before spending the insurance money. Then she seemed to get flustered and repeated what had become a familiar refrain. She didn't want to make any trouble. She hadn't meant to do anything wrong. I told her that it looked to me like it was the welfare office—and not her—who had done something wrong. I said I would try to get the county to drop the matter, but I thought we might have to go to a hearing, finally, to win. . . .

I could tell that Mrs. G. felt pressure from me to ask for a hearing, but she also seemed angry at the welfare office for asking her to pay for their mistake. I said that it was her decision, and not mine, whether to ask for the hearing, and reassured her that I would do my best to settle the matter, no matter what she decided. I also told her she could drop the hearing request at any time, for any reason, before or even after the event. When she nervously agreed to file the hearing request, I didn't second-guess her decision.

My negotiations failed. The county took the position that the worker should have suspended Mrs. G.'s AFDC as soon as the client had reported the insurance payment. This mistake was "regrettable," but it didn't shift the blame for the overpayment. Mrs. G.—and not the county—had received more welfare money than she was entitled to. End of discussion. I then appealed to state officials. They asked if the county would concede that the worker told Mrs. G. she was free to spend her insurance award as she pleased. When county officials refused, and the details of this conversation did not show up in the client's case file, the state declined to intervene. Mrs. G. then had to drop the matter or gear up for a hearing. After a lot of hesitation, she decided to go forward.

Mrs. G. brought all five of her girls to my office to prepare for the hearing. Our first task was to decide on a strategy for the argument. I told her that I saw two stories we could tell. The first was the story she had told me. It was the "estoppel" story, the story of the wrong advice she got from her worker about spending the insurance check. The second story was one that I had come up with from reading the law. The state had laid the groundwork for this story when it opted for the "life necessities" waiver permitted by federal regulations. If a client could show that she had spent the sum to avert a crisis situation, then it would be considered "unavailable" as income, and her AFDC benefits would not be suspended. I didn't like this second story very much, and I wasn't sure that Mrs. G. would want to go along with it. How could I ask her to distinguish "life necessities" from mere luxuries, when she was keeping five children alive on three hundred dollars a month, and when she had been given no voice in the calculus that had determined her "needs."

Yet I felt that the necessities story might work at the hearing, while "estoppel" would unite the county and state against us. According to legal aid's welfare specialist in the state capital, state officials didn't like the lump sum rule. It made more paper work for the counties. And, by knocking families off the federally financed AFDC program, the rule increased the pressure on state and county-funded relief programs. But the only way the state could get around the rule without being subject to federal sanctions was through the necessities exception. Behind the scenes, state officials were saying to our welfare specialist that they intended to interpret the exception broadly. In addition to this inside information that state officials would prefer the necessities tale, I knew from experience that they would feel comfortable with the role that story gave to Mrs. G. It would place her on her knees, asking for pity as she described how hard she was struggling to make ends meet. ...

This bind was familiar to me as a poverty lawyer. I felt it most strongly in disability hearings, when I would counsel clients to describe themselves as totally helpless in order to convince the court that they met the statutory definition of disability. But I had faced it in AFDC work as well, when I taught women to present themselves as abandoned, depleted of resources, and encumbered by children to qualify for relief. I taught them to say yes to the degrading terms of "income security," as it was called—invasions of sexual privacy, disruptions of kin-ties, the forced choice of one sibling's welfare over another's. Lawyers had tried to challenge these conditions, but for the most part the courts had confirmed that the system could take such license with its women. After all, poor women were free to say no to welfare if they weren't pleased with its terms.

As I contemplated my role as an advocate, I felt again the familiar sense that I had been taken. Here I was, asking Mrs. G. to trust me, talking with her about our conspiring together to beat the system and strategizing together to change it. Here I was, thinking that what I was doing was educative and empowering or at least supportive of those agendas, when all my efforts worked, in the end, only to teach her to submit to the system in all of the complex ways that it demanded.

In the moment it took for these old thoughts to flit through my mind, Mrs. G. and her children sat patiently in front of me, fidgeting, waiting for me to speak. My focus returned to them and the immediate crisis they faced if their AFDC benefits were cut. What story should we tell at the hearing, I wondered out loud. How should we decide? Mechanically at first, I began to describe to her our "options."

When I explained the necessities story, Mrs. G. said she might get confused trying to remember what all she had bought with the money. Why did they need to know those things anyway? I could tell she was getting angry. I wondered if two months of benefits—six hundred dollars—was worth it. Maybe paying it back made more sense. I reminded her that we didn't have to tell this story at the hearing, and in fact, we didn't have to go to the hearing at all. Although I was trying to choose my words carefully, I felt myself saying too much. Why had I even raised the question of which story to tell? It was a tactical decision—not the kind of issue that clients were supposed to decide. Why hadn't I just told her to answer the questions that I chose to ask?

Mrs. G. asked me what to do. I said I wanted to see the welfare office admit their mistake, but I was concerned that if we tried to make them, we would lose. Mrs. G. said she still felt like she'd been treated unfairly but—in the next breath—"I didn't mean to do anything wrong."

Why couldn't we tell both stories? With this simple question, I lost all pretense of strategic subtlety or control. I said sure.

I asked for the list she had promised to make of all the things she bought with the insurance money. Kotex, I thought, would speak for itself, but why, I asked, had she needed to get the girls new shoes? She explained that the girls' old shoes were pretty much torn up, so bad that the other kids would make fun of them at school. Could she bring in the old shoes? She said she could.

We rehearsed her testimony, first about her conversation with her worker regarding the insurance award and then about the Kotex and the shoes. Maybe the hearing wouldn't be too bad for Mrs. G., especially if I could help her see it all as strategy, rather than the kind of talking she could do with people she could trust. She had to distance herself at the hearing. She shouldn't expect them to go away from it understanding why she was angry, or what she needed, or what her life was like. The hearing was their territory. The most she could hope for was to take it over for a moment, leading them to act out her agenda. Conspiracy was the theme she must keep repeating as she dutifully played her role.

We spent the next half hour rehearsing the hearing. By the end, she seemed reasonably comfortable with her part. Then we practiced the cross-examination, the ugly questions that—even though everyone conceded to be irrelevant—still always seemed to get asked ... questions about her children, their fathers, how long she had been on welfare, why she wasn't working instead. This was the part of these sessions that I disliked the most. We practiced me objecting and her staying quiet and trying to stay composed. By the end of our meeting, the whole thing was holding together, more or less.

The hearing itself was in a small conference room at the welfare office. Mrs. G. arrived with her two oldest daughters and five boxes of shoes. When we got there the state hearing officer and the county AFDC director were already seated at the hearing table in lively conversation. The AFDC director was a youngish man with sandy hair and a beard. He didn't seem like a bureaucrat until he started talking. I knew most of the hearing officers who came to the county, but this one, a pale, greying man who slouched in his chair, was new to me. I started feeling uneasy as I rehearsed how I would plead this troubling case to a stranger.

We took our seats across the table from the AFDC director. The hearing officer set up a portable tape recorder and got out his bible. Mrs. G.'s AFDC worker, an African American woman about her age, entered through a side door and took a seat next to her boss. The hearing officer turned on the recorder, read his obligatory opening remarks, and asked all the witnesses to rise and repeat before god that they intended to tell the truth. Mrs. G. and her worker complied.

The officer then turned the matter over to me. I gave a brief account of the background events and then began to question Mrs. G. First I asked her about the insurance proceeds. She explained how she had received an insurance check of about six hundred dollars following a car accident in which she and her oldest daughter had been slightly injured. She said that the insurance company had already paid the medical bills and the lawyer; the last six hundred dollars was for her and her daughter to spend however they wanted. I asked her if she had shown the check to her AFDC worker before she cashed it. She stammered. I repeated the question. She said she may have taken the check to the welfare office before she cashed it, but she couldn't remember for sure. She didn't know if she had gotten a chance to talk to anyone about it. Her worker was always real busy.

Armed with the worker's own sketchy notation of the conversation in the case file, I began to cross-examine my client, coaxing her memory about the event we had discussed so many times before. I asked if she remembered her worker telling her anything about how she could spend the money. Mrs. G. seemed to be getting more uncomfortable. It was quite a predicament for her, after all. If she "remembered" what her worker had told her, would her story expose mismanagement in the welfare office, or merely scapegoat another Black woman, who was not too much better off than herself?

When she repeated that she couldn't remember, I decided to leave the estoppel story for the moment. Maybe I could think of a way to return to it later. I moved on to the life necessities issue. I asked Mrs. G. to recount, as best she could, exactly how she had spent the insurance money. She showed me the receipts she had kept for the furniture payments and I put them into evidence. She explained that she was buying a couple of big mattresses for the kids and a new kitchen table. She said she had also bought some food—some frozen meat and several boxes of Kotex for all the girls. The others in the room shifted uneasily in their chairs. Then she said she had also bought her daughters some clothes and some shoes. She had the cash register receipt for the purchase.

Choosing my words carefully, I asked why she had needed to buy the new shoes. She looked at me for a moment with an expression that I couldn't read. Then she stated, quite emphatically, that they were Sunday shoes that she had bought with the money. The girls already had everyday shoes to wear to school, but she had wanted them to have nice shoes for church too. She said no more than two or three sentences, but her voice sounded different—stronger, more composed—than I had known from her before. When she finished speaking the room was silent, except for the incessant hum of the tape machine on the table and the fluorescent lights overhead. In that moment, I felt the boundaries of our "conspiracy" shift. Suddenly I was on the outside, with the folks on the other side of the table, the welfare director and the hearing officer. The only person I could not locate in this new alignment was Mrs. G.'s welfare worker.

I didn't ask Mrs. G. to pull out the children's old shoes, as we'd rehearsed. Nor did I make my "life necessities" argument. My lawyer's language couldn't add anything to what she had said. They would have to figure out for themselves why buying Sunday shoes for her children—and saying it—was indeed a "life necessity" for this woman. After the hearing, Mrs. G. seemed elated. She asked me how she had done at the hearing and I told her that I thought she was great. I warned her, though, that we could never be sure, in this game, who was winning, or even what side anyone was on.

We lost the hearing and immediately petitioned for review by the chief hearing officer. I wasn't sure of the theory we'd argue, but I wanted to keep the case open until I figured out what we could do.

Three days after the appeal was filed, the county welfare director called me unexpectedly, to tell me that the county had decided to withdraw its overpayment claim against Mrs. G. He explained that on a careful review of its own records, the county had decided that it wouldn't be "fair" to make Mrs. G. pay the money back. I said I was relieved to hear that they had decided, finally, to come to a sensible result in the case. I was sorry they hadn't done so earlier. I then said something about how confusing the lump sum rule was and how Mrs. G.'s worker had checked with her supervisor before telling Mrs. G. it was all right to spend the insurance money. I said I was sure that the screw up was not anyone's fault. He mumbled a bureaucratic pleasantry and we hung up.

When I told Mrs. G. that she had won, she said she had just wanted to "do the right thing," and that she hoped they understood that she'd never meant to do anything wrong. I repeated that they were the ones who had made the mistake. Though I wasn't sure exactly what was going on inside the welfare office, at least this crisis was over.

B. THE TERRAIN

... I will identify three dominant themes, all of them linked, sometimes subtly, to Mrs. G.'s social identity as poor, Black, and female. The first theme is *intimidation*. Mrs. G. did not feel that she could risk speaking her mind freely to welfare officials. She lived in a community in which the social hierarchy had a caste-like rigidity. As a poor Black woman, her position at the bottom accorded her virtually no social or political power. She depended on welfare to survive and did not expect this situation to change in the future. She was simply not situated to take action that might displease her superiors. The second theme is *humiliation*. Even if Mrs. G. could find the courage to speak out at the hearing, her words were not likely to be heard as legitimate, because of the language she had learned to speak as a poor woman of color, and because of the kind of person that racist and gendered imagery portrayed her to be. The final theme is *objectification*. Because Mrs. G. had little voice in the political process that set the substantive terms of her welfare eligibility, the issues that she was constrained to talk about at the hearing bore little relation to her own feelings about the meaning and fairness of the state's action. ...

1. *Why Did Mrs. G. Return to the Lawyer?* The lawyer[143] thought she understood the answer to this question. In her view, Mrs. G.'s life had taught her that to be safe, she must submit to her superiors. Mrs. G. was faced with conflicting commands from the welfare agency and the legal aid office. So, like the archetypical woman, shaped to mold herself to male desire, Mrs. G. said "yes" to everything the Man asked. She said yes when the lawyer asked her to go through with a hearing, yes again when the fraud investigator asked her to drop it, and yes once more when the lawyer demanded her apology. In the lawyer's view, this excess of acquiescence had a sad, but straightforward meaning. It marked Mrs. G.'s lack of social power: this woman could not risk having a point of view of her own.

Yet the lawyer was not situated to see the whole story. Though she aspired to stand beside Mrs. G. as an equal, she also sought to guard her own status—and the modicum of social power that it gave her. She *saw* Mrs. G. as a victim because that was the role she needed her client to occupy to support her own social status. For if Mrs. G. was indeed silenced by the violence around her, she would then be dependent on the lawyer's expertise and protection, and therefore compliant to the lawyer's will. With such clients, the lawyer could feel quite secure of her power, and complacent about the value of her work.

But Mrs. G.'s survival skills were more complex, more subtle, than the lawyer dared to recognize. There might be another meaning to Mrs. G.'s ambivalence about what she wanted to do. Perhaps she was *playing* with the compliance that all of her superiors demanded. By acquiescing to both of the system's opposed orders, she was surely protecting herself from the risks of defiance. But she was also undermining the value—to them—of her own submission. By refusing to claim any ground as her own, she made it impossible for others to subdue her will.

Self-negation may not have been the *only* meaning that Mrs. G. felt positioned to claim. She finally *came back* to the lawyer, repudiated the settlement, determined to pursue her case. Was this merely one more deft move between two bureaucrats, searching them both for strategic advantage while secretly mocking the rhetoric of both spheres? Or did Mrs. G. finally get fed up at the unfairness of the welfare, and at her own endless submission? When she returned to the lawyer, she was offered a bargain. She might get money, and some limited protection from the welfare, if she went along with the hearing plan. But she might have also heard the lawyer to promise something different from

---

143. As I begin this critique of the lawyer's perspective, I must note the ambiguity of my own position in this project. As Mrs. G.'s lawyer, I appeared in her story. Yet I also wrote that story, and I now prepare to read it. The reader should ask what feelings and events I might have left out of the narrative of Mrs. G. because I was not situated to perceive them. Although this reading purports to comment on how the lawyer's viewpoint was limited in the story, my interpretation of the lawyer's limitations is itself shaped by my own present social location and concerns. What questions does this reading pose to the story, and what issues does my reading conceal from view?

this *quid pro quo.* In her talk of rights and justice, the lawyer offered Mrs. G. not just money, but also vindication. In going forward with the hearing, was Mrs. G. simply making a street-wise calculation to play the game the lawyer offered? Or was she also giving voice to a faint hope—a hope that one day she might really have the legal protections she needed to take part in the shaping of justice?

2. *Why Did Mrs. G. Depart from her Script?* The lawyer had scripted Mrs. G. as a victim. That was the only strategy for the hearing that the lawyer, within the constraints of her own social position, could imagine for Mrs. G. She had warned her client to play the victim if she wanted to win. Mrs. G. learned her lines. She came to the hearing well-rehearsed in the lawyer's strategy. But in the hearing, she did not play. When she was cued to perform, without any signal to her lawyer she abandoned their script.

The lawyer shared with Mrs. G. the oppression of gender, but was placed above Mrs. G. in the social hierarchies of race and class. The lawyer was paid by the same people who paid for welfare, the federal government. Both programs were part of a social agenda of assisting, but also controlling, the poor. Though the lawyer had worked hard to identify with Mrs. G., she was also sworn, and paid, to defend the basic constitution of the *status quo.* When Mrs. G. "misbehaved" at the hearing, when she failed to talk on cue and then refused to keep quiet, Mrs. G. pointed to the ambiguity of the legal aid lawyer's social role. Through her defiant actions, Mrs. G. told the lawyer that a conspiracy with a double agent is inevitably going to prove an unstable alliance.

The lawyer had tried to "collaborate" with Mrs. G. in devising an advocacy plan. Yet the terms of that "dialogue" excluded Mrs. G.'s voice. Mrs. G. was a better strategist than the lawyer—more daring, more subtle, more fluent—in her own home terrain. She knew the psychology, the culture, and the politics of the white people who controlled her community. She knew how to read, and sometimes control, her masters' motivations; she had to command this knowledge—this intuition—to survive. The lawyer had learned intuition as a woman, but in a much more private sphere. She was an outsider to the county, and to Mrs. G.'s social world. Mrs. G.'s superior sense of the landscape posed a subtle threat to the lawyer's expertise. Sensing this threat, the lawyer steered their strategic "discussion" into the sphere of her own expert knowledge. By limiting the very definition of "strategy" to the manipulation of legal doctrine, she invited Mrs. G. to respond to her questions with silence. And, indeed, Mrs. G. did not talk freely when the lawyer was devising their game-plan. Rather, Mrs. G. waited until the hearing to act out her own intuitions. Although she surely had not plotted those actions in advance, she came up with moves at the hearing which threw everyone else off their guard, and may have proved her the better *legal* strategist of the lawyer-client pair.

The disarming "strategy" that Mrs. G. improvised at the hearing was to appear to *abandon* strategy entirely. For a moment she stepped out of the role of the supplicant. She ignored the doctrinal pigeonholes that would fragment her voice. She put aside all that the lawyer told her the audience wanted to hear. Instead, when asked to point a finger at her caseworker, she was silent. When asked about "life necessities," she explained that she had used her money to meet *her own* needs. She had bought her children Sunday shoes.

a. Her Silence Before her Caseworker. When the lawyer asked Mrs. G. about the conversation with her caseworker regarding the insurance payments, Mrs. G. had nothing to say. The lawyer, smarting from her own rejection, felt that Mrs. G. was protecting a vulnerable Black sister with her silence—at her own, and her lawyer's expense. But perhaps something else was going on. Unlike Mrs. G., the caseworker had earned self-respect in the system. Mrs. G. and her like— desperately poor, with no formal schooling, burdened by too many children, "abandoned" by their men—cast a stigma on this woman because of the common color of their skin. Did this woman command a different kind of power over Mrs. G. than the white masters—a power that felt like shame, rather than fear? Perhaps Mrs. G. was not willing to flaunt her own degradation before this woman, as the lawyer demanded. Perhaps she was not willing to grovel—pointing fingers, showing off tattered shoes, listing each of her petty expenses—before this distant, disapproving sister. Perhaps Mrs. G.'s silence before this other Black woman, and her talk about Sunday shoes, expressed a demand—and an affirmation—of her own dignity.

b. Her Talk about Sunday Shoes. When Mrs. G. talked about Sunday shoes, she was talking about a life necessity. For subordinated communities, physical necessities do not meet the minimum require- ments for a human life. Rather, subordinated groups must create cultural practices through which they can elaborate an autonomous, oppositional consciousness. Without shared rituals for sustaining their survival and motivating their resistance, subordinated groups run the risk of total domination—of losing the *will* to use their human powers to subvert their oppressor's control over them. Religion, spirituality, the social institution of the Black Church, has been one such self-affirming cultural practice for the communities of African American slaves, and remains central to the expression of Black identity and group conscious- ness today. By naming Sunday shoes as a life necessity, Mrs. G. was speaking to the importance of this cultural practice in her life, a truth that the system's categories did not comprehend.

At the same time that Mrs. G.'s statement affirmed the church, it condemned the welfare system. By rejecting the welfare's definition of life necessities, she asserted her need to have a say about *the criteria* for identifying her needs. Her statement was a demand for meaningful participation in the political conversations in which her needs are contested and defined. In the present welfare system, poor women—the objects of welfare—are structurally excluded from those conversations. When Mrs. G. insisted on her need to say for herself what her "life necessities" might be, she expanded, for a moment, the accepted boundaries of those conversations.

Mrs. G.'s statement also spoke to a third dimension of her "life necessity." When Mrs. G. talked about buying Sunday shoes, she defied the rules of legal rhetoric—the rule of relevancy, the rule against "rambling," the unwritten rule that told her to speak like a victim if she wanted to win. Had Mrs. G. spoken the language that was proper for her in the setting, her relevant, logical, submissive, hyper-correct responses to their questions might have been comprehended. But, by dutifully speaking the language of an institution from which subordinated groups have historically been excluded and in which Mrs. G. felt herself to have no stake, her voice would have repeated, and legitimated, the very social and cultural patterns and priorities that had kept her down. Had she been a *respectful* participant in the legal ritual, Mrs. G. would have articulated someone else's need, or pleasure, rather than her own.

Mrs. G. did not boycott the hearing altogether. Rather, in her moment of misbehavior, she may have been standing her ground within it. Although she appeared, at first, to be deferring to the system's categories and rules, when she finally spoke, she animated those categories with her own experience. She stretched the category of "life necessity" to express her own values, and turned it around to critique the welfare's systemic disregard of her own point of view. By talking about Sunday shoes, Mrs. G. claimed, for one fragile moment, what was perhaps her most basic "life necessity." She claimed a position of equality in the speech community—an equal power to take part in the *making* of language, the making of shared categories, norms, and institutions—as she spoke through that language about her needs.

When Mrs. G. claimed this power, she affirmed the feminist insight that the dominant languages do *not* construct a closed system, from which there can be no escape. Although dominant groups may control the *social institutions* that regulate these languages, those groups cannot control the *capacity* of subordinated peoples to speak. Thus, women have evaded complete domination through their *practice* of speaking, like Mrs. G. spoke at her hearing, from their own intuitions and their own experience. ...

3. *How Was Mrs. G.'s Voice Heard?* The third question that the story raises is the ending. The story tells us that the hearing officer ruled against Mrs. G., and then the county welfare department decided to drop the case, restoring her full stipend. But the text does not say how the men across the table experienced the hearing, or why the county eventually gave in. Did Mrs. G.'s paradoxical "strategy" disarm her audience? Did she draw a response from her audience that was different—more compelling—than the pity that her lawyer had wanted to play upon? Did her presentation of herself as an independent, church-going woman, who would exercise her own judgment, and was willing to say what she needed—did these qualities make the men fear her, respect

her, regard her for a moment as a person, rather than a case? Did they feel a moment of anger—about the ultimately powerless roles that they were assigned to play in the bureaucracy that regulated all of their lives? Were these men moved, by the hearing, to snatch her case from the computer and subject it to their own human judgment? If this is indeed what happened—and we do not know—would Mrs. G., in retrospect, have wished the story to end that way? Or was this moment of benign discretion a double-edged precedent—more dangerous to her people than the computer's reliable indifference?

We do not know why the county decided to drop Mrs. G.'s case. What we do know, however, is that after the hearing Mrs. G. remained a Black, single mother on welfare—poor, dependent, despised. Mrs. G.'s unruly participation at her hearing was itself political action. Yet it was an act that did little to change the harsh landscape which constricts Mrs. G. from more sustained and more effective political participation. Substantial change in that landscape will come only as such fragile moments of dignity are supported and validated by the law. . . .

Notes and Questions

1. Because of her location at the intersection of race, gender, and class structures of oppression, Mrs. G. had to develop a special set of skills to negotiate her way through the legal and bureaucratic morass of our public benefits system, not to mention the skills needed to meet the challenge of daily survival as a single mother of five daughters living in poverty. Lucie White asks us to appreciate those skills, to try to understand how they are deployed, and to challenge the processes and assumptions of law that reinforce imagery which subordinates Mrs. G. How might different lawyers adapt their practices and legal strategies to incorporate White's insights? What are the risks of encouraging Mrs. G. to speak for herself from her understandings? What are the risks of shaping her understandings into arguments based on pre-existing legal categories?

2. Winning or losing the benefits in this hearing had real, urgent, material consequences in Mrs. G and her daughters' lives. Did Mrs. G. win? Why do you think this case turned out as it did? Can lawyers strategize with clients by depending upon the factors/reasons that affected the result in this case?

3. Professor White's analysis in *Mrs. G.* seeks to empower clients by listening closely to their stories and adapting legal strategies from the perspectives of clients' needs and experiences while struggling against patterns of subordination. Ruth Buchanan and Louise Trubek list the central tenets of this kind of alternative lawyering as:

> HUMANIZE: resist reduction of client stories to legal categories; frame issues in human terms.

> POLITICIZE: use critical legal theory to provide insight into the contingent nature of client disempowerment; apply feminist and antiracist analysis to help resist marginalization of client voices.

COLLABORATE: encourage participation of clients and client groups in practice decisions; attempt to dismantle the lawyer/client hierarchy.

STRATEGIZE: seek to access client experiences regarding strategies for struggle and resistance; develop a healthy skepticism regarding traditional advocacy arenas; continually re-evaluate advocacy effectiveness from a client perspective.

ORGANIZE: encourage organization and collective efforts by clients; work with existing social movements and client groups.

Ruth Buchanan & Louise G. Trubek, *Resistances and Possibilities: A Critical and Practical Look at Public Interest Lawyering,* 19 N.Y.U.Rev. of L. & Soc.Change 687, 691 (1992).

4. In a more recent article, Professor White encourages us to rethink strategies for addressing welfare. Lucie E. White, *No Exit: Rethinking "Welfare Dependency" From a Different Ground,* 81 Geo.L.J. 1961 (1993). After rechallenging the myth that "welfare causes poverty," she again uses narrative to bring to life the stories and experiences of two different women who are welfare dependent. Just as Mrs. G.'s story contains multiple layers of insights, so do the stories of Elaine Preston and Barbara Sutton. By telling their stories and sharing their hopes and despairs, White illustrates the lived context of welfare dependency and the double binds that women on welfare face—shame if they stay on welfare or violence if they leave.

> Whenever I listen intently to poor women talk about their lives, I hear stories of violence: the violence of racism and class bias that they remember—and expect—from school; the violence of industrial hazards, brain-deadening routines, repressive discipline, and sexual harassment that they face in the few available jobs; and the violence inherent in the bargain when they seek to secure their children's futures through a man. Poor women are thus trapped in a no-win predicament. They face shame if they stay on welfare. Yet the 'exits' they are offered are really traps, for rather than providing opportunities, these exits repeatedly expose them to violence.

Id. at 1989. Lucie White chastises mainstream welfare scholarship and practice for failing to dislodge the myth that welfare causes poverty, for using statistics alone instead of attending to real stories of women's lives to discover how these women are locked into recurring double binds, for perpetuating rhetoric and institutions that do violence, and for failing to prioritize and address issues of violence (physical, economic, and psychic) in poor women's lives. White's attention to these women's stories has created different knowledge about the causes of welfare dependency, and because of this knowledge, we must rethink the ways we practice poverty law and organize for social change. Starting from the bottom, the material conditions and concrete lives of poor women, White develops strategies and theories for welfare lawyering, rather than imposing abstract theories about welfare from above, to give meaning to the lives of existing women.

5. Political mobilization. Peter Gabel and Paul Harris offer a model of alternative or critical lawyering for social change that explicitly includes political mobilization.

PETER GABEL & PAUL HARRIS, BUILDING POWER AND BREAKING IMAGES: CRITICAL LEGAL THEORY AND THE PRACTICE OF LAW

11 N.Y.U.Rev. of L. & Soc.Change 369 (1983).

I. A Power-Oriented Approach to Law Practice

A first principle of a "counter-hegemonic" legal practice must be to subordinate the goal of getting people their rights to the goal of building an authentic or unalienated political consciousness. This obviously does not mean that one should not try to win one's cases; nor does it necessarily mean that we should not continue to organize groups by appealing to rights. . . .

A legal strategy that goes beyond rights-consciousness is one that focuses upon expanding political consciousness through using the legal system to increase people's sense of personal and political power. This can mean many different things depending upon the political visibility of any given case and the specific social and legal context within which a case arises. But in any context, a "power" rather than a "rights" approach to law practice should be guided by three general objectives that are as applicable to minor personal injury cases as to major cases involving important social issues. First, the lawyer should seek to develop a relationship of genuine equality and mutual respect with her client. Second, the lawyer should conduct herself in a way that demystifies the symbolic authority of the State. . . . Third, the lawyer should always attempt to reshape the way legal conflicts are represented in the law, revealing the limiting character of legal ideology and bringing out the true socioeconomic and political foundations of legal disputes. Reaching these objectives may have a transformative impact not only upon the lawyer and client working in concert, but also upon others who come into contact with the case, including the client's friends and family, courtroom participants such as jurors, stenographers, and public observers, and, in some cases, thousands or even millions of people who follow high-visibility political cases through the media. Of course, any particular lawyer's actions in a single case cannot lead to the development of an anti-hierarchical social movement; we believe, however, that if lawyers as a group begin to organize themselves around the realization of these goals, their impact on the culture as a whole can be much greater than they currently believe is possible. . . .

II. Counterpressure in High-Visibility Political Cases

Although a central objective of this article is to argue that all legal cases are potentially empowering, the classic political case remains one that receives widespread public attention because it emerges from a social conflict that has already achieved high visibility in the public consciousness. Examples of such cases in recent years include the political trials that arose out of the student and antiwar movements, and the many Supreme Court cases that have emerged from the civil rights and women's movements. Such cases contain unique possibilities and also difficulties for the lawyers and clients involved in them, because the aim is not only to win on the legal issues raised by the case, but to speak for the movement itself. Precisely because the State's objective is in part to defuse the political energy that has given rise to the case, the legal issue is often one that deflects attention from and even denies the political nature of the conflict.

A. The Chicago Eight Trial

Perhaps the clearest example of this "deflection" was the so-called "conspiracy" trial of the Chicago Eight, in which the issue as defined by the prosecutor was whether the defendants who had helped to organize the antiwar demonstrations outside the Democratic National Convention in 1968 had conspired to cross state lines with the intent to incite a riot. The political meaning of the demonstrations was to challenge the morality of the Vietnam War and the political process that served to justify it, but this meaning was, of course, legally irrelevant to the determination of whether the alleged conspiracy had taken place.

Using a case like this to increase the power of an existing political movement requires a systematic refusal to accept the limiting boundaries which the State seeks to impose on the conflict. Had the lawyers and clients in the Chicago Eight trial presented a legal defense in a normal professional way, they would have deferred to the authority of Judge Hoffman and politely tried to show, perhaps with success, that the defendants did not "intend" to incite a riot or did not "conspire" to cross state lines to do so. But the lawyers and clients understood very well that even a legal victory on these terms would have meant a political defeat for their movement. They understood that the prosecutor's real purpose was to channel the political struggle in the streets into an official public chamber, to recharacterize the protestors as hooligans, and to substitute a narrow and depoliticized legal description of the meaning of the Chicago events for their true meaning. In this context State power consists not so much in the use of direct force, but in the use of the sanctity of the legal process to recast the meaning of the disruption that took place.

In concert with their courageous clients, William Kunstler and Leonard Weinglass were able to reverse the government's strategy and cause it to backfire, seizing upon the media's coverage of the trial to strengthen the resistance that had begun in the streets. By openly flaunting the hierarchical norms of the courtroom and ridiculing the judge, the prosecutor, and the nature of the charges themselves, they successfully rejected the very forms of authority upon which the legitimacy of the war itself depended. As Judge Hoffman gradually lost the capacity to control "his" room, he was transformed on national television from a learned figure worthy of great respect into a vindictive old man wearing a funny black tunic. In the absence of an underlying popular movement, the tactic of showing continuous contempt for the proceedings might simply have been an unproductive form of "acting out." But within its concrete historical context, this tactic was the most effective way to affirm to millions of supporters following the trial that their version of the meaning of the Chicago protests was right and could not be eroded by the State's appeal to a mass belief in authoritarian imagery.

B. The Inez Garcia Trial

The importance of this kind of symbolic resistance was demonstrated in a somewhat different, although equally powerful, way in the two murder trials of Inez Garcia, which took place almost ten years later during an intense period in the rise of the women's movement. While the Chicago Eight defense reveals the way that a total refusal to recognize the legitimacy of legal authority can in some circumstances be politically effective, the Inez Garcia trials show that it is sometimes possible to infuse an existing "nonpolitical" legal defense with unique and powerful political meaning.

Inez Garcia shot and killed one of the men who helped to rape her. Twenty minutes after the rape she looked for and found the two men; as one pulled out a knife she killed him and shot at the other as he was running away. At her first trial facing a first-degree murder charge, she was represented by an excellent male criminal lawyer. He defended her on the grounds of "impaired consciousness," a psychiatric defense which argued that Garcia was suffering from a temporary loss of conscious control over her behavior. If successful, such an approach provided a complete defense to murder. The trial strategy was secondarily aimed at achieving a conviction on a lesser included offense, such as second-degree murder or manslaughter. This strategy was somewhat successful from a legal point of view, as Garcia was found guilty of second-degree murder and given a sentence less severe than the one she would have received for a first-degree conviction.

Politically, however, the defense was a failure: it contradicted the defendant's belief in the rightness of her own act, and it failed to place Garcia's conduct in the context of a rising women's movement that was demanding recognition of the violent effect of rape and sexual harassment upon women. In her defensive and apologetic posture, Garcia was humiliated by psychiatric testimony that exposed her personal life in a denigrating way, and offended by the argument, made in her defense, that she was "sleepwalking" and unconscious of what she was doing. The contradiction between this legal characterization of her conduct and her true feelings erupted on the stand when she testified: "I took my gun, I loaded it, and I went out after them.... I am not sorry that I did it. The only thing I am sorry about is that I missed Luis." Earlier in the trial, Garcia had reacted violently to the judge's decision to disallow testimony about the emotional trauma of rape. She leaped up from the counsel table and said: "Why don't you just find me guilty? Just send me to jail.... I killed the fucking guy because he raped me!" Obviously, after that, the jury could not accept the attempted portrayal of Garcia as a demure and innocent woman who was so overcome that she could not be held responsible for her acts.

Garcia's conviction was reversed on appeal because of an improper jury instruction. In the retrial she was represented by radical-feminist attorney Susan Jordan. The defense was a creative combination of the traditional rules of self-defense and the historical reality of the victimization of women by men. The task Jordan faced was to translate the male-oriented rule of self-defense into a form that would capture the real experience of a woman facing possible attack by a man. She also had to combat, within the confines of the courtroom, the sexist myths that would influence the jurors.

The rule of self-defense is based on one's right to use reasonable force if, and only if, one reasonably perceives that there will be an imminent attack. The heart of the defense is the defendant's state of mind—it is necessary to convince a jury that the defendant acted in a reasonable manner given the circumstances.

In Garcia's situation, the juror's understanding of whether Garcia acted "reasonably" would almost certainly be influenced by cultural myths about the act of rape. The rape myths are that women invite it, that they encourage it, and they like it, and that ultimately the rape is their own fault. Jordan directly confronted these stereotypes by the creative use of voir dire. The jurors were questioned individually, one by one in the judge's chambers. Each juror was asked questions which were designed to bring out any underlying sexist stereotypes. Although this was a painful process, initially opposed by the judge, and irritating to some jurors, the process paid off. The final jury of ten men and two women was able to view the rape not as a sexual act caused by male-female flirting, but rather as a violent assault. This view of rape as an act of violence was key to the acceptance of the self-defense theory.

Jordan also faced the problem of Garcia's obvious anger at the men who raped her. If this anger was viewed by the jury as the motive for her shooting, then it would negate self-defense and lead to a verdict of manslaughter. The defense, therefore, attempted to show that the anger was a justified and reasonable response to her rape. Expert witnesses testified to the psychological effects of rape, especially a rape committed on a latina, Catholic woman. Instead of the traditional tactic of trying to hide the woman's anger, the defense affirmed this anger and explained it in human terms which broke through the male prejudices embodied in the law's traditional view of the reasonable person. The result was a complete acquittal.

The two trials of Inez Garcia demonstrate that in the right circumstances it is possible to win a case with a political approach when a more conventional legal approach would fail. Inez Garcia took the action that she did at a time when the women's movement was actively challenging the forms of patriarchal domination characteristic of man-woman relations throughout the social structure, and the central symbol of this domination was the act of forcible rape itself. With a male attorney in her first trial in effect apologizing for her action and the anger that produced it, Garcia was separated from the movement supporting her, and indeed from her own self. In pleading "impaired consciousness" she was forced to deny the legitimacy of her own action and simultaneously the legitimacy of the "unreasonable" rage that women throughout the country were expressing in response to their social powerlessness in relation to men. The form of the first trial turned Garcia into an isolated object of the legal system, a mere "defendant" requesting mercy from a "masculine" legal structure. Even a victory in the first trial would have had negative political consequences because it would have affirmed the wrongness of both her action and the feeling that provoked it, while legitimizing the authority of a benevolent State.

The most important feature of the second trial was that it reversed the power relations upon which the first trial was premised. The defense both affirmed the validity of Garcia's action, and allowed Jordan to join Garcia as co-advocate for a vast popular movement, to speak to the jury not as a State-licensed technician "representing" an abstract "defendant," but as a woman standing together with another woman. Together, the two women were able to put the act of rape itself on trial and to address the jurors, not as "jurors" but as human beings, about the meaning of being a woman in contemporary society. The effect of this was to transform the courtroom into a popular tribunal and to divest the prosecutor and the judge (who, as men, could not abstract themselves entirely from the evident signs of their own gender) of some of the symbolic authority upon which the legitimacy of the "legal form" of the proceeding depended. This shift in the vectors of power within the room also allowed the jurors to escape their own reification, to discover themselves as politically responsible for making a human, rather than a merely formal, decision based on an application of existing law. Thus the conduct of the second trial, coupled with the widespread publicity attendant to it, served to expand the power of the movement from which the political basis of the case derived, and to delegitimate the apparent necessity of existing legal consciousness. This last point deserves special emphasis, for breaking through the sedimented authoritarian forms of a legal proceeding in an overtly political case has radical implications beyond those of the particular case itself: it signifies that the existing order is *merely possible,* and that people have the freedom and power to act upon it. In the special context of a public trial, such action demonstrates the living disintegration of symbolic State power in a heavily ritualized setting, one that is normally a principal medium for the transmission of authoritarian imagery.

III. COUNTERPRESSURE IN LOW-VISIBILITY POLITICAL CASES

In 1971 the Latin community in San Francisco's Mission District was experiencing "brown power" and intense organizing by radical and liberal groups. The most effective radical organization was called "Los Siete" ("The Seven"), named after seven young men who had been acquitted of murdering a policeman after a long, contested trial. Los Siete ran a community clinic, organized a formidable labor caucus, pushed for community control of police, and published a community newspaper.

Los Siete's members were often harassed by police who operated out of the then infamous Mission police station. On a busy shopping day, two of Los Siete's most active members, a latin man and a black woman, were selling their newspaper *Basta Ya* on the sidewalk in front of the largest department store in the Mission. The store manager called the police. When the police arrived they berated the young man, called him "wetback" and told him to go back to Mexico. The police confiscated the papers and arrested both the man and the woman for trespass, obstructing the sidewalk, and resisting arrest.

There was no publicity of the arrest. The store owners saw the arrest as a vindication of their right of private property. The police viewed it as a demonstration of their power in the Mission district and a warning to community groups. The district attorney's office treated the case as a routine misdemeanor. The defendants felt the arrests had been an act of intimidation and racism. The woman was treated as a prostitute at the City Jail, examined for venereal disease and put in quarantine for two days while awaiting the results of the test. The excuse given for such treatment was that she had been charged with obstructing the sidewalk, an offense associated with prostitution.

Los Siete asked the Community Law Collective, a local law office which acted as "house counsel" to many community organizations, to defend their members and to help them develop a legal-political analysis of the case. The attorneys explained that although there was a First Amendment issue present, it was doubtful that such a right could be vindicated at the lower court level. At trial, it would be the defendants' testimony against the testimony of two policemen, a security guard, and possibly the store manager. Even though the defendants had sold their newspapers on the sidewalk without harassing store customers, the State's witnesses would place them on store property obstructing customers, and the police would swear the latin man had pushed them and refused arrest. The jury would be almost all white and predisposed toward the State's witnesses. If the trial was before one of the few liberal municipal court judges, the defendants might receive thirty days in jail if convicted; if before one of the many conservatives, the sentence would probably be six months in jail. If, on the other hand, the defendants were to plead guilty, the district attorney would drop all the charges except trespass, and would offer a sixty-day suspended sentence.

If the lawyers had acted as apolitical professionals in this situation, they almost certainly would have advised their clients to plea bargain. First, it makes sense to accept probation in the face of a likely jail sentence. Second, preparation and trial would be quite time-consuming and remuneration would be small. But for the lawyers to have given such "normal" advice in this context would have made them mere extensions of the system. It is not in the interests of the State in this situation to send defendants to jail and risk an increase of organized anger in the community. Rather, the State's strategy is to break the spirit and limit the options of the community movement. It is the plea bargain which best accomplishes this purpose, by simultaneously vindicating the police, legitimating the store owner's property rights, and making community activists feel powerless and humiliated. Moreover, in offering defendants a six-month suspended sentence, the State is also offering them a two-year probation period, the obvious effect of which is to inhibit any future activism. In this context the plea bargain becomes the iron fist in the velvet glove, and the defense lawyer who passively participates in arranging such an outcome becomes partly responsible for its consequences.

Understanding the dangers of "copping a plea," the lawyers and clients attempted to define what was really at issue and to explore a radical approach to the case. The issue was the exercise of political power, in the form of selling *Basta Ya* on the streets of the Mission community. Selling the newspaper served three purposes. First, the person-to-person contact was an effective organizing tool for Los Siete, helping them to build support for their community programs. Second, the street-corner sales were the primary means of distributing the paper and therefore of getting the information in the paper out to the community. Third, the very act of selling their paper in the streets of the Mission district made the activists feel some power in the face of overwhelming police authority, and the sight of young latinos passing out their radical newspaper helped to create a vague but important sense of indigenous power in the community residents as well. To maintain this sense of power it seemed necessary to reject the psychological defeat inherent in the plea bargain, and to risk a trial.

The tasks facing the lawyers in this case were, first, to empower their clients and Los Siete as an organization and, second, to win the trial. Both goals would be furthered by an overtly political defense, the first because a political defense would insist that the defendants were right to be reaching out to the community; the second because this particular trial could be won only by challenging the narrow "legal" definition of their action as criminal obstruction and trespass.

The lawyers' first tactic was to go on the offensive by filing a motion to suppress the seized newspapers on the grounds that the arrest and seizure violated the First Amendment. This tactic was no different from one that any good defense lawyer would use once plea bargaining had been rejected, but here the purpose was not so much to vindicate a legal right as such, but rather to force the State to *defend* its actions. Surprisingly, the municipal court granted the motion, much to the irritation of the district attorney, who was then forced into the defensive posture of filing an appeal. The defense lawyers asked a young corporate attorney interested in "pro bono" work to prepare the appeal. The coalition of community lawyers and corporate lawyer increased the ideological pressure on the district attorney's office. Although the corporate attorney wrote an excellent brief and argued the case, the municipal court decision was reversed.

Next came the trial plan. The first strategic issue was whether to try to pack the courtroom with community people. Traditional lawyers are wary of this tactic for fear that the presence of third world and "radical" people will frighten the jury and create subconscious hostility. However, lawyers can often use crowded courtrooms to their advantage by dealing with the jury's anxiety and hostility toward the community presence in voir dire, and by openly discussing any negative preconceptions the jurors might have in opening and/or closing arguments. Due to a lack of publicity it was not possible in this case to fill the courtroom with community supporters, but enough were present to prevent the defendants from feeling isolated.

The second issue related to the clients' participation in the preparation and conduct of the trial. In the traditional view of the lawyer-client relationship, the lawyer is defined as the professional who "handles" all legal aspects of the case without client participation. By treating the client as someone who cannot understand the conduct of her own trial, the traditional approach increases the client's sense of powerlessness in the face of the intimidating spectacle going on in the courtroom. In this case the lawyers took the opposite approach, asking the clients to take an active part in all aspects of the case where prior legal training was not absolutely required. Thus the defendants wrote voir dire questions and assisted in the selection of jurors. The lawyers discussed each aspect of the case, explaining their tactics and incorporating many of the suggestions of the clients. In this manner the clients began to feel some control over the process which the State had forced them into.

As for the trial itself, a traditional approach would have been to argue the client's version of the facts against the State's version, relying on a reasonable-doubt defense and keeping the content of the newspaper itself out of evidence. A more liberal approach would have been to focus on the First Amendment aspects of the case, emphasizing the abstract right of dissenters to freedom of speech. The radical approach was to stress the political realities involved; to admit and defend the true nature of *Basta Ya,* and to expose the police department's racism and its attempts to harass and intimidate members of Los Siete.

The trial ended successfully for the defendants despite the judge's persistent attempts to ridicule the attorneys and to prohibit their making any mention of the First Amendment. Instead of feeling that they had won by disguising their politics through either the traditional or liberal approaches, the defendants felt a sense of power and truth because the political meaning of their actions had been presented and vindicated. After the trial the defendants went back with other members of Los Siete to distribute newspapers in the same location, while the police and storeowner looked on. "Basta Ya" means "Enough Already." The case delivered to the arresting officers, the local police station, and the conservative merchants a clear message: if you mess with Los Siete, they have the spirit and resources to hit back.

Low-visibility cases that contain political elements, such as *Basta Ya,* are presented in courtrooms throughout the country on a frequent basis. What is critical to understand is that one can transform a "solely criminal" case into a political case by making a few simple changes in approach and technique. This is possible because the courtroom is a small, closed, intensified experience for the jury and for the participants. Everything that takes place is magnified. Since the district attorney and judge will almost always define the case as nonpolitical, and will attempt to create an atmosphere of neutral application of objective laws, any injection of political and social reality will have a powerful impact. Using the *Basta Ya* trial, we can look at voir dire, opening statement and cross examination to illuminate this analysis.

The two young lawyers in the *Basta Ya* trial had a combined experience of less than four trials. They could not carry off a week-long antiracist voir dire as Charles Garry did in many of the Black Panther cases; their clients faced only misdemeanors and there was very little visible community support in the courtroom itself. An extensive voir dire in this context may have been viewed as overkill. However, it was simple to ask a few questions that had the effect of setting a political tone to the trial. For example, the first juror was asked the following: "The community newspaper that was being passed out was called *Basta Ya,* which means 'Enough Already!' Have you ever heard of it?" Since the juror's answer was no, the next question, spoken with enough clarity and strength to grab the attention of all the jurors, was, "*Basta Ya* has articles very critical of the police for harassing latinos and Mission residents. Would that prejudice you against Raul Flores?" By the fourth or fifth juror, this question became shortened to, "Would the articles criticizing police brutality make it hard for you to evaluate the evidence with an open mind?" One of the jurors, an older Italian man, was asked the following series of questions: "Mr. Flores speaks both English and Spanish. Are you familiar with people who have the ability to speak two languages?" Answer: "Of course; in my family, my wife and I, and son do." Question: "Do you take pride in your heritage, your culture?" Answer: "Very much. It's important." Question: "Would you think badly of Mr. Flores if, when he testifies, he speaks with a heavy Spanish accent?" Answer: "No, not if I can understand him." These types of questions give jurors some understanding of the racial and political issues behind the formal charges.

In opening statement, one need not give a political lecture to the jury, nor are most judges likely to allow such an approach. However, a few sentences can inform both the jury and the judge as to the actual nature of the case. For example, the following was one of two or three political comments in the *Basta Ya* opening statement: "Raul Flores will take the stand and testify. You will see that he is 23–years old, married, with one small child. He has been active for many years in community groups, militantly organizing against police abuse and brutality in the Mission district." At the very least, this type of statement puts the jury on notice as to the political context of the trial.

Cross-examination is the most overrated aspect of the trial. In a low-visibility case it is quite difficult for a lawyer to be able to expose the racism and bias of police officers. Consequently, one must try to shed light on that bias rather than attempt to tear the mask off.

Question: "Officer, you are assigned to the Mission police station, correct?" Answer: "Yes." Question: "For two years you have worked out of the Mission station, right?" Answer: "That's right." Question: "You've seen people selling *Basta Ya* up and down the streets of the Mission, haven't you?" Answer: "Yes, I have." Question: "And you have seen *Basta Ya* in the little newsboxes on the corners?" Answer: "I've noticed them occasionally." Question: "Before you arrested Mr. Flores and confiscated his papers, you were aware that the front page photo and headline were about police brutality in the Mission, weren't you?" Answer: "No, I don't think I was aware of that." These questions gave the jury some insight into the political motivations of the police, even though they did not fit the romanticized notion of a great political cross-examination.

One does not have to be defending the Chicago Eight, or Inez Garcia, to bring political reality into the courtroom. One does not have to be a William Kunstler or a Susan Jordan to use the above examples in trial. If we remember that behind each case there is a social reality that the law is trying to hide and suppress, we can find acceptable and practical methods to politicize our cases.

IV. COUNTERPRESSURE IN "NONPOLITICAL" CASES

... The vast majority of legal cases do not, however, have this immediate potential for public impact. Ordinary divorce, personal injury cases, or unemployment hearings are political in that they involve the influence of large social forces upon individual lives, but they are not normally experienced as such....

A. Discovering the Common Thread

Here are some examples of potential alternative practices that would have as their objective the politicization of non-political cases:

1. A family law practice might be organized with the aim of politicizing issues the State currently characterizes as purely private or personal in nature. Such a practice could include any or all of the following elements: (a) creating new legal forms to support nontraditional relationships that challenge the idea that lasting love and intimacy are available only within isolated "family units" (this is perhaps the most political aspect of the gay-rights movement); (b) developing a holistic multi-service center providing medical and psychological assistance to families breaking down under the strain of such social forces as stress at the workplace, unemployment, and the privatization of personal life; (c) developing new approaches to traditional divorce and child-custody cases to make the process of separation as educational and empowering as possible (including, for example, the use of face-to-face mediation instead of lawyer-to-lawyer adversary proceedings, and group-forming strategies

like the pro se divorce clinic in which women and/or men can discover their common experience of being imprisoned within traditional family roles while working together to change their status). ...

4. In a landlord-tenant practice that primarily consists of fighting evictions on a case-by-case basis, lawyers can politicize cases by encouraging organizing efforts among tenants and by simply suggesting that people discuss their common difficulties *as tenants*. Such a suggestion helps reveal that the political issue at the root of landlord-tenant conflicts is not whether tenants "need more rights," but rather what the destructive effects of the housing market itself are on people's communities and home lives....

Obviously, these examples are both simplistic and overly utopian if conceived as isolated attempts by individual lawyers. But if hundreds of lawyers begin to form networks that make the development of this kind of practice their self-conscious aim, they will have a real impact, not so much from the instrumental gains that they will make in individual cases, but from their contribution to the development of an authentic politics. If *every* dispute is founded ultimately upon conflicts and contradictions within the system as a whole, every such dispute raises the potential for thematizing in both reflection and collective action the relationship between private life and public totality. The activity of engaging in this politicization of legal practice is the activity of realizing the liberating politics of a future, more humane society in the present. It is the experience of engaging in this form of politics that is the true source of its transformative power.

B. The Politicization of the Courtroom

It is not an exaggeration to say that the single most powerful collective image of political authority is that of the courtroom. The robed judge who sits elevated from the gathering, the official and hushed character of the legal proceeding, the architecture of the room, the complex procedural technicalities—all of these and many other features of the courtroom ritual serve to reinculcate the political authority of the State, and through it the legitimacy of the socioeconomic order as a whole. Because the social power of hierarchies in the private sphere depends upon the continuing acceptance of the political authority that the courtroom encodes and symbolizes, a conscious effort to undermine the sanctity of the courtroom can become an important strategy....

The strategy proposed here is a more widespread practice of much longer duration, through which a great many lawyers in every kind of case make it a part of their political work to "gently" deconstruct the courtrooms in their local communities, and in so doing contribute to eroding the symbolic power of the State's authority from the bottom up....

1. Several years ago Stephanie Kline, a radical healthworker, was falsely charged with murder and possession of explosives. Bail was set at $75,000, and her lawyer moved to have it reduced. In the Oakland Municipal Courts there is a "prisoner's dock" adjoining the holding cell,

located to the right or left of the judge's elevated bench. At a bail hearing crowded with Kline's supporters, the bailiff escorted Kline to her dock to the right of the judge. Several yards away to the front-left of the judge sat her defense lawyer. Between them was the district attorney's table, located to the front-right of the judge. The defense lawyer asked the judge to allow the defendant to come over and sit with him. The judge refused. Defense counsel then got up and walked between the D.A. and the judge to the prisoner's dock. Neither the bailiff nor the judge stopped him. He argued for reduction of bail standing next to his client, a location which required the judge to turn to her right to hear the plea. The D.A. argued from his table. ...

Many lawyers assume that it is dangerous to be political in the courtroom because it will reduce their chances of winning. This is incorrect as a general principle, particularly if "political" is understood to mean demonstrating the underlying social reality of the case. Although there are undoubtedly many instances when a traditional legalistic approach is the most appropriate course of action, it is also true that, as a general rule, judges, prosecutors, and lawyers feel a loss of power when the roles within which they exercise control are revealed to be artificial and manipulative. The greater the extent to which conditioned images of the courtroom are undermined by honest spontaneity and moral authenticity in speech and action, the more likely it is that the jury will react to the totality of the event with a free and human response.

C. The Deprofessionalization of the Lawyer–Client Relationship

If a political lawyer can recoup her being from the role into which she has fallen and see the system as it really is, her practice can become a source of political strength for herself and her clients, and a source of opportunity to further the development of a true political or class consciousness. If the legal system is understood as nothing more than people in rooms who deploy their power through authoritarian symbols and imaginary laws, every social conflict that is channeled into such a room becomes an opportunity to challenge the dominant consciousness in a public setting. ...

V. Conclusion

Everything that we have said in this essay depends for its effectiveness on the development of a *movement* of lawyers who meet regularly to further develop the ideas that we have begun to present here, and who give one another the strength to take the risks that a truly politicized law practice requires. The possibility of utilizing social conflict to transform the legal arena from its current moribund state into an arena where a struggle for consciousness is waged obviously cannot be realized through the efforts of isolated practitioners. ...

Any transformative movement of lawyers must thus begin with the formation of small working groups, where lawyers who already know each other can begin to discuss what possibilities exist in their local communities for delegitimating legal work, and how they can develop a sense of collective support for one another's efforts. The general objective of such groups should be to break through the privatization of ordinary legal work, so that an alternative form of law practice like the one that we have begun to describe begins to achieve a degree of public legitimacy—so that, for example, a small group of lawyers that forms in Norman, Oklahoma, can know that there are other groups of lawyers in Ann Arbor or San Francisco who are trying to realize the same or similar objectives.

Notes and Questions

1. What role ought lawyers take with respect to political organizing and media campaigns? If these activities are rightfully part of a lawyer's work, should law schools offer courses in them? For two additional articles on political mobilization strategies, see Lucie White, *To Learn and Teach: Lessons from Driefrontein on Lawyering and Power,* 1988 Wisc. L.Rev. 699 and Lucie White, *Mobilization on the Margins of the Lawsuit" Making Space for Clients to Speak,* 16 N.Y.U. L. & Soc. Change 535 (1987-8).

2. One important step to changing the practice of law is changing the teaching of law. Several recent symposia offer ways to rethink legal education and the role of law schools and lawyers in addressing issues of social justice. Symposium, *The Justice Mission of American Law Schools,* 40 Cleve.St.L.Rev. (1992); Symposium, *Civic and Legal Education,* 45 Stan. L.Rev. (1993); Symposium, *Critical Theories and Legal Ethics,* 81 Geo.L.J. (1993); Symposium: *Legal Education,* 91 Mich.L.Rev. (1993); Symposium, *Women in Legal Education—Pedagogy, Law, Theory, and Practice,* 38 J.Legal Educ. (1988). Have issues of justice, fairness and equality been the focus of your legal education? Has your law school experience addressed the issues that you considered important when you first entered law school? Have you gained the knowledge, skills, and professional training you desired? Have you been challenged to think in new ways and to reach new understandings about law and justice? Think about what an ideal law school curriculum and experience should offer to prospective lawyers.

3. An indispensable and powerful book on alternative lawyering practice is Gerald P. Lopez, Rebellious Lawyering: One Chicano's Vision of Progressive Law Practice (Westview Press, 1992), which includes the following chapters: The Rebellious Idea of Lawyering Against Subordination; A Non–Profit Law Office in Transition; A Young Lawyer in a Small For–Profit Law Firm; A Lay Lawyer at Work; and Beyond Orthodox Organizing.

2. Creative applications of theories about power/privilege and strategies for social change in law

Below we have collected a small sampling of ways in which insights about naming, categorizing, power and privilege have been used to change legal approaches to social and political problems. These few examples, selected from a wide range of possibilities, are meant to whet your appetite for creative lawyering. Although this section comes at the end of this book, rather than dessert, consider this the hors d'oeuvre to a forthcoming meal of a lifetime of creative lawyering and progressive struggles for justice through law.

a. *Sexual Harassment and Sexism*

Catharine MacKinnon has been one of the most creative forces in reconceptualizing categories of legal thought to reflect her theories about gender and domination. In the late 1970s she took the previously undifferentiated sex-based experiences of oppression in the workplace and named them as sexual harassment. Catharine A. MacKinnon, The Sexual Harassment of Working Women (Yale U. Press, 1979). Once there was a way to speak about these experiences—once they had a name or label—and once they were connected to sex, Professor Mac-Kinnon recategorized their harms from annoyances and stresses that women had to tolerate in order to earn a paycheck to sex discrimination, remediable through Title VII and other anti-discrimination laws.

Inspired by new understandings about sexual harassment, other lawyers have worked in creative ways to reconceptualize harassing conduct that harms women. Some courts have reasoned that in order to appropriately assess whether conduct created a hostile environment for purposes of sexual harassment, it is necessary to use a "reasonable woman" standard or the perspective of people of the same gender as the plaintiff. *See e.g.* Ellison v. Brady, 924 F.2d 872 (9th Cir.1991). Justices like Marie Garibaldi of the New Jersey Supreme Court illustrate how to address gender power dynamics while articulating legal standards to be used in sexual harassment cases under their state laws.

LEHMANN v. TOYS 'R' US

Supreme Court of New Jersey, 1993.
132 N.J. 587, 626 A.2d 445, 453 & 457–59.

GARIBALDI, J.

To state a claim for hostile work environment sexual harassment, a female plaintiff must allege conduct that occurred because of her sex and that a reasonable woman would consider sufficiently severe or pervasive to alter the conditions of employment and create an intimidating, hostile, or offensive working environment. For the purposes of establishing and examining a cause of action, the test can be broken down into four prongs: the complained-of conduct (1) would not have occurred but for the employee's gender; and it was (2) severe or pervasive enough to make a (3) reasonable woman believe that (4) the conditions of employment are altered and the working environment is hostile or abusive. However, the second, third, and fourth prongs, while separable to some extent, are interdependent. One cannot inquire whether the alleged conduct was "severe or pervasive" without knowing how severe or pervasive it must be. The answer to that question lies in the other prongs: the conduct must be severe or pervasive enough to make a reasonable woman believe that the conditions of employment are altered and her working environment is hostile.

In this case, we discuss the standard assuming a female plaintiff, because in both the present case and the majority of cases, the plaintiff is a woman. However, the standard we announce today applies to sexual harassment of women by men, men by women, men by men, and women by women. The LAD protects both men and women and bars both heterosexual and homosexual harassment. The only difference in the standard would be that a male plaintiff would have to allege conduct that a reasonable man would believe altered the conditions of his employment and created a working environment that was hostile to men. . . .

VI. THE REASONABLE WOMAN STANDARD

In evaluating whether the harassment alleged was sufficiently severe or pervasive to alter the conditions of employment and to create a hostile or intimidating work environment for a female plaintiff, the finder of fact shall consider the question from the perspective of a reasonable woman. If the plaintiff is male, the perspective used shall be that of a reasonable man. We choose an objective and gender-specific perspective for a number of reasons.

We choose an objective standard, first, because as we explained above, the LAD is not primarily a tort scheme but rather is aimed at eradicating discriminatory conduct. An objective reasonableness standard better focuses the court's attention on the nature and legality of the conduct rather than on the reaction of the individual plaintiff, which is more relevant to damages.

Secondly, an objective standard provides flexibility. As we noted above, much conduct that would have been considered acceptable twenty or thirty years ago would be considered sexual harassment today. As community standards evolve, the standard of what a reasonable woman would consider harassment will also evolve.

However, incorporating community standards through the use of a reasonableness standard brings dangers against which courts must guard. We emphasize that the LAD is remedial legislation. Its very purpose is to change existing standards of conduct. Thus, the reasonableness requirement must not be used to hold that the prevailing level of discrimination is per se reasonable, or that a reasonable woman would expect sexual harassment on entering a historically male-dominated workplace. The LAD is designed to remediate conditions of hostility and discrimination, not to preserve and immunize pre-existing hostile work environments.

Thirdly, we choose an objective rather than a subjective viewpoint because the purpose of the LAD is to eliminate real discrimination and harassment. "It would not serve the goals of gender equality to credit a perspective that was pretextual or wholly idiosyncratic." Kathryn Abrams, Gender Discrimination and the Transformation of Workplace Norms, 42 Vand.L.Rev. 1183, 1210 (1989). A hypersensitive employee might have an idiosyncratic response to conduct that is not, objectively viewed, harassing. Allegations of such non-harassing conduct do not state a claim, even if the idiosyncratic plaintiff perceives her workplace to be hostile, because the complained-of conduct, objectively viewed, is not harassment, and the workplace, objectively viewed, is not hostile.

Conversely, an extraordinarily tough and resilient plaintiff might face harassing conduct that was, objectively viewed, sufficiently severe or pervasive to make the working environment hostile or intimidating, but because of her toughness, she might not personally find the workplace hostile or intimidating. Under our objective standard, such a plaintiff would state a claim even if she personally did not experience the workplace as hostile or intimidating. Sexual harassment is illegal even if the victim is strong enough not to be injured. Because such tough employees are perhaps the most likely to be strong enough to challenge harassers, the remedial purposes of the LAD are furthered by permitting claims by emotionally resilient plaintiffs without regard to subjective injury.

Of course, the subjective reaction of the plaintiff and her individual injuries remain relevant to compensatory damages. However, a plaintiff's subjective response is not an element of a hostile work environment sexual harassment cause of action.

We emphasize that only claims based on the idiosyncratic response of a hypersensitive plaintiff to conduct that is not objectively harassing would be barred by the reasonable woman standard. The category of reasonable women is diverse and includes both sensitive and tough people. A woman is not unreasonable merely because she falls toward the more sensitive side of the broad spectrum of reasonableness. Nor should "reasonable" be read as the opposite of "emotional." Perhaps because "reasonable" contains the word "reason," some have interpreted reasonableness as requiring a Vulcan-like rationality and absence of feeling. The reasonable woman standard should not be used to reject as unreasonable an emotional response to sexual harassment. On the contrary, such a response is normal and common. Only an idiosyncratic response of a hypersensitive plaintiff to conduct that a reasonable woman would not find harassing is excluded by the reasonable woman standard.

We turn now to our reasons for choosing a gender-specific standard. We believe that in order to fairly evaluate claims of sexual harassment, courts and finders of fact must recognize and respect the difference between male and female perspectives on sexual harassment. The reasonable person standard glosses over that difference, which is important here, and it also has a tendency to be male-biased, due to the tendency of courts and our society in general to view the male perspective as the objective or normative one.

Although there is far from a uniform female perspective on sexual harassment, nonetheless, the research and literature on sexual harassment suggest that there are differences in the way sexual conduct on the job is perceived by men and women. Kathryn Abrams argues that men consider sexual comments and conduct as "comparatively harmless amusement." Abrams, supra, 42 Vand.L.Rev. at 1203 (citing Barbara

Gutek, Sex and the Workplace 47–54 (1985)). When sexual comments or conduct are directed at them, men are apt to find it harmless and perhaps even flattering, but they are unlikely to consider it insulting or intimidating. Id. at 1206. Women, on the other hand, are more likely to find sexual conduct and comments in the workplace offensive and intimidating. Ibid. Abrams is speaking here only about heterosexual sexual harassment; she notes that "[t]hese conclusions might be different if a man were harassed by a gay male employer or supervisor." Id. at 1206 n. 97. Indeed, our general observation of a current social debate suggests to us that many men find the prospect of sexual harassment by other men extremely insulting and intimidating and not at all a "comparatively harmless amusement."

Two societal realities may underlie the difference in male and female perspectives. First, women live in a world in which the possibility of sexual violence is ever-present. Given that background, women may find sexual conduct in an inappropriate setting threatening. As the Ellison court perceptively wrote, because women are disproportionately victims of rape and sexual assault, women have a stronger incentive to be concerned with sexual behavior. Women who are victims of mild forms of sexual harassment may understandably worry whether a harasser's conduct is merely a prelude to violent sexual assault. Men, who are rarely victims of sexual assault, may view sexual conduct in a vacuum without a full appreciation of the social setting or the underlying threat of violence that a woman may perceive.

Second, in many areas of the workforce, women still represent a minority and are relatively recent entrants into the field. Because of their predominantly junior and minority status, for some women it is more difficult than it is for men to win credibility and respect from employers, coworkers, and clients or customers. That can make women's position in the workplace marginal or precarious from the start. Sexual harassment operates to further discredit the female employee by treating her as a sexual object rather than as a credible co-worker. That can both undermine the woman's self-confidence and interfere with her ability to be perceived by others as a capable worker with the potential to advance and succeed. Abrams, supra, 42 Vand.L.Rev. at 1208–09. Because of women's different status in the workplace, conduct that may be "just a joke" for men may have far more serious implications for women.

Those and other differences between the experiences of men and women shape the different perspectives of men and women. Finders of fact applying the gender–specific reasonableness standard must understand and respect those different perspectives.

––––––––

In *Robinson v. Jacksonville Shipyards, Inc.,* 760 F.Supp. 1486 (M.D.Fla.1991), the court found that a female welder was subjected to sexual harassment in the workplace in part due to the presence of pornographic posters and explicit sexual comments by coworkers.

Cynthia Grant Bowman has shifted MacKinnon's insights about the workplace to experiences of women along city streets and in other public places. Cynthia Grant Bowman, *Street Harassment and the Informal Ghettoization of Women,* 106 Harv.L.Rev. 517 (1993).

Opponents of sexism can learn about innovative approaches to law and uses of the media from Lori Peterson, a young, newly-minted attorney from Minnesota. Right out of law school she opened her own firm with two friends, and within a month she was representing several women employees of the Stroh Brewing Company who sued Stroh's for sexual harassment, in part based on its Old Milwaukee Beer Swedish Bikini Team advertising campaign in which a cadre of bikini clad models in blond wigs parachuted down to a group of beer-drinking men to the caption of "It doesn't get any better than this." Peterson argued that the commercials represented a corporate culture that demeaned and objectified women, a culture that contributed to a hostile work environment for women employees by encouraging male coworkers' abuse. *Haston v. The Stroh Brewery Co.,* No. C1–91–12990 (D.Minn. Filed Nov. 8, 1991). Two years later she settled the suit for an undisclosed amount a month before trial. Jill Hodges & Tony Kennedy, *Stroh's Settles Harassment Suit by Women Employees,* Star Tribune, Dec. 2, 1993, News, at A01. Peterson has also filed suit against Hooters of America restaurant chain in the Mall of America for sexual harassment of waitresses by customers based on the uniforms they are forced to wear by the corporation. Randy Furst, *Relentless Attorney Makes her Mark Hunting Sex Harassment,* Star Tribune, May 26, 1993, News, at A01.

There seems to be a growing willingness of judges to write about the history of sexism and discrimination against women. We have included excerpts from two such opinions below to show how once judges are sensitized to issues of subordination, power and privilege, they can include those ideas in their written opinions and legal reasoning. For example, Justice Levine wrote about Myra Bradwell and Lavinia Goodell in her special concurrence in a sex discrimination case, where she concludes that sex discrimination in employment can, in and of itself, be sufficiently outrageous conduct to make out a prima facie case of intentional infliction of emotional distress. Justice Spector also wrote specially to address issues of sexism and the ways that the legal system discriminates against women in the excerpt from her Twyman v. Twyman dissent below.

SWENSON v. NORTHERN CROP INSURANCE CO.

Supreme Court of North Dakota, 1993.
498 N.W.2d 174, 187.

LEVINE, J., concurring specially.

I join in the majority opinion, while registering but one small difference. I am not prepared to say in this case, that sex discrimination in obtaining employment or a promotion, without more, may not constitute sufficiently outrageous conduct to raise a jury question. With that difference noted, I concur in the rest of the opinion authored by former Chief Justice Erickstad.

Discrimination "deprives persons of their individual dignity...." Roberts v. United States Jaycees, 468 U.S. 609, 625 (1984). Sex discrimination is based on "archaic and overbroad assumptions" about the needs and capacities of women, sterotypical notions that "often bear no relationship to [a person's] actual abilities." Id. 468 U.S. at 625. There are countless examples of the exclusion of women from all walks of life because of the biased view that women are less able than men. Mississippi University for Women v. Hogan, 458 U.S. 718, 725 n. 10 (1982). One strikes close to home.

Myra Bradwell could not practice law.[1] Bradwell v. Illinois, 16 Wall 130, 21 L.Ed. 442 (1873). It may be that no reasonable jury in 1873 would have found Bradwell's exclusion outrageous. But, surely, the same cannot be said about juries in 1993. Fortunately, former custom does not prevent present practice from constituting extreme and outrageous conduct. See Alcorn v. Anbro Engineering, Inc., 468 P.2d 216, 219 n. 4 (Cal.1970) [racial epithets by one in position of authority states a claim for relief for the intentional infliction of emotional distress].

The outrageous conduct necessary to prove the intentional infliction of emotional distress is conduct that is so extreme in degree "as to go beyond all bounds of decency and to be regarded as atrocious, and utterly intolerable in a civilized community." Restatement (Second) of Torts

---

1. Ms. Bradwell had lots of company. Her sister-in-arms, Lavinia Goodell, met the same fate in Wisconsin in 1876. The Application of Miss Lavinia Goodell, 39 Wis. 232 (1876). Goodell's case commands special attention as a paradigm of conventional thinking about women. Chief Justice Ryan, in a unanimous opinion for himself and the two justices who then comprised the Wisconsin Supreme Court, denied Goodell's application squarely on the basis of her sex. He explained, in excruciating detail, the common law tradition of excluding women from the profession of law, because: "The law of nature destines and qualifies the female sex for the bearing and nurture of the children of our race and for the custody of the homes of the world and their maintenance in love and honor. And all life-long callings of women, inconsistent with these radical and sacred duties of their sex, as is the profession of the law, are departures from the order of nature; and when voluntary, treason against it...." As for lawyerly skills, women were found sorely deficient: "There are many employments in life not unfit for female character. The profession of the law is surely not one of these. The peculiar qualities of woman-

hood, its gentle graces, its quick sensibility, its tender susceptibility, its purity, its delicacy, its emotional impulses, its subordination of hard reason to sympathetic feeling are surely not qualifications for forensic strife. Nature has tempered woman as little for the juridical conflicts of the court room, as for the physical conflicts of the battle field. Womanhood is moulded for gentler and better things...." One might ask, but I won't, whether women's record of accomplishments in "the juridical conflicts of the court room" does not pierce Chief Justice Ryan and the common law's view, shared by a few others, that women are not qualified for the battlefield. Actually, given Chief Justice Ryan's sentiment that the practice of law is filled with "all that is selfish and malicious, knavish and criminal, coarse and brutal, repulsive and obscene ...," it is small wonder anyone would willingly undertake it! Over three years later, Goodell reapplied for admission to practice before the Wisconsin Supreme Court. Application of Goodell, 48 Wis. 693, 81 N.W. 551 (1879). The Court, enlarged to five members, granted her application. Chief Justice Ryan dissented!

§ 46 comment d (1965). The conduct must be, to use the vernacular, "really gross." It must substantially offend community notions of acceptable conduct. Grandchamp v. United Air Lines, 854 F.2d 381 (10th Cir.1988).

Is sex discrimination fairly regarded as "atrocious and utterly intolerable in a civilized community"? The answer must derive not alone from the act of sex discrimination but from the impact of that act on its victim. Sex discrimination debases, devalues and despoils. When we cannot do anything to overcome another's criticism, hatred or contempt, we are, in effect, struck twice: first, by the act and, second and equally devastating, by the realization that we are helpless to undo that act, overcome it or change it. This is particularly true in a workplace. See Robinson v. Jacksonville Shipyards, Inc., 760 F.Supp. 1486, 1505–07 (M.D.Fla.1991). As the majority points out, sex discrimination in the workplace constitutes an abuse of power by one in a superior position over one who is vulnerable and powerless. As children, we learned that lightning does not strike twice. As adults, we must conclude that discrimination surely does. An employee, like Swenson, who is eliminated solely because of her sex is laid low, first by the irrational, discriminatory conduct and then, by the inability to do anything about it. Indeed, victims, like Swenson, often need reassurance that it is not their fault that employers have discriminated against them. See Susan Martin, Sexual Harassment: The Link Joining Gender Stratification, Sexuality and Women's Economic Status, in Women: A Feminist Perspective 57, 62 (Jo Freeman ed., 4th ed. 1989). Discrimination is not a tale of hurt feelings, unkind behavior or inconsiderate conduct by one against another. Compare Muchow v. Lindblad, 435 N.W.2d 918 (N.D.1989). That it may insult is irrelevant; that it strips its victim of self-esteem, self-confidence and self-realization is the nub of its evil and the stuff of its outrageousness. As a subscriber to Oliver Wendell Holmes' belief that experience (not logic) fuels the engine of the law, and as a member of a class that has been subjected to discrimination, I find it difficult to understand how, at least, some members of the jury, whom we would all agree were reasonable members of their community, would not agree that sex discrimination, like race discrimination, goes beyond all bounds of decency and is truly atrocious and utterly intolerable in a civilized community. Compare Wendy Pollack, Sexual Harassment: Women's Experience vs. Legal Definitions, 13 Harvard Women's L.J. 35, 53 (Sp.1990) [legal concept of reasonable "man" standard or gender-neutral standard does not work in sexual harassment cases because it fails to recognize "male dominance" within "the larger phenomenon of gender hierarchy."].

And it is the jury that determines whether the challenged conduct is outrageous. E.g., Dreith v. National Football League, 777 F.Supp. 832 (D.Colo.1991). The court only decides the preliminary issue whether reasonable persons could differ on whether the conduct is outrageous. Id. It seems to me that if reasonable judges can disagree on whether or not sex discrimination is outrageous, then reasonable jurors can, too.

They should be given the opportunity to consider the question and plaintiff should be given the opportunity to educate, persuade and convince the jury in this case, that the alleged sex discrimination has no place in our society and is outrageous, extreme and wholly intolerable. The jury can take into account our changing social mores, the development of civil-rights law, and plaintiff's susceptibility as a member of a vulnerable class which has been historically discriminated against, to decide whether the conduct, that is, the sex discrimination, directed at plaintiff, constitutes the outrageous conduct necessary for plaintiff to prevail. See Contreras v. Crown Zellerbach Corp., 88 Wash.2d 735, 565 P.2d 1173 (1977). Only then will there be a fair resolution of the question of whether defendant's conduct substantially offends the community's notions of acceptable conduct. And that answer will be better provided by the representatives of the parties' community, the jurors, who likely have a keener aptness for judging their community's mores than either the trial court or this court.

The Supreme Court held in Bradwell that a statute describing "persons" who could practice law excluded females. That interpretation, however, must be viewed in the context of the legal culture of the time with its cabal of customary beliefs and complex of tradition about women and their separate sphere. The exclusion of women rested on the belief that men, simply because they were men, belonged in the public sphere rife with power and status, and women, in the private sphere—the home. See generally, Debra L. Rhode, The "No–Problem" Problem: Feminist Challenges and Cultural Change, 100 Yale L.J. 1731 (1991) [describing nineteenth-century-separate-spheres ideology]. Myra Bradwell could not practice law because of that prevailing view, espoused by Justice Bradley in his concurring opinion, that women did not have the "special skill and confidence" required of lawyers, because of women's "peculiar characteristics, destiny, and mission. . . ." Bradwell, supra at 16 Wall 142. Fortunately, that stereotypical notion of women's "proper place" was abandoned and women in increasing numbers now engage in the practice of law. Inaugurating this State's tradition, Helen Hamilton, the first woman graduate of the University of North Dakota School of Law, was described in information published in honor of her graduating class of 1905: "She with all the charm of woman, She with all the breadth of man." See U.N.D. Law Women's Caucus Pamphlet, Eleventh Annual Helen Hamilton Day, Mar. 4, 1993.

Today, if Helen Hamilton, charm and breadth notwithstanding, were unable to get a position because of sex discrimination, she would at least have the opportunity to right that wrong by having her day in court. She should be able to get to the jury with evidence of sex discrimination, defendant's intent or reckless disregard and her severe emotional distress and she should be able to prevail if she establishes those three elements of the tort by a preponderance of the evidence. To do that, she will have to have successfully eliminated from the jury those folks who just don't get it. It may well be that stereotypes about the "proper place" of women and their need for special treatment, like old soldiers, have not died. The jury can tell us if they have faded away.

TWYMAN v. TWYMAN

Supreme Court of Texas, 1993.
855 S.W.2d 619, 640.

SPECTOR, J. dissenting:

Over five years ago, a trial court issued a divorce decree that included an award to Sheila Twyman of $15,000 for the years of abuse she had suffered at the hands of her husband. At the time, the award was consistent with prevailing Texas law. Today, the plurality sets aside the trial court's award and sends Sheila Twyman back to start the process over in a new trial. Because justice for Sheila Twyman has been both delayed and denied, I dissent.

I.

At trial, Sheila testified that her husband, William Twyman, introduced bondage activities into their relationship after their marriage. Sheila told William that she could not endure these activities because of the trauma of having been raped several years earlier. She also informed William that she had been cut with a knife during the rape, and had been placed in fear for her life. Although William understood that Sheila equated bondage with her prior experience of being raped, he told Sheila that if she would not satisfy his desires by engaging in bondage, there would be no future to their marriage.

As a result, Sheila experienced "utter despair" and "devastation," as well as physical problems—weight loss and, after one encounter, prolonged bleeding that necessitated gynecological treatment. The pain and humiliation of the bondage activity caused her to seek help from three professional counselors.

The trial court found that William "engaged in a continuing course of conduct of attempting to coerce [Sheila] to join in his practices of 'bondage' by continually asserting that [their] marriage could be saved only by [Sheila] participating with [William] in his practices of 'bondage.'" The trial court also determined that Sheila's suffering was certainly foreseeable from William's continuing course of conduct, "in light of his existing knowledge of her long-existing emotional state, which was caused by her having been forcibly raped prior to their marriage." Finally, the trial court found that Sheila's mental anguish was a direct proximate result of William's sexual practices.

Based on the pleadings, evidence, and arguments, the trial court concluded that the facts and the law supported Sheila's recovery of $15,000 for William's negligent infliction of emotional distress. The court of appeals, in an opinion by Justice Gammage, affirmed the trial court's judgment under prevailing tort law and noted that this court had expressly approved the recovery of damages on a negligence claim in a divorce action.   790 S.W.2d 819, 823 (citing Price v. Price, 732 S.W.2d 316 (Tex.1987)).

This court, however, has now rejected Texas law established to provide redress for injuries of the kind inflicted by William Twyman. While allowing some tort claims to be brought in a divorce action, the plurality forbids recovery for negligent infliction of emotional distress, and insists that Sheila Twyman proceed on a theory of intentional infliction of emotional distress.

II.

Today's decision is handed down contemporaneously with the overruling of the motion for rehearing in Boyles v. Kerr, 855 S.W.2d 593 (Tex.1993), in which this court reversed a judgment in favor of a woman who was surreptitiously videotaped during intercourse, then subjected to humiliation and ridicule when the tape was displayed to others.   In Boyles, as in this case, a majority of this court has determined that severe, negligently-inflicted emotional distress does not warrant judicial relief—no matter how intolerable the injurious conduct.   The reasoning originally articulated in Boyles, and now implied in this case, is that "[t]ort law cannot and should not attempt to provide redress for every instance of rude, insensitive, or distasteful behavior"; providing such relief, the Boyles majority explained, "would dignify most disputes far beyond their social importance."   36 Tex.S.Ct.J. 231, 233–234 (Dec. 2, 1992).

Neither of these cases involves "rude, insensitive, or distasteful behavior"; they involve grossly offensive conduct that was appropriately found to warrant judicial relief.   The decision in Boyles overturns well-reasoned case law, and I strongly agree with the dissenting opinion in that case.   For the same reasons, I strongly disagree with the plurality here; the rule embodied in Boyles is no less objectionable when applied to the facts of this case.   Sheila Twyman is entitled to recover the amount awarded by the trial court for the injuries inflicted by her husband.

III.

It is no coincidence that both this cause and Boyles involve serious emotional distress claims asserted by women against men.   From the beginning, tort recovery for infliction of emotional distress has developed primarily as a means of compensating women for injuries inflicted by men insensitive to the harm caused by their conduct.   In "[t]he leading case which broke through the shackles," a man amused himself by falsely informing a woman that her husband had been gravely injured, causing a serious and permanent shock to her nervous system.   Wilkinson v. Downton, 2 Q.B.D. 57 (1897).   Similarly, in the watershed Texas case, a man severely beat two others in the presence of a pregnant woman, who suffered a miscarriage as a result of her emotional distress.   Hill v. Kimball, 76 Tex. 210, 13 S.W. 59 (1890).   By World War II, the pattern was well-established: one survey of psychic injury claims found that the ratio of female to male plaintiffs was five to one.   Hubert

Winston Smith, Relation of Emotions to Injury and Disease: Legal Liability for Psychic Stimuli, 30 Va.L.Rev. 193 (1944).

Even today, when emotional distress claims by both sexes have become more widely accepted, women's claims against men predominate. Of the thirty-four Texas cases cited by the plurality—all decided since 1987—women's claims outnumbered men's by a ratio of five to four; and only four of the thirty-four involved any female defendants. Of those cases involving relations between two individuals—with no corporations involved—five involved a woman's claim against a man; none involved a man's claim against a woman.

I do not argue that women alone have an interest in recovery for emotional distress. However, since the overwhelming majority of emotional distress claims have arisen from harmful conduct by men, rather than women, I do argue that men have had a disproportionate interest in downplaying such claims.

Like the struggle for women's rights, the movement toward recovery for emotional distress has been long and tortuous. See Peter A. Bell, The Bell Tolls: Toward Full Tort Recovery for Psychic Injury, 36 U.Fla.L.Rev. 333, 336–40 (1984). In the judicial system dominated by men, emotional distress claims have historically been marginalized: The law of torts values physical security and property more highly than emotional security and human relationships. This apparently gender-neutral hierarchy of values has privileged men, as the traditional owners and managers of property, and has burdened women, to whom the emotional work of maintaining human relationships has commonly been assigned. The law has often failed to compensate women for recurring harms—serious though they may be in the lives of women—for which there is no precise masculine analogue. Martha Chamallas and Linda K. Kerber, Women, Mothers, and the Law of Fright: A History, 88 Mich. L.Rev. 814 (1990). Even Prosser recognizes the role of gender in the historical treatment of claims like that involved in Hill v. Kimball: It is not difficult to discover in the earlier opinions a distinctly masculine astonishment that any woman should ever allow herself to be frightened or shocked into a miscarriage. W. Page Keeton et al., Prosser and Keeton on the Law of Torts § 12, at 55–56 (5th ed. 1984).

Displaying a comparable "masculine astonishment," the dissenting opinion by Justice Hecht insists that, with a few possible exceptions, women have played no distinct part in the development of tort recovery for emotional distress. As a general matter, Justice Hecht questions how a legal system dominated by men could develop a tort to compensate women even while marginalizing women's claims. The answer is amply illustrated by the present case: to provide some appearance of relief for Sheila Twyman, the court recognizes the tort of intentional infliction of emotional distress; but in doing so, it restricts her to a theory which, as Justice Hecht observes, is "seldom successful." 855 S.W.2d at 631. . . .

[Spector's telling of the history of emotional distress claims in Texas, which responds specifically to Justice Hecht, is omitted. Citing the last in the line of cases, she explains:] [A]s in so many of the other cases, the evolution of the law regarding emotional distress claims did enable a female to recover for emotional harm inflicted by men. This fact does not reflect a charitable desire to help women; it reflects the fact that the serious emotional distress claims usually involved injuries inflicted by men upon women.

Given this history, the plurality's emphatic rejection of infliction of emotional distress claims based on negligence is especially troubling. Today, when the widespread mistreatment of women is being documented throughout the country—for instance, in the areas of sexual harassment and domestic violence—a majority of this court takes a step backward and abolishes one way of righting this grievous wrong.

IV.

Rather than dismissing Sheila's claim outright, the plurality remands this cause to the trial court to allow Sheila to seek recovery under an alternative theory. I agree that Sheila is entitled to pursue a claim based upon intentional infliction of emotional distress, as set out in section 46 of the Restatement (2d) of Torts.

However, in restricting recovery for emotional distress to claims based upon intent, the plurality, joined by Justice Gonzalez's concurring opinion, demonstrates a basic misunderstanding of claims like those presented by Susan Kerr and Sheila Twyman. While recognizing that recovery should be allowed for conduct intended to inflict injury, the plurality fails to acknowledge the severe emotional distress often caused unintentionally.

This court has previously made clear that the distinguishing feature of an intentional tort is "the specific intent to inflict injury." Reed Tool Co. v. Copelin, 689 S.W.2d 404, 406 (Tex.1985) (citing Restatement (2d) of Torts s 8A (1965)); see also Rodriguez v. Naylor Indus., 763 S.W.2d 411, 412 (Tex.1988). This definition of an "intentional" injury is echoed in the portion of the Restatement governing intentional infliction of emotional distress: The rule stated in this Section applies where the actor desires to inflict severe emotional distress, and also where he knows that such distress is certain, or substantially certain, to result from his conduct. Restatement (2d) of Torts § 46 cmt. i (1965).

Unfortunately, in many cases, severe emotional distress is caused by an actor who does not actually desire to inflict severe emotional distress, and who is even oblivious to the fact that such distress is certain, or substantially certain, to result from his conduct. It may well be the case, for example, that William Twyman never actually intended to inflict emotional distress upon Sheila, and never expected the injury that his conduct caused. Rather, he may have insisted on bondage activities solely for the purpose of satisfying his own desires. Similarly, Dan Boyles may have videotaped his activities with Susan Kerr not for the purpose of injuring her, but rather for the purpose of amusing himself and his friends.

I do not argue, as the plurality asserts, that "the emotional harm William caused was foreseeable but not substantially certain to occur." 855 S.W.2d at 624. I do argue, though, that Sheila's recovery for William's conduct should not depend upon proof of William's sensitivity. To apply a standard based on intent is to excuse William's conduct so long as he believed his actions were harmless.

Brutish behavior that causes severe injury, even though unintentionally, should not be trivialized. Foreclosing recovery for such behavior may prevent litigation of frivolous claims; but it also denies redress in exactly those instances where it is most needed.

b. *Pornography and Violence Against Women*

Professor MacKinnon, in collaboration with Andrea Dworkin, has also worked to recategorize our understandings about pornography from an issue of free speech to an issue of civil rights. Catharine A. Mac-Kinnon, Only Words (Harvard U. Press, 1993); Toward a Feminist Theory of the State (Harvard U. Press, 1989); Feminism Unmodified: Discourses on Life and Law (Harvard U. Press, 1987). MacKinnon's work and legal strategies reveal the enormous power of naming and categorizing. Although the legislation with civil remedies that Mac-Kinnon and Dworkin drafted for the City of Indianapolis was declared unconstitutional in American Booksellers Association v. Hudnut, 771 F.2d 323 (7th Cir.1985), affirmed mem. 475 U.S. 1001, 106 S.Ct. 1172, 89 L.Ed.2d 291 (1986), rehearing denied 475 U.S. 1132, 106 S.Ct. 1664, 90 L.Ed.2d 206 (1986), a MacKinnon–Dworkin based anti-pornography statute that criminalizes certain pornography was upheld in Canada in Regina v. Butler, 89 D.L.R.4th 449 (S.C.C.1992).

MacKinnon and Dworkin's insight about the civil rights violation of pornography has informed the Senate version of the Violence Against Women Act (VAWA) of 1993, which the Senate passed as part of its crime bill in November 1993. Title III of the Senate version of the VAWA states:

VIOLENCE AGAINST WOMEN ACT
S. 11

SEC. 301. SHORT TITLE. This title may be cited as the "Civil Rights Remedies for Gender–Motivated Violence Act".

SEC. 302. CIVIL RIGHTS. (a) Findings.—The Congress finds that—(1) crimes motivated by the victim's gender constitute bias crimes in violation of the victim's right to be free from discrimination on the basis of gender; (2) current law provides a civil rights remedy for gender crimes committed in the workplace, but not for gender crimes committed on the street or in the home; (3) State and Federal criminal laws do not adequately protect against the bias element of gender-motivated crimes, which separates these crimes from acts of random violence, nor do those laws adequately provide victims of gender-motivated crimes the opportunity to vindicate their interests; (4) existing bias and discrimination in the criminal justice system often deprives victims of gender-motivated crimes of equal protection of the laws and the redress to which they are entitled; (5) gender-motivated violence has a substantial adverse effect on interstate commerce, by deterring potential victims from traveling interstate, from engaging in employment in interstate business, and from transacting with business, and in places involved, in interstate commerce; (6) gender-motivated violence has a substantial adverse effect on interstate commerce, by diminishing national productivity, increasing medical and other costs, and decreasing the supply of and the demand for interstate products; (7) a Federal civil rights action as specified in this section is necessary to guarantee equal protection of the laws and to reduce the substantial adverse effects of gender-motivated violence on interstate commerce; and (8) victims of gender-motivated violence have a right to equal protection of the laws, including a system of justice that is unaffected by bias or discrimination and that, at every relevant stage, treats such crimes as seriously as other violent crimes.

(b) Right To Be Free From Crimes Of Violence.—All persons within the United States shall have the right to be free from crimes of violence motivated by gender (as defined in subsection (d)).

(c) Cause of Action.—A person (including a person who acts under color of any statute, ordinance, regulation, custom, or usage of any State) who commits a crime of violence motivated by gender and thus deprives another of the right declared in subsection (b) shall be liable to the party injured, in an action for the recovery of compensatory and punitive damages, injunctive and declaratory relief, and such other relief as a court may deem appropriate.

(d) Definitions.—For purposes of this section—(1) the term "crime of violence motivated by gender" means a crime of violence committed because of gender or on the basis of gender; and due, at least in part, to an animus based on the victim's gender; (2) the term "crime of violence" means—(A) an act or series of acts that would constitute a felony against the person or that would constitute a felony against property if the conduct presents a serious risk of physical injury to another . . .; and (B) includes an act or series of acts that would constitute a felony described in subparagraph (A) but for the relationship between the person who takes such action and the individual against whom such action is taken.

(e) Limitation and Procedures.—(1) Limitation.—Nothing in this section entitles a person to a cause of action under subsection (c) for random acts of violence unrelated to gender or for acts that cannot be demonstrated, by a preponderance of the evidence, to be motivated by gender (within the meaning of subsection (d)). (subsections 2–5 omitted.)

S. 11, S.Rep. No. 138, 103rd Cong., 1st Sess.1993, 1993 WL 355617 (Sept. 10, 1993). The House of Representatives also passed a Violence

Against Women Act as part of its crime bill, but that version does not include a civil rights remedy.

In September 1994, The Violent Crime Control and Law Enforcement Act of 1994 became law. It contains the Civil Rights Remedies for Gender–Motivated Violence Act, 42 U.S.C.A. § 13981, 108 Stat. 1796, which is identical to the Senate bill, except that the "findings" section was changed to a "purpose" section as follows:

> SEC. 40302. CIVIL RIGHTS. (a) PURPOSE.—Pursuant to the affirmative power of Congress to enact this subtitle under section 5 of the Fourteenth Amendment to the Constitution, as well as under section 8 of Article I of the Constitution, it is the purpose of this subtitle to protect the civil rights of victims of gender motivated violence and to promote public safety, health, and activities affecting interstate commerce by establishing a Federal civil rights cause of action for victims of crimes of violence motivated by gender.

For a couple of the many interesting writings examining a civil remedy and/or "hate crime" approach to violence against women, see Brande Stellings, *The Public Harm of Private Violence: Rape, Sex Discrimination and Citizenship,* 28 Harv. C.R.–C.L. L.Rev. 185 (1993); Marguerite Angelari, *Hate Crime Statutes: A Promising Tool for Fighting Violence Against Women,* 2 Am.U.J. Gender & Law 63 (1994); Elizabeth A. Pendo, *Recognizing Violence Against Women: Gender and the Hate Crimes Statistics Act,* 17 Harv. Women's L.J. 157 (1994).

Massachusetts State Attorney General Scott Harshbarger, in a 1994 precedent-setting case, used a state civil rights law prohibiting hate-motivated behavior to obtain a preliminary injunction from a superior court against a man who had battered his wife and three girlfriends. Although protective or restraining orders are available to women threatened by intimate violence, this is the first time a gender-bias statute was used to get a preliminary injunction, violation of which could result in up to ten years in the state penitentiary. Nancie L. Katz, *Rights Law Invoked in Battering Case,* The Washington Post, April 28, 1994, at A05.

c. Environmental Racism

As with sexual harassment, naming was important to the development of strategies to defeat and remedy environmental racism. Creative lawyering and social activism, rejecting a color-blind approach to assessing the impact of environmental regulation, has led to "analyzing environmental policies and activities from the perspective of the subordinating impact on racial groups" along with challenging the "substantive distributional impacts of those rules in practice and the substantive blindness in the production of rules that lead to racially subordinating activities," whether unconscious or not. Gerald Torres, *Introduction: Understanding Environmental Racism,* Symposium: Race, Class, and Environmental Regulation, 63 U.Colo.L.Rev. 839, 840 (1992). In 1983 the General Accounting Office found that three out of four commercial hazardous waste landfills in EPA Region IV in the southeastern United

States were in predominantly black communities. U.S. General Accounting Office, Siting of Hazardous Waste Landfills and their Correlation with Racial and Economic Status of Surrounding Communities, 1983. A 1987 study determined that the major factor related to the presence of hazardous wastes in residential communities throughout the United States is race. Commission for Racial Justice, United Church of Christ, Toxic Wastes and Race in the United States (1987). See Robert Bullard, Unequal Protection: Environmental Justice and Communities of Color (Sierra Club, 1994); Bunyan Bryant & Paul Mohai, eds, Race and the Incidence of Environmental Hazards: A Time for Discourse (Westview Press, 1992); Sheila Foster, *Race(ial) Matters: The Quest for Environmental Justice*, 20 Ecology L.Q. 721 (1993); Paul Mohai & Bunyan Bryant, *Environmental Injustice: Weighing Race and Class as Factors in the Distribution of Environmental Hazards*, 63 U.Colo.L.Rev. 921 (1992); Luke Cole, *Remedies for Environmental Racism: A View From the Field*, 90 Mich.L.Rev. 1991 (1992); Rachel D. Godsil, Note, *Remedying Environmental Racism*, 90 Mich.L.Rev. 394 (1991). In several cases lawyers have tried to shift the paradigm from traditional environmental criteria for decisions about where to locate hazardous waste to a civil rights oriented discrimination analysis. So far no civil rights or equal protection strategies based on statistical evidence of discrimination have prevailed in challenging siting decisions, because courts have sought direct evidence of racial animus or discriminatory intent. *See e.g.* East Bibb Twiggs Neighborhood Ass'n v. Macon–Bibb County Planning and Zoning Commission, 706 F.Supp. 880 (M.D.Ga. 1989), affirmed, 896 F.2d 1264 (11th Cir.1989); Bean v. Southwestern Waste Management Corp., 482 F.Supp. 673 (S.D.Tex.1979). In addition to using sophisticated arguments for reinterpreting intent under an equal protection analysis in cases where environmental racism is "unconscious," see Charles Lawrence, *The Id, the Ego and Equal Protection: Reckoning with Unconscious Racism*, 39 Stan.L.Rev. 317 (1987), lawyers must think creatively about getting courts to recognize the ways in which environmental policies reproduce patterns of racial subordination and race-based harms. As these theories, litigation, and public advocacy strategies develop, other creative lawyers can opt for traditional tort, toxic tort, and nuisance approaches to inhibit further encroachments on communities of color. Pamela Duncan, *Environmental Racism: Recognition, Litigation, and Alleviation*, 6 Tul.Envtl.L.Rev. 317 (1993).

Similarly, challenges to racial segregation in education and housing provide ample creative opportunities for progressive lawyers.

d. Reparations and Remedies for Racist Violence

Although non-legal literature and politics involved African–American claims for reparations for the violence and harms of slavery since Reconstruction, in 1973 Boris Bittker published a book proposing a legal solution using 42 U.S.C. § 1983 to develop a reparations program. Boris I. Bittker, The Case for Black Reparations (1973). In the 1980s, Derrick Bell and Mari Matsuda explored the possibility of racial reparations programs with different degrees of confidence in their possible success. Derrick Bell, And We Are Not Saved (Basic Books, 1987); Mari Matsuda, *Looking to the Bottom: Critical Legal Studies and Reparations,* 22 Harv.C.R.–C.L.L.Rev. 323 (1987). Professor Matsuda's article creates compelling legal arguments for the use of racial reparations remedies and is quite inspiring.

The courts have not been particularly hospitable to claims for reparations, but there has been moderate legislative success, at least for Japanese–Americans interned during World War II. In Hohri v. United States, 586 F.Supp. 769 (D.C.C.1984), affirmed in part and reversed in part 782 F.2d 227 (D.C.Cir.1986), vacated and remanded 482 U.S. 64 (1987), nineteen Japanese–American internees or their living representatives brought a class action suit against the United States seeking money damages and a declaratory judgment for the harms they suffered during the Japanese–American internment in World War II. The litigation went up to the Supreme Court, which only discussed jurisdictional issues, and back down to a different court of appeals who ultimately affirmed the district court's dismissal of the class action on statute of limitations and sovereign immunity grounds. Hohri v. United States, 847 F.2d 779 (Fed.Cir.1988), cert. denied 488 U.S. 925, 109 S.Ct. 307, 102 L.Ed.2d 326 (1988). In the meantime, the Congress created a commission to study the internment of Japanese–Americans and then in response to the commission's findings of constitutional rights violations, enacted the Civil Liberties Act of 1988, 50 App. U.S.C.A. §§ 1989–1989d, 102 Stat. 903, which President Reagan signed. The Act contained an apology to U.S. citizens and resident aliens of Japanese ancestry who were evacuated, relocated, and interned during World War II, and it provided for $20,000 payments as reparations. Congress appropriated $500 million annually to pay the $1.25 billion in reparations. Under the Act's priority scheme, the elderly are paid first. Civil Liberties Act Amendments of 1992, Pub.L. No. 102–371.

Using this as a model, Representative John Conyers introduced a bill in the House of Representatives in 1989 and again in 1991 to create a commission to study slavery and racial discrimination against African–Americans, hoping eventually to get a similar act remedying these past harms. Commission to Study Reparation Proposals for African Americans Act, H.R. 3745, 101st Cong., 1st Sess. (1989) and H.R. 1684, 102d Cong., 1st Sess. (1991). So far, he has not been successful in Congress, but other states have adopted resolutions supporting his bill. Most recently, in a stunning victory for racial justice, the Florida Legislature passed a $2.1 million claims bill to pay survivors of the Rosewood arson and massacre, in which white racist violence wiped out the entire Black settlement there more than 70 years ago. *Florida Legislature To Pay $2.1 Million to Victims of 1923 Racist Massacre in Rosewood,* Jet, April 25, 1994, p. 12. Survivors will receive up to $150,000 each and scholarships will be created for descendants.

In 1993 two more powerful articles addressed the use of reparations as a remedy for racially motivated harms. Rhonda V. Magee, Note, *The*

Master's Tools, From the Bottom Up: Responses to African American Reparations Theory in Mainstream and Outsider Remedies Discourse, 79 Va.L.Rev. 863 (1993) (proposing a "cultural equity" theory including a variety of remedies, such as separate African–American universities, affirmative action and integration, and reparations); Vincene Verdun, *If The Shoe Fits, Wear It: An Analysis of Reparations to African Americans,* 67 Tul.L.Rev. 597 (1993). These legal analyses can be used to inform progressive lawyering efforts.

In a different approach to reparations for racial violence, Morris Dees, of the Southern Poverty Law Center, brought a lawsuit against the United Klans of America (KKK) on behalf of Beulah Mae Donald for the lynching of her 19 year old son, Michael, in 1981. He has written extensively about the case in Morris Dees with Steve Fieffer, A Season for Justice (Charles Scribner's Sons, 1991). Donald was awarded seven million dollars by an all-white jury. The Klan was forced to deed to her its new 7400 square foot building in Tuscaloosa in order to pay the judgment. After the judgment, the United Klans of America went bankrupt. In addition, Dees' work on this case led to the eventual prosecution of a Klan member for murder. Talk about stunning victories. Dees has performed a similar feat by suing neo-Nazi skinheads for damages. Morris Dees, Hate on Trial (Villard Books, 1993).

Tort and civil rights actions for compensatory and punitive damages provide an important avenue for creative lawyering. Many tort theorists and practitioners recognize that tort actions can be about social justice and civil rights. Some of the sex-based violence of the pharmaceutical industries has been addressed by litigation against producers of the Dalkon Shield and DES. *See, e.g.* Miles Lord, *The Dalkon Shield Litigation: Revised Annotated Reprimand by Chief Judge Miles W. Lord,* 9 Hamline L.Rev. 7 (1986). Accord, Leslie Bender, *An Overview of Feminist Torts Scholarship,* 78 Cornell L.Rev. 575 (1993); Thomas Koenig & Michael Rustad, *His and Her Tort Reform: Gender Injustice in Disguise,* 70 U.Wash.L.Rev. (forthcoming, 1995); Joan Steinman, *A Legal Sampler: Women, Medical Care, and Mass Tort Litigation,* 68 Chi.–Kent L.Rev. 409 (1992).

e. Hate Speech on Campuses

Because of increased incidents of hate speech on university campuses as our student bodies become more diverse, some universities have attempted to adopt codes prohibiting or regulating speech that victimizes historically subordinated groups. In a blow to this effort, codes at Michigan and Wisconsin universities were ruled unconstitutionally vague and overbroad. Doe v. University of Michigan, 721 F.Supp. 852 (E.D.Mich.1989); UWM Post, Inc. v. Board of Regents of Univ. of Wisconsin, 774 F.Supp. 1163 (E.D.Wis.1991). Private universities are not bound by the first amendment in the same way as public universities, because they do not represent the authority of the state. To address the disparity between student speech rights at public and private universities, California enacted the 1992 Leonard Law, which gives students the same free speech rights on campus that they have off campus. Nine students at Stanford, a private university, have filed a lawsuit in Santa Clara County Superior Court challenging the school's hate speech policy that prohibits "personal vilification of students on the basis of their sex, race, color, handicap, religion, sexual orientation, or national and ethnic origin." Ben Wildavsky, *War of Words over Stanford's Speech Rule,* San Francisco Chronicle, May 4, 1994, at A14.

A body of legal literature, far too extensive to name, has developed to discuss the conflict on campuses between absolutist first amendment free speech positions and equality issues about participation by and the meaningful citizenship of historically subordinated people. No doubt the traditional first amendment-based anti-censorship, marketplace of ideas, more-good-speech-will-beat-out-bad-speech kinds of arguments are familiar to you, because they traditionally are a core part of our constitutional law training. *See e.g.,* Nadine Strossen, *Regulating Racist Speech on Campus: A Modest Proposal?,* 1990 Duke L.J. 484. Less familiar may be arguments about how free speech rights as granted in the United States tend to privilege speakers already privileged by race, class, gender, and sexuality (even if those speakers are expressing unpopular ideas) and arguments based on the creative approaches taken by critical race scholars and others.

In a recent collection of essays entitled Words That Wound: Critical Race Theory, Assaultive Speech, and the First Amendment (Westview Press, 1993), Mari Matsuda, Charles Lawrence, Richard Delgado, and Kimberlé Crenshaw use insights about power, privilege and law and creative shifting of traditional legal categorical thinking to propose appropriate responses to hate speech which respect the victim's story and address the victim's harms.

For example, Charles Lawrence reinterprets *Brown v. Board of Education,* 347 U.S. 483, 74 S.Ct. 686, 98 L.Ed. 873 (1954), reading it as a case about regulating speech and symbolic messages, in addition to its being a case about equal educational opportunity.

CHARLES R. LAWRENCE, III, IF HE HOLLERS LET HIM GO: REGULATING RACIST SPEECH ON CAMPUS

in Words That Wound 53, 59 (Westview 1993).

Brown can also be read more broadly to articulate a principle central to any substantive understanding of the equal protection clause, the foundation on which all anti-discrimination law rests. This is a principle of equal citizenship. Under that principle, "Every individual is presumptively entitled to be treated by the organized society as a respected, responsible, and participating member." The principle further requires the affirmative disestablishment of societal practices that treat people as members of an inferior or dependent caste, as unworthy to participate in the larger community. The holding *Brown*—that racially segregated schools violate the equal protection clause—reflects the fact that segregation amounts to a demeaning, caste-creating practice. The prevention of stigma was at the core of the Supreme Court's unanimous decision in *Brown* . . . .

The key to this understanding of *Brown* is that the practice of segregation, the practice the Court held inherently unconstitutional, was *speech.* *Brown* held that segregation is unconstitutional not simply because the physical separation of Black and white children is bad or because resources were distributed unequally among Black and white schools. *Brown* held that segregated schools were unconstitutional primarily because of the *message* segregation conveys—the message that Black children are an untouchable caste, unfit to be educated with white children. Segregation serves its purpose by conveying an idea. It stamps a badge of inferiority upon Blacks, and this badge communicates a message to others in the community. . . . Therefore, *Brown* may be read as regulating the content of racist speech. As a regulation of racist speech, the decision is an exception to the usual rule that regulation of speech content is presumed unconstitutional.

————

From this analysis he concludes that the prohibition of certain racist speech on university campuses may be consistent with the constitution and even justified by current first amendment doctrine by analogy to captive audiences.

Mari Matsuda criticizes state action and first amendment doctrines as legal protection of racism and rebukes judges and lawyers for their lack of imagination in responding to victims of racist hate speech. Mari Matsuda, *Public Response to Racist Speech: Considering the Victim's Story* 17, 47, in Words That Wound, supra. After telling a series of stories about real life experiences of people being victimized by racist speech, Matsuda suggests that certain racist hate speech can be outlawed consistent with a growing international law consensus and with first amendment principles. Richard Delgado, who originally opened this critique of the first amendment's apparent impotence in addressing racial insults with a 1982 article from which this collaborative book has borrowed its name, opts for a tort-based remedy. Richard Delgado, *Words That Wound: A Tort Action for Racial Insults, Epithets, and Name Calling* 89, in Words That Wound, supra.

Last but not least, Kimberlé Crenshaw looks at the attempt to silence hateful speech from a very different perspective—one in which she sees racism as the motivation for silencing, rather than a true concern about the speech's victims. Kimberlé Williams Crenshaw, *Beyond Racism and Misogyny: Black Feminism and 2 Live Crew* 111, in Words That Wound, *supra.* Finding herself again at the intersection of race and gender politics, Crenshaw reveals the awkward place that government attempts to censor misogynist and obscene rap music leave black feminists.   Applying methods that require the analysis of issues in their specific contexts with a sensitivity to race, gender, and other power dynamics, she reluctantly opts to support the black musicians against the state whose motivation for acting can only be seen as having a racial cast, but to work within African–American communities to undermine and squelch misogynist lyrics and attitudes.

CONCLUSION

To seek justice and promote equality through law, we must discover ways to disrupt law's existing patterns of power and privilege, whether they stem from biologically or culturally constructed notions about race, class, gender, sexuality, disability, age, ethnicity and national origin. We can begin by questioning law's role and function, its underlying assumptions and unspoken norms, and its rhetoric of difference and domination. We must learn to see beyond law's artificially created categories and restrictive definitions of relevance. We need constantly to inquire about who is being excluded from law's protection and perspectives.

In a published opening address to the Third National Conference on Women of Color and the Law, Professor Mari Matsuda advises lawyers and law students to work in coalitions to develop adequate legal theories of subordination which can be used in transformative ways in our quest for justice. Matsuda, Beside My Sister, Facing the Enemy: Legal Theory Out of Coalition, 43 Stan.L.Rev. 1183 (1991). She argues that work in coalitions is essential to success, because oppressive structures are so interdependent that unless they are all eradicated, others will grow back in new places. Coalition work is the only way to get to the roots.

Working in coalitions is difficult. There are walls of distrust that must be scaled. There are histories of pain and offenses that must be addressed. Different experiences and perspectives must be listened to carefully and respectfully. Coalition participants must open themselves up and be vulnerable in order to succeed. As Bernice Johnson Reagon said

> Coalition work ... is some of the most dangerous work you can do. And you shouldn't look for comfort. Some people will come to a coalition and they rate the success of the coalition on whether or not they feel good when they get there. They're not looking for a coalition; they're looking for a home! ... You don't get a lot of food in a coalition. You don't get fed a lot ... In a coalition you have to give, and it is different from your home. You can't stay there all the time. You go to the coalition for a few hours and then you go back [home]. It is very important not to confuse them—home and coalition.

Reagon, Coalition Politics: Turning the Century 356, 359–60, in HOME GIRLS: A BLACK FEMINIST ANTHOLOGY (Barbara Smith, ed., Kitchen Table: Women of Color Press, 1983).

Although home and homogeneity are safer and more comfortable, Reagon says home cannot protect you from oppression. Coalition work can. Through coalition work we can best determine how and where to act to change oppressions within the legal system and we can generate the people-power to make a difference.

Coalition work requires thinking about interdependencies. One way to hone one's sensitivities to the interdependencies and relationships of structures of power is to "ask the other question."   Mari Matsuda explains:

> The way I try to understand the interconnection of all forms of subordination is through a method I call "ask the other question." When I see something that looks racist, I ask, "Where is the patriarchy in this?" When I see something that looks sexist, I ask, "Where is the heterosexism in this?" When I see something that looks homophobic, I ask, "Where are the class interests in this?" Working in coalition forces us to look for both the obvious and non-obvious relationships of domination, helping us to realize that no form of subordination ever stands alone.

Matsuda, supra at 1189.

Lawyering for justice has its frustrations, because often the legal system seems committed to reproducing patterns of unevenly distributed privilege and power. But, if you keep your "Eyes on the Prize," and you build coalitions with other lawyers and community members who are engaged in this struggle, you can spend your career in law working for justice, remedying unfairness, helping people to live with dignity and hope, and influencing our legal culture to move toward a better social order that offers a higher quality of life for everyone. You can contribute to this work in any area of law that interests you, whether direct delivery of legal services to the poor or any career choice across the spectrum of legal work, including corporate and tax practice. Lawyering for justice affords you an opportunity to be creative and passionate about your work. You can help make legal concepts like "civil rights" as rich as Alice Walker's interpretation of "Silver Writes." Maybe you can even make the world a place where her daring young man can crash all barriers at once.

*

Index

References are to Pages

---

†